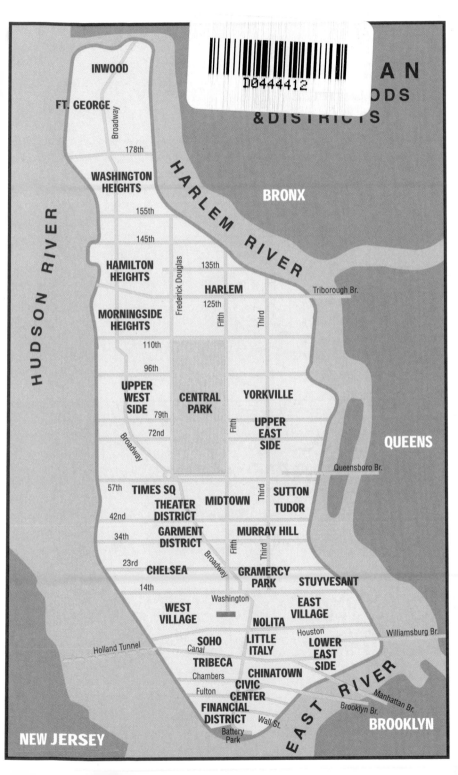

MANHATTAN NEIGHBORHOODS & DISTRICTS

INWOOD

FT. GEORGE

Broadway

178th

WASHINGTON HEIGHTS

BRONX

HARLEM RIVER

HUDSON RIVER

155th

145th

HAMILTON HEIGHTS

Frederick Douglas

135th

HARLEM

Triborough Br.

MORNINGSIDE HEIGHTS

125th

Fifth

Third

110th

96th

UPPER WEST SIDE

79th

CENTRAL PARK

YORKVILLE

Fifth

UPPER EAST SIDE

72nd

Broadway

QUEENS

Queensboro Br.

57th

TIMES SQ

THEATER DISTRICT

42nd

MIDTOWN

Third

SUTTON

TUDOR

GARMENT DISTRICT

34th

MURRAY HILL

23rd

CHELSEA

Fifth

Third

Broadway

GRAMERCY PARK

STUYVESANT

14th

WEST VILLAGE

Washington

EAST VILLAGE

NOLITA

Houston

Williamsburg Br.

SOHO

Canal

LITTLE ITALY

LOWER EAST SIDE

Holland Tunnel

TRIBECA

Chambers

CHINATOWN

CIVIC CENTER

EAST RIVER

Fulton

FINANCIAL DISTRICT

Wall St.

Manhattan Br.

Brooklyn Br.

Battery Park

BROOKLYN

NEW JERSEY

D0444412

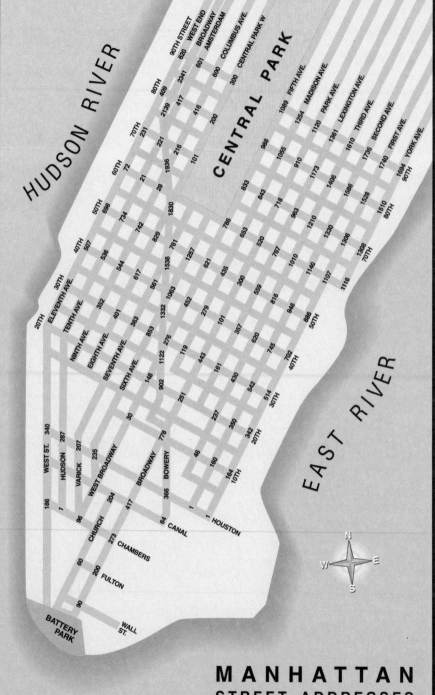

MANHATTAN
STREET ADDRESSES

GERRY FRANK'S

Where to
Find It,
Buy It,
Eat It
in
New York

GERRY FRANK'S

Where to Find It, Buy It, Eat It in New York

Gerry's Frankly Speaking, Inc.

P.O. Box 2225
Salem, OR 97308
503/585-8411
800/NYC-BOOK (800/692-2665)
Fax: 503/585-1076
E-mail: gerry@teleport.com
www.gerrysfranklyspeaking.com

Gerry Frank's Where to Find It, Buy It, Eat It in New York
Copyright (c) 1980, 1981, 1983, 1985, 1987, 1989, 1991,
1993, 1995, 1997, 1999, 2001, 2003, 2005, 2007, 2009
by Gerald W. Frank.

Printed in the United States of America
Library of Congress Catalog Card Number 80-7802

ISBN (13): 978-1-879333-20-8
ISBN (10): 1-879333-20-1

First Edition 1980
Second Edition 1981
Third Edition 1983
Fourth Edition 1985
Fifth Edition 1987
Sixth Edition 1989
Seventh Edition 1991
Eighth Edition 1993
Ninth Edition 1995
Tenth Edition 1997
Eleventh Edition 1999
Twelfth Edition 2001
Thirteenth Edition 2003
Fourteenth Edition 2005
Fifteenth Edition 2007
Sixteenth Edition 2009

No fees were paid or services rendered in exchange for inclusion in this book.

Although every effort was made to ensure that all information was accurate and up-to-date at the time of publication, neither the publisher or the author can be held responsible for any errors, omissions, or adverse consequences resulting from the use of such information.

It is recommended that you call ahead to verify the information contained in individual business listings.

Contents

III. WHERE TO FIND IT: MUSEUMS, TOURS, TICKETS, AND MORE

IV. WHERE TO FIND IT: NEW YORK'S BEST FOOD SHOPS

V. WHERE TO FIND IT: NEW YORK'S BEST SERVICES

VI. WHERE TO BUY IT: NEW YORK'S BEST STORES

VII. WHERE TO "EXTRAS"

Exclusive! Specialty Boxes

Note: You will find boxed information appearing throughout the pages of this book. These are tidbits of interesting and helpful information beyond the major write-ups. The following is a subject listing of these boxes in the order in which they appear, chapter by chapter, followed by the page number.

From the Author . . .

Dear Readers,

I've said it before and I'll say it again and again: New York is the most exciting, interesting, and diverse city in the world! Whether you're a native New Yorker, a seasoned traveler who has been here often, or someone visiting the city for the very first time, New York offers boundless things to see, do, buy, and eat. That is why I wrote **Where to Find It, Buy It, Eat It in New York**.

This book has its origins in my upbringing in a family that owned department stores and my subsequent association with U.S. Senator Mark O. Hatfield, from my home state of Oregon. Our Meier & Frank department store chain had a buying office in New York, so it was my privilege and pleasure to accompany my father as a young lad on many buying trips. When I became involved in the business, I made countless solo excursions to choose inventory and further explore this exciting place so far from my Oregon roots. Alas, the family business was sold to a conglomerate, and I found myself looking for new challenges.

I helped my friend Mark Hatfield run his successful campaigns for Oregon governor, beginning a professional association and friendship that continued through two gubernatorial terms and five terms in the U.S. Senate. I followed Mark to Washington, where I became his Chief of Staff.

I loved the work but not the city, where there was no getting away from 24/7 politics. My habit was to fly home to Oregon every other weekend and head up to Manhattan on the alternate weekends. I got to know the city so well that numerous people began asking my advice about where to stay, eat, shop, and be entertained. Then someone said, "Gerry, you should write a book on New York City." The rest is history.

To say I was wet behind the ears about authoring and marketing a book is an understatement. To my way of thinking, I had a fine product but was chagrinned to learn that no one in the publishing world seemed to care! I was faced with either letting the manuscript languish in a desk drawer or publish it myself. And so I became a self-published author who has sold over a million copies of my own book. Needless to say, I am very gratified.

New Yorkers tell me that they keep the latest edition nearby to find things in their own city. I've heard variations on the line "I've lived in New York all my life and never knew about..." many, many times. New Yorkers often refer to **Where to Find It . . .** as their "bible," and what a compliment that is! It's a wonderful resource for everyday and esoteric items alike, as well as for tourists who want to hit the highlights on a short visit. You will notice the absence of some familiar restaurants and businesses in this edition. The ravages of the financial downturn have caused the demise of hundreds of Manhattan businesses. However, new businesses are taking root and many are listed in this new edition.

The changes I've seen! New York has evolved from a financially broken, seamy, and dangerous city to one that proudly holds her head high. It's been through the devastating 9/11 attack, only to rise again and be stronger than ever. Neighborhoods have been widely gentrified.

This is a personal book where I give my opinions. There is no advertising, and no one pays for a mention. Since I conceived this book—yes, I feel as though this is my baby!—some 30 years ago, it's grown and matured. I do most of my own research, but I have built a team to make it all happen. Cheryl Johnson has been with me on this project since its conception and knows more about the ins and outs of putting a book together than I do. Her husband, Jim, acts as her assistant. Linda Chase has begun with this edition as text researcher for particular chapters, along with any number of loose-end details that come her way. Parke Puterbaugh, thankfully, remains my superb editor. Talented graphic artist Nancy Chamberlain marks this 16th edition with her second **Where to Find It . . .** book cover. Tom and Carole Stinski are typesetters extraordinaire and incredibly conscientious about producing the best possible book. My executive assistant, Linda Wooters, has been with me 17 years, sustaining a friendship as well as a professional relationship. She oversees the many facets of my life, as well as helping coordinate the production of this book.

The ever-changing face of New York keeps this electric city interesting and provocative. Whether you are extremely familiar with the city or a total newcomer, I hope you will experience some "ah-ha" moments as you turn the pages. I still love New York. I hope you do, too!

Gerry Frank.

Gerry Frank

I. In and Around the World's Greatest City

GETTING TO NEW YORK

New York is a popular destination for tourists from around the world. Whether you are a first-time tourist or a regular visitor, you're in for a wonderful treat. Planes, trains, and automobiles convey about 46 million visitors a year to Manhattan.

Three major airports serve New York City, and 110 million passengers annually pass through them on 80 carriers. **LaGuardia Airport** is most frequently used for domestic flights. **John F. Kennedy International Airport** has both domestic and international flights, as does **Newark Liberty International Airport**, located across the Hudson River in New Jersey.

Area Airports

Keep these contacts handy for information on airport parking, ground transportation, driving directions to the airports, airline information, passenger paging, AirTrain, shuttles, and the lost and found department.

Kennedy (718/244-4444, www.panynj.gov/aviation/jfkframe.htm)
LaGuardia (718/533-3400, www.panynj.gov/aviation/lgaframe.htm)
Newark Liberty (973/961-6000, www.panynj.gov/aviation/
ewrframe.htm)

The most common means of traveling between these airports and Manhattan are by taxicab, shuttle bus, and car or limousine service. Ground transportation representatives at each airport are pros at recommending the best way to reach your destination. Public transportation is usually the least expensive alternative but may take the longest time; and you will have to load and unload your own luggage and may have to make one or more transfers. Shared-ride vans, such as SuperShuttle, offer door-to-door service, which may make for a lengthy trip into the city. Taxicabs are readily available, and if there are two or more in your party, can be a good deal. To forgo the chaos of taxicabs and mass transit (but pay a bit more), arrange for a private car or limousine—you'll arrive in style and have someone else schlep your luggage.

Amtrak runs in and out of Pennsylvania Station (commonly referred to as **Penn Station**), a major subway hub located beneath Madison Square Garden between 31st and 33rd streets and Seventh and Eighth avenues. While service is concentrated between Washington, D.C. and Boston on the

Acela Express, long- and short-distance trains from all across the country and some Canadian cities also stop at Penn Station.

The station is open 24/7 and tickets can be purchased anytime from the Quik-Trak machines. Hours for the staffed ticket office and checked baggage are from 5:10 a.m. until 9:40 p.m. An enclosed waiting area for ticketed Amtrak passengers is located in the middle of the main concourse. Be prepared! This is the busiest train station in North America, and it's not a place you will want to spend any more time than necessary. (Call Amtrak at 800/872-7245 or go to www.amtrak.com for fare and schedule information.)

MetroNorth commuter trains run in and out of **Grand Central Terminal**, making frequent stops along the way to destinations such as Poughkeepsie and Brewster, New York and New Haven, Connecticut. For schedule information, call 800/638-7646, go to www.mta.info/mnr, or stop by a ticket booth at Grand Central Terminal, 42nd Street at Vanderbilt Avenue.

While traveling is expensive, bus travel remains a relative bargain. In addition to Greyhound, several express bus companies operate regularly between New York City and Washington, Boston, Philadelphia, and other cities on the East Coast and beyond. Bus fares remain more economical than air or train fares. Amenities vary by operator. Some offer reserved seats, discounts for frequent riders, Wi-Fi, and TVs, but you're on your own for food and beverage. Be sure to check details carefully. Many buses depart from **Port Authority Bus Terminal** (between Eighth and Ninth avenues from 40th to 42nd streets). Among the operators: Boltbus, www.boltbus.com; DC2NY, 202/332-2691, www.dc2ny.com; Greyhound Bus, 212/971-6300, www.greyhound.com; Megabus, 877/462-6342, www.megabus.com; Neon Bus, 800/752-4841, www.neonbus.com; Peter Pan Bus, 800/343-9999, www.peterpanbus.com; and Today's Bus, 718/386-5533, www.todaysbus.com.

If you don't have to drive in New York, then don't! The fact that most New Yorkers don't own cars should tell you something. Traffic congestion, extremely aggressive drivers, unbelievably complicated on-street parking regulations—not to mention pricey towaways and parking fines—are among the reasons to avoid driving. If you must get behind the wheel, then consult a good map or use a GPS, Mapquest, or some other means to get a clear view of where you're heading. Don't forget to buckle up!

Attention Older Visitors!

If you have trouble climbing long flights of stairs, avoid the subway! Most stations have steep stairways and few have elevators. Buses, on the other hand, can kneel to ease access from the curb, and newer ones have ramps instead of stairs. By law, taxi drivers are required to help disabled passengers and cannot start the meter until passengers are safely settled.

GETTING AROUND NEW YORK

Compared to most of the world's large cities, Manhattan is much easier to navigate, mainly because it is an island and therefore relatively compact. Here are some tips on getting around:

WALKING—This is still my favorite mode of travel in the city. For one thing, the people watching is great! By walking, you will also feel less guilty about having a meal at one of the eateries along your route. Going in a north-south direction, 20 blocks are the equivalent of one mile. Most east-west blocks are much longer. Walking is fast, cheap, and the most interesting way to explore the diverse neighborhoods. If you need directions along the way, duck into a shop or ask one of New York's finest. Many New Yorkers are also willing to aid a perplexed tourist pondering a map, but exercise caution when talking with strangers.

SUBWAY—Millions of people ride the subway every day. It's relatively inexpensive, and it's the fastest way to travel between Upper and Lower Manhattan. With the MetroCard system, you can buy a single ride; a 1-, 7-, or 14-day Fun Pass; or a 30-day unlimited ride card, which is accepted on both the subway and bus systems. Cards can be purchased at subway station booths, many neighborhood merchants, and MetroCard vending machines. All machines accept credit cards and ATM/debit cards, and larger machines also accept currency. Station booths take cash only. Up to three children under 44 inches tall can ride free with a fare-paying adult on buses and subways.

Spend a bit of time familiarizing yourself with the brochure for subway routes, and don't be afraid to ask where to catch the subway and which train to take. Once in the station, listen carefully, as train numbers and stations are recited quickly and often unintelligibly. Visit MTA's Trip Planner (www.tripplanner.mta.info), an online travel itinerary service for subway, bus, and walking directions.

All Manhattan subway stations are underground, and are almost always on a corner marked by signs with a big "M" or "MTA." Although the subway system operates 24 hours a day, not all station entrances are accessible at all times or have full-time agents. Trains generally run every two to five minutes during rush hours, every five to ten minutes during midday, every five to 15 minutes in the evening, and about every 20 minutes between midnight and 6:30 a.m. As you might guess, subway cars are very crowded during rush hours, even though additional cars are often in use.

Once you've passed through the turnstiles and are inside a station, you can transfer between lines or ride for as long as you like. With a MetroCard, you can transfer for free onto a bus within two hours with the same card—or anytime you want if you're using an unlimited-ride card. Station names are printed on the walls of the stations and announced inside subway cars. Pay close attention at all times so you don't miss your stop. Subway cars usually have at least one map posted. The newest cars have strip maps that show stops along the line, with a digital readout of the upcoming stop and an announcement of the current and next stations.

The MTA has a full list of Rules of Conduct, and I'd like to add some common-sense suggestions to make your subway journey safe and pleasant:

- Don't ride late at night or very early in the morning, especially if you're alone.
- Don't enter deserted stations.
- Don't ride in an empty car. At times of low ridership, try to find the car with the conductor—usually in the middle of the train.
- Don't wear flashy jewelry.
- Don't wander around aimlessly.
- Don't stand too close to the tracks; always wait behind the yellow line.

- Don't use subway station bathrooms.
- Do stand in the designated off-hours waiting area if you're riding at an off-peak hour so you are in view of an attendant.
- Do watch your wallet or purse, particularly in crowded cars, and don't flash cash when purchasing a MetroCard or at any time.

If you have questions or problems regarding the subway or bus systems, contact the Metropolitan Transit Authority (MTA) at 718/330-1234 between 6 a.m. and 10 p.m. every day or consult the MTA website (www.mta.info). You'll find schedules, locate the nearest bus stops or subway stations, be informed of travel advisories, and determine fares. There's also an automated "plan a route" option. Follow the prompts, provide your starting and ending locations, answer a couple of questions, and bus and/or subway lines will be suggested, as well as estimated travel time.

BUSES—Buses operate above ground with bus stops at street corners. Look for a round blue sign with a white bus outline. Many are accompanied by a "Guide-A-Ride" information box with a route map and schedule. Not all stops have bus shelters. As you board a bus, double check the destination and be ready to dip your MetroCard into the farebox. If you don't have a MetroCard, deposit coins for the fare and ask the driver for a transfer to another bus. Since buses do not accept currency, be prepared to carry quarters; otherwise, you might be begging your fellow passengers for change to pay your fare. Follow the route map on the bus or check with the bus operator if you have questions about your destination. You'll have an opportunity to check out the city, as buses offer a slower ride through town.

A number of buses run on express routes with limited stops, mainly during weekday rush hours. For safety, late-night and early-morning riders can request a dropoff at non-scheduled bus stops. Many museums, attractions, and major stores include the nearest bus stops and subway lines with their address information. Maps and brochures are readily available throughout the area. Buses are wheelchair accessible and friendly to those who have problems navigating stairs.

Don't Try to Get a Cab at 5 p.m.!

As ridiculous as it sounds, the hardest time of day to catch a cab is late afternoon—right around quitting time and just before dinner. Why? Because cab drivers typically work 12-hour shifts, and 4:30 or 5 p.m. ends the day shift. If you're making early dinner reservations or need to be somewhere in late afternoon, plan accordingly.

TAXIS—All officially licensed medallion taxicabs in New York are yellow, have the words "NYC Taxi" and fare information written on the side doors, and post their medallion numbers in a box on the roof. There are many unregulated "cars for hire" (known as gypsy cabs) that are not legally allowed pickups south of 96th Street, although some will try to do so anyway. Avoid this mode of transportation as they operate by their own rules, set arbitrary rates, and you will have no recourse in case of problems.

The Taxi and Limousine Commission (TLC) has mandated that all drivers be required to accept major credit and debit cards and that cabs be equipped to process such transactions. A word of warning: scrutinize your credit card receipt before leaving a taxi. Some drivers include a tip, and uninformed passengers may add a tip on top of that, resulting in inadvertent double-tipping. If you want to register a complaint or compliment, or to report lost or found items, make note of the driver's name and medallion number and contact the Taxi and Limousine Commission at 40 Rector Street, New York, NY 10006; 212/639-9675 or 311 (locally); or www.nyc. gov/taxi.

Your first encounter with a New York taxi may be at an airport. Legitimate taxi lines form in front of most terminals; follow signs to Ground Transportation. Cab rides into Manhattan are a flat rate from Kennedy and metered fares from LaGuardia or Newark. Allow about an hour between Kennedy and anywhere in Manhattan and expect to pay about $45, plus bridge or tunnel toll and tip. A cab trip between LaGuardia and midtown will take about half an hour and cost about $30, plus bridge toll and tip. Allow as long as an hour between Newark and Manhattan and plan to pay more—as much as $70, plus a $15 surcharge and tolls. Cab fares begin at $2.50 the moment you get in, and then you're charged 40 cents for each additional unit, which is each one-fifth of a mile while traveling or each minute while stopped in traffic or at stoplights. There is also a late-evening and early-morning surcharge and a weekday evening peak-hour surcharge. Standard tipping is 15 to 20% of the price of the trip.

Enlist the aid of employees at your hotel, restaurant, or other accommodating businesses to call a cab. If you're on your own, look for the lighted middle number on the roof of the cab, which indicates availability. If the light is off, the cabbie already has a fare or is off-duty. Stand on the corner and raise your arm to flag a taxi. You may observe the creative lengths to which some New Yorkers will go to hail a cab. When giving the address or your destination to your driver, it's helpful to also provide the cross street. The familiar yellow taxis operate 24/7 and generally accommodate no more than four passengers. For safety's sake, always enter and exit curbside.

New York City Taxi and Limousine Commission's Taxi Rider's Bill of Rights

As a taxi rider, you have the right to:
- go to any destination in New York City, Westchester County, Nassau County, or Newark Airport.
- decide the route taken, be it the most direct route or one of your choice.
- a safe and courteous driver who obeys all traffic laws.
- a knowledgeable driver who speaks English and knows city geography.
- air conditioning or heat upon request.
- a noise-free trip without gratuitous horn honking or radio.
- clean, smoke- and scent-free air.
- working seatbelts for all passengers.
- a taxicab with a clean interior, exterior, and partition.
- be accompanied by a service animal.
- a driver who does not use a cell phone while driving.
- decline to tip for poor service.

CAR SERVICES—The countless number of black Lincoln Town Cars and other distinctive black sedans whizzing through Manhattan may carry a celebrity, politician, businessperson, savvy tourists, or folks headed out for a special occasion. These cars are not reserved for just the elite. Unlike the yellow taxis, for-hire car services are by reservation only and generally charge by the hour or trip. Fares are not regulated by the Taxi and Limousine Commission and vary among the many competitive companies. Be sure to agree on a price and method of payment before settling in for a ride.

To forgo the chaos of taxicabs and mass transit, arrange for a private car or limousine prior to your arrival at one of the area airports. Last-minute reservations can also be made at the ground transportation desks or self-service kiosks, but you may have to wait awhile. Your hotel concierge or bellman will also be able to arrange for a car to drive you around the city for business or pleasure or back to the airport. See the service section of this book for my recommendations.

Be Careful About Rides!
Under no circumstances should you follow someone who approaches to ask if you need a taxi or limousine. The crowd offering taxis and limousines can be quite daunting, and their offers may seem tempting if the airport is jammed; however, you'll end up paying far more than you should and will have absolutely no recourse.

DRIVING—If you're driving in or through New York City, know where you're going and have an alternate route in mind. Be patient and try to avoid the daily rush hours, the city-declared "gridlock day warning," Sunday afternoons, and holidays.

Tune in to an all-news format AM radio station, such as 1010 WINS, for timely traffic updates. Using hand-held mobile phones while driving is prohibited, and fines are levied on violators. Most streets are one-way, though there are a few crosstown two-way streets. Obey the directional signs and be aware that streets are often closed for special events or construction. Speaking of signs, pay heed to those mandating no turn on red, no parking, no honking, no turning during certain hours, and fire hydrant and crosswalk zones, or you may wind up paying steep fines. Pedestrians do not always confine their crossing to crosswalks, so keep an eye open for jaywalkers and audacious bike messengers, who often go against the traffic flow.

Hop Stop
If you know where you want to go, but aren't sure how to get there, log on to www.hopstop.com for directions to any street address in New York and New Jersey via subway, bus, or on foot and the expected cost for a taxi. This great website also includes itineraries proposed by readers and tips on where to go (and where not to go). Other cities are listed as well.

PARKING—Parking a car in Manhattan can be very costly. Hotel parking fees are sky high, if available, and empty on-street metered parking spots are rare. Before you claim a spot, look for red-and-white parking signs listing restrictions, which are located on both sides of a street. Be aware of tow-away zones; no parking, no standing, and no stopping signs; and street cleaning rules that ban parking on alternate sides of a street on certain days. Meters accept quarters—lots of them. "Muni-meters" control several parking spots and, in addition to quarters, accept the MuniCard.

Municipal and private parking garages are plentiful, and the rules are confusing. Read the fine print. Also verify rates, after-hours accessibility, and form of payment before leaving your car or keys. It's possible to search for a parking garage near your destination and compare rates by visiting www.bestparking.com. Calling 311 will yield information on parking and towed vehicles. PDAs (personal data assistants) may be of help as well.

BICYCLING—Every day an estimated 131,000 people ride bicycles to work in New York City. The city has implemented designated bicycle lanes that move in the same direction as traffic. If there is no separate lane, use extreme caution when sharing the roadway with cars and trucks. Bikes are not permitted on city buses and allowed only in the rear cars of subways (except during rush hours).

Some buildings provide bike storage, and some employers allow riders to store bikes in their offices. Avoid chaining your bike to anything (sign posts, parking meters, fences, railings, grates) except bike racks. If you do so, you may rack up a fine. Invest in a heavy-duty, theft-deterrent lock, as New York City bike thieves are notoriously quick and nimble. Wear a helmet!

Cycling Manhattan

For exercise and seeing the sights, biking is a fun mode of transportation. Places to rent bikes, helmets, and accessories are conveniently located:

Central Park Boathouse Bike Rental (Central Park, 212/517-2233, www.thecentralparkboathouse.com): for use in Central Park only

Champion Bikes (896 Amsterdam Ave, 212/662-2690): repair work

Pedal Pusher Bike Shop (1306 Second Ave, 212-288-5592, www.pedalpusherbikeshop.com): closed Tuesdays, recorded audio-guide tours

Toga Bikes (110 West End Ave, 212/799-9625; 1153 First Ave, 212/759-0002 and **Gotham Bikes** (112 West Broadway, 212/732-2453, www.togabikes.com): New York's oldest bike retailer

---

GETTING TO KNOW NEW YORK

Reference to New York can have several different meanings. The state of New York is the third most populated state in the country. The county of New York is the most populated county in New York State. New York City, consisting of all five boroughs, is the most populated city in the United States. In this book, New York City, "the city," and Manhattan are used interchangeably and all mean the same thing: the borough of Manhattan. Manhattan is one of the four New York City boroughs that are islands. The fifth borough, The Bronx, is attached to the mainland.

A Little History

Native Americans were the first known residents of this area. Italian explorer Giovanni da Verrazano (as in the Verrazano Narrows Bridge) sailed into New York Harbor in 1524 and discovered Manhattan for his French patron, King Francis I. In 1609, Henry Hudson, a trader for the Dutch East India Company, entered the harbor and navigated the river that now bears his name. The first permanent European settlement in Manhattan, a Dutch trading post called Nieuw Amsterdam, was established just a few years later at the southern tip of the island, where Battery Park is today. It's true that the Dutch East India Company bought the area from local Indians for inexpensive beads, cloth, and other trinkets, but the two sides had vastly different understandings of what the agreement meant. It was renamed New York in 1664 after the British gained control. In the early 1800s, 60,000 New Yorkers lived mainly on the southern tip of Manhattan, with the rest of the island encompassing country estates, fertile farmland, thick forests, and wilderness. New York's historical museums depict life on the island from the days before automobiles, skyscrapers, and millions of people.

John Randall, Jr. was instrumental in developing an organizational plan for New York City's undeveloped land. The system is referred to as the Randall Plan and encompasses the area from about present-day 14th Street north to 155th Street. Take a look at the map at the front of this book, and you'll see a neatly aligned north-south, east-west grid. Below 14th, many streets take off in different directions—a remnant of Manhattan's rural past. Broadway heads northwest from 14th Street. It was once a footpath and is actually one of our nation's longest streets, reaching all the way to the state capital of Albany, some 160 miles away. Though the Randall Plan proved efficient, one major drawback ultimately cost the city millions of dollars, since little space was set aside for public parks.

Key to Addresses

All Manhattan's east-west streets are numbered, as are many of its north-south avenues. In general, most avenues are one-way and alternately northbound and southbound. Most streets are one-way as well; the even-numbered ones tend to be eastbound, and the odd-numbered ones are westbound. A few major east-west thoroughfares accommodate two-way traffic.

Thanks to the Internet, MapQuest, GPS, Palm Pilots, iPhones, and other high-tech information devices, pinpointing an address in Manhattan can be a snap. Phone directories and other publications generally include cross-street information as part of an address listing. If you're stuck finding a location with only the street address, here's a reliable system that will get you in close proximity:

AVENUES—If you have a numerical address on one of the north-south avenues, drop the last number, divide the remainder by two, and add or subtract the number indicated to find the corresponding cross streets. For example, to find 620 Avenue of the Americas: 62/2 = 31 - 12 = 19th Street

Avenue A, B, C, or D .... Add 3
First Avenue .... Add 3
Second Avenue .... Add 3

Third Avenue ....Add 10
Lexington Avenue ....Add 22
Fourth Avenue/Park Avenue South ....Add 8
Park Avenue ....Add 35
Madison Avenue .... Add 26
Fifth Avenue
• addresses up to 200 ....Add 13
• between 201 and 400 ....Add 16
• between 401 and 600 ....Add 18
• between 601 and 774 ....Add 20
• between 775 and 1286 ....Subtract 18
• between 1289 and 1500 ....Add 45
• addresses up to 2000 ....Add 24
Avenue of the Americas/Sixth Avenue ......Subtract 12
Lenox Avenue/Malcolm X Boulevard ....Add 110
Seventh Avenue ....Add 12
Adam Clayton Powell, Jr. Boulevard ....Add 20
Broadway
• addresses up to 754 are below 8th Street
• between 754 and 858 ....Subtract 29
• between 859 and 958 ....Subtract 25
• addresses above 1000 ....Subtract 30
Eighth Avenue .... Add 10
Ninth Avenue ....Add 13
Columbus Avenue ....Add 60
Tenth Avenue ....Add 14
Amsterdam Avenue..Add 60
Eleventh Avenue ....Add 15
West End Avenue ....Add 60
Convent Avenue ....Add 127
St. Nicholas Avenue ....Add 110
Manhattan Avenue ....Add 100
Edgecombe Avenue ....Add 134
Fort Washington Avenue ....Add 158

Five Area Codes and 11 Digits!

The expanding use of phone lines for cell phones, computers, FAX machines, and other gadgets necessitates four area codes for Manhattan—the long-familiar 212, as well as 917, 347, and 646. New York's other four boroughs share 718 area code. Whether you're calling across the street or to Staten Island, all calls require dialing 11 digits: the numeral 1, plus the area code and phone number.

Central Park West and Riverside Drive have formulas of their own. To find the cross street for a building on Central Park West, divide the address by 10 and add 60. To find the cross street for a building on Riverside Drive up to 165th Street, divide the address by 10 and add 72.

Because certain addresses—particularly those on Fifth, Madison, and Park avenues—are thought to be prestigious, many buildings use them even if the entrances are actually on a side street. This is most common in midtown and along Fifth Avenue on the Upper East Side. So if you can't find an address, look around the corner.

CROSS STREETS—Numbered cross streets run east-west. Addresses on them are easy to find. Allow for a little variation below 23rd Street (because Madison, Eleventh, and Twelfth avenues have yet to begin) and throughout the city whenever Broadway is involved.

EAST SIDE
1 to 49 .... between Fifth Avenue and Madison Avenue
50 to 99................. between Madison Avenue and Park Avenue
100 to 149............ between Park Avenue and Lexington Avenue
150 to 199............ between Lexington Avenue and Third Avenue
200 to 299............ between Third Avenue and Second Avenue
300 to 399............ between Second Avenue and First Avenue
400 to 499............ between First Avenue and York Avenue
500 to 599............ between Avenue A and Avenue B

WEST SIDE BELOW 59th STREET
1 to 99 .... between Fifth Avenue and Avenue of the Americas
100 to 199............ between Avenue of the Americas and Seventh Avenue
200 to 299............ between Seventh Avenue and Eighth Avenue
300 to 399............ between Eighth Avenue and Ninth Avenue
400 to 499............ between Ninth Avenue and Tenth Avenue
500 to 599............ between Tenth Avenue and Eleventh Avenue
600 and up............ between Eleventh Avenue and Twelfth Avenue

WEST SIDE ABOVE 59th STREET
1 to 99 ....between Central Park West and Columbus Avenue
100 to 199.......... between Columbus Avenue and Amsterdam Avenue
200 to 299 .... between Amsterdam Avenue and West End Avenue
300 and up............ between West End Avenue and Riverside Drive

Odd-numbered addresses on east-west streets are on the north (uptown) side, while even-numbered ones are on the south (downtown) side.

Avenue Smarts

Are you looking for Fourth Avenue? It may be the shortest numbered north-south avenue in the city. Fourth Avenue lies between Astor Place and East 14th Street, where it runs into Union Square and becomes Park Avenue. Blame the railroads for the confusion.

Avenue A resembles a dotted line. What started out as Avenue A from Houston Street all the way uptown under the Randall Plan (see page 8) has undergone name changes. If you see Asser Levy Place, Sutton Place, York Avenue, and Pleasant Avenue, you'll be able to get your bearings—First Avenue is one block west.

Neighborhoods

Manhattan is composed of many diverse neighborhoods whose names and boundaries change from time to time. There are no hard and fast rules defining neighborhood borders, which are influenced by economics and demographics. Upper Manhattan refers to the area above 59th Street, which runs along the southern border of Central Park. Midtown Manhattan refers to the area between 34th and 59th streets. The West Side refers to everything west of Fifth Avenue. Likewise, the East Side refers to the area east of Fifth Avenue. Downtown and Lower Manhattan refer to everything below 14th Street. The area between midtown and downtown is made up of roughly ten neighborhoods. (The map at the front of this book is a quick guide to these areas.) I encourage you to visit as many neighborhoods as possible to experience the city's exhilarating sights, sounds, flavors, and people.

INWOOD AND WASHINGTON HEIGHTS—This racially and ethnically mixed residential neighborhood is now primarily Dominican. During the Revolutionary War, it was home to George Washington's forces. The Morris-Jumel Mansion served as Washington's headquarters. There are several beautiful parks in this northernmost section of Manhattan, including Fort Tryon Park (which boasts The Cloisters Museum and Gardens), Inwood Hill Park, and Isham Park. Other points of interest are the Dyckman House (the last remaining Dutch colonial-era farmhouse in Manhattan), Audubon Terrace, Children's Museum of the Native American, USA Track and Field Hall of Fame, and the Little Red Lighthouse (made famous in a 1940's children's book). The Dominican populace is reflected in bodegas, clubs, street vendors, food carts, and ever-audible music. Life in this area is depicted in the Broadway musical *In the Heights*.

Marble Hill is actually the northernmost neighborhood of Manhattan, but it is no longer *on* Manhattan Island, due to the construction of the Harlem River Ship Channel. For this reason, it is now considered part of The Bronx.

HARLEM—The neighborhoods of Hamilton Heights, Astor Row, Sugar Hill, East Harlem, and Central Harlem all fall within the area known as Harlem. Residents of East Harlem are predominantly Latino, and the remaining population of Harlem is mainly African-American. Harlem is known worldwide as a center of African-American music, politics, and culture. It has experienced a renaissance over time, with much to offer residents and visitors. Because of the neighborhood diversity, there are equally assorted dining, shopping, and entertainment venues. You'll find the City College of New York, Hamilton Grange, St. Nicholas Park, the impressive Museum of the City of New York, the Schomburg Center for Research in Black Culture, the world-famous Apollo Theater, the Classical Theatre of Harlem, and the Dance Theater of Harlem. Former President Bill Clinton's foundation office is located on West 125th Street. Many of our nation's notables have resided here: George and Ira Gershwin, F. Scott Fitzgerald, Thurgood Marshall, Kareem Abdul-Jabbar, Harry Houdini, and Adam Clayton Powell, Jr. (for whom a boulevard is named).

MORNINGSIDE HEIGHTS—Since the 1890s, this small and vibrant area along the Hudson River has been known as Morningside Heights. Some people now consider Morningside Heights an extension of the Upper West Side, and others refer to this area as SoHa (South of *Ha*rlem) and incorporate SoHa into their business names. Tom's Restaurant (112th and Broadway) gained notoriety from the popular *Seinfield* television series. (The exterior was shown as Monk's Cafe.) Colleges and institutions proliferate: Barnard College, Columbia University, the Manhattan School of Music, Teachers College, Cathedral Church of St. John the Divine, Riverside

Church, St. Luke's Hospital, and the Jewish Theological Seminary of America. Riverside Park stretches for four glorious miles along the river and offers abundant recreational opportunities. These include a boat marina and monuments, the most famous of which is Grant's Tomb. Check out the variety of dining options: Max SoHa (trattoria), Kitchenette (home cooking), Havana Central at the West End (classic Cuban), and the Hungarian Pastry Shop (Old World bakery).

Harlem as a destination? You bet! This area is rich in culture, history, and architecture.

The Brownstone (24 E 125th St, 212/996-7980): women's boutique with local designers

Carol's Daughter (24 W 125th St, 212/828-6757): skin-care products

Champs (208 W 125th St, 212/280-0296): sporting goods

Demolition Depot (216 E 125th St, 212/860-1138): antiques, architectural

Duke Ellington Circle (110th St at Fifth Ave): a statue of Sir Duke posed next to a concert grand piano

Grandma's Place (84 W 120th St, 212/360-6776): books and toys

Harlem Is Home Tours (917/583-4109 or 212/658-9160): walking and specialty tours highlighting music, culture, and jazz

Hats by Bunn (2283 Seventh Ave, 212/694-3593): stylish head toppers

Hue-Man Bookstore and Cafe (2319 Frederick Douglass Blvd, 212/665-7400): African-American children's books

Malcolm Shabazz Harlem Market, a.k.a. **"African Market"** (52 W 116th St, 212/987-8131): traditional crafts and textiles

Renaissance Cigar Emporium (1825 Madison Ave, 212/348-7028): walk-in humidor and private lockers

The Winery (2166 Eighth Ave, 212/222-4866): wine boutique

UPPER WEST SIDE—This is a largely residential area, crowded with ethnically and racially mixed families and children. The apartment buildings facing Central Park have long been considered some of the most desirable in the city for the breathtaking views and coveted location. This area is frequently seen on TV shows and in movies; the magnificent Dakota and Ansonia apartment buildings, as well as the area's unique restaurants and shops, have had recognizable roles.

To say there are lots of quirky and nationally known shops on the Upper West Side is an understatement. Restaurants for every taste, budget, and ethnicity abound, many of them open around the clock. Everything is accessible: banks, gyms, cleaners, museums, churches, and schools. Directly across Central Park West is the green expanse of Central Park, as well as time-honored restaurant, Tavern on the Green. Some other notable destinations are Zabar's (among my favorite gourmet shops), ABC Studios, the New-York Historical Society, and the American Museum of Natural History. Lincoln Center encompasses more than a square block and is the cultural gem of this area. Midtown Manhattan and the Upper West Side share Columbus

Circle. The Shops at Columbus Circle draw people to the Time-Warner Center for upscale shopping and award-winning dining. The vibrant Museum of Arts and Design is also a magnet.

UPPER EAST SIDE—The Upper East Side is directly east of Central Park. This is a prestigious old-money residential neighborhood with more than its share of sophisticated art museums and galleries, posh boutiques, and fine restaurants and cafes. This area has been home to the Vanderbilts, Rockefellers, Carnegies, and Kennedys, and has rightfully earned such monikers as "Millionaires Row" and the "Silk Stocking District." It is still home to expensive apartment buildings, former mansions, and foreign consulates. The cost of living continues to be among the highest in the United States, even in the current economy. Affluent luxury shoppers enjoy superb selections of fine jewelry, multi-carated baubles, furs and other high-end goods right in their tony backyard. Exclusive private schools reflect the desire for superior education (and status). Hunter College, Cornell University Medical School, New York Presbyterian Hospital, and the Mount Sinai School of Medicine all call this prominent neighborhood home.

Many chic international designers have boutiques in the area. Bloomingdale's and Barneys have been fixtures on the retail front for decades. The Upper East Side has the greatest concentration of museums and galleries in the city, including the Cooper-Hewitt National Design Museum, the Metropolitan Museum of Art, the Solomon R. Guggenheim Museum, the Whitney Museum of American Art, and the Americas Society Gallery. The Asia Society

---

New York Districts

These distinctive districts are uniquely New York City:

Crystal District—The five-block stretch of Madison Avenue between 58th and 63rd streets is home to Steuben, Swarovski, Baccarat, Daum, and Lalique.

Diamond District—Jewelers and gem-cutters are concentrated on 47th Street between Fifth Avenue and Avenue of the Americas.

Financial District (a.k.a. "Wall Street")—Banks, investment firms, and stock markets are headquartered south of City Hall down to Exchange Place. The heart is the corner of Wall and Broad streets.

Garment District—From Fifth Avenue to Ninth Avenue and between 34th and 42nd streets is the fashion center. Since the early 1900s, this has been the hub of fashion design, although much production long ago moved offshore.

Museum Mile—Some of New York's finest museums are strung along Fifth Avenue from 82nd Street to 105th Street.

Theater District—Renowned on- and off-Broadway theaters are scattered from Avenue of the Americas to Tenth Avenue between 42nd and 53rd streets.

Honorable mentions include the Flower District on Avenue of the Americas between 28th and 29th streets; a cluster of kitchen-supply stores along The Bowery, north of Delancey and Grand streets; and stylish women's shoe stores on 8th Street between Fifth Avenue and Avenue of the Americas.

is headquartered here, as is the mayor's official abode, Gracie Mansion. This is an area to stroll for fascinating architecture, celebrity spotting, and colorful window and patio gardens.

MIDTOWN—Many people associate midtown Manhattan with Times Square's convergence of bright lights and towering buildings, but there's much more. The core of midtown comprises theaters, hotels, offices, restaurants, and retailers. Famous names include Tiffany's, F.A.O. Schwarz, Saks Fifth Avenue, Macy's, Lord & Taylor, Bergdorf Goodman, and Niketown, which share the avenues with smaller stores and sidewalk vendors. Midtown landmarks worth visiting are Carnegie Hall, Rockefeller Center, St. Patrick's Cathedral, Trump Tower, the Chrysler Building, New York Public Library, Grand Central Terminal, Radio City Music Hall, and bustling Bryant Park. Closer to the East River is Turtle Bay, home to the United Nations and luxurious residences. Well-appointed and spacious environs are constructed in the Sutton Place and Beekman Place areas, with abundant greenspaces and parks. The area is alive with great restaurants, cafes, specialty eateries, and nightclubs.

CLINTON—Some folks still refer to this area as Hell's Kitchen, while others prefer the newer and more descriptive alternative Midtown West. It is no longer the dangerous and violent region of the past, but instead an upscale neighborhood of diverse residents. Many actors live here because it's close to Broadway theaters. Restaurant Row, on 46th Street, has a profusion of appealing dining options. Ethnic grocers, bakers, butchers, and other food shops coexist with offices, car dealerships, horse stables, and myriad small shops. Each day tens of thousands of people pass through the Port Authority Bus Terminal (and past the bigger-than-life statue of Jackie Gleason's TV character, bus driver Ralph Kramden) and the Lincoln Tunnel. On the west side of the Henry Hudson Parkway are passenger ship terminals, Circle Line Cruises, and the Intrepid Sea-Air-Space Museum.

MURRAY HILL AND KIPS BAY—These are primarily residential areas with essential businesses that cater to apartment complexes and institutions. Several blocks along the East River are dominated by New York University Medical Center and its associated schools, Bellevue Hospital (the oldest public hospital in America) and the Veterans Administration Medical Center. Culturally, the Morgan Library Museum and Scandinavia House— The Nordic Center in America—are of interest.

CHELSEA—Big box stores have made their mark in this largely residential multicultural neighborhood, which is noteworthy for art galleries, clothing boutiques, small hotels, rocking nightclubs, and extraordinary restaurants. The former noisy, grimy industrial buildings have morphed into luxury lofts mixed with apartment complexes. The Fashion Institute of Technology, the School of Visual Arts, and the High School of Fashion Industries are convenient to the nearby Garment District. The Chelsea Piers development and the Hudson River Park Waterfront Promenade occupy the western border of Chelsea and offer abundant recreational activities. Foodies are attracted to the Chelsea Market, which has over 20 food-related shops. The offices of TV's Food Network are also in this complex. The General Theological Seminary of the Episcopal Church, the Center for Jewish History, the Rubin Museum of Art, the Chelsea Art Museum, and the Joyce Theater also call Chelsea home. Madison Square Garden, built atop Penn Station, has been a mainstay for decades and continues to draw thousands to concerts and sporting events.

FLATIRON DISTRICT—The flatiron-shaped building on Fifth Avenue at Broadway is the inspiration for the name of this district. Over the years it has also been referred to as Ladies' Mile, the Photo District, and the Toy District. Other notable buildings are the MetLife Tower, the Woolworth Building, and the New York State Supreme Court building. Major retailers and their brightly illuminated storefronts dress up the streets, and contemporary residential condominiums have joined the scene. In the shadow of the Flatiron Building is Madison Square (not to be confused with Madison Square Garden), a landscaped park with statues. Warm-weather favorites here are the Shake Shack and outdoor concerts.

GRAMERCY—This area has long been one of the city's most elegant, with some streets that are reminiscent of old London. Gramercy Park is a small private park accessible only to key-holding tenants of apartment buildings facing the gated Eden. A few blocks away is the very public Union Square; look for the *Metronome* artwork, which is actually a timepiece. Definitely don't miss the Greenmarket, a favorite farmers market, open seasonally. Stuyvesant Town and Peter Cooper Village are very large private planned communities with multi-storied residential buildings.

A Few Words About Attire

While life is much more casual than in previous times, most New Yorkers don't wander around midtown, shop in Bloomingdale's, frequent nice restaurants, or attend the Broadway theater wearing cutoff shorts and tank tops—and neither should tourists and visitors. Moreover, a few restaurants still require a jacket and tie for men, and women are expected to wear a nice dressy outfit. Call ahead if you're uncertain of dress codes.

MEATPACKING DISTRICT—Slaughterhouses and meatpacking plants, as well as many illicit activities, used to define this area. Now this neighborhood incorporates high-end boutiques, romantic restaurants, and fascinating nightlife along its crooked streets.

GREENWICH VILLAGE—Beatniks, jazz clubs, and folk artists in the 1950s and 1960s brought Greenwich Village into the public eye. Coffeehouses, experimental theaters, underground jazz clubs, and comedy clubs are still popular, and now boutiques share the buildings. Many middle-class families reside in mid-rise apartments, 19th-century rowhouses, and family walkups. Streets are generally named rather than numbered, and the grid layout found throughout the city basically doesn't exist here. Washington Square is a well-known gathering spot, and its impressive stone arch and central water fountain are often photographed. It has also been the site of numerous riots and rallies. Families and students from New York University use the park for rest and relaxation. People play chess, checkers, or other games. Not surprisingly, the Village has been home to many artists and political figures, such as Edgar Allan Poe, Allen Ginsberg, Bob Dylan, and Abbie Hoffman.

EAST VILLAGE—Within the East Village are Alphabet City, The Bowery, St. Mark's Place, Little India, and Loisaida. Similar to Greenwich Village, the East Village proffers offbeat and colorful nightclubs, commerce, and people. Outdoor activities come to life in Tompkins Square, the East River Park (along FDR Drive), the Toyota Children's Learning Garden, and other community gardens. Cooper-Union and The Bowery Poetry Club offer a flavor of the neighborhood's past. It's not difficult to imagine Lenny Bruce as a resident. Check out the Astor Place Theater for the Blue Man Group. The East Village is also home to some notable off-Broadway productions.

SOHO—Soho offers energy and charisma. This neighborhood is named for the area South of Houston. The old buildings are embellished with cast-iron works in intricate patterns. Tourists and assertive vendors interact on the sidewalks, haggling over jewelry and souvenir pieces. Other folks patronize the eclectic mix of trendy shops, boutiques, art galleries, and eating places. Businesses stay open late to cater to the weekend and after-work crowds. Buildings are shorter and streets are narrower than uptown.

TRIBECA—Thousands of cars pass through Tribeca each day via the Holland Tunnel. The name of this neighborhood is reflected by its shape—i.e., the Triangle Below Canal Street. It has become another trendy residential neighborhood and is a favorite for on-location filming. Enjoy a tranquil respite at Washington Market Park. The Tribeca Film Center, founded by Robert DeNiro, mixes well with resident artists, local entertainment, and antique stores.

Where Is Little Italy?

Yes, it still exists—sort of. As Chinatown and Nolita expand and the few remaining Italian immigrants move elsewhere, Little Italy lives on really only for tourists. Mulberry Street (known to locals as Via San Gennaro) around Grand Street is still home to a few Italian restaurants and stores. But like the Garment District and the bookstores of Fifth Avenue, Little Italy is largely just a memory.

CHINATOWN—The periphery of Chinatown continues to creep into surrounding neighborhoods, including Little Italy, expanding this bustling area. Various dialects of Chinese are spoken freely and the street signs are bilingual. Just about any consumer product made in China (and what isn't?) is sold here. Prices are noisily negotiated in jam-packed shops along overcrowded Canal Street. Plenty of authentic restaurants and groceries can be found and tastefully enjoyed. To learn more about this culture, check out the Museum of Chinese in the Americas and the Kim Lau Memorial Arch in Chatham Square. Beware of vendors offering to sell the latest DVDs, brand-name watches, or handbags. The infamous underground economy attracts both bargain-seeking shoppers and law enforcement.

NOLITA—Short for North of Little Italy, Nolita is one of New York's smaller neighborhoods, sandwiched between Soho, Noho, and Little Italy. Vibrant restaurants, galleries, and boutiques delight residents and visitors. A longtime favorite, Ray's Restaurant and Pizzeria, is on Prince Street. The gilded figure of Puck (Shakespeare's mischievous sprite) keeps watch on the Puck Building, on Lafayette Street.

LOWER EAST SIDE—This large area encompasses the Cooperative Village and parts of The Bowery and Chinatown. Again, the perimeters change, but there are still vestiges of Jewish heritage, as demonstrated in the Lower East Side Tenement Museum and the Eldridge Street Synagogue. Other worship centers are the Hare Krishna temple, the Bialystoker Synagogue, and a mosque, which are representative of the varied immigrant populations. Some businesses are closed for Shabbat on Friday afternoon and Saturday, Sunday remains the Jewish shopping day. Visit the famous Katz's Delicatessen for a real kosher meal to experience this unique local flavor. Hip nightclubs, a wide range of new restaurants, and ever-changing fashion boutiques have replaced some of the dilapidated housing, although some of the tenements are still occupied by new arrivals to the States. The East River Park provides a long, green swath under the Williamsburg Bridge that is host to several ball fields.

LOWER MANHATTAN—The southernmost and oldest part of Manhattan includes the Financial District, the Civic Center, downtown, and Battery Park City—just about everything south of Chambers Street. From the canyons and skyscrapers of Wall Street, this area is hectic. Small family-owned shops are nestled next to major chain stores, along with intimate restaurants. Ground Zero, the emotionally moving site of the World Trade Center buildings that were destroyed in the terrorist attacks of September 11, 2001, is now burgeoning with new construction. The somber tone lingers at New York Fire Department Engine and Ladder Company 10, just south on Liberty Street. The lineup of imposing structures and museums is impressive: the Woolworth Building, the beautifully restored and landscaped City Hall, the Federal Reserve Bank, the Vietnam Veterans Memorial, the Skyscraper Museum, the Museum of the American Indian, Trinity Church, the Federal Hall National Memorial, Fraunces Tavern Museum, and the Museum of American Financial History. The South Street Seaport complex extends alongside the East River, just south of the Brooklyn Bridge. If the weather is nice, plan a stroll, walk, or bike ride over the bridge. Battery Park City is yet another planned residential area of high-rise apartment buildings whose residents are treated to fabulous views of Battery Park and Castle Clinton National Monument, the Statue of Liberty, Ellis Island, and the Staten Island Ferry.

WHAT TO EXPECT

New York is surprisingly clean and safe and much easier to navigate than most people expect. The good news is that it is remarkably livable for its size, and the crime rate has plummeted from the early 1990s. The New York Police Department has a strong 24/7 presence on the streets, on the water, and in the air. Anytime there is a gathering—and there is always something going on in the city—the NYPD is visible. Feel comfortable about approaching officers with questions about directions or anything else. A call to 911 will aid you in an emergency, while 311 (in the city) will put you in touch with the police department for non-emergency issues.

That being said, keep in mind these common sense "don'ts":
- Don't display big wads of money or flashy watches and jewelry. In fact, avoid taking them with you. Leave most of your cash and all of your valuables at home or in the hotel safe.
- Don't use ATMs when no one else is around.

- Don't leave ATMs until you've put your money in a wallet and then put the wallet in your pocket or purse.
- Don't keep your wallet in your back pocket unless it's buttoned. Better yet, carry your wallet in a front pocket, along with keys and other important items.
- Don't wear your purse slung over one shoulder. Instead, put the strap over your head and keep your purse in front of you or to the side.
- Don't doze off on the subway or bus.
- Don't jog in Central Park or anywhere else after dark.
- Don't let yourself believe that staying in "good" neighborhoods protects you from crime. The only time I was ever mugged was on Park Avenue at 62nd Street, and you can't find a better neighborhood than that!
- Don't let anybody in your hotel room, even if they claim to work for the hotel, unless you've specifically asked them to come or have checked with the front desk to verify their authenticity.
- Don't talk to strangers who try to strike up a conversation unless you're sure of their motivation.
- Don't ever leave bags unattended. If you're going to put a bag or backpack on the floor at a restaurant or bathroom stall, put your foot or a leg of your chair through the strap.
- Don't hang your purse or anything else on the back of the door in a public bathroom stall.
- Don't walk around with your mouth open, camera slung over your shoulder and map visible, while saying things like, "Gee, honey, we sure don't have buildings this tall back home!"
- Don't be afraid to cross the street if a situation doesn't feel right. Shout for help if somebody is bothering you, or approach a policeman or friendly store worker.
- Don't make eye contact with panhandlers, and *never* give them money.
- Move away from unattended packages and immediately report any suspicious items or behavior to authorities.

A final word of warning: watch where you walk. Manhattan has an incredible amount of traffic, and the struggle among cars, taxis, trucks, buses, and pedestrians is constant. It may sound silly to repeat a warning from childhood, but look both ways before stepping into the street, wherever you are.

If you're traveling with a group or family, it's always a good idea to plan a meeting place in case you get separated. If there's an emergency, call 911.

Average temperatures range from highs in the 30s and 40s in December, January, and February (snow is always a possibility) to highs in the 80s and 90s in June, July, and August (when the humidity can be daunting).

TIPPING AND OTHER EXPENSES

No doubt about it: New York can be expensive. Basic hotels can cost upwards from $200 a night. An average dinner at a respectable restaurant will run about $25 (without cocktails or wine). Theater tickets are at least $100. Look for discounts and coupons in publications, on the Internet, and through membership organizations. Elsewhere in this book you'll discover less expensive alternatives and suggestions for free events and activities.

Tipping is expected in many instances. Keep $1 bills handy, as you'll burn through them. You won't be exposing all of your cash if you keep singles separated from larger bills. An easy way to figure out the tip on a restaurant tab is to double the tax, which is 8.375%.

Tipping Guide

Airports
Skycap —$1 to $1.50 a bag (more if the bag is big or heavy)
Taxi drivers—10% to 15% of the fare

Hotels
Doorman—$1 to $2 a bag; $1 to $2 for hailing a taxi
Bellhop—$1 to $2 a bag, depending on size and weight; $1 to $2 for deliveries to your room
Concierge—$5 to $20 for special services like securing hard-to-get theater tickets and restaurant reservations
Housekeeper—$3 to $4 a night; for extra service, an additional $1 to $2
Room service attendant—15% to 18% of the bill (before taxes)
Parking valet—$2

Restaurant
Coat check—$1 an item
Maitre d'—$10 to $100 (depending on the occasion, restaurant, and level of service you wish to receive, given before being seated)
Wait staff—15% to 20% of the bill before taxes
Sommelier—15% of the wine bill
Bartender—$1 to $2 per drink, or 10% to 15% of tab
Restroom attendant—50 cents to $1 for handing you a towel or if using any products or cosmetics

---

Checklists

Planning ahead for your trip will help alleviate stress. Read the sections of this book, call ahead, and order tickets well in advance when appropriate; some activities and events are seasonal.

When traveling remember these essentials:
- a government-issued picture ID card
- student ID card, if applicable (which will earn you student discounts)
- AARP or similar identification, if you qualify for a senior discount
- medications
- tickets for travel or events
- comfortable walking shoes
- umbrella and raincoat (or warm coat, scarf, boots, and gloves)
- opera glasses, if you're heading to the theater

Most hotels provide in-room coffeemakers (with coffee), irons, and hairdryers, and they also supply small amounts of shampoo, lotion, soap, and mending kits. In-room Internet connections are frequently available, as are in-room safes. Organize your credit cards and cash before leaving the room. Use a secure pocket or money belt. Ladies, be especially mindful of your handbag and do not wear gaudy jewelry.

Carry a small bag or tote with these daily essentials:
- cellular phone (some may have GPS capability)

- address and phone numbers of places you plan to visit and directions to get there
- maps of the bus and subway systems with an unlimited-use MetroCard
- tissues
- list of public bathrooms in the areas you'll be visiting
- loose change and small bills
- small notepad and pen
- weather-appropriate accessories: sunglasses, sunscreen, and water bottle or umbrella and gloves

Finally, don't forget this book!

Plan Your Day!

New York City is a big and crowded place. At times it is difficult to get around due to weather, street fairs, construction, motorcades, and the like. Plan your day before heading out. You will save a lot of time, money, and wear and tear on your feet and psyche.

II. Where to Eat It: Manhattan a la Carte

Since economic conditions are affecting almost every family in this country, how, when, and where diners go out to eat has become more important than ever. New York is no exception, as many folks in this metropolis have had to change their eating habits. That said, it is still the best restaurant city in the world!

Now more than ever, diners want value for their food dollar, no matter what their economic status. No longer are restaurants targeted just for reasons of trendiness and social standing. Inflated food and wine prices are not acceptable. Poor service, dirty surroundings, and unpleasant greetings are simply not tolerated.

I have visited thousands of New York restaurants, and I continue to eat my way around this city. My comments in this book are as up-to-date as possible and are meant to be helpful to New Yorkers and tourists alike when deciding where to go for a meal. From inexpensive to over-the-moon, there's a New York restaurant to fit your mood and budget.

These restaurant reviews, like everything in this book, reflect my opinions. Restaurants that try to inflate their standing by claiming not to take reservations for six weeks irritate me, as do those that don't pay attention to details like clean menus and spotless bathrooms. Moreover, I don't care how good the food is if the staff is uninformed or snooty. You don't need to bother patronizing these places since there are, literally, hundreds of alternatives.

An unpleasant attitude sometimes permeates Manhattan's better (read: more expensive) restaurants. Chefs have stepped out of their kitchens to become celebrities in their own right. There's nothing wrong with this, as many chefs deserve recognition! But when establishments project an attitude of doing patrons favors by allowing them to come to their "house" to eat, then they need to take another look at themselves. People come to enjoy food and shouldn't be made to feel like beggars pleading for admission to some hallowed room. Reservationists can be unpleasant. Restaurant greeters are often young ladies more interested in showing their wares than ushering diners to tables, and they're obviously in need of a session with "Miss Manners." The bottom line is that we are paying guests and we deservedly expect—especially given the prices—to be treated with warmth and consideration.

I like restaurants that emphasize quality food, good service, and reasonable prices. One of my absolutes is warm, fresh bread. The good news is that lots of restaurants exhibit all of these qualities, although "reasonable" is a relative term when it comes to New York menu prices and clearly depends on what is being served. At the right restaurant, an expensive meal is worth every penny! Some of my favorites are old-timers: restaurants that have been around for years and know how to do things to perfection. Some are newcomers striving to find a following with tapas, barbecue, or whatever the hottest trend happens to be.

The following pages include hundreds of restaurants that I consider worth your time and money. They range from casual to upscale. Before reading my recommendations, please keep the following in mind when dining in New York:

- New York dining habits are more akin to those in Europe than elsewhere in the country. Prime dinner time is 8 p.m., and many people are still eating at 10 p.m.
- Reservations matter! Make them, confirm them, honor them, and don't forget to be particularly nice to the person who takes your information.
- Dress appropriately. Like everywhere, New York is much less formal than it used to be, but several restaurants still have dress codes (see box on page 149) and many others have basic expectations of appropriate attire. Please don't wear a ballcap into any restaurant!
- *Old* doesn't necessarily mean *tired*. Some of the best restaurants in New York have been around for years. Value their longevity, and don't overlook them just because they're not trendy. Class is timeless.
- Eat where the locals eat. Explore areas like the Lower East Side and the East Village.
- Ask wine stewards and waiters for suggestions, but be wary of high-priced daily specials and don't order expensive bottled water. New York's drinking water is among the best in the country.
- Tip appropriately. A good rule of thumb is to double the tax (8.375% x 2). For really good service, tip between 20% and 25%.

In the following pages, you'll find a list of restaurants by neighborhood, as well as extensive lists of places that I think offer the best in a given food category. In addition, I've written scores of full-length reviews, beginning on page 81. Those restaurants fall into four price ranges, based on the cost of an appetizer and entrée (but not including drinks):

- Inexpensive: $15 and under per person
- Moderate: $16 to $34 per person
- Moderately expensive: $35 to $45 per person
- Expensive: $46 and up per person

If you have a particularly good or bad dining experience, don't hesitate to talk with the owner or manager. And by all means, please let me know, too, as I value the input of my readers tremendously. The same goes for suggesting your favorite restaurants.

Bon appetit!

Quick Reference Guide

Note: Restaurants are listed in this reference guide by neighborhood. The type of cuisine and the word "Sunday," if they are open on that day, follows each address.

CENTRAL PARK AREA

BLT Market (Ritz-Carlton New York, Central Park, 1430 Ave of the Americas): American, Sunday

Landmarc (Time Warner Center, 10 Columbus Circle, 3rd floor): American, Sunday

Sarabeth's (40 Central Park S): American/Continental, Sunday

South Gate (Jumeirah Essex House Hotel, 154 Central Park S): American, Sunday

Tavern on the Green (Central Park W at 67th St): Continental, Sunday

CHELSEA/WEST CHELSEA

Bobo (181 W 10th St): Contemporary French/Bistro, Sunday

Cook Shop (156 Tenth Ave): American, Sunday

Da Umberto (107 W 17th St): Italian

Del Posto (85 Tenth Ave): Italian, Sunday

Gascogne (158 Eighth Ave): French, Sunday

Klee Brasserie (200 Ninth Ave): Austrian, Sunday

La Bottega (Maritime Hotel, 88 Ninth Ave): Italian, Sunday

La Lunchonette (130 Tenth Ave): French, Sunday

Moran's Chelsea (146 Tenth Ave): American, Sunday

Porters New York (216 Seventh Ave): American, Sunday

T Salon (Chelsea Market, 75 Ninth Ave): Teahouse, Sunday

Trestle on Tenth (242 Tenth Ave): Swiss, Sunday

202 (Chelsea Market, 75 Ninth Ave): Mediterranean, Sunday

CHINATOWN

Golden Unicorn (18 East Broadway): Chinese, Sunday

EAST HARLEM

Rao's (455 E 114th St): Italian

EAST SIDE/UPPER EAST SIDE

Arabelle (Hotel Plaza Athenee, 37 E 64th St): Continental, Sunday

bar.vetro (222 E 58th St): Italian

Bistro 60 (37 E 60th St): French, Sunday

Bravo Gianni (230 E 63rd St): Italian, Sunday

Cafe Boulud (20 E 76th St): French, Sunday

Cafe d'Alsace (1695 Second Ave): Alsatian, Sunday

Cafe Sabarsky (Neue Galerie, 1048 Fifth Ave): Vietnamese, Sunday

Cucina Vivolo (138 E 74th St): Italian

Daniel (60 E 65th St): French

David Burke Townhouse (133 E 61st St): New American, Sunday

Demarchelier (50 E 86th St): French, Sunday

Elio's (1621 Second Ave): Italian, Sunday

Etats-Unis (242 E 81st St): American, Sunday

Fred's at Barneys New York (660 Madison Ave, 9th floor): American, Sunday

Geisha (33 E 61st St): Japanese
Gino (780 Lexington Ave): Italian, Sunday
Il Riccio (152 E 79th St): Italian, Sunday
Il Vagabondo (351 E 62nd St): Italian, Sunday
Jackson Hole Burgers (several locations): Burgers, Sunday
Jacques Brasserie (204 E 85th St): French, Sunday
John's Pizzeria (408 E 64th St): Italian, Sunday
King's Carriage House (251 E 82nd St): Continental, Sunday
Land Thai Kitchen (1565 Second Ave): Thai, Sunday
L'Atelier de Joël Robuchon (Four Seasons Hotel New York, 57 E 57th
  St): French, Sunday
Le Boeuf à la Mode (539 E 81st St): French
Le Refuge (166 E 82nd St): French, Sunday
Nicola's (146 E 84th St): Italian, Sunday
Our Place (1444 Third Ave): Chinese, Sunday
Paola's (Hotel Wales, 1295 Madison Ave): Italian, Sunday
Park Avenue Spring/Summer/Autumn/Winter (100 E 63rd St):
  American, Sunday
Pinocchio (1748 First Ave): Italian, Sunday
Post House (Lowell Hotel, 28 E 63rd St): Steak, Sunday
Primavera (1578 First Ave): Italian, Sunday
Sarabeth's (1295 Madison Ave): American/Continental, Sunday
Sarabeth's at the Whitney (Whitney Museum of American Art, 945
  Madison Ave): American/Continental, Sunday
Serendipity 3 (225 E 60th St): American, Sunday
Sette Mezzo (969 Lexington Ave): Italian, Sunday
Sfoglia (1402 Lexington Ave): Northern Italian, Sunday
Sistina (1555 Second Ave): Italian, Sunday
Spigolo (1561 Second Ave): Italian, Sunday
Taste (1413 Third Ave): American, Sunday
Tony's DiNapoli (1606 Second Ave): Italian, Sunday
Vinegar Factory (431 E 91st St): American, Sunday
Vivolo (140 E 74th St): Italian

EAST VILLAGE

Gyu-Kaku (34 Cooper Square): Japanese, Sunday
Hearth (403 E 12th St): American, Sunday
I Coppi (432 E 9th St): Italian, Sunday
Jack's Luxury Oyster Bar (101 Second Ave): Seafood

FLATIRON DISTRICT/GRAMERCY PARK/LOWER BROADWAY/UNION SQUARE

A Voce (41 Madison Ave): Italian, Sunday
Blue Smoke (116 E 27th St): Barbecue, Sunday
Blue Water Grill (31 Union Square W): Seafood, Sunday
City Bakery (3 W 18 St): Bakery/Cafe, Sunday
Craft (43 E 19th St): American, Sunday
Dévi (8 E 18th St): Indian, Sunday
Eleven Madison Park (11 Madison Ave): French/American
Gramercy Tavern (42 E 20th St): American, Sunday
Hill Country (30 W 26th St): Barbecue, Sunday
Irving Mill (116 E 16th St): American, Sunday
La Petite Auberge (116 Lexington Ave): French, Sunday
MetroCafe & Wine Bar (32 E 21st St): American, Sunday

Olives New York (W New York Union Square, 201 Park Ave S): Continental, Sunday
Rolf's (281 Third Ave): German, Sunday
Rosa Mexicano (9 E 18th St): Mexican, Sunday
Tabla (11 Madison Ave): Indian, Sunday
Tocqueville Restaurant (1 E 15th St): American, Sunday
Union Square Cafe (21 E 16th St): American, Sunday
Veritas (43 E 20th St): Continental, Sunday

GREENWICH VILLAGE/WEST VILLAGE

Babbo (110 Waverly Pl): Italian, Sunday
Blue Hill (75 Washington Pl): American, Sunday
Blue Ribbon Bakery (35 Downing St): American, Sunday
Cafe Cluny (284 W 12th St): French/American, Sunday
Camaje (85 MacDougal St): French, Sunday
Chez Jacqueline (72 MacDougal St): French, Sunday
Cowgirl (519 Hudson St): Southwestern, Sunday
Double Crown (316 Bowery): British Empire, Sunday
Five Points (31 Great Jones St): Mediterranean, Sunday
Gavroche (212 W 14th St): French, Sunday
Gonzo (140 W 13th St): Italian, Sunday
Good (89 Greenwich Ave): American, Sunday
Gotham Bar & Grill (12 E 12th St): American, Sunday
Il Mulino (86 W 3rd St): Italian
John's Pizzeria (278 Bleecker St): Italian, Sunday
Juice Generation (171 W 4th St): Health, Sunday
La Ripaille (605 Hudson St): French, Sunday
Le Gigot (18 Cornelia St): French, Sunday
Little Owl (90 Bedford St): New American, Sunday
Market Table (54 Carmine St): American, Sunday
Minetta Tavern (113 MacDougal St): French Bistro, Sunday
Morandi (211 Waverly Pl): Italian, Sunday
The New French (522 Hudson St): New French, Sunday
One if by Land, Two if by Sea (17 Barrow St): Continental, Sunday
Paris Commune (99 Bank St): French, Sunday
Perilla (9 Jones St): New American, Sunday
Pó (31 Cornelia St): Italian, Sunday
(The Famous) Ray's Pizza of Greenwich Village (465 Ave of the Americas): Pizza, Sunday
Rocco's Pastry Shop & Espresso Cafe (243 Bleecker St): Bakery/Cafe, Sunday
Scarpetta (355 W 14th St): Italian, Sunday
Smith's (79 MacDougal St): American
Strip House (13 E 12th St): Steak, Sunday
Tartine (253 W 11th St): Continental, Sunday
Wallsé (344 W 11th St): Austrian, Sunday
Waverly Inn & Garden (16 Bank St): Continental, Sunday

LOWER EAST SIDE

Allen & Delancey (115 Allen St): American, Sunday
Broadway East (171 East Broadway): American, Sunday
Clinton St. Baking Co. & Restaurant (4 Clinton St): American, Sunday
Freeman's (Freeman Alley): Continental, Sunday

Katz's Delicatessen (205 E Houston St): Deli, Sunday
Primehouse New York (381 Park Ave S): Steak, Sunday
Resto (111 E 29th St): Belgian, Sunday
Schiller's Liquor Bar (131 Rivington St): American, Sunday
Thor (Hotel on Rivington, 107 Rivington St): Central European, Sunday

MEATPACKING DISTRICT

Macelleria (48 Gansevoort St): Italian, Sunday
Pastis (9 Ninth Ave): French, Sunday
Spice Market (403 W 13th St): Asian, Sunday
Valbella (421 W 13th St): Northern Italian

MIDTOWN EAST

Adour Alain Ducasse (St. Regis New York, 2 E 55th St): French, Sunday
Alto (11 E 53rd St): Italian
Aquavit (65 E 55th St): Scandinavian, Sunday
Artisanal (2 Park Ave): Bistro/Brasserie, Sunday
BLT Steak (106 E 57th St): Steak
Bottega del Vino (7 E 59th St): Italian, Sunday
Brasserie (100 E 53rd St): French, Sunday
Butterfield 8 (5 E 38th St): American, Sunday
Cafe Centro (MetLife Building, 200 Park Ave): Continental
Capital Grille (Chrysler Center, 155 E 42nd St): Steak, Sunday
Chin Chin (216 E 49th St): Chinese, Sunday
Convivio (45 Tudor City Pl): Italian, Sunday
Cucina & Co. (MetLife Building, 200 Park Ave, lobby): Italian
Delegates Dining Room (United Nations, First Ave at 45th St, 4th floor): Continental
Dining Commons (City University of New York Graduate Center, 365 Fifth Ave): American
Docks Oyster Bar and Seafood Grill (633 Third Ave): Seafood, Sunday
El Parador Cafe (325 E 34th St): Mexican, Sunday
57 (Four Seasons Hotel New York, 57 E 57th St, lobby level): American, Sunday
Four Seasons (99 E 52nd St): Continental
Frank's Trattoria (371 First Ave): Italian, Sunday
Fresco by Scotto (34 E 52nd St): Italian
Grand Central Oyster Bar Restaurant (Grand Central Terminal, 42nd St at Vanderbilt Ave, lower level): Seafood
Hatsuhana (17 E 48th St and 237 Park Ave): Japanese
Il Postino (337 E 49th St): Italian, Sunday
La Grenouille (3 E 52nd St): French
Le Cirque (1 Beacon Court, 151 E 58th St): French
Le Périgord (405 E 52nd St): French, Sunday
Les Halles (411 Park Ave S): French, Sunday
Maloney & Porcelli (37 E 50th St): American, Sunday
Marchi's (251 E 31st St): Italian
The Morgan Dining Room (225 Madison Ave): New American, Sunday
Morton's of Chicago (551 Fifth Ave): Steak, Sunday
Mr. K's (570 Lexington Ave): Chinese, Sunday
Naples 45 (MetLife Building, 200 Park Ave): Italian
Palm One (837 Second Ave): Steak

Palm Too (840 Second Ave): Steak, Sunday
Park Avenue Bistro (377 Park Ave S): French
Pershing Square (90 E 42nd St): American, Sunday
Pietro's (232 E 43rd St): Italian
P.J. Clarke's (915 Third Ave): American/Bistro, Sunday
Pump Energy Food (several locations): Health, Sunday
Rare Bar & Grill (Shelburne Murray Hill Hotel, 303 Lexington Ave): American, Sunday
Ristorante Grifone (244 E 46th St): Italian
Rosa Mexicano (1063 First Ave): Mexican, Sunday
San Pietro (18 E 54th St): Italian
Sarabeth's at Lord & Taylor (424 Fifth Ave): American/Continental, Sunday
2nd Avenue Deli (162 E 33rd St): Deli, Sunday
Shun Lee Palace (155 E 55th St): Chinese, Sunday
Smith & Wollensky (797 Third Ave): Steak, Sunday
Sparks Steakhouse (210 E 46th St): Steak
Tao (42 E 58th St): Asian, Sunday
Turkish Kitchen (386 Third Ave): Turkish, Sunday
Vong (200 E 54th St): Thai, Sunday
Water Club (500 E 30th St): American, Sunday

MIDTOWN WEST

Abboccato (136 W 55th St): Italian, Sunday
Bar Americain (152 W 52nd St): American, Sunday
Beacon (25 W 56th St): American, Sunday
Ben Benson's Steak House (123 W 52nd St): Steak, Sunday
Benoit (60 W 55th St): French
Bond 45 (154 W 45th St): Italian, Sunday
Brasserie 8½ (9 W 57th St): French, Sunday
Brasserie Ruhlmann (45 Rockefeller Plaza): French, Sunday
Brooklyn Diner USA (212 W 57th St): Eclectic, Sunday
Bryant Park Grill (25 W 40th St): American/Continental, Sunday
Carmine's (200 W 44th St): Italian, Sunday
Carnegie Delicatessen and Restaurant (854 Seventh Ave): Deli, Sunday
Del Frisco's Double Eagle Steak House (McGraw-Hill Building, 1221 Ave of the Americas): Steak, Sunday
Gaby (Sofitel New York, 44 W 45th St): French, Sunday
Il Gattopardo (33 W 54th St): Italian, Sunday
Keens Steakhouse (72 W 36th St): American, Sunday
Le Bernardin (155 W 51st St): French
Mangia e Bevi (800 Ninth Ave): Italian, Sunday
McCormick & Schmick's (1285 Ave of the Americas): Seafood, Sunday
Michael's (24 W 55th St): California cuisine
Museum of Modern Art (9 W 53rd St): Continental, Sunday
Nobu 57 (40 W 57th St): Japanese, Sunday
Oceana (McGraw-Hill Building, 1221 Ave of the Americas): Seafood
Osteria del Circo (120 W 55th St): Italian, Sunday
Our Place Shanghai Tea Garden (141 E 55th St): Chinese, Sunday
Palm West Side (250 W 50th St): Steak, Sunday
Patsy's (236 W 56th St): Italian, Sunday
Pump Energy Food (40 W 55th St and 112 W 38th St): Health, Sunday

Quality Meats (57 W 58th St): New American/Steak, Sunday
Redeye Grill (890 Seventh Ave): American, Sunday
Remi (145 W 53rd St): Italian, Sunday
Round Table (Algonquin Hotel, 59 W 44th St, lobby level): American, Sunday
Rue 57 (60 W 57th St): French, Sunday
The Sea Grill (19 W 49th St): Seafood
Tony's DiNapoli (147 W 43rd St): Italian, Sunday
Trattoria dell'Arte (900 Seventh Ave): Italian, Sunday
21 Club (21 W 52nd St): American
Uncle Jack's Steakhouse (440 Ninth Ave and 44 W 56th St): Steak, Sunday
Woo Chon (10 W 36th St): Korean, Sunday

SOHO/LITTLE ITALY

Balthazar (80 Spring St): French, Sunday
Barmarche (14 Spring St): New American, Sunday
Bistro les Amis (180 Spring St): French, Sunday
Blue Ribbon Brasserie (97 Sullivan St): Eclectic, Sunday
Butter (415 Lafayette St): New American
Chinatown Brasserie (380 Lafayette St): Chinese, Sunday
Country Cafe (69 Thompson St): French/Moroccan, Sunday
Cupping Room Cafe (359 West Broadway): American, Sunday
Giorgione (307 Spring St): Italian, Sunday
Il Cortile (125 Mulberry St): Italian, Sunday
Kittichai (60 Thompson St): Thai, Sunday
Le Jardin Bistro (25 Cleveland Pl): French, Sunday
Mezzogiorno (195 Spring St): Italian, Sunday
Onieal's Grand Street (174 Grand St): Continental, Sunday
Raoul's (180 Prince St): French/Bistro, Sunday
Savore (200 Spring St): Italian, Sunday
Spring Street Natural Restaurant (62 Spring St): Health, Sunday
Woo Lae Oak Soho (148 Mercer St): Korean, Sunday

THEATER DISTRICT/TIMES SQUARE

Barbetta (321 W 46th St): Italian
Brooklyn Diner USA (155 W 43rd St): Eclectic, Sunday
db Bistro Moderne (55 W 44th St): French, Sunday
Ellen's Stardust Diner (1650 Broadway): Diner, Sunday
John's Pizzeria (260 W 44th St): Italian, Sunday
Juice Generation (644 Ninth Ave): Health, Sunday
Le Rivage (340 W 46th St): French, Sunday
Orso (322 W 46th St): Italian, Sunday
Ruby Foo's (1626 Broadway): Chinese, Sunday

TRIBECA/DOWNTOWN/FINANCIAL DISTRICT

Acappella (1 Hudson St): Italian, Sunday
Blaue Gans (139 Duane St): Austrian/German, Sunday
Bouley (163 Duane St): French/American, Sunday
Bouley Market (120 West Broadway): Deli/Bakery, Sunday
Bridge Cafe (279 Water St): American, Sunday
BrushStroke (30 Hudson St): Japanese
Capsouto Frères (451 Washington St): French, Sunday

Cercle Rouge (241 West Broadway): French, Sunday
Chanterelle (2 Harrison St): French, Sunday
Corton (239 West Broadway): French
Delmonico's (56 Beaver St): Steak
Il Bagatto (192 E 2nd St): Italian, Sunday
Landmarc (179 West Broadway): American, Sunday
Mai House (186 Franklin St): Vietnamese
MarkJoseph Steakhouse (261 Water St): Steak
Nobu New York/Nobu Next Door (105 Hudson St): Japanese, Sunday
P.J. Clarke's on the Hudson (4 World Financial Center): American/ Bistro, Sunday
Pump Energy Food (80 Pine St): Health, Sunday
Scalini Fedeli (165 Duane St): Italian
Tribeca Grill (375 Greenwich St): American, Sunday
2 West (Ritz-Carlton New York, Battery Park, 2 West St): American, Sunday
Upstairs at Bouley (130 West Broadway): Eclectic, Sunday
Walker's (16 N Moore St): Pub, Sunday

WEST SIDE/UPPER WEST SIDE/LINCOLN CENTER

Alouette (2588 Broadway): French, Sunday
Bar Boulud (1900 Broadway): French, Sunday
Big Nick's (2175 Broadway): Burgers/Pizza, Sunday
Carmine's (2450 Broadway): Italian, Sunday
'Cesca (164 W 75th St): Continental, Sunday
Eighty One (Excelsior Hotel, 45 W 81st St): Modern American, Sunday
Fairway Cafe & Steakhouse (2127 Broadway, upstairs): American, Sunday
Gabriel's Bar & Restaurant (11 W 60th St): Italian
Good Enough to Eat (483 Amsterdam Ave): American, Sunday
Jackson Hole Burgers (517 Columbus Ave): Burgers, Sunday
Jean Georges (Trump International Hotel and Tower, 1 Central Park W): Continental, Sunday
Juice Generation (117 W 72nd St and 2730 Broadway): Health, Sunday
La Boite en Bois (75 W 68th St): French, Sunday
Land Thai Kitchen (450 Amsterdam Ave): Thai, Sunday
Métisse (239 W 105th St): French, Sunday
Ocean Grill (384 Columbus Ave): Seafood, Sunday
Ouest (2315 Broadway): American, Sunday
Picholine (35 W 64th St): French Mediterranean
P.J. Clarke's at Lincoln Square (44 W 63rd St): American/Bistro, Sunday
Rosa Mexicano (61 Columbus Ave): Mexican, Sunday
Sarabeth's (423 Amsterdam Ave): American/Continental, Sunday
Shun Lee Cafe/Shun Lee West (43 W 65th St): Chinese, Sunday
Telepan (72 W 69th St): New American, Sunday

OUTSIDE MANHATTAN
Brooklyn
  Peter Luger Steak House (178 Broadway, at Driggs Ave): Steakhouse, Sunday
  River Cafe (1 Water St, foot of Brooklyn Bridge): American, Sunday
Queens
  Park Side (107-01 Corona Ave, at 51st Ave): Italian, Sunday

An Exclusive List: Hundreds of the Best Taste Treats in New York City (Eat-In and Takeout)

Antipasto bar: **Da Umberto** (107 W 17th St) and **Trattoria dell'Arte** (900 Seventh Ave)

Appetizers, gourmet: **Russ & Daughters** (179 E Houston St)

Apple crisp: **Corner Cafe & Bakery** (1645 Third Ave, 1659 Third Ave, and 2328 Broadway)

Apple ring (holidays or special order): **Lafayette** (26 Greenwich Ave)

Artichoke: **Gusto** (60 Greenwich Ave) and **La Lunchonette** (130 Tenth Ave)

Bacon: **Kitchenette** (156 Chambers St and 1272 Amsterdam Ave)

Baguettes: **Amy's Bread** (75 Ninth Ave, 250 Bleecker St, and 672 Ninth Ave)

Bakery goods, kosher: **Crumbs** (321½ Amsterdam Ave and other locations)

Banana split: **Blue Ribbon Bakery** (33 Downing St)

Baskets, gift and corporate: **Manhattan Fruitier** (105 E 29th St) and **Petrossian Cafe & Boutique** (911 Seventh Ave)

Bean curd: **Fong Inn Too** (46 Mott St)

Beef, cut to order (affordable): **Florence Meat Market** (5 Jones St)

Beef, fillet of (when available): **King's Carriage House** (251 E 82nd St)

Beef and veal (premium): **Lobel's Prime Meats** (1096 Madison Ave)

Beef Wellington: **One if by Land, Two if by Sea** (17 Barrow St)

Belgian nut squares: **Duane Park Patisserie** (179 Duane St)

Bialys: **Kossar's Bialys** (367 Grand St)

Blintzes: **Cafe Edison** (228 W 47th St) and **Veselka** (144 Second Ave)

Boeuf Bourguignon (menu special): **Country Cafe** (69 Thompson St)

Bomboloncini (fried doughnuts with fillings): **Osteria del Circo** (120 W 55th St)

Bonbons: **Teuscher Chocolates** (620 Fifth Ave and 25 E 61st St)

Bouillabaisse: **Pearl Oyster Bar** (18 Cornelia St)

Bratwurst: **Schaller & Weber** (1654 Second Ave)

Bread: **Del Posto** (85 Tenth Ave)

Bread, banana: **O Mai** (158 Ninth Ave)

Bread, chocolate cherry: **Amy's Bread** (75 Ninth Ave, 672 Ninth Ave, and 250 Bleecker St)

Bread, focaccia: **Falai Panetteria** (79 Clinton St)

Bread, garlic: **BLT Market** (Ritz-Carlton New York, 1430 Ave of the Americas)

Bread, Indian: **Dawat** (210 E 58th St)

Bread, Irish soda: **Zabar's** (2245 Broadway)

Bread, Semolina raisin fennel: **Amy's Bread** (75 Ninth Ave, 672 Ninth Ave, and 250 Bleecker St)

Bread, sourdough *boule* (small round loaf): **Silver Moon Bakery** (2740 Broadway)

Bread, whole wheat: **Dean & Deluca** (560 Broadway and 1150 Madison Ave)

Brownies: **Fat Witch Bakery** (75 Ninth Ave), **Sarabeth's** (1295 Madison Ave, 423 Amsterdam Ave, and 40 Central Park S), **Sarabeth's at the Whitney** (945 Madison Ave), and **Sarabeth's Bakery** (75 Ninth Ave)

Buns, sticky: **Amy's Bread** (75 Ninth Ave, 672 Ninth Ave, and 250 Bleecker St) and **William Greenberg Jr. Desserts** (1100 Madison Ave)

Burritos: **Benny's Burritos** (113 Greenwich Ave and 93 Ave A), **Harry's Burrito Junction** (241 Columbus Ave), and **La Esquina** (106 Kenmare St)

Cacik (homemade yogurt with diced cucumber): **Turkish Kitchen** (386 Third Ave)

Cake: **E.A.T.** (1064 Madison Ave) and **Ferrara Bakery and Cafe** (195 Grand St)

Cake, anniversary: **Luxee** (6 Clinton St)

Cake, Belgian chocolate: **King's Carriage House** (251 E 82nd St)

Cake, carrot: **Carrot Top Pastries** (3931 Broadway and 5025 Broadway)

Cake, chocolate: **Blue Ribbon** (97 Sullivan St), **Cafe Lalo** (201 W 83rd St), **Hard Rock Cafe** (1501 Broadway), **Moishe's Bakery** (115 Second Ave), **Serendipity 3** (225 E 60th St), and **Soutine Bakery** (104 W 70th St)

Cake, chocolate raspberry: **Caffe Roma** (385 Broome St)

Cake, white coconut and meringue: **Magnolia Bakery** (401 Bleecker St, 200 Columbus Ave, and 1240 Ave of the Americas)

Calzone: **Little Italy Gourmet Pizza** (55 W 45th St)

Candy, Asian: **Aji Ichiban** (167 Hester St)

Candy (butter crunch): **Mondel Chocolates** (2913 Broadway)

Candy (jelly beans): **Myzel Chocolates** (140 W 55th St)

Cannelloni: **Giambelli** (46 E 50th St) and **Piemonte Homemade Ravioli Company** (190 Grand St)

Cannolis: **De Robertis Pastry Shop & Caffe** (176 First Ave)

Caramels: **Fifth Avenue Chocolatiere** (693 Third Ave)

Casadielles (walnut- and honey-fried pastry): **El Quinto Pino** (401 W 24th St)

Cassoulet (seasonal): **L'Absinthe** (227 E 67th St), and **La Sirene** (558½ Broome St)

Caviar: **Caviar Russe** (538 Madison Ave), **Firebird** (365 W 46th St), **Petrossian Cafe & Boutique** (911 Seventh Ave), **Petrossian Restaurant** (182 W 58th St), and **Sable's Smoked Fish** (1489 Second Ave)

Caviar (best prices): **Russ & Daughters** (179 E Houston St) and **Zabar's** (2245 Broadway)

Caviar, Urbani: **Cucina & Co.** (Macy's, 151 W 34th St, cellar)

Ceviche (marinated seafood): **Rosa Mexicano** (1063 First Ave, 61 Columbus Ave, and 9 E 18th St)

Champagne: **Flute** (40 E 20th St and 205 W 54th St), **Garnet Liquor** (929 Lexington Ave), and **Gotham Wines** (2517 Broadway)

Charcuterie: **Dean & Deluca** (560 Broadway and 1150 Madison Ave) and **Irving Mill** (116 E 16th St)

Cheese, mozzarella: **Di Palo Fine Food** (200 Grand St), **Joe's Dairy** (156 Sullivan St), and **Russo's Mozzarella and Pasta** (344 E 11th St)

Cheese, ricotta: **Alleva Dairy** (188 Grand St) and **Russo's Mozzarella and Pasta** (344 E 11th St)

Cheese selection: **Dean & Deluca** (560 Broadway and 1150 Madison Ave), **Grace's Marketplace** (1237 Third Ave), **Murray's Cheese Shop** (254 Bleecker St), **Obikà Mozzarella Bar** (590 Madison Ave),

Saxelby Cheesemongers (120 Essex St), and **Zabar's** (2245 Broadway),

Cheesecake: **Corner Cafe & Bakery** (1645 Third Ave, 1659 Third Ave, and 2328 Broadway), **D'Aiuto Pastry** (405 Eighth Ave), **Mitchel London Foods** (22-A E 65th St), **S&S Cheesecake** (222 W 238th St, The Bronx), and **Two Little Red Hens** (1652 Second Ave)

Cheesecake, combination fruit: **Eileen's Special Cheesecake** (17 Cleveland Pl)

Cheesecake, ricotta: **Primavera** (1578 First Ave)

Chicken, beggar's (order in advance): **Shun Lee Palace** (155 E 55th St) and **Shun Lee West** (43 W 65th St)

Chicken, Dijon: **Zabar's** (2245 Broadway)

Chicken, fried: **Blue Ribbon Sushi** (308 W 58th St) and **Rao's** (455 E 11th St)

Chicken, grilled: **Da Nico** (164 Mulberry St)

Chicken, Indian: **Curry in a Hurry** (119 Lexington Ave) and **Pakistan Tea House** (176 Church St)

Chicken, Murray's free-roaming: sold in top-quality meat markets all over the city

Chicken, parmesan: **Il Mulino** (86 W 3rd St)

Chicken, roasted: **David Burke Townhouse** (133 E 61st St) and **Mitchel London Foods** (22-A E 65th St)

Chicken hash: **21 Club** (21 W 52nd St)

Chicken-in-a-pot: **Fine & Schapiro** (138 W 72nd St)

Chicken Kiev with foie gras sauce: **Picholine** (35 W 64th St)

Chicken salad: **China Grill** (60 W 53rd St)

Chili: **Manhattan Chili Company** (Grand Central Terminal, 42nd St at Vanderbilt Ave, lower level)

Chinese grocery market: **Kam Man** (200 Canal St)

Chocolate drinks: **MarieBelle New York** (762 Madison Ave and 484 Broome St)

Chocolate eclairs: **Patisserie Claude** (187 W 4th St)

Chocolates: **Kee's Chocolates** (80 Thompson St), **La Maison du Chocolat** (1018 Madison Ave, 30 Rockefeller Plaza, and 63 Wall St), **MarieBelle New York** (762 Madison Ave and 484 Broome St), and **Pierre Marcolini Chocolatier** (485 Park Ave)

Chorizo bocadillo (pork sausage baguette): **Bar Carrera** (175 Second Ave)

Clambake: **Clambakes by Jim Sanford** (205 W 95th St; call 212/865-8976)

Clam chowder: **Aquagrill** (210 Spring St) and **Dovetail** (103 W 77th St)

Clam chowder, New England: **Pearl Oyster Bar** (18 Cornelia St)

Clams: **Frank's Trattoria** (371 First Ave) and **Umberto's Clam House** (178 Mulberry St)

Cocas (flatbread pizzas from Catalonia): **Pipa** (ABC Carpet and Home, 38 E 19th St)

Coffee, iced: **Oren's Daily Roast** (1144 Lexington Ave and other locations)

Coffee beans: **Porto Rico Importing Company** (201 Bleecker St, 107 Thompson St, and 40½ St. Marks Pl) and **Zabar's** (2245 Broadway)

Cookies, butter: **CBK of New York** (337 E 81st St, 212/794-3383; by appointment)

Cookies, chocolate chip: **City Bakery** (3 W 18th St), **Downtown**

Cookie Co. (646/486-3585, www.downtowncookie.com), **Hampton Chutney Co.** (68 Prince St), **Jacques Torres Chocolate** (350 Hudson St), **Levain Bakery** (167 W 74th St), and **Ruby et Violette** (457 W 50th St)

Cookies, chocolate with walnuts: **Sarabeth's** (423 Amsterdam Ave, 1295 Madison Ave, and 40 Central Park S), **Sarabeth's at the Whitney** (945 Madison Ave), and **Sarabeth's Bakery** (75 Ninth Ave)

Cookies, chocolate hazelnut: **De Robertis Pastry Shop & Caffe** (176 First Ave)

Cookies, chocolate turtles: **Corner Cafe & Bakery** (1645 Third Ave, 1659 Third Ave, and 2328 Broadway)

Corn on the cob, grilled: **Cafe Habana** (17 Prince St)

Cornbread: **Moishe's Bakery** (115 Second Ave) and **107 West** (2787 Broadway)

Corned beef: **Katz's Delicatessen** (205 E Houston St)

Corned beef hash: **Carnegie Delicatessen and Restaurant** (854 Seventh Ave)

Cotton candy: **Four Seasons** (99 E 52nd St)

Crab: **Pisacane Midtown** (940 First Ave)

Crab, soft shell (seasonal): **New York Noodle Town** (28½ Bowery)

Crab cakes: **Acme Bar & Grill** (9 Great Jones St)

Crab claws, stone: **Shelly's New York** (41 W 57th St)

Cream puffs: **Choux Factory** (865 First Ave)

Crème brûlée: **Barbetta** (321 W 46th St) and **Tribeca Grill** (375 Greenwich St)

Croissants: **Almondine** (85 Water St, Brooklyn), **City Bakery** (3 W 18th St), **Le Pain Quotidien** (100 Grand St, 1131 Madison Ave, and other locations), **Patisserie Claude** (187 W 4th St), and **Rheon Cafe** (189 Spring St)

Croissants, almond: **Butterfield Market** (1114 Lexington Ave) and **Di Fiore Marquet** (15 E 12th St)

Croquettes: **Kyo Ya** (94 E 7th St) and **Tia Pol** (205 Tenth Ave)

Crudo (raw fish, Italian-style): **Esca** (402 W 43rd St)

Cupcakes: **Amy's Bread** (672 Ninth Ave, 75 Ninth Ave, and 250 Bleecker St), **Billy's Bakery** (184 Ninth Ave), **Butter Lane** (123 E 7th St), **Buttercup Bake Shop** (973 Second Ave), **Crumbs** (321½ Amsterdam Ave and other locations), **Cupcake Cafe** (545 Ninth Ave and 18 W 18th St), **Kitchenette** (1272 Amsterdam Ave), **Magnolia Bakery** (401 Bleecker St and 200 Columbus Ave), **Make My Cake** (121 St. Nicholas Ave and 2380 Adam Clayton Powell, Jr. Blvd), **Mitchel London Foods** (22-A E 65th St), **Out of the Kitchen** (420 Hudson St), **Sugar Sweet Sunshine Bakery** (126 Rivington St), and **William Greenberg Jr. Desserts** (1100 Madison Ave)

Curry: **Baluchis** (193 Spring St), **Brick Lane Curry House** (306-308 E 6th St), **Curry-Ya** (214 E 10th St), **Dhaba** (108 Lexington Ave), and **Tabla and Bread Bar** (11 Madison Ave)

Dates, piggyback: **Pipa** (ABC Carpet & Home, 38 E 19th St)

Delicatessen assortment: **Dean & Deluca** (560 Broadway and 1150 Madison Ave), **Grace's Marketplace** (1237 Third Ave), and **Zabar's** (2245 Broadway)

Dessert, chocolate: **ChikaLicious** (203 E 10th St) and **Max Brenner: Chocolate by the Bald Man** (841 Broadway and 141 Second Ave)

Dessert, frozen low-fat: **Tasti D-Lite** (1115 Lexington Ave and other locations)

Dessert, Japanese: **Kyotofu** (705 Ninth Ave)

Dessert tasting, chocolate: **Del Posto** (85 Tenth Ave)

Doughnuts: **Hearth** (403 E 12th St; seasonal), **Krispy Kreme** (1497 Third Ave and other locations), and **Sullivan Street Bakery** (533 W 47th St)

Doughnuts, whole wheat: **Cupcake Cafe** (545 Ninth Ave and 18 W 18th St)

Duck, barbecue: **Big Wong King** (67 Mott St)

Duck, Beijing: **Shun Lee Palace** (155 E 55th St)

Duck, braised: **Quatorze Bis** (323 E 79th St)

Duck, broiled: **Apple Restaurant** (17 Waverly Pl)

Duck, corned (appetizer): **wd-50** (50 Clinton St)

Duck, Peking: **Home's Kitchen** (22 E 21st St), **Our Place** (1444 Third Ave), **Peking Duck House Restaurant** (28 Mott St), **Shun Lee Palace** (155 E 55th St), and **Shun Lee West** (43 W 65th St)

Duck, roasted: **Four Seasons** (99 E 52nd St)

Duck, shepherd's pie: **Balthazar** (80 Spring St)

Duck, tea-smoked: **Grand Sichuan NY** (227 Lexington Ave and other locations)

Dumpling soup: **Shanghai Cafe** (100 Mott St)

Dumplings: **Chin Chin** (216 E 49th St), **Good Dumpling House** (214 Grand St), **Excellent Dumpling House** (111 Lafayette St), **Joe's Shanghai** (9 Pell St), and **Peking Duck House Restaurant** (28 Mott St)

Dumplings, crispy fried: **Nice Green Bo** (66 Bayard St)

Dumplings, pork and crab: **Grand Sichuan International** (229 Ninth Ave and other locations)

Dumplings, pork: **Sheng Wang** (27 Eldridge St)

Egg cream: **Carnegie Delicatessen and Restaurant** (854 Seventh Ave), **EJ's Luncheonette** (447 Amsterdam Ave and 1271 Third Ave), and **Soda Shop** (125 Chambers St)

Eggs, Alsatian *en cocotte* (baked eggs): **August** (359 Bleecker St)

Eggs, fresh Jersey: stands at 72 E 7th St (Thurs only: 7-5:30) and 1750 Second Ave

Eggs, fried duck: **Casa Mono** (52 Irving Pl)

Eggs, poached: **Blaue Gans** (139 Duane St)

Eggs, Scotch: **Myers of Keswick** (634 Hudson St)

Eggs, soft-boiled: **Le Pain Quotidien** (100 Grand St, 1131 Madison Ave, and other locations)

Empanadas: **Ruben's** (64 Fulton St, 76 Nassau St, and 149 Church St) and **Il Buco** (47 Bond St)

Escargots: **Artisanal** (2 Park Ave)

Espresso: **Caffe Dante** (79-81 MacDougal St), **Caffe Reggio** (119 MacDougal St), and **Ninth Street Espresso** (700 E 9th St)

Falafel (fried ball from chickpeas): **Alfanoose** (8 Maiden Lane), **Horus Cafe** (93 Ave B), **Sahara East** (184 First Ave), and **Taïm** (222 Waverly Pl)

Finocchiona (type of salami): **Salumeria Rosi** (283 Amsterdam Ave)

Fish, fresh: **Citarella** (1313 Third Ave, 2135 Broadway, 424 Ave of the Americas, and 461 W 125th St)

Fish, grilled: **Estiatorio Milos** (125 W 55th St)
Fish, smoked: **Russ & Daughters** (179 E Houston St) and **Barney Greengrass** (541 Amsterdam Ave)
Fish (Chilean sea bass, when available): **Cellini** (65 E 54th St)
Fish (flounder): **Soto** (357 Ave of the Americas)
Fish (halibut): **Le Bernardin** (155 W 51st St)
Fish (pickled herring): **Sable's Smoked Fish** (1489 Second Ave)
Fish (salmon fillets): **Sea Breeze Market** (541 Ninth Ave)
Fish (salmon, smoked): **Aquavit** (65 E 55th St), **Murray's Sturgeon Shop** (2429 Broadway), and **Sable's Smoked Fish** (1489 Second Ave)
Fish (sturgeon): **Barney Greengrass** (541 Amsterdam Ave) and **Sable's Smoked Fish** (1489 Second Ave)
Fish (tuna steak): **Gotham Bar & Grill** (12 E 12th St) and **Union Square Cafe** (21 E 16th St)
Fish (turbot, seasonal): **Jean Georges** (Trump International Hotel and Tower, 1 Central Park W)
Fish and chips: **A Salt & Battery** (112 Greenwich Ave), **BLT Fish and Fish Shack** (21 W 17th St), **Finnegan's Wake** (1361 First Ave), **Telephone Bar & Grill** (149 Second Ave), and **West Branch** (2178 Broadway)
Flatbreads: **Kalustyan's** (123 Lexington Ave)
Foie gras: **Balthazar** (80 Spring St), **Daniel** (60 E 65th St), **Gascogne** (158 Eighth Ave), **Le Bernardin** (155 W 51st St), **Le Périgord** (405 E 52nd St), and **Veritas** (43 E 20th St)
Fondue: **La Bonne Soupe** (48 W 55th St)
French fries: **Atomic Wings** (528 Ninth Ave), **Cafe de Bruxelles** (118 Greenwich Ave), **Cafe Loup** (105 W 13th St), **The Harrison** (355 Greenwich St; cooked in duck fat), **Market Cafe** (496 Ninth Ave), **Michael's** (24 W 55th St), **Pastis** (9 Ninth Ave), and **Petite Abeille** (466 Hudson St and other locations)
Fries, steak: **Balthazar** (80 Spring St) and **Montparnasse** (230 E 51st St)
Frites (potato fries with mayonnaise): **Pommes Frites** (123 Second Ave) and **Vol de Nuit** (148 W 4th St)
Fruit dessert plate: **Primavera** (1578 First Ave)
Game: **Da Umberto** (107 W 17th St) and **Ottomanelli & Sons** (285 Bleecker St)
Gelati: **Caffe Dante** (79-81 MacDougal St), **Ciao Bella Cafe** (27 E 92nd St), and **Il Laboratorio del Gelato** (95 Orchard St)
Gingerbread house (Christmas season only; requires one week notice): **Chez le Chef** (127 Lexington Ave)
Gnocchi, potato: **Hearth** (403 E 12th St)
Goat, roasted baby (by request): **Primavera** (1578 First Ave)
Gourmet food: **Eli's Manhattan** (1411 Third Ave), **Grace's Marketplace** (1237 Third Ave), and **Zabar's** (2245 Broadway)
Groceries, specialty: **Gourmet Garage** (453 Broome St, 301 E 64th St, 2567 Broadway, 117 Seventh Ave S, and 1245 Park Ave)
Guacamole: **Manhattan Chili Company** (Grand Central Terminal, 42nd St at Vanderbilt Ave, lower level) and **Rosa Mexicano** (1063 First Ave and other locations)
Haggis (Scottish pudding made of sheep innards): **St. Andrew's** (140 W 46th St)

Hamburgers: **Beacon** (25 W 56th St), **burger joint at Le Parker Meridien Hotel** (119 W 56th St), **Corner Bistro** (331 W 4th St), **db Bistro Moderne** (55 W 44th St), **Jackson Hole Burgers** (232 E 64th St and other locations), **Little Owl** (90 Bedford St), and **Shake Shack** (Madison Square Park and 366 Columbus Ave)

Hamburgers, Roquefort: **Burger Heaven** (9 E 53rd St)

Hamburgers (Kobe beef patties and hormone-free sirloin): **Zaitzeff** (72 Nassau St and 18 Ave B)

Hash: **BarBao** (100 W 82nd St)

Hen, Cornish: **Lorenzo and Maria's Kitchen** (1418 Third Ave)

Heros: **Italian Food Center** (186 Grand St) and **Manganaro's Hero Boy** (492 Ninth Ave)

Heros, sausage: **Manganaro Grosseria Italiana** (488 Ninth Ave)

Hominy, fried spiced: **Cook Shop** (156 Tenth Ave)

Horseradish, kosher: **The Pickle Guys** (49 Essex St)

Hot chocolate: **City Bakery** (3 W 18th St), **Jacques Torres Chocolate** (350 Hudson St and 285 Amsterdam Ave), **MarieBelle New York** (762 Madison Ave and 484 Broome St), and **Vosges Haut-Chocolat** (132 Spring St and 1100 Madison Ave)

Hot chocolate, frozen: **Serendipity 3** (225 E 60th St)

Ice cream: **Petrossian Cafe & Boutique** (911 Seventh Ave), **Petrossian Restaurant** (182 W 58th St), and **Serendipity 3** (225 E 60th St)

Ice cream, caramel: **Gramercy Tavern** (42 E 20th St)

Ice cream sundaes: **Brooklyn Diner USA** (212 W 57th St) and **Serendipity 3** (225 E 60th St)

Ice cream sundae, sesame: **Bôi** (246 E 44th St)

Indian snacks: **Lassi** (28 Greenwich Ave)

Jambalaya: **107 West** (2787 Broadway)

Juice, fresh-squeezed: **Candle Cafe** (1307 Third Ave)

Kebabs: **Ariana Afghan Kebab** (787 Ninth Ave), **Turkish Cuisine** (631 Ninth Ave), and **Turkish Kitchen** (386 Third Ave)

Knishes: **Murray's Sturgeon Shop** (2429 Broadway) and **Yonah Schimmel's Knishes** (137 E Houston St)

Kobe beef: **L'Atelier de Joël Rubuchon** (57 E 57th St)

Lamb, leg of: **Dovetail** (103 W 77th St)

Lamb, rack of: **Gotham Bar & Grill** (12 E 12th St) and **Shun Lee Palace** (155 E 55th St)

Lamb shank: **Market Table** (54 Carmine St) and **Molyvos** (871 Seventh Ave)

Lasagna: **Insieme** (777 Seventh Ave) and **Via Emilia** (47 E 21st St)

Latkes: **Just Like Mother's** (110-60 Queens Blvd, Forest Hills, Queens)

Lemonade, freshly squeezed: **Lexington Candy Shop** (1226 Lexington Ave) and **Pyramida** (401 E 78th St)

Liver, chopped: **Fischer Brothers** (230 W 72nd St) and **Sammy's Roumanian Steakhouse** (157 Chrystie St)

Liverwurst: **The Modern** (Museum of Modern Art, 9 W 53rd St)

Lobster: **Blue Ribbon Sushi** (119 Sullivan St), **Docks Oyster Bar and Seafood Grill** (633 Third Ave), and **Smith's** (79 MacDougal St)

Lobster, poached: **per se** (10 Columbus Circle)

Lobster roll: **BLT Fish & Fish Shack** (21 W 17th St) and **Pearl Oyster Bar** (18 Cornelia St)

Lollipops, cheesecake: **David Burke Townhouse** (133 E 61st St)

Macaroni and cheese: **S'mac** (345 E 12th St)

Marinara sauce: **Patsy's** (236 W 56th St)

Marshmallows: **Three Tarts** (164 Ninth Ave)

Meat (best service): **Jefferson Market** (450 Ave of the Americas)

Meat (German deli-style cold-cuts): **Schaller & Weber** (1654 Second Ave)

Meat and poultry (best prices): **Empire Purveyors** (883 First Ave)

Meatballs: **Il Gattopardo** (33 W 54th St)

Meatloaf (Sunday special): **Ouest** (2315 Broadway)

Meatloaf, bison: **Ted's Montana Grill** (110 W 51st St)

Meze (Turkish tapas-like appetizer): **Beyoglu** (1431 Third Ave)

Milkshakes: **Comfort Diner** (214 E 45th St) and **Brgr** (287 Seventh Ave)

Moussaka: **Periyali** (35 W 20th St)

Mücver (zucchini pancakes): **Turkuaz Restaurant** (2637 Broadway)

Muffins: **Between the Bread** (145 W 55th St) and **The Muffins Shop** (222 Columbus Ave)

Muffins, pear-walnut: **Soutine Bakery** (104 W 70th St)

Mushrooms, wild: **Grace's Marketplace** (1237 Third Ave)

Mussels: **Flex Mussels** (174 E 82nd St) and **Jubilee** (347 E 54th St)

Mutton chops: **Keens Steakhouse** (72 W 36th St)

Nachos: **Benny's Burritos** (113 Greenwich Ave and 93 Ave A)

Napoleons: **Ecco** (124 Chambers St)

Natural foods: **Whole Foods Market** (10 Columbus Circle and other locations)

Noodles: **Food Sing 88** (2 East Broadway), **Golden Bridge** (50 Bowery), **Je'Bon Noodle House** (15 St. Mark's Pl), **Kampuchea** (78 Rivington St), **Kelley and Ping** (127 Greene St), **Kong Kee Food** (240 Grand St), **Matsugen** (241 Church St), **Momofuku Noodle Bar** (171 First Ave), **Republic** (37 Union Sq W), **Sammy's Noodle Shop & Grill** (453 Ave of the Americas), **Sheng Wang** (27 Eldridge St), **Shun Lee Palace** (155 E 55th St), **Soba Nippon** (19 W 52nd St), and **Ten Ren's Tea Time** (79 Mott St)

Nuts: **A.L. Bazzini Co.** (339 Greenwich St)

Oatmeal: **Sarabeth's** (1295 Madison Ave, 423 Amsterdam Ave, and 40 Central Park S), and **Sarabeth's at the Whitney** (945 Madison Ave)

Olive oils: **Oliviers & Co.** (249 Bleecker St and 412 Lexington Ave)

Olives: **International Grocery** (543 Ninth Ave)

Onion rings: **Cornerstone Grill** (327 Greenwich St) and **Home Restaurant** (20 Cornelia St)

Organic ingredients: **Gusto Organics** (519 Ave of the Americas)

Oyster stew: **Grand Central Oyster Bar Restaurant** (Grand Central Terminal, 42nd St at Vanderbilt Ave, lower level)

Oysters: **Aquagrill** (210 Spring St)

Oysters, wood-roasted: **Beacon** (25 W 56th St)

Paella (saffron-flavored Spanish rice dish): **Boqueria** (53 W 19th St and 171 Spring St), **Sevilla** (62 Charles St), and **Socarrat Paella Bar** (259 W 19th St)

Pajun (Asian pancake): **Han Bat** (53 W 35th St)
Pancakes: **Clinton St. Baking Co. & Restaurant** (4 Clinton St), **Friend of a Farmer** (77 Irving Pl) and **Vinegar Factory** (431 E 91st St; weekend brunch)
Pancakes, kimchi: **Dok Suni's** (119 First Ave)
Pancakes, potato: **Rolf's** (281 Third Ave)
Pancakes, raspberry: **Veselka** (144 Second Ave)
Panini: **'ino** (21 Bedford St) and **'inoteca** (98 Rivington St)
Panna cotta: **Gramercy Tavern** (42 E 20th St) and **Union Square Cafe** (21 E 16th St)
Pasta: **Arqua** (281 Church St), **Bottino** (246 Tenth Ave), **Caffe Buon Gusto** (236 E 77th St), **Convivio** (45 Tudor City Pl), **dell'anima** (38 Eighth Ave), **Del Posto** (85 Tenth Ave), **Esca** (402 W 43rd St), **Fresco by Scotto** (34 E 52nd St), **Gabriel's Bar & Restaurant** (11 W 60th St), **Il Valentino** (330 E 56th St), **Insieme** (777 Seventh Ave), **L'Artusi** (228 W 10th St), **Paola's** (1295 Madison Ave), **Pasta Presto** (959 Second Ave), **Piano Due** (151 W 51st St), **Pinocchio** (1748 First Ave), **Remi** (145 W 53rd St), **Roberto Passon** (741 Ninth Ave), **Scarpetta** (355 W 14th St), **Teodora** (141 E 57th St), and **Todaro Bros**. (555 Second Ave)
Pasta (inexpensive): **LaMarca** (161 E 22nd St)
Pasta, angel hair: **Piemonte Homemade Ravioli Company** (190 Grand St) and **Nanni** (146 E 46th St)
Pastrami: **Artie's Delicatessen** (2290 Broadway), **Carnegie Delicatessen and Restaurant** (854 Seventh Ave), and **Katz's Delicatessen** (205 E Houston St)
Pastries: **Financier Patisserie** (3-4 World Financial Center, 62 Stone St, and 35 Cedar St)
Pastries, French: **La Bergamote** (169 Ninth Ave)
Pastries, Hungarian: **Hungarian Pastry Shop** (1030 Amsterdam Ave)
Pastries, Italian: **LaBella Ferrara Pastry** (108-110 Mulberry St) and **Rocco's Pastry Shop & Espresso Cafe** (243 Bleecker St)
Pastries, Japanese (traditional): **Minimoto Kitchoan** (608 Fifth Ave)
Paté: **Zabar's** (2245 Broadway)
Peanut butter: **Peanut Butter & Co.** (240 Sullivan St)
Pickle plate (seasonal): **Momofuku Noodle Bar** (171 First Ave)
Pickled-herring sampler: **Smörgas Chef** (53 Stone St)
Pickles (including kosher): **The Pickle Guys** (49 Essex St)
Pickles, sour or half-sour: **Russ & Daughters** (179 E Houston St)
Pie, apple: **William Greenberg Jr. Desserts** (1100 Madison Ave) and **Corner Cafe & Bakery** (1645 Third Ave, 1659 Third Ave, and 2328 Broadway)
Pie, banana cream: **Sarabeth's** (423 Amsterdam Ave, 1295 Madison Ave, and 40 Central Park S), and **Sarabeth's at the Whitney** (945 Madison Ave)
Pie, cheddar-crust apple (autumn only): **Little Pie Company** (424 W 43rd St and 107 E 42nd St, at Grand Central Terminal)
Pie, clam: **Lombardi's** (32 Spring St)
Pie, key lime: **Little Pie Company** (424 W 43rd St and 107 E 42nd St, at Grand Central Terminal) and **Union Square Cafe** (21 E 16th St)
Pie, pecan: **Magnolia Bakery** (401 Bleecker St and 200 Columbus Ave)

Pie, walnut sour-cream apple: **Little Pie Company** (424 W 43rd St and 107 E 42nd St, at Grand Central Terminal)

Pies: **E.A.T.** (1064 Madison Ave)

Pig, roast suckling: **Eleven Madison Park** (11 Madison Ave)

Pistachios: **A.L. Bazzini Co.** (339 Greenwich St)

Pizza (by the slice): **Pizza 33** (489 Third Ave)

Pizza, artichoke: **Artichoke Basille's Pizza & Brewery** (328 E 14th St) and **Di Fara Pizzeria** (1424 Ave J, Brooklyn)

Pizza, cheese: **Lombardi's** (32 Spring St)

Pizza, designer: **Paper Moon Milano** (39 E 58th St)

Pizza, gourmet: **apizz** (217 Eldridge St)

Pizza, grilled: **Gonzo** (140 W 13th St)

Pizza, Neapolitan: **Sal's & Carmine's Pizza** (2671 Broadway) and **Stromboli Pizzeria** (112 University Pl)

Pizza, sausage: **Franny's** (295 Flatbush Ave, Brooklyn)

Pizza, *stracciatella* (piled with fresh arugula): **Co.** (230 Ninth Ave)

Polenta, mushroom: **La Focaccia** (51 Bank St)

Popovers: **Popover Cafe** (551 Amsterdam Ave)

Pork, barbecue: **Big Wong King** (67 Mott St)

Pork, braised: **Daniel** (60 E 65th St)

Pork buns: **Lung Moon Bakery** (83 Mulberry St) and **Momofuku Ssäm Bar** (207 Second Ave)

Pork, European-style cured: **Salumeria Biellese** (376 Eighth Ave)

Pork belly: **Adour Alain Ducasse** (2 E 55th St)

Pork shank: **Maloney & Porcelli** (37 E 50th St)

Potato chips: **Vinegar Factory** (431 E 91st St)

Potatoes, mashed: **Mama's Food Shop** (200 E 3rd St) and **Union Square Cafe** (21 E 16th St)

Potatoes, *pecorino* (cheese from ewe's milk): **Convivio** (45 Tudor City Pl)

Pot-au-feu (boiled beef and vegetables): **Brasserie 44** (44 W 44th St), **L'Absinthe** (227 E 67th St), and **Parigot** (155 Grand St)

Preserves, homemade: **Spoon** (17 W 20th St)

Pretzels, hand-dipped chocolate: **Evelyn's Chocolates** (29 John St)

Prime rib: **Smith & Wollensky** (797 Third Ave)

Produce, fresh: **Fairway Market** (2127 Broadway and 2328 Twelfth Ave)

Prosciutto: **Salumeria Rosi** (283 Amsterdam Ave)

Pudding, rice: **Rice to Riches** (37 Spring St)

Ravioli: **Bruno Ravioli** (2204 Broadway and other locations), **Di Palo Fine Food** (200 Grand St), **Osteria del Circo** (120 W 55th St), and **Piemonte Homemade Ravioli Company** (190 Grand St)

Ravioli, foie gras: **Scarpetta** (355 W 14th St)

Ravioli, steamed Vietnamese: **Indochine** (430 Lafayette St)

Ribs: **Baby Buddha** (753 Washington St), **Brother Jimmy's BBQ** (1485 Second Ave), **RUB BBQ** (208 W 23rd St), **Ruby Foo's** (1626 Broadway), and **Sylvia's** (328 Lenox Ave)

Ribs, braised short beef: **Daniel** (60 E 65th St) and **Scarpetta** (355 W 14th St)

Rice: **Rice** (292 Elizabeth St and 115 Lexington Ave)

Rice, fried: **Ollie's Noodle Shop and Grill** (1991 Broadway and other locations)

Risotto: **Four Seasons** (99 E 52nd St) and **Risotteria** (270 Bleecker St)

Rugelach: **Margaret Palca Bakes** (191 Columbia St, Brooklyn) and **Ruthy's Cheesecake and Rugelach Bakery** (75 Ninth Ave)

Sake: **Sakagura** (211 E 43rd St)

Salad, Caesar: **Pearl Oyster Bar** (18 Cornelia St) and **Post House** (28 E 63rd St)

Salad, egg: **Murray's Sturgeon Shop** (2429 Broadway)

Salad, lobster: **Sable's Smoked Fish** (1489 Second Ave)

Salad, red beet: **Roberto Passon** (741 Ninth Ave)

Salad, seafood: **Gotham Bar & Grill** (12 E 12th St)

Salad, tuna: **Cosi Sandwich Bar** (841 Broadway and other locations), **Murray's Sturgeon Shop** (2429 Broadway), and **Todaro Bros.** (555 Second Ave)

Salad, warm white bean: **Caffe Grazie** (26 E 84th St)

Salad, whitefish: **Barney Greengrass** (541 Amsterdam Ave)

Salad bar: **Azure** (830 Third Ave) and **City Bakery** (3 W 18th St)

Salumi (Italian meat products): **Salumeria Biellese** (376-378 Eighth Ave)

Sandwich, avocado (Thursday special): **Olives** (120 Prince St)

Sandwich, bacon, lettuce, and tomato (BLT): **Di Fiore Marquet** (15 E 12th St), **Eisenberg's Sandwich Shop** (174 Fifth Ave), and **Good** (89 Greenwich Ave)

Sandwich, *bánh mì* (Vietnamese hoagie): **Nicky's Vietnamese Sandwiches** (150 E 2nd St)

Sandwich, cheese-steak: **BB Sandwich Bar** (120 W 3rd St), **Carl's Steaks** (79 Chambers St), **99 Miles to Philly** (94 Third Ave), and **Wogie's Bar & Grill** (39 Greenwich Ave)

Sandwich, chicken: **Ranch 1** (5 W 46th St and other locations)

Sandwich, Cuban: **Margon Restaurant** (136 W 46th St)

Sandwich, flatbread: **Cosi Sandwich Bar** (841 Broadway and other locations)

Sandwich, French dip: **Sandwich Planet** (534 Ninth Ave)

Sandwich, grilled cheese: **Resto** (111 E 29th St) and **Say Cheese** (649 Ninth Ave)

Sandwich, loin of pork: **Bottino** (246 Tenth Ave)

Sandwich, pastrami on rye: **Katz's Delicatessen** (205 E Houston St)

Sandwich, po' boy: **Two Boots** (42 Ave A and other locations)

Sandwich, pork: **Porchetta** (110 E 7th St)

Sandwich, pulled pork: **Hard Rock Cafe** (1501 Broadway)

Sandwich, turkey: **Viand Coffee Shop** (2130 Broadway, 300 E 86th St, 673 Madison Ave, and 1011 Madison Ave)

Sandwich, whitefish salad: **Russ & Daughters** (179 E Houston St)

Sandwiches (many varieties): **Call Cuisine** (1032 First Ave) and **'wichcraft** (555 Fifth Ave and other locations)

Sashimi: **Sakagura** (211 E 43rd St)

Sauerkraut: **Katz's Delicatessen** (205 E Houston St)

Sausage, blood: **Bar Carrera** (175 Second Ave) and **Buenos Aires** (513 E 6th St)

Sausage, freshly made (over 40 kinds; selection varies daily): **Salumeria Biellese** (376-378 Eighth Ave)

Sausage, German: **Hill Country** (30 W 26th St)

Scallops: **Le Bernardin** (155 W 51st St)

Schnecken (cinnamon yeast pastry roll-ups): **William Greenberg Jr. Desserts** (1100 Madison Ave)

Scones: **Mangia** (50 W 57th St), **The Muffins Shop** (222 Columbus Ave), and **Tea & Sympathy** (108 Greenwich Ave)

Seafood dinners: **Le Bernardin** (155 W 51st St)

Shabu-shabu (Japanese hot pot): **Swish Cafe & Shabu Shabu** (88 W 3rd St)

Shabu-shabu, foie gras (occasionally): **Masa** (10 Columbus Circle, 4th floor)

Shrimp, grilled: **Periyali** (35 W 20th St)

Sliders (mini burgers): **Little Owl** (90 Bedford St)

Smoothies: **Juice Generation** (644 Ninth Ave and other locations)

Sorbet: **La Boite en Bois** (75 W 68th St) and **La Maison du Chocolat** (1018 Madison Ave, 30 Rockefeller Plaza, and 63 Wall St; summer only)

Soufflés: **Capsouto Frères** (451 Washington St), **Gilt** (New York Palace Hotel, 455 Madison Ave), **Gordon Ramsay at the London** (151 W 54th St), and **La Grenouille** (3 E 52nd St)

Soup: **Sheng Wang** (27 Eldridge St)

Soup, black bean: **Union Square Cafe** (21 E 16th St)

Soup, chestnut and fennel (seasonally): **Picholine** (35 W 64th St)

Soup, chicken: **Brooklyn Diner USA** (212 W 57th St and 155 W 43rd St), **Bubby's** (120 Hudson St), **Carnegie Delicatessen and Restaurant** (854 Seventh Ave), and **Fred's** (Barneys New York, 660 Madison Ave)

Soup, Chinese noodle (won ton): **New Chao Chow** (111 Mott St)

Soup, duck: **Kelley and Ping** (127 Greene St)

Soup, French onion: **Casanis** (81 Ludlow St), **La Bonne Soupe** (48 W 55th St), and **Le Singe Vert** (160 Seventh Ave)

Soup, hot and sour: **Shun Lee Cafe** (43 W 65th St)

Soup, hot yogurt (special): **Beyoglu** (1431 Third Ave)

Soup, *kimchi chigae* (spicy stew with beef, tofu, and pork): **Do Hwa** (55 Carmine St)

Soup, matzoh ball: **Blue Ribbon Bakery** (33 Downing St) and **2nd Avenue Deli** (162 E 33rd St)

Soup, minestrone: **Il Vagabondo** (351 E 62nd St) and **Trattoria Spaghetto** (232 Bleecker St)

Soup, pumpkin (seasonal): **Mesa Grill** (102 Fifth Ave)

Soup, split pea: **Cafe Edison** (228 W 47th St) and **Joe Jr.** (167 Third Ave)

Soup, tomato: **Sarabeth's** (423 Amsterdam Ave, 1295 Madison Ave, 40 Central Park S), and **Sarabeth's at the Whitney** (945 Madison Ave)

Soybeans: **Soy** (102 Suffolk St)

Spices: **Aphrodisia** (264 Bleecker St), **International Grocery** (543 Ninth Ave), and **Kalustyan's** (123 Lexington Ave)

Spinach pies, Greek: **Poseidon Bakery** (629 Ninth Ave)

Spring rolls: **Pho Grand** (277-C Grand St)

Spring rolls, crab: **Vong** (200 E 54th St)

Squab, roasted stuffed (seasonally): **Corton** (239 West Broadway) and **Daniel** (60 E 65th St)

Steak, Cajun rib: **Morton's of Chicago** (551 Fifth Ave) and **Post House** (28 E 63rd St)

Steak, hanger: **The Harrison** (355 Greenwich St) and **South Gate** (Jumeirah Essex House, 154 Central Park S)

Steak, pepper: **Chez Josephine** (414 W 42nd St)

Steak, Porterhouse: **Morton's of Chicago** (551 Fifth Ave), **Peter Luger Steak House** (178 Broadway), and **Porters New York** (216 Seventh Ave)

Steak tartare: **21 Club** (21 W 52nd St)
Stew, *kimchi*: **Momofuku Noodle Bar** (171 First Ave)
String beans, Chinese-style: **Tang Tang** (1328 Third Ave)
Strudel: **Cafe Sabarsky** (1048 Fifth Ave, at Neue Galerie) and **The Modern** (9 W 53rd St, at Museum of Modern Art)
Sweetbreads: **Casa Mono & Bar Jamone** (52 Irving Place)
Swordfish, charbroiled: **Morton's of Chicago** (551 Fifth Ave)
Tacos: **Gabriela's** (688 Columbus Ave), **Maya** (1191 First Ave), **Mexicana Mama** (525 Hudson St), and **Rosa Mexicano** (1063 First Ave, 61 Columbus Ave, and 9 E 18th St)
Tacos, fish: **Mercadito** (179 Ave B)
Taffy, Atlantic City: **BLT Market** (1430 Ave of the Americas)
Tapas: **Bar Carrera** (175 Second Ave), **Boqueria** (53 W 19th St and 171 Spring St), **Casa Mono & Bar Jamone** (52 Irving Pl), **El Quinto Pino** (401 W 24th St), **Flor de Sol** (361 Greenwich St), **Las Ramblas** (170 W 4th St), **Ñ** (33 Crosby St), **Oliva** (161 E Houston St), **Pipa** (38 E 19th St, at ABC Carpet & Home), **Solera** (216 E 53rd St), **Tia Pol** (205 Tenth Ave), and **Xunta** (174 First Ave)
Tart, apple: **Gotham Bar & Grill** (12 E 12th St), **Di Fiore Marquet** (15 E 12th St), and **Quatorze Bis** (323 E 79th St)
Tart, dessert: **Le Bernardin** (155 W 51st St)
Tart, fruit: **Ceci-Cela** (55 Spring St)
Tart, fruit and vegetable: **Once Upon a Tart** (135 Sullivan St) and **Spoon** (17 W 20th St)
Tart, lemon: **Margot Patisserie** (2109 Broadway)
Tartines: **Le Pain Quotidien** (100 Grand St, 1131 Madison Ave, and other locations)
Tartufo: **Bianca** (5 Bleecker St), **Il Corallo Trattoria** (172-176 Prince St), **Il Vagabondo** (351 E 62nd St), and **Sette Mezzo** (969 Lexington Ave)
Tea, green: **Ito En** (822 Madison Ave)
Tea, loose (over 100 kinds!): **Alice's Tea Cup** (102 W 73rd St)
Tempura: **Inagiku** (111 E 49th St, at Waldorf-Astoria Hotel)
Tequila: **Dos Caminos** (373 Park Ave S, 825 Third Ave, and 475 West Broadway)
Tiramisu: **Biricchino** (260 W 29th St), **Caffe Dante** (79 MacDougal St), and **Mezzogiorno** (195 Spring St)
Tonkatsu (pork chops, Japanese-style): **Katsu-Hama** (11 E 47th St)
Torte, Sacher (special order): **Duane Park Patisserie** (179 Duane St)
Tortillas, corn: **Pure Food and Wine** (54 Irving Pl)
Tripe *alla parmigiana*: **Babbo** (110 Waverly Pl)
Vegan foods: **Whole Earth Bakery & Kitchen** (130 St. Mark's Pl)
Vegetarian items: **Hudson Falafel** (516 Hudson St), **Natural Gourmet Institute** (48 W 21st St), and **Vegetarian Paradise 2** (144 W 4th St)
Venison (seasonal): **Chanterelle** (2 Harrison St)
Waffles, Belgian: **Cafe de Bruxelles** (118 Greenwich Ave), **Le Pain Quotidien** (100 Grand St, 1131 Madison Ave, and other locations), and **Petite Abeille** (46 Hudson St and other locations)
Waffles, pumpkin: **Sarabeth's** (1295 Madison Ave, 423 Amsterdam Ave, and 40 Central Park S), **Sarabeth's at Lord & Taylor** (424 Fifth Ave), and **Sarabeth's at the Whitney** (945 Madison Ave)

Wagashi (sweet confections): **Minimoto Kitchoan** (608 Fifth Ave)
Whiskeys, malt: **SoHo Wines & Spirits** (461 West Broadway)
Wine, French: **Park Avenue Liquors** (292 Madison Ave) and **Quality House** (2 Park Ave)
Wine, German: **First Avenue Wines & Spirits** (383 First Ave)
Yogurt, frozen: **Pinkberry** (330 W 58th St)

BAGELS

Absolute Bagels (2788 Broadway)
Bagels on the Square (7 Carmine St)
BagelWorks (1229 First Ave)
Barney Greengrass (541 Amsterdam Ave)
Ess-a-Bagel (359 First Ave and 831 Third Ave)
H&H Bagels (2239 Broadway and 639 W 46th St)
H&H Midtown Bagels East (1551 Second Ave)
Lenny's (2601 Broadway)
Murray's Bagels (500 Ave of the Americas)

BARBECUE

Big Wong King (67 Mott St): Chinese style
Blue Smoke (116 E 27th St)
Bone Lick Park (75 Greenwich Ave): ribs and pork smoked over fruit woods and hickory
Brother Jimmy's BBQ (428 Amsterdam Ave and other locations): ribs, sandwiches, good sauce
Daisy May's BBQ USA (623 Eleventh Ave)
Dallas BBQ (1265 Third Ave, 27 W 72nd St, 132 Second Ave, and other locations): big and busy
Dinosaur BBQ (646 W 131st St)
Great NY Noodletown (28 Bowery St): Order a whole pig in advance.
Hill Country (30 W 26th St): live music
Kam Man (200 Canal St): Chinese barbeque
Kang Suh (1250 Broadway)
RUB BBQ (208 W 23rd St)
Shun Lee Cafe (43 W 65th St): classy Chinese
Sylvia's (328 Lenox Ave): reputation better than the food
Virgil's Real Barbecue (152 W 44th St): big, brassy, mass production
Wildwood Barbeque (225 Park Ave S): all-natural meats
Woo Chon (8-10 W 36th St): Korean

BARS FOR SENIORS

Bar Room at the Modern (Museum of Modern Art, 9 W 53rd St)
Bemelmans Bar (Carlyle Hotel, 35 E 76th St)
Blue Bar (Algonquin Hotel, 59 W 44th St)
Carnegie Club (156 W 56th St)
King Cole Bar (St. Regis New York, 2 E 55th St)

BREAKFAST

For morning meal power scenes, hotels are the preferred locations. The biggest names:

Four Seasons Hotel New York: **L'Atelier de Joël Robuchon** (57 E 57th St): excellent pancakes

Jumeirah Essex House: **South Gate** (160 Central Park S)
Le Parker Meridien Hotel: **Norma's** (118 W 57th St)
Loews Regency Hotel: **540 Park Restaurant** (540 Park Ave)
Paramount Hotel: **The Mezzanine** (235 W 46th St)
Peninsula New York Hotel: **Fives** (700 Fifth Ave)
Royalton Hotel: **Brasserie 44** (44 W 44th St)

Other restaurants serving excellent or interesting breakfasts:

Amy Ruth's (113 W 116th St)
Balthazar (80 Spring St)
Bar Breton (254 Fifth Ave)
Big Wong King (67 Mott St): Chinese breakfast
BLT Market (Ritz-Carlton New York, Central Park, 1430 Ave of the Americas)
Bouley Market (120 West Broadway)
Brasserie (100 E 53rd St)
Bubby's (120 Hudson St)
Burger Heaven (9 E 53rd St)
Cafe Cluny (284 W 12th St)
Carnegie Delicatessen and Restaurant (854 Seventh Ave)
Ceci-Cela (55 Spring St)
City Bakery (3 W 18th St)
Country (Carlton on Madison Avenue, 88 Madison Ave)
Cucina & Co. (MetLife Building, 200 Park Ave)
Dishes (48 Grand Central Station, 42nd St at Vanderbilt Ave, lower concourse)
E.A.T. (1064 Madison Ave)
EJ's Luncheonette (447 Amsterdam Ave and 1271 Third Ave)
El Malecon (764 Amsterdam Ave): Latin American breakfast
Ellen's Stardust Diner (1650 Broadway)
Fairway Market (2127 Broadway)
Falai Panetteria (79 Clinton St): early-bird crowd
Fitzer's (Fitzpatrick Manhattan Hotel, 687 Lexington Ave)
Friend of a Farmer (77 Irving Pl)
Grey Dog's Coffee (33 Carmine St and 90 University Pl)
Heartbeat (W New York Hotel, 149 E 49th St)
Katz's Delicatessen (205 E Houston St)
Kitchenette (156 Chambers St)
Michael's (24 W 55th St)
Morandi (211 Waverly Pl): Italian breakfast
New York Luncheonette (135 E 50th St)
Nice Matin (201 W 79th St)
Nios (Muse Hotel, 130 W 46th St)
NoHo Star (330 Lafayette St)
Once Upon a Tart (135 Sullivan St)
Pastis (9 Ninth Ave): haven for weekday breakfasts in the Meatpacking District
Pigalle (790 Eighth Ave)
Pink Tea Cup (42 Grove St): country breakfasts
Popover Cafe (551 Amsterdam Ave)
Rue 57 (60 W 57th St)
Sarabeth's (423 Amsterdam Ave, 1295 Madison Ave, and 40 Central

Park S), **Sarabeth's at Lord & Taylor** (424 Fifth Ave), and **Sara-beth's at the Whitney** (945 Madison Ave)
Sarabeth's Bakery (75 Ninth Ave)
Schiller's Liquor Bar (131 Rivington St)
2nd Avenue Deli (162 E 33rd St)
Soda Shop (125 Chambers St)
Tramway Coffee Shop (1143 Second Ave)
202 (75 Ninth Ave): French toast
Veselka (144 Second Ave)
Viand Coffee Shop (300 E 86th St, 673 Madison Ave, 2130 Broadway, and 1011 Madison Ave): crowded, but great value
Viet-Nam Banh Mi So 1 (369 Broome St)
Whole Foods Market (10 Columbus Circle, 250 Seventh Ave, 4 Union Square S, and 95 E Houston St)

BRUNCH

Alias (76 Clinton St)
Aquagrill (210 Spring St)
Aquavit (65 E 55th St): all-you-can-eat Swedish brunch on Sunday
Arium (31 Little W 12th St): tea salon and cafe in the Meatpacking District
Balthazar (80 Spring St)
Barney Greengrass (541 Amsterdam Ave)
Beacon (25 W 56th St)
Blue Ribbon Bakery (35 Downing St)
Cafe Habana (17 Prince St)
Cafe Lalo (201 W 83rd St)
Calle Ocho (446 Columbus Ave)
Candle 79 (154 E 79th St)
Capsouto Frères (451 Washington St)
Church Lounge (2 Ave of the Americas)
Clinton St. Baking Co. & Restaurant (4 Clinton St)
Cook Shop (156 Tenth Ave)
Cupping Room Cafe (359 West Broadway)
Danal (59 Fifth Ave): luscious French toast
David Burke Townhouse (133 E 61st St)
Five Points (31 Great Jones St)
Freeman's (Freeman Alley, off Rivington St bet Bowery and Chrystie St)
Friend of a Farmer (77 Irving Pl)
Good (89 Greenwich Ave)
Good Enough to Eat (483 Amsterdam Ave)
Isabella's (359 Columbus Ave)
Kittichai (60 Thompson St)
Klee Brasserie (200 Ninth Ave)
La Ripaille (605 Hudson St)
Morandi (211 Waverly Pl)
Nice Matin (201 W 79th St)
Odeon (145 West Broadway)
Olives New York (W New York, 201 Park Ave S)
Paris Commune (99 Bank St): bohemian West Village bistro
Park Avenue Spring/Summer/Autumn/Winter (100 E 63rd St)
Petite Abeille (466 Hudson St)
Pig 'n Whistle (922 Third Ave): traditional Irish breakfast

Popover Cafe (551 Amsterdam Ave)
Prune (54 E 1st St): inspired weekend brunch
Quantum Leap Natural Food (203 First Ave)
River Cafe (1 Water Street, Brooklyn)
Sarabeth's (1295 Madison Ave, 423 Amsterdam Ave, and 40 Central Park
   S), **Sarabeth's at Lord & Taylor** (424 Fifth Ave), and **Sarabeth's
   at the Whitney** (945 Madison Ave)
South Gate (Jumeirah Essex House, 160 Central Park S)
Spring Street Natural Restaurant (62 Spring St)
Sylvia's (328 Lenox Ave)
Tartine (253 W 11th St)
Tavern on the Green (Central Park W at 67th St): for entertaining out-
   of-town guests
Tribeca Grill (375 Greenwich St)
202 (75 Ninth Ave)
Vinegar Factory (431 E 91st St)
Wallsé (344 W 11th St)
Water Club (500 E 30th St)

BURGERS

Bar 89 (89 Mercer St)
Big Nick's (2175 Broadway): You'll love it!
BLT Burger (470 Ave of the Americas)
Blue Ribbon Bakery (35 Downing St)
Blue Smoke (116 E 27th St)
Brasserie 44 (Royalton Hotel, 44 W 44th St)
Brasserie 360 (200 E 60th St)
Brgr (287 Seventh Ave)
Burger Heaven (20 E 49th St, 536 Madison Ave, 9 E 53rd St, 291
   Madison Ave, and 804 Lexington Ave)
burger joint at Le Parker Meridien Hotel (119 W 56th St)
Burger Shoppe (30 Water St)
Burgers and Cupcakes (265 W 23rd St)
Cafe de Bruxelles (118 Greenwich Ave)
Chelsea Grill (675 Ninth Ave)
Corner Bistro (331 W 4th St)
db Bistro Moderne (City Club Hotel, 55 W 44th St)
Fanelli's Cafe (94 Prince St)
Five Guys (43 W 55th St and other locations)
5 Napkin Burger (630 Ninth Ave)
Great Jones Cafe (54 Great Jones St)
Hard Rock Cafe (1501 Broadway)
Home Restaurant (20 Cornelia St)
Irving Mill (116 E 16th St)
J.G. Melon (1291 Third Ave)
Jackson Hole Burgers (232 E 64th St, 521 Third Ave, 1611 Second Ave,
   1270 Madison Ave, and 517 Columbus Ave)
Keens Steakhouse (72 W 36th St)
Knickerbocker Bar and Grill (33 University Pl)
Little Owl (90 Bedford St)
Market Table (54 Carmine St)
McDonald's (160 Broadway): atypically classy

MetroCafe & Wine Bar (32 E 21st St)
Odeon (145 West Broadway)
Old Town Bar and Restaurant (45 E 18th St)
P.J. Clarke's (915 Third Ave)
Pastis (9 Ninth Ave)
Patroon (160 E 46th St)
Paul's Palace (131 Second Ave)
Pop Burger (58-60 Ninth Ave)
Popover Cafe (551 Amsterdam Ave)
Prime Burger Cafe (56 Ninth Ave)
Rare Bar & Grill (Shelburne Murray Hill Hotel, 303 Lexington Ave)
Resto (111 E 29th St)
Rodeo Bar (375 Third Ave)
Royale (157 Ave C)
Rue 57 (60 W 57th St)
Shake Shack (Madison Square Park and 366 Columbus Ave)
Soup Burg (1095 Lexington Ave)
Stand (24 E 12th St)
21 Club (21 W 52nd St)
Union Square Cafe (21 E 16th St)
Waverly Inn & Garden (16 Bank St)
White Horse Tavern (567 Hudson St)
Wollensky's Grill (201 E 49th St)
Zaitzeff (72 Nassau St)

CHEAP EATS

Alias (76 Clinton St)
Alouette (2588 Broadway)
Back Stage Eatery (579 Fifth Ave)
Bereket (187 E Houston St)
Beyoglu (1431 Third Ave)
Big Nick's (2175 Broadway)
Boqueria (171 Spring St)
Bouchon Bakery (10 Columbus Circle, 3rd floor)
Buddakan (75 Ninth Ave)
burger joint at Le Parker Meridien Hotel (119 W 56th St)
Cafe Cafe (470 Broome St)
Cafe de Bruxelles (118 Greenwich Ave)
Cafe Edison (Hotel Edison, 228 W 47th St)
Cafe Lalo (201 W 83rd St)
Cafe Orlin (41 St. Mark's Pl)
Cafe Riazor (245 W 16th St)
Caffe Vivaldi (32 Jones St)
Carmine's (2450 Broadway and 200 W 44th St)
Casa Adela (66 Ave C)
Casa Havana (190 Eighth Ave)
Chatham Restaurant (9 Chatham Square)
Chickpea (210 E 14th St)
City Bakery (3 W 18th St)
Corner Bistro (331 W 4th St)
Cosette (163 E 33rd St)
Cucina Stagionale (289 Bleecker St)

Cupcake Cafe (545 Ninth Ave and 18 W 18th St)
Curry & Curry (153 E 33rd St)
Dakshin Indian Bistro (1713 First Ave)
Danal (59 Fifth Ave)
David Burke at Bloomingdale's (150 E 59th St)
Degustation (239 E 5th St)
Dining Commons (City University of New York Graduate Center, 365 Fifth Ave, 8th floor)
East Village Cheese (40 Third Ave)
Edgar's Cafe (255 W 84th St)
Euzkadi (108 E 4th St)
Fatty Crab (643 Hudson St and 2170 Broadway)
First Avenue Coffee Shop (1433 First Ave)
Frank (88 Second Ave)
Frankie's Spuntino (17 Clinton St)
Go Sushi (3 Greenwich Ave)
Golden Unicorn (18 East Broadway)
Grand Sichuan International (15 Seventh Ave and other locations)
Grano Trattoria (21 Greenwich Ave)
Gray's Papaya (402 Ave of the Americas, 539 Eighth Ave, and 2090 Broadway)
Hallo Berlin (624 Tenth Ave)
Havana New York (27 W 38th St)
Home Restaurant (20 Cornelia St)
Il Bagatto (192 E 2nd St)
Ivo & Lulu (558 Broome St)
Ivy's Cafe (154 W 72nd St)
Jasmine (1619 Second Ave)
Jean Claude (137 Sullivan St)
John's Pizzeria (278 Bleecker St and other locations)
Katz's Delicatessen (205 E Houston St)
Kennedy's Restaurant (327 W 57th St)
Kitchenette (156 Chambers St)
Lil' Frankie's Pizza (19 First Ave)
Little Havana (30 Cornelia St)
Luke's Bar & Grill (1394 Third Ave)
McDonald's (160 Broadway and other locations)
Nam (110 Reade St)
107 West (2787 Broadway)
Pakistan Tea House (176 Church St)
Paul's Palace (131 Second Ave)
Peep (177 Prince St)
Pho Bang (157 Mott St)
Pigalle (790 Eighth Ave)
Pinch, Pizza by the Inch (474 Columbus Ave)
Pommes Frites (123 Second Ave)
Popover Cafe (551 Amsterdam Ave)
Pret à Manger (530 Seventh Ave and other locations)
Prime Burger (5 E 51st St)
The Redhead (349 E 13th St)
Saigon Grill (91-93 University Pl)
Sapporo (152 W 49th St)

Sau Voi Corp (101-105 Lafayette St)
Sirtaj (36 W 26th St)
The Smith (55 Third Ave)
Sosa Borella (832 Eighth Ave)
Spring Street Natural Restaurant (62 Spring St)
Supper (156 E 2nd St)
Suzie's (163 Bleecker St)
Sylvia's (328 Lenox Ave)
Tanti Baci Caffe (163 W 10th St)
Tartine (253 W 11th St)
Tavern on Jane (31 Eighth Ave)
Tea & Sympathy (108 Greenwich Ave)
Tiny's Giant Sandwich Shop (129 Rivington St)
Tossed (295 Park Ave S)
Turkish Cuisine (631 Ninth Ave)
Uncle Moe's (14 W 19th St)
Urban Roots (51 Ave A)
Vanessa's Dumpling House (118-A Eldridge St)
Veselka (144 Second Ave)
Viand Coffee Shop (300 E 86th St, 673 Madison Ave, 2130 Broadway, and 1011 Madison Ave)
'wichcraft (555 Fifth Ave and other locations)
Yakitori Totto (251 W 55th St)
Zum Schneider (107-109 Ave C)

CHEESE PLATES

Artisanal (2 Park Ave)
Chanterelle (2 Harrison St)
craftbar (900 Broadway)
Daniel (60 E 65th St)
Eleven Madison Park (11 Madison Ave)
Gramercy Tavern (42 E 20th St)
Jean Georges (Trump International Hotel and Tower, 1 Central Park W)
La Grenouille (3 E 52nd St)
Le Cirque (1 Beacon Court, 151 E 58th St)
The Morgan Dining Room (Morgan Library and Museum, 225 Madison Ave)
Osteria del Circo (120 W 55th St)
Picholine (35 W 64th St)
Solera (216 E 53rd St)
Telepan (72 W 69th St)
Wallsé (344 W 11th St)

COFFEEHOUSES

Aroma Espresso Bar (145 Greene St)
Cafe Lalo (201 W 83rd St)
Caffe Dante (79-81 MacDougal St)
Caffe Roma (385 Broome St)
City Bakery (3 W 18th St)
Cupcake Cafe (545 Ninth Ave and 18 W 18th St)
Cupping Room Cafe (359 West Broadway)
Ferrara Bakery and Cafe (195 Grand St)

French Roast (78 W 11th St and 2340 Broadway)
Hungarian Pastry Shop (1030 Amsterdam Ave)
Irving Farm Coffee Company (56 Seventh Ave)
Jack's Stir Brewed Coffee (138 W 10th St)
La Colombe Torrefaction (319 Church St)
Le Pain Quotidien (1131 Madison Ave; 38 E 19th St, at ABC Carpet Home; and other locations)
Once Upon a Tart (135 Sullivan St)
Oren's Daily Roast (1144 Lexington Ave and other locations)
Sarabeth's (1295 Madison Ave, 423 Amsterdam Ave, and 40 Central Park S), **Sarabeth's at Lord & Taylor** (424 Fifth Ave), and **Sarabeth's at the Whitney** (945 Madison Ave)
Sensuous Bean (66 W 70th St)
71 Irving Place (71 Irving Pl)
Starbucks (numerous locations)
Veselka (144 Second Ave)

DELIS AND QUICK LUNCHES

Artie's Delicatessen (2290 Broadway)
Back Stage III (807 Lexington Ave)
Balthazar (80 Spring St)
Barney Greengrass (541 Amsterdam Ave)
Ben's Kosher Deli (209 W 38th St)
Bread (20 Spring St)
Breadstix Cafe (254 Eighth Ave)
Carnegie Delicatessen and Restaurant (854 Seventh Ave)
Charles St. Food (144 Seventh Ave S)
City Market Cafe (551 Madison Ave)
Dil-E Punjab (170 Ninth Ave)
Dishes (6 E 45th St; Grand Central Terminal, 42nd St at Vanderbilt Ave; and 399 Park Ave)
E.A.T. (1064 Madison Ave)
Ess-a-Bagel (831 Third Ave and 359 First Ave)
Fine & Schapiro (138 W 72nd St)
Food Exchange (120 E 59th St)
Garden of Eden (7 E 14th St, 2780 Broadway, and 162 W 23rd St)
Grace's Marketplace (1237 Third Ave)
Juice Generation (644 Ninth Ave and other locations)
Junior's (Grand Central Terminal, 42nd St at Vanderbilt Ave, lower level)
Katz's Delicatessen (205 E Houston St)
Likitsakos Market (1174 Lexington Ave)
M&O Market (124 Thompson St)
Out of the Kitchen (420 Hudson St)
RUB BBQ (208 W 23rd St)
Samad's (2867 Broadway)
Sarabeth's (1295 Madison Ave, 423 Amsterdam Ave, and 40 Central Park S)
Sarabeth's Bakery (75 Ninth Ave)
Sarge's Deli (548 Third Ave)
Village Farm & Grocery (146 Second Ave)
Zabar's (2245 Broadway)

DESSERTS

Asiate (Mandarin Oriental New York, 80 Columbus Circle, 35th floor)
Babycakes (248 Broome St)
Bouley (120 West Broadway)
Cafe Lalo (201 W 83rd St)
Cafe Sabarsky (Neue Galerie, 1048 Fifth Ave)
ChikaLicious (203 E 10th St)
Cupcake Cafe (545 Ninth Ave and 18 W 18th St)
David Burke Townhouse (133 E 61st St)
Egg Custard King Two Cafe (271 Grand St)
Ferrara Bakery and Cafe (195 Grand St)
Gramercy Tavern (42 E 20th St)
Hearth (403 E 12th St)
Il Laboratorio del Gelato (95 Orchard St)
Jacques Torres Chocolate (350 Hudson St, 285 Amsterdam Ave, and
    66 Water St, Brooklyn)
Jean Georges (Trump International Hotel and Tower, 1 Central Park W)
Lady M Cake Boutique (41 E 78th St)
Luxee (6 Clinton St)
Magnolia Bakery (401 Bleecker St, 200 Columbus Ave, and 1240 Ave of
    the Americas)
Once Upon a Tart (135 Sullivan St)
Petrossian Restaurant (182 W 58th St)
Rocco (181 Thompson St)
Schiller's Liquor Bar (131 Rivington St)
Serendipity 3 (225 E 60th St)
202 (75 Ninth Ave)
Veniero's (342 E 11th St)
wd-50 (50 Clinton St)
Zabar's Cafe (2245 Broadway)

DIM SUM

The serving of small tea pastries called *dim sum* originated in Hong Kong and has become a delicious Chinatown institution. Although dim sum is usually eaten for brunch, some restaurants also serve it as an appetizer. Dim sum items are rolled over to your table on carts, and you simply point at whatever looks good. This eliminates the language barrier and encourages experimentation. When you're finished, the small plates you've accumulated are counted and the bill is drawn up accordingly. Here are some of the most popular dim sum dishes:

- *Cha Siu Bow* (steamed barbecued pork buns)
- *Cha Siu So* (flaky buns)
- *Chun Guen* (spring rolls)
- *Dai Tze Gau* (steamed scallop and shrimp dumplings)
- *Don Ta* (baked custard tarts)
- *Dow Sah Bow* (sweet bean paste-filled buns)
- Fancy Fans (meat-filled pot-sticker triangles)
- *Four-Color Siu Mai* (meat-and-vegetable-filled dumplings)
- *Gau Choi Gau* (pan-browned chive and shrimp dumplings)
- *Gee Cheung Fun* (steamed rice-noodle rolls)
- *Gee Yoke Go* (savory pork triangles)

- *Ha Gau* (shrimp dumplings)
- *Jow Ha Gok* (shrimp turnovers)
- *Pot Sticker Kou The* (meat-filled dumplings)
- *Satay Gai Tran* (chicken satay)
- *Siu Mai* (steamed pork dumplings)
- *Tzay Ha* (fried shrimp ball on sugarcane)

For the most authentic and delicious dim sum in New York, try these:

Chinatown Brasserie (380 Lafayette St)
Dim Sum Go Go (5 East Broadway)
Golden Unicorn (18 East Broadway): an especially fine selection
HSF (46 Bowery)
Jing Fong (20 Elizabeth St)
Mandarin Court (61 Mott St)
Oriental Garden (14 Elizabeth St)
Our Place (141 E 55th St and 1444 Third Ave)
Ping's Seafood (22 Mott St)
Ruby Foo's (1626 Broadway)
Shun Lee Cafe (43 W 65th St)

DINERS

Brooklyn Diner USA (212 W 57th St and 155 W 43rd St): outstanding
City Diner (2441 Broadway): retro-elegant
Ellen's Stardust Diner (1650 Broadway)
Empire Diner (210 Tenth Ave)
Hudson Diner (468 Hudson St)
Skylight Diner (402 W 34th St)

DINING SOLO

Some of these restaurants have dining counters, while others are tranquil and suitable for single diners:

Aquavit (65 E 55th St)
Babbo (110 Waverly Pl)
Cafe de Bruxelles (118 Greenwich Ave)
Cafe S.F.A. (Saks Fifth Avenue, 611 Fifth Ave)
Carnegie Delicatessen and Restaurant (854 Seventh Ave)
Caviar Russe (538 Madison Ave)
Chez Napoléon (365 W 50th St)
Cupcake Cafe (545 Ninth Ave and 18 W 18th St)
Elephant & Castle (68 Greenwich Ave)
Gotham Bar & Grill (12 E 12th St)
Grand Central Oyster Bar Restaurant (Grand Central Terminal, 42nd St at Vanderbilt Ave, lower level)
J.G. Melon (1291 Third Ave)
Jackson Hole Burgers (232 E 64th St, 521 Third Ave, 1611 Second Ave, 517 Columbus Ave, and 1270 Madison Ave)
Joe's Shanghai (9 Pell St)
Kitchenette (156 Chambers St)
La Bonne Soupe (48 W 55th St)
La Caridad 78 (2199 Broadway)
Naples 45 (MetLife Building, 200 Park Ave)

Pepolino (281 West Broadway)
Raoul's (180 Prince St)
Republic (37 Union Square W)
Sarabeth's (1295 Madison Ave, 423 Amsterdam Ave, 40 Central Park S),
    Sarabeth's at Lord & Taylor (424 Fifth Ave), and **Sarabeth's at**
    the Whitney (945 Madison Ave)
Trattoria dell'Arte (900 Seventh Ave)
Union Square Cafe (21 E 16th St)
Viand Coffee Shop (300 E 86th St, 673 Madison Ave, 1011 Madison Ave,
    and 2130 Broadway)

DON'T BOTHER

Too many restaurants spoil the real reasons for dining out, which is to get
a good meal in a comfortable setting at a fair price. With so many great
choices in Manhattan, why waste time and money on mediocre ones? Some
restaurants on the following list are well known and popular, but I feel you
can get better value elsewhere.

Angelo's of Mulberry Street: The portrait of President Reagan is their
    only claim to fame.
B Bar & Grill: The servers are as disinterested as you will be in the food.
Bice: very noisy, very unimpressive
BLT Prime: With its high noise level and mediocre food, it's not up to the
    standards of its sister operations, BLT Steak and BLT Fish.
Café des Artistes: The paintings remain appealing, but the beauty of the
    food has faded.
Chiam: charming in every way except the most important – the food
Cipriani Downtown: expensive journey to Italy
City Crab: The amateurish service and mediocre food are enough to make
    anyone crabby.
City Grill: big menu, big crowd, not so big taste
Crispo: The anticipation is far better than the reality.
Cru: This room has had its ups and downs, and the present operation is one
    of the downs.
Cub Room: needs a lot of mothering
Giorgio's of Gramercy: utterly unmemorable
Giovanni Venti Cinque: haughty treatment and high prices
Island Burgers and Shakes: overpraised, unattractive hole-in-the wall
Kefi: Despite considerable hype, it is very ordinary with a menu that does
    not have general appeal. Unappetizing service, too, like putting a dirty fork
    back on the table.
La Mirabelle: nice people, but tired menu and surroundings
Le Veau d'Or: Heaven help the stranger.
LUPA: very uneven in both food and service
Metrazur: The train left a long time ago!
Michael Jordan's The Steak House N.Y.C.: No slam dunk here; the
    place is grossly overhyped.
Mickey Mantle's: a strikeout
Nello: Skimpy portions, overextended menu, and exorbitant prices com-
    bine to make this Madison Avenue cafe a real ripoff.
Old Homestead: *Old* is the best description.

Perry Street: Jean-Georges Vongerichten lives upstairs, but his guests downstairs are not treated to his usual greatness in food, atmosphere, or service in this disappointingly spare room.
Philippe: expensive Chinese dishes, inexcusably bad service
Rothmann's Steakhouse & Grill: Why waste bucks at this amateurish operation?
Savoy: uncomfortably cute, unappealing plates
Shula's Steak House: A famous name on the door doesn't guarantee a great meal. The prices are ridiculous and the place is dull.
Stage Deli: This place is rather unattractive, the smell is unappealing, and the food is, in many cases, quite unacceptable.
Swifty's: unpleasant greeting, snobby atmosphere
Triomphe: small in size, value, and service
Village: uninspired cooking in an uninspired space
Wolfgang's Steakhouse: Wolfgang Zwiener (formerly of Peter Luger) now has his own place, but it doesn't quite make the grade.

EATING AT THE BAR OR PUB

Aquagrill (210 Spring St)
Babbo (110 Waverly Pl)
Bar Blanc (142 W 10th St)
Beacon (25 W 56th St)
Bread Bar (11 Madison Ave)
Cafe de Bruxelles (118 Greenwich Ave)
China Grill (60 W 53rd St)
Cipriani Dolci (Grand Central Terminal, 42nd St at Vanderbilt Ave)
Del Posto (85 Tenth Ave)
Delmonico's (56 Beaver St)
Emerald Inn (205 Columbus Ave): good choice before an event at Lincoln Center
Fanelli's Cafe (94 Prince St)
Five Points (31 Great Jones St)
Gotham Bar & Grill (12 E 12th St)
Gramercy Tavern (42 E 20th St)
Hallo Berlin (624 Tenth Ave)
Keens Steakhouse (72 W 36th St)
Mesa Grill (102 Fifth Ave)
The Monkey Bar (Elysee Hotel, 60 E 54th St)
Old Town Bar and Restaurant (45 E 18th St)
Patroon (160 E 46th St)
Penang (127 W 72nd St)
Picholine (35 W 64th St)
Redeye Grill (890 Seventh Ave)
Union Square Cafe (21 E 16th St)
Wollensky's Grill (201 E 49th St)

FAMILY-STYLE DINING

Carmine's (2450 Broadway and 200 W 44th St)
China Grill (60 W 53rd St)
Phoenix Garden (242 E 40th St)
Piccolo Angolo (621 Hudson St)
Ruby Foo's (1626 Broadway)

Sambuca (20 W 72nd St)
Tao (42 E 58th St)
Tony's DiNapoli (1606 Second Ave)

FIRESIDE

Alta (64 W 10th St)
Beppe (45 E 22nd St)
Cornelia Street Cafe (29 Cornelia St)
I Trulli (122 E 27th St)
Keens Steakhouse (72 W 36th St)
Molly's Pub and Shebeen (287 Third Ave)
Moran's Chelsea (146 Tenth Ave)
One if by Land, Two if by Sea (17 Barrow St)
Shaffer City Oyster Bar & Grill (5 W 21st St)
21 Club (21 W 52nd St): cocktail lounge
Vivolo (140 E 74th St)
Water's Edge (44th Dr at East River, Queens)
Waverly Inn & Garden (16 Bank St)
wd-50 (50 Clinton St)

FOREIGN FAVORS

Some of these commendable ethnic establishments do not have full write-ups in this chapter. Here are the best of the more exotic eateries, arranged by cuisine:

Afghan: **Afghan Kebab House** (1345 Second Ave)

African: **Nomad** (78 Second Ave), **Xai Xai** (365 W 51st St), and **Zere-oué** (13 E 37th St)

Argentine: **Chimichurri Grill** (609 Ninth Ave) and **Sosa Borella** (832 Eighth Ave)

Asian: **Lucky Cheng's** (24 First Ave)

Australian: **Eight Mile Creek** (240 Mulberry St), **Public** (210 Elizabeth St), and **Tuck Shop** (68 E 1st St)

Austrian: **Cafe Sabarsky** (Neue Galerie, 1048 Fifth Ave), **Klee Brasserie** (200 Ninth Ave), **Seasonal Restaurant & Weinbar** (132 W 58th St), and **Wallsé** (344 W 11th St)

Belgian: **Cafe de Bruxelles** (118 Greenwich Ave), **Petite Abeille** (466 Hudson St), and **Resto** (111 E 29th St)

Brazilian: **Churrascaria Plataforma** (316 W 49th St), **Churrascaria Tribeca** (221 West Broadway), **Circus** (132 E 61st St), **Emporium Brazil** (15 W 46th St), and **Ipanema** (13 W 46th St)

Caribbean: **Ideya** (349 West Broadway) and **Negril Village** (70 W 3rd St)

Chilean: **Pomaire** (371 W 46th St)

Chinese: **Au Mandarin** (200-250 Vesey St), **Baby Buddha** (753 Washington St), **Big Wong King** (67 Mott St), **Chin Chin** (216 E 49th St), **China Fun** (246 Columbus Ave), **Chinatown Brasserie** (380 Lafayette St), **Flor de Mayo** (483 Amsterdam Ave and 2651 Broadway), **Golden Unicorn** (18 East Broadway), **Grand Sichuan International** (229 Ninth Ave), **Hong Kong Station** (128 Hester St), **Hop Lee** (16 Mott St), **HSF** (46 Bowery), **Jing Fong** (20 Elizabeth St), **Joe's Ginger** (25 Pell St), **Joe's Shanghai** (9 Pell St), **Mr. K's** (570 Lexington Ave), **New Bo Ky** (80 Bayard St), **New Green Bo** (66 Bayard St), **Oriental Garden** (14 Elizabeth St), **Ping's Seafood** (22 Mott St), **Shang** (187 Orchard St), **Shanghai Cuisine** (89-91 Bayard St), **Shun Lee Palace** (155 E 55th St), **Shun Lee West** (43 W 65th St), **Tang Pavilion** (65 W 55th St), and **Wu Liang Ye** (36 W 48th St)

Cuban: **Cabana** (1022 Third Ave), **Cafecito** (185 Ave C), **Cafe Con Leche** (424 Amsterdam Ave), **Cafe Habana** (17 Prince St), **La Caridad 78** (2199 Broadway), **Little Havana** (30 Cornelia St), and **Victor's Cafe** (236 W 52nd St)

East European: **Petrossian Restaurant** (182 W 58th St), **Sammy's Roumanian Steakhouse** (157 Chrystie St), and **Veselka** (144 Second Ave)

Ethiopian: **Meskerem** (468 W 47th St) and **Queen of Sheba** (650 Tenth Ave)

Filipino: **Elvie's Turo-Turo** (214 First Ave)

French: see restaurant write-ups (beginning on page 81)

German: **August** (359 Bleecker St), **Hallo Berlin** (624 Tenth Ave), **Heidelberg Restaurant** (1648 Second Ave), **Loreley** (7 Rivington St), **Rolf's** (281 Third Ave), and **Zum Schneider** (107-109 Ave C)

Greek: **Ammos** (52 Vanderbilt Ave), **Anthos** (36 W 52nd St), **Avra** (141 E 48th St), **Estiatorio Milos** (125 W 55th St), **Gus' Place** (192 Bleecker St), **Ithaka** (308 E 86th St), **Kellari Taverna** (19 W 44th St), **Likitsakos Market** (1174 Lexington Ave), **Molyvos** (871 Seventh Ave), **Periyali** (35 W 20th St), **Persephone** (115 E 60th St), **Pylos** (128 E 7th St), **Snack** (105 Thompson St), **Thalassa** (179 Franklin St), **Uncle Nick's** (747 Ninth Ave), and **Viand Coffee Shop** (300 E 86th St, 673 Madison Ave, 1011 Madison Ave, and 2130 Broadway)

Indian: **Banjara** (97 First Ave), **Bay Leaf** (49 W 56th St), **Bombay Talkie** (189 Ninth Ave), **Brick Lane Curry House** (306-308 E 6th St), **Bukhara Grill** (217 E 49th St), **Chola** (232 E 58th St), **Darbar** (152 E 46th St), **Dawat** (210 E 58th St), **Dévi** (8 E 18th St), **Haveli** (100 Second Ave), **Indian Bread Co.** (194 Bleecker St), **Indus Valley** (2636 Broadway), **Jewel of India** (15 W 44th St), **Minar** (5 W 31st St), **Salaam Bombay** (317 Greenwich St), **Surya** (302 Bleecker St), **Tabla** (11 Madison Ave), **Taj Mahal** (318 E 6th St), **Tamarind** (41-43 E 22nd St), **Utsav** (1185 Ave of the Americas), and **Yuva** (230 E 58th St)

Indonesian: **Bali Nusa Indah** (651 Ninth Ave)

Irish: **Eamonn's Bar & Grill** (9 E 45th St), **Neary's** (358 E 57th St), and **Spotted Pig** (314 W 11th St)

Italian: see restaurant write-ups (beginning on page 81)

Japanese: **Benihana** (47 W 56th St), **Bond Street** (6 Bond St), **Curry-Ya** (214 E 10th St), **Donguri** (309 E 83rd St), **Hakubai** (Kitano Hotel, 66 Park Ave), **Hatsuhana** (237 Park Ave and 17 E 48th St), **Inagiku** (Waldorf-Astoria, 111 E 49th St), **Ito En** (822 Madison Ave), **Japonica** (100 University Pl), **Jewel Bako** (239 E 5th St), **Kuruma Zushi** (7 E 47th St), **Kyotofu** (705 Ninth Ave), **Kyo Ya** (94 E 7th St), **Menchanko-Tei** (131 E 45th St), **Minimoto Kitchoan** (608 Fifth Ave), **Nobu New York** and **Nobu Next Door** (105 Hudson St), **Omen** (113 Thompson St), **Ono** (18 Ninth Ave), **Ozu** (566 Amsterdam Ave), **Sakagura** (211 E 43rd St), **Seo** (249 E 49th St), **Soto** (357 Ave of the Americas), **Sugiyama** (251 W 55th St), **Sumile Sushi** (154 W 13th

St), **Sushi Yasuda** (204 E 43rd St), **SushiSamba 7** (245 Park Ave S and 87 Seventh Ave S), and **Tori Shin** (1193 First Ave)

Korean: **Cho Dang Gol** (55 W 35th St), **Do Hwa** (55 Carmine St), **Dok Suni's** (119 First Ave), **Gahm Mi Oak** (43 W 32nd St), **Hangawi** (12 E 32nd St), **Kang Suh** (1250 Broadway), **Kori** (253 Church St), **Kum Gang San** (49 W 32nd St), **New York Kom Tang** (32 W 32nd St), **Persimmon** (277 E 10th St), **Won Jo** (23 W 32nd St), **Woo Chon** (8-10 W 36th St), and **Woo Lae Oak Soho** (148 Mercer St)

Lebanese: **Al Bustan** (319 E 53rd St)

Malaysian: **Fatty Crab** (643 Hudson St), **New Malaysia Restaurant** (46-48 Bowery), and **Penang** (127 W 72nd St)

Mediterranean: **Antique Garage** (41 Mercer St), **L'Orange Bleue** (430 Broome St), **Zanzibar** (645 Ninth Ave), and **Zerza Bar** (308 E 6th St)

Mexican: **Centrico** (211 West Broadway), **Dos Caminos Soho** (475 West Broadway), **El Parador Cafe** (325 E 34th St), **Fresco Tortillas** (766 Ninth Ave), **La Esquina** (106 Kenmare St), **La Superior** (295 Berry St, Brooklyn), **Los Dados** (73 Gansevoort St), **Mama Mexico** (2672 Broadway), **Maya** (1191 First Ave), **Mexicana Mama** (525 Hudson St), **Mexican Radio** (19 Cleveland Pl), **Pampano** (209 E 49th St), **Rinconcito Mexicano** (307 W 39th St), **Rosa Mexicano** (1063 First Ave and 61 Columbus Ave), **Toloache** (251 W 50th St), **Tortilla Flats** (767 Washington St), and **Tulcingo del Valle Restaurant** (665 Tenth Ave)

Middle Eastern: **Bread and Olive** (24 W 45th St), **Cleopatra's Needle** (2485 Broadway), and **Moustache** (90 Bedford St and 265 E 10th St)

Moroccan: **Cafe Mogador** (101 St. Mark's Pl)

Pan-Latino: **Calle Ocho** (446 Columbus Ave) and **Paladar** (161 Ludlow St)

Persian: **Persepolis** (1407 Second Ave) and **Shalizar** (1420 Third Ave)

Portuguese: **Alfama** (551 Hudson St), **Macao Trading Company** (311 Church St), **O Lavrador** (138-40 101st Ave, Queens), and **Pao** (322 Spring St)

Puerto Rican: **La Taza de Oro** (96 Eighth Ave)

Russian: **Firebird** (365 W 46th St), **Russian Samovar** (256 W 52nd St), and **Uncle Vanya** (315 W 54th St)

Scandinavian: **Aquavit** (65 E 55th St) and **Smörgås Chef** (Scandinavia House Galleries, 58 Park Ave)

Scottish: **St. Andrew's** (140 W 46th St)

Southwestern: **Agave** (140 Seventh Ave S) and **Mesa Grill** (102 Fifth Ave)

Spanish: **Boqueria Soho** (171 Spring St), **Cafe Español** (172 Bleecker St), **Cafe Riazor** (245 W 16th St), **El Faro** (823 Greenwich St), **La Fonda Del Sol** (MetLife Building, 200 Park Ave), **Mercat** (45 Bond St), **Olé Restaurant** (434 Second Ave), **Pamplona** (37 E 28th St), **Pipa** (ABC Carpet & Home, 38 E 19th St), **Solera** (216 E 53rd St), **Tio Pepe** (168 W 4th St), and **Toledo** (6 E 36th St)

Thai: **Holy Basil** (149 Second Ave), **Peep** (177 Prince St), **Pongsri Thai** (106 Bayard St), **Regional Thai Sa-Woy** (1479 First Ave), **Rhong-Tiam** (541 LaGuardia Pl), **Royal Siam Thai** (240 Eighth Ave), **Siam Grill** (592 Ninth Ave), **Thailand Restaurant** (106 Bayard St), **Topaz** (127 W 56th St), and **Vong** (200 E 54th St)

Tibetan: **Tibetan Kitchen** (444 Third Ave) and **Tsampa** (212 E 9th St)

Turkish: **Ali Baba** (212 E 34th St), **Beyoglu** (1431 Third Ave), **Dervish**

Turkish (146 W 47th St), **Pasha** (70 W 71st St), **Pera Mediter-
ranean Brasserie** (303 Madison Ave), **Sip Sak** (928 Second Ave),
Turkish Cuisine (631 Ninth Ave), **Turkish Kitchen** (386 Third
Ave), **Üsküdar** (1405 Second Ave), and **Zeytin** (519 Columbus Ave)
Vietnamese: **BarBao** (100 W 82nd St), **Le Colonial** (149 E 57th St),
Mekong (18 King St), **Nha Trang** (87 Baxter St), **Pho Viet Huong**
(73 Mulberry St), and **Saigon Grill** (91-93 University Pl and 620 Am-
sterdam Ave)

FRENCH BISTROS
Balthazar (80 Spring St)
Bar Tabac (128 Smith St, Brooklyn)
Cafe Boulud (20 E 76th St)
Cafe Charbon (170 Orchard St)
Cafe Luxembourg (200 W 70th St)
Flea Market Cafe (131 Ave A)
Jean Claude (137 Sullivan St)
JoJo (160 E 64th St)
Le Gigot (18 Cornelia St)
Le Jardin Bistro (25 Cleveland Pl)
Pastis (9 Ninth Ave)
Raoul's (180 Prince St)
Rue 57 (60 W 57th St)

GAME
Game is generally offered in winter months or by special request.
Aquavit (65 E 55th St)
Babbo (110 Waverly Pl)
Barbetta (321 W 46th St)
Blue Hill (75 Washington Pl)
Cafe Boulud (20 E 76th St)
Chanterelle (2 Harrison St)
Daniel (60 E 65th St)
Eleven Madison Park (11 Madison Ave)
Felidia (243 E 58th St)
Four Seasons (99 E 52nd St)
Gascogne (158 Eighth Ave)
Il Mulino (86 W 3rd St)
Jean Georges (Trump International Hotel and Tower, 1 Central Park W)
La Grenouille (3 E 52nd St)
Le Périgord (405 E 52nd St)
Mesa Grill (102 Fifth Ave)
Ouest (2315 Broadway)
Picholine (35 W 64th St)
Primavera (1578 First Ave)
River Cafe (1 Water St, Brooklyn)
Tocqueville Restaurant (1 E 15th St)
Union Square Cafe (21 E 16th St)

GREENMARKET RESTAURANTS
Chefs at these restaurants routinely create their menus with fresh ingredients from the Greenmarkets (see separate write-up Chapter IV, page 252).

BLT Market (Ritz-Carlton Hotel, 1430 Ave of the Americas)
Blue Hill (75 Washington Pl)
Cook Shop (156 Tenth Ave)
Craft (43 E 19th St)
Market Table (54 Carmine St)
Sfoglia (1402 Lexington Ave)
Telepan (72 W 69th St)

HEALTHY FARE

Angelica Kitchen (300 E 12th St): organic and vegan
Candle 79 (154 E 79th St)
Dine by Design (252 Elizabeth St): upscale caterer
Four Seasons (99 E 52nd St): expensive
Gobo (401 Ave of the Americas and 1426 Third Ave)
Hangawi (12 E 32nd St)
Josie's Restaurant (300 Amsterdam Ave)
Popover Cafe (551 Amsterdam Ave)
Pure Food and Wine (54 Irving Pl)
Quantum Leap Natural Food (226 Thompson St and 203 First Ave)
Spring Street Natural Restaurant (62 Spring St): your best bet
Zen Palate (663 Ninth Ave and other locations)

HOTEL DINING

Manhattan hotel dining has regained some of its glow of long ago. No longer are on-premises eateries just for the convenience of registered guests. Now they are destinations for those who desire a less trendy scene with inviting, elegant atmosphere. Noteworthy choices include:

Algonquin Hotel (59 W 44th St): **Round Table** and **Oak Room** (evening cabaret)
Carlton on Madison Avenue (88 Madison Ave): **Country**
Carlyle Hotel (35 E 76th St): **Restaurant Carlyle** (overpriced)
City Club Hotel (55 W 44th St): **db Bistro Moderne** (Daniel Boulud's urbane bar-restaurant)
Elysee Hotel (60 E 54th St): **The Monkey Bar** (great history and eclectic menu with Asian flair)
Four Seasons Hotel New York (57 E 57th St): **L'Atelier de Joël Robuchon**
Hilton New York (1335 Ave of the Americas): **New York Marketplace** (casual, deli-like) and **Etrusca** (Italian, dinner only)
Hilton Times Square (234 W 42nd St): **Restaurant Above** and **Pinnacle Bar** (breathtaking views, creative American menu with Italian accents)
Hotel Gansevoort (18 Ninth Ave): **Ono Restaurant**
Hotel on Rivington (107 Rivington St): **Thor** (one of downtown's most fashionable scenes)
Inn at Irving Place (56 Irving Pl): **Casa Mono, Cibar Lounge,** and **Lady Mendl's Tea Salon** (very proper)
Jumeirah Essex House (160 Central Park S): **South Gate** ("occasion" dining)
Kimberly Hotel (145 E 50th St): **Ferro's Restaurant** (classic steakhouse)
Kitano Hotel (66 Park Ave): **Hakubai** (Japanese) and **Garden Cafe**

Le Parker Meridien Hotel (118 W 57th St): **burger joint** (lobby), **Norma's** (breakfast and brunch), and **Seppi's** (classic French bistro)

Library Hotel (299 Madison Ave): **Madison and Vine**

Loews Regency Hotel (540 Park Ave): **540 Park Restaurant** (power scene) and **The Library** (informal)

London NYC (151 W 54th St): **Maze** (casual) and **Gordon Ramsay** (fine dining)

Lowell Hotel (28 E 63rd St): **Pembroke Room** and **Post House** (very good meat and potatoes)

Mandarin Oriental New York (80 Columbus Circle): **Asiate**

Millennium Broadway and Premier Tower (145 W 44th St): **Restaurant Charlotte** (American menu)

New York Helmsley (212 E 42nd St): **Mindy's**

New York Marriott Downtown (85 West St): **85 West** (American)

New York Marriott Marquis (1535 Broadway): **Encore Restaurant**, **Katen Sushi Bar** (Japanese cuisine with modern decor), and **The View** (revolving top-floor eatery with New York-centric menu)

New York Palace Hotel (455 Madison Ave): **Gilt** and **Istana** (lobby)

Pierre Hotel (2 E 61st St): **Le Caprice** (stately and beautiful)

Plaza Athenee (37 E 64th St): **Arabelle** (dignified)

Ritz-Carlton New York, Battery Park (2 West St): **2 West** (New American)

Ritz-Carlton New York, Central Park (50 Central Park S): **BLT Market**

Royalton Hotel (44 W 44th St): **Brasserie 44** (chic, popular with publishing moguls)

St. Regis New York (2 E 55th St): **Adour Alain Ducasse** and **Astor Court** (you can't do better)

Shelburne Murray Hill Hotel (303 Lexington Ave): **Rare Bar & Grill** (elegant burger spot)

Sheraton Manhattan Hotel (790 Seventh Ave): **Russo's Steak & Pasta**

Sheraton New York Hotel and Towers (811 Seventh Ave): **Avenue** (cafe) and **Hudson's Market**

Shoreham Hotel (33 W 55th St): **Shoreham Bar and Restaurant**

Soho Grand Hotel (310 West Broadway): **Grand Bar & Lounge** (upscale bar menu) and **The Galleria**

Trump International Hotel and Tower (1 Central Park W): **Jean Georges** (The Donald's personal gem)

Waldorf-Astoria (301 Park Ave): **Bull & Bear** (British atmosphere), **Inagiku** (Japanese), **Oscar's** (cafeteria), and **Peacock Alley Restaurant**

Wales (1295 Madison Ave): **Sarabeth's** (delightful) and **Joanna's** (Italian)

Warwick (65 W 54th St): **Murals on 54**

W New York (541 Lexington Ave): **Heartbeat** (breakfast)

W New York-Times Square (1567 Broadway): **Blue Fin** (seafood)

KOSHER

Kosher dining experiences in New York City run the gamut from elegant restaurants with celebrity chefs to the falafel stand outside Rockefeller Center and the kosher hot dog stand at Shea Stadium. Note: *Especially* with kosher dining, call ahead to make sure restaurants are open.

Abigael's on Broadway (1407 Broadway)

Cafe K (8 E 48th St): This may be the busiest lunch spot in New York City.

Cafe Roma Pizza (854 Amsterdam Ave)

Cafe Weissman (Jewish Museum, 1109 Fifth Ave): This museum was the old Felix Warburg mansion, and this intimate spot in the basement is a kosher oasis on Museum Row.

Caravan of Dreams (405 E 6th St): natural, raw, and vegetarian East Village kosher restaurant

Circa (22 W 33rd St): This upscale cafeteria lunch location has everything from sushi to create-your-own salads and hot lasagna—all delicious!

Colbeh (43 W 39th St)

Darna (600 Columbus Ave): Darna's accents are Moroccan/Middle Eastern couscous with a splash of Moroccan decor

Diamond Dairy (4 W 47th St, mezzanine): Watching the diamond trade is worth the cost of a meal here (at affordable old-time prices!), and the Jewish-mother cooking style will warm your insides and make you nostalgic. Even if it's July, get the chicken soup!

Dougie's Express (74 W 47th St): The ribs are as good as kosher gets, and the original store has spawned a franchise.

Eden Wok (43 E 34th St): great kosher Chinese restaurant with sushi bar

Estihana (221 W 79th St): closest kosher choice to the Museum of Natural History

Galil (1252 Lexington Ave): a small Israeli meat restaurant with surprisingly large portions of Middle Eastern specialties

Jerusalem II (1375 Broadway): Crowds keep coming back to one of the first and best pizza, falafel, and salad bar emporiums in town.

Le Marais (150 W 46th St): This French steakhouse, which has a butcher store in the front, sets the kosher standard.

Mendy's Galleria (115 E 57th St): huge portions, fantastic food, and friendly service

Mendy's Rockefeller Plaza (30 Rockefeller Plaza)

My Most Favorite Food (120 W 45th St): Expensive pasta, fish, salads, and desserts are all delectable.

Tevere (155 E 84th St): old family Italian/Jewish recipes and great traditions

Va Bene (1589 Second Ave): superb pastas

Yonah Schimmel's Knishes (137 E Houston St): Schimmel started serving knishes 150 years ago to immigrants, and it's still in business.

LATE HOURS

The city that never sleeps . . .

Balthazar (80 Spring St)

Baraonda (1439 Second Ave)

Bereket (187 E Houston St)

Big Arc Chicken (233 First Ave)

Big Nick's (2175 Broadway)

Blue Ribbon (97 Sullivan St)

Blue Ribbon Sushi (119 Sullivan St and 278 Fifth Ave)

Cafeteria (119 Seventh Ave)

Cafe Lalo (201 W 83rd St)

Carnegie Delicatessen and Restaurant (854 Seventh Ave)

Cozy Soup 'n' Burger (739 Broadway)

dell'anima (38 Eighth Ave)

Empire Diner (210 Tenth Ave)

Fatty Crab (643 Hudson St)
Frank (88 Second Ave)
French Roast (78 W 11th St and 2340 Broadway)
Fuleen Seafood (11 Division St)
Gam Mee Oak (43 W 32nd St)
Gray's Papaya (2090 Broadway)
Great NY Noodletown (28 Bowery)
Green Kitchen (1477 First Ave)
Han Bat (53 W 35th St)
Kum Gang San (49 W 32nd St)
Landmarc (10 Columbus Circle)
L'Express (249 Park Ave S)
Mas Farmhouse (39 Downing St)
Merkato 55 (55 Gansevoort St)
Momofuku Ssäm Bar (207 Second Ave)
Odessa (119 Ave A)
Pastis (9 Ninth Ave)
P.J. Clarke's (915 Third Ave)
Raoul's (180 Prince St)
Rose Bar (Gramercy Park Hotel, 2 Lexington Ave): reservations a must
Sarge's Deli (548 Third Ave)
Spotted Pig (314 W 11th St)
Suzie Wong (547 W 27th St)
Veselka (144 Second Ave)
Viand Coffee Shop (2130 Broadway)
Wollensky's Grill (201 E 49th St)
Won Jo (23 W 32nd St)

MUNCHING AT THE MUSEUMS

Even some of the smallest museums have cafes. Often these are upscale spots where you can rest your feet and get a surprisingly good bite to eat. Be forewarned that they are usually quite expensive. Some of the best:

American Folk Art Museum (45 W 53rd St): **Cafe**
Asia Society (Park Ave at 70th St): **Garden Court Cafe**
Dahesh Museum (580 Madison Ave): **Cafe Opaline**
Guggenheim Museum (1071 Fifth Ave): **Museum Cafe**
Jewish Museum (1109 Fifth Ave): **Cafe Weissman**
Metropolitan Museum of Art (1000 Fifth Ave): **Cafeteria** (basement) and **Petrie Court Cafe and Wine Bar** (looks onto Central Park)
The Morgan Library and Museum (225 Madison Ave): **The Morgan Dining Room**
Museum of Modern Art (9 W 53rd St): **The Modern**
Neue Galerie (1048 Fifth Ave): **Cafe Sabarsky**
Rubin Museum of Art (150 W 17th St): **Cafe at the RMA**
Scandinavia House Galleries (58 Park Ave): **Smörgås Chef**
Whitney Museum of American Art (945 Madison Ave): **Sarabeth's at the Whitney**

OLD-TIMERS

1783: **Fraunces Tavern** (54 Pearl St)
1794: **Bridge Cafe** (279 Water St)

1864: **Pete's Tavern** (129 E 18th St)
1868: **Old Homestead** (56 Ninth Ave)
1885: **Keens Steakhouse** (72 W 36th St)
1887: **Peter Luger Steak House** (178 Broadway, Brooklyn)
1888: **Katz's Delicatessen** (205 E Houston St)
1890: **P.J. Clarke's** (915 Third Ave)
1906: **Barbetta** (321 W 46th St)
1913: **Grand Central Oyster Bar Restaurant** (Grand Central Terminal, 42nd St at Vanderbilt Ave, lower level)
1920: **Waverly Inn & Garden** (16 Bank St)
1926: **Palm One** (837 Second Ave)
1927: **Minetta Tavern** (113 MacDougal St)
1929: **21 Club** (21 W 52nd St)

Food Tips from Distant Lands

- **Chinese**: The most popular Chinese cuisines are Cantonese (heavy on fish, dim sum a specialty); Chiu Chow (thick shark's fin soup, sliced goose, China's "Sicilian" cuisine); Hakka (salted, use of innards); Hunan (spicy, try fried chicken with chili); Peking (Peking duck and beggar's chicken are the best known); Shanghai (freshwater hairy crab is very popular); and Szechuan (spiciest of all, simmering and smoking are common cooking methods).
- **Indian**: Northern Indian food features wheat bread and curries. Fish and chicken are cooked in a tandoor clay oven. Indian food is not necessarily hot and spicy.
- **Indonesian**: Satays of chicken and beef, skewered and served with peanut sauce, are the main dishes.
- **Japanese**: Most popular foods are sushi (raw fish atop vinegared rice), sashimi (slices of raw fish), tempura (deep-fried vegetables and seafood), and teppanyaki (beef, seafood, garlic, and veggies cooked on a central griddle). Sake (rice wine) and Japanese beers such as Sapporo make good accompanying beverages.
- **Korean**: Table-top griddles are used for barbecuing beef slices for a dish called *bulgogi*.
- **Malaysian**: The best-known dish is *laska*, a creamy, coconut-based soup with noodles, shrimp, and chicken.
- **Singaporean**: This cross-cultural cuisine favors fried *mee* (thick yellow noodles) and satays (skewered and barbecued meat). Coconut is featured in sweet rice cakes and *laska*.
- **Taiwanese**: Fish and other seafoods are cooked in hot pots and enhanced with chili- and sesame-flavored oil condiments.
- **Thai**: Thai food can be very spicy! The national dish is *tom yum gung*, a soup made with chili, lemon grass, and coriander that is topped with shrimp, chicken, or squid.
- **Vietnamese**: You'll find French-inspired dishes like fried frog legs, sausage, and salami cold-cuts platters. Spring rolls wrapped in lettuce leaves are traditional.

OUTDOOR DINING

Aquagrill (210 Spring St)
Barbetta (321 W 46th St): garden
Barolo (398 West Broadway)
Bello Giardino (71 W 71st St)
Blue Water Grill (31 Union Sq W)
Bottino (246 Tenth Ave)
Bread Bar (11 Madison Ave)
Bryant Park Grill (25 W 40th St)
Cafe Centro (200 Park Ave)
Cafe St. Bart's (109 E 50th St)
Caffe Dante (79-81 MacDougal St)
Cascina (647 Ninth Ave)
Cavo (42-18 31st Ave, Queens)
Central Park Boathouse (Central Park at E 72nd St)
Da Nico (164 Mulberry St)
Da Silvano (260 Ave of the Americas)
Druids (736 Tenth Ave)
DuMont (432 Union Ave, Brooklyn)
Empire Diner (210 Tenth Ave)
Financier Patisserie (62 Stone St)
5 Ninth (5 Ninth Ave)
Fragole (394 Court St)
Gascogne (158 Eighth Ave)
Gavroche (212 W 14th St)
Gigino (Wagner Park, 20 Battery Pl)
Grocery (288 Smith, Brooklyn)
Grotto (100 Forsyth St)
Home Restaurant (20 Cornelia St)
I Trulli (122 E 27th St)
Il Gattopardo (33 W 54th St)
Jackson Hole Burgers (232 E 64th St, 1611 Second Ave, and 517 Columbus Ave)
Le Jardin Bistro (25 Cleveland Pl)
Mezzogiorno (195 Spring St)
Moda Restaurant (135 W 52nd St)
New Leaf Cafe (Fort Tryon Park, 1 Margaret Corbin Dr)
Nice Matin (201 W 79th St)
Nougatine (Trump International Hotel and Tower, 1 Central Park W)
Ono (Hotel Gansevoort, 18 Ninth Ave)
Pampano (209 E 49th St, 2nd floor terrace)
Paradou (8 Little West 12th St)
Pastis (9 Ninth Ave)
Patroon (160 E 46th St, 3rd floor)
Pete's Tavern (129 E 18th St)
Porters New York (216 Seventh Ave)
Pure Food and Wine (54 Irving Pl)
River Cafe (1 Water St, Brooklyn)
Roc Restaurant (190-A Duane St)
Rock Center Cafe/The Rink Bar (Rockefeller Center, 20 W 50th St)
San Pietro (18 E 54th St)

79th Street Boat Basin Cafe (Riverside Park at 79th St; seasonal)
Shake Shack (Madison Square Park and 366 Columbus Ave; seasonal)
Sheep Meadow Cafe (Central Park W at 69th St; seasonal)
SouthWest NY (225 Liberty St)
Spring Street Natural Restaurant (62 Spring St)
SushiSamba 7 (87 Seventh Ave S)
Tartine (253 W 11th St)
Tavern on the Green (Central Park W at 67th St)
Terrace 5 (Museum of Modern Art, 11 W 53rd St)
Terrace in the Sky (400 W 119th St)
Trattoria dell'Arte (900 Seventh Ave)
Water Club (East River at 30th St, upstairs)
Waverly Inn & Garden (16 Bank St)
White Horse Tavern (567 Hudson St)
World Yacht Cruises (Pier 81, 41st St at Hudson River)
Yaffa Cafe (97 St. Mark's Pl)

OUTDOOR DRINKS

Bull McCabe's (29 St. Mark's Pl)
Casimir (103-105 Ave B)
Chelsea Brewing Company (Pier 59, West St at 18th St)
Finnegan's Wake (1361 First Ave)
Hallo Berlin (624 Tenth Ave)
Iris and B. Gerald Cantor Roof Garden (Metropolitan Museum of
  Art, 1000 Fifth Ave)
Metro Grill Roof Garden (Hotel Metro, 45 W 35th St)
O'Flaherty's Ale House (334 W 46th St)
Revival (129 E 15th St)
Ryan's Irish Pub (151 Second Ave)
Sweet & Vicious (5 Spring St)
White Horse Tavern (567 Hudson St)

OYSTER BARS

Blue Ribbon (97 Sullivan St)
Docks Oyster Bar and Seafood Grill (633 Third Ave)
Grand Central Oyster Bar Restaurant (Grand Central Terminal,
  42nd St at Vanderbilt Ave, lower level)
Pearl Oyster Bar (18 Cornelia St)
Shaffer City Oyster Bar & Grill (5 W 21st St)

PERSONAL FAVORITES

Babbo (110 Waverly Pl): fabulous food
Balthazar (80 Spring St): really fun atmosphere
Barbetta (321 W 46th St): What a classy operation.
Blue Ribbon (97 Sullivan St): great value
Bouley (163 Duane St): It doesn't come any better.
Brooklyn Diner USA (212 W 57th St and 155 W 43rd St): satisfying
  meals all day
Chanterelle (2 Harrison St): always first-class
Cucina & Co. (MetLife Building, 200 Park Ave, lobby): great quick meal
Del Posto (85 Tenth Ave): very classy service

40 Carrots (Bloomingdale's, 1000 Third Ave, metro level): nice atmosphere, great menu, wonderful coffee yogurt
Golden Unicorn (18 East Broadway): great Chinese platters
Gotham Bar & Grill (12 E 12th St): Everything is good.
Gramercy Tavern (42 E 20th St): quintessential New York
Il Mulino (86 W 3rd St): Italian heaven!
Jackson Hole Burgers (232 E 64th St, 521 Third Ave, 1611 Second Ave, 1270 Madison Ave, and 517 Columbus Ave): best burgers
La Grenouille (3 E 52nd St): beautiful
Le Périgord (405 E 52nd St): impeccable
McCormick & Schmicks (1285 Ave of the Americas): fresh seafood
The Modern (Museum of Modern Art, 9 W 53rd St): great setting
Nobu New York (105 Hudson St): Japanese food at its best
One if by Land, Two if by Sea (17 Barrow St): romantic
Park Side (107-01 Corona Ave, Queens): Come here to eat!
Piccolo Angolo (621 Hudson St): like family
Post House (Lowell Hotel, 28 E 63rd St): macho meals
Primavera (1578 First Ave): superb service
River Cafe (1 Water St, East River, Brooklyn): Oh, that view!
Sfoglia (1402 Lexington Ave): wonderful bread
Shake Shack (Madison Square Park and 366 Columbus Ave): I love the shakes.
Smith & Wollensky (797 Third Ave): old-time flavor
Union Square Cafe (21 E 16th St): justly famous

PIZZA

Accademia di Vino (1081 Third Ave)
Adrienne's Pizzabar (86 Pearl St and 154 Stone St)
Angelo's Pizzeria (117 W 57th St)
apizz (217 Eldridge St)
Artichoke Basille's Pizza & Brewery (328 E 14th St): really good
Arturo's Coal Oven Pizza (106 W Houston St)
Beacon (25 W 56th St)
Bella Vita (211 W 43rd St)
Co. (230 Ninth Ave): baker Jim Lahey's restaurant debut
Da Ciro (229 Lexington Ave)
Da Nico (164 Mulberry St)
Denino's (524 Port Richmond Ave, Staten Island)
Famous Ben's Pizza (177 Spring St)
Fred's at Barneys New York (660 Madison Ave)
Giorgione (307 Spring St)
Grandaisy Bakery (73 Sullivan St)
Grimaldi's (19 Old Fulton St, Brooklyn)
Il Corallo Trattoria (176 Prince St)
Joe's Pizza (7 Carmine St)
John's Pizzeria (278 Bleecker St and other locations)
Lazzara's Pizza Cafe (221 W 38th St, upstairs)
Lil' Frankie's Pizza (19 First Ave)
Lombardi's (32 Spring St)
Luca Lounge (220 Ave B)
Luigi's (1701 First Ave)
Mezzogiorno (195 Spring St)

Naples 45 (MetLife Building, 200 Park Ave)
Nick & Toni's Cafe (100 W 67th St)
Nick's Pizza (1814 Second Ave)
Orso (322 W 46th St)
Osteria del Circo (120 W 55th St)
Patsy's (2287 First Ave)
(The Famous) **Ray's Pizza of Greenwich Village** (465 Ave of the Americas)
Sal's & Carmine's Pizza (2671 Broadway)
Serafina (29 E 61st St and 38 E 58th St)
Stromboli Pizzeria (112 University Pl)
Totonno Pizzeria Napolitano (1544 Second Ave)
Trattoria dell'Arte (900 Seventh Ave)
Two Boots (42 Ave A, 74 Bleecker St, and other locations)
Una Pizza Napoletana (349 E 12th St)
Vinny Vincenz (231 First Ave)

POWER MEALS

Balthazar (80 Spring St)
Ben Benson's Steak House (123 W 52nd St)
Cafe Boulud (20 E 76th St)
Cafe Pierre (Pierre Hotel, 2 E 61st St)
Daniel (60 E 65th St)
Da Silvano (260 Ave of the Americas)
Delmonico's (56 Beaver St)
Del Posto (85 Tenth Ave)
540 Park Restaurant (Loews Regency Hotel, 540 Park Ave)
Fives (Peninsula New York Hotel, 700 Fifth Ave)
Four Seasons (99 E 52nd St)
Gabriel's Bar & Restaurant (11 W 60th St)
Gotham Bar & Grill (12 E 12th St)
Il Mulino (86 W 3rd St)
Jean Georges (Trump International Hotel and Tower, 1 Central Park W)
La Grenouille (3 E 52nd St)
Le Bernardin (155 W 51st St)
Maloney & Porcelli (37 E 50th St)
Michael's (24 W 55th St)
The Monkey Bar (Elysee Hotel, 60 E 54th St)
Morton's of Chicago (551 Fifth Ave)
Nobu New York and **Nobu Next Door** (105 Hudson St)
Palm One (837 Second Ave)
Park Avenue Spring/Summer/Autumn/Winter (100 E 63rd St)
Primavera (1578 First Ave)
Rao's (455 E 114th St)
Restaurant Carlyle (Carlyle Hotel, 35 E 76th St)
Sette Mezzo (969 Lexington Ave)
Smith & Wollensky (797 Third Ave)
21 Club (21 W 52nd St)

PRE-THEATER

Let your waiter know when you are first seated that you will be attending the theater so that service can be adjusted accordingly. If it is raining, allow extra time for getting a taxi. Some restaurants have specially priced pre-theater dinners.

Aquavit (65 E 55th St)
Arqua (281 Church St)
Barbetta (321 W 46th St)
Beacon (25 W 56th St)
Becco (355 W 46th St)
Blue Fin (W New York-Times Square, 1567 Broadway)
Brasserie 44 (Royalton Hotel, 44 W 44th St)
Cafe Un Deux Trois (123 W 44th St)
Carmine's (2450 Broadway and 200 W 44th St)
Centolire (1167 Madison Ave)
Chez Josephine (414 W 42nd St)
Dawat (210 E 58th St)
Esca (402 W 43rd St)
Firebird (365 W 46th St)
Four Seasons (99 E 52nd St)
Gino (780 Lexington Ave)
Hearth (403 E 12th St)
Hell's Kitchen (679 Ninth Ave)
Indochine (430 Lafayette St)
La Boite en Bois (75 W 68th St)
L'Atelier de Joël Robuchon (Four Seasons Hotel New York, 57 E 57th St)
Marchi's (251 E 31st St)
Momofuku Noodle Bar (171 First Ave)
Ollie's Noodle Shop and Grill (411 W 42nd St, 2315 Broadway, and 1991 Broadway)
Orso (322 W 46th St)
Picholine (35 W 64th St)
Red Cat (227 Tenth Ave)
Sandwich Planet (534 Ninth Ave)
South Gate (Jumeirah Essex House, 160 Central Park S)
Spice Market (403 W 13th St)
Tavern on the Green (Central Park W at 67th St)
Telepan (72 W 69th St)
Thalia (828 Eighth Ave)

PUBS AND GOOD BARS

Angels Share (8 Stuyvesant St)
Anotheroom (249 West Broadway)
Apothéke (9 Doyers St)
APT (419 W 13th St): hidden
Arlene's Grocery (95 Stanton St)
Ava Lounge (Dream Hotel, 210 W 55th St): rooftop
Back Page Sports Bar (1472 Third Ave): football
Balcony Bar (Metropolitan Museum of Art, 1000 Fifth Ave): culture
Baraonda (1439 Second Ave): international
Bar Blanc (142 W 10th St): actually a food-first establishment
Bar East (1733 First Ave): down-to-earth
Bar 89 (89 Mercer St): renowned for unisex glass bathrooms

Bar 44 (Royalton Hotel, 44 W 44th St): fireside in the lobby lounge
Bar 12:31 (Hotel Chandler, 12 E 31st St): cozy
Barrow's Pub (463 Hudson St)
Bar Seine (Hotel Plaza Athenee, 37 E 64th St)
Beer Table (427 Seventh Ave, Brooklyn): congenial and tasteful
Bemelmans Bar (Carlyle Hotel, 35 E 76th St): old-school hotel bar
Bill's Gay Nineties (57 E 54th St)
Birdland (315 W 44th St): jazz
Blarney Rock Pub (137 W 33rd St): Irish all the way
Blind Pig (233 E 14th St): nightly sports action on nine huge TV screens
Blue Note (131 W 3rd St): lots of talent here
Blue Ribbon Downing Street Bar (34 Downing St): sip and be seen
Blue Seats (157 Ludlow St): sports bar with 62 flat-screen TVs
Bobo (181 W 10th St)
Bookmarks Lounge (Library Hotel, 299 Madison Ave): roof bar
Boqueria Soho (171 Spring St): tapas bar
Bowery Electric (327 Bowery): dance to DJs
Brandy Library (25 N Moore St): fine liquor
Bread Bar (11 Madison Ave): fancy bar menu
Bridge Cafe (279 Water St): elevated pub grub
Brother Jimmy's Bait Shack (1644 Third Ave): football
Bull & Bear (Waldorf-Astoria, 301 Park Ave)
Bungalow 8 (515 W 27th St): celeb watering hole
Burp Castle (41 E 7th St): a hundred international bottles and a dozen taps focusing on Belgian beers
Butterfield 8 (5 E 38th St): unassuming pub and lounge
Camaradas El Barrio (2241 First Ave): Spanish Harlem happy-hour location
Campbell Apartment (Grand Central Terminal, 42nd St at Vanderbilt Ave, off West Balcony): unique
Carnegie Club (156 W 56th St): jazz ensembles
Cellar Bar (Bryant Park Hotel, 40 W 40th St): hotel bar
Chelsea Brewing Company (Pier 59, West St at 18th St): big place, big steaks
Chibi's Bar (238 Mott St): Japanese hideaway
Corner Bistro (331 W 4th St): eat
d.b.a. N.Y.C. (41 First Ave): relaxed place with an expanded bar list, including 130 single-malt Scotches and 50 tequilas
The Delancey (168 Delancey St): rooftop
Dempsey's Pub (61 Second Ave)
Dive Bar (732 Amsterdam Ave)
Dublin 6 (575 Hudson St)
Duvet (45 W 21st St): perfect for an office party
Eamonn's Bar & Grill (9 E 45th St): Irish
Ear Inn (326 Spring St)
El Quinto Pino (401 W 24th St): tapas bar
Eleven Madison Park (11 Madison Ave)
Emerald Inn (205 Columbus Ave): friendly Irish pub
Employees Only (510 Hudson St): focus on fresh ingredients and rejuvenated classics
ESPN Zone (1472 Broadway): sports

Feinstein's at Loews Regency Hotel (540 Park Ave): sophisticated cocktail-sipping and people watching
Flatiron Lounge (37 W 19th St): plush banquettes, Manhattan's best Manhattans
40/40 Club (6 W 25th St): sports
Four Seasons Hotel 57 Bar (57 E 57th St)
Freeman's (Freeman Alley)
Ginger Man (11 E 36th St): huge beer selection for finance types
Gramercy Tavern (42 E 20th St)
Grand Bar & Lounge (Soho Grand Hotel, 310 West Broadway)
Heartland Brewery (1285 Ave of the Americas, 35 Union Square W, and other locations): Try the charcoal stout.
Heights Cafe (84 Montague St, Brooklyn)
Hotel Roger Williams (131 Madison Ave)
Hudson Bar & Books (636 Hudson St): reading
Jeremy's Ale House (228 Front St)
Jimmy's Corner (140 W 44th St)
Jimmy's No. 43 (43 E 7th St): beyond bar food
John Street Bar & Grill (17 John St): spacious rec room
Keens Steakhouse (72 W 36th St)
King Cole Bar (St. Regis New York, 2 E 55th St)
Landmark Tavern (626 Eleventh Ave): 19th-century decor
Lenox Lounge (288 Malcolm X Blvd): Harlem lounge and jazz club
The Library (Loews Regency Hotel, 540 Park Ave): class
Little Branch (20 Seventh Ave S): perfectly calibrated cocktails in subterranean venue
Living Room (W New York-Times Square, 1567 Broadway): tourists
Lobby Lounge (Mandarin Oriental New York, 80 Columbus Circle, 35th floor): phenomenal Central Park views
Macao Trading Company (311 Church St)
McCormack's (365 Third Ave): soccer and football
McQuaid's Public House (589 Eleventh Ave)
Mercer Kitchen (99 Prince St): celebrity watching
Molly's Pub and Shebeen (287 Third Ave): Irish
The Monkey Bar (Elysee Hotel, 60 E 54th St)
Morgan's Bar (237 Madison Ave): great ambience
Mustang Sally's (324 Seventh Ave): basketball
No Idea (30 E 20th St)
North Square Lounge (Washington Square Hotel, 103 Waverly Pl)
Oak Room (Algonquin Hotel, 59 W 44th St)
Oasis (W New York, 541 Lexington Ave, lobby level)
Old Town Bar and Restaurant (45 E 18th St): burgers
P.J. Clarke's (915 Third Ave)
The Park (118 Tenth Ave): people watching
Parlour (250 W 86th St)
Peculier Pub (145 Bleecker St): 400 beers!
Pegu Club (77 W Houston St): inventive twist on cocktails
Peter McManus Cafe (152 Seventh Ave)
Pete's Tavern (129 E 18th St): New York's oldest continuously operating pub
Pianos (158 Ludlow St): busy
Pinetree Lodge (326 E 35th St): pleasingly grungy garden

Play-by-Play (4 Penn Plaza): sports
Puck Fair (298 Lafayette St): Irish
Rao's (455 E 114th St)
Rock Center Cafe (Rockefeller Plaza, 20 W 50th St): Watch the ice-skaters.
Rose Bar (Gramercy Park Hotel, 2 Lexington Ave)
Rudy's Bar & Grill (627 Ninth Ave)
Rusty Knot (425 West St)
Sakagura (211 E 43rd St): Japanese restaurant bar
Salon de Ning (Peninsula New York Hotel, 700 Fifth Ave): rooftop bar with view of the Museum of Modern Art's Sculpture Garden
Session 73 (1359 First Ave): live music
79th Street Boat Basin Cafe (79th St at Hudson River, Riverside Park): view with a bar (seasonally)
Ship of Fools (1590 Second Ave): football
Slaughtered Lamb Pub (182 W 4th St): Drink and dine by the fire.
Smith's Bar & Restaurant (701 Eighth Ave): Drink standing up.
Smoke Jazz Club & Lounge (2751 Broadway): best jazz bar
Spotted Pig (314 W 11th St): London-style gastro-pub
Spuyten Duyvil (359 Metropolitan Ave, Brooklyn): Yes, it is in Brooklyn, but it is one of the best beer bars around.
Stone Street Tavern (52 Stone St): relaxed spot for post-trading beers
Subway Inn (143 E 60th St): cheapo
Swift Hibernian Lounge (34 E 4th St): 26 beers on tap
Tonic and the Met Lounge (727 Seventh Ave): boxing
Tonic East (411 Third Ave): rooftop
Trailer Park Lounge (271 W 23rd St): turkey burgers
The View (New York Marriott Marquis, 1535 Broadway): rotating rooftop views
Water Street Restaurant and Lounge (66 Water St, Brooklyn): bar, restaurant, club, gallery
Waterfront Ale House (540 Second Ave): great Belgian beer, good food
The Whiskey (1567 Broadway): see and be seen
White Star (21 Essex St)
Wollensky's Grill (201 E 49th St)
Xunta (174 First Ave): tapas bar
Zinc Bar (82 W 3rd St): good music

ROMANTIC

Barbetta (321 W 46th St)
Blue Hill (75 Washington Pl)
Bouley (163 Duane St)
Bridge Cafe (279 Water St)
Caffe Reggio (119 MacDougal St)
Caffe Vivaldi (32 Jones St)
Capsouto Frères (451 Washington St)
Chanterelle (2 Harrison St)
Chez Josephine (414 W 42nd St)
Danal (59 Fifth Ave)
Erminia (250 E 83rd St)
Firebird (365 W 46th St)
Four Seasons (99 E 52nd St)

I Trulli (122 E 27th St)
Il Buco (47 Bond St)
Il Cortile (125 Mulberry St)
Jean Georges (Trump International Hotel and Tower, 1 Central Park W)
King Cole Bar (St. Regis New York, 2 E 55th St)
Lady Mendl's Tea Salon (Inn at Irving Place, 56 Irving Pl)
La Grenouille (3 E 52nd St)
Le Périgord (405 E 52nd St)
One if by Land, Two if by Sea (17 Barrow St)
Paola's (1295 Madison Ave)
Primavera (1578 First Ave)
River Cafe (1 Water St, Brooklyn)
Scalinatella (201 E 61st St)
Spice Market (403 W 13th St)
Tavern on the Green, Crystal Room (Central Park W and 67th St)
Water Club (30th St at East River)
Water's Edge (44th Dr at East River, Queens)

SANDWICHES

Alidoro (105 Sullivan St)
Amy's Bread (75 Ninth Ave, 672 Ninth Ave, and 250 Bleecker St)
Baoguette (61 Lexington Ave)
Bread Market & Cafe (1290 Ave of the Americas)
Cafe Gitane (242 Mott St)
Call Cuisine (1032 First Ave)
Carnegie Delicatessen and Restaurant (854 Seventh Ave)
City Bakery (3 W 18th St)
Cosi Sandwich Bar (841 Broadway and other locations)
Cucina & Co. (MetLife Building, 200 Park Ave)
Deb's (200 Varick St)
Defonte (261 Third Ave): over-the-top heros
E.A.T. (1064 Madison Ave)
Eisenberg's Sandwich Shop (174 Fifth Ave)
Faicco's (260 Bleecker St)
Good and Plenty to Go (410 W 43rd St)
'ino (21 Bedford St)
'inoteca (323 Third Ave)
Italian Food Center (186 Grand St)
Manganaro's Hero Boy (492 Ninth Ave)
Mangia (50 W 57th St)
Nicky's Vietnamese Sandwiches (150 E 2nd St)
Once Upon a Tart (135 Sullivan St)
Piada (3 Clinton St): Italian
Popover Cafe (551 Amsterdam Ave)
Porchetta (110 E 7th St)
Salumeria Biellese (376-378 Eighth Ave)
Sandwich Planet (534 Ninth Ave)
Shorty's (576 Ninth Ave)
Sosa Borella (832 Eighth Ave)
Sullivan Street Bakery (533 W 47th St)
Swich (104 Eighth Ave)
Telephone Bar & Grill (149 Second Ave)

Terramare (22 E 65th St)
Todaro Bros. (555 Second Ave)
Union Square Cafe (21 E 16th St)
'wichcraft (555 Fifth Ave and other locations)

SEAFOOD

Aquagrill (210 Spring St)
Aquavit (65 E 55th St)
BLT Fish and Fish Shack (21 W 17th St)
Blue Fin (W New York-Times Square, 1567 Broadway)
Blue Ribbon (97 Sullivan St)
Blue Water Grill (31 Union Square W)
Bridge Cafe (279 Water St)
Docks Oyster Bar and Seafood Grill (633 Third Ave)
Ed's Lobster Bar (222 Lafayette St)
Esca (402 W 43rd St)
Estiatorio Milos (125 W 55th St)
Grand Central Oyster Bar Restaurant (Grand Central Terminal, 42nd St at Vanderbilt Ave, lower level)
Jack's Luxury Oyster Bar (101 Second Ave)
John Dory (85 Tenth Ave)
Kuruma Zushi (7 E 47th St)
Le Bernardin (155 W 51st St)
Lure Fishbar (142 Mercer St)
Mary's Fish Camp (64 Charles St)
McCormick & Schmick's (1285 Ave of the Americas)
Mermaid Inn (568 Amsterdam Ave and 96 Second Ave)
Ocean Grill (384 Columbus Ave)
Oceana (55 E 54th St)
Oriental Garden (14 Elizabeth St)
Pearl Oyster Bar (18 Cornelia St)
Primola (1226 Second Ave)
Remi (145 W 53rd St)
The Sea Grill (19 W 49th St)
Shelly's New York (41 W 57th St)
Trata Estiatorio (1331 Second Ave)
Westville (210 W 10th St)

SHOPPING BREAKS

To replenish your energy, here are some good places to eat in the major Manhattan stores:

ABC Carpet & Home (888 Broadway, 212/473-3000): **ABC Simple** (Jean-Georges Vongerichten's green restaurant), **Le Pain Quotidien** (bakery & cafe), and **Pipa** (South American)
Barneys New York (660 Madison Ave, 212/833-2200): **Fred's** (upscale)
Bergdorf Goodman (men's store, 745 Fifth Ave, 212/753-7300): **Bar 3**
Bergdorf Goodman (women's store, 754 Fifth Ave, 212/753-7300): **BG Restaurant** (7th floor) and **Goodman** (plaza level)
Bloomingdale's (1000 Third Ave, 212/705-2000): **B Cafe** (6th floor), **Flip** (lower level), **40 Carrots** (metro level), and **Le Train Bleu** (6th floor)
Bodum Cafe & Home Store (413 W 14th St, 212/367-9125)

Lord & Taylor (424 Fifth Ave, 212/391-3344): **Sarabeth's** (5th floor)
Macy's (151 W 34th St, 212/695-4400): **Au Bon Pain** (street level and 8th floor), **Cucina Express Marketplace** (cellar level), **Grill Restaurant & Bar** (cellar level), and **Starbucks** (3rd floor)
Saks Fifth Avenue (611 Fifth Ave, 212/753-4000): **Cafe S.F.A.** (8th floor, tasty and classy)
Takashimaya (693 Fifth Ave, 212/350-0100): **Tea Box Cafe** (lower level, Oriental flavor)

Are you feeling under the weather? How about a bowl of chicken soup? Some of the best bowls in the city are served at these comfort food specialists.

Artie's Delicatessen (2290 Broadway)
Brooklyn Diner USA (212 W 57th St)
Carnegie Delicatessen and Restaurant (854 Seventh Ave)
Fine & Schapiro (138 W 72nd St)
Kitchenette (156 Chambers St)
2nd Avenue Deli (162 E 33rd St)
Zabar's (2245 Broadway): Saul Zabar himself is there to make sure it tastes just like his grandmother's.

SOUTHERN FLAVORS AND SOUL FOOD

Acme Bar & Grill (9 Great Jones St)
Amy Ruth's (113 W 116th St)
Ashford and Simpson's Sugar Bar (254 W 72nd St)
Brother Jimmy's BBQ (1485 Second Ave)
Bubby's (120 Hudson St)
Great Jones Cafe (54 Great Jones St)
Londel's Supper Club (2620 Frederick Douglass Blvd)
Miss Maude's Spoonbread Too (547 Lenox Ave)
107 West (2787 Broadway)
Pink Tea Cup (42 Grove St)
Shark Bar (307 Amsterdam Ave)
Sister's Cuisine (47 E 124th St)
Sylvia's (328 Lenox Ave)

STEAKS

Angelo and Maxie's (233 Park Ave S): reasonable prices
Ben Benson's Steak House (123 W 52nd St)
Bistro le Steak (1309 Third Ave): inexpensive and good
BLT Steak (106 E 57th St)
Bull & Bear (Waldorf-Astoria, 301 Park Ave)
Capital Grille (155 E 42nd St)
Churrascaria Plataforma (Belvedere Hotel, 316 W 49th St)
craftsteak (85 Tenth Ave)
Del Frisco's Double Eagle Steak House (1221 Ave of the Americas)
Frankie and Johnnie's (269 W 45th St)
Gallagher's Steak House (228 W 52nd St)
Keens Steakhouse (72 W 36th St)

Le Marais (150 W 46th St): kosher
Maloney & Porcelli (37 E 50th St)
MarkJoseph Steakhouse (261 Water St)
Morton's of Chicago (551 Fifth Ave)
Palm One, Palm Too, and Palm West Side (837 Second Ave, 840 Second Ave, and 250 W 50th St)
Patroon (160 E 46th St): outrageously expensive
Peter Luger Steak House (178 Broadway, Brooklyn): a tradition since 1887
Pietro's (232 E 43rd St)
Porters New York (216 Seventh Ave)
Post House (Lowell Hotel, 28 E 63rd St)
Primehouse New York (381 Park Ave)
Quality Meats (57 W 58th St)
Ruth's Chris Steak House (148 W 51st St)
Smith & Wollensky (797 Third Ave)
Sparks Steakhouse (210 E 46th St)
Strip House (13 E 12th St)

SUSHI

In the early 1980s, sushi bars became the trendy new *haute cuisine* of the fashionable set. To this day, New Yorkers love to wrap their chopsticks around succulent slivers of raw or cooked seafood on rice. Although many are content to order assortments concocted by the chef, true aficionados prefer to select by the piece. To tailor your next sushi platter to your own taste, here's what you need to know:

- *Amaebi* (sweet shrimp)
- *Anago* (sea eel)
- *California roll* (avocado and crab)
- *Hamachi* (yellowtail)
- *Hirame* (halibut)
- *Ika* (squid)
- *Ikura* (salmon roe)
- *Kappa maki* (cucumber roll)
- *Maguro* (tuna)
- *Nizakana* (cooked fish)
- *Saba* (mackerel)
- *Sake* (salmon)
- *Tekka maki* (tuna roll)
- *Toro* (fatty tuna)
- *Umeshiso maki* (plum roll)
- *Unagi* (freshwater eel)
- *Uni* (sea urchin)

Give any of these a try for sushi:

Aki (181 W 4th St)
Avenue A Sushi (103 Ave A)
Blue Ribbon Sushi (119 Sullivan St)
Bond Street (6 Bond St)
Geisha (33 E 61st St)
Hatsuhana (17 E 48th St)

Inagiku (Waldorf-Astoria, 301 Park Ave)
Japonica (100 University Pl)
Jewel Bako (239 E 5th St)
Kai (Ito En, 822 Madison Ave)
Kuruma Zushi (7 E 47th St, 2nd floor)
Kyo Ya (94 E 7th St)
Masa (10 Columbus Circle, 4th floor)
Matsugen (241 Church St)
Megu (62 Thomas St)
Nippon (155 E 52nd St)
Nobu New York and **Nobu Next Door** (105 Hudson St)
Ruby Foo's (1626 Broadway)
Sapporo East (164 First Ave)
Shabu-Tatsu (216 E 10th St)
Sugiyama (251 W 55th St)
Sushi a Go-Go (1900 Broadway)
Sushi-Azabu (428 Greenwich St)
Sushi Hana (1501 Second Ave)
Sushi of Gari (347 W 46th St, 370 Columbus Ave, and 402 E 78th St)
Sushi Seki (1143 First Ave)
Sushi Yasuda (204 E 43rd St)
Sushi Zen (108 W 44th St)
Sushiden (19 E 49th St and 123 W 49th St)
SushiSamba 7 (87 Seventh Ave and 245 Park Ave)
Takahachi (85 Ave A)
Tomoe Sushi (172 Thompson St)
Tsuki (1410 First Ave)
Ushi Wakamaru (136 W Houston St)
Yama (38 Carmine St and 122 E 17th St)

TAKEOUT

Balthazar (80 Spring St)
Beacon (25 W 56th St)
Bread (20 Spring St)
Cafe Español (172 Bleecker St)
City Market Cafe (551 Madison Ave)
City 75 (75 Rockefeller Plaza)
Cucina Vivolo (138 E 74th St)
Dean & Deluca (560 Broadway and 1150 Madison Ave)
Demarchelier (50 E 86th St)
Food Passion (1200 Lexington Ave)
Jacques Brasserie (204-206 E 85th St)
Jubilee (347 E 54th St)
Just Salad (320 Park Ave, 134 W 37th St, and 100 Maiden Lane)
L'Absinthe (227 E 67th St)
Lorenzo and Maria's Kitchen (1418 Third Ave)
Maria Pia (319 W 51st St)
Molyvos (871 Seventh Ave)
Murray's Cheese Shop (254 Bleecker St)
Pepe Verde (559 Hudson St)
RUB BBQ (208 W 23rd St)
Sarabeth's Bakery (75 Ninth Ave)

Schiller's Liquor Bar (131 Rivington St)
Sushi a Go-Go (1900 Broadway)
Sushi Zen (108 W 44th St)
Tio Pepe (168 W 4th St)
Tossed (295 Park Ave S)
Turkuaz Restaurant (2637 Broadway)
Virgil's Real Barbecue (152 W 44th St)

TEATIME

Thé Adoré (17 E 13th St)
Alice's Tea Cup (102 W 73rd St, 156 E 64th St, and 220 E 81st St)
Astor Court (St. Regis New York, 2 E 55th St)
Bar Seine (Hotel Plaza Athenee, 37 E 64th St)
Cafe S.F.A. (Saks Fifth Avenue, 611 Fifth Ave, 8th floor)
Carlyle Hotel Gallery (35 E 76th St)
Cha-an (230 E 9th St, 2nd floor)
Danal (59 Fifth Ave)
Gotham Lounge (Peninsula New York Hotel, 700 Fifth Ave)
Ito En (822 Madison Ave)
King's Carriage House (251 E 82nd St)
Lady Mendl's Tea Salon (56 Irving Pl)
McNally Jackson Book Store and Tea House (50 Prince St)
The Morgan Dining Room (The Morgan Library & Museum, 225 Madison Ave): in the cafe
Pembroke Room (Lowell Hotel, 28 E 63rd St)
Podunk (231 E 5th St)
Rotunda (Pierre Hotel, 2 E 61st St)
Sant Ambroeus (1000 Madison Ave and 259 W 4th St)
Sarabeth's (1295 Madison Ave, 423 Amsterdam Ave, and 40 Central Park S), **Sarabeth's at Lord & Taylor** (424 Fifth Ave), and **Sarabeth's at the Whitney** (945 Madison Ave)
T Salon (Chelsea Market, 75 Ninth Ave)
Tea & Sympathy (108 Greenwich Ave)
Tea Box Cafe (Takashimaya, 693 Fifth Ave)
Teany (90 Rivington St)
Ty Lounge (Four Seasons Hotel New York, 57 E 57th St)
Yaffa's Tea Room (19 Harrison St)

TOP-RATED

Adour Alain Ducasse (St. Regis New York, 2 E 55th St)
Allen & Delancey (115 Allen St)
Babbo (110 Waverly Pl)
Barbetta (321 W 46th St)
Blue Ribbon Sushi (119 Sullivan St)
Bouley (163 Duane St)
Cafe Boulud (20 E 76th St)
Chanterelle (2 Harrison St)
Craft (43 E 19th St)
Daniel (60 E 65th St)
Del Posto (85 Tenth Ave)
Eleven Madison Park (11 Madison Ave)
Four Seasons (99 E 52nd St)

Gilt (New York Palace Hotel, 455 Madison Ave)
Gotham Bar & Grill (12 E 12th St)
Gramercy Tavern (42 E 20th St)
Il Mulino (86 W 3rd St)
Insieme (777 Seventh Ave)
Jean Georges (Trump International Hotel and Tower, 1 Central Park W)
Kyo Ya (94 E 7th St)
La Grenouille (3 E 52nd St)
Le Bernardin (155 W 51st St)
Le Périgord (405 E 52nd St)
Mas Farmhouse (39 Downing St)
Masa (Time Warner Center, 10 Columbus Circle, 4th floor)
Momofuku Ko (163 First Ave)
Nobu New York and **Nobu Next Door** (105 Hudson St)
Nobu 57 (40 W 57th St)
Oceana (55 E 54th St)
Park Avenue Spring/Summer/Autumn/Winter (100 E 63rd St)
per se (Time Warner Center, 10 Columbus Circle, 4th floor)
Peter Luger Steak House (178 Broadway, Brooklyn)
Post House (Lowell Hotel, 28 E 63rd St)
Primavera (1578 First Ave)
Public (210 Elizabeth St)
River Cafe (1 Water St, Brooklyn)
Sasabune (401 E 73rd St)
Scarpetta (355 W 14th St)
Sugiyama (251 W 55th St)
Sushi of Gari (402 E 78th St)
Sushi Seki (1143 First Ave)
Sushi Yasuda (204 E 43rd St)
Union Square Cafe (21 E 16th St)
Veritas (43 E 20th St)

VEGETARIAN OFFERINGS

Angelica Kitchen (300 E 12th St)
Barbetta (321 W 46th St)
Benny's Burritos (113 Greenwich Ave and 93 Ave A)
Blossom (187 Ninth Ave)
Candle Cafe (1307 Third Ave)
Caravan of Dreams (405 E 6th St)
Chennai Garden (129 E 27th St)
Chola (232 E 58th St)
Counter (105 First Ave)
Dévi (8 E 18th St)
Dirt Candy (430 E 9th St)
Gobo (1426 Third Ave)
Green Table (Chelsea Market, 75 Ninth Ave)
Hangawi (12 E 32nd St)
Maoz Vegetarian (38 Union Square E)
Monte's Trattoria (97 MacDougal St)
Pure Food and Wine (54 Irving Pl)
Quantum Leap Natural Food (226 Thompson St and 203 First Ave)
Quintessence (263 E 10th St)

Rice (292 Elizabeth St and 115 Lexington Ave)
Salute! Restaurant and Bar (270 Madison Ave)
Snack (105 Thompson St)
Souen (28 E 13th St and 210 Ave of the Americas)
Spring Street Natural Restaurant (62 Spring St)
Surya (302 Bleecker St)
Two Boots (42 Ave A and other locations)
Vatan (409 Third Ave)
Vegetarian Paradise 2 (144 W 4th St)
Village Natural (46 Greenwich Ave)
Whole Earth Bakery & Kitchen (130 St. Mark's Pl)
Zen Palate (633 Ninth Ave and other locations)

VIEW

Alma (187 Columbia St, Brooklyn): magical rooftop garden
Asiate (Mandarin Oriental New York, Time Warner Center, 80 Columbus
  Circle, 35th floor)
Delegates Dining Room (United Nations, First Ave at 45th St, 4th
  floor)
Empire Hotel Rooftop (44 W 63rd St): 12th floor offers view of Lin-
  coln Center
Metropolitan Museum of Art (1000 Fifth Ave): rooftop bar
Peninsula New York Hotel (700 Fifth Ave): rooftop terrace bar and
  lounge with stunning views of Fifth Avenue
per se (Time Warner Center, 10 Columbus Circle, 4th floor)
River Cafe (1 Water St, Brooklyn): A window seat affords that breath-
  taking view of the downtown Manhattan skyline you've always seen on
  postcards and in movies.
Tavern on the Green (Central Park W at 67th St): Magical!
Top of the Tower (Beekman Tower Hotel, 3 Mitchell Pl): an art deco
  penthouse delight
The View (New York Marriott Marquis, 1535 Broadway): revolves high
  above Times Square
Water Club (30th St at East River): Savor the view with Sunday brunch.
World Yacht Cruises (Pier 81, 41st St at Hudson River): Manhattan
  from the water

Don't be confused by the name of this restaurant. **Delicatessen**
(54 Prince St, 212/226-0211) is open for breakfast, lunch, and dinner,
and serves comfort food with an international influence. With classic
ingredients, the all-time favorites include meatloaf, fish and chips, and
grilled mahi-mahi. For dessert, try Ovaltine pudding parfait or dunk a
homemade chocolate chip cookie in a cool glass of milk. A glass-ceiling
courtyard doubles as a lounge and private event room.

WINE BARS
Ara (24 Ninth Ave)
Artisanal (2 Park Ave)
Bin No. 220 (220 Front St)

Blue Ribbon Downing Street Bar (34 Downing St): 300-bottle wine
   list
Bottega del Vino (7 E 59th St)
Cafe Katja (79 Orchard St): Austrian wines and nibbles
Cafe Notte (1626 Second Ave): wine and coffee bar
Casellula (401 W 52nd St): extensive cheeses and superb tasting menu
Cavatappo (1728 Second Ave)
Centovini (25 W Houston St)
Enoteca I Trulli (122 E 27th St)
Epistrophy (200 Mott St): romantic
Gottino (52 Greenwich Ave): exceptional wines and snacks
I Tre Merli (463 West Broadway)
Il Posto Accanto (190 E 2nd St)
'inoteca (98 Rivington St)
Jadis (42 Rivington St)
MetroCafe & Wine Bar (32 E 21st St)
Monday Room (210 Elizabeth St)
Morrell Wine Bar & Cafe (1 Rockefeller Plaza)
Paradou (8 Little West 12th St)
Pata Negra (345 E 12th St): Spanish hams and cheeses
Proseccheria at Pasticcio (447 Third Ave)
Pudding Stones (1457 Third Ave)
Solex (103 First Ave): extensive wine list and unusual tarts, pot pies, and
   quiches
Ten Degrees (121 St. Mark's Pl)
Terroir (413 E 12th St): 50 wines by the glass
Turks and Frogs (323 W 11th St)
Veritas (43 E 20th St)
Wined Up (913 Broadway, 2nd floor)
Xicala Wine & Tapas Bar (151-B Elizabeth St)

I've done my best to provide you with accurate and helpful informa-
tion, but things inevitably change. An important tip before heading to
any restaurant is to call ahead in order to avoid disappointment and to
save yourself an unsuccessful visit. Why?
   • Even the best restaurants come and go.
   • Locations sometimes change.
   • Days and hours of operation can change.
   • Many restaurants encourage reservations.
So have fun choosing, and enjoy your New York dining experience!

New York Restaurants: The Best in Every Price Category

ABBOCCATO
136 W 55th St (bet Ave of the Americas and Seventh Ave)
Breakfast: Daily; Lunch: Mon-Sat; Dinner: Daily   212/265-4000
Expensive   www.abboccato.com

The Livanos family is known and respected on the New York restaurant scene. They own this elegant Italian dining spot, which serves some traditional (as if you are really in Italy) plates, so expect big things—especially if you like rather fussy Italian dishes. Personally, I like a simple approach, so I found some items a bit overwhelming but nonetheless very good. Most of the appetizers, especially the pastas, are excellent, and the breadsticks are fabulous! The *branzino*, crispy veal sweetbreads, sweet potato ravioli, and grilled baby lamb chops, are all noteworthy. The dessert menu, including homemade gelati, is a dream. However dreamy the dining experience, the sizable tab will wake you up.

ACAPPELLA
1 Hudson St (bet West Broadway and Chambers St)   212/240-0163
Lunch: Mon-Fri; Dinner: Daily   www.acappella-restaurant.com
Moderately expensive

Acappella is a classy, upscale—in atmosphere, food, and pricing—Tribeca dining room with a highly professional staff that provides a very special dining experience. It's a good place for a romantic interlude, for an important business lunch, or to experiment with some unique Northern Italian dishes. You'll find homemade pastas, risotto, calamari, fish, veal scaloppine, veal chops, Kobe beef, breaded breast of chicken, and prime steak on the menu. For dessert, splurge on the homemade Italian cheesecake or chocolate truffle torte.

If a great selection of small plates tempts you, try **Atria** (13-15 W 54th St, 212/262-4600, www.atrianyc.com). What a choice: oysters Rockefeller, crisp calamari, salt-stone-grilled prawns, coconut-crusted lobster, seared sea scallops, *weisswurst* and *haendlmaier* mustard, and much more. A couple of these platters, shared with your partner, are not only fun eating but also won't break the bank. Of course, larger plates are also available.

ADOUR ALAIN DUCASSE
St. Regis New York   212/710-2277
2 E 55th St (bet Fifth and Madison Ave)   www.adourstregis.com
Dinner: Daily
Expensive to very expensive

Alain Ducasse's experiences in New York have been much like a roller coaster, up and down, but never without a thrill here and there. His time at the venerable Essex House created a lot of chatter, but not much to endear himself to his diners. Now there is another dining adventure, elegant and grand. The menu and service are exceptional, and so are the prices. Whether savvy diners will be willing to pay top prices for lamb or cod with the

Ducasse touch remains to be seen. Pork *tournedos* are delicious, as is lobster Thermidor. But the real shining stars here are the extensive and expensive wine list—one of the most complete in Manhattan—and the fabulous desserts. If money is truly no object, splurge and enjoy yourself.

ALLEN & DELANCEY

115 Allen St (at Delancey St)	212/253-5400
Dinner: Daily	www.allenanddelancey.net
Moderately expensive to expensive	

Delancey Street has long been a linchpin of the Lower East Side, while Allen Street was best known for a series of small necktie stores that sold their wares at deep discounts. Now one of the most interesting and best newish restaurants in the city is located in this fabled area. Allen & Delancey is a bustling house that has been attractively decorated with all manner of unusual objects. The place is warm and compelling, with a small bar and very noisy main dining area. The food makes up for any shortfalls in atmosphere, and the American menu will please the most particular diners. Superb appetizers like carmelized bone marrow and caviar or French fingerlings with prosciutto shavings are delicious. The entree menu includes several seafood dishes, chicken, meat, and an unusual plate of beef, red cabbage, and potato puree. The desserts really caught my eye (and taste): chocolate peanut butter tart, sweet cream French toast, and warm blood-orange pudding cake.

The Lower East Side has an amazing restaurant scene. One of the cleanest and best—so good it's worth a trip from uptown—is **Falai** (68 Clinton St, 212/253-1960). The cuisine is Italian, the outdoor patio is highly inviting, the homemade breads are among the best I have ever tasted, and the profiteroles are to die for. The sorbets are also first-class. **Falai Panetteria** (79 Clinton St, 212/777-8956), a tiny satellite operation just across the street, is a good spot for quick takeout or eat-in soups, pastas, salads, and paninis.

ALOUETTE

2588 Broadway (bet 97th and 98th St)	212/222-6808
Dinner: Daily	www.alouettenyc.com
Moderate	

Looking for a bustling eatery on the Upper West Side with reasonable prices and good food? Alouette meets the criteria and is made even more desirable by a friendly and helpful staff. Seating is provided in smallish quarters on the street floor, and more tables are available on the mezzanine. You'll find many French specialities to start: *paté de foie gras de canard*, onion soup *gratinee,* escargots, and a delicious warm goat-cheese *tartelette.* Seafood dishes are available, but Alouette really shines in the steak category. Hanger steak and sirloin are excellent choices, with superb *pommes frites* (as you would expect) and a coconut-infused spinach side dish. Pretend you are in Paris and enjoy the cheese plate for dessert.

ALTO

11 E 53rd St (bet Fifth and Madison Ave)	212/308-1099
Lunch: Mon-Fri; Dinner: Mon-Sat	www.altorestaurant.com
Moderately expensive	

If you can find this rather hidden room, then expect to enjoy a classy Italian meal. I happen to be a great soup lover. Their offerings are first-rate, and if the puree of mushroom is available, then by all means order it. Lots of pastas are offered; their hand-cut semolina spaghetti is a house favorite. Pricey entrees are heavy on the seafood side. Sirloin of beef is delicious and worth the hefty tab. Cheese plates are a dime a dozen in Manhattan, but Alto's is especially tasty. For dessert try honey crisp apple tart with caramel gelato.

Dim sum is available almost any hour at **Ollie's** (1991 Broadway, 212/595-8181). A selection of reasonably priced steamed "Chinese healthy" dishes is offered. This is a good family restaurant.

AQUAVIT
65 E 55th St (bet Park and Madison Ave)   212/307-7311
Lunch: Mon-Fri (Sat in cafe only); Dinner: Daily; Brunch: Sun
Moderately expensive   www.aquavit.org

If you are looking for a true Scandinavian experience, you can't do better than Aquavit. Owner Hakan Swahn and chef Marcus Samuelsson have put together a first-class establishment. The tab will likely be sizable, but you can reduce it somewhat by dining in the more informal cafe, which serves the same wonderful food. The atmosphere is conducive to classy dining; they prefer that gentlemen wear jackets. The raw shell plate, lobster roll, or foie gras *ganache* will get the meal off to a great start. The seafood offerings —salmon, halibut, trout, and more—are the pride of the house. You'll find typical Scandinavian dishes, like gravlax and Swedish meatballs, served in the cafe. Hearty appetites will enjoy the seafood stew. My dessert suggestion is the signature Arctic Circle parfait.

ARABELLE
Hotel Plaza Athenee
37 E 64th St (bet Madison and Park Ave)   212/606-4647
Breakfast: Daily; Lunch: Tues-Sun; Dinner: Tues-Sat; Brunch: Sun
Moderately expensive to expensive   www.arabellerestaurant.com

Dining in this attractive room is a civilized experience. It is elegant and charming, and the adjacent lounge is one of the classiest places in Manhattan. For starters, try real French onion soup (in the lounge) or sauteed Hudson Valley foie gras. If you still have room, entree winners include pan-roasted Atlantic halibut, dumplings, beef tenderloin, and a tasty Maine lobster salad. By all means try the warm valrhona chocolate cake for dessert. The wait staff is unusually attentive and professional.

ARTISANAL
2 Park Ave (at 32nd St)   212/725-8585
Lunch: Mon-Fri; Dinner: Daily; Brunch: Sat, Sun
Moderate to moderately expensive   www.artisanalbistro.com

You'll be surprised how good the beef and chicken are here! Imagine a combination bistro, brasserie, and *fromagerie*, and you'll have a clear picture of this exciting operation. Being a cheese lover, I found the menu and attractive in-house takeout cheese counter first-rate. The crab and avocado salad is a wonderful way to start. Pricey seafood platters include lobster, clams, scallops, oysters, shrimp, sea urchin, and more. Several fondues are offered, including a classic Swiss and a wonderful Stilton and Sauterne. Seafood specialties include soft-shell crabs (in summer), cod, and Dover sole. Heartier appetites will be sated by grilled lamb chops, several steak items, and daily offerings. For dessert, cruise the cheese counter and load your plate from a selection of 250 of the world's finest. Seating is comfortable in the spacious room, service is highly informed and refined, and the energy level is high. Great wine selection, too!

Chinatown is a fascinating place to visit. It's fun just wandering in and out of the neighborhood shops, restaurants, and unique amusements of this busy place. Here are some of the best for eating:

Big Wong King (67 Mott St, 212/964-0540): barbecue
New Green Bo (66 Bayard St, 212/625-2359): Shanghai cuisine
Oriental Garden (14 Elizabeth St, 212/619-0085): fresh fish
Ping's Seafood (22 Mott St, 212/602-9988): great meal

A VOCE
41 Madison Ave (at 26th St)   212/545-8555
Lunch: Mon-Fri: Dinner: Daily   www.avocerestaurant.com
Moderate

The name means "word of mouth," and word got out quickly! A Voce is a busy place, with talented chef Missy Robbins. The setting is rather cold, but the vast windows opening up on a terrace, great in the nice weather, do soften the place. Like so many of the hot restaurants, this one is overbearingly noisy, but good food makes up for any discomfort. The attractive wait staff is well rehearsed on how to sell. I was impressed with the mature greeting by the restaurant manager, so different than the snotty and unschooled persons one encounters too often these days at the door in Manhattan eateries. By all means, finish your meal with the vanilla custard doughnuts (*bomboloni*) served with chocolate sauce.

BABBO
110 Waverly Pl (at Washington Square)   212/777-0303
Dinner: Daily   www.babbonyc.com
Moderate to moderately expensive

Surely you have heard about Babbo! For many years 110 Waverly Place has been one of my favorite dining addresses. First it was the legendary Coach House, and now it is the magnificent Italian watering spot Babbo, which means "daddy" in the native tongue. It has become one of the most respected houses of fine Italian dining in New York, and this reservation is one of the toughest in Manhattan. The townhouse setting is warm and comfortable, the service is highly professional, and an evening at Babbo is one you will savor for a long time! Most everything is good, but I especially recommend sweetbreads, grilled ribeye steak for two, and beef cheek ravioli. Wonderful desserts might include chocolate hazelnut cake, saffron panna cotta, pistachio and chocolate *semifreddo*, and the ever-popular cheese plate. Best of all is the assortment of homemade gelati and sorbetti.

BALTHAZAR
80 Spring St (at Crosby St)   212/965-1414
Breakfast: Daily; Lunch: Mon-Fri; Dinner: Daily; Brunch: Sat, Sun
Moderate   www.balthazarny.com

Balthazar is a popular destination at any time of the day (or night, as they serve late). The setting—with old mirrors, ceiling fans, and a yellow tin roof—is unique, and the food is quite good, considering the size of the operation. The personnel are harried but well-trained, and you will not wait for your water glass to be filled. Excellent bakery items shine at breakfast; be sure to pick up some tasty bread next door at their bakery on your way out. At lunch and dinner you can enjoy delicious seasonal salads, sandwiches, cheeses, paninis, fabulous French onion soup, *brandade*, escargots, steak *frites*, and an abundant seafood selection (including a seafood bar). For dessert the *tarte tatin* is a must. This brasserie is fun and different, and its takeout menu is a plus.

Asiate (Mandarin Oriental New York, 80 Columbus Circle, 212/805-8881) is a beautifully situated and well-appointed room. However, I do not feel the hefty prices are warranted.

BAR AMERICAIN
152 W 52nd St (bet Ave of the Americas and Seventh Ave)
Lunch: Mon-Fri; Dinner: Daily; Brunch: Sat, Sun   212/265-9700
Moderately expensive to expensive   www.baramericain.com

Bar Americain is indeed almost purely American. It can perhaps best be described as an American brasserie. The setting is large, occupying a space that was once the Judson Grill. The decor is a bit offbeat; however, chef Bobby Flay has made the room come alive. The food quality and attentive, professional service make this a good bet. The cocktails are numerous and interesting. To start, an eye-catching raw bar is stocked with oysters, clams, lobsters, and more. One could make a meal on the appetizers. Vidalia onion soup with blistered Vermont cheddar cheese is superb. The same holds true for crawfish and Dungeness crab griddle cakes. For entrees: cioppino, duck (with dirty wild rice), and rack of pork are worth a try. Five steak dishes are offered. Don't pass up a side of hot potato chips with blue cheese sauce. Take extra time to study the excellent dessert menu!

BARBETTA
321 W 46th St (bet Eighth and Ninth Ave)   212/246-9171
Lunch, Dinner, Supper: Tues-Sat   www.barbettarestaurant.com
Moderate to moderately expensive

Barbetta is one of those special places you'll find only in New York! Owner Laura Maioglio is a very special person, as well. It is an elegant restaurant serving *Piemontese* cuisine. Piemonte is located in northern Italy, and the cuisine reflects that charming part of the country. You can dine here in European elegance. One of New York's oldest restaurants, Barbetta celebrated its 100th anniversary in 2006. Amazingly, it is still owned by the family that founded it. One of the special attractions is dining alfresco in the garden during the summer. The main dining room and private party rooms are magnificent! They offer an a la carte luncheon menu, as well as a three-course pre-theater dinner menu. Six to eight choices are offered at each course, and service is expeditious, so that you can make opening curtain. After 8 p.m. you can enjoy a leisurely dinner with *crespelle* (almost a meal in itself), handmade ravioli, or the fabulous quail's nest of *fonduta* with white truffles. Barbetta specializes in fish and game dishes, which vary daily. Try squab prepared with hazelnuts and chestnuts. Other selections include rabbit, beef braised in red wine with polenta, and delicious rack of venison. Sixteen desserts are prepared daily, including several chocolate offerings; an assortment of cakes, tarts, and fruits; and panna cotta that's among the best in the city. Barbetta's extraordinary wine list features 1,650 bottles.

Time Warner Center Restaurants

The exclusive address of the **Time Warner Center** (10 Columbus Circle) is home to upscale shops, markets, and restaurants. As you would expect, the variety is wide and prices are generally expensive. **Bouchon Bakery** (212/823-9366, American/French) and **Landmarc** (212/823-6123, French) are both on the third floor. **Masa** and the more modest **Bar Masa** (212/823-9800, Japanese), **per Se** (212/823-9335, American/French), and **Porter House New York** (212/823-9500) have stylish dining facilities on the fourth floor. All are open for dinner, and most serve lunch. Call well in advance for reservations.

BAR BOULUD
1900 Broadway (bet 63rd and 64th St)   212/595-0303
Lunch: Mon-Fri; Dinner: Daily; Brunch: Sat, Sun   www.barboulud.com
Moderate

In a handy location just across Broadway from Lincoln Center, this sleek room features attractive table settings and a huge bar. With direction from Daniel Boulud, a menu has been crafted featuring a number of his favorites. You'll find hearty soups, patés, salads, and sandwiches. The housemade ham and *guérande* butter sandwich is delicious. For heavier fare, you'll find salmon, steaks, sausages, and chicken with a distinctive French flavor. Charcuterie specialties are available daily, with vegetables to accompany. A good showing of cheeses, ice creams, sorbets, and rich chocolate treats are featured for dessert. This is an obvious winner for the "ladies who lunch."

BARMARCHE
14 Spring St (at Elizabeth St)   212/219-2399
Lunch: Tues-Sun; Dinner: Daily; Brunch: Sat, Sun   www.barmarche.net
Moderate

Spring Street is full of small, cozy, and interesting places to dine. The area is called Nolita (shortland for "north of Little Italy"). One of the best stops hereabouts is Barmarche, where the folks are very friendly, the food is excellent, the price is right, and the atmosphere is appealing. You'll find a number of small plates, like a small pizza or chilled oysters, along with fresh salads, sandwiches, taquitos, and one of the best burgers in the city. The garlic fries served alongside the burgers are crisp, non-greasy, and delicious. Barmarche also does catering and is available for parties.

BEACON
25 W 56th St (bet Fifth Ave and Ave of the Americas)
Lunch: Mon-Fri; Dinner: Daily; Brunch: Sun   212/332-0500
Moderately expensive   www.beaconnyc.com

In a huge space divided into intimate sections, Beacon serves tasty dishes cooked over an open fire. If you can get seated near the open kitchen ("the pit"), it is a fascinating show. With over 200 seats and an expansive menu for lunch and dinner, the staff is well trained to provide superior service. Over a dozen appetizers (from wood-roasted bone marrow to oysters on the half shell), sandwiches, salads, steaks, chops, seafood, and pasta are available at noon. Menu offerings increase at night. The wood-roasted chops and veal dishes are special. Dessert soufflés add a festive end to a great meal.

BEN BENSON'S STEAK HOUSE
123 W 52nd St (bet Ave of the Americas and Seventh Ave)
Lunch: Mon-Fri; Dinner: Daily   212/581-8888
Moderately expensive   www.benbensons.com

For years Ben Benson's has been a favorite of the meat-and-potato set, and with justification. The atmosphere is macho-clubby, and the food is uniformly good. Unlike some other steakhouses, service is courteous and efficient. The menu is what you would expect: sirloin and T-bone steaks, filet mignon, prime rib, chops, and the like. But Ben Benson's also offers seafood, chicken, calves liver, and chopped steak. A special steak-style veal chop offers 22 ounces of delicious indulgence. The soups are outstanding! Wonderful potatoes, onion rings, or healthy spinach will complete the stomach-filling experience. Daily lunch specials include lobster cakes, grilled chicken breast, roast beef hash, and chicken pot pie. Just don't come looking for bargains. Ben treats you well, and you will pay well in return!

Café Borgia (161 Prince St, 212/677-1850) is legendary for its coffees, lattes, teas, and sandwiches. It is always packed with a high-energy crowd of all ages. Prices are modest and the place is really fun!

BENOIT
60 W 55th St (bet Fifth Ave and Ave of the Americas)   646/943-7373
Lunch, Dinner: Mon-Sat   www.benoitny.com
Moderately expensive

In an attractive room that has seen its share of ups and downs over the years, master foodie Alain Ducasse has designed a charming bistro with special touches only the French can create. One immediately notices the warm greeting, very professional service, and interesting diners. What to eat? It is like going to heaven by way of France! The *paté en croute* (an 1892 recipe) is fabulous; a charcuterie and paté selection is varied and filling. "Ladies who lunch" will delight in the *quenelles de brochet*, and *Rachou cassoulet* is sensational. At lunch, feast on escargots, lobster ravioli, and chocolate soufflé. Portions are huge! Take your time and savor the atmosphere as well as the platters.

BIG NICK'S
2175 Broadway (at 77th St)   212/362-9238
Daily: 24 hours   www.bignicksnyc.com
Inexpensive

This unfancy, inexpensive place offers good food at low prices. Breakfasts are super, and they serve lots of salads and sandwiches for lunch. The burgers are sensational. There is a special selection for the diet-conscious. Filo pastries and meat, cheese, and spinach pies are all specialties. Pizzas and baked potatoes are served any way you want, or try delicious cakes and pies, homemade baklava, and Greek yogurt. Service is friendly, and they offer free delivery. Big Nick's has been at it since 1962 with virtually no publicity.

BISTRO LES AMIS
180 Spring St (at Thompson St)   212/226-8645
Lunch, Dinner: Daily   www.bistrolesamis.com
Moderate

Bistro les Amis is a delightful bistro worth stopping by in the middle of a Soho shopping trip or gallery excursion. In the warmer months, doors open onto the sidewalk, and the passing parade is almost as inviting as the varied menu. French onion soup with gruyere is a must, and salmon marinated with fresh dill and herbs is just as good. Lunch entrees include sandwiches and fresh salads. In the evening, seafood and steak dishes are available. The steak *frites* with herb butter are first-class. There's nothing very fancy about this bistro—just good food with an extra touch of friendly service.

> **Bianca** (5 Bleecker St, 212/260-4666), is a small Italian neighborhood restaurant that has gotten a lot of attention. The lasagna is great, the mashed potatoes are sinful, and the *tartufo is* almost the real thing. The tab is modest. Take cash, as credit cards are not accepted.

BISTRO 60
37 E 60th St (at Madison Ave)   212/230-1350
Lunch, Dinner: Daily; Brunch: Sun   www.bistro60.com
Moderate

With a typical French menu and a delightful outdoor space to enjoy in nice weather, Bistro 60 is a welcome stopping place for weary shoppers who have been trekking the streets of the Upper East Side. Salads are appealing, particularly a wonderful red and yellow beet dish with goat cheese. Of course you'll find oysters, snails with garlic butter, wild mushrooms in puff pastry, artichokes with vinaigrette dressing, and smoked salmon with caviar on the bill of fare. For hearty diners, the steak tartare, Long Island duck, or mussels in white wine sauce are suggested. It is always nice to find a place like Bistro 60, where you can get a satisfying meal in the middle of the afternoon.

BLAUE GANS
139 Duane St (bet Church St and West Broadway)
Lunch: Mon-Fri; Dinner: Daily; Brunch: Sat, Sun   212/571-8880
Moderate to moderately expensive   www.kg-ny.com

The space may be familiar to you, as it used to house Le Zinc. However, the food at Blaue Gans ("Blue Goose") is very different! Chef Kurt Guten-brunner lives up to his heritage with an Austro-German bistro that offers delicious platters like red cabbage and good salad, smoked trout, goulash, vegetable strudel, wiener schnitzel, *käsekrainer* (with sauerkraut), blood sausage, and *Kavalierspitz* (boiled beef shoulder) served with fabulous creamed spinach. *Tafelspitz* (boiled beef) is Austria's national dish, and it, too, is available. I am a great lover of Vienna, especially the fabulous Sacher torte, which is a tradition in this great city. Unfortunately, Blaue Gans' Sacher torte falls far short of fabulous. Instead, go for the Salzburger nockerl, a warm dessert soufflé that's jazzed up with tart huckleberries. The folks here are delightful, which makes the meal even more memorable.

Budget-Friendly Restaurants

The economy has taken a big bite out of dining-out budgets, but people still want to dine on appetizing fare. Here are some tasty and affordable alternatives to the high-priced restaurants:

Gelato—**Dessert Club, ChikaLicious** (203 E 10th St, 212/475-0929): try soft-serve

Indian—**Chennai Garden** (129 E 27th St, 212/689-1999): plentiful combination dinner

Organic food—**Cook Shop** (156 Tenth Ave, 212/924-4440): food from local farms

Pasta—**Pepe Rosso to Go** (149 Sullivan St, 212/677-4555): authentic and cheap

Rotisserie chicken—**Pio Pio** (1746 First Ave, 212/426-5800): Peruvian style

---

BLT MARKET

Ritz-Carlton New York, Central Park   212/521-6125
1430 Ave of the Americas (at 59th St)   www.bltmarket.com
Breakfast: Daily; Lunch: Mon-Sat; Dinner: Daily
Expensive (breakfast is moderate)

Laurent Tourondel has a series of BLT operations around the city (Prime, Fish, Burger, Steak), with BLT Market being one of the most unique. It is in a classy location, with farmyard scenes and objects adorning the room. The menu changes with the season, and fresh produce is the theme of the meals. You'll find unusual combinations and very different tastes—and you'll pay mightily for them. I found the place a tad snooty, with obviously well-heeled business types and elderly gentlemen trying to impress their partners or clients. The best part of the meal is the baguette of fresh garlic bread delivered in a paper bag. The roasted Jamison Farm lamb loin is truly delicious, too.

BLT STEAK

106 E 57th St (bet Park and Lexington Ave)   212/752-7470
Lunch: Mon-Fri; Dinner: Mon-Sat   www.bltsteak.com
Moderately expensive to expensive

No, BLT does not stand for the popular bacon, lettuce, and tomato sandwich. It stands for Bistro Laurent Tourondel, and chef Tourondel's considerable talents in the kitchen have made this French/American steakhouse one of the best in Manhattan. The delicious popovers served at the start absolutely melt in your mouth! Most of the pricey salads are big and healthy, and the soups are filling and hearty. Save room for the main show: hanger steak, Kobe flat-iron steak, filets, New York strip steak, and more. You have your choice of eight great sauces to accompany the meat entree. Also on the menu: fish, shellfish, and potatoes done seven different ways. (I could make an entire meal of BLT's potato choices!) The rack of lamb is superb. Chocolate tart smothered with creamy ice cream is one of the best desserts in Manhattan or anywhere.

BLUE HILL
75 Washington Pl (bet Ave of the Americas and MacDougal St)
Dinner: Daily   212/539-1776
Moderate to moderately expensive   www.bluehillfarm.com

Dramatic it is not. Comfortable it is—barely. Solid it is—in spades. Blue Hill is named for a farm in the Berkshires inhabited by a member of the owner's family. The restaurant reflects the chef's solid upbringing with David Bouley. The limited menu, with only a half dozen appetizers and entrees, includes some spectacular standouts and changes periodically. Poached duck is a specialty. The crabmeat salad, if available, is top rate. If your evening plans involve intimate conversation, forget Blue Hill, as eavesdropping is inevitable. The chocolate bread pudding ("chocolate silk") is really the only dessert worth the calories.

For a really superb experience, make reservations up to two months in advance for **Blue Hill at Stone Barns** (914/366-9600, www.blue hillstonebarns.com). It is located 30 miles north of the city at the Stone Barns Center for Food and Agriculture in Pocantico Hills, New York. Only 80 guests are accommodated nightly in what was once a cow barn. Executive chef Dan Barber presides over a kitchen that serves a *prix fixe* Sunday dinner from $95 to $125.

BLUE RIBBON BAKERY
35 Downing St (at Bedford St)
Lunch, Dinner: Daily; Brunch: Sat, Sun   212/337-0404
Moderate   www.blueribbonrestaurants.com

The rustic breads at this cafe and bakery are excellent, and there is so much more. Downstairs, customers may dine in a fantastic grotto-like atmosphere, complete with two small dining rooms, a wine cellar, and wonderful fresh-bread aroma. The upstairs and downstairs menus feature sandwiches, steaks, seafood, cheeses, grilled items, veggies, and yummy desserts (including profiteroles).

BLUE RIBBON BRASSERIE
97 Sullivan St (bet Spring and Prince St)   212/274-0404
Daily: 4 p.m.-4 a.m.   www.blueribbonrestaurants.com
Moderate

Blue Ribbon is one of the most popular spots in Soho, with a bustling bar scene and people lining up for its limited number of tables. Regulars savor the exceptional food in this unpretentious restaurant. There is a raw bar to attract seafood lovers, along with clams, lobster, crab, boiled crawfish, and the house special "Blue Ribbon Royale" appetizer plate. One can choose from two dozen appetizers, including barbequed ribs, smoked trout, caviar, and chicken wings. Entrees are just as wide-ranging: sweetbreads, catfish, tofu ravioli, fried chicken and mashed potatoes, burgers, and more. How the smallish kitchen can turn out so many dishes is amazing, but they certainly do it well. Don't come for a relaxed evening; this is strictly an all-American culinary experience. Those who experience hunger pangs after midnight appreciate the late hours. Try the excellent sushi at their nearby **Blue Ribbon Sushi** (119 Sullivan St, 212/343-0404). Then there is the **Blue Ribbon Sushi Bar & Grill** (308 W 58th St, 212/397-0404), in the Columbus Hotel. The sushi menu is expanded, with a wide variety of popular cold and hot dishes, all expectedly very good. This location also offers traditional or Japanese breakfast and Sunday brunch.

Here's a bar that is both an attraction and a thriving watering hole. The story of the **Campbell Apartment**, located off the West Balcony of Grand Central Terminal (42nd St at Vanderbilt Ave, 212/953-0409), is a fascinating one. The space was once the private office of John Campbell, a very wealthy financier. In its heyday, these classy digs had a butler and some of the most expensive furnishings available. Even jaded New Yorkers like to tell stores about this fellow and that room. It is surely worth a visit!

BLUE SMOKE
116 E 27th St (bet Lexington Ave and Park Ave S)   212/447-7733
Lunch, Dinner: Daily; Brunch: Sat, Sun   www.bluesmoke.com
Moderate

With Blue Smoke, Danny Meyer filled a real void in the Manhattan dining scene, satisfying legions of barbecue lovers who found it difficult to get authentic down-home ribs in the Big Apple. In addition to ribs, you'll find chili, smoked beef brisket, tasty sandwiches, pit-baked beans, and more. Blue Smoke is not just a barbecue place, but a full-fledged scene, with an ultra-busy bar attracting fun-loving trendsetters.

BLUE WATER GRILL
31 Union Square W (at 16th St)   212/675-9500
Lunch, Dinner: Daily; Brunch: Sun   www.brguestrestaurants.com
Moderate

This seafood restaurant really knows the ocean and all the edible creatures that inhabit it! Blue Water Grill is a highly professional operation (except for their phone system). Superbly trained personnel operate in a building that once served as a bank and is now a very bustling restaurant. Wonderful appetizers may include lobster bisque, grilled baby octopus, and Maryland crab cakes. Tuna, salmon, and swordfish are prepared several ways. Lobsters and oysters (several dozen varieties) are fresh and tasty. For those who want to stick to shore foods, there are pastas, chicken dishes, and grilled filet mignon. A half dozen sensibly priced desserts include a seasonal fruit plate and warm valrhona chocolate cake with vanilla ice cream.

BOBO
181 W 10th St (at Seventh Ave)   212/488-2626
Dinner: Daily; Brunch: Sat, Sun   www.bobonyc.com
Moderately expensive

Tucked away in an unassuming building just off Seventh Avenue, Bobo is a warm and charming place to dine, but insist on eating upstairs. Attentive service, sizeable portions, and quite good food make this a rather romantic dining spot. Menu favorites include local, New England, and West Coast oysters, and a number of tasty appetizers that are heavy on the seafood side —like scallop *crudo* or Maine crab (when in season). Again, the entrees feature seafood dishes with bass, cod, and skate usually available. Braised short ribs are delicious. A number of desserts are available. Eight cheeses are listed at reasonable prices.

> For a quick meal, head over to **Camaje** (85 MacDougal St, 212/673-8184), which is a great bistro. Ask owner Abigail Hitchcock about her cooking classes.

BOND 45
154 W 45th St (bet Ave of the Americas and Seventh Ave)
Breakfast: Mon-Sat; Lunch, Dinner: Daily; Brunch: Sat   212/869-4545
Moderate to moderately expensive   www.bond45.com

In the middle of the Theater District, busy restaurateur Shelly Fireman has created another huge dining hall. Billed as an Italian steak and seafood room, Bond 45 is named for the old Bond men's store that used to occupy this site. If it's Italian, Bond 45 has it! The antipasto bar at the entrance makes a mouth-watering beginning. Beyond that, there are salads, mozzarella, carpaccio dishes, oysters, clams, cured meats, pastas, steaks, and so on. An abundance of wait personnel ensures prompt service. Be advised that the dessert selection doesn't live up to the rest of the fare.

BOTTEGA DEL VINO
7 E 59th St (bet Fifth and Madison Ave)
Breakfast, Lunch, Dinner: Daily   212/223-3028
Moderately expensive   www.bottegadelvinonyc.com

This is a serious restaurant that serves serious food. Translated: don't come expecting bargains or typical Italian fare. The location is handy for those visiting or living on the Upper East Side. Service is very professional. All the dishes I tried were good, especially the steaks. If risotto with shrimp and asparagus tips is on the menu, go for it! The signature dish, risotto Amarone (as in Amarone wine), lives up to its reputation. Desserts are tasty and filling, and the cheese selection is excellent.

BOULEY
163 Duane St (at Hudson St)   212/964-2525
Lunch, Dinner: Daily
Expensive

BOULEY MARKET
120 West Broadway (at Duane St) 212/219-1011
Daily: 7:30 a.m.-8:30 p.m.

UPSTAIRS AT BOULEY
130 West Broadway (at Duane St) 212/608-5829
Lunch, Dinner: Daily; Brunch: Sat, Sun

BRUSHSTROKE
30 Hudson St

BOULEY TEST KITCHEN
88 West Broadway (at Chambers St), 5th floor 212/964-2525

BOULEY PRODUCTION KITCHEN
160 Varick St www.davidbouley.com

There is no end to the culinary genius of David Bouley, one of the most celebrated chefs in the United States. His flagship restaurant, **Bouley**, is one of Manhattan's finest dining venues, with superb French fare and service. It is definitely an "occasion" destination. Located under vaulted red arches, **Bouley Market** provides a selection of artisanal cheeses, hot- and cold-prepared foods to go, salads and Bouley bakery items. This is a self-serve operation that can be enjoyed in the adjacent tea room by day and the wine bar by night. **Upstairs at Bouley** is David's casual dining spot, featuring some of the best burgers in town. Visiting chefs display their talents at the **Bouley Test Kitchen**, used for catered events and cooking classes. **Bouley Production Kitchen** (debuting in fall 2009) is designed around a fully intact *art nouveau* bakery, which you can observe from the mezzanine while dining. **BrushStroke** is another David Bouley project targeted for late 2009. It will showcase Bouley's passion for Japanese cuisine, featuring the best of Japan's offerings, from sushi to Kaiseki menus.

Burp Castle (41 E 7th St, 212/982-4576)—Excuse me! What a name! This is not your usual noisy beer hall. Murals depicting the Middle Ages embellish the walls; hence, the castle theme. The Belgian beer selection is much larger than you'd expect in this small bar, and it varies with what is currently on tap. Conversation is encouraged, although rambunctious talkers are quieted. *Pomme frites* (from around the corner) are served Monday, Wednesday, and Sunday during happy hour. If you miss out, it's acceptable to bring in your own food.

BRASSERIE
100 E 53rd St (bet Park and Lexington Ave) 212/751-4840
Breakfast, Lunch: Mon-Fri; Dinner: Daily; Brunch: Sat, Sun
Moderate www.patinagroup.com

For those who like big, brassy, fun dining spots that serve very good food, Brasserie is a New York tradition. What was once a round-the-clock operation now keeps handy late hours (Mon-Thurs till 11 p.m., Fri, Sat till midnight, Sun till 10 p.m.) in very attractive quarters: a grand staircase fit for a fashion show with sexy lighting and a bar that offers all manner of goodies. Much of the food has a French flair, but there is more: well-prepared grill dishes, short ribs, grilled bass, scallops, crab cakes, *pot-au-feu*, steamed mussels with *frites*, and daily specials. Favorites include good old-fashioned onion soup, burgers, and salad niçoise. For dessert, try the chocolate *beignets*.

BRASSERIE 8½
9 W 57th St (bet Fifth Ave and Ave of the Americas)   212/829-0812
Lunch: Mon-Fri; Dinner: Daily; Brunch: Sun   www.patinagroup.com
Moderately expensive

The interior and the dining are both dramatic at Brasserie 8½. Descending a long spiral staircase, you enter a spectacular room filled with comfy chairs, an attractive bar, a wall of Léger stained glass, and a collection of signed Matisse prints. Even the tableware is pleasing. Main-course winners include crab cakes, roast chicken, grilled sea scallops, grilled veggie salad, and Maine lobster salad. Specials are offered daily. Sunday brunch is worth a visit. Great desserts might include chocolate soufflé with malt ice cream. Three private rooms are available for special events.

The Big Apple also boasts some big restaurants. New York's top chefs and restaurateurs keep pumping up the square footage of their newest outposts. Bigger is not necessarily better, but at most of these operations, size and quality coexist just fine.

Buddakan (75 Ninth Ave, 212/989-6699): 368 seats
Del Posto (85 Tenth Ave, 212/497-8090): very good indeed; 700 seats
Morimoto (88 Tenth Ave, 212/989-8883): you'll like it; 369 seats
Nobu 57 (40 W 57th St, 212/757-3000): done with style and grace; 300 seats
Rosa Mexicano (9 E 18th St, 212/533-3350): tasty South of the Border treats; 350 seats
Tao (42 E 58th St, 212/888-2288): Asian bistro; 300 seats

BRASSERIE RUHLMANN
45 Rockefeller Plaza (enter on 50th St, bet Fifth Ave
    and Ave of the Americas)   212/974-2020
Lunch, Dinner: Mon-Sat: Brunch: Sun   www.brasserieruhlmann.com
Moderate to moderately expensive

This is *the* place for steak tartare! The attraction is the location: right in the heart of the midtown shopping area. The large room (232 seats) is bold and classy, the service is highly professional, and you are greeted with genuine enthusiasm. Some signature dishes: for lunch, roasted free-range chicken; for dinner, Dover sole; and for dessert, hazelnut *Paris-brest*. You will also appreciate designer Emile-Jacques Ruhlmann's red art-deco interior. Brasserie Ruhlmann opens early and closes late.

BRAVO GIANNI
230 E 63rd St (bet Second and Third Ave)   212/752-7272
Lunch: Mon-Fri; Dinner: Daily   www.bravogianni.com
Moderately expensive

Fans of Bravo Gianni—and there are many—may be upset that I've spoiled their secret by including it in this book. It's so comfortable and the food so good that they don't want it to become overcrowded and spoiled. But it doesn't look like there's any real danger of that happening as long as Gianni himself is on the job. The not-too-large room is pleasantly appointed, with beautiful plants on every table. The atmosphere is intimate. And what tastes await you! You can't go wrong with any of the antipasto selections or soups. They have the best ravioli in town. No one does *tortellini alla panna*, *ravioli alla Genovese*, or roast baby lamb better, either. I can recommend every dish on the menu, with top billing going to the fish dishes and rack of lamb. Marvelous desserts, many of them made in-house, will surely tempt you. Legions of loyal customers come back again and again, and it's easy to see why.

In these money-saving times, New Yorkers are lining up to fill their lunch plates with items from a growing number of attractive and well-stocked delis and buffets. They offer eat-in or takeout sandwiches, soups, drinks (including smoothies), huge salad bars, hot entrees, and a good selection of desserts. The advantages are obvious: quick service, reasonable prices, and tasty food.

Here are some I recommend:

Amy's Bread (75 Ninth Ave, 212/462-4338)
Azure (830 Third Ave, 212/486-8080)
Balthazar (80 Spring St, 212/965-1785)
Ben's Kosher Deli (209 W 38th St, 212/398-2367)
Bonsignour Cafe (35 Jane St, 212/229-9700)
Breadstix Cafe (254 Eighth Ave, 212/243-8444)
Churrascaria Plataforma (behind Belvedere Hotel, 316 W 49th St, 212/245-0505)
City Bakery (3 W 18th St, 212/366-1414)
City Market Cafe (551 Madison Ave, 212/572-9800)
Clinton St. Baking Co. & Restaurant (4 Clinton St, 646/602-6263)
Food Exchange (120 E 59th St, 212/759-0656)
Food Passion (1200 Lexington Ave, 212/861-2766)
Garden of Eden (162 W 23rd St, 212/675-6300; 7 E 14th St, 212/255-4200; and 2780 Broadway, 212/222-7300)
Juice Generation (171 W 4th St, 212/242-0440 and other locations)
Just Salad (320 Park Ave, 212/244-1111; 134 W 37th St, 212/244-1111; and 100 Maiden Lane, 212/244-1111)
Mangia (50 W 57th St, 212/582-5882; 16 E 48th St, 212/754-7600; and 22 W 23rd St, 212/647-0200)
Maoz Vegetarian (38 Union Square E, 212/260-1988)
North Village Deli Emporium (78 Eighth Ave, 212/229-0887)
Quantum Leap Natural Foods (203 First Ave, 212/673-9848)

BRIDGE CAFE

279 Water St (beneath Brooklyn Bridge)   212/227-3344
Lunch: Mon-Fri; Dinner: Daily; Brunch: Sun   www.bridgecafenyc.com
Moderate

The Bridge Cafe—located north of South Street Seaport beneath the Brooklyn Bridge—has been operating since 1794, making it the oldest drinking establishment in the city. Over the decades—nay, over the centuries!—it has housed its share of brothels and saloons. Start with the popular Bridge Cafe salad. Other great dishes include buffalo steak, lobster pot pie, and vegetable strata. There is nothing fancy about this place—just good food and especially pleasant personnel. Don't leave without trying the old-fashioned butterscotch pudding. On Sunday, the French toast will get you off to a great start.

BROADWAY EAST
171 East Broadway (near Rutgers St)   212/228-3100
Dinner: Daily; Brunch: Sat, Sun   www.broadwayeast.com
Moderate to moderately expensive

Come to Broadway East for dinner and stay to party downstairs at **B. East**—or just make this a party destination. Cuisine is American, with a nod to vegan and vegetarian diets at prices that won't break the bank. There's an abbreviated late-night menu for the merrymakers in the nightclub-cum-speakeasy.

Enjoy a very satisfying weekend brunch at **Cafe de Bruxelles** (118 Greenwich Ave, 212/206-1830). What to order? Belgian waffles, of course, which come with delicious Belgian fries and a green salad.

BROOKLYN DINER USA
212 W 57th St (bet Broadway and Seventh Ave)   212/977-1957
155 W 43rd St (bet Broadway and Ave of the Americas)
Breakfast, Lunch, Dinner, Late Supper: Daily   212/265-5400
Moderate   www.brooklyndiner.com

Brooklyn Diner USA (which is located in Manhattan) is worth a visit. With all-day dining, an expansive menu, pleasant personnel, better-than-average diner food, and reasonable prices, these places are winners. You can find just about anything your heart desires: breakfast fare, sandwiches (the cheeseburger is a must), salads, hearty lunch and dinner plates, homemade desserts, and good drinks. Their muffins are moist, flavorful, and outrageously good. A tile floor and comfortable booths add to the authentic diner ambience.

BRYANT PARK GRILL
25 W 40th St (bet Fifth Ave and Ave of the Americas)
Lunch: Mon-Fri; Dinner: Daily; Brunch: Sat, Sun   212/840-6500
Moderate   www.arkrestaurants.com

This place is one of Manhattan's most charming American grills. A handy location in midtown, a refreshing view of Bryant Park, and a sensible, family-friendly menu make this a popular destination. Although the menu changes with the seasons, one can count on a good selection of soups, salads, steak, and seafood items at lunch and dinner. A $35 *prix fixe* pre-theater menu is available from 5 to 7 daily with three courses—handy for those going to shows nearby. The a la carte weekend brunch is popular, too. Personnel are friendly and child-oriented.

BUTTER
415 Lafayette St (bet 4th St and Astor Pl)   212/253-2828
Dinner: Mon-Sat   www.butterrestaurant.com
Moderately expensive

Noisy and fun, Butter prides itself on churning out exceptional dishes. The appetizer menu includes lobster rolls, delicious foie gras, and fresh salads. For entrees, any of the seafood dishes and the outstanding grilled organic ribeye are good. They do braised beef shanks well, too! The upside-down apple crisp will appeal to your sweet tooth, and the warm banana bread is a good choice, if it's on the menu. A tasting menu is also offered.

BUTTERFIELD 8
5 E 38th St (bet Fifth and Madison Ave)   212/679-0646
Lunch, Dinner: Daily   www.butterfield8nyc.com
Moderate

Old-time New Yorkers will remember Butterfield 8 as a classy telephone prefix. This nostalgic phrase was revived as an attractive, busy retreat serving American fare. The atmosphere is strictly old-time New York, and so is the food: Caesar and Cobb salads, cheese-steak sandwiches, Angus burgers, oysters, and seared ahi tuna steaks. There's even macaroni and cheese. What's for dessert? New York-style cheesecake, of course! A young, attractive wait staff makes visiting here a pleasure.

> **Cafe Lalo** (201 W 83rd St, 212/496-6031) is a madhouse at all hours. For delicious, reasonably priced sandwiches and other light meals, this room is first-rate. The dessert selection can only be described as awesome!

CAFE BOULUD
20 E 76th St (at Madison Ave)   212/772-2600
Lunch: Tues-Sat; Dinner: Daily; Brunch: Sun   www.danielnyc.com
Moderately expensive

Boulud is a famous name in Manhattan food circles. If you are one of the "ladies who lunch" or like to look at those who do, then this is the place for you. The food is quite good, though the room is rather drab and I sometimes find the attitude haughty. Once seated, however, you'll enjoy the innovative menu. There are always vegetarian selections, world cuisines (every season highlights a different area), traditional French classics and country cooking, and menu items inspired by the "rhythm of the seasons." A three-course *prix fixe* menu is available at lunch, and there is a tasting menu for dinner. Evening prices are higher, but remember this place belongs to the Daniel Boulud, one of the nation's best chefs. Unfortunately he isn't in the kitchen at Cafe Boulud, because he is busy doing great things at his flagship restaurant, Daniel.

CAFE CENTRO
MetLife Building
200 Park Ave (45th St at Vanderbilt Ave)   212/818-1222
Lunch: Mon-Fri; Dinner: Mon-Sat   www.patinagroup.com
Moderate

A grand cafe reminiscent of Paris in the 1930s, New York's Cafe Centro offers a classic Parisian brasserie menu. Guests are greeted by a gas-fired rotisserie and a beautiful open kitchen that's spotlessly clean and efficient. For starters, crusty French bread is laid out in front of you. A raw bar is featured. One can always find such favorites as light and tasty chicken pie *bisteeya* (with almonds, raisins, and orange-flower essence). Other specialties include a hefty seafood platter, excellent steaks and French fries, sea bass, penne pasta, and moist, flavorful roast chicken. The pastry chef turns out a variety of changing desserts: New York State apple strudel, ricotta *beignets*, mocha torte, and a sampler plate of cookies. Adjoining the dining room is a busy beer bar that serves light sandwiches and appetizers.

CAFE CLUNY
284 W 12th St (at 4th St)   212/255-6900
Breakfast, Lunch: Mon-Fri; Dinner: Daily; Brunch: Sat, Sun
Moderate to moderately expensive   www.cafecluny.com

On hard-to-find West 12th Street, Cafe Cluny is worth tracking down. You can drop by at any hour and be assured of very good food at sensible prices. Sandwiches and salads are the order of the day at noon. A pricier dinner menu features chicken, beef, and short-rib entrees. Daily specials are offered for both lunch and dinner.

French Specialties

Bouillabaisse: French seafood stew
Confit: goose, duck, or pork that has been salted, cooked, and preserved in its own fat
Coulis: a thick, smooth sauce, usually made from vegetables but sometimes from fruit
En croute: anything baked in a buttery pastry crust or hollowed-out slice of toast
Foie gras: duck or goose liver, usually made into paté
Tartare: finely chopped and seasoned raw beef, often served as an appetizer

---

CAFE D'ALSACE
1695 Second Ave (at 88th St)   212/722-5133
Lunch: Mon-Fri; Dinner: Daily; Brunch: Sat, Sun www.cafedalsace.com
Moderate

When dress and noise level are not important and kids may be in your party, Cafe d'Alsace is a good choice for dining on the Upper East Side. The menu is large and varied: quiches (excellent!), sandwiches, sausages served with sauerkraut, salads, steaks, *charcroute*, and a full brunch selection. Their burger includes onions braised in Riesling. Young helpers provide informed service. The chef features Alsatian specialties, including Alsatian sugar cookies for dessert. If bistro ambience appeals to you, then check out this charmer. Adults, this place stocks over 110 varieties of beer, and a beer sommelier is on hand to help make a selection.

CAFE SABARSKY
Neue Galerie
1048 Fifth Ave (at 86th St)   212/288-0665
Breakfast, Lunch: Wed-Mon; Dinner: Thurs-Sun
Moderate   www.cafesabarsky.com

The setting is quaint, the personnel are gracious, the prices are right, and the German-Austrian food is delicious. For breakfast, try Sabarsky *Frühstück* (Viennese mélange, orange juice, soft-boiled eggs, and Bavarian ham). Lunch and dinner selections include pea soup with mint, paprika sausage salad, crepes with smoked trout, Bavarian sausage, späetzle with mushrooms and peas, and Hungarian beef goulash. Cafe Sabarsky also serves sandwiches, sensational sweets (like Viennese dark chocolate cake and apple strudel), Viennese coffees, and much more. Cafe Sabarsky is crowded, so come early and expect a wait! Music is offered Friday through Sunday.

Eat at the Bar

To save on your dining tab, try eating at the bar, where smaller portions and lower prices are generally offered. Granted, the surroundings are not as intimate or glamorous as the main dining rooms, but the food is just as good.

In this regard I recommend **Gordon Ramsay at the London** (London NYC Hotel, 151 W 54th St, 212/468-8888; dinner Tuesday through Saturday). **The London Bar** is *the* place to be seated here. You'll find tasty delights from across the pond that are superbly prepared with polished service to match.

Picholine (35 W 64th St, 212/724-8585; dinner daily) is another great place to experience the food by taking advantage of bar seating. At Picholine, chef/proprietor Terrance Brennan has refined his culinary talents with goodies like paella spring rolls. Don't miss the Picholine cheese carts! Finally, the desserts at both Picholine and the London Bar are worth a visit in themselves.

CAMAJE
85 MacDougal St (bet Bleecker and Houston St)   212/673-8184
Daily: noon-midnight; Brunch: Sat, Sun   www.camaje.com
Inexpensive

Abigail Hitchcock knows how to cook a great meal. In tiny quarters (capacity 24 or so), this cozy French bistro may evoke memories of some wonderful little place you may have discovered in Paris. Camaje is one of those New York restaurants relatively few know about, yet those who do return often. From the moment delicious, crusty bread arrives through the serving of excellent homemade desserts, everything is wholesome and tasty. There's three-onion soup *gratinee*, a half-dozen sandwiches, crostini, small plates, meat and fish entrees, and veggie side dishes. You can create your own three-ingredient crepe. Try one of their crepes *sucrées* for dessert; my favorite is a chocolate ice cream crepe with caramel sauce. Another plus is the large selection of quality teas. Cooking classes are offered three times a week. Several times a month diners are offered a four-course dinner with wine and entertainment. Reservations are necessary.

CAPITAL GRILLE
Chrysler Center, Trylon Towers
155 E 42nd St (bet Lexington and Third Ave)   212/953-2000
Lunch: Mon-Fri; Dinner: Daily   www.thecapitalgrille.com
Moderately expensive

Hungry for lobster bisque? Start here! With all the top-drawer steak-houses in Manhattan, it's amazing they are all so busy. This one is stunningly decorated with Philip Johnson's glass-and-steel pyramids. The room exudes comfort and congeniality, and this is underscored by a welcoming, pleasant, efficient, and informed wait staff. Some say this is a Republican establishment, but no one asks for political affiliation and I found them to be super-nice to everyone. The midtown location is handy, the menu is full of the usual appetizers, soups, and salads (a good bet for lunch), and the dry-aged steaks and chops are fabulous. Desserts are good—I liked the flourless chocolate espresso cake—but not overly memorable.

For a bit of nostalgia and perhaps a taste of caviar, venison, borscht, chicken Kiev, or beef Stroganoff, try the famous **Russian Tea Room** (150 W 57th St, 212/581-7100). It is open weekdays for lunch, brunch on the weekend, and dinner every night. It's colorful but expensive, and the food is not great, with service leaving a lot to be desired.

CAPSOUTO FRÈRES
451 Washington St (south of Canal St; entrance at 135 Watts St)
Lunch: Tues-Fri; Dinner: Daily; Brunch: Sat, Sun   212/966-4900
Moderate   www.capsoutofreres.com

In 1891, when the Landmark Building was constructed, this was an "in" area. Now it is hot all over again, the building is still a beauty, and Capsouto Frères (which is housed within) just gets better and better. Serving contemporary French cuisine, three brothers operate this classic establishment, complete with ceiling fans, wooden tables, good cheer, and tasty plates. An assortment of savory soufflés is very popular. At noon a special *prix fixe* lunch is offered, or you can order from an a la carte menu laden with salads, fish, meat, and pasta dishes. In the evening more of the same is served along with quail, duckling, and first-rate sirloin steak. They are known for their signature dessert soufflés. This bistro is a great setting for a casual evening with good friends who like to live it up!

CARMINE'S
2450 Broadway (bet 90th and 91st St)   212/362-2200
Lunch, Dinner: Daily
200 W 44th St (bet Seventh and Eighth Ave)   212/221-3800
Lunch, Dinner: Daily   www.carminesnyc.com
Moderate

Time to treat the gang or the whole family? Call Carmine's for reservations and show up famished. You will be treated to Southern Italian-style family dining with huge portions and zesty seasonings. The platters are delicious and filling. Show up early if your party numbers less than six, as they will not reserve tables for smaller parties after 7 p.m. Menu choices run the gamut of pastas, chicken, veal, seafood, and tasty Italian appetizers (such as calamari). Wall signs explain the offerings. There is also a delivery menu.

CARNEGIE DELICATESSEN AND RESTAURANT
854 Seventh Ave (at 55th St)   212/757-2245, 800/334-5606
Breakfast, Lunch, Dinner: Daily (6:30 a.m-4 a.m.)
Moderate   www.carnegiedeli.com

There's no city on earth with delis that compare to New York's, and Carnegie Delicatessen and Restaurant is one of the best. Its location in the middle of a busy hotel district makes it perfect for midnight snacks. Everything is made on-premises, with free delivery between 7 a.m. and 2 a.m. inside a five-block radius. Making your food choice is difficult, but I say your favorite Jewish mother didn't make chicken soup better than Carnegie's homemade variety. Order it with matzo balls, golden noodles, rice, *kreplach*, or *kasha*. Beyond soup, there are great blintzes, open-faced hot sandwiches and other sandwiches galore, including a very juicy burger with all the trimmings. You'll find lots of fish entrees, corned beef, pastrami, and rare roast beef. There is an unequalled choice of egg dishes, salads, and numerous side orders of everything from hot baked potatoes to potato pancakes. Desserts cover everything from A to Z—even Jell-O—and outrageous New York cheesecake is served plain or topped with strawberries, blueberries, or cherries. Bring cash as they don't take credit cards.

You had better make a reservation if you're headed to **L'Artusi** (228 W 10th St, 212/255-5757). The limited space fills up quickly, especially prime seats observing the busy, open kitchen. The list of attractions includes reasonable prices, Italian wines, and just plain good food: raw bar, cheese counter, beef, poultry, pasta dishes, and delectable desserts. L'Artusi is a high-energy establishment that offers late-night dining.

CERCLE ROUGE
241 West Broadway (bet Walker and White St)
Lunch: Mon-Fri; Dinner: Daily; Brunch: Sat, Sun   212/226-6174
Moderate   www.cerclerougeresto.com

Classic bistro dishes are available in a true French setting at Cercle Rouge. Other features include a kid-friendly Saturday and Sunday brunch with a magician, a spacious outdoor terrace, and private party facilities. A grand shellfish platter, a number of mussel and oyster entrees, and a large cheese selection are among the specialties.

'CESCA
164 W 75th St (at Amsterdam Ave)   212/787-6300
Dinner: Daily; Brunch: Sun   www.cescanyc.com
Moderate to moderately expensive

You'll love 'Cesca's atmosphere, situated in a former hotel lobby that is both intimate and attractive. The wait staff is highly skilled and accommodating, and the food is deliciously Italian from start to finish. The menu changes often, but the dishes are uniformly well done. Superb Italian bread adds to the meal. One of the most pleasant and economical ways to enjoy a place like 'Cesca is to build your dinner around the cheese boards. The regional cheeses of Italy are all spectacular.

CHANTERELLE
2 Harrison St (at Hudson St)   212/966-6960
Lunch: Thurs-Sat; Dinner: Tues-Sun   www.chanterellenyc.com
Expensive

For nearly three decades I have been a great admirer of Chanterelle. Karen and David Waltuck have created something unique and special for Manhattan diners. All the ingredients are here: magnificent decor, extremely professional service, wonderful food, and owners who look after every detail. Of course, nothing this good comes cheaply, and Chanterelle's dinners can be tough on the pocketbook. However, the *prix fixe* lunch is a real deal. The menu changes often, so there are many featured items. Ask Karen (who is out front) or David (in the kitchen) to suggest a menu. The seafood dishes are especially tasty. Their grilled seafood sausage is rightly famous. If you have any room after this, then you might try the superb cheese selection. A mousse, soufflé, or an unusual flavor of ice cream are great dessert choices, and Chanterelle's petit fours (served with coffee) make all others seem mundane.

Megu (62 Thomas St, 212/964-7777, www.megunyc.com) absolutely deserves top billing as a Japanese restaurant. The theme is pricey modern Japanese. The selection of dinner dishes, the adept service, and the romantic and compelling atmosphere add up to a truly superb dining experience. Of course, there is sushi in abundance, but the star of the menu is thin slices of Kobe beef that one can cook over a hot rock. The Japanese version of a Caesar salad is delicious. Even the desserts (yes, in a Japanese restaurant) are plentiful and fanciful.

CHEZ JACQUELINE
72 MacDougal St (bet Bleecker and Houston St)   212/505-0727
Dinner: Daily; Brunch: Sat, Sun   www.chezjacqueline.com
Moderate

Chez Jacqueline is a very popular neighborhood French bistro, and no wonder. The atmosphere and service are appealingly relaxed. All ages seem to be happy here: young lovers hold hands, and seniors have just as good a time on a special evening out. Popular appetizers are fish soup, escargots, and goat-cheese salad. As you might expect from a French house, the loin dishes are excellent. My favorite is hearty beef stew in red wine, tomato, and carrot sauce. For dessert, try the caramelized apple tart.

CHINATOWN BRASSERIE
380 Lafayette St (at Great Jones St)   212/533-7000
Lunch (dim sum): Daily; Dinner: Daily
Moderate   www.chinatownbrasserie.com

Here's a welcome addition to New York's Chinese restaurant scene! This place is big, attractive, energetic, and well-organized. Moreover, it serves really delicious food, mostly with an Oriental accent. You'll find wraps, salads, soups, crispy rolls, fish, meat, and chicken dishes. Their dim sum is truly first-rate and cooked to order. Peking duck with Mandarin pancakes is a specialty. Of course there are plenty of rice and noodle dishes, along with standards like General Tso's chicken. There is even a good dessert: butterscotch and banana trifle. A sexy downstairs bar space is available for private parties. Service is quick and efficient.

CHIN CHIN
216 E 49th St (bet Second and Third Ave)   212/888-4555
Lunch: Mon-Fri; Dinner: Daily   www.chinchinny.com
Moderate to moderately expensive

Chin Chin is a Chinese restaurant whose classy ambience and price reflect a superior cooking style. There are two rooms and a garden in back. The soups and barbecued spare ribs are terrific starters. Chin Chin house specialties include Grand Marnier prawns and orange beef. I'd concentrate on the seafood dishes, though you might also try the wonderful Peking duck dinner, with choice of soup, crispy duck skin with pancakes, fried rice, poached spinach, and homemade sorbet and ice cream. The menu is similar at lunch and dinner. A reasonable *prix fixe* lunch is available.

Here are a couple of recommendations for Scottish fare: **Brandy Library** (25 N Moore St, 212/226-5545) and **St. Andrew's Pub** (140 W 46th St, 212/840-8413). You might even find haggis—sheep innards, an acquired taste—on the menu!

CITY BAKERY
3 W 18th St (at Fifth Ave)   212/366-1414
Breakfast, Lunch: Daily   www.thecitybakery.com
Moderate

Your taste buds will begin to tingle the moment you walk into the bustling City Bakery—which is really not a bakery but a buffet operation. Your eyes and stomach will savor the fresh-looking salad bar, tempting hot entrees, hearty sandwiches, yummy pastries, chocolate room, and much more. I am impressed with the well-trained personnel, who keep displays well stocked, tables clean, and checkout counters running efficiently. For a casual, moderately priced meal in unfancy surroundings, this is a good deal.

CLINTON ST. BAKING CO. & RESTAURANT
4 Clinton St (at Houston St)   646/602-6263
Breakfast, Lunch, Dinner: Mon-Sat; Brunch: Sat, Sun
Moderate   www.greatbiscuits.com
Come here for New York's best pancakes! Their hot buttered cider is famous, too. Clinton Street may be a bit out of the way—it's on the Lower East Side—but the trip is worth it if you want wholesome food at very reasonable prices. At breakfast you will find homemade granola, French toast, great pancakes, biscuit sandwiches, omelets, and more. For lunch, homemade soups, salads, eggs, and sandwiches are featured. The evening menu includes delicious homemade potato chips, oysters, butcher's salad, halibut, macaroni and cheese, rib steak, and garlic chicken. Homemade cakes

and pastries are available all day. Extra thick shakes, sundaes, and sodas are a feature of their fountain. The atmosphere may be a bit dull, but the food certainly isn't. A large takeout menu is available.

CONVIVIO
45 Tudor City Place (at 42nd St)	212/599-5045
Lunch: Mon-Fri; Dinner: Daily	www.convivionyc.com
Moderately expensive	

What was once L'Impero, a charming room, is now even more appealing and considerably brighter as Convivio. In a setting that breathes relaxation, a meal here is a welcome relief from the hurly-burly of city life. Dishes with a distinct Southern Italian flavor dominate the menu, with prices dropping a bit to fit current economic conditions. Bring an appetite, because chef Michael White has created some spectacular pastas: buffalo ricotta gnocchi, *maccheroni* (pancetta, pecorino, scallion, and eggs), and spaghetti with clams, leeks, and white wine like you have never tasted before. There are also tomato braised short ribs, grilled lamb chops, a delicious Sicilian seafood soup. Desserts are right on target: novel gelatos and sorbets, zesty Southern Italian cheeses, and a special chocolate cake. The wait staff seem genuinely happy to tell you about their store of goodies.

> Call ahead to find their location, or simply look for the **Treats Truck** (212/691-5226, www.treatstruck.com), which wanders the streets of Manhattan vending delicious goodies. Treats also offers special orders, catering, and delivery to your door!

COOK SHOP
156 Tenth Ave (at 20th St)	212/924-4440
Breakfast, Lunch: Mon-Fri; Dinner: Daily; Brunch: Sat, Sun	
Moderate to moderately expensive	www.cookshopny.com

It's no mystery why this place is always packed! The Cook Shop is one of the most pleasant dining venues on the far West Side, with really great food (featuring mainly organic food from local farms), efficient service, and a fun atmosphere. Their "Little Gems" salad is one of the best I have ever tasted. Stone oven-cooked whole fish, baby chicken, and soft-shell crabs are also delicious main courses. Oysters by the piece are also available. For dessert, there is a nice selection of cheeses, but the really loaded butter-pecan ice cream sundae is worth a visit in itself.

CORTON
239 West Broadway (at Walker St)	212/219-2777
Dinner: Mon-Sat	www.cortonnyc.com
Expensive to very expensive	

Drew Nieporent is a rightful legend in the Manhattan food world. He knows the city and the restaurant biz, and he is on the job seemingly round the clock, making sure his establishments are top-notch. The name Corton derives from a fine Burgundy. Not surprisingly, the restaurant offers a modern French menu and fits this superlative classification to perfection. With the help of talented chef and co-owner Paul Liebrandt, Drew has created a classic room, charming in its simplicity, with superbly trained personnel serving innovative, delicious food. There is a *prix fixe* three-course offering, as well as a multi-course tasting menu. The seasonal salad is unusual, not overfilling, healthy, and luscious. Turbot, chicken, lobster, beef, or any other entree on the *carte du jour* will arrive with a stunning look and a fine, memorable taste to savor. The desserts are good, although not brilliant, with the exceptions of the chocolate fondant and the caramel brioche. Your tab will reflect Corton's absolutely first-class cuisine, ambience, and expertise. My hat is off again to Drew for presenting Manhattan with another spectacular dining experience.

Make mine a double—burger that is! Sometimes the most satisfying meal is a large, juicy, double cheeseburger. These joints add their own special touches to one of America's favorite foods:

Black Iron Burger Shop (540 E 5th St, 212/677-6067): kitchen open late

City Burger (1410 Broadway, 212/997-7770): fresh ground-steak burgers

Five Guys (43 W 55th St, 212/459-9600 and 269 Bleecker St, 212/367-9200): worth the calories; a Virginia-based chain

Flip (Bloomingdale's, 1000 Third Ave, 212/705-2993): Choose your own combination.

Shake Shack (Madison Square Park at 23rd St, 212/889-6600 and 366 Columbus Ave, 646/747-8770): a New York City experience brought to you by the extraordinary Danny Meyer

Txikito (240 Ninth Ave, 212/242-4730): Basque-inspired ingredients

---

COUNTRY CAFE
69 Thompson St (bet Spring and Broome St)   212/966-5417
Lunch, Dinner: Mon-Fri; Brunch: Sat, Sun
Moderate

You have to know what you're looking for to find this tiny Soho establishment. Once inside, you'll appreciate the no-nonsense approach to Moroccan and French country dining. The service and atmosphere could easily be transplanted to any small village in Europe. The menu would fit right in as well, with items like homemade country paté with onion and fruit chutney, vegetable couscous, snails in garlic butter, sea bass, and one of the city's best steaks *au poivre* with real homemade French fries. The pressed chicken dish is fabulous. I love the informality of the place, the sizable portions, and the obvious delight the young staff takes in showing guests what it is like to be treated by some real homebodies. *Bon appetit!*

COWGIRL
519 Hudson St (at 10th St)   212/633-1133
Breakfast, Lunch: Daily; Dinner: Daily; Brunch: Sat, Sun
Inexpensive to moderate   www.cowgirlnyc.com

Colorful and busy, Cowgirl is Manhattan's version of Texas chuckwagon cuisine. The menu is varied, with something for everyone: burgers, fajitas, enchiladas, chilis, chicken, steak, sausages, catfish, and macaroni and cheese. Kids love the place! Portions are large and quite tasty, the wait staff enters into the fun, and the tab is accommodating, too. The smoked BBQ ribs are a specialty. They are bathed in a delicious sauce and served with really tasty

BBQ beans and slaw. Ask for the ice cream "baked potato" for dessert: vanilla ice cream shaped like a spud, with heaps of hot fudge, chopped pecans, and a pat of butter (which is really frosting). If that sounds like a bit much, you can opt for a slice of pecan or key lime pie.

CRAFT

43 E 19th St (bet Park Ave S and Broadway)   212/780-0880
Dinner: Daily   www.craftrestaurant.com
Expensive

Craft is utterly unique and worth visiting for a number of reasons. The atmosphere is conducive to good eating, and the help is particularly friendly. The way you order is even unique. Everything is a la carte. The menu is divided into sections: fish and shellfish, meats, vegetables, mushrooms, potatoes, grains, and beans. You can put together any combination you find appealing, and the plates won't overwhelm your appetite. Chef-owner Tom Colicchio came from the Gramercy Tavern, and his expertise shows. The dessert selection is great: wonderful cheeses, pastries, custards, fruits, ice creams, and sorbets (with many sauces available). If you're not terribly hungry or there are picky eaters in the group, head to Craft. **Craftbar** (900 Broadway, 212/461-4300), its sister operation, is more casual, with a contemporary New American menu and composed dinner plates.

In my youth I wanted to be a "soda jerk"! For a trip down memory lane, visit the **Soda Shop** (125 Chambers St, 212/571-1100) to satisfy such cravings. In addition to a fabulous white marble bar (originally from the Plaza Hotel), you'll find great sodas, only-in-New York egg creams, and rich milkshakes.

CUCINA & CO.

MetLife Building
200 Park Ave (45th St at Vanderbilt Ave), lobby   212/682-2700
Breakfast, Lunch, Dinner: Mon-Fri   www.patinagroup.com
Takeout: Mon-Fri (7 a.m.-9 p.m.)
Moderate

Hidden among three hyped restaurants (Tropica, Naples 45, and Cafe Centro) in the bowels of the huge MetLife Building, Cucina & Co. is a treasure. The takeout counter is one of the best in mid-Manhattan, displaying all sorts of prepared foods, sandwiches, salads, great cookies and cakes, breads, and whatever else you might want to take home or to the office. Adjoining is a bustling, crowded cafe that serves first-class food at reasonable prices for such a prime location. You will find delicious burgers (served on sesame brioche rolls), baked pastas, quiches, seafood, health food dishes, and a good selection of dessert items. The service is fast and the personnel highly professional. They have to be in order to serve so many people during rush hours! I heartily recommend this place, especially for lunch. Two other Cucina & Co. locations (30 Rockefeller Center, 212/332-7630 and Macy's Cellar, 151 W 34th St, 212/868-2388) occupy similarly prime Manhattan locales and offer the same quality of food and service. Unlike the MetLife location, the other two are open daily.

CUPPING ROOM CAFE
359 West Broadway (bet Broome and Grand St)   212/925-2898
Breakfast, Lunch: Mon-Fri; Dinner: Daily; Brunch: Sat, Sun
Moderate   www.cuppingroomcafe.com

It is easy to see why the Cupping Room Cafe is one of the most popular places in Soho to meet and dine. In a noisy, convivial atmosphere, with a bar where you can drink and/or eat, all the news of the area is exchanged. The diverse comfort-food offerings at lunch and dinner include pastas, seafood, chicken, steaks, and vegetarian dishes. But breakfast and brunch are where they really shine: freshly baked pastries, fruit and cheese, waffles, pancakes, wonderful French toast, and eggs and omelets. Eggs Benedict can be custom-made from their Benedict bar. For lighter dining, there are soups, sandwiches, burgers, and salads. Ask about daily dessert items; most are delicious, fresh, reasonably priced, and caloric. Live R&B, jazz, or world music is performed Wednesday through Saturday nights for a small cover charge.

Traditional French diners won't want to miss **Chez Napoléon** (365 W 50th St, 212/265-6980, www.cheznapoleon.com), where two smallish dining rooms house unusual wall pieces and French lore. The patés, blood sausage, and frog legs are legendary. The staff and clientele are justly famous, too. This is family dining at its best!

DANIEL
60 E 65th St (bet Madison and Park Ave)   212/288-0033
Dinner: Mon-Sat   www.danielnyc.com
Expensive

Every detail of this superb dining palace is a work of art, especially the dishes placed in front of you. If you are ready to have an absolutely superb dining experience and money doesn't matter, then join the often long waiting list for a table in the newly freshened space, which is a treat for the eyes as well as the stomach. Daniel Boulud deserves to feel immensely proud of his four-star, classical French Country restaurant. The wait staff is highly professional and knowledgeable. Signature dishes change seasonally on the contemporary French menu. It might be a duo of roasted beef tenderloin and braised short ribs (the best I have ever tasted), swordfish, sole, or tuna. Desserts are works of art, especially the chocolate creations. Don't miss the cheese selection! Every time I visit this restaurant I don't want the meal to end, and I can't think of a higher compliment.

DA UMBERTO
107 W 17th St (at Ave of the Americas)   212/989-0303
Lunch: Mon-Fri; Dinner: Mon-Sat   www.daumbertonyc.com
Moderate to moderately expensive

This Tuscan trattoria appeals to the senses of serious Italian diners. A groaning table of inviting antipasto dishes greets guests. One could easily make an entire meal just from this selection. All of the platters look so fresh and healthy! Owner Vittorio Assante is around much of the time, ensuring that the service is as good as the food. One can look into the glass-framed kitchen at the rear to see how real professionals work. You'll see well-prepared pastas, fish, veal, game (in season), and chicken. Your waiter will have many specials to detail. If you have room, chocolate truffle cake and tiramisu are the best of the dessert selections.

DAVID BURKE TOWNHOUSE
133 E 61st St (bet Park and Lexington Ave)   212/813-2121
Lunch: Mon-Fri; Dinner: Daily; Brunch: Sat, Sun
Moderately expensive   www.davidburketownhouse.com

Let's start at the end! To me, this establishment from famed chef David Burke really shines with its desserts. Butterscotch panna cotta, coconut layer cake, and petit fours are all created by an excellent pastry chef. Of course, there are other attractions at this spot, which is popular with ladies. If I had to choose one word to describe the place, it would be *fussy*. Their chef's salad is absolutely the best I have ever tasted. I also like the way bread is served: warm, in a small pan, like a muffin. The menu changes periodically. A white limousine is parked outside for smokers!

Save room for decadent desserts at one of these places!
Adour Alain Ducasse (2 E 55th St, 212/710-2277): dark chocolate sorbet
ChikaLicious (203 E 10th St, 212/995-9511): chiffon-like cheese-cake
Dovetail (103 W 77th St, 212/362-3800): bread pudding
Le Cirque (151 E 58th St, 212/644-0202): "Floating Island"

DB BISTRO MODERNE
55 W 44th St (bet Fifth Ave and Ave of the Americas)   212/391-2400
Breakfast: Daily; Lunch: Mon-Sat; Dinner: Daily   www.danielnyc.com
Moderate to moderately expensive

Renowned restaurant impressario Daniel Boulud's db Bistro Moderne is, for him, a more casual dining experience. Even burgers are served, and they are very good; at $32, they should be! Of course, this is no ordinary hamburger. It is ground sirloin filled with short ribs, foie gras, and black truffles, served on a parmesan bun and accompanied by delicious, light *pommes soufflés* in a silver cup. Diners have their choice of two rooms with a communal table that is comfortable for singles between them. The menu offers several items in each category of fish, charcuterie, and meats. For dessert, the cheese selection is a real winner, as are any of Daniel's specialties that use berries and other fresh fruit.

DELEGATES DINING ROOM
United Nations
First Ave at 45th St, 4th floor   212/963-7626
Lunch: Mon-Fri   www.aramark-un.com
Moderate

Don't let the name or security measures keep you away! The public can enjoy the international food and special atmosphere at the U.N. Delegates Dining Room. Conversations at adjoining tables are conducted in almost every language. The setting is charming, overlooking the East River. The room is large and airy, the service polite and informed. There is a large selection of appetizers, soups, salads, entrees, and desserts on the daily "Delegates Buffet." All of the dishes are attractively presented and very tasty. A huge table of salads, baked specialties, seafoods, meats, vegetables, cheeses, desserts, and fruits await the hungry noontime diner. Some rules apply: jackets are required, jeans and sneakers are prohibited, and a photo ID is needed. Well-behaved children (no toddlers) are welcome with an adult. There isn't a more appetizing complete daily buffet available in New York. Reservations are a must.

DELMONICO'S

56 Beaver St (at William St)   212/509-1144
Lunch: Mon-Fri; Dinner: Mon-Sat   www.delmonicosny.com
Moderately expensive

You've heard and read about Manhattan's Financial District, but if you want a real feel for the area and the people who make it tick, have a meal at Delmonico's. It is truly a New York institution. The atmosphere is old-time New York, but with a very appropriate renovated flair. As you might imagine, service is highly professional. The wine cellar is filled with a huge selection of the world's best vintages. Private dining is also offered. The Delmonico steak (a boneless ribeye that originated here) and other prime meat cuts are house specialties, with accompaniments like famous Delmonico potatoes (whose recipe was created here many years ago). Delmonico steaks may be served elsewhere, but the authentic item is found only at the namesake restaurant. Don't be afraid to try chicken, duck, eggs Benedict, lobster Newberg, rack of lamb, or tuna here, either. All are made from tried and true recipes. Daily specials are featured. Small plates include reasonably priced salads and sandwiches available in the adjoining Grill Room. By all means try Baked Alaska, the signature dessert. The cheese selection is superb as well. This is Manhattan's original fine-dining restaurant, dating from 1837. After over a century of presenting gourmet plates, Delmonico's is back on top!

> The line forms in all types of weather for **EJ's Luncheonette** (1271 Third Ave, 212/472-0600), where breakfast, lunch, and dinner are served daily. You'll find great flapjacks, waffles, omelets, sandwiches, burgers, baked items, salads, and everything in between. In addition to a huge menu, especially at breakfast, you'll enjoy the very reasonable prices. Free delivery, too!

DEL FRISCO'S DOUBLE EAGLE STEAK HOUSE

McGraw-Hill Building
1221 Ave of the Americas (at 49th St)   212/575-5129
Lunch: Mon-Fri; Dinner: Daily   www.delfriscos.com
Expensive

Del Frisco's provides a good meal with accommodating service in a setting where both the ceiling and prices are high. Fresh, warm bread is brought to the table as you enjoy a seafood appetizer or great beefsteak tomato and sliced onion salad. Steaks, chops, veal dishes, and lobster are all first-rate, while accompanying side dishes are large and uneven. In-house desserts include bread pudding with Jack Daniel's sauce, crisp chocolate soufflé cake with raspberries, and strawberries Romanoff with vanilla ice cream. All are winners. This establishment is inviting, except when it comes to price. Isn't $19.95 for a shrimp cocktail a bit steep? To be frank, I've also found myself wondering whether every dish is freshly cooked for each diner.

DEL POSTO
85 Tenth Ave (bet 15th and 16th St)   212/497-8090
Lunch: Wed, Fri; Dinner: Daily   www.delposto.com
Expensive

It's big and bold! No question about it, Del Posto is an "occasion" restaurant. Mario Batali has shown what can be done with good taste. Afterward, diners may feel their wallets have become a bit thinner, but they will long remember the experience of dining here. The room is warm, with adequate space between tables, a huge staff, informed service, and beautiful china. Some dishes are prepared tableside. The wine steward dutifully tastes from each bottle before it is presented to the guest. Bread baskets are superb. Soothing piano music will calm those who arrive after a harried day. All of these touches speak to this class operation. What to order? *Garganelli verdi al ragu Bolognese*, *Del Posto agnolotti dal plin*, or for dessert, the chocolate ricotta Tartino—all are exceptional. Leave room for the fine selection of complimentary after-dinner cookies. Private party spaces on the balcony level provide an enchanting view of the professional proceedings below. (Note: You can save a few bucks by eating at the bar.)

Stone Street, located between Broad and Whitehall streets in the Financial District, is particularly pleasant for eating outdoors in nice weather. My top suggestions:

Adrienne's Pizzabar (54 Stone St, 212/248-3838)
Stone Street Tavern (52 Stone St, 212/785-5658)
Ulysses (58 Stone St, 212/482-0400)

DEMARCHELIER
50 E 86th St (at Madison Ave)   212/249-6300
Lunch, Dinner: Daily; Brunch: Sun   www.demarchelierrestaurant.com
Moderate

Drop in on Friday for delicious bouillabaisse! For years diners have come to this French bistro for two reasons: good food and no pretense. If you like solid French fare like artichokes and asparagus in season, crusty bread, *paté de campagne*, and salad *niçoise*, you will love Demarchelier. Steak dishes are also a specialty. Service is extremely efficient and prompt—ideal if you are in a lunch rush. Takeout dishes are available, too.

DÉVI
8 E 18th St (bet Broadway and Fifth Ave)   212/691-1300
Lunch: Mon-Fri; Dinner: Daily   www.devinyc.com
Moderate to moderately expensive

You can't do better than Dévi for Indian food. The setting is very attractive—colorful, yet understated, and small enough to be inviting. The excellent food lives up to the setting. A full vegetarian selection is offered. Seafood, poultry, and meat dishes are featured. Lamb-stuffed tandoori chicken is a favorite entree. For those who really know Indian food, the side dishes are very special (like slaws, spiced spinach sauce with mushrooms, and wonderful Indian bread). A full menu of unusual desserts is presented: Indian ice cream, crispy saffron bread pudding, fig cake, and much more. The staff is attentive, polite, and helpful.

DINING COMMONS
City University of New York Graduate Center
365 Fifth Ave (at 34th St) 212/817-7953
Breakfast (1st floor), Lunch (8th floor): Mon-Fri
Inexpensive

The Dining Commons offers excellent food in comfortable surroundings at affordable prices. Continental breakfasts featuring muffins, Danishes, croissants, bagels, and more are available. Lunches feature deli sandwiches, salads, and some hot entrees. It is possible to eat heartily for under $10, and both eat-in and takeout are available. The facility is open to faculty, students, and the general public. This is no run-of-the-mill fast-food operation. Restaurant Associates does a particularly good job of offering tasty, adequate portions without fancy touches.

> **Commerce** (50 Commerce St, 212/524-2301, www.commerce restaurant.com) is a moderately priced delight, full of atmosphere, nice people, and really good contemporary American food with Asian, French, and Italian accents. Whether your dish is cassoulet, fettucini, or Maine lobster, it will be delicious. And don't leave without trying the chocolate soufflé.

DOCKS OYSTER BAR AND SEAFOOD GRILL
633 Third Ave (at 40th St) 212/986-8080
Lunch: Mon-Fri; Dinner: Daily; Brunch: Sat, Sun
Moderate www.docksoysterbar.com

At Dock's you'll find fresh swordfish, lobster, tuna, Norwegian salmon, red snapper, and other seafood specials that change with the season. Crab cakes are outstanding. At dinner the raw bar offers four oyster and two clam selections. For a lighter meal, try steamers in beer broth or mussels in tomato and garlic. Delicious smoked sturgeon and whitefish are available. Docks has a special New England clambake on Sunday and Monday nights. The atmosphere is congenial, and so are the professional waiters.

DOUBLE CROWN
316 Bowery (at Bleecker St) 212/254-0350
Dinner: Daily; Brunch: Sat, Sun www.doublecrown-nyc.com
Moderate

If you are a dyed-in-the-wool Anglophile, you'll love this place! You can start with raw oysters, pigs in a wet blanket, duck steamed bun, or braised pork belly. Then on to a delicious endive and stilton salad, cured Scottish salmon, or crispy drunken quail. For the main course, try steamed snapper, pheasant and licorice pie, bangers and mash, or elk Wellington. The English tradition of a Sunday roast lives on here. For the solo diner, there is a large communal table. The place reeks of British atmosphere, including friendly servers.

EIGHTY ONE
Excelsior Hotel
45 W 81st St (bet Central Park West and Columbus Ave)
Dinner: Daily; Brunch: Sun   212/873-8181
Expensive   www.81nyc.com

It is amazing how quickly word spreads, particularly on the Upper West Side, when a great restaurant makes a play for the thousands who live in this area. Be aware that Eighty One is hidden in the back spaces of the Excelsior Hotel with no outside sign. The room is cozy and comfortable, the noise level tolerable, and the personnel friendly (if not a bit overbearing). The food is delicious and unusual. Appetizers might include a *foie gras* dish or a number of seafood combinations. Veal rack, short ribs, and chicken all make satisfying entrees. A large dessert menu, prepared by executive pastry chef John Miele, boasts such luxuries as bittersweet chocolate and hazelnut *millefeuille*. For your sake I hope it is on the menu when you visit. The downside is pricing. Yes, I know the quality of the dishes is very good, but entrees costing nearly $40 seems a bit excessive.

If you are looking for a noisy and fun spot for a meal or snack after a show, I'd suggest **Seppi's** (123 W 56th St, 212/708-7444). This bit of Paris in midtown Manhattan adjoins Le Parker Meridien Hotel and is just right for late dining (till 2 a.m.!). You'll find typical French appetizers, omelets, pastas, fish, meat, and sandwiches. Saturday and Sunday brunches are a specialty.

ELEVEN MADISON PARK
11 Madison Ave (at 24th St)   212/889-0905
Lunch: Mon-Fri; Dinner: Mon-Sat   www.elevenmadisonpark.com
Expensive

Another fine Danny Meyer operation! In a soaring space previously used for business meetings, he's crafted an attractive dining room with an intimate bar and several private rooms. Swiss chef Daniel Humm offers a very special, intensely flavored, contemporary French menu that changes frequently. The food is delicious! When you visit, be sure to tour the building and study the archival photos throughout.

ELIO'S
1621 Second Ave (at 84th St)   212/772-2242
Dinner: Daily
Moderate to moderately expensive

For years Elio's has been *the* classic clubby Upper East Side dining room for those who are recognizable, as well as those who aspire to be. They have gone organic. In not so fancy surroundings, with waiters who greet regulars as if they are part of the family, tasty platters of beef carpaccio, clams, mussels, stuffed mushrooms, and minestrone are offered as starters. Lots of spaghetti and risotto dishes follow, along with seafood (their specialty), liver, scaloppine, and the usual Italian assortment. For dessert, try the delicious sorbets. Although half the fun is watching the not-so-subtle eye contact among diners, the food is excellent, and it is easy to see why Elio's remains a neighborhood favorite.

ELLEN'S STARDUST DINER

1650 Broadway (at 51st St)   212/956-5151
Breakfast, Lunch, Dinner: Daily   www.ellensstardustdiner.com
Inexpensive to moderate

Come here for good food and a singing wait staff! Ellen's fits right into the theater neighborhood. A casual, fun, and noisy spot, it serves satisfying food the traditional American way. Trains are the theme of the decor. A track circles the balcony, with a locomotive and cars that would thrill any railroad buff. The breakfast menu includes bagels and muffins, along with tasty buttermilk pancakes, Belgian waffles, French toast, and omelets. For the rest of the day, comfort foods are the order: salads and sandwiches, burgers, chicken pot pie, meatloaf, barbecue baby back ribs, turkey, and steak. Don't forget the egg creams, shakes, malts, and a nice selection of caloric desserts, and be sure to ask that your shake be made "thick"! Delivery is available.

Here are two notable indoor *Biergartens* (beer gardens):
Hallo Berlin (626 Tenth Ave, 212/977-1944 and 744 Ninth Ave, 212/333-2372)
Zum Schneider (107 Ave C, 212/598-1098)

EL PARADOR CAFE

325 E 34th St (bet First and Second Ave)   212/679-6812
Lunch, Dinner: Daily   www.elparadorcafe.com
Moderate

Having been in business for five decades, El Parador is the granddaddy of New York's Mexican restaurants. Delicious Mexican food is served in a fun atmosphere at down-to-earth prices. Moreover, these are some of the nicest folks in the city. Warm tortilla chips arrive at your table while you study the list of specialties. There are quesadillas, Spanish sausages, and black bean soup to start; delicious shrimp and chicken dishes follow. Create your own tacos and tostaditas, or try stuffed jalapenos. El Parador has over 50 brands of premium tequila, and they concoct what many consider the best margaritas in New York.

ETATS-UNIS

242 E 81st St (bet Second and Third Ave)   212/517-8826
Dinner: Daily   www.etatsunisrestaurant.com
Moderate to moderately expensive

Etats-Unis is like a large family dining room. There are only 14 tables and a busy kitchen where owner Luca Pecora works to produce some of the best food this side of your grandmother's kitchen! Appetizers, entrees, and desserts change every evening and are always delicious. It's very wholesome food, not cute or fancy, and served professionally in portions that are substantial but not overwhelming. Fresh homemade bread is an attraction. Try date pudding or chocolate soufflé for dessert. The tab is not cheap, but in order to support an operation with limited hours and few tables, the folks at Etats-Unis must make every meal count. A bar/cafe across the street by the same name is open for lunch and dinner. Both locations are available for private parties.

FAIRWAY CAFE & STEAKHOUSE
2127 Broadway (at 74th St), upstairs   212/595-1888
Breakfast and Lunch: Daily (as Fairway Cafe);
Dinner: Daily (after 5:30 p.m., as Fairway Steakhouse)
Moderate   www.fairwaymarket.com

Most folks know of Fairway as a busy market. Take the stairway by the entrance, however, and you'll find a rather bare-bones room that serves unbelievably good food—much of it of the comfort variety—at comfortable prices. Breakfasts include eggs, pancakes, omelets, smoked salmon, and the like. The luncheon soups, salads, and sandwiches are extremely good values for the quality offered. Evening brings a modestly priced steakhouse, with complete steak dinners—your choice of cut, plus salad, soup, and vegetables—for $40. There are chops, rack of lamb, short ribs, fish, chicken, even spaghetti and pizza. All desserts are only $5. An extensive catering menu is available.

I firmly believe that a meal at one of the quiet, elegant, old-time Manhattan restaurants can be an exceptional treat. When you consider the quality of your meal, the service you receive, and the atmosphere, I am convinced that you get *more* than your money's worth. I have several strong recommendations for just such an experience. These houses are superb!

DeGrezia (231 E 50th St, bet Second and Third Ave, 212/750-5353): Italian

Le Périgord (405 E 52nd St, bet First Ave and East River, 212/755-6244): French

Primavera (1578 First Ave, at 82nd St, 212/861-8608): Italian

---

57
Four Seasons Hotel New York
57 E 57th St (bet Park and Madison Ave), lobby level   212/758-5757
Breakfast, Lunch: Daily; Brunch: Sat, Sun   www.fourseasons.com
Moderate to moderately expensive

When the name Four Seasons is on the door, you can be assured that the service inside is something special. So it is at 57, one of Manhattan's star hotel dining rooms. The room is highlighted by handsome cherry floors with mahogany inlays, ceilings of Danish beechwood, and bronze chandeliers. The tabletops match the floor in material and design. Served in an informal yet elegant atmosphere, the food has the authority of classic American cooking. The menu changes by season, featuring some exceptionally well-thought-out pasta entrees. Salads and fish are good lunch choices. Taste and personal attention, not the ego of a famous chef, are what makes this room tick. A thoughtful touch is the offer of rapid service for "power breakfast" guests.

FIVE POINTS
31 Great Jones St (bet Lafayette St and Bowery)   212/253-5700
Lunch: Mon-Fri; Dinner: Daily; Brunch: Sat, Sun
Moderate   www.fivepointsrestaurant.com

In a charming, busy, and inviting space, Five Points serves some of the best food in New York at prices that won't make you squirm! For years this has deservedly been one of the most popular rooms in downtown Manhattan. A wonderful choice of appetizers awaits: oysters, marinated olives, roasted mussels, crab cakes, a great wood oven pizzette, and many more. For the main course, a number of pastas are featured, along with seafood dishes (bass and sea scallops), plus a delicious pork shoulder. Order the hot fudge sundae, if offered. Sunday brunch brings homemade cakes and biscuits, egg dishes from the wood oven, plus melt-in-your-mouth pancakes. Five Points has one of the most diverse brunch menus in the city. No wonder they are always packed!

Cheap Expensive Food

Cheap expensive food is a real oxymoron! To experience the best of New York's chefs at a fraction of the cost of dinner in their spendy restaurants, look at these lunch alternatives:

Aquavit Cafe (65 E 55th St, 212/307-7311): $22 smorgasbord plate
Jean Georges (1 Central Park West, 212/299-3900): $28 for the *prix fixe* lunch; $24 at Cafe Nougatine
Picholine (35 W 64th St, 212/724-8585): one-course tasting plate, $15; three-selection tasting flight, $20

FOUR SEASONS
99 E 52nd St (bet Park and Lexington Ave)   212/754-9494
Lunch: Mon-Fri; Dinner: Mon-Sat   www.fourseasonsrestaurant.com
Expensive

Four Seasons is elegant and awe-inspiring in its simplicity and charm. Two separate dining areas—the Grill Room and the Pool Room—have different menus and appeal. *Prix fixe* and a la carte menus are available in both rooms. The house is celebrating its 50th birthday by offering a $59 three-course *prix fixe* menu. The dark suits (translation: business and media heavy hitters) congregate at noon in the Grill Room, where the waiters know them by name and menu preferences (great salads, a wonderful duck entree, steak tartare, burgers). The Pool Room, set beside an actual marble pool, is more romantic and feminine. Society mavens and couples who want to dine with the stars are made to feel at home with superb service. The dessert menu can only be described as obscene; individual soufflés are a splendid treat.

FRANK'S TRATTORIA
371 First Ave (bet 21st and 22nd St)   212/677-2991
Lunch, Dinner: Daily
Inexpensive

It's true in New York, just as it is elsewhere in the country, that no one knows great, cheap places to eat better than the boys in blue. Manhattan's finest are some of the best customers of this modest trattoria, and it is easy to see why. The menu runs the gamut of Florentine dishes. Each is prepared to order and served piping hot (as is the bread, which is always a good sign). There is a large seafood selection, plus steaks, chops, and chicken. You can choose from over 20 pizzas, served whole or by the piece. Everyone here is informal and friendly, and Frank is delighted that the good word about his place has spread beyond the neighborhood regulars.

FRED'S AT BARNEYS NEW YORK
660 Madison Ave (at 60th St), 9th floor   212/833-2200
Lunch, Dinner: Daily; Brunch: Sat, Sun   www.barneys.com
Moderate to moderately expensive

It would be a tossup as to which is better at Fred's—the food or the people watching—where the "beautiful people" definitely like to see and be seen. You'll find the dishes ample and delicious (and they should be, at the prices charged). Selections include seafood dishes, pastas, salads, pizzas, and sandwiches. Tasty French fries are served Belgian-style. There's no shortage of selections or calories on the dessert menu. I just wonder if all those skinny model types really finish their meals! I find it hard to say good things about Barneys these days, but their restaurant is first-class.

Across the street from Madison Square Garden and Penn Station is a colorful watering hole and eating destination with the amusing name **Fat Annie's Truck Stop** (131 W 33rd St, 212/695-1122). You'll find a lively crowd, good drinks, and low-priced blue-plate specials.

FREEMAN'S
Freeman Alley (at Rivington St)   212/420-0012
Breakfast, Lunch: Mon-Fri; Dinner: Daily; Brunch: Sat, Sun
Moderate   www.freemansrestaurant.com

Unique is the word here! You don't want to miss Freeman's—even though it is almost impossible to locate. It used to be a halfway house. Freeman's is crowded, noisy, and unpretentious. It has extra-friendly service personnel, clean restrooms, a great bar and bartender, and a nice kitchen. But most of all, it has really delicious food. You must start with "Devils on Horseback": Stilton-stuffed prunes wrapped in bacon and served piping hot. Then there is a delicious hot artichoke dip with crisp bread. (All the breads are excellent.) The roasted pork loin and seared filet mignon are outstanding. A dish of marinated beets with dill is special. Desserts are just okay, but a visit here is so unique you can overlook your sweet tooth! Reservations can only be made for parties of six or more.

FRESCO BY SCOTTO
34 E 52nd St (bet Madison and Park Ave)   212/935-3434
Lunch: Mon-Fri; Dinner: Mon-Sat   www.frescobyscotto.com
Moderate to moderately expensive

For the past 16 years, Fresco by Scotto has become a midtown Manhattan tradition for lunch and dinner. Owned and operated by the naturally hospitable Scotto family, the restaurant is often referred to as the "NBC Commissary." Dining here has been made even more interesting with the addition of several items: potato and zucchini chips with gorgonzola cheese, chicken meat balls, and *pappardelle* with duck and wild mushroom ragu. Fresco offers countless meat and fish dishes, scrumptious pastas, and homemade *bomboloni* for dessert. Executive chef Stephen Santoro, former chef instructor at the Culinary Institute of America, is ingredient-driven and inspired by the changing seasons. **Fresco *on the go*** (40 E 52nd St, 212/754-2700) offers homemade muffins and pancakes, sticky buns, and eggs to order for breakfast. At noon, delicious sandwiches, pizzas, soups, salads, and homemade pastas are available at this next-door facility and a new downtown location (114 Pearl St, 212/635-5000).

GABRIEL'S BAR & RESTAURANT
11 W 60th St (bet Broadway and Columbus Ave)   212/956-4600
Lunch: Mon-Sat; Dinner: Mon-Sat   www.gabrielsbarandrest.com
Moderate

Gabriel's is a winner for dining in the Lincoln Center area. You are greeted by Gabriel Aiello, an extremely friendly host, as "Gabriel ... Gabriel" plays in the background. And what good food and drink! Delicious bread. Fresh peach or blueberry *bellinis*. A fine assortment of Italian appetizers. Then on to first-class pastas (like *tagliatelle* with peppers), chicken, steaks, and wood-grilled seafood dishes. The in-house gelati creations are among New York's best, as is the flourless chocolate torte. To cap it all off, Gabriel's offers more than a dozen unusual teas (like peach melba, raspberry, and French vanilla). Gabriel doesn't have to blow his own horn; his satisfied customers are happy to do it for him! Private party facilities are available.

You don't have to sacrifice a nice meal if you're enjoying delicious cocktails or wine at these watering holes:

Brandy Library (25 N Moore St, 212/226-5545): classic cocktails, bite-sized foods

Employees Only (510 Hudson St, 212/242-3021): skillful bartenders, full dinner menu and lighter late-night fare

Pegu Club (77 W Hudson St, 212/473-7348): creative martinis, Asian-inspired small plates

Terroir (413 E 12th St, 646/602-1300): wine bar with a fun, eclectic menu

---

GABY
Sofitel New York
44 W 45th St (bet Fifth Ave and Ave of the Americas)   212/782-3040
Breakfast, Lunch, Dinner: Daily   www.gabynyrestaurant.com
Moderate

Gaby is a convenient stop in busy midtown Manhattan that's open from early morning until late in the evening. The cuisine is French, fused with Asian, Latin, and African flavors. Foie gras and snails are popular starters. The French onion soup has a double cheese crust. For a quick and satisfying lunch, order a 30-minute meal served Bento box-style, or enjoy quiche or one of the daily specials. However, the real star is the traditional crème brûlée—just about the best in the city.

GASCOGNE
158 Eighth Ave (at 18th St)   212/675-6564
Lunch: Tues-Fri; Dinner: Daily; Brunch: Sat, Sun
Moderate   www.gascognenyc.com

Hearty appetites will delight in the southwestern French cooking at this intimate, unaffected Chelsea bistro. The capable and friendly waiters will happily explain the fine points of the rather limited menu. Salads are popular. Foie gras lovers will be in heaven. The main-course menu features duck, cassoulet, quail, and roasted rabbit. Seafood dishes are especially tasty. All desserts are made in-house and show imagination. There are sorbets, fruit tarts, soufflés, and some unusual ice cream flavors (prune, Armagnac, and chocolate mint). A small dining area is available downstairs. The garden is charming. If you are longing for a satisfying French dining experience, look at the pre-theater *prix fixe* menu. By the way, Gascony is the only region in the world where Armagnac, a brandy distilled from wine, is produced.

If you have a special craving for a sandwich, then make your way to **Eisenberg's Sandwich Shop** (174 Fifth Ave, 212/675-5096). Since 1929 they have been putting the most delicious sandwiches together, and the selection will please most everyone. Prices are moderate, and party platters are available.

GAVROCHE
212 W 14th St (bet Seventh and Eighth Ave)   212/647-8553
Lunch: Tues-Fri; Dinner: Daily; Brunch: Sun   www.gavroche-ny.com
Moderate

This unpretentious establishment, hidden on West 14th Street, serves some of the tastiest French country food in the city. There is no pretense, just good, solid French cuisine prepared by individuals who were brought up across the ocean. The bread is served warm, the salads are served cold, and the bountiful entrees will satisfy the most exacting palate. A three-course *prix fixe* lunch for $20 is a great bargain. By the way, Gavroche is ideal for solo diners who want a reasonably priced meal.

GEISHA
33 E 61st St (bet Park and Madison Ave)   212/813-1113
Lunch: Mon-Fri; Dinner: Mon-Sat   www.geisharestaurant.com
Moderately expensive to expensive

Sushi is the star here, but Geisha also does well with other modern-day Asian offerings. You can choose from an assortment of menu items. The excellent sushi rolls include caterpillar roll (saltwater eel, cucumber, and avocado) and the signature Geisha roll (served with lobster honey miso dressing and *shiso* vinaigrette). The house is divided into a downstairs lounge and dining area and upstairs dining room, plus an adjacent *tatami* (family) room decorated with rich kimono fabrics. Main courses run the gamut from skate, salmon, halibut, and cod to filet mignon and rack of lamb. A number of tasty salads are just right for lunch. Unlike the desserts, the collection of green teas is special. A private party room is available.

GINO
780 Lexington Ave (at 61st St)   212/758-4466
Lunch, Dinner: Daily
Moderate

Gino is a New York institution where the ubiquitous crowd will immediately clue you into the fact that the food is great. Why? Because this Italian restaurant is filled with native New Yorkers. You'll see no tourist buses out front. The menu has been the same for years: a large selection of popular dishes (over 30 entrees!) from antipasto to soup and pasta to fish. There are daily specials, but you only have to taste such regulars as chicken *alla* Capri, Italian sausages with peppers, or scampis *alla* Gino to get hooked. Gino's staff has been here forever, taking care of patrons in an informed, fatherly manner. The best part comes when the tab is presented. East Side rents are always climbing, but Gino has resisted price hikes by taking cash only and serving delicious food that keeps the tables full. Reservations are not accepted, so come early.

How does a light, inexpensive French lunch sound? I have found a great place for just that: **Frederick's Downtown** (637 Hudson St, 212/488-4200). Open every day for lunch, with outdoor seating available, this is a pleasant place to enjoy a thrifty noon meal with friends. You'll find goodies like homemade gazpacho, platters of raw vegetables, a super selection of cheeses, huge sandwiches with really crispy French fries, pizzas, pastas, steaks, seafood, and more. It's almost like being in Paris!

GIORGIONE
307 Spring St (bet Greenwich and Hudson St)　　　212/352-2269
Lunch: Mon-Fri; Dinner: Daily　　　www.giorgionenyc.com
Moderate

When the name Deluca (as in Dean & Deluca) is involved, you know it is a quality operation. Giorgio Deluca is one of the partners in this attractive, high-tech establishment, which features shiny metal-top tables and an inviting pizza oven that turns out some of the best pies in the area. This is a very personal restaurant, with Italian dishes like you'd find in mother's kitchen in the Old Country: carpaccio, prosciutto, ravioli, risotto, and linguine. The minestrone is as good as I have ever tasted. Pizzas come in eight presentations. A raw bar is also available. Finish with a platter of tasty Italian cheeses or pick from the appealing dessert trolley.

GOLDEN UNICORN
18 East Broadway (at Catherine St)
Breakfast, Lunch, Dinner, Dim Sum: Daily　　　212/941-0911
Inexpensive　　　www.goldenunicornrestaurant.com

Golden Unicorn prepares the best dim sum outside of Peking! This bustling, two-floor, Hong Kong-style Chinese restaurant serves delicious dim sum every day of the week. Besides delicacies from the rolling carts, diners may choose from a wide variety of Cantonese dishes off the regular menu. Pan-fried noodle dishes, rice noodles, and noodles in soup are house specialties. Despite the size of the establishment (they can accommodate over 500 diners), you will be amazed at the fast service, cleanliness, and prices. This is one of the best values in Chinatown.

GONZO
140 W 13th St (bet Ave of the Americas and Seventh Ave)
Dinner: Daily　　　212/645-4606
Moderate

In today's world, what diners really want is tasty food, decent atmosphere, and competent service. All of this is available at Gonzo, a popular spot in Manhattan. Seating is available at the bar and in the smallish, attractive back room. Grilled pizzas are big and modestly priced. There are also chopped salads, sliced meat and cheese plates, real Italian pastas, and a nice selection of meat and fish entrees. My choices: braised short ribs of beef (the meat literally falls off the bone) and grilled whole fish (which varies each day). A dozen or more side-dish offerings, many of them grilled, will satisfy veggie lovers. Chef-owner Donna Scotto knows what the younger crowd likes and caters to them.

GOOD
89 Greenwich Ave (bet Bank and 12th St)
Lunch: Tues-Fri; Dinner: Daily; Brunch: Sat, Sun   212/691-8080
Moderate   www.goodrestaurantnyc.com

Good is a casual, friendly, take-your-time establishment. It is a popular destination for locals, especially for brunch. The solid, contemporary American fare is served by very friendly personnel. The brunch menu highlight is the "Good Breakfast": a heaping plate of eggs with a choice of pancakes, home fries, and bacon or sausage. Burgers are tasty, and house-smoked pulled pork is a good bet for dinner.

Looking for quick takeout downtown? Look no further than **Olives** (120 Prince St, 212/941-0111), which is one of the best. The soups, salads, and sandwiches are all delicious and reasonably priced. Sample sandwiches include Olives' hero (copa, salami, marinated onions, and more), mozzarella, smoked turkey, ancho chili-rubbed steak, and grilled chicken breast. This place is a winner!

GOOD ENOUGH TO EAT
483 Amsterdam Ave (at 83rd St)   212/496-0163
Breakfast, Lunch: Mon-Fri; Dinner: Daily; Brunch: Sat, Sun
Inexpensive   www.goodenoughtoeat.com

New York is a weekend breakfast and brunch town, and you cannot do better than Good Enough to Eat in both categories. Savor the apple pancakes, four-grain pancakes with walnuts and fresh bananas, and chocolate chip and coconut pancakes. Additional offerings: French toast, waffles, a dozen kinds of omelets, scrambled egg dishes, corned beef hash, real Irish oatmeal, fresh-squeezed orange juice, and homemade sausage. The lunches in this homey and noisy room—with a tile floor and wooden tables and bar —feature inexpensive and delicious salads, burgers (juicy and delicious), pizzas, and sandwiches. More of the same is served for dinner, plus meatloaf, turkey, pork chops, fish, and roast chicken plates. A children's menu is available for lunch and dinner, and an outdoor cafe is popular when the weather is nice. This is comfort food at its best, all the way through wonderful homemade pies, cakes, and ice creams.

GOTHAM BAR & GRILL
12 E 12th St (bet Fifth Ave and University Pl)   212/620-4020
Lunch: Mon-Fri; Dinner: Daily   www.gothambarandgrill.com
Moderately expensive

The Gotham is a must! Since 1984 it has been recognized as one of New York's best. Dining here can be summed up in one word: *exciting!* It is not inexpensive, but every meal I have had has been worth the tab—and there is a really good *prix fixe* lunch deal. You may also eat at the bar. Alfred Portale is one of the most talented chefs in the city. The modern, spacious, high-ceilinged space is broken by direct spot lighting on the tables. Fresh plants lend a bit of color. There are great salads (try the seafood), excellent free-range chicken, and superior grilled salmon and roast cod. Each entree is well seasoned, attractively presented, and delicious. The rack of lamb is one of the tastiest in town. Desserts are all made in-house; try the carrot cake or unique ice cream flavors.

> There's lots of interest in Cuban cuisine these days. One of the best places in Manhattan for such staples as paella and Havana-style bar-becued ribs is **Havana Central** (22 E 17th St, 212/414-4999). Jeremy Merrin, a hands-on partner, welcomes diners with counter service at lunch and tables at dinner. The price is right, and vegetarians will feel at home.

GRAMERCY TAVERN
42 E 20th St (bet Park Ave S and Broadway)   212/477-0777
Lunch: Mon-Fri; Dinner: Daily   www.gramercytavern.com
Expensive

Every detail has been honed to perfection at Gramercy Tavern, and the public has responded. This is a *very* busy place. The space is unusually attractive, the servers are highly trained, and the food is excellent. The ceiling is a work of art, the private party room is magnificent, and there is not a bad seat in the house. Chef Michael Anthony, has created an American menu. Both regular and vegetarian tasting menus are available. You'll enjoy a superior offering of cheeses, sorbets, and ice creams for dessert. This is a great place for a party!

GRAND CENTRAL OYSTER BAR RESTAURANT
Grand Central Terminal (42nd St at Vanderbilt Ave), lower level
Lunch, Dinner: Mon-Sat   212/490-6650
Moderate   www.oysterbarny.com

Native New Yorkers are familiar with the nearly century-old institution that is the Oyster Bar at Grand Central. This midtown destination has been restored and is once again popular with commuters and residents. (They serve over 2,000 folks a day!) The young help are accommodating, and the drain on the pocketbook is minimal. The menu boasts more than 72 seafood items (with special daily entrees), about 30 varieties of oysters, a superb oyster stew, clam chowder (Manhattan and New England styles), oyster pan roast, bouillabaisse, *coquille St. Jacques*, Maryland crab cakes (Wednesday special), Maine lobsters, 75 wines by the glass, and marvelous homemade desserts.

GYU-KAKU

34 Cooper Square (bet 5th and 6th St)   212/475-2989
Lunch: Mon-Sat; Dinner: Daily   www.gyu-kaku.com
Moderate to moderately expensive

A fun experience and very tasty food is the best way to describe this Japanese barbecue restaurant. After a gracious greeting, you are seated at tables with a burner in the center. Then you carefully examine a lengthy menu of appetizers, salads, soups, beef tongue, *kalbi* (short ribs), *harami* (outside skirt), *yaki shabu* (belly), ribeye, filet mignon, intestines, vegetables, rice, noodles, and more. Accommodating servers will help with your choices and give instructions on how to cook the various items. The Kobe beef slices are marvelous, as are the lamb and seafood dishes. Tender pieces of lobster tail are a treat. If you order fresh orange juice, they will squeeze it right at the table! Japanese restaurants are generally not great for desserts, but it's worth getting your hands and face gooey with the S'mores dish at Gyu-Kaku.

HATSUHANA

17 E 48th St (bet Fifth and Madison Ave)   212/355-3345
237 Park Ave (at 46th St)   212/661-3400
Lunch, Dinner: Mon-Fri (Dinner on Sat at 48th St location)
Moderate   www.hatsuhana.com

Hatsuhana has a longstanding reputation as one of the best sushi houses in Manhattan. One can sit at a table or the sushi bar and get equal attention from the informed help. There are several dozen appetizers, including broiled eel in cucumber wrap and chopped fatty tuna with aged soybeans. Next try salmon teriyaki or any number of tuna or sushi dishes. Forget about desserts and concentrate on the exotic appetizer and main-dish offerings.

Desserts from Around the World

Chinese—**Double Crispy Bakery** (230 Grand St, 212/966-6929): doughnuts on a stick

Greek—**Poseidon Bakery** (629 Ninth Ave, 212/757-6173): *galakto-boureko* (rich custard pastry)

Indian—**Spice Corner** (135 Lexington Ave, 212/689-5182): *kalakand* (solidified sweetened milk and cheese)

Italy—**A Voce** (41 Madison Ave, 212/545-8555): *bomboloni*

Japan—**Riingo** (205 E 45th St, 212/867-4200): green-tea doughnuts

Latin—**Casa Adela** (66 Ave C, 212/473-1882): flan custard

Middle Eastern—**Alfanoose** (8 Maiden Lane, 212/528-4669): *baklava*

Senegalese—**Dibiterie Cheikh** (231 W 116th St, 212/663-0717): *thiakry* (sour cream with spices)

HEARTH

403 E 12th St (at First Ave)   646/602-1300
Dinner: Daily   www.restauranthearth.com
Moderately expensive

In a cozy atmosphere in the East Village, with an open kitchen and pleasant personnel, Hearth is one of those places where the clientele seem more focused on their dining companions than the food. Nevertheless, the New American/Tuscan dishes are done well, even if the prices are a bit inflated. The black sea bass, guinea hen, and sirloin steak are very popular. The menu changes daily. All in all, it's a good place to bring a must-impress date—but avoid the unattractive back room. Just down the block visit their wine bar, **Terroir** (413 E 12th St, 646/602-1300; open late, closed Sunday).

HILL COUNTRY
30 W 26th St (bet Broadway and Ave of the Americas)   212/255-4544
Lunch, Dinner: Daily   www.hillcountryny.com
Moderate

This unusual spot is modeled after the old-fashioned meat markets of Central Texas, with an ambience and aroma that will bring joy to barbecue fans. Informal dining is available at tables scattered around the premises. Separate stands offer meat dishes (like brisket, pork spare ribs, whole chicken, Texas sausage), sandwiches, beans, macaroni and cheese, corn pudding, salads, and produce. Lemon bars, banana cream pudding, and bourbon pecan pie are popular desserts. Live music is featured Wednesday through Saturday. Delivery service is offered, and party platters are arranged for office parties. New York is not a great barbecue town, but this place does its best to bring some of the flavors of Texas to the Big Apple.

> A midtown spot that is not very exciting but does have good Italian food is **Fiorini** (209 E 56th St, 212/308-0830, www.fiorinirestaurant. com). Why these folks don't add a bit of pizzazz to their operation is hard to understand!

I COPPI
432 E 9th St (bet First Ave and Ave A)   212/254-2263
Dinner: Daily; Brunch: Sat, Sun   www.icoppinyc.com
Moderate

The husband and wife team of Lorella Innocenti and John Brennan have created a charming Tuscan restaurant where tasty food matches the appealing East Village atmosphere. They have imported talent from the Old Country to ensure that the breads are authentic. A brick pizza oven adds a special touch. The menu changes seasonally. Outstanding brunch dishes (spring through fall) may include Tuscan-style omelets and thin egg noodles with *bolognese* sauce. Pastas, grilled striped bass, and grilled sirloin steak make excellent dinner choices. Save room for gelati, sorbet, or Tuscan cheese for dessert. The heated and canopied outdoor garden is especially inviting. There's no need to rush uptown to fancier and pricier Tuscan restaurants, as I Coppi is as professional and authentic as I have found anywhere in the city.

IL BAGATTO
192 E 2nd St (bet Ave A and B)   212/228-0977
Dinner: Tues-Sun (closed Aug)   212/228-3703 (delivery)
Inexpensive   www.ilbagatto.com

One of Manhattan's best bargains, Il Bagatto is the place to come if you're feeling adventurous. Housed in tiny digs in an area you would hardly call compelling, this is an extremely popular Italian trattoria. The owners have discovered the rules of success: being on the job and ensuring that every dish tastes just like it came out of mama's kitchen. About a dozen tables upstairs and in the lounge are always filled, so it's best to call ahead for reservations. There's delicious spaghetti, homemade gnocchi with spinach, tortellini with meat sauce (made from a secret recipe), and wonderful tagliolini with seafood in a light tomato sauce. Other menu offerings include chicken, carpaccio, and salads, and there are always a few daily specials. They deliver, too. The adjacent wine bar serves both food and drink.

IL CORTILE
125 Mulberry St (bet Canal and Hester St)   212/226-6060
Lunch, Dinner: Daily   www.ilcortile.com
Moderate

Here is a good reason to visit Little Italy! While the area is more for tourists than serious diners, there are some exceptions. Il Cortile is an oasis of tasty Italian fare in an attractive and romantic setting. A bright and airy garden area in the rear is the most pleasant part of the restaurant. The menu is typically Italian, with entree listings that include fish, chicken, and veal dishes, plus excellent spaghetti, fettuccine, and ravioli. Sauteed vegetables like bitter broccoli, hot peppers, mushrooms, spinach, and green beans are specialties of the house. Service is excellent and expeditious, and the waiters zip around like they are on roller skates. If you can fight through the gawking visitors, you will find Il Cortile worth the effort!

> If you are looking for a true American bistro with a menu full of items you would put on your "most wanted" list, then I would suggest a visit to **The Harrison** (355 Greenwich St, 212/274-9310). Seasonal house favorites are crispy shrimp, strip steak, and duck-fat fries. The country-inn atmosphere is more about civility than excitement. At the Harrison, diners take greater pleasure from the tastes than the hype.

IL GATTOPARDO
33 W 54th St (bet Fifth Ave and Ave of the Americas)   212/246-0412
Lunch, Dinner: Daily   www.ilgattopardonyc.com
Expensive

This place appeals to serious gourmets, as food and service leave little to be desired. The room is not fancy; it is, in fact, rather claustrophobic. In good weather, the outdoor seating is charming, as is dining in the greenhouse setting. The interesting and varying appetizers may include beef and veal meatballs wrapped in cabbage, scallops, and shrimp salad. Among the many pastas, homemade *scialatielli* is delicious. Main-course highlights include Neapolitan meatloaf, herb-crusted rack of lamb, fish and shellfish stew, and much more. If your favorite dish is not on the menu, then ask in advance and they'll make it for you. For dessert, warm chocolate cake with ice cream is sinfully good.

IL MULINO

86 W 3rd St (bet Sullivan and Thompson St)   212/673-3783
Lunch: Mon-Fri; Dinner: Mon-Sat   www.ilmulino.com
Moderately expensive

Il Mulino is a New York experience not to be missed! Never mind that reservations usually must be made a month or so in advance. Never mind that it's always crowded, the noise level is intolerable, and the waiters nearly knock you down as you wait to be seated. It's all part of the ambience at Il Mulino, one of New York's best Italian restaurants. Your greeting is usually "Hi, boss," which gives you the distinct impression that the staff is accustomed to catering to members of the, uh, "family." When your waiter finally comes around, he'll reel off a lengthy list of evening specials with glazed eyes. A beautiful, mouth-watering display of these specials is arrayed on a huge entrance table. After you're seated, the waiter delivers one antipasto after another while he talks you into ordering one of the fabulous veal dishes with portions bountiful enough to feed King Kong. *Osso buco* is a favorite dish. By the time you finish one of the luscious desserts, you'll know why every seat in the small, simple dining room is kept warm all evening.

IL POSTINO

337 E 49th St (bet First and Second Ave)   212/688-0033
Lunch: Mon-Sat; Dinner: Daily   www.ilpostinorestaurant.com
Expensive

It is nice to splurge on occasion, if what you get is worth the extra bucks. Il Postino does have rather hefty prices, but the offerings rival the best in Manhattan! The setting is comfortable and not showy. You'll be impressed by the captains, who can recite a lengthy list of specials without hesitation. You have your choice of ground-level tables or a slightly raised balcony; the latter feels more comfortable to me. An extraordinarily tasty bread dish and assorted small appetizer plates get things off to a good start. Sensational pastas like linguine with three kinds of clams or tagliolini with mushrooms should not be missed. Chicken in a baked crust is very satisfying, and roasted loin of veal for two is also top-grade. The authentic Italian sorbets finish a memorable gourmet experience. Incidentally, lunch is equally tasty and easier on the wallet.

IL RICCIO

152 E 79th St (bet Third and Lexington Ave)   212/639-9111
Lunch, Dinner: Daily   www.ilriccionyc.com
Moderate

There's nothing fancy here—just good Italian fare. Il Riccio is consistent, so you can count on leaving satisfied and well fed. Spaghetti with crabmeat and fresh tomato is one of my favorites. So is thinly sliced beef with truffled pecorino cheese and breaded rack of veal. Also offered are Dover sole and grilled sardines with broccoli, along with other seasonal specials. The patio is a small, comfortable place to dine in nice weather. Service is unfailingly pleasant. Fruit tarts are homemade and delicious, and marinated peaches (when available) are the signature dessert.

IL VAGABONDO
351 E 62nd St (bet First and Second Ave)   212/832-9221
Lunch: Mon-Fri; Dinner: Daily
Inexpensive

Il Vagabondo is a good spot to recommend to your visiting friends, and many folks consider it their favorite restaurant! This bustling house has been popular with New Yorkers in the know since 1965. The atmosphere is strictly old-time, complete with white tablecloths, four busy rooms, and an even busier bar. There is spaghetti, ravioli, and absolutely marvelous veal and chicken *parmigiana*. There is no pretense at this place, which is a terrific spot for office parties. You will see happy faces, compliments of a delicious meal and reasonable bill. Save room for the Bocce Ball Dessert (*tartufo*). Il Vagabondo, you see, is the only restaurant in New York with an indoor bocce court!

> Yes, I know this is a Manhattan guidebook! However, there are a couple of places in the neighboring Brooklyn borough that I want to include. I was intrigued in name alone by the **General Greene** (229 De Kalb Ave, at Clermont Ave, 718-222-1510), and stopped in to investigate. If you're in the Fort Greene neighborhood for dinner or brunch on Saturday or Sunday, give it a try. The place is clean and busy, and you'll see lots of young people enjoying small dishes. Radishes and anchovies, chicken Cobb salad, scalloped potatoes, and creamed spinach are all uniformly tasty and well worth the modest tab. The only downside in my experience was a rude, unfriendly manager; hopefully, that situation has been remedied. Another Brooklyn find is **Franny's** (295 Flatbush Ave, Prospect Heights, 718/230-0221), where you won't go wrong with the super pizzas and salads.

IRVING MILL
116 E 16th St (bet Irving Place and Union Square E)   212/254-1600
Dinner: Daily; Brunch: Sun   www.irvingmill.com
Moderate to moderately expensive

Owner Sergio Riva has put together one of the most appealing new houses in Manhattan. Most everything about this place is inviting—the personal service, decor, tasty food, reasonable prices, and ambience. Pork dishes are a big thing here: pulled pork sandwiches, *charcroute* plate, even pig's ear salad. But there is much more! I'd strongly recommend the roasted whole chicken (for two), which comes with macaroni and cheese and pork rinds. Also, the Irving Mill burger is a winner; it's not inexpensive, but worth every dollar! Seafood lovers will enjoy the sauteed sturgeon or seasonal catch. My favorite desserts include wonderful apple fritters with cinnamon ice cream and *crème fraiche* panna cotta.

JACK'S LUXURY OYSTER BAR
101 Second Ave (bet 5th and 6th St)   212/253-7848
Dinner: Mon-Sat
Moderate to moderately expensive

Jack and Grace Lamb oversee their small operation with a tiny bar that's a fun place. You can enjoy fresh oysters (done four ways), excellent poached lobster, littleneck clams, and more. In some cases, smaller *is* better.

JACKSON HOLE BURGERS

232 E 64th St (bet Second and Third Ave)	212/371-7187
521 Third Ave (at 35th St)	212/679-3264
1611 Second Ave (at 84th St)	212/737-8788
1270 Madison Ave (at 91st St)	212/427-2820
517 Columbus Ave (at 85th St)	212/362-5177

Breakfast, Brunch, Lunch, Dinner: Daily   www.jacksonholeburgers.com
Inexpensive

Jackson Hole is my favorite burger destination! You might think that a burger is a burger. But having done hamburger taste tests all over the city, I can attest that this is the best. Each one weighs at least seven juicy, delicious ounces. You can get all kinds: pizza burger, Swiss burger, English burger, or a Baldouni burger (mushrooms, fried onions, and American cheese). Or try an omelet, a Mexican item, a salad, or grilled chicken breast. The atmosphere isn't fancy, but once you sink your teeth into a Jackson Hole burger, accompanied by great onion rings or French fries and a homemade dessert, you'll see why I'm so enthusiastic (as is former President Bill Clinton). Breakfast or brunch is also served. Check with each location, as service varies. Free delivery and catering are available.

Egg Cream

A New York invention, the egg cream is generally credited to Louis Auster, a Jewish immigrant who owned a candy store at Stanton and Cannon streets during the early part of the 20th century. Mostly to amuse himself, he started mixing carbonated water, sugar, and cocoa until he concocted a drink he liked. It was such a hit that the famous fountain operation of Schraft's reportedly offered him $20,000 for the recipe. Auster wouldn't sell and secretly continued making his own syrup in the back room of his store. When he died, his recipe went with him. Some years later, Herman Fox created another chocolate syrup, which he called Fox's U-Bet. To this day Fox's brand is regarded as the definitive egg cream syrup.

JACQUES BRASSERIE

204 E 85th St (bet Second and Third Ave)	212/327-2272
Lunch, Dinner: Daily; Brunch: Sat, Sun	www.jacquesnyc.com

Moderate

It is easy to understand why this bistro is so popular with folks in the neighborhood. It is cozy, friendly, and moderately priced, and they serve great food. In addition, Jacques himself is one of the friendliest proprietors in town. All of the classic French dishes are available: onion soup, steak *au poivre,* crème brûlée, cheeses, and a wonderful chocolate soufflé with Tahitian vanilla ice cream. There are also outstanding seafood dishes, including mussels prepared six ways. Moreover, this bistro is intimate, making it a great place for private parties.

JEAN GEORGES

Trump International Hotel and Tower
1 Central Park West (bet 60th and 61st St)   212/299-3900
Breakfast: Daily (in cafe); Lunch: Mon-Fri;   www.jean-georges.com
Dinner: Mon-Sat; Brunch: Sun
Very expensive

A treat for the senses! Jean-Georges Vongerichten has created a French dining experience in a setting that can only be described as cool, calm, and calculating. I mean *calculating* in the sense that one is put into a frame of mind to sample *haute cuisine* at its best in a very formal dining room that's awash with personnel. The New French Asian menu changes seasonally. Come ready to be educated! In keeping with any operation bearing the Trump name, the hype at Jean Georges continues. But to be honest, if price is unimportant, you can't do better. The cafe, **Nougatine**, is a bit less intimidating and is open daily for breakfast, lunch, and dinner.

If you've ever doubted the delectability of "health foods," then check out the highly popular **Just Salad** (320 Park Ave, 134 W 37th St, and 100 Maiden Lane; 212/244-1111, www.justsalad.com). A dozen salads are made to order as you watch; all are very fresh and well-priced. You'll also find a dozen wraps and soups. Delivery is available.

JOHN'S PIZZERIA

278 Bleecker St (bet Ave of the Americas and Seventh Ave)
                                                   212/243-1680
260 W 44th St (bet Eighth Ave and Broadway)   212/391-7560
408 E 64th St (bet First and York Ave)   212/935-2895
Daily: 11:30 a.m. to 11:30 p.m.
Moderate   www.johnspizzerianyc.com

These are not ordinary pizzas! Pete Castelotti (there is no John) is known as the "Baron of Bleecker Street." However, he also brought his John's Pizzerias to the Upper West Side and the Upper East Side so that more New Yorkers could taste some of the best brick-oven pizzas in the city. John's offers 54 (count 'em) varieties, from cheese and tomatoes to a gut-busting extravaganza of cheese, tomatoes, anchovies, sausage, peppers, meatballs, onions, and mushrooms. John's does appetizers, salads, sandwiches, homemade spaghetti, cheese ravioli, and manicotti well, too. Things are higher-class uptown; in fact, the enormous 44th Street pizzeria occupies a former church.

Lunch can be a power meal with clients or a grab-and-go affair to get you by until dinner. If the latter is your choice, check out these ethnic midtown street-food vendors:

Bangladeshi: **Biryani cart** (SW corner of 46th St, at Ave of the Americas)
Cuban: **Margon** (136 W 46th St, 212/354-5013)
Indian: **Food Court** (1013 Ave of the Americas, 212/840-3767)
Japanese: **Cafe Zaiya** (18 E 41st St, 212/779-0600)
Korean: **Woorijip** (12 W 32nd St, 212/244-1115)

JUICE GENERATION
171 W 4th St (bet Ave of the Americas and Seventh Ave)
Mon-Fri: 8-8; Sat, Sun: 9-9   212/242-0440

644 Ninth Ave (bet 45th and 46th St)   212/541-5600
117 W 72nd St (bet Broadway and Columbus Ave)   212/579-0400
2730 Broadway (bet 104th and 105th St)   212/531-3111
Mon-Sat: 8 a.m.-9 p.m.; Sun: 9-9   www.juicegeneration.com

Juice Generation is a healthy choice for quick, delicious eating. *Fresh* and *local* are the key concepts here. Whenever possible, area farmers provide fresh fruits and vegetables, wheatgrass, and dairy products for Juice Generation's smoothies, sandwiches, salads, and organic soups—many of which are vegetarian. For added punch, choose a refreshing drink that will boost energy, immunity, and promote weight loss. Poultry, fish, and veggie sandwiches are served on whole-grain breads with low-fat condiment options.

Located up in Morningside Heights, the **Hungarian Pastry Shop** (1030 Amsterdam Ave, 212/866-4230) is a cafe *and* bakery! The wonderful cakes are only part of the appeal. The cafe serves all sorts of waist-expanding items, along with delicious Viennese coffee.

KATZ'S DELICATESSEN
205 E Houston St (at Ludlow St)   212/254-2246
Mon, Tues: 8 a.m.-9:45 p.m.; Wed, Thurs: 8 a.m.-10:45 p.m.;
Fri, Sat: 8 a.m.-2:45 a.m.; Sun: 8 a.m.-10:45 p.m.   www.katzdeli.com
Inexpensive

Established in 1888, Katz's Delicatessen is the oldest and largest deli in Manhattan. If you're experiencing hunger pangs on the Lower East Side, try Katz's. It is a super place with hand-carved and overstuffed sandwiches that are among the best in town. Mainstays include pastrami, hot dogs, corned beef, and potato pancakes. Prices are reasonable. Go right up to the counter and order—it is fun watching the no-nonsense operators slicing and fixing—or sit at a table where a seasoned waiter will take care of you. Try dill pickles and sauerkraut with your sandwich. Incidentally, Katz's is a perfect place to sample the unique (and disappearing) lowbrow "charm" of the Lower East Side. While you wait for a table or discover that the salt and pepper containers are empty and the catsup is missing, you'll know what I mean. Catering (at attractive rates) and private party facilities are available.

KEENS STEAKHOUSE
72 W 36th St (bet Fifth Ave and Ave of the Americas)
Lunch: Mon-Fri; Dinner: Daily   212/947-3636
Moderate   www.keens.com

One of the most reliable long-time Manhattan restaurants is Keens Steakhouse, a unique New York institution. I can remember coming here decades ago, when those in the garment trade made Keens their lunch headquarters. This has not changed. Keens still has the same attractions: the bar reeks of atmosphere, and there are great party facilities and fine food to match. Keens has been a fixture in the Herald Square area since 1885. For some time it was for "gentlemen only," and although it still has a masculine atmosphere, ladies are made to feel comfortable and welcome. The famous mutton chop with mint is the house specialty, but other delicious dishes include steak, lamb, fish, and lobster. They do single-malt Scotch tastings from fall through spring and stock one of the largest collections in New York. If you have a meat-and-potato lover in your party, this is the place to come. Make sure to save a little room for the deep-dish apple pie.

KING'S CARRIAGE HOUSE
251 E 82nd St (bet Second and Third Ave)   212/734-5490
Lunch, Dinner: Daily; Tea: Daily (at 3)   www.kingscarriagehouse.com
Moderately expensive

Even some folks in the immediate neighborhood are unaware of this sleeper. King's is indeed an old carriage house, remade into a charming two-story dining salon that your mother-in-law will love. The ambience is Irish manor house, and the menu changes every evening. In a quaint setting with real wooden floors, you dine by candlelight in a very civilized atmosphere. The luncheon menu stays the same: salads, sandwiches, and lighter fare. Afternoon tea is a treat. The continental menu changes nightly and may feature grilled items (like loin of lamb). On Sundays, it is a roast dinner (leg of lamb, loin of pork, chicken, or tenderloin of beef). The $49 *prix fixe* menu is a really good value. I found the Stilton cheese with a nightcap of ruby port absolutely perfect for dessert. Chocolate truffle cake and rhubarb tart are excellent, too.

Restaurateur Peter Poulakakos has brought family-style Italian dining to the Financial District. **Harry's Italian** (2 Gold St, 212/747-0797) serves Italian staples like pasta, chicken, and veal dishes—large portions at affordable prices.

KITTICHAI
60 Thompson St (at Broome St)
Lunch: Mon-Fri: Dinner: Daily; Brunch: Sat, Sun   212/219-2000
Moderately expensive   www.kittichairestaurant.com

Kittichai serves real Thai food! One's eyes rest as much on the table-ware, the black-draped service personnel, and the fish tank as on the food. As is true in most Thai restaurants, seafood is high on the list. Marinated monkfish is a splendid starter, and the seafood soup is a must on a cold evening. The salad of banana blossoms, artichokes, and roasted chili was a pleaser at my table. Don't overlook the chocolate (cocoa powder) baby back ribs marinated in Thai spices. For entrees, Chilean sea bass and wok-fried chicken with roasted cashew nuts are winners. Kittichai's curries are exceptional. Honestly, I found this place a bit much, both in attitude and dishes, but you do get a peek at the mystique of Thailand.

KLEE BRASSERIE
200 Ninth Ave (at 22nd St)
Lunch: Tues-Sun: Dinner: Daily; Brunch: Sat, Sun   212/633-8033
Moderate   www.kleebrasserie.com
Enjoy a bit of Austrian atmosphere in a sparklingly clean room. You can

also enjoy a well-selected cheese platter, some thin-crust pizzas, Tyrolean macaroni and cheese, a Kobe beef hot dog, or traditional weiner schnitzel. In the evening, duckling from the stone wood-fired oven, steaks from the mesquite grill, a good choice of pastas that change daily, and many of the lunch items are available. For dessert? Sacher torte, of course!

Italian Specialties

Bruschetta: slices of crispy garlic bread, usually topped with tomatoes and basil

Carpaccio: thin shavings of raw beef topped with olive oil and lemon juice or mayonnaise

Risotto: creamy, rice-like pasta, often mixed with shellfish and/or vegetables

Saltimbocca: Thinly sliced veal topped with prosciutto and sage is sauteed in butter and slow-simmered in white wine. The name means "jumps in your mouth."

Zabaglione: dessert sauce or custard made with egg yolks, marsala, and sugar; also known as *sabayon* in France

---

LA BOITE EN BOIS
75 W 68th St (at Columbus Ave)   212/874-2705
Lunch: Mon-Sat; Dinner: Daily; Brunch: Sun   www.laboitenyc.com
Moderate

You don't have to pronounce the name of this French restaurant properly to have a good time! It packs them in every evening for obvious reasons: delicious food, personal service, and moderate prices. Salads are unusual, and the country paté is a great beginner. For an entree, I recommend filet of snapper, roast chicken with herbs, or *pot-au-feu*. The atmosphere is intimate, and all the niceties of service are operative from start to finish. The French toast at brunch is a treat. Desserts are made in-house; try one of their sorbets. Since La Boite en Bois is small and popular, call ahead for reservations.

The things I like to hear least at restaurants:

"Are you guys doing okay?"

"Have a seat in the bar until your table is ready."

"Sorry, we can't accommodate you tonight." Spoken when the place is half-empty.

From the server: "This dish is my favorite."

When paying with cash: "Do you need change?"

"Are you still working on that?"

LA BOTTEGA
Maritime Hotel   212/243-8400
88 Ninth Ave (at 17th St)   www.themaritimehotel.com
Breakfast, Lunch, Dinner: Daily; Brunch: Sat, Sun
Moderate

In nice weather, outside dining at La Bottega is very pleasant. At other times, the inside restaurant seating at this downtown hotel offers a relaxing setting for business meetings. The food is basic Italian, moderately priced, with no surprises. Pizzas, pastas, and salads are the main offerings. Sliced prosciutto with seasonal fruit is one of the best light dishes. Several flavors of gelato are on the dessert menu.

> The West Village has an upscale trattoria in **Centro Vinoteca** (74 Seventh Ave, 212/367-7470). This busy establishment serves lunch and dinner daily, as well as weekend brunch. Menu items are plentiful, as are the portions. *Piccolini* (small plates) are tasty options. If it is on the brunch menu when you visit, try the egg, fennel sausage, and fontina sandwich on a fennel raisin roll. No matter what time you are there, save room for a cannoli with pistachios and orange sauce—*mmm!*

LA GRENOUILLE
3 E 52nd St (bet Fifth and Madison Ave)   212/752-1495
Lunch: Tues-Sat; Dinner: Mon-Sat   www.la-grenouille.com
Expensive

Put on your finest clothes if you're going to dine at La Grenouille, a special place that must be seen to be believed. Beautiful, fresh-cut flowers herald a unique, not-to-be-forgotten dining experience. The food is as great as the atmosphere, and although prices are high, La Grenouille is worth every penny. Celebrity-watching adds to the fun. You'll see most of the famous faces at the front of the room. The professional staff serves a complete French menu. Be sure to try the cold hors d'oeuvres, which are a specialty of the house, as are the lobster dishes, sea bass, and poached chicken. Nowhere in New York are sauces any better. Don't miss the superb dessert soufflés. The tables are close together, but what difference does it make when the people at your elbows are so interesting?

LA LUNCHONETTE
130 Tenth Ave (at 18th St)   212/675-0342
Lunch, Dinner: Daily
Inexpensive to moderate

La Lunchonette proves that you don't have to be fancy to succeed, as long as you serve good food. In an unlikely location, this popular spot offers some of the tastiest French dishes around: snails, sauteed portobello mushrooms, and lobster bisque to start, and omelets, grilled lamb sausage, sauteed calves liver, and more for entrees. On Sunday evening, live music is a feature. You'll be pleasantly surprised when the bill comes!

LANDMARC
Time Warner Center
10 Columbus Circle (at 60th St), 3rd floor   212/823-6123
Breakfast, Lunch, Dinner: Daily
179 West Broadway (bet Leonard and Worth St)   212/343-3883
Breakfast: Daily; Lunch: Mon-Fri; Dinner: Daily; Brunch: Sat, Sun
Moderate   www.landmarc-restaurant.com

Big menu, very tasty food, accommodating staff—what more could you want? Seafood entrees include grilled salmon, tuna, and monkfish. Pork chops and roasted chicken are excellent. Daily pasta specials are available, and steaks with French fries are a specialty. Delicious fresh salads are a lunch favorite. Looking for a novel entree? Try the crispy sweetbreads or popular mussels with a selection of sauces. Both locations are crowded and offer high-energy dining.

LAND THAI KITCHEN

1565 Second Ave (bet 81st and 82nd St)	212/439-1847
450 Amsterdam Ave (at 82nd St)	212/501-8121
Lunch, dinner: Daily	www.landthaikitchen.com
Moderate	

Come here for well-prepared and -presented Thai food at good prices. The brief menu offers about a dozen noodle and rice dishes and combinations from the wok. Other entree offerings are fish, steak, and duck breast, all served with jasmine rice. Appetizers, salads, and side dishes round out the menu. The chef is known for spicy sauces; ask your server to have the heat of the dish turned up or down to suit your taste. Delivery and takeout are available.

Light up! Smoking Places

Nowadays, you will get the boot in most New York bars if you try to have a smoke. However, there are a few places left where you can legally light up, toss back a drink, and grab a meal.

Carnegie Club (156 W 56th St, 212/957-9676): cigar bar and jazz

Circa Tabac (32 Watts St, 212/941-1781): over 200 brands of cigarettes

Club Macanudo (26 E 63rd St, 212/752-8200): private humidors

Florio's Grill & Cigar Bar (192 Grand St, 212/226-7610): nice selection of cigars

Hudson Bar & Books (636 Hudson St, 212/229-2642): seminars and special events

Lexington Bar & Books (1020 Lexington Ave, 212/717-3902): jackets preferred

Merchants, N.Y. (1125 First Ave, 212/832-1551): sophisticated environs

---

LA PETITE AUBERGE

116 Lexington Ave (at 28th St)	212/689-5003
Lunch: Mon-Fri: Dinner: Daily	www.lapetiteaubergeny.com
Moderate	

Genuine French cooking is not easily found in this area, but this smallish, unpretentious restaurant is worth a casual lunch or dinner visit. Friendly personnel will lead you through the usual French favorites: onion soup, escargots, frog legs, roast duck, filet mignon, rack of lamb, and filet of sole. Delicious soufflés are the best way to finish a satisfying meal.

LA RIPAILLE

605 Hudson St (at 12th St)   212/255-4406
Lunch, Dinner: Daily; Brunch: Sat, Sun   www.laripaille.com
Moderate

This small, bright, Parisian-style bistro in the West Village (complete with fireplace) makes a cozy spot for an informal meal. You might want to enjoy a cocktail on the lovely outdoor terrace. The chef puts his heart into every dish. Entrees are done to perfection; the seafood is always fresh, and they do an excellent job with rack of lamb and duck *magret*. White chocolate is a house favorite; at least half of the dessert offerings use it as an ingredient. Rave notices from New York gourmets are proudly displayed at the front of the room.

L'ATELIER DE JOËL ROBUCHON

Four Seasons Hotel New York
57 E 57th St (bet Madison and Park Ave)   212/350-6658
Dinner: Daily   www.fourseasons.com
Very expensive

This one falls in the "if it is expensive, it must be great" category. Well, it *is* very expensive, and I would classify it as very good—but certainly not worth the price. If the occasion is something highly special, then go ahead and give it a try. I'd recommend sitting at the counter, as the service is much better than at the tables and the personnel seem more anxious to please. The greeting, like that at so many New York restaurants, is haughty. However, if you do get a chance to meet the manager, she is a gem and very gracious. The menu is full of delicacies like caviar and foie gras—spendy, but done with great class and eye appeal. Flavors abound here, and you may never have experienced some of them before. Frog legs, lobster, and sea bass are all memorable dishes, and there is a tasting menu. Even the burger —actually, two small ones, complete with foie gras and all the trimmings—is delicious. Desserts are varied and outrageously expensive. The molten chocolate cake is probably the best. Is L'Atelier de Joël Robuchon excessive? Yes. Is dining here an event? Definitely.

LE BERNARDIN

155 W 51st St (at Seventh Ave)   212/489-1515
Lunch: Mon-Fri; Dinner: Mon-Sat   www.le-bernardin.com
Expensive

You surely have heard of this seafood palace! There has to be one restaurant that tops every list, and for seafood Le Bernardin holds that spot. Co-owner Maguy LeCoze and executive chef Eric Ripert make this house extremely attractive to the eye and very satisfying to the stomach. Wonderfully fresh oysters and clams make a great start. Whatever your heart desires from the ocean is represented on the entree menu. What distinguishes La Bernardin is presentation. Signature dishes change nightly and might include yellowfish tuna (appetizer), monkfish, halibut, and skate. *Prix fixe* lunch is $68; dinner is $109. The dessert menu usually includes a cheese assortment, superb chocolate dishes, and unusual ice creams. A tasting menu is also available.

LE BOEUF À LA MODE

539 E 81st St (bet York and East End Ave)   212/249-1473
Dinner: Mon-Sat   www.leboeufalamode.net
Moderately expensive

My idea of a perfect restaurant is Le Boeuf à la Mode. This Upper East Side French bistro has been pleasing New Yorkers for decades. The owners know the recipe for success: warm, comfortable surroundings; pleasant, informed service; outstanding, reliable food; and prices that will not decimate one's pocketbook. The classic French fare includes snails in garlic butter, sauteed shrimp, onion soup, outstanding grilled baby lamb chops, and filet mignon. To top it off, the dessert cart is so appetizing you'll want to order one of each item! Visit Le Boeuf à la Mode and you'll feel as if you've taken a trip to Paris.

Some Money-Saving Tips

- Eat out at lunchtime rather than dinner . . . or eat a Sunday supper.
- Eat at the bar, where the menu is less expensive.
- Eat a few appetizers rather than a main entree.
- Don't drink bottled water.
- Don't go for the expensive wines. Some less expensive bottles are just as good!
- Don't go for the entree specials, which are often overpriced.
- Don't feel that you must have a dessert.
- The first main dish listed on a menu is usually the most profitable.
- Be sure to "check your check."

LE CIRQUE

1 Beacon Court
151 E 58th St (bet Lexington and Third Ave)   212/644-0202
Lunch: Mon-Fri; Dinner: Mon-Sat   www.lecirque.com
Expensive

It's all about Sirio Maccioni! Probably no one on the Manhattan restaurant scene has more devoted followers than this charming gentleman. Now he has a difficult-to-find retreat that's frequented by fans looking for frog legs, *quenelles de brochet*, honey-glazed duck breast, and pig's feet. Most of all they want to be seen by the "swells" and get a kiss from Sirio himself. The food, under the direction of chef Craig Hopson, is absolutely superb. The atmosphere is what you would expect (classy, subdued, jackets required) as are the prices (expensive). If you want the same great food in a more relaxed setting, head to the wine lounge. Private facilities are also available. I love watching Sirio, who is the epitome of what a restaurateur owner should be.

LE GIGOT

18 Cornelia St (bet Bleecker and 4th St)
Lunch, Dinner: Tues-Sun; Brunch: Sat, Sun   212/627-3737
Moderate   www.legigotrestaurant.com

This is a charming, romantic 28-seat bistro in the bowels of the Village. Most taxi drivers have never heard of Cornelia Street, so allow extra time if you come by cab. Once you're here, the cozy atmosphere and warm hospitality of the ladies who greet and serve combines with hearty dishes that will please the most discerning diner. My suggestion for a memorable meal: *bouillabaisse* or, in winter, *le boeuf Bourguignon* (beef stew in red wine with shallots, bacon, carrots, mushrooms, and potatoes). Snails and patés make delicious starters. Tasty desserts like upside-down apple tarts and flambéed bananas with cognac are offered. Brunches are a specialty. Le Gigot is a lot less expensive than its counterpart in Paris, but just as appealing. Note: Only cash and American Express are accepted.

> **Norma's** (Le Parker Meridien Hotel, 118 W 57th St, 212/708-7460) is rightfully praised for having the best breakfast menu in Manhattan. Here are some sample offerings: blueberry and buttermilk pancakes, Johnny applecakes, crispy Belgian waffles with fresh fruit, crunchy pecan and macadamia-nut granola, a gooey four-cheese omelet, and an overstuffed croissant of smoked salmon and scrambled eggs. For exotic tastes, try the "Zillion Dollar" lobster frittata, with ten ounces of *sevruga* caviar. The price: $1,000. The budget version, with one ounce of caviar, goes for a mere $100.

LE JARDIN BISTRO

25 Cleveland Pl (bet Kenmare and Spring St)   212/343-9599
Lunch, Dinner: Daily; Brunch: Sat, Sun   www.lejardinbistro.com
Moderate

This charming downtown restaurant has thrived over the years because it is an excellent operation in every way. The setting, particularly by the garden, is homey and pleasant. The service is unobtrusive and friendly. The menu offers good value. You'll find many French favorites: onion soup, tuna tartare, niçoise salad, and more to start. For the main course, I'd suggest *bouillabaisse*, breast of duck, or rack of lamb. For dessert, Le Jardin's profiteroles (vanilla ice cream in puff pastry) are New York's best, mainly because of the fabulous chocolate sauce. A "Rotating Recession" *prix fixe* dinner menu—$29.99 for 3 courses and $24.99 for two courses—is offered Sunday through Thursday.

LE PÉRIGORD

405 E 52nd St (bet First Ave and East River)   212/755-6244
Lunch: Mon-Fri; Dinner: Daily   www.leperigord.com
Expensive

Don't miss this one! I love this place, which has been charming diners for over 45 years. *Civilized* is the word to describe Le Périgord. It is like dining in one of the great rooms of Manhattan in the "good old days," but with a distinctively modern presence. From gracious host Georges Briguet to the talented chef, everything is class personified. Gentlemen should wear jackets. Every captain and waiter has been trained to perfection. Fresh roses and Limoges dinner plates adorn each table. But this is just half the pleasure of the experience. Every dish—from the magnificent cold appetizer buffet that greets guests to the spectacular dessert cart—is tasty and memorable. You may order a la carte, of course. Soups are outstanding. Dover sole melts in your mouth. A fine selection of game is available in winter. Roasted free-range chicken, served with the best potato dish I have ever tasted (*bleu de* gex potato gratin), should not be missed. The chocolate mousse is without equal in Manhattan. The luxurious setting of Le Périgord makes one appreciate what gracious dining on a special night out is all about.

LE REFUGE
166 E 82nd St (bet Third and Lexington Ave)   212/861-4505
Dinner: Daily   www.lerefugenyc.com
Moderate

In any other city, Le Refuge would be one of the hottest restaurants in town. But aside from folks in the neighborhood, few seem to have heard of it. This charming, three-room French country restaurant offers excellent food, professional service, and delightful surroundings. The front room is cozy and comfortable, and the rear sections provide nice views and pleasant accommodations. A back garden is open in the summer. This is another house where the owner is the chef, and as usual, it shows in the professionalism of the presentations. Specialties of the house: duck with fresh fruit, *bouillabaisse de crustaces*, and couscous Mediterranean with shrimp. Finish off your meal with crème brûlée, profiteroles, or chocolate truffle cake.

In an area known for wine bars, **Sorella** (95 Allen St, 212/274-9595, www.sorellanyc.com) is well worth a visit. Try fresh-baked *grissini* to start, then add a little something from the *qualcosina* menu of delicious small plates (risotto, crispy veal sweetbreads, and lamb ragu). Changing nightly is a two-course *prix fixe stasera abbiamo* menu. Wines are sold by the glass or bottle, and beer drinkers will find a selection of brews on tap or in bottles. This place is a taste of luxury, and it's affordable!

LE RIVAGE
340 W 46th St (bet Eighth and Ninth Ave)   212/765-7374
Lunch, Dinner: Daily   www.lerivagenyc.com
Moderate

Le Rivage is one of the survivors along the highly competitive "restaurant row" of 46th Street. They endure by serving French food that's well prepared and reasonably priced. Escargots, onion soup, *coq au vin rouge*, and peach melba are all delectable and well-presented. The atmosphere and pleasant attitude of the servers will put one in the proper frame of mind to enjoy a Broadway show.

LES HALLES
411 Park Ave S (bet 28th and 29th St)   212/679-4111
Daily: 7:30 a.m. to midnight   www.leshalles.net
Moderate

Come here anytime you are hungry! Les Halles has struck a responsive chord on the New York restaurant stage. No doubt that is because the brasserie provides tasty food in an appealing atmosphere at reasonable prices. Specialties like blood sausage with apples, lamb stew, and fillet of beef are served in hefty portions with fresh salad and delicious French fries. Harried waiters try their best to be polite and helpful, but they are not always successful, as tables turn over rapidly. If a week in Paris is more of a dream than a reality, then you might settle for mussels, snails, onion soup, and classic cassoulet at this busy establishment. The dessert selection is a disappointment, except for the crepes Suzette, prepared tableside. (Note: Les Halles' butcher shop, by the front door, is open daily.) The quieter **Les Halles Downtown** (15 John St, 212/285-8585) has much the same menu and offers ten mussel preparations.

LITTLE OWL
90 Bedford St (at Grove St)   212/741-4695
Lunch, Dinner: Daily; Brunch: Sat, Sun   www.thelittleowlnyc.com
Moderate

There's not much to look at but a lot to be satisfied with in the food category at Little Owl. With tiny tables and a capacity of only 32 diners, this corner establishment is a very personal place with a wait staff that is warm and eager to please. Every seasonal Mediterranean dish I tasted was excellent and reasonably priced. The mixed green salad was as delicious as any I have had in the city. Some outstanding entrees: potato gnocchi, crispy chicken, and grilled pork chops. Beans are a top side dish. The brunch menu is particularly attractive, with dishes like whole-wheat pancakes, gravy meatball sliders, yellowfin tuna, and bacon cheeseburger with spiced fries. Baked strawberry custard and brownie with praline coffee sauce are wonderful desserts, if available. Just one drawback: Little Owl is very popular, so reservations are a must.

This is one of Manhattan's best-kept secrets! If you are looking for atmosphere and the size of the check makes no difference, then go for dinner at **Bruno Jamais** (24 E 81st St, 212/396-3444). In the magnificent townhouse that once housed the famed Parioli Romanissimo restaurant, a room has been created that brings visions of dining in a European palace! Wine glasses hang from the ceiling, the service is hushed, many full-suited functionaries walk the floor, and the platters presented are attractive and tasty (if not particularly memorable). Music and dancing are available after dining. You'll see all ages here. Just hold on tight to your wallet!

MACELLERIA
48 Gansevoort St (at Greenwich St)
Lunch: Mon-Fri: Dinner: Daily; Brunch: Sat, Sun   212/741-2555
Moderately expensive   www.macelleriarestaurant.com

The Meatpacking District has certainly been spruced up in recent years. New restaurants and stores have transformed this once uninviting part of Manhattan. One of the brightest spots in the area is Macelleria, essentially a Northern Italian steakhouse with added attractions. The setting is what you might expect: masculine and unpretentious, with outside tables for nice-weather dining. Friendly and welcoming help make an excellent first impression. The menu is traditional, with some pleasant additions: fresh and filling salads, a number of pastas, chicken, veal, and duck. Steaks are the primary draw. They *are* very tasty, although the line that they are the "best in New York" is an exaggeration. I would highly recommend this spot for dinner with business partners after consummating a big deal. For private events, try the wine cellar or the chef's table—located in the meat locker!

MAI HOUSE

186 Franklin St (bet Hudson and Greenwich St)   212/431-0606
Dinner: Thurs-Sat   www.myriadrestaurantgroup.com
Moderate

This is not one of the many small, family-operated Vietnamese restaurants that are so popular because of their cheap prices. Mai House is definitely an upscale house, with many exotic Vietnamese specialties and a rather sophisticated atmosphere. Yes, there are spring rolls, but also barbecued quail and wild boar *nem* sausage for appetizers. Thinly sliced lemongrass short ribs are delicious, as are sweet-and-sour spicy red snapper and nuggets of cuttlefish. Traditionalists will find many kinds of noodles and rice. A glass of sake will finish off a tasty meal.

Looking for a lunch with tasty, interesting choices? I recommend **Devon & Blakely** (461 Fifth Ave and other locations, 212/684-4321) for their crab-cake sandwich and baked artichoke heart salad. Also on the lunch menu are more sandwiches, wraps, paninis, soups, quesadillas, and salads. Standard morning and afternoon fare includes muffins, pastries and other sweets, and a lengthy list of beverages. Devon & Blakely's six locations are open weekdays from 7 to 4 for takeout, delivery, and catering.

MALONEY & PORCELLI

37 E 50th St (bet Park and Madison Ave)   212/750-2233
Lunch: Mon-Fri; Dinner: Daily   www.maloneyandporcelli.com
Expensive

If your accountant wrangles you a nice tax refund, take him or her to Maloney & Porcelli! Most everything is expensive: the ambience, the platters, and (yes) the check. But the meat dishes—fabulous sirloin steaks and crackling pork shank—are wonderful. It is tempting to fill up on the great bread basket, but leave room for first-rate appetizers like oven-fired pizzas, crab cakes, and tuna tartare. Lobster dishes are a specialty, particularly the "Angry Lobster." An intriguing dessert selection is available. Their private dining room is a great facility for an office party or wedding reception.

MANGIA E BEVI

800 Ninth Ave (at 53rd St)   212/956-3976
Lunch, Dinner: Daily   www.mangiaebevirestaurant.com
Inexpensive to moderate

Dining on Ninth Avenue? Mangia e Bevi is a top choice for delicious food at unbelievably low prices (for Manhattan). The noise level is almost unbearable, the tables allow you to instantly become friendly with strangers, and the waiters are very casual yet surprisingly helpful. The abundant antipasto platter, overflowing with nearly a dozen choices, is a house specialty. This rustic trattoria also features a large selection of pastas, fish, meat dishes, salads, and a bevy of in-season veggies. Brick-oven pizza lovers will be in heaven with pleasing combinations and equally pleasing prices. There's nothing special about desserts, except for the homemade tiramisu. It is easy to see why this colorful spot is one of the most popular destinations along Ninth Avenue.

MARCHI'S
251 E 31st St (at Second Ave)   212/679-2494
Dinner: Mon-Sat (special hours for private parties)
Moderate   www.marchirestaurant.com

Marchi's has been a New York fixture since 1930, when it was established by the Marchi family in an attractive brownstone townhouse. Three sons are on hand, lending a homey flavor to the restaurant's three dining rooms and garden patio (a great spot for a private dinner). It's almost like eating at your favorite Italian family's home, especially since there are no menus. Bring a hearty appetite to take full advantage of a superb feast. The first course is a platter of antipasto—including radishes, *finocchio,* and Genoa salami—plus a salad of tuna, olives, and red cabbage. The second is an absolutely delicious homemade lasagna. The third is crispy deep-fried fish, light and tempting, served with beets and string beans. The entree is delicious roast chicken and veal served with fresh mushrooms and tossed salad. Dessert consists of fresh fruit, cheese, lemon fritters, and sensational *crostoli* (crisp fried twists sprinkled with powdered sugar). The tab is reasonable. Come to Marchi's for a unique, leisurely meal and an evening you will long remember. Experience a little taste of Italy in Marchi's garden, with the Empire State Building as your centerpiece. Unbelievable!

Attention Bloomingdale's shoppers! Dart across the street to **Brasserie 360** (200 E 60th St, 212/688-8688) if you are hungry. It's not fancy or gourmet, but the food is well-prepared, the price is right, and the place is always jumping.

MARKET TABLE
54 Carmine St (at Bedford St)
Lunch: Mon-Fri; Dinner: Daily; Brunch: Sat, Sun   212/255-2100
Moderate   www.markettablenyc.com

It is easy to see why this place is always packed. The food is excellent, the personnel polite and helpful, the prices moderate, and the atmosphere inviting. Comfort food is the name of the game here: crisp salads, hearty sandwiches, grilled chicken, strip steak, and more. The hamburgers alone are worth a visit; they are huge, juicy, and served with delicious fries. Risotto and lamb shanks are perfectly done. Great food and good value make Market Table a real winner.

MARKJOSEPH STEAKHOUSE
261 Water St (off Peck Slip)   212/277-0020
Lunch: Mon-Fri; Dinner: Mon-Sat   www.markjosephsteakhouse.com
Moderately expensive

A fun visit! If the trendy uptown steakhouses turn you off, then head downtown—with good directions, as Water Street turns into Pearl Street near this location—to a comfortable, homey neighborhood room that is high on quality meat (USDA prime dry-aged) and low on attitude. The room is filled with folks in casual garb, more intent on delving into a huge, juicy steak than wondering who's at the next table. If you're dining with a group, the seafood combination platter (lobster, shrimp, clams, calamari, and mussels) is a great place to start. Porterhouse steak and filet mignon are highly recommended. Baked and hash brown potatoes are great side dishes. At lunch, the half-pound burgers are wonderful, as is the signature steak sandwich. If there's still room for dessert, opt for *tartufo* or the MarkJoseph special. You'll be surprised at its contents!

MCCORMICK & SCHMICK'S
1285 Ave of the Americas (at 52nd St)   212/459-1222
Lunch: Mon-Sat; Dinner: Daily   www.mccormickandschmick.com
Moderate to moderately expensive

Since I live on the Pacific coast, I can recognize a great seafood house. Oregon-based McCormick & Schmick's seafood restaurant chain has an operation in Manhattan, and it is a dandy. The fresh seafood sheet (printed twice daily) lists over 30 treats from the world's waterways, all prepared with imagination and care. And the prices, unlike those at some of the so-called class seafood houses in Manhattan, are very much within reach of the average pocketbook. What's good and special: pan-fried Willapa Bay oysters, oysters on the half-shell, Massachusetts steamer clams, Atlantic salmon, and Dungeness crab legs sauteed with mushrooms, artichoke hearts, and sherry. Entrees run the geographical gamut from cashew-crusted Ecuadorian tilapia to Nantucket Bay scallops and Costa Rican mahi-mahi. There are also ample choices for non-seafood diners. Don't miss the dessert tray, which will complete a memorable meal!

> Leave it to superchef Jean-Georges Vongerichten to come up with another place that ranks among the best in its category. **Matsugen** (241 Church St, 212/925-0202) is a Japanese eatery that has superb sushi, tempura, shabu-shabu, and noodles that will please any discriminating palate. You'll dine in comfortable alcoves or at a communal table. On the plus side, you will find dozens of choices and delicious desserts (unique for a Japanese restaurant). On the minus side, the tab can be a bit hefty.

MÉTISSE
239 W 105th St (bet Amsterdam Ave and Broadway)
Lunch: Mon-Fri; Dinner: Daily; Brunch: Sat, Sun   212/666-8825
Moderate   www.metisserestaurant.com

This Upper West Side French bistro does all the good things you would expect, but it is the atmosphere that adds so much to a dinner at Métisse. The place is quiet and restful, the waiters unobtrusive, the cuisine satisfying, and the check reasonable. Imagine a $14 *prix fixe* luncheon, a $15 and $20 *prix fixe* brunch, and a $21 *prix fixe* dinner. Salads are fresh, and the varied entree selection includes seafood, steaks, and chops. For dessert, chocolate mousse will top off a fine meal. Come on Monday evening for the piano bar.

METROCAFE & WINE BAR
32 E 21st St (bet Park Ave S and Broadway)
Lunch: Mon-Fri; Dinner: Daily; Brunch: Sat, Sun   212/353-0800
Moderate   www.metrocafenyc.com

Reasonable pricing is the draw at MetroCafe. In addition to a complete menu, wine lovers will delight in 125 wines by the glass, 21 wine flights, plus beer and champagne flights. Other attractions: a good selection of Kobe burgers and steaks, and dim sum. You can dine on fresh salads, thin-crust pizzas, filling sandwiches, pastas, excellent chargrilled burgers, and a selection of comfort foods that include meatloaf, fish and chips, grilled chicken *paillard*, and grilled filet of salmon. Desserts are tasty, and the atmosphere is family-friendly. Takeout is also available.

MEZZOGIORNO
195 Spring St (near Ave of the Americas)   212/334-2112
Lunch, Dinner: Daily   www.mezzogiorno.com
Moderate

Florence, Italy, is one of the world's most charming cities, not only because of its abundance of great art, but also for the wonderful small restaurants on virtually every street corner. At Mezzogiorno, a Florence-style trattoria in New York, the food is comparably good (though some of the art is questionable). The place is busy and noisy, and tables are so close together that conversation is almost impossible. The decor is best described as "modern Florence." Check out the unusual writing on the ceiling, done by master fresco artist Pontormo. Better yet, keep your eyes on the food. The salad selection is outstanding, and their lasagna is one of Manhattan's best. Mezzogiorno is also famous for pizza. You'll find all the ingredients here for a wonderful make-believe evening in Florence.

For a quick and tasty bite, try **Certé** (20 W 55th St, 212/397-2020). You'll find breakfast items, fresh baked goods, sandwiches, health foods, good soups and burgers and pizzas. I especially like the selection of jumbo muffins.

MICHAEL'S
24 W 55th St (bet Fifth Ave and Ave of the Americas)
Breakfast, Lunch: Mon-Fri; Dinner: Mon-Sat   212/767-0555
Moderately expensive to expensive   www.michaelsnewyork.com

"A midtown scene" would best describe this very attractive restaurant, located conveniently for shoppers, business types, hotel visitors, and the like. Its several rooms are airy and pleasant, especially in nice weather. Service is professional and attentive. You'll see some familiar media faces, society types, important-looking business execs, and ordinary fat-walleted gawkers. The food is expensive: Michael's burger is tabbed around $36, and seafood dishes are even more. While it is overpriced, there is no question about the quality or presentation. Appetizers like clams, oysters, ravioli, and foie gras terrine are quite special. Perhaps the real treat is the fabulous Cobb salad, probably the best in New York. Prepare to splurge!

MINETTA TAVERN
113 MacDougal St (at Bleecker St)   212/475-3850
Dinner: Daily   www.minettatavernny.com
Moderate

A new look here! Keith McNally and his team are now running this long-time favorite as a French bistro, specializing in prime meat. Yet a careful renovation has preserved Minetta's ambience: vintage wall mural, red leather banquettes, framed photo gallery, and a long oak bar up front. Established in 1937, Minetta Tavern has been serving excellent Northern Italian food for generations in Greenwich Village. Located on the spot where Minetta Brook wandered through Manhattan in the early days, this tavern was made famous by Eddie "Minetta" Sieveri, a friend of many sports and stage stars of yesteryear. Comfort dishes like great burgers, pastas, and meat and potatoes are featured. Everyone is made to feel comfortable here. Late-nighters will appreciate the supper menu from midnight to 2 a.m. on weekends.

With so many Italian restaurants in the city, it is almost a full time job just keeping track of the new ones and those that have gone out of business. These old-timers are reliable, but not exciting: **Savore** (200 Spring St, 212/431-1212), for when you are shopping in Soho; and **Centolire** (1167 Madison Ave, 212/734-7711), a good stop when you need some relief from a Madison Avenue shopping spree.

MORANDI
211 Waverly Place (at Seventh Ave S)   212/627-7575
Breakfast, Lunch: Mon-Fri; Dinner: Daily; Brunch: Sat, Sun
Moderate   www.morandiny.com

Morandi is the ultimate restaurant for the Italian food lover who wants authentic dishes without a huge tab. The setting is comfortable and inviting, the service prompt, and the menu unbelievably complete. You'll find every antipasti, salad, and *primi* and *secondi piatti* you could imagine. The paninis are delicious. Pastas are the real thing! Daily specials are anticipated by regular customers. I'd recommend braised beef with polenta or meatballs with pine nuts and raisins. You can even come for a hearty Italian breakfast, with their delicious bread as an added treat. The homemade gelati is excellent.

MORAN'S CHELSEA
146 Tenth Ave (at 19th St)   212/627-3030
Lunch, Dinner: Daily; Brunch: Sat, Sun   www.moranschelsea.com
Moderate

In a building that's nearly 200 years old, Moran's has seen a lot of history, including time as a speakeasy and a Jewish lodging house during Prohibition days. The years have been kind to this exceptionally charming tavern, complete with fireplaces in every room, hardwood paneling, large and attractive party facilities, and a cozy bar. There is copper everywhere you look. The old tin ceiling adds a special dimension. Fresh seafood, aged chops, lobster, crab cakes, prime rib, and shepherd's pie are just a few of the specialties. You'll also find excellent burgers, fresh salads, and a few pastas. If you are looking for a unique venue for a group of up to 180, I strongly suggest checking out Moran's. The personnel are friendly and accommodating.

THE MORGAN DINING ROOM

225 Madison Ave (bet 36th and 37th St)   212/683-2130
Lunch: Tues-Fri; Dinner: Fri; Brunch: Sat, Sun   www.themorgan.org
Moderate

The Morgan Library & Museum is a grand place to visit, and you can extend the experience by dining in the cozy room where J.P. Morgan himself broke bread. It is a great place to meet friends, and the tab is surprisingly friendly. First courses include house-cured salmon, salads, and tarts. Among the tasty entrees are large salads, chicken fricassee, and pastas. Director Paul Huyck has assembled a friendly wait staff.

Asian Specialties

Dim sum: a whole meal of succulent nibblers, such as steamed dumplings, shrimp balls, and savory pastries

Egg foo yung: thick, savory pancakes made of eggs, vegetables, and meat, often slathered with a rich, broth-based sauce

General Tso's chicken: breaded, deep-fried chicken chunks tossed in a spicy-sweet sauce

Moo shu: stir-fried shredded meat, vegetables, and seasonings, scrambled with eggs and rolled (usually by the diner) inside thin pancakes

Peking duck: Air is pumped beneath a duck's skin, then the bird is coated with honey and hung up until the skin dries and hardens. The duck is roasted, cut into pieces, and served with scallions and pancakes or steamed buns.

Sashimi: sliced raw fish served with *daikon* (Japanese radish), wasabi (Japanese horseradish), pickled ginger, and soy sauce

Sukiyaki: stir-fried pieces of meat (and sometimes vegetables, noodles, or tofu) flavored with soy sauce, *dashi* (Japanese fish stock), and *mirin* (sweet rice wine)

Sushi: raw fish or vegetables served atop vinegared rice or inside rolls wrapped in *nori* (sheets of dried seaweed)

Tempura: fried, battered seafood and vegetables

Teriyaki: a sauce of rice wine, soy sauce, sugar, and seasonings that is used to marinate beef or chicken, which is then grilled or stir-fried

---

MORTON'S OF CHICAGO

551 Fifth Ave (at 45th St)   212/972-3315
Lunch: Mon-Fri; Dinner: Daily   www.mortons.com
Moderately expensive to expensive

Every member of the highly efficient staff at this franchised, high-end steakhouse has been trained in the Morton's manner. At the start of your meal, you are shown a cart with sample entree items: various cuts of beef, lobster, and whatever else happens to be featured. Every dish is fully explained. Appetizers are heavy in the seafood department. Shrimp, oysters, smoked salmon, sea scallops, and salads are attractive and appetizing. The steaks and chops are so tender you can cut them with a fork. They arrive promptly, too, which is not the case in many steakhouses. There are several potato choices, including wonderful hash browns. Sauteed spinach with mushrooms and steamed broccoli and asparagus are fresh and tasty. Top it all off with a delicious soufflé—chocolate, Grand Marnier, lemon, or rasp-berry—that's large enough for two hungry diners. A busy bar (which serves bar bites) and function rooms are added attractions at Morton's.

MR. K'S

570 Lexington Ave (at 51st St)   212/583-1668
Lunch, Dinner: Daily   www.mrksnyc.com
Moderately expensive to expensive

Mr. K's is a very classy Chinese dining room where high-powered politi-cos and famous celebrities come to dine. All manner of goodies will whet the appetite: Shanghai spring rolls, dumplings, and a delicious seafood dish of sauteed crab, shrimp, and scallops. Of course, there is chicken and corn chowder; in my opinion, no Chinese dinner is complete without it. What else? Share an assortment of plates with your table partners: lemon chicken, Peking duck, honey-braised pork ribs, sesame beef, crispy sea bass, and sesame prawns with shiitake mushrooms. If you like spicy dishes, go for the firecracker prawns with Szechuan sauce!

Go to this place for sizeable portions at low prices. **Mama's Food Shop** (200 E 3rd St, 212/777-4425) is an inexpensive and tasty des-tination for homemade dishes like meatloaf, grilled salmon, and fried, roasted, and grilled chicken. Sides include mashed potatoes, macaroni and cheese, honey-glazed sweet potatoes, green beans, Swiss chard, and turnips. Don't miss the banana cream pie! Takeout, delivery, and cater-ing are available.

MUSEUM OF MODERN ART

9 W 53rd St (bet Fifth Ave and Ave of the Americas)   212/333-1220
The Modern (dining room)   www.themodernnyc.com
Lunch: Daily; Dinner: Mon-Sat
Bar Room
Lunch, Dinner: Daily
Cafe 2 and Terrace 5: museum hours
Moderate to moderately expensive (The Modern and Bar Room)

Both the Museum of Modern Art and its dining venues are special New York treats. Under the expert eye of top restaurateur Danny Meyer, the museum features four unique dining venues. **The Modern** dining room is top-drawer and formal (gentlemen are asked to wear coats), with a grand view of the sculpture garden. The *prix fixe* menu features creative multi-course French cuisine. Next door is the **Bar Room**, where food is a bit less expensive but equally tasty and not quite so fancy. The *tarte flambé* is worth a visit in itself. You'll find over 30 menu items. **Cafe 2** and **Terrace 5** are on the upper floors and appeal mainly to families visiting the museum, with some dishes aimed at quick service and kids.

NAPLES 45

MetLife Building, 200 Park Ave (entrance on 45th St)   212/972-7001
Breakfast, Lunch, Dinner: Mon-Fri   www.patinagroup.com
Moderate

This may well be the best pizza house in Manhattan! Absolutely delicious, authentic Neapolitan pizzas are made with *caputo* flour, imported from Southern Italy, and other tasty ingredients. Cooked in an oak-burning oven, they are a sight to behold and taste. You have your choice of individual ten-inch plates or their "Mezzo Metro," large enough to feed three or four persons. Other offerings include small dishes (like veal meatballs or fried calamari), pizza-bread sandwiches, soups, seafood, pastas, and salads. Takeout and delivery are available, as is patio dining in nice weather. The place is jammed!

THE NEW FRENCH
522 Hudson St (bet Charles and 10th St)   212/807-7357
Lunch, Dinner: Daily; Brunch: Sat, Sun
Moderate

Not often do I recommend a restaurant just because of one dish, but in the case of the New French, this is true. Their "New French Salad"—a combination of chopped romaine, radicchio, pear, gruyere, celery, carrots, gold beets, and red wine-pear vinaigrette—is an appealing luncheon or dinner treat. There is much more, too, like pizza *bianca*, sandwiches, crepes, curry, and burgers at lunch, and lamb, hanger steak, and mussels in the evening. Prices are reasonable. Try the bread pudding for dessert.

Esca (402 W 43rd St, 212/564-7272) is one of Manhattan's best seafood restaurants. The emphasis is on Southern Italian seafood and pastas. This attractive establishment in the Theater District is always crowded—and deservedly so.

NICOLA'S
146 E 84th St (bet Lexington and Third Ave)   212/249-9850
Dinner: Daily
Moderately expensive

Upper-crust New Yorkers who like a clubby atmosphere and good food —which are not often found together—love this place! At times the noise level rivals that of a Broadway opening. In a setting of rich wood with familiar framed faces on the walls, no-nonsense waiters serve delicious platters of pasta, veal, chicken, fish, and steak. The emphasis is Italian, and there are inviting daily specials in every category. Concentrate on the main part of your meal, as desserts show little imagination.

NOBU 57
40 W 57th St (bet Fifth Ave and Ave of the Americas)   212/757-3000
Lunch: Mon-Fri; Dinner: Daily   www.noburestaurants.com
NOBU NEW YORK
105 Hudson St (at Franklin St)   212/219-0500
Lunch: Mon-Fri; Dinner: Daily
NOBU NEXT DOOR
105 Hudson St (bet Franklin and N Moore St)   212/334-4445
Dinner: Daily
Expensive

Yes, these places are busy and expensive, but they are worth every penny and any frustrating wait for reservations. Nobu Matsuhisa has put together spectacular venues for those who love sushi and great Japanese food that's not too complex but unfailingly tasty. Because I like salty dishes, this menu appeals to me. I like the feel: at once classy and crowded, with an unmistakable party atmosphere. Sitting at the sushi bar allows you to watch the large, superbly trained staff perform like a symphony orchestra. A woodburning oven adds to the splendid array of dishes. The black cod is a standout. Dozens of sushi, sashimi, and sushi roll selections are available. Fresh, delicious salads abound. Leave room for the Bento Box dessert: warm chocolate fondant cake with green-tea ice cream. You're going to pay well for all these treats—especially if you have the Wagyu beef—but you'll go away relishing a very special dining experience.

Here's my answer to the quandary of so many desserts but so little time: **Luxee** (6 Clinton St, 212/375-1796, open daily except Monday). Pastry chef Yoshie Shirakawa has created deliciously adorned desserts, taking tiramisu to new heights. Even ice cream gets jazzed up by being served in a crepe cup. For special occasions, the decadent Strawberry Field cake incorporates whipped cream and meringue, but the sinful *Chocolat Chocolat*, made with Valrhona chocolate, is definitely over the top. Weekdays are special between 3:00 and 6:00 p.m., when guests can enjoy the cake buffet. One price includes servings of any or all of the delectable cakes from the takeout section, plus a beverage of choice.

OCEAN GRILL
384 Columbus Ave (bet 78th and 79th Ave)
Lunch: Mon-Sat; Dinner: Daily; Brunch: Sun   212/579-2300
Moderate   www.brguestrestaurants.com

Ocean Grill is one of the few good seafood restaurants on the Upper West Side. In nice weather, watching the passing parade from an outside table is fun. Quite popular with young professionals, the place is noisy, too. The food is good (not great), with littleneck clams topping the list. For a party, chilled shellfish platters—offering a selection of lobster, clams, oysters, shrimp, and more—are appropriate. The grill turns out Scottish salmon, bigeye tuna, mahi-mahi, and wild striped bass. Other attractions include crab cakes, lobster bisque, and seafood Cobb salad. For brunch, seasonal quiches and blueberry and buttermilk pancakes are good bets.

OCEANA
McGraw-Hill Building, 1221 Ave of the Americas (at 49th St)
Lunch: Mon-Fri; Dinner: Mon-Sat   212/759-5941
Expensive   www.oceanarestaurant.com

When you finally save enough money to afford a cruise, you want to do it right and book passage on a really fabulous ship. Well, the same holds true if you want a really first-rate seafood meal. Oceana is just that kind of place. This midtown townhouse offers several floors of classy dining. The menu changes frequently, and the seafood catches are so fresh they practically swim to the table. For entrees I suggest herb-rubbed Scottish salmon, taro-wrapped pompano, or Nova Scotia lobster with wild mushrooms and pro-sciutto. The homemade potato gnocchi is a blue-ribbon winner! Cocoa panna cotta and browned-butter cheesecake are delectable desserts!

OLIVES NEW YORK
W New York Union Square
201 Park Ave S (at 17th St)   212/353-8345
Breakfast: Daily; Lunch: Mon-Fri; Dinner: Daily; Brunch: Sat, Sun
Moderate   www.toddenglish.com

For yuppies, this is *the* place! The trendy crowd seems to like the New England influence of Todd English's open-kitchen charmer. A spirited and jazzy atmosphere combines with superbly trained personnel and great food to make a pleasant dining experience. Portions are big, with delicious pastas high on the list. If your tastes are not too fancy, the burgers are very good and the peanut butter pancakes at brunch are "to die for."

ONE IF BY LAND, TWO IF BY SEA
17 Barrow St (bet Seventh Ave and 4th St)   212/228-0822
Dinner: Daily; Brunch: Sun   www.oneifbyland.com
Expensive

The candlelight, fireplace, flowers, and background piano music all add to the ambience of this romantic room. One if by Land, Two if by Sea is housed in an 18th-century carriage house once owned by Aaron Burr. Allow extra time to find this place, as Barrow Street (one of the West Village's most charming) is generally unknown to taxi drivers, and there's no sign out front! Tables at the front of the balcony are particularly appealing. You can't go wrong with rack of lamb or duck breast. Individual beef Wellington is usually excellent, as is spice-roasted lobster. A *prix fixe* five-course tasting menu is available. Their classic crème brûlée is a favorite dessert, and brioche French toast served at brunch is quite tasty. Some reviewers have down-graded this house, but I still think it has great charm.

ONIEAL'S GRAND STREET
174 Grand St (bet Lafayette and Mulberry St)   212/941-9119
Lunch, Dinner, Late Night Menu: Daily; Brunch: Sat, Sun
Moderate   www.onieals.com

This legendary and historic speakeasy, with its secret tunnel to the old police headquarters, evokes memories of days long past. Housed beneath a 150-year-old hand-carved mahogany ceiling, this bar, lounge, and restaurant is reminiscent of another time. Onieal's achieved additional celebrity as a backdrop on HBO's *Sex and the City*. They serve one of the best burgers in town. You'll find marinated grilled yellowfin tuna, Cobb salad, hanger steak *au poivre*, risotto, and more. For dessert, try the Four Devils chocolate cake (named after the four devils intricately carved on the ceiling). Service at Onieal's is friendly and efficient.

ORSO
322 W 46th St (bet Eighth and Ninth Ave)   212/489-7212
Lunch, Dinner: Daily; Brunch: Sun   www.orsorestaurant.com
Moderate

This restaurant features the same menu all day long, which is great for those with unusual dining hours and handy for theatergoers. Orso is one of the most popular places on midtown's "restaurant row," so if you're planning a six o'clock dinner, be sure to make reservations. The smallish room is cozy and comfortable. It's watched over by a portrait of Orso, a Venetian dog who is the mascot for this Italian bistro. The kitchen is open in the back, allowing diners to see the experienced staff at work. The changing menu offers many good appetizers, including cold roast veal and grilled eggplant salad. A variety of pizzas and some excellent pasta dishes are also offered. For an entree, you can't go wrong with the popular sauteed calves liver. The strawberry tiramisu, one of many homemade desserts, will finish off a great meal. A special Sunday brunch menu is available.

Jacket Required—and Leave the Sneakers at Home

Several exclusive restaurants still impose a dress code that require men to wear jackets while dining. If you show up without one, don't be surprised if they discreetly loan one to you.

Bouley: jacket required, no sneakers
Cafe Carlyle: jacket required
Daniel: jacket required
Jean Georges: jacket required
La Grenouille: jacket required
Le Bernardin: jacket required
Le Cirque: jacket required; bar area less formal
Le Périgord: jacket preferred
The Modern: jacket required
per se: jacket required; no jeans, sneakers, or shorts
Picholine: jacket preferred
River Cafe: jacket required
21 Club: jacket required and tie preferred; no jeans, sneakers, or shorts

---

OSTERIA DEL CIRCO
120 W 55th St (bet Ave of the Americas and Seventh Ave)
Lunch: Mon-Fri; Dinner: Daily   212/265-3636
Moderately expensive   www.osteriadelcirco.com

Were it not for the fact that the owners are the sons of Sirio Maccioni (the legendary restaurateur of Le Cirque fame), this establishment might just be written off as another Italian restaurant. But here we have three brothers—Mario, Marco, and Mauro (and mother Egidiana)—operating a classy establishment with a friendly, circus-themed ambience, atypical Italian menu, and a touch of Le Cirque's magic. The tastiest items include great pizzas and salads, satisfying soups, and unusual pastas. A unique dessert is an Italian favorite called *bomboloncini:* small vanilla-, chocolate- and marmalade-filled doughnuts.

OUEST
2315 Broadway (at 84th St)   212/580-8700
Dinner: Daily; Brunch: Sun   www.ouestny.com
Moderate

Ouest is overflowing with happy locals enjoying one of the best rooms in the city. The comfortable booths, open kitchen, cozy (if dark and noisy) balcony, and pleasant serving staff combine to make Thomas Valenti's jewel first-class. This is not surprising, as Valenti gained experience at Alison on Dominick St. and Butterfield 8 on the Upper East Side. The bistro menu is just as inviting as the semicircular tables, with appetizer choices like smoked duck breast with crispy eggs and bitter greens, goat cheese ravioli, and several fresh salads. The braised short ribs and lamb shanks melt in your mouth. Nightly specials include meatloaf on Sunday. From delicious warm bread at the start to rich chocolate cake for dessert, the whole experience at Ouest is pure pleasure.

OUR PLACE
1444 Third Ave (at 82nd St)
Lunch: Mon-Sat; Dinner: Daily; Brunch: Sat, Sun   212/288-4888
Moderate   www.ourplaceuptown.com

Our Place is not a typical Chinese restaurant. Classy service, moderate prices, and delicious food have been its trademarks for many years. Appreciative Upper East Siders keep its two spotlessly clean dining rooms filled for nearly every meal. Single diners obviously feel comfortable and enjoy the atmosphere. You'll find many of your favorite Chinese dishes on the menu. I've enjoyed wonton soup, moo shu pork, tangerine beef, Szechuan chicken, duck-wrapped lettuce with pine nuts, and home-style chicken casserole. Free delivery is offered in a wide area. Prices are as comfortable as the chairs.

> Diners with sophisticated tastes will enjoy the menus at **Dovetail** (103 W 77th St, 212/362-3800) and **Bar Blanc** (142 W 10th St, 212/255-2330). Both of these houses were instantly popular with foodies, but things have now quieted down a bit.

OUR PLACE SHANGHAI TEA GARDEN
141 E 55th St (bet Lexington and Third Ave)   212/753-3900
Lunch, Dinner: Daily   www.ourplace-teagarden.com
Moderate

Shanghai flavors are a bit more complex than other Chinese dishes, and that holds true at this clean, first-rate Oriental room. Shanghai specialties include "Lion's Head" (giant meatballs and vegetable hearts in brown sauce), sauteed squid, and Shanghai-style braised pork shoulder. Besides the Shanghai-style specialties, there are more typical Chinese items, with an excellent assortment of dumplings, soups, and chicken and duck dishes. Their barbecued honey spare ribs are the best in the city. Service is highly efficient and professional. You can take the family out for a tasty, reasonably priced meal at Our Place.

PALM ONE
837 Second Ave (at 44th St)   212/687-2953
Lunch: Mon-Fri; Dinner: Mon-Sat

PALM TOO
840 Second Ave (at 44th St)   212/697-5198
Lunch: Mon-Fri; Dinner: Daily

PALM WEST SIDE
250 W 50th St (bet Eighth Ave and Broadway)   212/333-7256
Lunch: Mon-Sat; Dinner: Daily   www.thepalm.com
Expensive

Even with the glut of new steakhouses in Manhattan, steak and lobster lovers still have a special place in their hearts for the Palm (a.k.a. Palm One), which started as a speakeasy in 1926. All three locations have much the same atmosphere. They're noted for huge, delicious steaks, chops, and lobsters. Don't miss the terrific Palm fries (homemade potato chips) or onion rings. Daily specials vary among the Palm locations. These are earthy spots, so don't get too dressed up. Indolent waiters are part of the scene.

You're sure to smile when you step through the doors of **The Smile** (26 Bond St, www.thesmilenyc.com). In addition to a limited menu of tasty breakfast, brunch, and lunch selections, the enterprising proprietors sell merchandise also serving as the eclectic decor.

PAOLA'S
Hotel Wales
1295 Madison Ave (at 92nd St)   212/794-1890
Lunch, Dinner: Daily; Brunch: Sun   www.paolasrestaurant.com
Moderate

Here's a wonderful place in the Hotel Wales for a romantic evening! The Italian home cooking is first-class, with Paola overseeing the kitchen. Great filled pastas, superb veal dishes, and tasty hot vegetables (like baby artichoke hearts) are house specialties. Be advised that they don't spare on the garlic! Top off your reasonably priced meal with a rich chocolate mousse.

PARIS COMMUNE
99 Bank St (at Greenwich St)
Lunch: Mon-Fri; Dinner: Daily; Brunch: Sat, Sun   212/929-0509
Moderate   www.pariscommune.net

There is a new attraction at Paris Commune: the Rouge Wine Bar. This restaurant is a popular gathering spot in the West Village, where regulars outnumber visitors every night. The French/Continental menu includes pastas, salads, steaks, and seafood. The staff is prompt and efficient. Dining by candlelight is a big attraction. The weekend brunch features spectacular French toast, along with the usual fare. Delicious dishes include vegetable frittata and their famous gingerbread. Homemade cheesecakes are good and rich. Check out the $10 lunch specials and recession dinner specials.

PARK AVENUE BISTRO
377 Park Ave S (bet 26th and 27th St)   212/689-1360
Lunch: Mon-Fri; Dinner: Mon-Sat   www.parkavenuebistronyc.com
Moderate

Having relocated across the street from its original location, the Park Avenue Bistro is full of smiling faces. This small, homey jewel specializes in authentic French cuisine from the Provence region. From the start, when warm and tasty bread is placed before you, to the finishing touch of rich and

luscious homemade desserts (like vanilla bread pudding), you are surrounded by attentive service and magnificent food. Don't miss the hanger
steak or lamb stew. Young artists are spotlighted in the ever-changing gallery.
A professional team runs this house, and it shows.

PARK AVENUE SPRING/SUMMER/AUTUMN/ WINTER
100 E 63rd St (at Park Ave)
Lunch: Mon-Fri; Dinner: Daily; Brunch: Sat, Sun   212/644-1900
Moderately expensive   www.parkavenuenyc.com

This is one of the most interesting restaurant concepts I've ever seen.
Each season Park Avenue is totally transformed by cuisine, decor, and beverages. Even the name reflects the current season. Chef Craig Koketsu
incorporates fresh produce in his contemporary American menus.

Alas! I can remember, as can many thousands of New Yorkers and
visitors, when the Plaza Hotel was *the* center of social life in Manhattan. Unfortunately, that is no longer true. (See the Plaza Hotel writeup
in the Services section of this edition.) One of the great places to dine
in the heyday of the hotel was the **Oak Room and Bar** (Central
Park S at Fifth Ave, 212/758-7777). Now this facility, still with a lot of
nostalgic charm—and great views from the bar—is under different
management and ownership than the hotel. The platters are quite
good, though not exceptional, with the real reason for dining here
being the atmosphere. Hold onto your pocketbook and tuck a hand-
kerchief in your pocket to wipe the tears away as you pine for the
"good old days."

PARK SIDE
107-01 Corona Ave (51st Ave at 108th St, Corona, Queens)
Lunch, Dinner: Daily   718/271-9274
Moderate   www.parksiderestaurant.com

Talk about fun! Do you want to show someone who claims to know
everything about New York a place he or she likely hasn't heard about?
Would you like to eat on your way to or from LaGuardia or Kennedy Airport? Do you want a special meal in an unusual setting? Well, all of the above
are excellent reasons to visit Park Side, in Queens. I've included this restaurant that isn't in Manhattan because it *is* exceptional. This is a first-class, spotlessly clean restaurant that serves wonderful Italian food at very affordable
prices. Start with garlic bread and then choose from two dozen kinds of
pasta and an opulent array of fish, steak, veal, and poultry dishes. The meat
is all prime-cut and fresh—nothing frozen. You'll also find polite, knowledgeable waiters in an informal atmosphere. Get a table in the garden room or
the Marilyn Monroe room upstairs. Eat to your heart's content, and then be
pleasantly surprised at the tab.

PASTIS
9 Ninth Ave (at Little West 12th St)   212/929-4844
Breakfast, Lunch: Mon-Fri; Dinner: Daily; Brunch: Sat, Sun
Moderate   www.pastisny.com

In what was once a garage, a large area has been gutted and converted into a bar and dining space with touches that make it look as though it has been around for a long time. Keith McNally, who knows how to present a restaurant, has turned this Meatpacking District warehouse into one of the most high-energy rooms in Manhattan. The dining room, if you can get in, serves reasonably good food to hordes who love the unbelievable noise level and classic bistro fare. A nice touch is a long table in the center of the dining space for singles and others who do not want to wait in the reservation line. The menu includes oysters on the half shell, omelets, shell-fish stew, roast lobster, sauteed chicken, braised beef, patés, good French fries, and their "Floating Island" dessert. The first question you will ask is "How did they cram all these people into this place?" After a few minutes, you'll understand that the crowd is part of the attraction. Pastis offers delivery, too.

Small restaurants, diners, and delis are usually colorful places to take a meal. Since the quarters are generally quite close, it's inevitable to eavesdrop on the staff's dialogue. They seem to have a language all their own. Here are some examples, along with their meanings:

Hockey puck: a well-done hamburger
Kill it: overcook a food item
Pittsburgh rare: burnt outside, rare inside
Rollup: silverware folded into a napkin (usually linen, but can be paper)
SOS: sauce on side
The Man (a.k.a. **the Boogie Man**): health inspector
Throw or toss a pie: to make a pizza
Window: a shelf (usually heated) where food is placed after preparation for delivery to a table

---

PATSY'S
236 W 56th St (bet Broadway and Eighth Ave)   212/247-3491
Lunch, Dinner: Daily   www.patsys.com
Moderate

For over half a century, the Scognamillo family has operated this popular eatery, specializing in Neapolitan cuisine. At present, the son and a grandson are taking care of the front of the house, while another grandson is following the family tradition in the kitchen. "Patsy" was an immigrant gentleman chef whose nickname graces this bilevel restaurant. Each floor has its own cozy atmosphere and convenient kitchen. The family makes sure that every party is treated with courtesy and concern, as if they are in a private home. A full Italian menu includes a special soup and seafood entree each day. If you can't find what you like among the two dozen pasta choices, you are in deep trouble! There are also *prix fixe* lunch and dinner (pre-theater) menus, which are very convenient if you are headed to Lincoln Center, Carnegie Hall, or the Theater District.

PERILLA
9 Jones St (bet Bleecker and 4th St)   212/929-6868
Dinner: Daily; Brunch: Sat, Sun   www.perillanyc.com
Moderate to moderately expensive

There is something very satisfying about having a leisurely brunch on a weekend in the Village, and for this, Perilla is a really good bet. Of course, there are nightly dinners, too, with equal quality in both food and service. Perilla's New American menu has a variety of flavors. For brunch, blueberry and buckwheat pancakes are worthy of a visit. For the more adventurous, order the celery seed-crusted fried oysters. I found the dessert offerings to be particularly appealing. The cheese selection is excellent and reasonably priced. How about a maple crème caramel or vanilla-scented doughnut with apple compote filling and pumpkin Bavarian cream? What a way to go!

> Without question, the best barbecued spare ribs in Manhattan can be found at **Pig Heaven** (1540 Second Ave, 212/744-4333). The rest of the menu is basic Chinese, and most dishes are quite good. The place is spotlessly clean. For an event sure to impressive your guests, I can't imagine a better centerpiece than Pig Heaven's ribs! Free delivery is available on the East Side from 60th Street to 95th Street.

PERSHING SQUARE
90 E 42nd St (at Park Ave)
Breakfast, Lunch, Dinner: Daily; Brunch: Sat, Sun   212/286-9600
Moderate   www.pershingsquare.com

In a space opposite Grand Central Station, Pershing Square serves throngs of hungry local and traveling New Yorkers. The odd-shaped room is full of energy and conversation, much of it relating to the broad variety of menu offerings. For those who missed breakfast before boarding their train, Pershing Square offers Irish oatmeal, eggs Benedict, vanilla-bean brioche French toast, and great buttermilk pancakes. Omelets are a specialty. Lunch and dinner items include seafood dishes, boneless beef short ribs, roast chicken, steaks, and pastas. The grilled hamburger with a selection of cheeses and crisp steak fries is a winner any time of day. Seafood dishes—like seared sea scallops with saffron orzo and tomato cream sauce, and pan-seared Atlantic salmon—are popular for dinner. Try chocolate mousse cake for dessert. A friendly wait staff and an attractive bar are pluses.

PETER LUGER STEAK HOUSE
178 Broadway (at Driggs Ave), Brooklyn   718/387-7400
Lunch, Dinner: Daily   www.peterluger.com
Expensive

Peter Luger's reputation is sometimes larger than the restaurant itself! Folks don't come for the ambience or service, but if it's steak you want, you simply can't do better. The menu makes it simple: your choices are steak for one, two, three, or four. The creamed spinach and steak sauce (which they now sell by the bottle) are out of this world. Tell your waiter to go easy on the whipped cream if you order dessert. Peter Luger is only a stone's throw from Manhattan (take the first right off the Williamsburg Bridge), and the staff is accustomed to ordering cabs. Making reservations well in advance is suggested.

PICHOLINE
35 W 64th St (bet Broadway and Central Park West)   212/724-8585
Dinner: Tues-Sat   www.picholinenyc.com
Moderately expensive to expensive

Terrance Brennan is a workhorse, and it shows in his attractive restaurant. The warm atmosphere is a perfect backdrop for the seasonal, Mediterranean-inspired plates. The many positives include outstanding service, perfectly done fish dishes, superbly prepared game, and daily classic cuisine specials. The wine room and small private party room are fabulous settings for a memorable evening. I always look forward to the magnificent cheese dessert cart. Jackets are preferred for gentlemen. A new *Menu d' Economie* hits the wallet just right.

Gilt (455 Madison Ave, 212/891-8100) is located in the New York Palace Hotel. The setting is magnificent—the 19th-century Villard Mansion was once the home of the legendary Le Cirque. Executive chef Justin Bogle oversees Gilt's New American cuisine, and the dishes are as elegant as the surroundings. Choose from an extensive wine list (some pricey, some reasonable). Three dozen carefully selected whole-leaf teas, including rare and unusual finds, are offered. Dinner is served Tuesday through Saturday; the bar is open daily with a tasty bar-food menu. The chocolate soufflé dessert is aptly named "Gilty Pleasure."

PIETRO'S
232 E 43rd St (bet Second and Third Ave)   212/682-9760
Lunch: Mon-Fri; Dinner: Mon-Sat (closed Sat in summer)
Expensive   www.pietros.com

Pietro's is a steakhouse featuring Northern Italian cuisine. Everything is cooked to order. The menu includes great salads (they claim to make New York's best Caesar salad), steaks, chops, seafood, chicken, and an enormous selection of veal dishes. Tell your companions not to bother dressing up. Bring an appetite, however, because portions are huge. Although they're best known for steaks, you will also find abundant chicken and veal selections (marsala, cacciatore, scaloppine, piccata, *francaise,* etc.) and nine potato dishes. Prices border on expensive and the place is boisterous, but you'll certainly get your money's worth. By the way, Pietro's is very child-friendly.

PINOCCHIO
1748 First Ave (bet 90th and 91st St)   212/828-5810
Lunch: Sun; Dinner: Tues-Sun
Moderate

Come here for serious Italian dining. Mark Petrillo presides over this unpretentious 12-table etablishment on the Upper East Side, where wonderful home-style Italian food is served. There are numerous specials every night, and I'd suggest letting the boss order for you. You'll always find great pastas, like cheese-filled ravioli, tortellini Pinocchio (meat-filled tortellini with cream, peas, and prosciutto), several spaghetti dishes, and fettuccine alfredo. The room is available for private parties at both lunch and dinner.

P.J. CLARKE'S
915 Third Ave (at 55th St)   212/317-1616
Lunch, Dinner: Daily; Brunch: Sun

P.J. CLARKE'S ON THE HUDSON
4 World Financial Center (at Vesey St)   212/285-1500
Lunch, Dinner: Daily; Brunch: Sat, Sun

P.J. CLARKE'S AT LINCOLN SQUARE
44 W 63rd St   212/957-9700
Lunch, Dinner: Daily; Brunch: Sat, Sun   www.pjclarkes.com
Moderate

P.J. Clarke's can rightfully be called a Manhattan institution. Every day at lunch and dinner, regulars are joined by hordes of visitors guzzling at the bar, eyeing the raw bar, or fighting for a table. No one is disappointed with the sizable platters, great burgers, and fresh seafood. Service is highly professional, and the price is right. Upstairs at the Third Avenue location, you'll be taken with the decor at **The Sidecar**, which has its own kitchen and entrance. All patrons at P.J. Clarke's on the Hudson have a stunning view of New York Harbor and the Statue of Liberty. A seasonal cafe alongside the marina is great for leisurely dining. The 63rd Street locale is a stellar venue for munchies after a performance at Lincoln Center.

Many good things contribute to the success of **Bread** (20 Spring St, 212/334-1015). Some customers eat in; others avoid the mob by taking advantage of the free local delivery (from 10:30 a.m. to midnight and to 1 a.m. on Friday and Saturday). The salads, pastas, hot plates, and sandwiches are big and delicious. And, the prices are right!

PÓ
31 Cornelia St (bet Bleecker and 4th St)   212/645-2189
Lunch: Wed-Sun; Dinner: Daily   www.porestaurant.com
Moderate

Steve Crane has found the formula for a successful eating establishment. The space is crowded, but tables are not on top of each other. The service is family-friendly, informed, and quick. The food is hearty, imaginative and exceptionally tasty. The prices are right. No wonder the place is always busy! As I have noted before, if the bread is good, chances are what follows will be also. Pó has crusty, fresh Italian bread. The pasta dishes—tagliatelle, tortellini, linguine, and a special or two—are huge. The tasting menus offer great value, with a six-course meal going for $52. Pastas and some heavier entrees (like grilled salmon) are available for lunch, along with inventive sandwiches like marinated portobello with roasted peppers. *Affogato*, an unusual and satisfying dessert, consists of coffee gelato in chilled cappuccino with chocolate and caramel sauces.

PORTERS NEW YORK
216 Seventh Ave (bet 22nd and 23rd St)   212/229-2878
Lunch: Mon-Fri; Dinner: Daily; Brunch: Sat, Sun
Moderate

No big name or trendy buzz at Porters, just good food in a clean and modest Chelsea location. It is very satisfying if you are looking for sensible, well-prepared food at affordable prices. At dinnertime, popular appetizers (such as filet mignon carpaccio), salads, shellfish stew, great burgers, and coconut-crusted salmon are available. They also offer a nice selection of steak and chicken dishes. Yukon mashed potatoes are a special side.

POST HOUSE
Lowell Hotel
28 E 63rd St 212/935-2888
Lunch: Mon-Fri; Dinner: Daily www.theposthouse.com
Moderately expensive

This Manhattan steakhouse is an "in" social and political hangout that serves excellent food in comfortable surroundings. The guest list usually includes many well-known names and recognizable faces. They are attracted by the good food, warm ambience, and daily specials. Hors d'oeuvres like crabmeat cocktail, lobster cocktail, and stone crab claws are available in season, but the major draws are steak and lobster. Prices for the latter are definitely not in the moderate category; ditto for lamb chops. However, the quality is excellent, and the cottage fries, fried zucchini, hash browns, and onion rings are superb. Save room for the chocolate treasure box (white and dark chocolate mousse with raspberry sauce). If you can walk out under your own steam after all this, you're doing well!

Mexican Specialties

Ceviche: citrus-marinated raw fish
Chilis rellenos: mild to spicy chili peppers stuffed with cheese and fried in egg batter
Chorizo: spicy pork sausage
Empanadas: meat-filled pastries surrounded by a fat-laden crust
Enchiladas: soft corn tortillas filled with meat, beans, vegetables, or cheese and topped with salsa and cheese
Fajitas: marinated beef, shrimp, chicken, and/or vegetables served with warm tortillas for wrapping by the diner
Paella: an elaborate saffron-flavored rice casserole with a variety of seafood and meats
Tamales: chopped meat and vegetables encased in cornmeal dough

---

PRIMAVERA
1578 First Ave (at 82nd St) 212/861-8608
Dinner: Daily www.primaveranyc.com
Expensive

Rave reviews on this one! Primavera is one of my favorite places, and it keeps getting better. Owner Nicola Civetta is the epitome of class, and his wife, Peggy, is equally charming. They know how to make guests feel at home and present a superb Italian meal. Don't come if you're in a hurry, as Primavera is geared toward relaxed dining. I could wax eloquently with descriptions of the dishes, but you can't go wrong no matter what you order. All the veal dishes are spectacular. Let Nicola choose for you, as there are specials every day. To top it all off, they have one of the most beautiful desserts anywhere: a gorgeous platter of seasonal fruit that is almost too attractive to eat. Primavera is always busy, so reservations are a must. A beautiful private party room is available.

PRIMEHOUSE NEW YORK
381 Park Ave S (at 27th St)   212/824-2600
Lunch: Mon-Fri; Dinner: Daily; Brunch: Sat, Sun
Moderately expensive to expensive   www.brguestrestaurants.com

Don't be put off by the size of Primehouse New York. The folks here are very accommodating, and the quality of the food is excellent. The portions are huge, and you'll likely be able to take home a doggy bag for next day's lunch. Yes, it is primarily a meat house, but there are other goodies: oysters, chicken breast, macaroni and cheese, and beer-battered onion rings. They have their own aging room (ask to see it). The classic filet mignon is terrific, and salads are another good bet. The place has a leathery, masculine feel, but is comfortable for a hand-holding couple. Bottom line: one of Manhattan's better steakhouses.

> Don't miss a visit to **Bubby's** (120 Hudson St, 212/219-0666). First of all, the regular menu items are tasty and reasonably priced. The Sunday brunch is delicious and a real scene for locals! Then there are the great pies: mile-high apple, sour cherry, key lime, and chocolate peanut butter. Homemade cakes, too! Delivery in Tribeca is free.

PUMP ENERGY FOOD
40 W 55th St (bet Fifth Ave and Ave of the Americas)   212/246-6844
275 Madison Ave (at 40th St)   212/697-7867
112 W 38th St (bet Broadway and Ave of the Americas) 212/764-2100
Crystal Pavilion, 805 Third Ave (at 50th St)   212/421-3055
31 E 21st St (bet Park Ave and Broadway)   212/253-7676
80 Pine St (at Pearl St)   212/785-1110
Breakfast: Mon-Fri; Lunch, Dinner: Daily; Brunch: Sat, Sun
Moderate   www.thepumpenergyfood.com

No, these are not gourmet restaurants! But with so many readers into health and fitness, I thought I would mention these healthy retreats, which feature good, tasty, and nutritious food at reasonable prices. The dozens of super-charged dishes are appropriately given names like Hercules (grilled chicken breast and lentil soup) and Hard Core (grilled turkey breast with soy sauce). Also on the menu are salads and toasted sandwiches, healthy sweet treats (no butter, oil, sugar, or salt), soups, chili, and healthy sides like hummus, brown rice, steamed spinach, and baked falafel. Free delivery is offered.

QUALITY MEATS
57 W 58th St (bet Fifth Ave and Ave of the Americas)   212/371-7777
Lunch: Mon-Fri; Dinner: Daily   www.qualitymeatsnyc.com
Moderately expensive to expensive

On the site of the former Manhattan Ocean Club, Michael Stillman—son of Smith & Wollensky boss Alan Stillman—operates "somewhat" of a steakhouse that's become popular with younger meat lovers. With a butcher-shop look on several levels, outstanding chef Craig Koketsu in the kitchen, and a wait staff that really know what they are doing, Quality Meats has all of the basics soundly covered. They have lots of oyster selections, stone crab claws in season, ample salads, and tasty appetizers (like steak tartare and smoked corn chowder). Entrees include a number of steaks (the filet is fantastic), roasted pork, rack of lamb, and fish. Don't pass up the pan-roasted crispy potatoes, gnocchi and cheese, sautéed spinach, and grilled asparagus. For dessert, the homemade ice creams are a treat (try the "coffee and doughnuts"). As if all of this weren't enough, the pie and tart selection is outstanding. The **Charcuterie Bar** offers individual items or a sampler plate as well. (P.S. Check out the very unique restrooms!)

Pure Food and Wine (54 Irving Pl, 212/477-1010) is New York's premier raw foods restaurant. The food is not quite raw—but nothing is cooked over 117 degrees, so as not to destroy the food's enzymes. You will find a tasty selection of soups, salads, lasagna, ravioli, pizzas, and other choices. There's a juice bar, and takeout is available. Reservations are strongly suggested.

RAO'S
455 E 114th St (at First Ave)   212/722-6709
Dinner: Mon-Fri   www.raos.com
No credit cards
Inexpensive

Don't be put off by rumors about Rao's, such as there being a two-month wait for reservations. If you want to go to Rao's—an intimate, old-time (1896) Italian restaurant—you should plan a bit in advance, however. The place is crowded all the time for two reasons: the food is great, and prices are ridiculously low. Don't walk or take a car; hail a taxi and get out in front of the restaurant, which is in Spanish Harlem. When you're ready to leave, they'll call a taxi. Frankie Pellegrino is a gregarious and charming host who makes guests feel right at home and will even sit at your table while you order. Be prepared for leisurely dining. While you're waiting, enjoy the excellent bread and warm atmosphere. Believe it or not, the Southern fried chicken (Rao's style) is absolutely superb and would be my number-one choice. (Hint: Try appearing unannounced at the door or call the same day, as tables are often available on the spur of the moment.)

RAOUL'S
180 Prince St (bet Sullivan and Thompson St)   212/966-3518
Dinner: Daily   www.raoulsrestaurant.com
Moderate

Old World touches here! There are dozens of good places to eat in Soho, and Raoul's is one of the best. This long, narrow restaurant used to be an old saloon. There are paper tablecloths and funky walls covered with a mishmash of posters, pictures, and calendars of every description. The bistro atmosphere is neighborly, friendly, and intimate; the prices are moderate; and the service is attentive. Attire on the trendy clientele runs the gamut from jeans to fur coats. The house favorites are steak *au poivre* and paté *maison*. Raoul's is a natural for those whose days begin when the rest of us are ready to hit the sack.

RARE BAR & GRILL

Shelburne Murray Hill Hotel   212/481-1999
303 Lexington Ave (at 37th St)   www.rarebarandgrill.com
Breakfast, Lunch, Dinner: Daily; Brunch: Sat, Sun
Moderate

If noise is your thing, you will be right at home at Rare. Inhabited by tables filled with yuppies and button-down business types, this restaurant literally vibrates with energy. The food is almost secondary to the scene, but the burgers are fabulous. You can get a classic burger or order one of their more exotic types: Mexican, foie gras, Kobe beef, barbecued pork, turkey scallion, crab, shrimp, and vegetable. They also serve a French fry tasting basket (cottage, shoestring, and sweet potato fries with dipping sauces), salads, soups, fried Oreos, and a huge banana split.

Gentlemen, an evening at **Robert's Steakhouse** (603 W 45 St, 212/245-0002) can be a memorable, if expensive, experience. The steaks are as good as can be found anywhere in the city, and the entertainment is exceptional. You won't find a place more fun than their Penthouse Executive Club!

(THE FAMOUS) RAY'S PIZZA OF GREENWICH VILLAGE

465 Ave of the Americas (at 11th St)   212/243-2253
Sun-Thurs: 11 a.m.-2 a.m.; Fri, Sat: 11 a.m.-3 a.m.
Inexpensive

In Manhattan, the name "Ray" is synonymous with pizza! Ray's is so popular that guests have had pizzas shipped to Midwestern relatives. No pizzeria in the Big Apple is better than this one, supposedly featuring the *real* Ray. The pizza is gourmet at its best, and you can create your own from the many toppings offered. You can have a fresh slice, whole pizza, or Sicilian square. You won't leave hungry, as pizzas are a generous 18 inches. Take-and-bake personal pizzas—ten-inch frozen cheese pies that are all natural and handmade—cook in your oven in just 12 minutes. Free delivery is available.

REDEYE GRILL

890 Seventh Ave (at 56th St)   212/541-9000
Lunch: Mon-Sat; Dinner: Daily; Brunch: Sun   www.redeyegrill.com
Moderately expensive

From the day it opened, the Redeye Grill has been a busy place! Owner Sheldon Fireman knows how to appeal to the eye, taking a cue from his successful Trattoria dell'Arte. Specialties include all shapes and sizes of shrimp (this is "the home of the dancing shrimp bar"), a huge seafood appetizer platter (at a huge price), grilled fish, and pastas. There's more: steaks, burgers, egg dishes, and sushi, and their famous Hollywood Cobb salad. The personnel are hip and helpful, but the scene is the major attraction. DJs spin music in the evenings, and outdoor terrace dining is available during spring, summer, and fall.

REMI
145 W 53rd St (bet Ave of the Americas and Seventh Ave)
Lunch, Dinner: Daily   212/581-4242
Moderate   www.remi-ny.com

Come here for the best seafood risotto in town! Remi operates in a spectacular space in midtown, handy to hotels and theaters. In an unusually long room dominated by a dramatic 120-foot Venetian wall painting by Paulin Paris, the food soars as high as the setting. In warm weather, the doors open up and diners can enjoy sitting at tables in the adjoining atrium. Waiters, chairs, and wall fabrics all match in attractive stripes. Antipasto like roasted quail wrapped in bacon (available seasonally) will get you off to a delicious start. Main dishes are not of the usual variety. The spaghetti, linguine, and ravioli (stuffed with such items as shrimp, ricotta, and vegetables) can match any house in Venice. Of course, there are fish and meat dishes for more mainstream appetites. The chocolate-raspberry mousse cake is superb. Paddle on down (Remi means "oars") for a first-class experience! Takeout and delivery are available.

RESTO
111 E 29th St (bet Lexington and Park Ave)   212/685-5585
Lunch: Mon-Fri; Dinner: Daily; Brunch: Sat, Sun   www.restonyc.com
Moderate

Resto is a winner for Belgian food lovers. Executive chef Robert Hellen has put together an affordable dining room that offers much more than the delicious burgers for which they have become famous. You will find small plates (like spiced lamb ribs, deviled eggs, and double-cooked *pori*) and a collection of house charcuterie. The housemade sausage is exceptional. If you are a fan of mussels, then enjoy Resto's several offerings.

If you are craving a great pork dinner, then a trip to tiny **Porchetta** (110 E 7th St, 212/777-2151) is a must. There is more, of course: great roast potatoes and a vegetarian dish. The ambience and delicious aroma will delight you. Whether you eat in or take out, you won't leave Porchetta hungry, sorry, or broke.

RISTORANTE GRIFONE
244 E 46th St (bet Second and Third Ave)   212/490-7275
Lunch: Mon-Fri; Dinner: Mon-Sat   www.grifonenyc.com
Moderate to moderately expensive

New Yorkers get so hyped up about trendy new places that they tend to forget about old-timers that quietly continue to do a good job. Grifone is one of those. If you are looking for an attractive, comfortable, and cozy place to dine—one with impeccable service and great food—then try Grifone. The menu is Northern Italian, and the many daily specials include a good selection of pasta, chicken, veal, fish, and beef dishes. A takeout menu is available as well. Quality never goes out of style. Just ask the neighborhood regulars who flock here year after year.

RIVER CAFE

1 Water St (Brooklyn Bridge), Brooklyn   718/522-5200
Lunch: Mon-Sat; Dinner: Daily; Brunch: Sun   www.rivercafe.com
Moderately expensive

The River Cafe isn't in Manhattan, but it *overlooks* Manhattan, and that's the main reason to come here. The view from the window tables is fantastic, awesome, romantic—you name it. There's no other skyline like it in the world. And so the River Cafe—just across the East River in the shadow of the Brooklyn Bridge—remains an extremely popular and sophisticated place. Call at least a week in advance to make reservations, and be sure to ask for a window table. This is a flag-waving special-occasion restaurant that's proud of its American cuisine. The seafood, lamb, and steak entrees are particularly good, and desserts are rich and fresh. The "Brooklyn Bridge" dessert, done in dark chocolate, is unforgettable.

ROCCO'S PASTRY SHOP & ESPRESSO CAFE

243 Bleecker St (at Fourth Ave and Carmine St)   212/242-6031
Sun-Thurs: 7:30 a.m.-midnight; Fri til 1a.m.; Sat til 1:30 a.m.
Moderate

You'll know you are near Rocco's by the tantalizing aromas lingering outside. Inside are tempting Italian goodies like crispy biscotti, *panettone*, cream- and fruit-filled pastries, freshly baked cookies, decadent cakes, and beautiful holiday indulgences. There are lots of choices for any time of the day: pastries for breakfast, lunch, or break treats; dinner or late-night desserts; and gelato for any reason. In addition to eating on premises and taking out, Rocco's offers many of these items through mail order.

Those ubiquitous food-vendor carts don't always serve palatable fare. One that does is **Sammy's Halal** (4th St and Broadway, and 4th St and Ave of the Americas). Join the lunchtime lineup for award-winning gyros or rice with dark-meat chicken. You control the spiciness with sauces of varying degrees of zest.

ROLF'S

281 Third Ave (at 22nd St)   212/477-4750
Lunch, Dinner: Daily   www.rolfsnyc.com
Moderate

In a city with few good German restaurants, Rolf's is worth remembering. It's a colorful destination where several dozen tables and wooden benches perfectly complement the eclectic decor. Faux Tiffany lampshades, old pictures, tiny lights, strings of beads, and what-have-you add up to a charming and comfortable setting for tasty German dishes. The schnitzels, goulash, sauerbraten, boiled beef, veal shanks, and bratwurst are served in ample portions with delicious potato pancakes and sauerkraut. German, apple, and potato pancakes come with applesauce on the side. For dessert, save room for homemade apple strudel or Black Forest cake.

ROSA MEXICANO

1063 First Ave (at 58th St)   212/753-7407
Dinner: Daily

61 Columbus Ave (at 62nd St)   212/977-7700
9 E 18th St (bet Fifth Ave and Broadway)   212/533-3350
Lunch: Mon-Fri; Dinner: Daily; Brunch: Sat, Sun
Moderate to moderately expensive   www.rosamexicano.com

This is, quite simply, classic Mexican cuisine. Start with the guacamole *en molcajete*; prepared fresh at the table, it is the best in town. There are also great appetizers, like small tortillas filled with sauteed shredded pork, small shrimp marinated in mustard and chili vinaigrette, and raviolis filled with sauteed chicken, tomato, and onion. Main-course entrees include huge, tasty crepes filled with shrimp and a multi-layered tortilla pie. Grilled specialties like beef short ribs and skewered marinated shrimp are tempting. Even the desserts are first-class. Choose from a traditional flan, Mexican spongecake, or mango with ice cream. The atmosphere at these three locations is friendly, the energy level high, and the dining top-drawer.

ROUND TABLE
Algonquin Hotel   212/840-6800
59 W 44th St (bet Fifth Ave and Ave of the Americas), lobby level
Breakfast: Daily; Lunch: Mon-Sat; Dinner: Daily; Brunch: Sun
Moderate to moderately expensive   www.algonquinhotel.com

The dishes here have seen a lot of history! At the Algonquin's famous Round Table, all manner of famous yesteryear personalities in the arts, business, and politics would meet to exchange stories and repartee. It is still alive and kicking! You can even reserve the famous table if your party numbers seven or more. The Round Table reeks of days past, but the food is very good and the servers will shower you with loving care. Don't expect anything fancy; just relax in the manner of the good old days.

RUBY FOO'S
1626 Broadway (at 49th St)   212/489-5600
Lunch, Dinner: Daily   www.brguestrestaurants.com
Moderate

Busy Ruby Foo's is billed as a dim sum and sushi palace, with the best dishes being in the latter category. However, if you and your tablemates share the roasted Peking duck, you will go home happy. There is a large selection of maki rolls: spicy tuna, fresh crabmeat, tempura shrimp, California (crab and avocado), and much more. Sushi platters are well-selected and great for a party. Hand rolls, soups, salads, and rice dishes are also featured. The crowd is hip, the noise level high, the food very good, and the value outstanding.

RUE 57
60 W 57th St (at Ave of the Americas)   212/307-5656
Breakfast, Lunch, Dinner: Daily; Brunch: Sat, Sun   www.rue57.com
Moderate (lunch) to moderately expensive (dinner)

With an extremely convenient location, friendly service, and pleasant atmosphere, this Parisian-style brasserie is one busy place. The menu encompasses soups and salads, oysters and clams, steaks, varied other entrees (like salmon, chicken, risotto, and ravioli), and daily specials. The young ones will enjoy the great burgers. Lovers of Japanese cuisine will find sushi, sashimi, maki, and temaki. Don't pass up the beefsteak tomato salad with onions and Roquefort!

SAN PIETRO
18 E 54th St (bet Fifth and Madison Ave)   212/753-9015
Lunch, Dinner: Mon-Sat   www.sanpietro.net
Moderately expensive

The Bruno brothers have brought the joys of Southern Italy to their
upscale restaurant, which is popular with society mavens and the well-to-do.
Fresh fruit and veggies are legendary, as is linguine with anchovy juice.
Spaghetti dishes and *scialatelli* are special, too. Fish, veal, and chicken dishes
are very well crafted. On the downside, waiters can be offhand and even
snooty if they think you're not a big tipper, and desserts leave a lot to be
desired. However, if you want to enjoy tasty Italian dishes while seeing how
the other half lives, San Pietro might be the ticket!

New York eating establishments have come to recognize that a
quick snack or meal is routine for lots of people. You can now find
excellent comfort-food stops all over Manhattan:

- Danny Meyer's **Shake Shack** (Madison Square Park, 23rd St bet
  Madison Ave and Broadway), is a popular seasonal place, with long
  lines in nice weather. And no wonder! Wonderful burgers, hot dogs,
  frozen custards, shakes, floats, and more are served. A year-round
  second location is now open on the Upper West Side (366 Columbus Ave, 646/747-8770).
- **Westville** (210 W 10th St and 173 Ave A) is a tiny stop with big flavors, serving salads, soups, burgers, hot dogs, sandwiches, complete
  platters, and yummy desserts. Brunch is served on weekends and
  holidays, with the usual bagel, egg, and breakfast dishes.
- Fast counter service is offered at **New York Burger Co.** (303
  Park Ave and 678 Ave of the Americas). Choices include excellent
  burgers and fries, fresh salads, smoothies, and other good choices.
  The crowds are a good indication that this is a tasty spot!

SARABETH'S
423 Amsterdam Ave (at 80th St)   212/496-6280
1295 Madison Ave (at 92nd St)   212/410-7335
Breakfast, Lunch, Dinner: Daily; Brunch: Sat, Sun

40 Central Park S (bet Fifth Ave and Ave of the Americas)
Breakfast, Lunch, Dinner: Daily; Brunch: Sat, Sun   212/826-5959
Moderate

SARABETH'S AT LORD & TAYLOR
424 Fifth Ave (at 39th St), 5th floor   212/827-5068
Lunch: Mon-Fri; Brunch: Sat, Sun

SARABETH'S AT THE WHITNEY
Whitney Museum of American Art
945 Madison Ave (bet 74th and 75th St)   212/570-3670
Lunch: Tues-Fri; Brunch: Sat, Sun   www.sarabeth.com
Moderate

I am reminded of the better English tearooms when visiting one of Sarabeth's locations. Swinging it is not. Reliable it is. The big draw is the home-

made quality of the dishes, including the baked items and excellent desserts. They also make gourmet preserves and sell them nationally. Menu choices include excellent omelets, porridge, and fresh fruit for breakfast; a fine assortment of light items for lunch; and fish, game, or meat dishes for dinner. The chocolate mousse cake, chocolate soufflé, warm berry bread pudding, and homemade ice cream are splendid desserts. Service is rapid and courteous. Look in on **Sarabeth's Bakery** at the Chelsea Market (75 Ninth Ave, 212/989-2424), too.

SAVORE
200 Spring St (at Sullivan St)   212/431-1212
Lunch, Dinner: Daily; Brunch: Sat, Sun   www.savorenyc.com
Moderate

Soho has no shortage of restaurants, some of them with a snooty attitude that's in keeping with the area. Savore has none of this. You come here for good, fresh food served in a casual and friendly atmosphere. It is a particularly attractive destination in nice weather, when tables are placed outside. The menu offers a large selection of pastas, like hand-cut spaghetti with basil and roasted tomato. In true Tuscan fashion, salads are served after the main course. I am partial to their crème brûlée, which features a wonderful coffee flavor.

> Avenue C now earns an "A" for dining. While Avenues A and B are still rather rough, Avenue C has a beguiling mix of Australian, Latin, Middle Eastern, and Vietnamese joints, along with some others that are a bit more conventional, including **Bao Noodles** (391 Second Ave, 212/725-7770). Don't bother dressing up for a visit to this neighborhood.

SCALINI FEDELI
165 Duane St (bet Greenwich and Hudson St)   212/528-0400
Lunch: Tues-Fri; Dinner: Mon-Sat   www.scalinifedeli.com
Expensive

This very upscale Italian restaurant is for those who want a truly classy and classic meal. The offerings are exotic: seared foie gras and roasted apples, soft egg-yolk ravioli with ricotta and spinach . . . and that's just to start! Then it's on to delicious braised short ribs of beef, breast of Muscovy duck, and wonderful tuna. Desserts are equally fabulous, like flourless chocolate cake (cooked to order) with a trio of gelati or warm caramelized apple tart in a baked phyllo crust. Luncheons are a bit lighter. *Prix fixe* dinner menus are the order of the day. As you look around this sedate establishment, note the relative youth of some of the gourmet diners. A private room in the wine cellar is available for parties.

SCARPETTA
355 W 14th St (at Ninth Ave)   212/691-0555
Dinner: Daily   www.scarpettanyc.com
Moderately expensive to expensive

This house is the baby of talented chef Scott Conant, who has given the Village neighborhood another venue that attracts folks from all over the city.

The setting is most appealing, with a retractable roof, high rafters, a very busy bar, and rows of light bulbs suspended in unique boxes. What you really come here for, though, is true Italian cooking, and that is exactly what you get. The breads are good enough for an entire meal. In fact, *scarpetta* refers to the Italian tradition of sopping up great sauces. Pastas are the chef's trademark; his spaghetti is especially marvelous. Other sure bets are black cod and melt-in-your-mouth braised short ribs of beef. Top it all off with wonderful key lime cheesecake. P.S. I dare you to find the almost hidden outdoor sign!

SCHILLER'S LIQUOR BAR
131 Rivington St (at Norfolk St)   212/260-4555
Breakfast, Lunch: Mon-Fri: Dinner: Daily (open late); Brunch: Sat, Sun
Moderate   www.schillersny.com

There is no place quite like Schiller's Liquor Bar in Manhattan. Keith McNally has created an unusual, fun, and deservedly popular munching and drinking spot in an area not renowned for exciting places. Schiller's Liquor Bar (that's the full name) joins a group of busy brasseries run by McNally. The atmosphere is rather Parisian and the service is informal, with much emphasis on the wine selection. Cheap, decent, and good vintages are offered and priced accordingly. They serve good Bibb lettuce salads, excellent burgers, Welsh rarebit, modestly priced steaks, rotisserie chicken, and daily specials. For those who lament the lack of good German food in Manhattan, call Schiller's to see what specials are on the menu. Sticky toffee pudding and chocolate cream pie are two of the better desserts. Takeout and delivery are also offered.

Oenophiles take note, as the following places have some of the best wine selections in the city.

A Voce (41 Madison Ave, 212/545-8555)
Babbo (110 Waverly Pl, 212/777-0303)
Balthazar (80 Spring St, 212/965-1414)
Compass (208 W 70th St, 212/875-8600)
Daniel (60 E 65th St, 212/288-0033)
Le Périgord (405 E 52nd St, 212/755-6244)
Primavera (1578 First Ave, 212/861-8608)
Union Square Cafe (21 E 16th St, 212/243-4020)
Veritas (43 E 20th St, 212/353-3700)

THE SEA GRILL
19 W 49th St (bet Fifth Ave and Ave of the Americas) 212/332-7610
Lunch: Mon-Fri; Dinner: Mon-Sat   www.theseagrillnyc.com
Moderately expensive

You'll pay for the setting as well as the food at this Rockefeller Center seafood house, which overlooks the ice-skating rink in winter and features open-air dining in nice weather. Take advantage of the seafood bar (clams, oysters, shrimp, mussels, crab, and lobster) to start. Well-prepared but somewhat pricey main courses include tasty crab cakes, salmon, and Nantucket bay scallops. I love the desserts! Offerings might include such delights as warm chocolate steamed pudding, warm apple tart, key lime pie, and "Palette of Sorbets." Rockefeller Center has been spruced up, and the Sea Grill is one of its gems. Now if they could just lighten up on the prices!

2ND AVENUE DELI
162 E 33rd St (bet Lexington and Third Ave)   212/689-9000
Daily: 6 a.m.-midnight (Fri til 4 a.m.)   www.2ndavedeli.com
Moderate

Even with a move from its well-established namesake location on Second Avenue, this famous deli continues to draw huge crowds who love the gigantic portions and quality plates. The atmosphere is made extra-friendly by long-time personnel, and the menu is complete with favorite kosher Jewish deli dishes. A visit here is a special treat. A plate of delicious crisp dill pickles is placed in front of you at the start. On my last visit, I consumed two plates—they were that good! Appetizers include chopped liver, meatballs, franks, and chicken wings. Soups include the favorite matzoh ball. There's also blintzes, potato pancakes, challah French toast, knishes, kugels, coleslaw, huge open (and closed) sandwiches, burgers, deli platters, and many beef entrees. Don't forget the chicken, fish, and steaks! I would rate this place as one of the very best delis in the city—or anywhere, for that matter. It can easily become habit forming!

Harlem has its share of respectable dining options.
Londel's Supper Club (2620 Frederick Douglass Blvd, 212/234-6114): jazz on weekends
Miss Maude's Spoonbread Too (547 Lenox Ave, 212/690-3100): pork chops and spoonbread, of course
Native (161 Lenox Ave, 212/665-2525): eclectic cuisine
Patsy's Pizzeria (2287-2291 First Ave, 212/534-9783): since 1933
Rao's (455 E 114th St, 212/722-6709): famous Italian landmark
Revival (2367 Frederick Douglass Blvd, 212/222-8338): soul food
Settepani (196 Lenox Ave, 917/492-4806): bakery specialties
Sylvia's (328 Lenox Ave, 212/996-0660): soul food and entertainment

---

SERENDIPITY 3
225 E 60th St (bet Second and Third Ave)   212/838-3531
Daily: 11:30 a.m.-midnight (Fri till 1 a.m., Sat till 2 a.m.)
Moderate   www.serendipity3.com

How does a "Golden Opulence Sundae" sound? It costs $1,000 and must be ordered a week in advance, but it actually contains edible gold leaf! The young and young-at-heart rate Serendipity 3 *numero uno* on their list of "in" places, as it has been for a half century. In an atmosphere of nostalgia set in a quaint, two-floor brownstone, this full-service restaurant offers a complete selection of delicious entrees, sandwiches, soups, salads, and pastas. The real treats are the fabulous desserts, including favorites like hot fudge sundaes and frozen hot chocolate (which can also be purchased in mix form to take home). The "Forbidden Broadway" ice cream sundae is awesome. An added pleasure is the opportunity to browse a shop loaded with trendy gifts, books, clothing, and accessories. If you are planning a special gathering for the teens in your clan, make Serendipity 3 the destination!

SETTE MEZZO
969 Lexington Ave (bet 70th and 71st St)   212/472-0400
Lunch, Dinner: Daily
Cash only
Moderate

This spot is the "hidden" favorite of Manhattan's elite business world. Sette Mezzo is small, professional, and busy, and it makes a great place for people-watching! There are no affectations in decor, service, or food preparation. This is strictly a business operation, with the emphasis on serving good food at reasonable prices. Don't worry about dressing up, as most diners come casually attired to enjoy a variety of Italian dishes done to perfection. In the evening, all of the grilled items are excellent. Fresh seafood is a specialty. Ask about the special pasta dishes for some marvelous combinations. For more traditional Italian plates, try veal chops, veal cutlets, stuffed baked chicken, or fried calamari and shrimp. Homemade desserts include several caloric cakes, tasty lemon tarts, sherbet, and ice cream.

> If you are in the mood for a great burger or hot dog and French fries, grab a friend and head to **Five Guys** (43 W 55th St, 212/459-9600). The place is a real New York experience: jumping, crowded, fun. The huge selection of free toppings is another plus.

SFOGLIA
1402 Lexington Ave (at 92nd St)   212/831-1402
Lunch: Tues-Sat; Dinner: Daily   www.sfogliarestaurant.com
Moderate

Pronounced *SFOG-lea* the name means uncut sheet of pasta. How appropriate for this rustic Italian eatery! Most folks would probably never notice this unassuming little trattoria on the Upper East Side, but believe me, you don't want to miss it! Of course, I was delighted when delicious warm bread arrived at the start. I could make a whole meal of this homemade, crusty treat. The place is rather bare bones, with several large tables where you might be seated with folks unknown. No problem! The food is so good you will quickly become best friends with the strangers at your elbows as you exchange bites. Proprietors and chefs Ron and Colleen Marnell-Suhanosky and their staff couldn't be friendlier. The menu changes every few weeks, but you will always find something good: fish, *papperdella*, meat, ravioli, chicken, *orata*, and more. You'll feel healthier just gazing upon the bowls of fruit or vegetables on the tables. Don't miss the cheese platter. Next door is **Tutto Sfoglia**, a "to go" outlet for Sfoglia pasta, sauces, breads, and other specialties.

SHUN LEE CAFE
Lunch: Sat, Sun; Dinner: Daily

SHUN LEE WEST
Lunch: Mon-Fri; Dinner: Daily; Brunch: Sat, Sun   212/595-8895
43 W 65th St (at Broadway)   ww.shunleewest.com
Moderate

Dim sum and street-food combinations are served in an informal setting at Shun Lee Cafe. It's a fun place where you can try some unusual and delicious Chinese dishes. A waiter comes to your table with a rolling cart and describes the various goodies. The offerings vary, but don't miss stuffed crab claws if they are available. Go on to the street-food items: delicious roast pork, barbecued spare ribs, a large selection of noodle and rice dishes and soups, and a menu full of mild and spicy entrees. Sauteed prawns with ginger and boneless duckling with walnut sauce are great choices. A vegetarian dish of shredded Chinese vegetables is cooked with rice noodles and served with a pancake (like moo shu pork, but without the meat). For heartier appetites, Shun Lee West—the excellent old Chinese restaurant that adjoins Shun Lee Cafe—is equally good. Some of the best Chinese food in Manhattan is served here. If you come with a crowd, family-style dining is available. Prices are a bit higher at the restaurant than in the cafe.

SHUN LEE PALACE
155 E 55th St (bet Lexington and Third Ave)　　　212/371-8844
Lunch, Dinner: Daily　　　　　　　　　　　　www.shunleepalace.com
Moderate to moderately expensive

There are all manner of Chinese restaurants in Manhattan: The colorful Chinatown variety. The mom-and-pop corner operations. The overly Americanized establishments. The grand Chinese dining rooms. Shun Lee Palace belongs in the last category, possessing a very classy, refined look. You are offered a delicious journey into the best of this historic cuisine. You can dine rather reasonably at lunch; a three-course *prix fixe* experience is available. Ordering from the menu (or through your captain) can be a bit pricier, but the platters are worth it. Specialties include beggar's chicken (24 hours advance notice required), curried prawns, and Beijing duck. There's much more, including casserole specials and spa cuisine. Yes, this is just about the closest thing Manhattan has to a real Chinese palace.

Sometimes we want more than a hearty drink when we step into a bar. We want a place with color and excitement, too! **Wilfie & Nell** (228 W 4th St, 212/242-2990) is just such a place. This place reeks of atmosphere, attracts a vibrant crowd, and serves good drinks. Delicious and sensibly priced snacks are offered for less than $10, too.

SISTINA
1555 Second Ave (at 80th St)　　　　　　　　　212/861-7660
Lunch, Dinner: Daily
Moderate

The philosophy of this family operation is that the joy is in the eating, not the surroundings, and for that they get top marks. Because the atmosphere is quite plain, one comes to Sistina for the food, and it can't be beat for classy Italian cooking. The specialty of the house is seafood; the Mediterranean red snapper and salmon are excellent dishes. There are also the usual choices of pasta, veal, and chicken, as well as daily specials.

SMITH & WOLLENSKY
797 Third Ave (at 49th St)　　　　　　　　　212/753-1530
Lunch, Dinner: Daily　　　　　　　　　　www.smithandwollensky.com
Moderate to moderately expensive

When visitors to the Big Apple want a taste of what this great city is all about, there is no better choice than Smith & Wollensky. There is an abundance of space (two floors) and talented, helpful personnel. I always grade a place on the quality of their bread, and Smith & Wollensky's is excellent. The lobster cocktail is one of the best in the city. Featured entrees include wonderful steaks (USDA prime, dry-aged and hand-butchered), prime rib, and lamb chops. Every man in the family will love the place, and the ladies will appreciate the special attention paid to them. Come here when you and your guests are really hungry.

SMITH'S
79 MacDougal St (bet Bleecker and Houston St)   212/260-0100
Dinner: Mon-Sat   www.smithsync.com
Moderate

With a limited menu and pleasant ambience, this is one of the better places to dine on busy MacDougal Street. The offerings change by season, and you'll find fresh items in the appetizers and starters, like green asparagus with peekytoe crab *bérnaise*. Entrees include seafood dishes like wild striped bass and mahi-mahi. Chicken, steak, lobster, and lamb dishes are uniformly delicious. What I really like about this place is the laid-back atmosphere and service. If you're in the mood for good food in tranquil environs, Smith's is a good choice.

The **Hard Rock Cafe** (1501 Broadway, at 44th St, 212/343-3355; Sun-Thurs: 11a.m.-12:30 a.m.; Fri, Sat: 11 a.m.-1:30 a.m.) draws visitors of all ages from around the world. Upstairs, you'll find Hard Rock clothing and souvenirs reflecting a New York theme. Downstairs, a 700-seat restaurant serves burgers, salads, and pastas. A unique outdoor space above the Hard Rock marquee hosts private parties.

SOUTH GATE
Jumeirah Essex House Hotel   212/484-5120
154 Central Park South (at 59th St)   www.154southgate.com
Breakfast, Lunch, Dinner: Daily
Expensive

This is definitely an "occasion" dining room. With a grand setting overlooking Central Park, fabulous wine collection, and plenty of breathing space, South Gate is a Manhattan jewel. The restaurant is entered from Central Park South. Superbly trained personnel make a meal in this dramatic room a dining treat for both Essex House guests and outside diners. Executive chef Kerry Heffernan's ever-changing menu offers such delicacies as Hudson Valley foie gras and flash-seared calamari to start. On to a nice selection of soups and salads, and tasty, warm bread. Well-prepared seafood, vegetarian, meat, and fowl plates are available. Butter-roasted lobster and braised and roasted rib of beef are outstanding. The pastry chef will have a number of tasty selections for you!

SPARKS STEAKHOUSE
210 E 46th St (bet Second and Third Ave)   212/687-4855
Lunch: Mon-Fri; Dinner: Mon-Sat   www.sparkssteakhouse.com
Moderately expensive

You come here to eat, period. This is a well-seasoned and popular beef restaurant with little ambience. For years, businessmen have made an evening at Sparks a must, and the house has not let time erode its reputation. You can choose from veal and lamb chops, beef scaloppine, and medallions of beef. There are a half-dozen steak items, like steak *fromage* (with Roquefort), prime sirloin, sliced steak with sauteed onions and peppers, and top-of-the-line filet mignon. Seafood dishes are another specialty. Rainbow trout, filet of tuna, and halibut steak are as good as you'll find in most seafood houses. The lobsters are enormous, delicious, and expensive. Skip the appetizers and desserts, and concentrate on the main dish. Private party rooms are available.

What is *momofuku*? It translates into "lucky peach," but in the dining arena it is the domain of chef David Chang.

His original **Momofuku Noodle Bar** (171 First Ave, 212/475-7899) is open daily for lunch and dinner. You'll find noodles, small dishes, and a large variety of small plates, with items changing by the season, plus heritage pork and shellfish offerings.

Momofuku Ssäm Bar (207 Second Ave, 212/254-3500) is open daily for lunch and dinner. This place first offers a choice of *ssäm* (a kind of wrap) or bowl, and then a protein (pork, chicken, beef, or tofu), followed by extras like beans or roasted onions. You won't go away hungry. Best description: earthy, Asian-accented meathead cuisine—whatever that means!

The 12-seat **Momofuku Ko** (163 First Ave) is one of the hardest restaurants in town to score a lunch or dinner reservation. Prices hover around $85 to $100 per plate for the multi-course meal. This is superb eclectic dining, if you have the patience to wait for a seat. No walk-ins; reservations are only accepted online (www.momofuku.com) seven days in advance. Good luck!

SPICE MARKET
403 W 13th St (at Ninth Ave)   212/675-2322
Lunch, Dinner: Daily   www.spicemarketnewyork.com
Moderate

For atmosphere and tasty upscale Asian street food, this is one of the city's hot dining spots. Located in the trendy Meatpacking District, Spice Market is a charming space with tables surrounding an open area that leads to an inviting downstairs bar. The decor is tasteful, while the food is different and exciting. The Vietnamese spring rolls are yummy, the salads are unusual and good, and the chicken skewer with peanut sauce is outstanding. Other wonderful dishes: striped bass or cod with Malaysian chili sauce; onion- and chili-crusted short ribs that melt in your mouth; and a large selection of vegetables, noodles, and rice. Desserts are even better. Thai jewels and fruits with fresh coconut snow—one of the most famous street desserts in Thailand—is a must. Other sweet selections: Ovaltine *kulfi* and a really fabulous chocolate and Vietnamese coffee tart served with ice cream.

SPIGOLO
1561 Second Ave (at 81st St)   212/744-1100
Dinner: Daily
Moderately expensive

Some Upper East Siders swear by this Italian house, perhaps because it is tiny and reservations are not easy to come by. I really don't know what all the raves are about. I found Spigolo to be good but not great. Seafood dishes at the start are quite flavorful, including clams, oysters, and salmon tartare. Braised lamb shank makes for a hearty and satisfying main dish, as does breast of veal served with delicious butternut squash puree. If its somewhat out-of-the-way location and having to wait days for a reservation aren't turnoffs, then go right ahead. Otherwise, this chapter is filled with numerous Italian eateries that do just as well—and many of them much better—for a far more reasonable price.

JAMES BEARD HOUSE
167 W 12th St (bet Ave of the Americas and Seventh Ave)
212/675-4984
www.jamesbeard.org

This is a real chefs' place! The legendary James Beard had roots in Oregon, so anything to do with his life is of special interest to this author. He was a familiar personality on the Oregon coast, where he delighted in serving the superb seafood for which the region is famous. When Beard died in 1985, his Greenwich Village brownstone was put on the market and purchased by a group headed by the late Julia Child. Now the home is run by the nonprofit James Beard Foundation as a food and wine archive, research facility, and gathering place. It is the nation's only such culinary center. There are nightly dinners at which some of our country's best regional chefs show off their substantial talents. For foodies, this is a great opportunity to have a one-on-one with some really interesting folks. Call for scheduled dinners.

SPRING STREET NATURAL RESTAURANT
62 Spring St (at Lafayette St)   212/966-0290
Breakfast, Lunch: Mon-Fri; Dinner: Daily; Brunch: Sat, Sun
Moderate   www.springstreetnatural.com

Before eating "naturally" became a big thing, Spring Street Natural Restaurant was a leader in the field. That tradition continues after 30 years. In attractive surroundings, the kitchen provides meals prepared with fresh, unprocessed foods, and most everything is cooked to order. Neighborhood residents are regular customers, so you know the food is top-quality. Specials are offered every day, with a wide variety of organic salads, pastas, vegetarian meals, free-range poultry, and fresh fish and seafood. Try wonderful roasted salmon with creamy risotto and baby asparagus stalks. Spring Street also produces great desserts, like chocolate walnut pie, honey raspberry blueberry pie, and honey pear pie. The last two are made without sugar and dairy products.

STRIP HOUSE
13 E 12th St (bet Fifth Ave and University Pl)   212/328-0000
Dinner: Daily   www.striphouse.com
Moderately expensive

Strip House offers a modern twist to the traditional steakhouse experience. Rich leather, plush fabrics, and dark red walls lined with photographs of sultry 1920s burlesque stars all create a seductive atmosphere. The innovative menu features prime cuts of wet-aged beef, all charred to perfection with signature seasoning. Flavorful sides like black truffle creamed spinach, goose-fat potatoes, and creamed corn with crispy pancetta complement the entrees. Decadent desserts include a 24-layer chocolate cake.

TABLA
11 Madison Ave (at 25th St)   212/889-0667
Dining Room (upstairs)   www.tablany.com
Lunch: Mon-Fri; Dinner: Daily

Bread Bar (downstairs)
Lunch: Mon-Sat: Dinner: Daily
Moderate (downstairs) to expensive (upstairs)

Here is yet another of Danny Meyer's unique restaurants! Upstairs you will now find American food infused with Indian spices. Dinner is *prix fixe* only, while lunch is both a la carte and *prix fixe*. Downstairs features homestyle Indian cooking with an a la carte menu and *prix fixe* options. For those who like a taste of India without going overboard, this is a first-class operation in every way.

> **The John Dory** (85 Tenth Ave, 212/929-4948) is making its mark as one of Manhattan's better seafood houses. At the start you have a choice of five different breads. Most everything about his place, including the accommodating staff, is first-class. Another good bet in the seafood category is **Fishtail by David Burke** (135 E 62nd St, 2123/754-1300). There is much to appreciate here: the fish decor, the fact that this is a "natural seafood restaurant," and the great variety of dishes. Winners include the raw bar, sashimi, crispy crab cakes, and swordfish steak. Cheesecake lollipops make a novel dessert.

TAO
42 E 58th St (bet Madison and Park Ave)   212/888-2288
Lunch: Mon-Fri; Dinner: Daily   www.taorestaurant.com
Moderate

There's no place quite like this! Tao is billed as an Asian bistro, but it is much more than that. In a huge space that once served as a theater, a dramatic dining setting has been created with a huge Buddha looking down as you enjoy wonderful food at reasonable prices. Hordes of diners can be accommodated on two levels; a sushi bar and several regular bars are also available. Reservations are strongly recommended, as thirtysomethings make Tao their headquarters. A number of small plates are available to start, including Thai stuffed shrimp and squab lettuce wraps. Save room for a delicious Kobe beef steak, filet mignon cooked at your table in a hot pot, or a marvelous wok-seared New York sirloin with shiitake mushrooms that melts in your mouth. A $24 *prix fixe* lunch is offered daily. For dessert, try the molten chocolate cake with coconut ice cream.

TARTINE
253 W 11th St (at 4th St)   212/229-2611
Lunch: Wed-Fri; Dinner: Daily; Brunch: Sat-Tues
Moderate

Read carefully! Tartine will be your kind of place if you don't mind: (1) waiting outside in the rain, cold, or heat; (2) bringing your own drinks; (3) paying cash; and (4) having your used fork laid back down in front of you for the next course. All of this, of course, is secondary to the fact that this tiny place (about 20 chairs) serves some of the tastiest dishes in the Village. There are soups, salads, quiches, and omelets, plus chicken, meat, and fish entrees at pleasing prices. French fries are a treat. Desserts and pastries are baked on-premises. For about half the price of what you would pay uptown, you can finish your meal with splendid custard-filled tarts, a fabulous hazelnut-covered chocolate ganache, strawberry shortcake, or thinly sliced warm apples with cinnamon on puff pastry with ice cream. There is always a wait at dinner—a good sign, since neighborhood folks know the best spots. If you want wine, you are encouraged to bring your own.

> Whenever hunger hits, remember this name: **Cafeteria** (119 Seventh Ave, 212/414-1717). Not only is good food served at attractive prices, but they are open 24 hours a day, seven days a week. The place is always humming with customers.

TASTE
1413 Third Ave (at 80th St)   212/717-9798
Dinner: Daily; Brunch: Sat, Sun   www.elizabar.com
Moderate (Taste Cafe) to moderately expensive (Taste)

When it comes to quality food (with prices to match), there is no equal in Manhattan to Eli Zabar. Taste has all the pluses and minuses you've come to expect from this gentleman. Dinners change nightly and feature such winners as sauteed duck livers, roasted artichoke hearts, wild Pacific salmon, pork chops, and quail. A wine bar serves good wines that aren't *too* expensive by the glass. With Zabar's market just below, Taste must be offering really fresh food. As you would expect from a Zabar operation, the breads are superb. The more informal, self-service **Taste Cafe** serves breakfast, lunch, and weekend brunch.

TAVERN ON THE GREEN
Central Park West at 67th St
Lunch: Mon-Fri; Dinner: Daily; Brunch: Sat, Sun   212/873-3200
Moderate to moderately expensive   www.tavernonthegreen.com

Tavern on the Green is a destination attraction. The setting in Central Park, with lights twinkling in nearby trees and glamorous indoor fixtures, makes for dining experiences that residents and visitors alike never forget. Even though the operation is big and busy, the food and service are usually first-rate. Chef Brian Young has a huge job keeping this hopping place happily organized. If you are planning an evening that must be extra special, make reservations in the **Crystal Room**. Your out-of-town relatives will love it! Seasonal menus can be viewed online.

TELEPAN
72 W 69th St (at Columbus Ave)   212/580-4300
Lunch: Wed-Fri; Dinner: Daily; Brunch: Sat, Sun   www.telepan-ny.com
Moderate to moderately expensive

When you have overloaded on the flashy dining scene, step back and be Bill Telepan's guest. Everything about this place—surroundings, menu, and service—reflects the laid-back personality of chef/owner Telepan. It is a quiet and reliable restaurant enhancing the Upper West Side for more mature diners. Local ingredients are featured on the changing menu. Order the spring vegetables bread soup, if it's on the menu; it could make an entire meal. There are worthy egg dishes, soft-shell crab, organic chicken, and braised short ribs with garlic potato puree. Steamed chocolate cake with caramel ice cream and chocolate sauce is properly sinful.

THOR
Hotel on Rivington
107 Rivington St (bet Essex and Ludlow St)   212/796-8040
Breakfast: Daily; Lunch: Mon-Fri; Dinner: Daily; Brunch: Sat, Sun
Moderate to moderately expensive   www.hotelonrivington.com

Would you believe a first-class hotel and restaurant on Rivington Street on the Lower East Side? With a French-American flavor, dramatic atmosphere, and one of the nicest wait staffs in the city, Thor is worth a special evening. Tastings of a number of cold and hot plates are encouraged. You'll find specialties like fried baby artichoke salad and honey and lavender tomato confit. Plenty of fish and meat dishes are available, and the oven-carmelized filet of cod is delicious. Be sure to save room for warm flourless dark-chocolate cake.

TOCQUEVILLE RESTAURANT
1 E 15th St (bet Union Square W and Fifth Ave)
Lunch: Mon-Sat; Dinner: Daily; Brunch: Sun   212/647-1515
Moderately expensive   www.tocquevillerestaurant.com

Marco Moreira and wife Jo-Ann Makovitzky have moved their pride-and-joy restaurant into a larger, more elegant location. Innovative dishes are featured on a constantly changing menu. At lunchtime, a *prix fixe* menu is offered. Your entree might be 60-second seared dry-aged sirloin, followed by a wonderful apple tart dessert. You will enjoy an absolutely fabulous meal made all the more pleasant by a well-trained and accommodating staff. Homemade brioche, rosemary, and French rolls are so good you must be careful not to ruin your appetite. The locale affords room for private dining (up to 25 people) and a bar area where you can enjoy drinks and snacks or order from the full menu. This talented pair also operates **Catering by Tocqueville**, a catering service accessible via the restaurant's phone number. Personal food delivery is a given, but they can also take care of rental items, flowers, photographers, and professional service staff.

TONY'S DINAPOLI

1606 Second Ave (at 83rd St)   212/861-8686
Dinner: Daily (open at 2 p.m. on Sat, Sun)
147 W 43rd St (bet Broadway and Ave of the Americas)
Lunch, Dinner: Daily   212/221-0100
Moderate   www.tonysnyc.com

Tony's is not to be missed for great family-style dining. The kids will love it, as will your hungry spouse. The place is colorful, noisy, and busy. The 43rd Street location in Times Square is a bit more subdued. Huge platters of appetizers, delicious salads, pastas, chicken and veal dishes, broiled items, and seafood come piping hot and ready for the whole crew to dig into. Individual side portions can now be requested as well. Most everyone finds that they can't eat it all, so you'll see lots of take-home boxes exiting these locations. Even the dessert menu is gigantic: cheesecakes, strawberry shortcake, sundaes, sorbets, and *tartufo* (almost the real thing). Sheer fun, believe me!

Conveniently located across from Bryant Park, **Zeytinz Fine Food Market Place** (24 W 40th St, 212/575-8080) offers gourmet sandwiches, wraps, paninis, pizzas, soups, and salads. You can also try something from the cold buffet, sushi bar, or grill. Zeytinz offers specialty drinks like lattes and smoothies, a large selection of breakfast items, and custom-made cakes, tarts, and cookies. Catering, gift baskets, and delivery are available.

TRATTORIA DELL'ARTE

900 Seventh Ave (at 57th St)
Lunch, Dinner: Daily; Brunch: Sun   212/245-9800
Moderate   www.trattoriadellarte.com

The natives already know about Trattoria Dell'Arte, as the place is bursting at the seams every evening. A casual cafe is at the front, seats are available at the antipasto bar in the center, and the dining room is in the rear. One would be hard-pressed to name a place at any price with tastier Italian food. The antipasto selection is large, fresh, and inviting; you can choose a platter with various accompaniments. There are daily specials, superb pasta dishes, grilled fish and meats, and salads. Wonderful pizzas are available every day. The atmosphere and personnel are warm and pleasant. I recommend this place without reservation—although you'd better have one if you want to sit in the dining room. An outdoor sidewalk cafe provides seating during the warmer months.

TRESTLE ON TENTH

242 Tenth Ave (at 24th St)
Breakfast, Lunch, Dinner: Daily; Brunch: Sat, Sun   212/645-5659
Moderate   www.trestleontenth.com

Employing a restrained Swiss accent, this house does well with a seasonal menu of chicken, lamb saddle, veal kidneys, pork loin, braised beef short ribs, and superb *crépinette* (pulled pork shoulder). I always enjoy a light and tasty butter lettuce salad to start. Here it is made with crispy bacon and a delicious buttermilk dressing. Cured meats and aged cheeses are also featured.

A *nusstorte* (pie) with walnuts and caramel is a reliable dessert. The folks are down-to-earth and the atmosphere unpretentious.

TRIBECA GRILL
375 Greenwich St (at Franklin St)
Lunch: Mon-Fri; Dinner: Daily; Brunch: Sun   212/941-3900
Moderate   www.myriadrestaurantgroup.com/tribecagrill

It hardly seems possible this place will celebrate its 20th birthday in 2010. Please note the address is Greenwich *Street*, not Avenue. The setting is a huge old coffee-roasting house in Tribeca. The inspiration is Robert DeNiro. The bar comes from the old Maxwell's Plum restaurant. The kitchen is first-class. The genius is savvy Drew Nieporent. Put it all together, and you have a winner. No wonder the people-watching is so good here! Guests enjoy a spacious bar and dining area, a fabulous private screening room upstairs, a collection of paintings by actor Robert DeNiro, and banquet facilities for private parties. The food is stylish and wholesome. Excellent salads, seafood, veal, steak, and first-rate pastas are house favorites. One of the top dishes is seared tuna with sesame noodles. The tarts, tortes, and mousses also rate with the best. Their world-class wine list (1,500 selections!) has received the Grand Award from *Wine Spectator Magazine*.

Named for talented chef Wylie Dufresne, **wd-50** (50 Clinton St, 212/477-2900) is open Wednesday through Sunday for dinner. The room is attractive, with good lighting, unique restrooms, and a dramatic semi-open kitchen. Much of the fare is delicious. However, unless you are a contemporary gourmet who enjoys unusual dishes served with equally unusual accompaniments—like pork belly with black soybeans and turnips—I would suggest heading elsewhere.

T SALON
Chelsea Market
75 Ninth Ave (bet 15th and 16th St)
Breakfast, Lunch, Dinner: Daily   212/243-2259
Moderate   www.tsalon.com

Given all the renewed interest in teas, the unusual and enchanting T Salon is sure to captivate tea addicts, as well as those who just want to experiment on an occasional basis. You will find green teas (light colored Oriental tea with a delicate taste), oolong teas (distinctive peach flavor), and black teas (heavy, deep flavor and rich amber color), as well as white and red teas. Tea blending is a specialty. Miriam Novalle, the T Salon's guru, has brewed up some changes. Besides pastries and fruit, a full vegan menu is offered, including soups, salads, spring rolls, and lasagna. A day's advance notification is required for "proper afternoon tea" with tea sandwiches. Look for a full bar and reasonably priced tea-making accessories, in addition to 320 varieties of tea. This is a unique destination for special events and private parties, besides a quiet cup of tea.

TURKISH KITCHEN
386 Third Ave (bet 27th and 28th St)
Lunch: Mon-Fri; Dinner: Daily; Brunch: Sun   212/679-6633
Moderate   www.turkishkitchen.com

Turkey is in! I mean both the country and the food. This Turkish delight has great food and is absolutely spotless. Moreover, the staff exudes charm! There are all kinds of Turkish specialties, like zucchini pancakes, *istim kebab* (baked lamb shanks wrapped with eggplant slices), hummus, and tasty baked and grilled fish dishes. You can wash it all down with sour cherry juice from Turkey or *cacik*, a homemade yogurt. This family-run Gramercy-area operation is one of the best.

21 CLUB
21 W 52nd St (bet Fifth Ave and Ave of the Americas)   212/582-7200
Lunch: Tues-Fri; Dinner: Tues-Sat (closed Sat in summer)
Expensive to very expensive   www.21club.com

Believe it or not, there is a new bar at 21! The operaton itself has been around for a long time, with a reputation as a place to see and be seen. I can remember fascinating lunches, here with my uncle, who was a daily diner. Alas, things have changed. Yes, there is still a gentleman at the door to give you the once over. Men's jackets are required and ties are encouraged (no jeans or sneakers). There are still 21 classics on the menu, even a not-so-lowly burger at $30. And the atmosphere is still quite special. But the tradition ends, as far as I am concerned. The service is haughty, and the food is just okay. If your out-of-town guests simply *must* see this place and you're feeling flush, then go; otherwise, the memories are better.

> Guaranteed good dining at places you may not have heard about:
> **Bar Boulud** (1990 Broadway, 212/595-0303)
> **Convivio** (45 Tudor City Place, 212/599-5045)
> **Corton** (239 West Broadway, 212/219-2777)
> **Scarpetta** (355 W 14th St, 212/691-0555)
> **Sfoglia** (1402 Lexington Ave, 212/831-1402)

202
Chelsea Market
75 Ninth Ave (bet 15th and 16th St)
Breakfast: Daily; Dinner: Tues-Sun; Brunch: Daily   646/638-1173
Moderate   www.nicolefarhi.com

This unique operation in the busy Chelsea Market—a cafe and a store all in one—is a good place to rest weary feet. You'll find full English breakfasts (bacon, sausage, mushrooms, and poached eggs), buttermilk pancakes, bagels, salads, tuna burgers, steaks, and more. The young personnel are very accommodating, and the platters are more than adequate. Adjoining is a rather sparse clothing and gift store that's worth browsing but not much more. The expensive duds are by designer Nicole Farhi.

2 WEST
Ritz-Carlton New York, Battery Park
2 West St (at Battery Pl)   917/790-2525
Breakfast, Lunch, Dinner: Daily; Brunch: Sun   www.ritzcarlton.com
Moderately expensive

The view is the thing here! The food is very good, but the edibles might be outclassed by the visual sights. The view of the park and water combines with gorgeous indoor glass pieces and artwork to make a memorable feast for the eyes. The serving pieces are attractive, too. When you merge all of this with extremely fast, informed service and good food, I have no complaints. This room is just one of the hotel's dining choices, all of them done to Ritz-Carlton's standards of perfection. You'll find a rich selection of plates carefully designed and presented with local ingredients. I like the dessert plate; the chocolate tart is exceptional.

UNCLE JACK'S STEAKHOUSE
440 Ninth Ave (at 34th St)   212/244-0005
44 W 56th St (bet Fifth Ave and Ave of the Americas) 212/245-1550
Lunch: Mon-Fri; Dinner: Daily   www.unclejacks.com
Moderate (lunch) to expensive (dinner)

Entering this atmospheric steakhouse is like going back decades in time. The hand-carved mahogany bar, the antique light fixtures, the blackboard menu, and the private Library Room (Ninth Avenue location) make the place comfortable and colorful. You will be well taken care of, as the wait staff and captains are right on the job. Uncle Jack's is one of the few steakhouses in Manhattan that specialize in Kobe beef, which is famous for its tenderness and flavor. The beef is aged for 21 days and cooked to perfection, and you can expect an equally grand price tag. Other menu items are what you would expect from a first-class steakhouse, and all are tasty and more comfortably priced. A Sommelier's Dinner, a feast of food and wine, is available for $99.95. For a gentlemen's evening out, a bachelor party, or office celebration, I can't imagine a more pleasant place. You can purchase Uncle Jack's bottled steak sauce for home use.

UNION SQUARE CAFE
21 E 16th St (bet Fifth Ave and Union Square W)   212/243-4020
Lunch, Dinner: Daily   www.unionsquarecafe.com
Moderate

The Stars and Stripes fly high at Union Square Cafe, a very popular American restaurant (albeit with an Italian soul). The clientele is as varied as the food. Conversations are often oriented toward the publishing world, as well-known authors and editors are often seated at lunch. The menu is creative, the staff unusually down-to-earth, and the prices very much within reason. Owner Danny Meyer offers such specialties as oysters Union Square, hot garlic potato chips, and wonderful black bean soup. For lunch, try the yellowfin tuna burger served on a homemade poppyseed roll or one of the great pastas. Dinner entrees from the grill are always delicious (tuna, shell steak, and veal). I come just for the warm banana tart with honey-vanilla ice cream and macadamia brittle! Try a light afternoon cheese plate at the bar.

VALBELLA
421 W 13th St (bet Ninth Ave and Washington St)   212/645-7777
Lunch: Mon-Fri; Dinner: Mon-Sat   www.valbellany.com
Moderate

In my opinion, service is the name of the game in today's highly competitive marketplace. Patronizing so many restaurants, I can immediately assess the service. At Valbella, it is top-notch. Wait staff don't stand around and talk—they are in constant motion and obviously well-trained. The Italian fare is also first-rate, featuring a decent selection of typical dishes. The pastas caught my eye: penne *alla* vodka, *cavatelli*, *trenette* (sautéed jumbo shrimp), fettuccine, risotto with wild mushrooms, and more. The almond-crusted lamb chops with roasted potatoes and vegetables is an especially delicious dish. Like most Italian houses, veal is also a specialty. The Chef Room is a private dining area that will seat 10 to 30 people.

VERITAS
43 E 20th St (at Park Ave S)   212/353-3700
Dinner: Daily   www.veritas-nyc.com
Moderately expensive

There are only 55 seats at Veritas, and all of them are kept warm at every meal. Getting to enjoy chef Grégory Pugin's seasonal creations is definitely worth any wait. The world-class wine cellar stocks over 3,500 selections, ranging from $18 to $100,000! Like the food, the room is done in superb taste; every color and surface spells quality. Top dishes include lobster *nage*, pimientos *del piquillo*, Wagyu filet, and squab roti. Chocolate soufflé is a must for dessert.

Touring Washington Heights? Stop by **New Caporal** (3772 Broadway, 212/862-8986) for great fried chicken; take home a rotisserie chicken from **La Fiesta Restaurante** (3797 Broadway, 212/281-2886); pick out some fresh produce at **Carniceria la Blanda** (3824 Broadway, 212/927-4860); or try the fresh fish at **Brother Fish Market** (3845 Broadway, 212/781-2680).

VINEGAR FACTORY
431 E 91st St (bet York and First Ave)   212/987-0885
Breakfast, Lunch, Dinner: Daily (cafe); Brunch: Sat, Sun (upstairs)
Moderate   www.elizabar.com

Savvy Upper East Siders quickly learned that weekend brunch at Eli Zabar's Vinegar Factory is unfailingly delicious. Taste buds spring to alertness as you wander the packed aisles of the Vinegar Factory (a great gourmet store) on your way upstairs to the cafe for Saturday or Sunday brunch. Don't expect bargain prices; after all, this is an Eli Zabar class operation. Quality is substantial. Wonderful breads (Eli is famous for them), a fresh salad bar, omelets, pizzas, pancakes, blintzes, and huge sandwiches are the order of the day; many are available as self-serve items. Your hungry teens will love the massive portions, and you'll appreciate the fast, friendly service.

CUCINA VIVOLO
138 E 74th St (at Lexington Ave)   212/717-4700

VIVOLO
140 E 74th St (bet Park and Lexington Ave)   212/737-3533
Lunch: Mon-Sat; Dinner: Mon-Sat

BAR.VETRO
222 E 58th St (bet Second and Third Ave)
Lunch: Mon-Fri; Dinner: Mon-Sat   212/308-0112
Moderate   www.vivolonyc.com

In 1977, Angelo Vivolo created a neighborhood classic from an old townhouse. Vivolo is a charming two-story restaurant with cozy fireplaces and professional service. Vivolo's success expanded to the Cucina specialty food shop and sensual bar.vetro. There are great things to eat at all three places. You can sit down and be pampered, have goodies ready for takeout, or place an order for delivery. The Cucina menu offers wonderful Italian specialty sandwiches made with all kinds of breads, as well as soups, cheeses, sweets, espresso, and cappuccino. In the restaurants proper, there are pastas, stuffed veal chops, and daily specials. Vivolo serves over 60 scaloppine preparations. Whichever Vivolo eatery you choose, save room for the cannoli *alla* Vivolo, a tasty version of the Italian classic.

VONG
200 E 54th St (bet Second and Third Ave)   212/486-9592
Lunch: Mon-Fri; Dinner: Daily   www.jean-georges.com
Moderate to moderately expensive

The atmosphere is Thai-inspired with romantic and appetizing overtones. Ladies will love the colors and lighting, and gentlemen will remember the great things Vong does with peanut and coconut sauces on their Thai/French fusion menu. I could make a meal of appetizers like chicken and coconut milk soup, prawn satay with oyster sauce, and raw tuna wrapped in rice paper. Order crispy squab or venison medallions, if available. A vegetarian menu is offered. For dessert, I suggest passionfruit sorbet or warm chocolate cake (upon request). Dining here is a lot cheaper than a week at Bangkok's Oriental Hotel and just as delicious!

> Great crepes (they call them *gallettes*), a busy bar scene, a great location—all this equals **Bar Breton** (254 Fifth Ave, 212/231-4999). There's more: super breakfasts (wonderful French toast), super burgers, and daily entree specials like delicious calves liver, chicken, and meat dishes. This place is a winner; it brings Brittany to the Big Apple!

WALKER'S
16 N Moore St (at Varick St)   212/941-0142
Lunch: Mon-Fri; Dinner: Daily; Brunch: Sat, Sun
Inexpensive

If you are looking for a glimpse of old Manhattan, you'll love Walker's. In three crowded rooms, at tables covered with plain white paper so that diners can doodle with crayons, hearty food is served at agreeable prices. The regular menu includes homemade soups, salads, omelets (create your own), sandwiches, and quiches. Burgers are big and satisfying. A dozen or so daily specials include fish and pasta dishes. For those coming from uptown, it is a bit of an undertaking to get here. For those in the neighborhood, it is easy to see why Walker's is a favorite, especially on Sunday jazz nights.

WALLSÉ
344 W 11th St (at Washington St)   212/352-2300
Dinner: Daily; Brunch: Sat, Sun   www.wallserestaurant.com
Moderate to moderately expensive

Vienna it is not, but Kurt Gutenbrunner brings a somewhat Austrian flavor to the West Village. The two dining rooms are sparse but comfortable. The staff is pleasant and helpful, adding to the dining experience. Appetizers like foie gras terrine and chestnut soup with Armagnac prunes are seasonal favorites. Yes, there is wiener schnitzel with potato-cucumber salad, and you can always hope that crispy cod strudel is on the menu. Great pastries for dessert: apple strudel, cheesecake, and Salzburger *nockerl*. The cheese selection is first-rate.

WATER CLUB
500 E 30th St (at East River)
Lunch: Mon-Sat; Dinner: Daily; Buffet Brunch: Sun   212/683-3333
Moderately expensive   www.thewaterclub.com

Warning! Do not fill up on the marvelous small scones that are made fresh and served warm. They are the best things you have ever tasted, but they will diminish your appetite for the excellent meal to follow. The Water Club presents a magnificent setting on the river. A large selection of seafood appetizers is available. Entrees include numerous fish dishes, plus meat and poultry items. Chocolate truffle cake will round off a special meal. The place is large and noisy, with a fun atmosphere that is ideal for special occasions. They also have excellent private party facilities. There is nightly piano music, as well as accommodations for a drink or light meal on the roof (weather permitting). Getting here from the north can be confusing. (Directions: Exit FDR Drive at 23rd Street and make two left turns.)

> The Bromberg brothers operate several winning restaurants. **Blue Ribbon Downing Street Bar** (34 Downing St, 212/691-0404, Dinner: Daily; Brunch: Sat, Sun) is right across the street from Blue Ribbon Bakery. With the Blue Ribbon name attached, you know the food will be first-class. Small plates, smoked meats, fish, and a good selection of wines and cognacs are featured.

WAVERLY INN & GARDEN
16 Bank St (bet 4th and Waverly St)   212/243-7900
Dinner: Daily
Moderately expensive to expensive

The Waverly Inn is owned by Graydon Carter, publisher and editor of *Vanity Fair*. Because it is his personal establishment, the average diner will find it difficult, if not impossible, to enjoy the tastes of a truly good restaurant in a most attractive space. That is because it is nearly impossible to reach Waverly Inn by phone to make a reservation. My best advice is to drop in early for dinner (they open at 6 p.m.), and you might be lucky enough to snare a table. You won't be disappointed. Small plates include oysters on the half shell, salads, salmon tartare, crab cakes, and more. Braised short ribs are a sensational entree. You might also choose a Waverly burger, several fish dishes, or grilled mussels. The surroundings are charming. In the garden room, a working fireplace adds to the ambience. Once seated, you'll find the service very professional, and they really seem happy to serve you.

WOO CHON

10 W 36th St (at Fifth Ave)   212/695-0676
Daily: 10:30 a.m.-2 a.m.   www.woochon.com
Moderate

Look at the hours they keep at Woo Chon! This Korean restaurant is sparkling clean, friendly, and inviting. For a group dinner, order a variety of beef, pork, and shrimp dishes and have fun grilling them at your table. The sizzling seafood pancake is a winner! Accompanying dishes add a special touch to your meal. In addition to marinated barbecue items, there are such tasty delights as Oriental noodles and vegetables, traditional Korean herbs and rice served in beef broth, a variety of noodle dishes, and dozens of other treats from the Far East. If you are unfamiliar with Korean food, the helpful personnel will explain the dishes and how to eat them.

Speakeasies and their illegal activities are long gone from Gotham, but there are a few places that still have the flavor of past decades:
Apothéke (9 Doyers St, 212/406-0400, www.apothekenyc.com)
Bill's Gay Nineties (57 E 54th St, 212/355-0243, www.billsnyc.com)
Fanelli's Cafe (94 Prince St, 212/226-9412, www.fanellicafe.com)
Macao Trading Company (311 Church St, 212/431-8642)
Onieal's Grand Street (174 Grand St, 212/941-9119, www.onieals. com)
21 Club (21 W 52nd St, 212/582-7200, www.21club.com)

WOO LAE OAK SOHO

148 Mercer St (bet Prince and Houston St)   212/925-8200
Lunch, Dinner: Daily   www.woolaeoaksoho.com
Moderate to moderately expensive

In attractive Soho surroundings, one can choose from a large selection of hot and cold appetizers, as well as traditional Korean specialties. The best include Dungeness crab wrapped in spinach crepes and tuna tartare served over sliced Asian pears. Rice and side dishes such as seasoned seaweed, radish *kimchi,* and raw garlic are also available. The big draws are the barbecued items, cooked right at your table. Slices of beef, short ribs, chicken, lamb, pork, scallops, shrimp, tuna, veggies, and much more are available for barbecuing. The personnel are very helpful to beginners and seem genuinely pleased when diners show interest in their unique menu.

There's lots to like about **Il Buco** (47 Bond St, 212/533-1932): a warm, comfortable, antique-filled ambience; delicious Italian fare featuring seasonal ingredients; an outstanding wine list with a good selection by the glass; and rooms for special occasions. The *formaggi* dessert menu is worth special mention for delicious cheese tastes from around the world.

III. Where to Find It: Museums, Tours, Tickets, and More

A Week in New York

"I'm going to be in New York for a week. What do you recommend that I do?" I've been asked that question a thousand times in the last 50 years, and I'm always torn about how to answer. You could spend an entire lifetime in New York and still never see and do everything this fabulous city has to offer. If you're here for a week, the first things you need to do are gather information and make some choices.

My advice is to pick one or two places you really want to visit each day and build your itinerary around them. Because New York is so big, I suggest limiting your daily itinerary to just one or two neighborhoods. Also check to be sure that places you want to visit will be open on that day before you get too far along in your planning. You'll need to know that the Metropolitan Museum of Art, for instance, is closed on Mondays and the Museum of Modern Art is closed on Tuesdays. Many museums and other tourist spots have reduced hours in the winter months. Of course, some activities are seasonal: ice skating in Rockefeller Plaza can be done only in winter, while Shakespeare in the Park is offered only in summer.

Every trip to New York is different, and each person will have a different list of favorites. If you have friends who know New York, by all means ask for their recommendations. The following itinerary for a week in New York combines my own favorites with some of the absolute "don't miss" classics. Whether you follow this outline, take a friend's suggestions, or make up your own, remember that part of the pleasure of New York is simply taking it all in at your leisure. Whatever else you do, spend a little time just walking around!

MONDAY: Getting Oriented

- Buy the current edition of *Time Out New York*, and read the various "This Week in New York" sections over coffee.
- Stop by **NYC & Company** (810 Seventh Ave, at 53rd St), the city's main tourist information center, to pick up maps and brochures and ask any questions you may have.
- Take a **Hop-On Hop-Off** bus tour of Manhattan (Gray Line New York Sightseeing, 777 Eighth Ave, between 47th and 48th St, 212/445-0848, 800/669-0051).

- Lunch at **Sfoglia** (1402 Lexington Ave).
- Walk along Madison Avenue in the 60s and 70s, checking out all the big-name boutiques.
- Take a walk through Central Park.
- Dinner in one of the restaurants at **Time Warner Center** (10 Columbus Circle).

TUESDAY: Museum Mile
- Breakfast at **Norma's** at Le Parker Meridien Hotel (118 W 57th St).
- **Cooper-Hewitt National Design Museum** (2 E 91st St).
- **Solomon R. Guggenheim Museum** (1071 Fifth Ave).
- Lunch at the cafeteria in the **Metropolitan Museum of Art** (Fifth Ave bet 80th and 84th St).
- **Metropolitan Museum of Art** (see above).
- **Whitney Museum of American Art** (945 Madison Ave).
- Visit **The Apple Store** (767 Fifth Ave).
- Dinner at **Tao** (42 E 58th St).
- Take in a show on **Broadway** or at a comedy club.

WEDNESDAY: Midtown
- Stroll through **Rockefeller Plaza** (Fifth Ave bet 49th and 51st St).
- Stop by **St. Patrick's Cathedral** (Fifth Ave at 51st St).
- Lunch at **Grand Central Oyster Bar Restaurant** (Grand Central Terminal).
- Take the 12:30 p.m. tour of **Grand Central Terminal**, offered only on Wednesday by the Municipal Art Society.
- Visit the **New York Public Library** (Fifth Ave bet 40th and 42nd St).
- Spend the afternoon touring the **Museum of Modern Art** (11 W 53rd St).
- Dinner at **The Modern** (in the Museum of Modern Art).

THURSDAY: Upper West Side
- Start the day with a nosh at **Zabar's** (2245 Broadway).
- Stop by the **Cathedral Church of St. John the Divine** (Amsterdam Ave at 112th St).
- Stock up on sweets at **Mondel Chocolates** (2913 Broadway).
- Lunch at **Cafe Lalo** (201 W 83rd St).
- Spend the afternoon at **The Cloisters** (Fort Tryon Park).
- Dinner at **Barbetta** (321 W 46th St).
- Go see a Broadway show. Get tickets well in advance from **Americana Tickets**, or try your luck at a **TKTS** booth.

FRIDAY: Lower Manhattan
- Take the first ferry from Battery Park to the **Statue of Liberty** and **Ellis Island**.
- Walk up the **Battery Park Esplanade**.
- Stop by **Ground Zero** (along Church St, between Barclay and Liberty St) and observe the site of the September 11, 2001, terrorist attack.
- Lunch at **Balthazar** (80 Spring St).
- Stop by **St. Paul's Chapel** (209 Broadway).
- Visit the **United Nations** (First Ave bet 42nd and 47th St).
- Take a leisurely late afternoon stroll on the **Brooklyn Bridge**.
- Dinner at the **River Cafe** (1 Water St, Brooklyn).

- Go see a performance at **Lincoln Center**.

SATURDAY: Chelsea and Soho
- Shop at **ABC Carpet & Home** (888 Broadway).
- Browse the **Strand Book Store** (828 Broadway).
- Go gallery hopping on and around West 22nd Street in Chelsea.
- Have a late morning brunch at **2nd Avenue Deli** (162 E 33rd St).
- Go gallery hopping and shopping on and around West Broadway in Soho.
- Dinner at **Cucina** (200 Park Ave).
- Take a late-evening elevator ride up to the observation deck of the **Empire State Building** (Fifth Ave bet 33rd and 34th St).
- Walk along Fifth Avenue.

SUNDAY: Lower East Side
- Lunch at **Katz's Delicatessen** (205 E Houston St).
- Take the noon tour at the **Lower East Side Tenement Museum** (108 Orchard St).
- Take the 1 p.m. walking tour of the Lower East Side, sponsored by the Lower East Side Tenement Museum (see above).
- Visit the remarkable **Eldridge Street Synagogue** (12 Eldridge St).
- Dinner at **Le Périgord** (405 E 52nd Ave).

Information on all places listed in these itineraries can be found in other sections of this book. Whatever else you do during your visit, I have two final pieces of advice:

- Get to know the subway system. It is generally safe, reliable, convenient, inexpensive (particularly if you get a seven-day pass), and by far the most efficient way to travel in New York, unless you have mobility issues. If you take cabs everywhere, you'll burn both money and time.
- Slow down. New Yorkers move very fast. It is fun to get into the flow of things, but it is also good to pause and take a look around. Don't get so focused on your destination that you fail to savor the journey. New York is a remarkable city! Enjoy!

Top Ten Places to Visit in New York

There are certain places in New York that everyone has on their "must visit" list. I've listed mine here, in alphabetical order, for easy reference. I've also noted whether admission is free or if there is a nominal ($1 to $5), reasonable ($6 to $19), or expensive ($20 and up) admission fee; taxes and add-ons are extra.

AMERICAN MUSEUM OF NATURAL HISTORY
Central Park West (bet 77th and 81st St)   212/769-5100
Daily 10-5:45   www.amnh.org

Founded in 1869, this remarkable museum has taught generations of New York children and out-of-town visitors alike about the remarkable diversity of our planet and the natural world around us. It is hard to over-state the size of this sprawling place: the museum, the Hayden Planetarium, and the Rose Center for Earth and Space have 45 permanent exhibition halls in 25 interconnected buildings covering almost 20 acres. The museum alone has more than 32 million artifacts and specimens.

Like several other museums of its size in New York, the American Museum of Natural History can seem overwhelming. My advice is to go to the information desk when you first arrive, get a floor plan, and then sit down and think about where you would like to go. If you're planning to see an IMAX movie or the Space Show at the Rose Center, be sure to note the time on your ticket and plan the other parts of your visit accordingly. While the constantly changing special exhibits are often fascinating, be aware that they are also often very crowded. So, too, are some of the permanent exhibits, including the Hall of Biodiversity, the Akeley Hall of African Mammals, the Milstein Hall of Ocean Life, and the Hall of Human Origins. However, exhibits on the Northwest Coast and other Native Americans, as well as Asian, African, and Central and South American cultures, are often entirely empty even on busy days and yet full of fascinating items. Between all of the fossils, minerals, skeletons, and insects, there's really something for everyone. Plan to stay for at least a couple hours.

Guided tours are available, as are four eateries and more gift shops than you can count. Admission fee charged (reasonable).

If you're a garden lover and are willing to venture out of the more traveled parts of Manhattan or into the outer boroughs, try these gems:
- **Brooklyn Botanic Gardens**: 1000 Washington Avenue, Brooklyn (718/623-7200, www.bbg.org)
- **Heather Garden**: Fort Tryon Park at Fort Washington Avenue in northern Manhattan (www.nycgovparks.org)
- **New York Botanical Garden**: Bronx River Parkway at Fordham Road, The Bronx (718/817-8700, www.nybg.org)
- **Wave Hill**: W 249th Street and Independence Avenue, The Bronx (718/549-3200, www.wavehill.org)

CENTRAL PARK
Fifth Ave to Central Park West from 59th to 110th St

This urban gem was designed in 1858 by Frederick Law Olmsted, the same landscape architect who designed the U.S. Capitol grounds in Washington, D.C. Central Park occupies a rectangle in the heart of Manhattan that's bounded by Fifth Avenue on the East Side and Central Park West on the West Side. Its 843 acres of grass, rocky outcroppings, ponds, trees, and paths stretch from 59th Street to 110th Street. Tennis courts, baseball diamonds, playgrounds, a couple restaurants, ice-skating (in winter), miniature golf (in summer), and even a castle are all here! Thanks to the Central Park Conservancy, a nonprofit organization that began managing the park in 1980, it is all clean, safe, and wonderfully accessible to the 25 million people who use it every year.

Regardless of season, the best way to experience Central Park is just to walk in it. (If you ever get lost, it helps to know that the first digits of the number plate on the lampposts correspond to the nearest cross street.) There's so much to see and do in the park that it's almost a city within the city. Just about every New Yorker has a favorite spot. Some of my favorites include **Conservancy Gardens** (just off Fifth Avenue and 105th Street),

The Boathouse (near 72nd Street on the east side), **Central Park Zoo** (just off Fifth Avenue at 64th Street), **Belvedere Castle** (mid-park near 79th Street), and **Strawberry Fields** (near Central Park West, between 71st and 74th streets). You can get one of those quintessential New York photos standing on the rock outcroppings just inside the park off 59th Street and Avenue of the Americas.

Another great way to experience Central Park is by attending an event there. Particularly in the summer, it's home to everything from free concerts by the New York Philharmonic and the Metropolitan Opera, Shakespeare in the Park performances, and all sorts of other cultural events. For a complete listing of events, walking tours, and other park activities, go to www.central parknyc.org.

Skyscrapers by the Numbers

We all know that the **Empire State Building** is the city's tallest building, soaring 102 floors (or 1,250 feet) to the sky. The other leaders, in order of height, are the **Chrysler Building** (77 floors), the **GE Building** (70 floors), **70 Pine Street** (67 floors), and the **MetLife Building**, the **Woolworth Building**, and **Trump Tower** (58 floors).

EMPIRE STATE BUILDING

350 Fifth Ave (bet 33rd and 34th St)   212/736-3100
Daily: 8 a.m.-2 a.m. (last elevator at 1:15 a.m.)   www.esbnyc.org

When people think of New York, this 102-story building is often the first image that comes to mind. Soaring above its neighbors just south of downtown, this skyscraper was built in 1931 and has defined the New York City skyline ever since. Sometimes confused with its shorter uptown neighbor, the Chrysler Building, the Empire State Building is the tallest building in the city. (In case you're wondering, there are 1,860 steps from bottom to top!)

Lots of tourists from all over the world and fans of movies like *King Kong*, *An Affair to Remember*, and *Sleepless in Seattle* simply can't come to New York without visiting this landmark and its observation deck on the 86th floor. On a clear day, you can almost see forever. But be advised that wait lines are long, the lobby is crowded, and the staff is alternately bored and rude. It's also worth noting that the ticket desk and line to go through security are actually on the second floor. The lobby on the first floor is kept clear for all the office workers who actually work in the Empire State Building. If you really have your heart set on a visit here, consider coming early in the morning or late at night, or buying advance tickets online. Tickets to the 102nd floor observatory or for **Skyride** (a simulated helicopter ride over New York) cost extra, and the former can only be purchased on the 86th floor. An ESB Express Pass, although pricey, for all ages will put you at the front of all three lines. Admission fee charged (reasonable).

FIFTH AVENUE

London. Paris. Tokyo. They all have fashionable streets with out-of-sight rents. But nowhere in the world is quite as fashionable or quite as expensive as New York's Fifth Avenue.

Fifth Avenue starts down in Greenwich Village at **Washington Square Park**, and the **Empire State Building** is on Fifth Avenue between 33rd and 34th streets. However, when tourists say they want to visit Fifth Avenue, they mean midtown and the Upper East Side.

The stretch of Fifth Avenue between 42nd Street and 59th Street is the heart of New York. It was once lined with mansions and is still home to some of the grandest and most recognizable buildings in the city. They include the mid-Manhattan branch of the **New York Public Library** (at 42nd St), **Rockefeller Center** (between 48th and 50th St), **Saks Fifth Avenue** (at 50th St), **St. Patrick's Cathedral** (at 51st St), **Tiffany & Company** (at 57th St), and the **Plaza Hotel** (at 59th St). Relative new-comers like **The Apple Store** (between 58th and 59th St), **Niketown** (at 57th St), **The NBA Store** (at 52nd St), **American Girl Place** (at 49th St), and the **Build-a-Bear Workshop** (at 46th St) suggest what a tourist mecca Fifth Avenue has become.

The stretch of Fifth Avenue between 59th Street and 110th Street runs along the east side of Central Park. You'll find the **Neue Galerie New York** (at 86th St), the **National Academy Museum & School of Fine Art** (between 89th and 90th St), the **Jewish Museum** (at 92nd St), the **Museum of the City of New York** (between 103rd and 104th St), and **El Museo del Barrio** (at 104th St). When it is completed in a few years, the **Museum for African Art** will extend Museum Mile all the way to the top of Central Park, at 110th Street.

Like much of New York, the best way to see Fifth Avenue is on foot. The sidewalks running along Central Park are a particular pleasure. There's no subway line running on Fifth Avenue, although there are lots of buses and cabs. Traffic on Fifth Avenue is one-way heading south. One more tip: Under no circumstances should you go into a store on Fifth Avenue in midtown with "going out of business" signs in the windows. They have a habit of going out of business regularly!

You can tell a real New Yorker from a wanna-be if he or she:

- Refuses to refer to Sixth Avenue as Avenue of the Americas.
- Refers to the MetLife Building as the PanAm Building.
- Has never been to either the Empire State Building or the Statue of Liberty.
- Has never bought a bagel at a grocery store.
- Doesn't flinch when the dinner bill exceeds $300 for two people but also knows where to get a perfectly good meal for under $20.
- Doesn't own a car but rents one on weekends to go to Ikea and Home Depot—or doesn't have a driver's license at all.
- Never eats dinner before 8 p.m.
- Knows the differences between Lombardi's and John's and has a strong opinion about whose pizza is better.
- Buys the Sunday *New York Times* on Saturday night.
- Keeps a bike in the living room.
- Gives directions to cab drivers.
- Never rides a bus—but if he or she did, would exit via the back door.
- Swipes a MetroCard through the reader and knows the "Proceed" or "Try Again" beep without looking at the screen.

GUGGENHEIM MUSEUM
1071 Fifth Ave (at 89th St)   212/423-3500
Fri-Wed: 10-5:45 (Fri till 7:45)   www.guggenheim.org

The Solomon R. Guggenheim Museum began in 1939 as the Museum of Non-Objective Painting. It was created to house the growing art collection of American industrialist Solomon Guggenheim. His collection included the work of such contemporaries as Vasily Kandinsky, Paul Klee, and Marc Chagall, and many of those original pieces form the backbone of this remarkable museum today. Of course the collection has grown tremendously since it incorporates work from artists ranging from late 19th-century impressionists to contemporary artists.

Although Guggenheim museums in Berlin, Venice, and Bilbao, Spain, showcase parts of the collection, the museum on Fifth Avenue is still *the* Guggenheim. In addition to the works displayed inside, people put this world-famous museum at the top of their itineraries because of its instantly recognizable building. It's an inverted ziggurat that looks a bit like a snail from the outside and allows visitors on the inside to wind their way through the collection rather than roaming in and out of rooms. The Guggenheim was designed by Frank Lloyd Wright and sits at the north end of Museum Mile, right across Fifth Avenue from Central Park. It opened in 1959 and underwent an extensive renovation for its 50th anniversary. Stand across the street to get the best architectural view.

In some ways, the breadth of the Guggenheim's collection rivals that of the Museum of Modern Art (in midtown) and the Metropolitan Museum of Art (a few blocks south on Fifth Avenue). But the great pleasure of the Guggenheim is that it's a bit smaller and more intimate than its famous cousins, giving art lovers time to linger. If 20th-century art is your passion, then there's no place you'll rather spend a day! Admission fee charged (reasonable).

LINCOLN CENTER   212/546-2656
Columbus Ave bet 62nd and 65th St   www.lincolncenter.org

Just as Museum Mile along Fifth Avenue is the most stunning concentration of art anywhere in the world, the 16-acre Lincoln Center campus may be the world's most stunning concentration of performing arts institutions. The **Julliard School of Music** is housed here, as are the **New York City Ballet**, the **New York City Opera**, the **Chamber Music Society of Lincoln Center**, the **New York Philharmonic**, and the **Metropolitan Opera**. There is also a branch of the **New York Public Library** devoted entirely to the performing arts.

A year-long celebration and major renovations to the campus marked Lincoln Center's 50th anniversary in 2009. If you want to peek inside some of the concert halls and other spaces here, daily tours are available (212/875-5350). You're also welcome to wander around and enjoy the fountains, open terraces, and other public spaces. Each of the several stops are well worth your time. And if you're interested in seeing one of the hundreds of performances that take place here every year, call the **Lincoln Center Events Hotline** (212/546-2656) for current information. Seeing a production at Lincoln Center is a special only-in-New-York treat!

METROPOLITAN MUSEUM OF ART

1000 Fifth Avenue (bet 80th and 84th St)   212/535-7710
Tues-Sun: 9:30-5:30; Fri-Sat: 9:30-9   www.metmuseum.org

Five thousand years of art. That's how the Metropolitan Museum of Art ("The Met," as its known to New Yorkers and art fans) describes its holdings. It's all here: Egyptian tombs. Greek sculptures. African masks. European and Japanese arms and armor. Vases from China. Early American furniture. Tiffany windows. Nineteenth-century costumes. Twentieth-century photography. And no matter how many times you visit or how much time you spend here, there's just no way you'll ever see it all. The depth and breadth of The Met's collection is unparalleled.

There are several ways to approach touring The Met. I suggest coming early on a weekday morning, getting a copy of the floor plan at the information desk, and figuring out a couple areas of the museum you want to visit over the course of a day. You can always break for lunch at one of the museum's several restaurants or end your day with a drink at **The Balcony Cafe and Bar**. Another alternative is taking a "Museum Highlights" tour, offered regularly in various languages. My favorite strategy is simply going where everyone else isn't. Crowds can be overwhelming on weekends and whenever there's a special exhibit. Buying advanced admission online is a good way to avoid long lines.

A favorite part of any Met visit for many people is a trip to one of the museum's many stores. Although you can now visit Met gift stores at LaGuardia and Kennedy airports, as well as at Rockefeller Plaza, it's more fun browsing the shops inside The Met itself. Admission fee charged (expensive). Same-day admission to **The Cloisters Museums and Gardens** in northern Manhattan's Fort Tryon Park is included.

MUSEUM OF MODERN ART

11 W 53rd St (bet Fifth Ave and Ave of the Americas) 212/708-9400
Wed-Mon: 10:30-5:30 (Fri till 8)   www.moma.org

This museum is itself a masterpiece, filled with glass and soaring spaces. On West 53rd Street just off Fifth Avenue in midtown, MoMA (pronounced MO-ma) is the leading museum in the world dedicated to modern art. Well over 150,000 pieces of art—paintings, prints, photography, sculpture—are housed here, along with a remarkable archive and film library. From Cezanne, van Gogh, Matisse, and Picasso to Jasper Johns, Jeff Koons, Georgia O'Keeffe, and Jackson Pollack, just about any artist you can imagine is represented. Indeed, MoMA's sleek galleries are a Who's Who of modern art history.

MoMA's curatorial departments include Architecture and Design; Drawings, Painting and Sculpture; Photography, Prints and Illustrated Books; Film; and Media. Pieces from each department are always on display in various collection galleries. In addition, MoMA has changing exhibitions and often hosts special traveling exhibitions. If you have time, I suggest starting on the sixth floor and working your way down. If you want a quick tour of some of the museum's most famous holdings—including van Gogh's *Starry Night*, Picasso's *Guitar*, Matisse's *Dance (1)*, and Andy Warhol's *Campbell's Soup Cans*—stop by the information desk and get a map.

A visit to this amazing place is not complete without a stop at the MoMA

Bookstore (just off the foyer on the first floor) and the MoMA Design Store (across the street). Although there is some overlap between the two stores, there are enough differences to make it well worth your time to peruse both, as well as lunch at either of the two cafes at MoMA or dinner at The Modern, a high-end restaurant. Admission fee charged (expensive). Some films carry an additional charge. Admission to PS 1, an affiliated museum in Long Island City, is free if you show your MoMA ticket stub within 30 days.

STATUE OF LIBERTY

New York Harbor (south of Battery Park)   212/363-3200
Daily: 9-5 (adjusted seasonally)   www.nps.gov/stli

They call her Lady Liberty. This 151-foot bronze statue of a woman holding a torch was created by Frederic-Auguste Bartholdi and given to the United States as a gift from France in 1886. Standing on Liberty Island in New York Harbor, it's probably the single most iconic sight in all of New York. For generations of immigrants who came through nearby Ellis Island, it was also the first real sight they had of this new land. The words from "The New Colossus," a poem written by Emma Lazarus to help raise money for the completion of the pedestal for this powerful monument, still expresses the most noble instincts of our country and the symbolism of the Statue of Liberty: "Give me your tired, your poor/Your huddled masses yearning to breathe free."

A trip out to Liberty Island and the Statue of Liberty will take the better part of a morning or afternoon, so plan accordingly. Both the Statue of Liberty and Ellis Island are run by the National Park Service. Visiting either or both requires a trip by boat from Battery Park. Head to Castle Clinton in Battery Park for tickets and detailed information, or buy your tickets in advance from www.statuecruises.com or by calling 877/ *LADYTIX*. Even if you have tickets, you'll need to wait in line for the next available boat. My advice: go early on a weekday and bring along lots of patience. Lady Liberty's crown was reopened to the public for the first time since September 11, 2001, on July 4th, 2009. Free admission; ferry ticket (reasonable) is required.

TIMES SQUARE

42nd St at Broadway and surrounding area   www.timessquarenyc.org

When I first starting writing this book, Times Square was synonymous with petty crime, prostitution, and filth. Not anymore. In fact, I find it hard to believe that the Times Square of yesteryear and the Times Square of the 21st century are the same place. Named for the original New York Times building and incorporating the neighborhood around 42nd Street and Broadway, Times Square is now a center of New York's burgeoning tourist industry. It's full of family-friendly restaurants, hotels, and entertainment venues. **Madame Toussaud's** wax museum; a **Toys "R" Us** superstore, complete with a real Ferris wheel; and **ESPN Zone** are just a few of the hundreds of family-oriented attractions that have sprouted up here. There's even a terrific tourist information center at 1560 Broadway (between 46th and 47th streets), and a long-awaited TKTS booth located under the red steps in Father Duffy Square at Broadway and 47th Street.

All of those changes do not, however, put Times Square at the top of my

"Top Ten" list of places to visit. The whole area is wildly crowded with out-of-towners. In fact, it's a bit like going to a big mall somewhere in the non-descript suburbs around the winter holidays, except that you have to deal with traffic and there are few bargains to be had.

Picnicking

A picnic in New York City can be as simple as takeout on a park bench, homemade sandwiches with a few extra goodies tossed in a backpack, or an elaborately catered affair with china, fine linens, and cushy chairs and tables. The locations are limitless—rooftops, parks, marinas, or gardens. Perhaps you already have a favorite spot. If not, check with the **New York City Department of Parks and Recreation** (www.nycgovparks.org) for a list of possibilities, including the available facilities. And what to eat? Chapter IV (Food Shops) is chock full of possibilities for filling a picnic basket. What a perfect way to spend a sunny day in the city!

The Best of the Rest

The previous "Top Ten" list includes the museums and sights everyone wants to see when they come to New York. Although many of the museums and sights on that list are definite "must-sees," they are by no means all there is to New York. In fact, some of *my* "must-sees" are less well known, smaller, or a bit off the beaten path. The following list includes what I consider to be among the crown jewels of this remarkable city.

AMERICAN FOLK ART MUSEUM
45 W 53rd St (at Ave of the Americas)   212/265-1040
Tues-Sun: 10:30-5:30 (Fri till 7:30)   www.folkartmuseum.org

The American Folk Art Museum's architecturally award-winning building is half the reason to visit this gem. A sleek and beautiful addition to midtown, it is filled with light and interesting spaces. The museum's collection of American paintings, textiles, and other folk art spans several centuries and is thoughtfully displayed in galleries and public spaces throughout the eight-story building. The museum's cafe and gift shop are excellent. The museum offers free live music Friday evenings in the atrium. Admission fee charged (reasonable).

BROOKLYN BRIDGE
near City Hall Park in Lower Manhattan

Spanning the East River, this spectacular suspension bridge links Lower Manhattan to Brooklyn. It took 15 years and two generations to build. After its designer, John Roebling, was killed in an accident, his son Washington and wife Emily took over the project. Pedestrians and bicyclists share the bridge's historic promenade; bicyclists have the north lane, pedestrians the south. To reach the bridge, go to the east side of City Hall Park, just off Broadway, and follow the signs. Sunset and sunrise are particularly beautiful times to take a stroll on the bridge, although it's open 24 hours a day.

CATHEDRAL CHURCH OF ST. JOHN THE DIVINE

1047 Amsterdam Ave (at 112th St)   212/316-7540
Mon-Sat: 7-6 (Sun till 7)   www.stjohndivine.org

Gracing Amsterdam Avenue on the east side of Columbia University, the Cathedral Church of St. John the Divine is one of the largest Christian houses of worship in the world. And it isn't even finished! Part Gothic, part Romanesque, and part Byzantine, this magnificent Episcopal cathedral is so big that the Statue of Liberty could easily fit inside the main sanctuary. For information about daily tours, call 212/932-7347. Admission is free, but donations are accepted and a minimal fee is charged for tours.

Ground Zero

Just the words *Ground Zero* evoke graphic scenes emblazoned in our collective memory of the terrorist attacks upon the twin towers of the World Trade Center on September 11, 2001. Tens of thousands worked here every day, and more than 3,000 people from over a hundred countries lost their lives on that fateful day. It's not a museum, and it feels odd to call it an attraction. In fact, despite groundbreaking in 2004 for a new Freedom Tower on the site, there's not much to see except the retaining wall that continues to hold back the Hudson River and a vast amount of empty space. But hundreds of thousands of people visiting New York every year stop to pay their respects. Church, Liberty, Barclay, and West streets form the boundaries of the site. Most visitors make a stop at the Wall of Heroes along Church Street. The glass-enclosed back wall of the World Financial Center, directly across West Street from Ground Zero, also offers a good view of the site.

The September 11 Families Association has created a **Tribute WTC Visitor Center** (120 Liberty St, between Greenwich and Church St). Family members, neighbors, and others directly affected by the events of September 11 lead tours of the site, and galleries display various items relating to the World Trade Center and those who died there. (For more information, go to www.tributewtc.org or call 212/393-9160.) A reasonable donation is requested.

Perhaps the most moving of the many other memorials is an exhibit inside **St. Paul's Chapel** called "Unwavering Spirit: Hope and Healing at Ground Zero." A gathering place for thousands fleeing the destruction on September 11, the chapel is located on Broadway between Fulton and Vesey streets. The exhibit is open Monday through Saturday from 10 to 6 and Sunday from 8 to 4. Admission is free.

THE CLOISTERS MUSEUMS AND GARDENS

Fort Tryon Park   212/923-3700
Tues-Sun: 9:30-5

Perhaps the finest medieval art museum in the world, this branch of the Metropolitan Museum of Art is also one of the quietest and most beautiful places in all of New York. Built at the far north end of the island on land donated by John D. Rockefeller, Jr., in the late 1930s, the museum incorporates large sections of cloisters and other medieval buildings brought from Europe. Tapestries, ivories, paintings, sculptures, and other decorative items are part of the spectacular collection on display. From the outdoor terrace, you can look out at the medieval gardens, the Hudson River, and the Palisades beyond, easily forgetting that you're in a 21st-century city. Admission fee charged (expensive). Same-day admission to the Metropolitan Museum of Art is included in the price.

New York-ese

Many places in America have their own special words and phrases that people from elsewhere don't understand. Here are some terms commonly heard in New York:

Bridge and tunnel crowd: a disparaging term for visitors from New Jersey; also "B&T crowd"

The City: shorthand for New York City

Coffee regular: coffee with milk and sugar

The FDR: Franklin Roosevelt Drive, an expressway running the length of Manhattan's East Side along the East River

Fuhgeddaboudit: "Forget about it," as in "Don't mention it." It can also mean "No way."

The Garden: Madison Square Garden

Houston: a street in lower Manhattan, pronounced *HOUSE-ton*

The Island: Long Island

The Met: the Metropolitan Opera or Metropolitan Museum of Art

Schlep: as a verb, to drag or haul something; as a noun, a jerk

Shmeer: a smear of cream cheese, usually on a bagel

Slice: a piece of pizza

Soda: any sweet carbonated beverage; short for "soda pop"

COOPER-HEWITT NATIONAL DESIGN MUSEUM
2 E 91st St (at Fifth Ave)   212/849-8400
Mon-Fri: 10-5; Sat: 10-6; Sun: noon-**6**   www.ndm.si.edu

Founded as the Cooper Union Museum for the Arts of Decoration in 1897, this remarkable institution became part of the Smithsonian Institution in 1967. Its exhibitions, covering 24 centuries of every facet of design, are consistently well conceived and interesting. But what I really love about the Cooper-Hewitt is that it's housed in Andrew Carnegie's 64-room mansion. The Great Hall and the gardens are particular pleasures! Incidentally, if you're interested in seeing how a few other of New York's wealthiest citizens lived a hundred years ago, take a trip to the Rockefeller Rooms, on the fifth floor of the Museum of the City of New York, and Mr. Morgan's Library and Study, at the Morgan Library and Museum. Admission fee charged (reasonable).

FRICK COLLECTION
1 E 70th St (at Fifth Ave)   212/288-0700
Tues-Sat: 10-6; Sun: 11-5   www.frick.org

This elegant mansion takes my breath away! Built by industrialist Henry Clay Frick almost a century ago to house his growing art collection, the Frick Collection is one of the last great mansions on Fifth Avenue and on the very top of my "must-see" list in New York. Gilbert Stuart's portrait of George Washington is here, as are works by Vermeer, Rembrandt, El Greco,

Goya, and masters ranging from the Italian Renaissance to the 19th century. But it isn't just the paintings that dazzle. Frick's collection also includes stunning Oriental rugs, Chinese porcelain, Limoge enamels, and a wide range of decorative arts that must be seen to be believed. Take time to wander, looking at everything from the paintings to the light fixtures to the rugs, and outside at the serene Garden Court. Take note: Children under 10 are not allowed into the Frick and children from age 10 to 16 must be accompanied by an adult. Admission fee charged (reasonable).

GRAND CENTRAL TERMINAL
42nd St bet Vanderbilt and Lexington Ave   212/340-2583
Daily: 5:30 a.m.-2:00 a.m.   www.grandcentralterminal.com

New York's past, present, and future come together in this marble palace. Opened in 1913, Grand Central is first and foremost a train station, home to hundreds of commuter trains that operate between Manhattan and points north in Westchester County and Connecticut. It also plays host to an upscale food market, dozens of shops featuring everything from toys to lingerie, and a great food court downstairs. (Stores and restaurants keep shorter hours.) You'll even find safe public bathrooms! Come in the Vanderbilt Avenue entrance and watch the action from the balcony. There's no charge to wander around the terminal.

JEWISH MUSEUM
1109 Fifth Ave (at 92nd St)   212/423-3200
Sat-Thurs: 11-5:45 (Thurs till 8)   www.thejewishmuseum.org

The Jewish Museum (an independent nonprofit organization) is housed in yet another grand Fifth Avenue mansion. This one was donated by Felix Warburg's widow in 1945. (Warburg was a Jewish philanthropist.) The museum houses the largest collection of Jewish art and Judaica in the United States, showcasing 4,000 articles of Jewish culture. Some pieces were rescued from European synagogues and Jewish communities before and during World War II. The heart of the museum is "Culture and Continuity: The Jewish Journey." This two-floor exhibit features 800 works from around the world. A visit to the museum's excellent gift shop or Celebrations, a smaller design shop in an adjacent brownstone, is well worth an extra half-hour. Admission fee charged (reasonable); free to everyone on Saturday.

LOWER EAST SIDE TENEMENT MUSEUM
108 Orchard St (bet Delancey and Broome St)   212/431-0233
Mon-Fri: 11-6 (Mon till 5:30); Sat-Sun: 10:45-6   www.tenement.org

Whether or not you're one of the hundreds of thousands of people in this country whose family traces its arrival in this country to the Lower East Side, a visit to this living history museum is another one of my "must-sees" in New York. Every tour starts at the visitors center and then crosses the street to the tenement building at 97 Orchard Street, where various apartments are frozen in time. Home to as many as 7,000 people from more than 20 nations between 1863 and 1935, this building is a living memorial to the hundreds of thousands of people who passed through the Lower East Side as immigrants to this country. A new guided tour is "The Moores: An Irish

Family in America." Depending on the tour, you'll encounter various immigrant families modeled on real people who lived in this building between the 1870s and the 1930s. A walking tour of the Lower East Side is also available on weekends in warmer months. Take time for the excellent 25-minute film about the history of immigration on the Lower East Side, which runs continuously at the visitors center. Take time to browse in the excellent gift shop, too. It costs nothing to enter the visitors center. Fee charged (reasonable) for tours; reservations strongly suggested.

MORGAN LIBRARY AND MUSEUM
225 Madison Ave (at 36th St)   212/685-0008
Tues-Thurs: 10:30-5; Fri: 10:30-9; Sat: 10:30-6; Sun: 11-6
www.themorgan.org

Two rooms make a visit to this out-of-the-way museum well warranted: Mr. Morgan's Library and Study. Designed in the early 20th century to house the astonishing collection amassed by Pierpont Morgan (an industrialist and financier), these two elegant rooms and their contents will transport you to another time and place. Just imagine yourself surrounded by these paintings, sculptures, furniture, books, architectural details, and textiles spanning many centuries and several continents! It's hard to believe anyone ever lived like this. Morgan's collection includes historical, artistic, literary, and musical works. The spaces in the rest of the museum, including an atrium and other galleries, are often crowded and feel a bit disjointed. However, this is a good place to eat. Admission fee charged (reasonable).

Real estate developers have had their hands in the demise or disfigurement of the Lower East Side tenements ever since immigration slowed in the 1920s. When they haven't been completely replaced by high-rises, drastic renovations have left these vestiges of mass immigration unrecognizable from their previous historical architecture. The National Trust for Historic Preservation has added this area, once one of the most crowded communities on Earth, to its endangered list. What was long a colorful shopping area has greatly changed. You'll not find the bargains or selections of past years, but a Sunday visit to Orchard Street is still an experience.

MUSEUM OF THE CITY OF NEW YORK
1220 Fifth Ave (bet 103rd and 104th St)   212/534-1672
Tues-Sun: 10-5   www.mcny.org

Why this museum and the New-York Historical Society don't merge their massive holdings and consolidate their operations is beyond me. Both are dedicated to preserving the history of New York from the earliest European settlement, and both have remarkable collections. For the casual visitor, the Museum of the City of New York is probably the more accessible of the two. It's certainly the most family friendly. With three floors of changing and permanent exhibits, the museum also offers an exceptional array of children's programs, lectures, classes, and other events. Admission fee charged (reasonable).

MUSEUM OF JEWISH HERITAGE: A LIVING MEMORIAL TO THE HOLOCAUST

36 Battery Place (inside Battery Park City)   646/437-4200
Sun-Tues: 10-5:45; Wed: 10-8; Thurs: 10-5:45;   www.mjhnyc.org
Fri: 10-5 (till 3 during EDT)

This remarkable and sometimes overlooked museum just north of Battery Park in Lower Manhattan manages to be not only a memorial to those who perished in the Holocaust but also a vibrant, life-affirming celebration of Jewish culture and its endurance. Using first-person narratives and a remarkably diverse collection, the museum's three-part permanent display tells the unfolding story of Jewish life a century ago, the persecution of Jews and the Holocaust, and modern Jewish life and renewal in the decades since. Both the cafe, which has amazing views of the Statue of Liberty and New York Harbor, and the museum's gift shop are worthy of a visit. Andy Goldsworthy's *Garden of Stone* outside the museum is a terrific spot to sit and think. Because of the sobering subject matter, this may not be a place to take young children, and all visitors should be prepared to take their time. Admission fee charged (reasonable).

Historic Churches and Synagogues

Because New York was a British colony for much of its early history, the city's lower half is full of historic Episcopal churches. They include **Trinity Church** (Broadway at Wall St); **St. Paul's Chapel**, the oldest church building in the city, dating from 1764 (Broadway between Fulton and Vesey St); **St. Mark's Church in-the-Bowery**, constructed on the site of Peter Stuyvesant's personal chapel in 1799 (10th St at Third Ave); **Grace Church** (Broadway between 10th and 11th St); and the **Church of the Transfiguration**, also known as "the Little Church Around the Corner" (Fifth Ave at 29th St).

Other historic houses of worship in Manhattan include **Abyssinian Baptist Church** (132 Odell Clark Pl), **Central Synagogue** (Lexington Ave at 55th St), **Marble Collegiate Church** (1 W 29th St), **Riverside Church** (490 Riverside Dr), the **Spanish and Portuguese Synagogue** (8 W 70th St), the **Bialystoker Synagogue** (7-11 Willet St), and **Temple Emanu-El** (1 E 65th St).

NEW YORK PUBLIC LIBRARY

455 Fifth Ave (bet 40th and 42nd St)   212/340-0833
Mon-Wed: 9-9; Thurs-Sat: 10-6; Sun: 1-5   www.nypl.org

This mid-Manhattan branch of the New York Public Library is a working library and has the largest collection of circulating and reference works in the entire system. It's also home to a wide range of public programs. But this isn't just any library! Located along Fifth Avenue, it's a "must-see" if you're in midtown. Standing guard out front are two stately lions, named Patience and Fortitude by former mayor Fiorello LaGuardia. Inside you'll find marble staircases, an excellent gift shop, the dramatic Rose Main Reading Room on the third floor (enhanced with Wi-Fi and laptop docking), an amazing map room on the first floor, and various gallery spaces. Stop by the information desk in the breathtaking lobby to find out about the frequent tours offered by the Friends of the New York Public Library. Free admission.

ROOSEVELT ISLAND
East River, between Manhattan and Queens

If you're a photographer looking for that perfect shot of the Manhattan skyline, a trip to Roosevelt Island should be at the top of your itinerary. At various times in its history, Roosevelt Island was known as Blackwell's Island and Welfare Island, and it's been home to prisons, hospitals, and asylums. Today this two-mile island in the middle of the East River is home to 18,000 residents, many of whom commute into Manhattan each day. Visitors come for the view, particularly from the tram and from the northwest tip of Lighthouse Park. The four-minute tram ride from Manhattan leaves from a small station at Second Avenue and 59th Street. The tram to Roosevelt Island runs daily from 6 a.m.-2 a.m. (Fri and Sat till 3:30 a.m.) for a nominal fare of $2.

> Because of ongoing security concerns, the **New York Stock Exchange** is no longer open to the public.

ST. PATRICK'S CATHEDRAL
Fifth Ave between 50th and 51st St   212/753-2261
Daily: 6:30 a.m.-8:30 p.m.   www.saintpatrickscathedral.org

Designed in the middle of the 19th century by famed architect James Renwick, Jr., this Gothic cathedral is a much-loved Fifth Avenue landmark and the largest Roman Catholic church in the United States. The main organ has over 9,000 pipes, and the sanctuary can seemingly seat half of Manhattan. Whether you're here for a service or just peeking inside, it's hard to overstate the beauty and elegance of St. Patrick's. Please remember that this is an active church. Mass is said several times each day, eight times on Sunday, and even more on Holy Days. You are welcome to come in and light a candle or just sit in silence. Here's a tip: the cathedral's steps along Fifth Avenue are one of the best places in New York for resting your feet and watching the world go by! Free admission.

STATEN ISLAND FERRY
Whitehall Ferry Terminal (at the foot of Whitehall St)
                                              www.siferry.com

Eight different ferries make 109 trips every day between Staten Island and the Whitehall Ferry Terminal on Manhattan's southern tip. The trip takes 25 minutes and covers five miles. And what a trip it is! Like the ferries that traverse Puget Sound near Seattle, the Staten Island ferries offer some of the very best views and a comfortable place to sit and take them in. Best of all, the Staten Island ferry is free! Just show up anytime of day or night and there will be a sailing again soon.

TRINITY CHURCH
74 Trinity Place (Broadway at Wall St)   212/602-0800
Museum: Mon-Fri: 9-11:45 and 1-3:45; Sat: 10-3:45; Sun 1-3:45
                                          www.trinitywallstreet.org

In the heart of lower Manhattan's Financial District, this is the third Episcopal church to occupy a site on land donated by King William III of England in 1698. This building was completed in 1846, although the headstones in the 2.5-acre graveyard date back to the late 17th century. Believe it or not, Trinity Church was the tallest building in Manhattan for most of the 19th century. Today it offers a small museum, guided tours, and concerts, in addition to daily worship services. Admission is free, but donations are accepted.

Outside Manhattan

Just because I've limited this guide to museums and sights in Manhattan doesn't mean that there aren't places in other boroughs worth exploring. The **New York Transit Museum** in Brooklyn (718/694-1600, www.mta.info/museum) should be at the top of the list for anyone interested in trains and subways. **The Brooklyn Museum** (718/638-5000, www.brooklynmuseum.org) is one of the country's most prestigious museums and has one of the best Egyptian collections in the world. The recently renovated and expanded **Bronx Museum of the Arts** (718/638-5000, www.brooklynmuseum.org) offers wonderful opportunities to see new and emerging artists through its Arts in the Marketplace program. The **New York Hall of Science** in Queens (718/699-0005, www.nyscience.org), the **Bronx Zoo** (718/367-1010, www.bronxzoo.org), and the **Liberty Science Center**, just across the Hudson River in New Jersey (201/200-1000, www.lsc.org), are all world-class destinations.

UNITED NATIONS
First Ave bet 42nd and 47th St   212/963-4440 (tours)
Building: daily: 9-5 (closed weekends in Jan and Feb) www.un.org/tours
Tours: Mon-Fri: 9:45-4:45

New York is a great American city, but it is also a great *international* city and the headquarters of the United Nations. The flags of 192 member nations fly along First Avenue in front of the General Assembly building, and many languages are spoken on the streets in this area as delegates come and go. You can visit the beautiful and peaceful grounds of the UN, wander through the changing exhibits in the large lobby, or go inside the main building for a tour. Whatever else you do, be sure to visit the stores in the basement, as well as the UN's very own post office. Fee charged for tours (reasonable); children must be at least five years of age. There is no charge to enter the building.

WHITNEY MUSEUM OF AMERICAN ART
945 Madison Ave (at 75th St)   212/570-3676
Wed-Thurs and Sat-Sun: 11-6; Fri: 1-9   www.whitney.org

The artist and art collector Gertrude Vanderbilt Whitney started this museum in 1931 with her personal collection of 20th-century art. It has grown in the years since (and moved twice) while remaining true to its mission of collecting and displaying modern American art. Of course, that mission means the Whitney's remarkable collection now spans more than a century and continues to expand. It includes the world's largest collections of Edward Hopper, Reginald Marsh, and Alexander Calder, as well as sculptures, paintings, drawings, media installations, and other works by established and emerging artists. A branch of Sarabeth's Kitchen, long a popular East Side restaurant, is located on the museum's lower level. Admission fee charged (reasonable).

Smaller Museums and Special Spots

AMERICAN NUMISMATIC SOCIETY
75 Varick St (at Canal St), 11th floor   212/571-4470
Mon-Fri: 10-4   www.numismatics.org

The American Numismatic Society moved to a new location in 2008, allowing visitors and members better access to the 800,000 coins, medals, paper currency, and other artifacts in their vast collection. There is a library and also a research area. On loan to the Federal Reserve Bank of New York is a fascinating display ("Drachmas, Doubloons, and Dollars: The History of Money") of some of the highlights of the society's collection. Free admission.

AMERICAS SOCIETY GALLERY
680 Park Ave (at 68th St)   212/249-8950
Wed-Sat: noon-6   www.americas-society.org

The Americas Society was founded in 1965 by David Rockefeller with the simple but important goal of furthering understanding between the Americas. The changing exhibitions in its small but elegant gallery space showcase the diverse work of artists from throughout the Americas. Free admission.

ASIA SOCIETY AND MUSEUM
725 Park Ave (at 70th St)   212/288-6400
Tues-Sun: 11-6 (Fri till 9)   www.asiasociety.org

Drawing upon private collections and its own extensive holdings of art from more than 30 Asia-Pacific nations, the Asia Society mounts changing exhibits of traditional and contemporary art. By all means visit the lovely Garden Court Cafe, and a boutique that stocks items by Asian and Asian-American designers. Admission fee charged (reasonable).

BARD GRADUATE CENTER
18 W 86th St (at Central Park West)   212/501-3000
Tues-Sun: 11-5 (Thurs till 8)   www.bgc.bard.edu

The Bard Graduate School is known around the world for its passionate commitment to the decorative arts, design, and culture. Its beautiful townhouse on the Upper West Side hosts several changing exhibits each year. Admission fee charged (nominal).

BRYANT PARK
Ave of the Americas bet 40th and 42nd St   www.bryantpark.org

This park symbolizes for me the remarkable transformation that has occurred throughout the city in the past 30 years. Long a place to be avoided, Bryant Park is now a thriving part of the city's life. Home to a wonderful carousel, an ice rink in winter, free movies in summer, and chess and backgammon games throughout the year, this urban jewel sits behind the New York Public Library. Have lunch, go to an event, or just wander through. Free Wi-Fi is provided.

CHELSEA ART MUSEUM
556 W 22nd St (at Eleventh Ave)   212/255-0719
Tues-Sat: 11-6 (Thurs till 8)   www.chelseaartmuseum.org

This museum is dedicated to showcasing the work of artists from the 20th and 21st centuries whose work is not as well known in the United States as it is in their home countries. It's a great stop if you're gallery-hopping in Chelsea. The Jean Miotte Foundation is also housed here. Admission fee charged (reasonable).

CHINA INSTITUTE
125 E 65th St (bet Lexington and Park Ave)   212/744-8181
Daily: 10-5 (Tues and Thurs till 8)   www.chinainstitute.org

This is the only not-for-profit gallery in New York (other than the Metropolitan Museum of Art) dedicated to showcasing the traditional art of China. Changing exhibits in this beautiful East Side townhouse are of consistently high quality. Admission fee charged (nominal).

You Can't Take It With You
If you are heading out for a day of gallery and museum hopping, take stock of what you are toting. Many institutions ban laptops, backpacks, luggage, and large shopping bags. Some establishments offer lockers or coat-check facilities for these items, but many refuse to store visitors' valuables.

DRAWING CENTER
35 Wooster St (bet Grand and Broome St)   212/219-2166
Tues-Fri: 10-6; Sat: 11-6   www.drawingcenter.org

Dedicated exclusively to showcasing contemporary and historical drawings, this Soho institution mounts highly regarded changing exhibitions. Free admission.

DYCKMAN FARMHOUSE MUSEUM
4881 Broadway (at 204th St)   212/304-9422
Wed-Sat: 11-4; Sun: noon-4   www.dyckmanfarmhouse.org

This is the last surviving example of the sort of farmhouse built all over New York well into the 19th century. It is a little time machine sitting on what was once Kingsbridge Road (now known as Broadway). There are some particularly good family programs. Admission fee charged (nominal).

EL MUSEO DEL BARRIO
1230 Fifth Ave (at 104th St)   212/831-7272
www.elmuseo.org

This museum is closed for renovation until late 2009. El Museo del Barrio means "Museum of the Neighborhood" in Spanish. It was founded by artists and community activists as a place to showcase the diverse art of Puerto Rico and Latin America. Call or check their website for the latest information.

FEDERAL HALL NATIONAL MEMORIAL
26 Wall St (bet Broad and William St)   212/825-6888
Mon-Fri: 9-5   www.nps.gov/feha

Everyone knows that Washington, D.C., is the nation's capital, but it didn't start out that way. In fact, George Washington was inaugurated on this spot in the first Federal Hall (torn down in 1812 and rebuilt in 1842), which served briefly as the U.S. Capitol. After extensive renovations, this National Park Service site hosts a small gallery and an information center largely focused on Lower Manhattan. Free admission.

FORBES MAGAZINE GALLERIES
62 Fifth Ave (at 12th St)   212/206-5548
Tues, Wed, Fri, Sat: 10-4   www.forbesgalleries.com

Tucked beside the lobby of the Forbes Magazine building, these little galleries showcase some of the diverse collections of the late Malcolm Forbes and his sons. You can see 10,000 toy soldiers and related figurines, 500 toy boats, and even a 1920 edition of the Landlord's Game—the forerunner of today's Monopoly. Gone are the eggs and other pieces from the House of Fabergé. Instead there are rotating exhibits. Free admission.

FRAUNCES TAVERN MUSEUM
54 Pearl St (at Broad St)   212/425-1778
Mon-Sat: noon-5   www.frauncestavernmuseum.org

Fraunces Tavern was a meeting place for the Sons of Liberty before the Revolutionary War and the site of General George Washington's farewell address to his officers after the war. Its history can be traced back to 1719 and it is the oldest surviving structure in Manhattan. The first floor still operates as a restaurant (call 212/968-1776 for reservations), while the second floor is dedicated to a museum focused largely on the Revolutionary War period. Admission fee charged (nominal).

HISPANIC SOCIETY OF AMERICA
Audubon Terrace (Broadway bet 155th and 156th St)   212/926-2234
Tues-Sat: 10-4:30   www.hispanicsociety.org

The former farm of naturalist John James Audubon seems like an unlikely place for the Hispanic Society of America, and a man named Archer Milton Huntington sounds like an unlikely benefactor. But the most significant collection of paintings, textiles, ceramics, photographs, and other items from the Iberian Peninsula and Latin America in North America indeed sits atop Audubon's farm and was largely assembled by Huntington. If you're interested in the subject, a trek up to this out-of-the-way spot will be well worth your time. An exceptional reference library is also housed here. Free admission.

INTERNATIONAL CENTER OF PHOTOGRAPHY
1133 Ave of the Americas (at 43rd St)   212/857-0000
Tues-Sun: 10-6   www.icp.org

If you like photography, this center for the study, preservation, and exhibition of photographic art is a "must-see." Beautiful gallery spaces and exceptionally well-conceived shows combine to make visiting here a real treat. Admission fee charged (reasonable).

INTREPID SEA, AIR & SPACE MUSEUM

Pier 86 (Twelfth Ave at 46th St)   212/245-0072, 877/957-7447
Mon-Fri: 10-5; Sat-Sun: 10-6   www.intrepidmuseum.org

This hugely popular museum is open once again. The complex comprises the 820-foot long aircraft carrier *Intrepid* (incorporating a theater, children's interactive zone, and the anchor chain room), the submarine *Growler*, and about 30 aircraft (including the *Concorde* and the A-12 *Blackbird* spy plane). Collections of uniforms, medals, photos, and all sorts of memorabilia associated with the sea, air, and space programs are seen throughout the bowels of the carrier. Allow plenty of time to take in the interactive exhibits. Admission fee charged (expensive); check for seasonal closures.

JAPAN SOCIETY GALLERY

333 E 47th St (bet First and Second Ave)   212/832-1155
Tues-Thurs: 11-6; Fri: 11-9; Sat-Sun: 11-5   www.japansociety.org

Founded in 1907, the Japan Society is a remarkable institution dedicated to furthering understanding between the United States and Japan. In addition to language classes, lecture series, films, and other programs, the society has a small but elegant gallery space that presents three exhibitions every year. Admission fee charged (reasonable).

Since 2003, emerging artists have shown their photography, works on paper, mixed media, and paintings at **Jen Bekman Gallery** (6 Spring St, 212/219-0166, www.jenbekman.com). Frequent exhibitions spotlight innovative new artists in this warm Soho gallery (Wed-Sat: noon-6 or by appointment). Another Bekman venture is **20x200**, which offers affordable limited-edition artwork online (www.20x200.com). Copies of two new high-quality prints are offered each week, starting at $20.

MERCHANT'S HOUSE MUSEUM

29 E 4th St (bet Lafayette St and Bowery)   212/777-1089
Thurs-Mon: 12-5   www.merchantshouse.com

Step back in time to an era when this part of town was considered the suburbs and New York was the country's leading port city. Built in 1832, this townhouse is a real time capsule, full of the furniture, clothes, and other items used by one of New York's wealthy merchant families. The servant call bells, the elegant four-poster beds, and the gas chandeliers are just a few of the many period details you'll find as you wander through this beautifully preserved family home (inside and out). This is the only home of its type from this period in New York City, and it is a National Historic Landmark. The backyard is a replica of a 19th-century garden, and it includes varietals from that era. Check the schedule for museum-hosted events. Admission fee charged (reasonable).

MORRIS-JUMEL MANSION

65 Jumel Terrace (bet 160th and 162nd St)   212/923-8008
Wed-Sun: 10-4   www.morrisjumel.org

George Washington used this mansion—located on a hill overlooking the Harlem River, Long Island Sound, the Hudson River, and the Palisades—as his headquarters at the beginning of the Revolutionary War. Built in 1765, its commanding views offered an important strategic position first to Washington and later to the British. When the British finally left, General Washington returned in 1790 for a dinner with a range of the country's founding fathers, including John Adams, Thomas Jefferson, and Alexander Hamilton. Several owners and much more history passed through these rooms in the intervening years, and most of the furniture—including a bed said to have belonged to Napoleon—dates from the 19th century. Admission fee charged (nominal).

MOUNT VERNON HOTEL MUSEUM AND GARDEN
421 E 61st St (between First and York Ave)   212/838-6878
Tues-Sun: 11-4 (Tues till 9 in June and July)   www.mvhm.org

Another time machine that's survived into the 21st century, this amazing little spot started life as a carriage house for a large estate. It served as a day hotel in the early 19th century and eventually became a private home. Now owned and lovingly preserved by the Colonial Dames of America, it's full of period pieces reflecting its years as a destination for day-trippers coming out to the country by boat or by carriage from Lower Manhattan. The Mount Vernon Hotel Museum and Garden (formerly known as the Abigail Adams Smith Museum) will transport you back 200 years. Tours are provided on request by wonderfully knowledgeable docents. Admission fee charged (nominal).

MUSEUM AT ELDRIDGE STREET
12 Eldridge Street (bet Canal and Division St)   212/219-0302
Sun-Thurs: 10-3   www.eldridgestreet.org

For decades after opening in 1887, the Eldridge Street Synagogue on the Lower East Side was a central part of the life of thousands of Eastern European Jewish immigrants. After it fell on hard times, which left it literally falling apart, a nonprofit organization was formed to restore its original grandeur and tell some of the stories that passed through these doors. Call or visit the website for details about public programs and tours. Admission fee charged for tour (reasonable).

MUSEUM OF AMERICAN FINANCE
48 Wall St (at William St)   212/908-4110
Mon-Fri: 10-4   www.moaf.org

This museum is appropriately sited in the building that once housed the Bank of New York, which was founded by Alexander Hamilton (who went on to become our nation's first Secretary of the Treasury). The largest exhibit focuses on New York's financial markets, which are located only a block or so away from this museum. Visitors explore the routes of check and credit card transactions, differences between financial institutions, and the Federal Reserve System. There's even a piggybank display! Various forms of money are exhibited, from the earliest tender to the latest currency with hidden anti-counterfeiting technology. Special events to reflect economic times are often scheduled. Admission fee charged (reasonable).

MUSEUM OF AMERICAN ILLUSTRATION
128 E 63rd St (bet Park and Lexington Ave)   212/838-2560
Tues: 10-8; Wed-Fri: 10-5; Sat: 12-4   www.societyillustrators.org

Changing exhibitions, including some from the Society of Illustrators' permanent collection, are housed in an elegant 1853 carriage house that today serves as the society's headquarters. Books, magazines, and posters are some of the items for sale in the museum shop. Free admission.

MUSEUM OF ARTS AND DESIGN
2 Columbus Circle (at Eighth Ave)   212/299-7777
Wed-Sun: 11-6 (Thurs till 9)   www.madmuseum.org

The museum, also known as MAD, occupies a recently redesigned building located in the spruced-up Columbus Circle. The concave exterior, covered with small glazed terra-cotta tiles, seemingly glitters at dusk. Inside are collections and exhibitions of contemporary objects created in clay, glass, wood, metal, and fiber (from the mid-20th century to present). The permanent collection numbers more than 2,000 such objects. The attractive store sells useful and decorative items. Admission fee charged (reasonable).

MUSEUM OF BIBLICAL ART
1865 Broadway (at 61st St)   212/408-1500
Tues-Sun: 10-6 (Thurs till 8)   www.mobia.org

This remodeled and expanded museum is the only one in the world dedicated to preserving and understanding art inspired and influenced by the Hebrew Scriptures and the Christian Testament. From ecclesiastical art to contemporary secular work, this fascinating museum offers a unique perspective on how the symbols and narratives of the Bible influence art and are often incorporated into it. Admission fee charged (reasonable).

Most galleries are open Tuesday through Saturday from 10 or 11 a.m. to 5 or 6 p.m. Some close for a few weeks in summer.

MUSEUM OF CHINESE IN THE AMERICAS
215 Centre St (bet Howard and Grand St)   212/619-4785
Mon-Fri: 11-5; Thurs: 11-9; Sat, Sun: 10-5   www.moca-nyc.org

A 2009 move to larger quarters enabled expansion of this fine museum. It is dedicated to telling and preserving the stories of Chinese immigrants to this country, through its historical exhibits, walking tours, and a Chinatown Film Project. Admission fee charged (reasonable).

MUSEUM AT FIT
Seventh Ave at 27th St   212/217-4560
Tues-Fri: noon-8   www.fitnyc.edu/museum

The Fashion Institute of Technology (FIT) is one of the world's leading fashion schools and a branch of the State University of New York. This little museum is dedicated to the art of fashion through exhibitions, programs, and publications. Color, texture, and design are front and center in this museum's changing exhibitions. Its intriguing collections include garments, accessories, textiles, and more than 4,000 pairs of shoes! Free admission.

MUSEUM OF SEX
233 Fifth Ave (at 27th St)   212/689-6337
Sun-Fri: 11-6:30; Sat: 11-8   www.museumofsex.com

Opened in 2002, this entire affair (excuse the pun) is a bit tawdry, appearing to run on a shoestring budget. However, if you're not shy about what can only be described as soft-core pornography, there's a lot to be learned about the history of sex and its influence on our culture. Admission fee charged (reasonable); no one under 18 is allowed in the museum.

NATIONAL ACADEMY MUSEUM & SCHOOL OF FINE ART
1083 Fifth Ave (bet 89th and 90th St)   212/369-4880
Wed-Thurs: noon-5; Fri-Sun: 11-6   www.nationalacademy.org

A name change from the National Academy of Design more accurately describes New York's oldest art school. Modeled after the Royal Academy of London, it has been among the city's leading art institutions since opening in 1825. Smaller than some of the other museums along Museum Mile, the National Academy Museum & School of Fine Art nonetheless is worth a stop if you're interested in 19th- and 20th-century American art. Dorothea Rockburne, Thomas Eakins, John Singer Sargent, Federic Church, and Jasper Johns are just a few members of the National Academy whose work is represented in the permanent collection. Admission fee charged (reasonable).

Photography

Some museums and galleries allow visitors to snap photos of famous works on display. Others have strict "no photography" policies and will send security officers to enforce their regulations. The same prohibition can even apply to sketching. Check the fine print online before you go or ask at the establishment. You may avoid an embarrassing situation.

NATIONAL MUSEUM OF THE AMERICAN INDIAN
1 Bowling Green (foot of Broadway)   212/514-3700
Daily: 10-5 (Thurs till 8)   www.nmai.si.edu

The George Gustav Heye Center (within the Alexander Hamilton Customs House) is home to one of three branches of the National Museum of the American Indian. Opened in 1994, this branch in Lower Manhattan offers changing exhibitions featuring items and works both old and new. (The largest branch is on the National Mall, in Washington, D.C.) Its two terrific gift shops are well worth a visit, as is the building itself. Take time to look up at the intricate details in the ceilings, especially in the rotunda and library, and to descend the exquisite (if a bit worn) staircase. Free admission.

NEUE GALERIE NEW YORK
1048 Fifth Ave (at 86th St)   212/628-6200
Thurs-Mon: 11-6   www.neuegalerie.org

Ronald Lauder and his longtime friend, the late Serge Sabarsky, loved German and Austrian art and design from the early 20th century and dreamed of opening a museum to showcase it. Lauder purchased this amazing building, once home to Mrs. Cornelius Vanderbilt III, in 1994 and transformed their dream into this first-class museum. Public tours are offered at

2 p.m. on Saturday and Sunday. Children under 12 are not welcome, and children from 12 to 16 must be accompanied by an adult. Admission fee charged (reasonable).

NEW-YORK HISTORICAL SOCIETY
170 Central Park West (bet 76th and 77th St)   212/873-3400
Tues-Sun: 10-6 (Fri till 8)   www.nyhistory.org

John James Audubon's watercolors for *Birds of America*, Thomas Cole's *The Course of Empire*, and more Tiffany lamps than you can imagine are just a few highlights of the New-York Historical Society. A visit to this *grande dame*—located just south of the American Museum of Natural History—is a great way to glimpse the city's past. The best part of this museum is the Henry Luce III Center for the Study of American Culture, located on the fourth floor. Brimming with thousands of pieces from the museum's vast permanent collection, it's like wandering through the city's attic. Admission fee charged (reasonable).

Haunted Manhattan

October 31 isn't the only time to celebrate ghostly apparitions. You may witness spirited occurrences at any time—friendly or otherwise!

- The headless ghost of actor George Frederick has been spotted at **St. Paul's Chapel** burial ground.
- **The Palace Theatre** supposedly boasts over 100 ghosts.
- Aaron Burr reputedly haunts the restaurant **One if by Land, Two if by Sea** (once his carriage house); flying dishes have been observed.
- The ghost of Bishop Dubois frequents the **Old St. Patrick's Cathedral**.
- Unexplained noises, voices, and footsteps occur at **Beth Israel Hospital**.
- The **Chelsea Hotel** gained notoriety from some of its guests and their activities. Still making the unearthly scene are Eugene O'Neill, Thomas Wolfe, and Sid Vicious. Beware of the elevator!

NEW YORK CITY FIRE MUSEUM
278 Spring St (bet Hudson and Varick St)   212/691-1303
Tues-Sat: 10-5; Sun: 10-4   www.nycfiremuseum.org

In a renovated 1904 firehouse, this fun museum is a "must-see" for anyone interested in firefighting. With hundreds of artifacts dating from the late 18th century, the collection is among the most extensive of its kind in the country. Highlights include leather fire buckets, hand-pumped fire engines, and a horse-drawn ladder wagon. Call ahead to make sure your visit won't coincide with that of a large school group. Admission fee charged (nominal).

NEW YORK CITY POLICE MUSEUM
100 Old Slip (bet Water and South St)   212/480-3100
Mon-Sat: 10-5   www.nycpolicemuseum.org

Located in New York's first precinct house, this museum is dedicated to preserving the long history of the New York City Police Department. Displays include a jail cell, famous criminals, vintage weapons, and a special memorial to the officers who died on September 11, 2001. A large gift shop is a hit with kids and adults alike. Admission fee charged (nominal).

NICHOLAS ROERICH MUSEUM
319 W 107th St (bet Broadway and Central Park West)
Tues-Sun: 2-5   212/864-7752
                                                        www.roerich.org

The late Nicholas Roerich was Russian, but in many ways he was a citizen of the world. He dedicated much of his life to convincing governments to protect art even in times of conflict. His own paintings, many done in (and of) the Himalayas, are on display at this unassuming townhouse near Columbia University. Free admission; contributions suggested.

The More Things Change . . .

The last peep shows have moved out of Times Square, and even the seafood merchants have moved out of the old Fulton Fish Market. However, some things in New York still haven't changed. If it's nostalgia you want, try the **Waldorf-Astoria** (301 Park Ave), **Radio City Music Hall** (Ave of the Americas at 50th St), the overpriced **21 Club** (21 W 52nd St), the **Grand Central Oyster Bar Restaurant** (Grand Central Terminal), or **McSorley's Old Ale House** (15 E 7th St). You might also check out some of the old-time shops on the Lower East Side, like **Katz's Delicatessen** (205 E Houston St).

PALEY CENTER FOR MEDIA
25 W 52nd St (bet Fifth Ave and Ave of the Americas)   212/621-6800
Tues-Sat: noon-6   www.paleycenter.org

Is there an episode of *The Brady Bunch* you've always wanted to show your kids? A segment of *The Ed Sullivan Show* you've always wanted to view again? What about the Nixon-Kennedy debates? Or that Mean Joe Greene Coca-Cola commercial? For folks who love television, this place is Nirvana. In addition to scheduled screenings, you can select from the library's more than 120,000 programs—spanning the history of radio and television— for your own viewing. There's no memorabilia here, just thousands of hours of programming. Admission fee charged (reasonable).

RADIO CITY MUSIC HALL
1260 Ave of the Americas (at 50th St)
            212/247-4777 (tour information), 800/745-3000 (tickets)
Daily: 11-3   www.radiocity.com

Part of Rockefeller Center, this Art Deco wonder was built in 1932 and seats more than 6,000 people. It's home to a world-famous Christmas show, complete with live animals; an equally fabulous Easter show; and varied productions throughout the year. Countless entertainers have performed here over the years, and you can soak up some of its storied history by looking up at the giant marquee. Admission fee charged (reasonable).

ROCK & ROLL HALL OF FAME ANNEX NYC

76 Mercer Street (bet Spring and Broome St)   646/786-6680
Tues-Thurs: 11-8:30; Fri-Sat: 11-10; Sun: 11-8   www.rockannex.com

With the addition of this amazing annex in Soho, there's no need to travel to Cleveland for immersion in rock and roll's greatest moments. Experience the lively sounds that shaped the history of modern music as you wander through the galleries and discover eclectic personal items from legendary artists: drumsticks, clothing, and other memorabilia. Tickets may be purchased in person, by phone, or online, and they come with specific entry times. Contact the museum to hear about special guest appearances or arrange for a private function. Admssion fee charged (expensive).

A 100-mile trip northwest of the city will bring you to the **Bethel Woods Center for the Arts** (866/781-2922, www.bethelwoods center.org), in Bethel, New York. On this historic site in 1969, the legendary **Woodstock Music and Art Fair**, more commonly and simply known as "Woodstock," was held. The muddy fields have been replaced with this spectacular multimedia museum, which chronicles the turbulent 1960s and focuses on the Woodstock experience. Concerts and performances are held in several indoor and outdoor venues.

ROCKEFELLER CENTER

Between Fifth Ave, Ave of the Americas, 49th St, and 50th St
Daily: 6:30 a.m.-midnight   212/332-6868
                                                www.rockefellercenter.com

A 30-building complex built as the Depression raged in the 1930s, Rockefeller Center is in some ways the anchor of midtown Manhattan. Technologies have come and gone, as radio gave way to television and now to all sorts of new media. Tenants and owners have come and gone, too, but this amazing complex is one of the few constants in this ever-changing city. Rockefeller Center includes Radio City Music Hall, NBC Studios, Channel Gardens, a world-famous ice-skating rink, a two-floor Metropolitan Museum of Art store, a post office (on the lower level, near the skating rink), and subway stop. You can shop on the lower level, wave to the folks back home outside the *Today Show*'s windows, have dinner while watching the ice skaters, or take a trip up to the "Top of the Rock" (212/332-6621, www.topofthe rocknyc.com), towering 70 floors above the street. You can even tour NBC Studios and Rockefeller Center. Go to the **NBC Experience Store** (on 49th St between Fifth Ave and Ave of the Americas) for schedules and prices. What I most like to do at Rockefeller Center, however, is simply walk around. It's like visiting an old friend! Fee charged for tours (reasonable).

ROSE MUSEUM AT CARNEGIE HALL

154 W 57th St (at Seventh Ave)   212/903-9629
Daily: 11-4:30 (closed July-Sept)   www.carnegiehall.org

If you're interested in the history of music in New York, this little upstairs museum—adjacent to Carnegie Hall and across and just down the street from the Steinway piano store—is a fun place to stop. Its permanent exhibit traces the history of Carnegie Hall from 1891. It's open to the public during the day and to evening concert-goers during intermission. Tours of Carnegie Hall, including the Isaac Stern Auditorium, are offered during the season (fall through spring); call or check their website for details. Free admission to museum; admission fee charged for tours (reasonable).

RUBIN MUSEUM OF ART
150 W 17th St (at Seventh Ave)   212/620-5000
Mon: 11-5; Wed: 11-7; Thurs: 11-5; Fri-Sun: 11-6 (Fri till 10)
                                                www.rmanyc.org

Paintings, sculptures, and textiles from the Himalayas and surrounding regions are displayed at the Rubin Museum of Art, an international center for the preservation and enjoyment of Himalayan art. Cultural events, collections, changing exhibitions, tours, and educational programs help further understanding of this region. Admission fee charged (reasonable).

SCANDINAVIA HOUSE GALLERIES
58 Park Ave (bet 37th and 38th St)   212/879-9779
Tues-Sat: noon-6   www.scandinaviahouse.org

This sleek building, just south of Grand Central Terminal, is home to the American-Scandinavian Foundation. Dedicated to building ties and improving understanding between the United States and the Nordic countries of Sweden, Denmark, Iceland, Norway, and Finland, the foundation offers films, children's programs, lectures, and more. Its galleries host changing art, design, and historical exhibitions. A small cafe, **Smörgås Chef**, a beautiful store, and well-designed public spaces make visiting here a real pleasure. Admission fee charged (nominal).

SKYSCRAPER MUSEUM
Ritz-Carlton New York, Battery Park
39 Battery Place (at West St), 1st floor   212/968-1961
Wed-Sun: noon-6   www.skyscraper.org

Where better to have a museum dedicated to the history and future of skyscrapers than New York City? Founded in 1996, this ironically small museum shares a building with the Ritz-Carlton New York, Battery Park at the southern end of Battery Park City. After four homes in six years, it seems to have settled into a permanent space. Admission fee charged (nominal).

SOUTH STREET SEAPORT MUSEUM
12 Fulton St (bet Water and South St)   212/748-8600
April-Dec: Tues-Sun: 10-6 (all galleries and ships);
Jan-March: reduced hours and access to ships
                                    www.southstreetseaportmuseum.org

Two centuries ago, New York was one of the world's most active ports. Even as recently as 1967—when the South Street Seaport Museum was founded—Fulton Street was synonymous with the Fulton Fish Market (which finally moved to The Bronx a couple of years ago). Little is left today except the history, and that's what you'll find as you explore the galleries and ships while wandering around this area. With its cobblestone streets, beautiful old boats, and salty breezes, it's easy to imagine that you've been transported to a different era. Admission fee charged (reasonable).

STUDIO MUSEUM IN HARLEM
144 W 125th St (bet Malcolm X and Adam Clayton Powell, Jr. Blvd)
Wed-Fri: 11-6; Sat: 10-6; Sun: noon-6   212/864-4500
                                          www.studiomuseum.org

Like the Museum of Chinese in the Americas, this wonderful place is both a museum and a vibrant part of the community. Recently expanded to include more gallery space and an auditorium, the Studio Museum displays the work of black artists from around the block and around the world. An Artist in Residence program, a wide range of programs for families and children, and film screenings are just a few ways the Studio Museum engages its audience and reaches into the community. Suggested admission fee charged (reasonable).

TIBET HOUSE
22 W 15th St (bet Fifth Ave and Ave of the Americas)   212/807-0563
Mon-Fri: 10-5   www.tibethouse.org

Founded at the request of the Dalai Lama, Tibet House is the center of efforts in the United States to present and preserve Tibetan culture. It has a small gallery space and offers changing exhibits showcasing contemporary and classical Tibetan art. Free admission; donations welcome.

The **New Museum of Contemporary Art** (235 Bowery, 212/219-1222, www.newmuseum.org) has finally found a permanent home. It is the first art museum constructed in downtown Manhattan, nestled among restaurant-supply businesses. This contemporary art museum is uniquely built as seven off-axis stacked rectangles. It features the stimulating works of artists from around the globe, in all media, including performances and technology art.

THEODORE ROOSEVELT BIRTHPLACE
28 E 20th St (bet Broadway and Park Ave)   212/260-1616
Tues-Sat: 9-5 (closed federal holidays)   www.nps.gov/thrb

This wonderful brownstone is a reconstruction of Theodore Roosevelt's childhood home. Operated by the National Park Service, it houses a small museum and various period rooms in the living quarters. Guided tours of the rooms are offered hourly between 10 and 4, except at noon. Admission fee charged (nominal).

UKRAINIAN MUSEUM
222 E 6th St (bet Second and Third Ave)   212/228-0110
Wed-Sun: 11:30-5   www.ukrainianmuseum.org

This museum in the heart of the East Village invites visitors to "discover the wonderful heritage of your parents and grandparents." Displaying folk art, costumes, paintings, and an amazing collection of *pysanky* (Ukrainian Easter eggs), this museum is a terrific cultural resource for anyone who wants to learn more about Ukrainian heritage—yours or otherwise. Admission fee charged (reasonable).

UNION SQUARE PARK
Between Broadway, Park Ave S, 14th St, and 17th St

Union Square Park is now home to the city's best known and largest Greenmarket (which is open on Monday, Wednesday, Friday, and Saturday). It's full of New Yorkers and tourists alike enjoying the beautifully renovated and surprisingly clean public spaces. The famous Union Square Cafe is just one of dozens of restaurants in the area.

Sailing Up, Sailing Down

The Hudson and East rivers, which have long been engines of commerce of this region, became very polluted in the second half of the 20th century and were little used when I first began writing this book over 30 years ago. No longer! Whether it's basic transportation or a nostalgic sail on a hundred-year-old schooner, there are many options for getting out on the water. They include:

The Adirondack—This 80-foot schooner is docked at the Chelsea Piers complex and is available for both public cruises and charters (646/336-5270, www.sail-nyc.com).

Bateaux New York—Also moored at the Chelsea Piers, this company's elegant glass boat has regularly scheduled lunch and dinner cruises, as well as sightseeing cruises (866/211-3805, www.bateauxnewyork.com).

Circle Line—In addition to their famous three-hour cruise around the island of Manhattan, this company runs the boats that go to and from the Statue of Liberty and Ellis Island, as well as a variety of other sightseeing and adventure cruises from several ports in the city. Thrill-seekers will like the *Shark Speedboat* (866/925-4631, www.circleline downtown.com).

New York Water Taxi—Based at South Street Seaport, this company's boats are all painted to look like old-fashioned taxis. Commuter boats and sightseeing tours are available (212/742-1969, www.nywater taxi.com).

New York Waterway—This company runs ferry service for commuters, as well as sightseeing boats for tourists, in New York Harbor and around the island of Manhattan (800/533-3779, www.nywaterway.com).

The Pioneer—This wonderful 1885 schooner is docked at South Street Seaport (212/748-8786, www.southstreetseaportmuseum.org). It takes regularly scheduled summer tours around New York Harbor.

The Ventura—This classic old yacht is docked at North Cove, near the World Financial Center in Battery Park City, as is the 1950 speedboat *Petrel* (212/786-1204, www.sailnewyork.com). The *Ventura* takes folks on regularly scheduled cruises in the summer. The *Petrel* is available for private charters for up to four people.

WEST SIDE JEWISH CENTER
347 W 34th Street (bet Eighth and Ninth Ave)   212/502-5291
Mon-Thurs: 9-5; Fri 9-1   www.westsidejewishcenter.org

In the early 1900s, New York claimed the largest Jewish population in the world, with immigrants from Germany, Russia, and Eastern Europe. The West Side Jewish Center synagogue and social center has been in this location for over 115 years. Services are offered daily, as well as for Shabbat and holidays. People of all ages engage in interesting classes, lectures, and social programs. This historic location is adjacent to Pennsylvania Station, Madison Square Garden, and the Jacob Javits Convention Center. It is truly a sanctuary with heart in the heart of the city. Tours and Sabbath meals can be arranged in advance. Free admission.

Isn't That Where . . .

New York is full of backdrops for movies and television shows. If you are a fan of shows like *The Sopranos*, *Gossip Girl*, or *Sex in the City*, one of the many tours offered by **On Location Tours** (212/683-2027, www.sceneontv.com) may be the highlight of your trip. Particularly popular with young people, these tours will take you to see where scenes from various movies and television shows were filmed. Bus tours take you to different places and focus on various topics. Children under 15 must be accompanied by an adult. Go to the website to learn about specific tours and prices. Advance reservations are required.

YANKEE STADIUM
1 E 161st St (at Jerome Ave)   718/579-4594
                                               www.yankees.com

The "House That Ruth Built"—that's Babe Ruth, the baseball legend—has been replaced with the new billion-dollar Yankee Stadium. The field dimensions remain the same, seats and legroom are more spacious, there are more eateries and team stores, more luxury and party suites, and the main scoreboard is seven times larger. The classic tour (between May and September) includes visits to the museum, Monument Park, dugouts, batting cages, and clubhouse. There are different hours for individual and small and large groups, depending on game-day schedule; it is therefore best to check the website or call for details. Admission fee charged (reasonable).

YESHIVA UNIVERSITY MUSEUM
15 W 16th St (at Fifth Ave)   212/294-8330
Tues-Thurs: 11-5; Sun 11-5   www.yumuseum.org

Part of the Center for Jewish History, this surprisingly large and vibrant museum houses an exceptional collection of paintings, books, artifacts, and other items relating to Jewish life, history, and culture. A trip here can be wonderfully rewarding, but be sure to check the hours, as the museum seems closed as often as its open. Admission fee charged (reasonable).

Galleries

When people think of viewing art, they often think only of museums. While the art museums in New York are exceptional, anyone interested in art ought to visit some commercial galleries, too. Galleries are places where potential buyers and admirers alike can look at the work of contemporary and 20th-century artists at their own pace and without charge. (A few galleries specialize in older works, too.) Let me stress "admirers alike." A lot of people are afraid to go into galleries because they think they'll be expected to buy something or be treated poorly if they don't know everything there is to know about art. That just isn't true, and an afternoon of gallery hopping can be a lot of fun.

First decide what kind of art you want to see. New York has long been considered the center of the contemporary art world, and it follows that the city is home to literally hundreds of galleries of all sizes and styles. In general, the more formal and conventional galleries are on or close to Madison Avenue on the Upper East Side and along 57th Street. (You'll need to look up to find a lot of them, particularly on 57th Street.) Some of the less formal, avant-garde galleries tend to be in Soho: on West Broadway, between Broome and Houston streets; on Greene Street, between Prince and Houston streets; and on Prince Street, between Greene Street and West Broadway. Some of the latter are also in Tribeca.

As a general rule, artists who have yet to be discovered go where the rents are lower, and then more established artists and galleries follow. Gallery hot spots include the west end of Chelsea, the northwest corner of the West Village (on and around West 14th Street), the Lower East Side (particularly on and around Rivington Street), and several parts of Brooklyn.

If you want to experience the diversity of the New York gallery scene, sample a couple of galleries in each neighborhood. The Art Dealers Association of America (212/488-5550, www.artdealers.org) is a terrific resource if you have particular artists or areas of interest in mind.

Galleries are typically known for the artists they showcase. If you are interested in the work of just one artist, the *New Yorker* and *New York* magazine contain listings of gallery shows arranged by artists' names. Be sure to look at the dates, as shows sometimes change quickly. *Time Out New York* has a list of galleries by neighborhood in its "Arts" section, complete with descriptions of current shows. The Friday and Sunday editions of the *New York Times* are also good resources.

Tours and Tour Operators

Whether you like to walk or ride, be part of a small group or with a whole herd, New York has a tour for you. While I definitely advocate getting out and exploring on your own at least part of the time you're in New York, there are lots of interesting tours that will take you places you either won't go or can't go by yourself.

If you're interested in having a tour organized for your group, **Doorway to Design** (212/229-0299, www.doorwaytodesign.com) and **Viewpoint International** (212/246-6000, www.viewpointinternational.com) are reputable companies that have been around for a long time. If you want a particular kind of tour or a guide with special skills or areas of expertise, contact the **Guides Association of New York** (212/969-0666, www.ganyc.org). The website has information about the city's licensed guides and their specialties, as well as practical details about the tours they offer. If you're looking for a really personalized introduction to New York, then get in touch with **Big Apple Greeter** (212/669-8159, www.bigapplegreeter.org). This nonprofit volunteer service is designed to hook visitors up with real New Yorkers, and is a great way to get an insider's view of the city for free.

If you're feeling a little overwhelmed by New York and want to see the sights from the safety and anonymity of a tour bus, **Gray Line** (212/445-0848, www.graylinenewyork.com) is your best bet. The company offers all sorts of different packages on its double-decker buses, including a three-day tour with trips to the Statue of Liberty and the Empire State Building, as well as a two-day hop-on and hop-off tour of over 50 stops all around New York. Prices vary, as do the lengths of the various tours. Another great way to get a quick and basic orientation is **Circle Line**'s three-hour cruise all the way around the island of Manhattan. The narration tends toward the corny, but you'll learn a lot, get some great photo opportunities, and really acquire a sense of New York as an island. Call 212/563-3200 or go to www.circle line42.com for more information.

If you want a personal orientation tour, try **My Kind of Town New York** (212/754-4500, 866/691-8687, www.mykindoftown.com). These private tours are undertaken in the comfort of a Mercedes Benz SUVs and tailored just for you.

Many of the museums and sights listed previously offer tours of their own collections or of surrounding neighborhoods. Just about any tour offered by the **Central Park Conservancy** is a personal favorite.

Following are places not mentioned in other parts of this book that offer particularly interesting or popular tours.

The **New York Landmarks Conservancy** has published several books detailing self-guided walking tours in Lower Manhattan, the Upper East Side, Harlem, and the Flatiron District. Call 212/995-5260 or go to www.nylandmarks.org for more information. If you specifically want to visit Harlem, I highly recommend **Harlem Spirituals** (212/391-0900, www.harlemspirituals.com).

CITY HALL

52 Chambers St (at Park Row)   212/788-2656
Tours: Mon-Fri: 9-5; reservations necessary   www.nyc.gov

Built in the early 19th century and still used as the City Hall for all five New York boroughs, this grand building is open for public tours by appointment. In addition to grand staircases, beautiful art, and a soaring rotunda, you'll get to visit the historic Governor's Room. Combined tours of City Hall and the nearby Tweed Courthouse are also available. Find out about availability and make tour reservations online. Free admission.

FEDERAL RESERVE BANK

33 Liberty St (bet Nassau and William St)   212/720-6130
Tours: Mon-Fri: 9:30, 10:30, 11:30, 1:30, 2:30 (reservations necessary)
                                                   www.newyorkfed.org

Billions of dollars of gold from more than 36 foreign central banks and international agencies are stashed in the Fed's vault in the bedrock of Manhattan Island. Daily tours of this incredible institution are free, but reservations must be made at least a week in advance. Be sure to look for the American Numismatic Society's display on the history of money. Free admission.

GRACIE MANSION
88th St at East End Ave   212/570-4751 or 311 (in New York)
Tours: Wed: 10, 11, 1, 2 (reservations necessary)   www.nyc.gov

Thanks to Fiorello LaGuardia, New York is one of the few cities in the U.S. with an official mayoral residence. Built in 1799, this historic mansion is one of the oldest continuously occupied homes in New York (well, sort of—current mayor Michael Bloomberg actually lives in an East Side townhouse). It's located in Carl Schurz Park, overlooking the East River. Admission fee charged (reasonable).

The knowledgeable guides at **Bike the Big Apple** (877/865-0078, www.bikethebigapple.com) put a different spin on seeing the sights. Of course you can cruise through Central Park and trendy nearby neighborhoods, but they'll also lead riders down the trails of high finance and Chinatown; on a journey in quest of brews, chocolates, and great views; across the East River to Roosevelt Island for an ethnic tour; or to check out the city lights on a twilight pedal across the Brooklyn Bridge after a swing through Lower Manhattan. Tour prices include bike and helmet rental fees.

MADISON SQUARE GARDEN
33rd St at Seventh Ave   212/465-5802
Tours: Daily: 11-3 (reservations necessary)   www.thegarden.com

If you've always wanted to see the New York Knicks' locker room, here's your chance. This historic arena in the heart of Manhattan is a little worn around the edges, but it still holds lots of great memories. Be forewarned that tour schedules are often abbreviated and access to certain areas may be limited because of events at "The Garden." Admission fee charged (reasonable).

METROPOLITAN OPERA
Lincoln Center (Columbus Ave at 64th St)   212/769-7020
Mon-Fri: 3:30; Sun: 1:30 and 3:30   www.metoperafamily.org
Tours: Oct-May during opera season

Even folks who don't care for opera will be wowed by this behind-the-scenes look at this country's most famous opera company. Visit the stage and get an up-close look at some of the costumes and sets. These popular 90-minute tours are offered by the Metropolitan Opera Guild, but times can change, so check the calendar on the guild's website. Plan well in advance, as tours often sell out. Admission fee charged (reasonable).

NBC STUDIOS
30 Rockefeller Plaza (49th St bet Fifth Ave and Ave
    of the Americas)   212/664-3700
Tours: Mon-Thurs: 8:30-4:30; Fri-Sat: 9:30-5:30; Sun: 9:30-4:30
                    www.nbcuniversalstore.com

NBC's studios are located in Rockefeller Center, right in the heart of midtown. If you want to take a look around the sets of the *Today Show*, *Saturday Night Live*, and other NBC television shows, here's your chance. Take note: the studios are often crowded, overhyped, and a bit chaotic, and children under six are not allowed on the tour. Admission fee charged (reasonable).

Walking Tours

Walking tours are another great way to get to know parts of New York you otherwise might overlook. *Time Out New York* lists scheduled walking tours in its "Around Town" section each week. Here are some tour guides.

BIG ONION WALKING TOURS
Tours: Daily (usually): times vary   212/439-1090
                                                        www.bigonion.com

Seth Kamil and his band of guides—most of them graduate students in American history—share their vast knowledge of New York through a wide array of walking tours. Among the most popular are the Multi-Ethnic Eating Tour, Lower East Side on Christmas Day, and Revolutionary New York. Check ahead for tour times, meeting places, and price. Some tours are free and require no reservation; others require both a reservation and fee.

JOYCE GOLD'S HISTORY TOURS OF NEW YORK
                                                        212/242-5762
                                        www.joycegoldhistorytours.com

Nowhere in the United States are past and present so closely quartered as in New York, and few people are better able to convey that simultaneous sense of timelessness and modernity than historian Joyce Gold. Her scheduled tours, which include such topics as Fifth Avenue Gold Coast and The Bowery—Entertainments High and Low, are usually given on weekends. Joyce personally leads all her public tours and is available for private tours as well. Reservations for her scheduled tours are not required. Fee charged (reasonable).

New York's first family of tour guides operates **Levy's Unique New York** (718/287-6177 or 877/NYC-LUNY; www.levysuniqueny. com). The clan, led by dad Mark, conducts educational and enlightening outings that are thoroughly entertaining and sometimes zany! Most popular is the half-day City Highlights tour. Other excursions are New York by Land and Sea, Bohemians and Beatniks of Greenwich Village, and Ethnic Eats—Nibbles and Noshes. There's even a narrated stroll across the Brooklyn Bridge. Tour times and costs vary; custom tours are available.

MUNICIPAL ART SOCIETY
Tour days and times vary   212/935-3960
                                                        www.mas.org

This terrific advocacy group offers a wide array of thematic and area-specific walking tours for people interested in the city's architecture and history. Most tours are led by historians. The diverse topics include downtown skyscrapers, the World Trade Center site, Hamilton Heights, Park Avenue, and various neighborhoods. Allow about an hour and a half for your tour. Fee charged (reasonable).

URBAN PARK RANGERS
Tours: Wed-Thurs (summer); daily during school breaks
212/360-2774 or 311 (in New York)
www.nycgovparks.org

The city's Department of Parks and Recreation employs Urban Park Rangers, who give wonderful weekend walking tours of Central Park and other parks throughout Manhattan and the outer boroughs. Many are designed for children or families. Go to the department's website and click "Things to Do" and "Urban Park Rangers" to get a full schedule of upcoming tours and other events. Free admission.

There are all types of sightseeing tours to the usual Manhattan tourist attractions. **Savory Sojourns** (212/691-7314, 888/972-8679, www.savorysojourns.com) has created a winning combination of learning about the neighborhoods while shopping, tasting, cooking, and dining at some of the well-known, as well as obscure destinations around town. You might find yourself shopping for chocolate truffles, trying your hand at filling cannolis, or discovering the latest fashion trends from an expert.

IV. Where to Find It: New York's Best Food Shops

If you're in New York for any length of time, you'll become acquainted with the art of *noshing* (Yiddish for snacking). Nearly every block has a tempting deli, bakery, or shop selling candy, cheese, wine, ice cream, or (my favorite) chocolate. Street vendors dispense all sorts of food and produce, many of them ethnic choices. Don't miss Greenmarkets, the Essex Street Market, and Chelsea Market. All of them carry a spectacular variety of produce, meats and seafood, cheeses, baked good—just about anything edible. Great food emporiums like Zabar's and Grace's Marketplace entice more than the appetite with housewares and unusual kitchen and gastronomic goodies. Stop and shop as you happen upon these Big Apple treasures. You'll enjoy the variety and fabulous tastes, and your friends will be delighted with your finds.

Asian

ASIA MARKET
71½ Mulberry St (bet Canal and Bayard St)   212/962-2020
Daily: 8-7

Fresh fruit and vegetables, plus exotic herbs and spices from all over Asia, are the main attractions at Asia Market. You'll find items from Thailand, Indonesia, Malaysia, the Philippines, Japan, and China, plus a staff ready to explain how to prepare dishes from these countries. Asia Market provides produce to some of New York's best restaurants.

Bakery Goods

AMY'S BREAD
672 Ninth Ave (Hell's Kitchen, bet 46th and 47th St)   212/977-2670
75 Ninth Ave (Chelsea Market, bet 15th and 16th St)   212/462-4338
250 Bleecker St (bet Carmine and Leroy St)   212/675-7802
Hours vary by store   www.amysbread.com

As the aroma of freshly baked bread and sweets drifts onto Ninth Avenue, locals and tourists line up outside of Amy's Hell's Kitchen location to sample the many treats for sale. An oasis in the heart of midtown,

Amy's Bread is a cross between a Parisian *boulangerie* and a cozy Midwestern kitchen. Of course, you should come for the bread—Amy's signature semolina with golden raisins and fennel, the green olive *picholine*, or a simple French baguette. Among the goodies are grilled sandwiches, sticky buns, old-fashioned double layer cakes, and decadent brownies. The staff provides consistent, friendly service.

Korea in New York

For a taste of Korea (literally) and to relish the culture, here are several businesses in Koreatown and on the Upper East Side that you should know about. The Korean business district is primarily on 32nd Street, between Fifth Avenue and Broadway.

Food

Hangawi (12 E 32nd St, 212/213-0077): vegetarian
Kunjip (9 W 32nd St, 212/216-9487): in the middle of Koreatown, open 24/7
Woo Lae Oak (148 Mercer St, 212/925-8200): famous table barbecue
Woorijip (12 W 32nd St, 212/244-1115): buffet, open 24/7

Korean culture

Kang Collection (9 E 82nd St, 212/734-1490): traditional art
KooNewYork (126 E 64th St, 2nd floor, 646/918-7030): gallery of high-quality classical and contemporary art; by appointment only
Korea Society (950 Third Ave, 8th floor, 212/759-7525)
Lee Young Hee Korean Museum (2 W 32nd St, Suite 301, 212/560-0722): traditional costumes and furnishings

---

ARON STREIT
150 Rivington St (bet Clinton and Suffolk St) 212/475-7000
Mon-Thurs: 9-4:30 www.streitsmatzos.com

Matzo is a thin, wafer-like unleavened bread. According to tradition, it came out of Egypt with Moses and the children of Israel when they had to flee so quickly there was no time to let the bread rise. Through the years, matzo was restricted to the time around Passover, and even when matzo production became automated, business shut down for a good deal of the year. But not today and not in New York. Streit (which is the only family-owned and operated matzo business in America) produces matzo throughout the year, pausing only on Saturday and Jewish holidays to clean the machines. Streit allows a peek at the production process, which is both mechanized and extremely primitive. Matzo is baked in enormous thin sheets that are later broken up. If you ask for a fresh batch, they might break it right off the production line. They also offer noodles, wafers, canned soups, potato products, Hanukkah items, and Jewish specialty dishes.

BANGKOK CENTER GROCERY
104 Mosco St (bet Mott and Mulberry St) 212/349-1979
Daily: 10-8 (Tues to 7) www.thai-grocery.com

You'll find a complete selection of Thai foods in this amazing store, including teas, sticky rice, rice noodles, Thai herbs and spices, frozen foods, and prepared foods you can take home for dinner. They also offer snacks, candies, beverages, magazines, and Asian cookware.

Glossary for Bread Lovers

Boule: round, domed bread
Baguette: long, thin loaf with soft interior and a crackly crust
Batard: short, slightly flattened baguette
Challah: braided white yeast bread
Ciabatta: flat, rectangular Northern Italian bread with an airy interior and chewy crust
Ficelle: extra-thin baguette
Focaccia: flat, dense, and tender bread flavored with olive oil; from Liguria
Fougasse: chewy-crusted, rather flat sourdough wheat bread from Provence
Integrale: Italian term for "whole wheat"
Miche: round sourdough French bread
Pain au levain: dense whole-wheat French sourdough bread with a very chewy crust
Pugliese: big, round bread with a dark crust and light, airy interior
Sourdough: bread made from cultured dough ("starter") that is used for leavening many bread batches

---

BILLY'S BAKERY
184 Ninth Ave (bet 21st and 22nd St)   212/647-9956
Mon-Thurs: 8:30 a.m.-10 p.m.; Fri, Sat: 8:30 a.m.-midnight;
Sun: 9 a.m.-10 p.m.   www.billysbakerynyc.com

You simply cannot leave this place without some of the delicacies offered: wonderful layer cakes (like red velvet cake), cheesecakes, icebox pies, cupcakes, bars, cookies, muffins, and much more. Items are made on-premises, and it is a very clean and professional operation. Special cake designs and inscriptions are available. A second Tribeca location will open in late 2009 at 75 Franklin Street.

Looking for really good baguettes? Here are some suggestions:
Balthazar Bakery (80 Spring St)
Silver Moon Bakery (2740 Broadway)
Sullivan Street Bakery (533 W 47th St)
Zabar's (2245 Broadway)

CAFE LALO
201 W 83rd St (at Amsterdam Ave)   212/496-6031
Mon-Thurs: 8 a.m.-2 a.m.; Fri: 8 a.m.-4 a.m.; Sat: 9 a.m.-4 a.m.;
Sun: 9 a.m-2 a.m.   www.cafelalo.com

In my opinion, this is the best dessert shop in town. You will be reminded of a fine European pastry shop as you enjoy delicious desserts with cappuccino, espresso, cordials, or other libations from the well-stocked bar. Cafe Lalo offers more than a hundred choices, including cakes, cheesecakes, tarts, pies, and connoisseur cheese platters. Yogurt and ice cream are also available, and soothing music makes every calorie go down sweetly. Breakfasts and brunches are a treat. Delivery is offered throughout Manhattan.

CAKES 'N SHAPES
466 W 51st St (at Tenth Ave)   212/629-5512
Hours by appointment   www.cakesnshapes.com

Let your imagination take over for the next occasion that calls for cakes or cookies. Furnish Edie Connolly with a picture of a person, place, book cover, company logo, or other favorite image, and she'll impose an edible likeness on a shortbread cookie. (Imagine—you can bite the head off of a politician or your boss and get away with it!) Free-form chocolate and vanilla pound cakes are also available. Some popular 3-D works of edible art: purses and clothing items, sports equipment, bodies, critters, and consumer products. Cookies are shippable. You can even send out edible Christmas cards!

New York is famous for great cheesecakes. Here are some of the best:

Eileen's Special Cheesecake (17 Cleveland Pl, 212/966-5585, 800/521-CAKE, www.eileenscheesecake.com)

Junior's (1515 Broadway, 212/302-2000, and Grand Central Terminal, 42nd St bet Vanderbilt and Lexington Ave, 212/586-4677, www. juniorscheesecake.com): The restaurant is on the lower level, and the bakery is on the main concourse, near Track 36.

New York New York Cheesecake (405 Eighth Ave, 212/564-7136)

Ruthy's Cheesecake and Rugelach Bakery (75 Ninth Ave, 212/463-8000)

Two Little Red Hens (1652 Second Ave, 212/452-0476, www.two littleredhens.com)

CORRADO BREAD & PASTRY
1361 Lexington Ave (at 90th St)   212/348-8943
Mon-Fri: 7 a.m.-8 p.m.; Sat: 8-7; Sun: 8-6   www.corradobread.com

If you're in the Lenox Hill area, then drop by this good-looking corner bakery, where the aromas are enticing. There are about 30 kinds of breads and rolls, yummy desserts, salads, and made-to-order sandwiches. Try a sandwich of smoked turkey on brioche or tuna on Jewish rye sandwich, and perhaps a decadent chocolate mousse raspberry tart. Outdoor cafe tables add a nice touch.

CREATIVE CAKES
400 E 74th St (at First Ave)   212/794-9811
Mon-Fri: 8-4:30; Sat: 9 a.m.-11 a.m.   www.creativecakesny.com

Being in the "creative cake" business myself, I know all about making special concoctions. Creative Cakes knows how to have fun using fine ingredients and ingenious patterns. Cake lovers are fans of the fudgy chocolate cake with buttercream icing and sensational designs. Among other things, Bill Schutz has replicated the U.S. Customs House in cake form for a Fourth of July celebration. Prices are reasonable, and these edible creations are sure to be a conversation piece at any party.

CUPCAKE KIDS!

150 W 10th St (bet Greenwich Ave and Waverly Pl)   646/789-5554
Hours by appointment   www.cupcakekids.com

Proprietor Jessi Walter loves kids and good food. She combines these passions into a business teaching cooking skills to students from age 2 to 16. The emphasis is on nutrition and well-balanced meals and snacks. Workshops are usually scheduled in different restaurants around the city; she'll even bring the fun, interactive event to your special venue. Basic, seasonal, or custom classes are ideal for birthday parties, scout or youth groups, field trips, camps, and play dates.

Downtown Cookie Co.

In this day and age, there's no need for a storefront to offer goods and services. Dan Guerrera founded Downtown Cookie Co. in 2008, and customers have found his business through the Internet and telephone (646/486-3585, www.downtowncookieco.com). Dan and crew bake scratch cookies (without additives or preservatives) and deliver them by messenger around the city. They will also ship cookies via FedEx anywhere in the continental U.S.

DESSERT DELIVERY

360 E 55th St (bet First and Second Ave)   212/838-5411
Mon-Fri: 9-6; Sat: 9-5   www.dessertdeliveryny.com

An unusual concept: Dessert Delivery sells only what they consider to be the best pastry items made in the city. Created by different chefs, there are chocolate-chip cookies, strawberry shortcakes, cakes and cupcakes, and lots more. Delivery service—they say within two hours—is offered without advance notification. For office parties or home celebrations, this is a very good bet. Bill Clinton and Donald Trump are among their customers!

D'AIUTO PASTRY

405 Eighth Ave (bet 30th and 31st St)   212/564-7136
Daily: 4 a.m.-8 p.m.

Just thinking about D'Aiuto makes me hungry! You'll find famous Baby Watson cheesecakes, plus 25 other cakes and pies baked fresh each day by three generations of bakers. Also featured are banana bread, cornbread, crumb cakes, cupcakes, cannolis, Mississippi mud cakes, pecan pies, banana cream pies, apple strudel, cookies, scones, eclairs, opera pastries, chocolate doughnuts, and much more.

DOUGHNUT PLANT

379 Grand St (bet Essex and Norfolk St)   212/505-3700
Tues-Sun: 6:30 a.m.-7 p.m. (or until doughnuts are gone)
                                  www.doughnutplant.com

Mark Isreal has come a long way since delivering doughnuts on his bicycle. Now he presides over an establishment that is truly unique, concocting fluffy, fresh organic doughnuts made with spring water. There are 26 flavors, including orange, banana with pecans, "Yankee" (blueberry pin stripes), and rosewater (yes, with fresh rose petals!). Square jelly doughnuts are available, too. Doughnuts are hand-cut, yeast-raised, and very large. They also serve cinnamon buns, sticky buns, blackout cake doughnuts, and such beverages as hot chocolate, chai tea, and organic coffee.

EUROPAN BAKERY CAFE
2503 Broadway (bet 93rd and 94th St)   212/222-5110
Daily: 24 hours
135 Columbus Ave (bet 65th and 66th St)   212/799-4100
Daily: 6 a.m.-midnight

Hunger pangs in the wee hours? Come here to assuage them! This bakery features delicious cakes, pastries, and cookies. There is more: pizzas, wraps, salads, sandwiches, deli goods, breakfast items (pancakes, eggs, French toast, Danishes, and jumbo bagels), paninis, and ice cream. Their selection of international wraps is outstanding.

FERRARA BAKERY AND CAFE
195 Grand St (bet Mulberry and Mott St)   212/226-6150
Daily: 8 a.m.-11:30 p.m. (Fri, Sat till 12:30 a.m.)   www.ferraracafe.com

This store in Little Italy is one of the biggest little *pasticcerias* in the world. The business deals in wholesale imports and other ventures, but their edible goodies could support the whole operation. The atmosphere would never suggest that this is anything but a very efficiently run Italian bakery. Open since 1892, Ferrara was likely America's first espresso bar.

At **Bagels on the Square** (7 Carmine St, 212/691-3041), just about every kind of bagel and cream cheese can be found here. It's a bagel lover's paradise!

GLASER'S BAKE SHOP
1670 First Ave (bet 87th and 88th St)   212/289-2562
Tues-Fri: 7-7; Sat: 8-7; Sun: 8-3
Closed July and part of Aug

If it's Sunday, it won't be hard to find Glaser's. The line frequently spills outside as people queue up to buy the Glaser family's fresh cakes and baked goods. One isn't enough of anything here. Customers typically walk out with arms bulging. The Glasers have run their shop as a family business since 1902 at this same location, and they're justifiably proud of their breads, brownies, cakes, cookies (try the chocolate chip!), and wedding cakes.

H&H BAGELS
2239 Broadway (at 80th St)   212/595-8000
639 W 46th St (bet Eleventh and Twelfth Ave)   212/765-7200
Daily: 24 hours   www.hhbagels.com

If you find yourself out and about in the middle of the night, you can get a fresh hot bagel without having to wait in H&H's long daytime line. Regardless of the hour, you can satisfy your hot bagel craving day or night at H&H, which bakes the best bagels in Manhattan. They ship worldwide; call 800/NY-BAGEL for mail order.

KOSSAR'S BIALYS
367 Grand St (at Essex St)   212/473-4810
Sun-Thurs: 6 a.m.-8 p.m.; Fri: 6-3:30   877-4-BIALYS
                                                    www.kossarsbialys.com

The *bialy* derives its name from Bialystok (in Poland), where they were first made. Kossar's brought the recipe over from Europe almost a century ago, and their bialys, bagels, horns, and onion boards are fresh from the oven. The taste is Old World and authentic. Payment is by cash only.

LADY M CAKE BOUTIQUE
41 E 78th St (at Madison Ave)   212/452-2222
Mon-Fri: 10-7; Sat: 11-7; Sun: 11-6   www.ladymconfections.com

For some of the area's most outstanding cakes—and they *should* be, at the prices charged—a visit to this house is a must. You'll find a dazzling selection of over 12 handmade cakes, which can be enjoyed in the small cafe (salads and sandwiches till 3 p.m.) or taken home. Special gift packaging for whole cakes is also available for an additional fee. Customers can enjoy tea while sampling goodies by the slice.

Bakers know that quality ingredients produce the best results. Try these brands of unsweetened chocolates in cookies, cakes, and brownies for extra-special treats and desserts:
Scharffen Berger: unsweetened pure dark chocolate
Callebaut: the number-one chocolate manufacturer in the world
Valrhona: French chocolate, currently available only in bulk quantities

---

LE PAIN QUOTIDIEN
1131 Madison Ave (bet 84th and 85th St)   212/327-4900
833 Lexington Ave (bet 63rd and 64th St)   212/755-5810
100 Grand St (at Mercer St)   212/625-9009
Numerous other locations   www.painquotidien.com
Hours vary by store

Le Pain Quotidien traces its roots to Brussels, Belgium. It is a country-style bakery with long communal tables that serves customers breakfast, lunch, and light afternoon meals. European breads and pastries are sold at the counter. The meals offered are simple and the service refined. You'll find delicious croissants, *pain au chocolate, brioche,* heaping bread baskets, Belgian sugar waffles, an unusual Tuscan platter, crisp salads, and a splendid board of French cheeses. They also make wonderful sandwiches, like Scottish smoked salmon with dill and Parisian ham with three mustards. Don't pass up the Belgian chocolate brownies!

LITTLE PIE COMPANY
424 W 43rd St (at Ninth Ave)   212/736-4780
Mon-Sat: 8-8; Sun: 10-7

107 E 42nd St (at Grand Central Terminal)   212/414-2324
Mon-Sat: 8 a.m.-9 p.m.; Sun: 8-6   www.littlepiecompany.com

Former actor Arnold Wilkerson started baking apple pastries for private orders in his own kitchen. He now operates a unique shop that makes hand-made pies and cakes using fresh seasonal fruits. Although they specialize in apple pie, they also make fresh peach, cherry, blueberry, and other all-American fruit-pie favorites, along with cream, meringue, and crumb pies. Stop by for a hot slice of pie a la mode and a cup of cider. Also available are delicious brownies, bars, muffins, cupcakes, fruit Danishes, applesauce carrot cakes, white coconut cake, chocolate cream pie, and cheescakes with wild blueberry, cherry, and orange toppings. No preservatives are used!

MAGNOLIA BAKERY
401 Bleecker St (at 11th St)   212/462-2572
Sun-Thurs: 9 a.m.-11:30 p.m.; Fri, Sat: 9 a.m.-12:30 a.m.

200 Columbus Ave (at 69th St)   212/724-8101
Sun-Thurs: 8 a.m.-10 p.m.; Fri, Sat: 8 a.m.-midnight

1240 Ave of the Americas (at 49th St)   212/767-1123
Mon-Thurs: 7 a.m.-10 p.m.; Fri: 7 a.m.-midnight;
Sat: 8 a.m-midnight; Sun: 8 a.m.-10 p.m.   www.magnoliabakery.com

What charming places! Everything is made on premises: layer cakes, pies, cupcakes, brownies, cookies, icebox desserts, and banana pudding. Birthday cakes are a specialty that come in various types and sizes. You won't go away hungry!

> Attention all bakers and cake decorators! **New York Cake & Baking Supply** (56 W 22nd St, 212/675-CAKE) is a treasure trove of cake and chocolate supplies. You'll find everything in the baking world at reasonable prices. You can browse conveniently at www.nycake.com and then phone, fax, or order online.

MOISHE'S HOMEMADE KOSHER BAKERY
115 Second Ave (bet 6th and 7th St)   212/505-8555
Sun-Thurs: 7 a.m.-9 p.m.; Fri: 7-6

Jewish bakery specialties are legendary, and they are done to perfection at Moishe's. The cornbread is prepared exactly as it was in the Old Country (and as it should be now); the pumpernickel is dark and moist; and the ryes are simply scrumptious. The cakes and pies are special, too! The charming owners run one of the best bakeries in the city, with the usual complement of bagels, bialys, cakes, and pastries. By all means try the challah; Moishe's produces the best in town. The chocolate layer cakes are also superb.

MURRAY'S BAGELS
500 Ave of the Americas (bet 12th and 13th St)   212/462-2830
242 Eighth Ave (bet 22nd and 23rd St)   646/638-1335
Hours vary by store

Eighteen varieties of delicious hand-rolled, kettle-boiled, and baked bagels are featured at Murray's, but there is much more. You'll also find smoked fish, spreads and schmears, deli items for sandwiches, plus soups and pastries. It's all available for eat-in, catering platters, and free delivery (within limits).

ORWASHER BAKERY
308 E 78th St (bet First and Second Ave)   212/288-6569
Mon-Sat: 8-7; Sun: 9-4   www.orwasherbakery.com

Orwasher's Bakery has served Manhattan's Upper East Side for nearly a century, and today they bake about 30 varieties of all-natural breads every day. Originally famous for its classic New York breads—rye, cinnamon raisin, and pumpernickel—Orwasher's now offers a complete line of classic European breads, such as Irish soda and ciabatta. Health-conscious customers will enjoy the hearth-baked whole wheat and multigrain breads. Owner Keith Cohen recently launched a line of artisan wine breads that are made with a natural starter created from fermenting wine grapes. These artisan breads have a slighty sour flavor, are extra crusty, and are shaped and baked downstairs in Orwasher's ancient brick oven. They pair perfectly with farm-stand vegetables, stews, cured or braised meats, and fine cheeses. The bakery carries a full line of classic pastries, as well as cupcakes, artisan cheeses, and superb coffee.

Show up with cookies or cupcakes from **Eleni's Cookies** (Chelsea Market, 75 Ninth Ave, 212/255-7990, www.elenis.com) and you'll be a hit at the next party or event. Make a bigger splash with personalized or themed treats, all individually iced and decorated.

POSEIDON BAKERY
629 Ninth Ave (bet 44th and 45th St)   212/757-6173
Tues-Sat: 9-7   www.poseidonbakery.com

Poseidon was founded in 1922 by Greek baker Demetrios Anagnostou. Today it is run by his great-grandson, Paul, to the same exacting standards, and tremendous pride is evident. When a customer peers over the counter and asks about something, the response is usually a long description and sometimes an invitation to taste. There is homemade baklava, strudel, *katalf*, *trigona*, *tiropita* (cheese pie), *spanakopita,* and *saragli*. Poseidon's handmade phyllo is world-renowned. They have cocktail-size frozen spinach, cheese, vegetable, and meat pies for home consumption or parties.

ROCCO'S PASTRY SHOP & ESPRESSO CAFE
243 Bleecker St (bet Carmine and Leroy St)   212/242-6031
Sun-Thurs: 7:30 a.m.-midnight; Fri: till 1 a.m.; Sat: till 1:30 a.m.
                                                www.roccospastry.com

You'll know you're near Rocco's by the tantalizing aromas lingering outside. Inside are tempting Italian goodies like crispy biscotti, *panettone*, cream- and fruit-filled pastries, freshly baked cookies, decadent cakes, and beautiful holiday indulgences. There are choices for any time of the day: pastries for breakfast, lunch or break treats, dinner or late-night desserts, and gelato for any reason. In addition to eating in and taking out, fans of Rocco's will be glad to know that many items are available for local pickup or mailed delivery.

SILVER MOON BAKERY
2740 Broadway (at 105th St)   212/866-4717
Mon-Fri: 7:30 a.m.-8 p.m.; Sat, Sun, holidays: 8:30-7
                                                www.silvermoonbakery.com

Silver Moon presents delicious French, German, and Italian breads, French pastries and cakes, tarts, macaroons, challah, brioche (fresh fruit, raspberry, raisin, and chocolate chip), muffins, scones, and more. You can also enjoy a sandwich, soup, or quiche and watch the passing parade. Birthday and wedding cakes are made-to-order, as are special holiday treats.

SOMETHING SWEET
177 First Ave (at 11th St)   212/533-9986
Daily: 8 a.m.-9 p.m.   www.somethingsweetpastry.com

Beautifully decorated cakes, luscious tarts, cookies, and more goods here are made of chocolate, filled with chocolate, and enrobed in chocolate. No wonder my sweet tooth works overtime here! Other delectable goodies include mango mousse cake, fruit tarts, Linzer cookies, and various flavored macaroons made with almond flour. Custom orders for weddings, anniversaries, birthdays, graduations, and other occasions are cheerfully accepted at this European-style bakery.

> Yes, there is such a thing as Indian fast food! Come try some at **Indian Bread Co.** (194 Bleecker St, 212/228-1909, www.indian breadco.com). Hours are Sun-Thurs: noon-11; Fri, Sat: noon-5 a.m.

SULLIVAN STREET BAKERY
533 W 47th St (bet Tenth and Eleventh Ave)   212/265-5580
Daily: 8-7   www.sullivanstreetbakery.com

Come here for fresh, crusty, warm loaves of French bread. This is also the place to go for really fresh, authentic Italian country bread. Their sourdough is served in a number of restaurants, so you know it is first-rate. Sullivan Street Bakery carries the only flatbread *pizza bianca romana* (Roman-style white pizza) in Manhattan. Raisin-walnut bread is another specialty. You'll find great sandwiches, too.

SYLVIA WEINSTOCK CAKES
273 Church St (bet Franklin and White St)   212/925-6698
Mon-Fri: 9-5 (by appointment)   www.sylviaweinstock.com

Sylvia Weinstock has been in the cake business since the 1980s, so she knows how to satisfy customers who want the very best. Lifelike floral decorations are her trademark. Although weddings are a specialty (two months notice is suggested), she will produce masterpieces—including hand-molded sugar figures and exquisitely carved cakes—for any occasion.

WHOLE EARTH BAKERY & KITCHEN
130 St. Mark's Pl (bet First Ave and Ave A)   212/677-7597
Daily: 10-10

This is a completely vegan establishment and perhaps the only Manhattan bakery that uses organic flours and organic, unprocessed sweeteners. They feature great pizza, lasagna, and soup, plus daily selections of savory foods. Catering is available.

YONAH SCHIMMEL'S KNISHES

137 E Houston St (bet First and Second Ave)   212/477-2858
Sun-Thurs: 9-7; Fri, Sat: 9 a.m.-midnight   www.knishery.com

Yonah Schimmel has been selling knishes since 1910, and the name is now legendary. He started out dispensing knishes among the pushcarts of the Lower East Side. A Yonah Schimmel knish is a unique experience. It doesn't look or taste anything like the mass-produced things sold at supermarkets, lunch stands, and New York ballgames. Yonah's knishes have a thin, flaky crust—almost like strudel dough—surrounding a hot, moist filling, and they are kosher. The best-selling filling is potato, but kasha (buckwheat), spinach, and a half-dozen others are also terrific. No two knishes come out exactly alike, since each is handmade. You can order online or by fax (212/477-2858) for delivery anywhere in the continental U.S.

Get in touch with **Manhattan Milk Co.** (917/843-0727; www. manhattanmilk.com) for fresh bottled milk (chocolate, too!), organic eggs, cases of water, juices, and other products. They'll deliver to your door, if you're home between 4 a.m. and 10 a.m. to accept delivery, or leave the order with your doorman at any time. These folks bring convenience to a new level, with service available anywhere in Manhattan.

Beverages

NEW YORK BEVERAGE WHOLESALERS

515 Bruckner Blvd (bet 149th and Austin Pl), The Bronx
Mon-Fri: 9-5; Sat: 9-4   212/831-4000, 718/401-7700
                                          www.nybeverage.com

The *buy*-words here are tremendous variety and great prices. This outfit has one of the largest retail beer selections in New York City, with over 500 brands available, plus sodas, mineral and natural waters, iced teas, and seltzers. They will deliver to your door, supply specialty imports, and work with you on any quantities needed. Call to place a delivery order. Don't forget the ice!

RIVERSIDE BEER AND SODA DISTRIBUTORS

2331 Twelfth Ave (at 133rd St)   212/234-3884
Mon-Sat: 9-6

This place mainly supplies wholesalers and large retail orders, but they are not averse to serving retail customers with cases or kegs of beer. Once you've made the trek up here, you might as well take advantage of the discount and buy in quantity.

British

MYERS OF KESWICK

634 Hudson St (bet Horatio and Jane St)   212/691-4194
Mon-Fri: 10-7; Sat: 10-6; Sun: noon-5   www.myersofkeswick.com

Peter and Irene Myers are to English food what Burberry, Church, and Laura Ashley are to English clothing. They've made it possible for you to visit "the village grocer" for imported staples and fresh, home-baked items you'd swear came from a kitchen in Soho—the London neighborhood, that is.

Among the tins, a shopper can find Heinz *treacle* sponge pudding, trifle mix, *ribena,* mushy peas, steak and kidney pie, Smarties, lemon barley water, chutneys, jams and preserves, and all the major English teas. Fresh goods include sausage rolls, Myers' pork pie, Scotch eggs, British bangers, and Cumberland sausages, all made fresh daily. Each month spotlights a different pie. There are also cheeses—the double Gloucester is outstanding!—and chocolates. For Anglophiles and expatriates alike, Myers of Keswick is a *luverly* treat.

Candy

DIVALICIOUS CHOCOLATE FOUNTAINS
365 Broome St (between Elizabeth and Moss St)   212/343-1243
Wed-Sun: 12-8   www.divaliciouschocolate.com

Being a chocoholic, I love this kind of business! Divalicious rents those wonderful machines that melt chocolate for users to dip fruits or sweets for a decadent treat. The fee depends upon the size of machine, duration of rental, dippables, and an attendant. The cafe also serves drinks and tasty treats (chocolate, of course) and stocks an impressive selection of *couverture* chocolates. They will cater school and corporate events, weddings, bar and bat mitzvahs, showers, trade shows, and more. Special events can be scheduled in the cafe, too.

Since 1894, **Veniero's** (342 E 11th St, 212/674-7070, www.venieros pastry.com) has been serving Italian pastries, cakes, and gelati to satisfied customers. The quarters still have many original details, including hand-stamped copper ceilings and etched glass doors.

DYLAN'S CANDY BAR
1011 Third Ave (at 60th St)   646/735-0078
Mon-Thurs: 10-9; Fri, Sat: 10 a.m.-11 p.m.; Sun: 11-8
                                                   www.dylanscandybar.com

Ralph Lauren's daughter, Dylan, has been a candy maven since 2001. This emporium is inundated with kids and grown-ups alike. All enjoy the old-fashioned soda fountain with custom-made ice cream flavors and the enormous selection of candies from around the world. These include jelly beans, gum, popcorn, nostalgic choices (Necco wafers, Pixy Stix, wax lips, Abba-Zabba bars), chocolates (decadent truffles, chocolate-covered goodies, bars, and brownie mixes), and lots more. The expanded fashion line includes colorful accessories, jewelry, and cute shirts for the whole family. Sweet dreams are assured with the candy-themed pajamas. The bath and body products feature tempting flavors like coconut bonbon, strawberry licorice, and chocolate cupcake.

ECONOMY CANDY
108 Rivington St (bet Essex and Ludlow St)   212/254-1531
Sun-Fri: 9-6; Sat: 10-5   800/352-4544 (outside New York)
                                                   www.economycandy.com

Since 1937, the same family has been selling everything from penny candies to beautiful gourmet gift baskets at Economy Candy. What a selection of dried fruits, candies, cookies, nuts, and chocolates—even sugar-free goodies! The best part is the price. You'll find much for your baking needs: cocoas, baking chocolate, and glazed fruits. Old-time favorites include Skybars, Mary Janes, candy buttons, and Ice Cubes. Mail orders are filled efficiently and promptly; an online catalog is available. This is a must-stop for holiday candy treats.

JACQUES TORRES CHOCOLATE
350 Hudson St (at King St)   212/414-2462
Mon-Sat: 9-7; Sun: 10-6   www.mrchocolate.com

You can watch those delicious Jacques Torres bars and other creations being made right before your eyes! In a hefty space that houses a factory, retail counter, and cafe, Jacques Torres will send the chocoholic in you to heaven.

> One of my favorite snacks is a fresh, juicy strawberry dipped in chocolate. You can watch them being made at **Godiva** (745 Seventh Ave, 212/921-2193, and other locations). Take home a few of these magnificent morsels for afternoon tea or a special dessert!

LA MAISON DU CHOCOLAT
1018 Madison Ave (bet 78th and 79th St)   212/744-7117
Mon-Sat: 10-7; Sun: noon-6

30 Rockefeller Plaza (49th St bet Fifth Ave and Ave of the Americas)
Mon-Fri: 9:30-7; Sat: 10-7; Sun: noon-6   212/265-9404

63 Wall St (bet Pearl and Hanover St)   212/952-1123
Mon-Fri: 9:30-7; Sat: 11-6   www.lamaisonduchocolat.com

What a place! Over 40 delicious variations of light and dark chocolates are available under one roof. They carry French truffles, plain and fancy champagnes, orangettes, chocolate-covered almonds, caramels, candied chestnuts (seasonal), and fruit paste. There's even a tea salon that serves pastries and drinks. Everything is made in Paris, and Manhattan's La Maison du Chocolat is the first branch outside of France. Prices are a cut above the candy-counter norm, but then so are exotic flavors like September raspberries, freshly grated ginger root, raisins flamed in rum, marzipan with pistachio and kirsh, and caramel butter.

LEONIDAS
485 Madison Ave (bet 51st and 52nd St)   212/980-2608
Mon-Fri: 9-7; Sat: 10-7; Sun: noon-6   www.leonidas-chocolate.com

This store sells and ships the famous Leonidas Belgian confections to those who appreciate exquisite sweets. Over 100 varieties of them—milk, white, and bittersweet chocolate pieces, chocolate orange peels, solid chocolate medallions, fabulous fresh cream fillings, truffle fillings, and marzipan—are flown in fresh every week. Leonidas' pralines are particularly sumptuous. Jacques Bergier, the genial general manager, can make the mouth water just describing this treasure trove. Best of all, prices are reasonable. Speaking of Leonidas, three retail locations of **Manon Cafe** (120 Broadway, 212/766-6100; 3 Hanover Square, 212/422-9600; and 74 Trinity Pl, 212/233-1111) serve Leonidas' Belgian chocolates, as well as coffee, espresso, cappuccino, sandwiches, and salads.

LI-LAC CHOCOLATES

40 Eighth Ave (at Jane St)   212/924-2280
Mon-Fri: 10-8; Sat: noon-8; Sun: noon-6

Grand Central Market Hall (Lexington Ave at 43rd St)   212/370-4866
Mon-Fri: 7 a.m.-9 p.m.; Sat: 10-7; Sun: 11-6   www.li-lacchocolates.com

Since 1923, Li-Lac has been *the* source for fine chocolate in Greenwich Village. Li-Lac's delicious chocolate fudge is made fresh every day, and their maple walnut fudge is every bit as good. Then there are pralines, mousses, French rolls, nuts, glacé fruits, and hand-dipped chocolates.

How about a chocolate tour? **New York Chocolate Tours** (917/292-0680, www.sweetwalks.com) will take you to delicious places that excite the heart (and taste buds) of every chocoholic! Several different tours are available; contact them for details of time and place. Private tours are available upon request.

MARIEBELLE NEW YORK

484 Broome St (bet West Broadway and Wooster St)   212/925-6999
762 Madison Ave (at 65th St)   212/249-4587
Daily: 11-7   www.mariebelle.com

Forget about the diet and rush down to MarieBelle. What awaits you is thick European hot chocolate, homemade cookies and biscuits, a cacao bar, and wines (Madison Ave location only). The exotic chocolate flavors are packed with class. What a great gift for chocoholics! Crepes, fondues, sandwiches, salads, and other light fare are available at the Cacao Bar. Small private events are a specialty.

MONDEL CHOCOLATES

2913 Broadway (at 114th St)   212/864-2111
Mon-Sat: 11-7; Sun: noon-6   www.mondelchocolates.com

Mondel has been a tasty gem in the neighborhood for over a half-century. Owner Florence Mondel's father founded the store. The aroma is fantastic! The chocolate-covered ginger, orange peel, nut barks, and turtles are especially good. I routinely order their nonpareils. A dietetic chocolate line is offered.

TEUSCHER CHOCOLATES OF SWITZERLAND

25 E 61st St (at Madison Ave)   212/751-8482
Mon-Sat: 10-6; Sun: noon-5   www.teuschermadison.com

620 Fifth Ave (Rockefeller Center)   212/246-4416
Mon-Sat: 10-6; Thurs: 10-7; Sun: noon-6   www.teuscherfifthavenue.com

If there was an award for "most elegant chocolate shop," it would go to Teuscher. These are not just chocolates; they're imported works of art.

Chocolates are shipped weekly from Switzerland. They are packed into stunning handmade boxes that add to the decor of many a customer's home. The truffles are almost obscenely good. The superb champagne truffle has a tiny dot of champagne cream in the center. The cocoa, nougat, butter-crunch, muscat, orange, and almond truffles all have their own little surprises. Truffles are the stars, but Teuscher's marzipan and praline chocolates are of similar high quality.

> I still like to go to real old-time places, especially this luncheonette. Established in 1925, **Lexington Candy Shop** (1226 Lexington Ave, 212/288-0057) continues to provide great breakfasts, burgers, ice cream, egg creams, and, of course, candy.

Catering, Delis, Food to Go

ABIGAIL KIRSCH
Chelsea Piers, Pier 60 (23rd St at Hudson River)   212/336-6060
Daily: 9-5 (by appointment)   www.abigailkirsch.com

Abigail Kirsch's food, service, decor, and tableware are of the very highest quality, and so is her pricing. But you will get your money's worth if it's a class event, wedding, corporate function, or intimate cocktail party that you are hosting. You will not have to worry about a single detail from this organization, since you are relying on over three decades of experience.

AGATA & VALENTINA
1505 First Ave (at 79th St)   212/452-0690
Daily: 8:30-8   www.agatavalentina.com

This is a very classy expanded gourmet shop with an ambience that will make you think you're in Sicily. There are good things to eat at every counter, with each one more tempting than the next. You'll love the great selection of gourmet dishes, bakery items, seafood, magnificent fresh vegetables, meats, cheeses, appetizers, candies, and gelati. Extra virgin olive oil is a house specialty.

> If you would like to shop where chefs stock up, consider visiting **Trufette** (a.k.a. **S.O.S. Chefs**, 104 Ave B, 212/505-5813). Among the interesting finds: many kinds of preserves, glazes, chocolates, truffles, mushrooms, foie gras, spices, flavored salts, nuts, vanilla beans, saffron, fennel pollen, and much more. It is a high-end discovery center!

AZURE
830 Third Ave (at 51st St)   212/486-8080
Daily: 24 hours

Azure's 125 feet of hot and cold offerings is quite a sight. What a salad bar! Of course, there is more: homemade soups, hot Italian sandwiches, stuffed baked potatoes, pizzas, sushi, and great muffins. Azure also offers healthy Mongolian grill fare.

Favorite Chocolate Shops of a Serious Chocoholic (Me!)

Bespoke Chocolates (6 Extra Pl, off E 1st St, 212/260-7103)
Charbonnel et Walker (Saks Fifth Avenue, 611 Fifth Ave, 8th floor, 212/588-0546)
Chocolate Bar (19 Eighth Ave, 212/366-1541)
Christopher Norman Chocolates (60 New St, 212/402-1243; also carried at Dean & Deluca and Whole Foods Markets)
Fifth Avenue Chocolatiere (693 Third Ave, 212/935-5454)
Jacques Torres Chocolate (350 Hudson St, 212/414-2462 and 285 Amsterdam Ave, 212/787-3256)
Kee's Chocolates (80 Thompson St, 212/334-3284)
La Bergamote (169 Ninth Ave, 212/627-9010)
L.A. Burdick Chocolates (800/229-2419): mail order or delivery
La Maison du Chocolat (1018 Madison Ave, 212/744-7117 and 30 Rockefeller Center, 212/265-9404)
Leonidas (485 Madison Ave, 212/980-2608 and at Manon Cafe locations)
Manhattan Fruitier (105 E 29th St, 212/686-0404)
MarieBelle New York (484 Broome St, 212/884-9707 and 762 Madison Avenue, 212/249-4585)
Martine's (400 E 82nd St, 212/744-6289 and at Bloomingdale's, 1000 Third Ave, 6th floor)
Max Brenner, Chocolate by the Bald Man (841 Broadway and 141 Second Ave, 212/388-0030)
Neuchatel Chocolates (55 E 52nd St, 212/759-1388)
Teuscher Chocolates of Switzerland (25 E 61st St, 212/751-8482 and 620 Fifth Ave, 212/246-4416
Vosges Haut-Chocolat (132 Spring St, 212/625-2929 and 1100 Madison Ave, 212/717-2929)

Here are New York's best restaurants for chocolate desserts:

Bar Room at The Modern (9 W 53rd St, 212/333-1220): hazelnut *dacquoise*
craft (43 E 19th St, 212/780-0880): chocolate soufflé
Jean Georges (1 Central Park W, 212/299-3900): warm, soft chocolate cake
Spotted Pig (314 W 11th St, 212/620-0393): flourless chocolate cake

BARNEY GREENGRASS
541 Amsterdam Ave (bet 86th and 87th St)   212/724-4707
Tues-Sun: 8-6 (takeout)   www.barneygreengrass.com
Tues-Fri: 8:30-4; Sat, Sun: 8:30-5 (restaurant)

Those who like sturgeon love Barney Greengrass! This family business has occupied the same locale since 1929. Barney has been succeeded by his grandson Gary, but the same quality gourmet smoked fish is still sold over the counter, just as it was in Barney's day. Greengrass lays claim to the title of "Sturgeon King," and few would dispute it. While sturgeon is indeed king, Greengrass also has other regal smoked-fish delicacies: Nova Scotia salmon, belly lox, and whitefish. There is more: caviar, pickled herring, pastrami salmon, and kippered-salmon salad. The dairy and deli line—including vegetable cream cheese, great homemade cheese blintzes, homemade salads and borscht, and a smashing Nova Scotia salmon with scrambled eggs and onions—is world-renowned. In fact, because so many customers couldn't wait to get home to unwrap their packages, Greengrass started a restaurant next door.

BARRAUD CATERERS

405 Broome St (at Centre St) 212/925-1334
Mon-Fri. 10-6 www.barraudcaterers.com

Owner Rosemary Howe has an interesting background. She was born in India and grew up British, and is therefore familiar with Indian and Anglo-Indian food. Her training in developing recipes is on the French side. Because she was raised in the tradition of afternoon tea, she knows finger sandwiches and all that goes with them. Her menus are unique. All breads are menu-specific, and every meal is customized from a lengthy list. A wine consultant is available, and consultations on table etiquette are given. Dinners that focus on cheese and wine are a specialty. This is a real hands-on operation, with Rosemary taking care of every detail of your brunch, tea, lunch, or dinner. She also features degustation (tasting) menus, paired with appropriate wines for each course.

Bazzini (339 Greenwich St, 212/334-1280, www.bazzininuts.com) is Tribeca's gourmet food emporium. You'll find a great showing of fine foods: meats, fish, produce, deli items, prepared foods to go, charcuterie, and more. There is an on-premises cafe. Knives and cutting boards are stocked. Nuts and dried fruits are a specialty. Delivery is available.

BUTTERFIELD MARKET

1114 Lexington Ave (bet 77th and 78th St) 212/288-7800
Mon-Fri: 7:30 a.m.-8 p.m.; Sat: 7:30-5:30; Sun: 8-5
www.butterfieldmarket.com

Upper East Siders have enjoyed the goodies at Butterfield for nearly a century. Highlights of this popular market include an excellent prepared-foods section, produce, a good selection of quality specialty items, tasty pastries, charcuterie, attractive gift baskets, a terrific cheese selection, and a diet-busting candy and sweets section. Catering is a feature, and service is personal and informed.

CHELSEA MARKET

75 Ninth Ave (bet 15th and 16th St) 212/243-6005
Mon-Sat: 8-8; Sun: 10-8 www.chelseamarket.com
Hours vary by store

In a complex of 18 former industrial buildings, including the old Nabisco Cookie Factory of the late 1800s, an 800-foot-long concourse houses one of the most unusual marketplaces in the city. The space is innovative, including a waterfall fed by an underground spring. Among the nearly two dozen shops, you'll find **Amy's Bread** (big selection, plus a cafe); **Bowery Kitchen Supplies** (kitchen buffs will go wild!); **Chelsea Market Baskets**; **Chelsea Wine Vault** (climate-controlled); **Cleaver Company** (catering and event planning); **Ronnybrook Farm Dairy** (fresh milk and eggs); **Buon Italia** (great Italian basics); **Hale & Hearty Soups** (dozens of varieties); **Imports from Marrakesh**; **The Lobster Place** (takeout seafood); **Sarabeth's Bakery**; **Manhattan Fruit Exchange** (for buying in bulk); **Chelsea Thai** (wholesale and takeout); **Morimoto New York** (Japanese fine dining); **Fat Witch Bakery** (brownies, goodies, gifts); and **Eleni's Cookies** (artfully iced sugar cookies, bagels, ice cream, and more). **Ruthy's Cheesecake and Rugelach Bakery** is outstanding!

DEAN & DELUCA
560 Broadway (at Prince St)   212/226-6800
Daily: 7 a.m.-8 p.m.
1150 Madison Ave (at 85th St)   212/717-0800
Daily: 8-8   www.deananddeluca.com

Dean & Deluca is one of the most recognizable names on the American epicurean scene. The flagship store in Soho offers an extraordinary array of local, national, and international culinary selections. Among the many temptations are fresh produce and flowers, fresh-baked breads and pastries, prepared dishes, a good showing of cheeses and charcuterie, and a selection of meats, poultry, and seafood. A bustling espresso bar serves coffee and cappuccino, as well as sweets and savories. This part of the business has been expanded into smaller cafes throughout the city. To complete a gourmet adventure, Dean & Deluca offers an assortment of housewares. They can also cater intimate gatherings and corporate events.

> Be sure to stop by **Blue Ribbon Bakery Market** (14 Bedford St, 212/337-0404). You'll find a yummy selection of famous Blue Ribbon breads—even toast with scrumptious toppings!

DELMONICO GOURMET FOOD MARKET
55 E 59th St (bet Madison and Park Ave)   212/751-5559
150 E 42nd St (at Lexington Ave)   212/661-0150
24 hours

Each of these markets has gourmet groceries, fresh produce, pastries, a bakery, a huge selection of cheeses, and much more. This is a good choice if you are planning a catered event for your office or home. I like the ultra-clean surroundings and accommodating help. Don't miss the charcuterie selection and salad bars.

EDIBLE ARRANGEMENTS
1788 Third Ave (at 99th St) and other locations   212/828-5858
Hours vary   www.ediblearrangements.com

These bouquets look good enough to eat—and, as the name indicates, you can do just that! A tasty assortment of fresh fruit is creatively displayed in vases, mugs, baskets, bowls, and novelty containers. This unique, healthy gift idea is ideal for desserts, centerpieces, showers, holidays, and almost any other occasion. Arrangements can be made even more delicious with all-natural fudge sauce for dipping. Convey a special message with a mylar balloon or plush bear.

ELI'S MANHATTAN
1411 Third Ave (bet 80th and 81st St)   212/717-8100
Daily: 7 a.m.-9 p.m.   www.elismanhattan.com

You know quality is foremost when the name Eli Zabar is attached. This is true at Eli's Manhattan, which carries dairy items, pastries, flowers, prepared foods, appetizers, smoked fish, coffee, wine and spirits, and gift baskets. Catering is available. Prices can be high, but so is quality. A self-service cafe called **Taste** (1413 Third Ave, 212/717-9798) offers breakfast and lunch, and then transforms into a full-service restaurant for dinner.

The Lower East Side's **Essex Street Market** (120 Essex Street, at Delancey St) has been a historic shopping destination since 1947. You'll find vendors of seafood, meats, ethnic groceries, baked goods, produce, and bulk-food items. The market also features specialty stores dispensing clothing, electronics, household goods, hardware, and religious items. No matter what you are looking for, Essex Street Market promises a unique shopping experience.

FAIRWAY
2127 Broadway (at 74th St)   212/595-1888
Daily: 6 a.m.-1 a.m.

2328 Twelfth Ave (at 133rd St)   212/234-3883
Daily: 8 a.m.-11 p.m.   www.fairwaymarket.com

The popular institution known as Fairway made its name with an incredible selection of fruits and vegetables. They offer produce in huge quantities at reasonable prices. The uptown store is newer and larger, stocking a wonderful array of cheeses, meats, bakery items, and more. Additions to the Broadway store include an on-premises bakery, the **Fairway Cafe and Steakhouse** (run by Mitchel London, executive chef), organically grown produce, expanded fish and meat departments, and a catering service. Fairway operates its own farm on Long Island and has developed relationships with area produce dealers. Both stores offer a full line of organic and natural grocery, health, and beauty items. There is an all-kosher bakery at the Twelfth Avenue location, in Harlem. As you make your rounds on the Upper West Side, you can't go wrong by carrying a Fairway bag on one arm and a Zabar's bag on the other!

FINE & SCHAPIRO
138 W 72nd St (bet Broadway and Columbus Ave)
Daily: 10-10   212/877-2874, 212/877-2721
                                     www.fineandschapiro. com

Ostensibly a kosher delicatessen and restaurant, Fine & Schapiro also offers great dinners for home consumption. Because of the high quality, they term themselves "the Rolls-Royce of delicatessens." That description is not hyperbole. Fine & Schapiro dispenses a complete line of cold cuts, hot and cold hors d'oeuvres, catering platters, and magnificent sandwiches—try the pastrami! Everything that issues from Fine & Schapiro is perfectly cooked and artistically arranged. The sandwiches are masterpieces; the aroma and taste are irresistible. Chicken in the pot and stuffed cabbage are among their best items.

GARDEN OF EDEN GOURMET MARKET

162 W 23rd St (bet Ave of the Americas and Seventh Ave)	
	212/675-6300
7 E 14th St (bet University Pl and Fifth Ave)	212/255-4200
2780 Broadway (bet 106th and 107th St)	212/222-7300
Mon-Sat: 7 a.m.-10 p.m.; Sun: 7 a.m.-9:30 p.m.	
	www.edengourmet.com

These stores are both farmers markets and gourmet shops! The food items are fresh, appetizing, and priced to please. Moreover, the stores are immaculate and well organized, and the personnel are exceptionally helpful. You'll find breads and bakery items, cheeses, veggies, meats, seafood, pastas, desserts, patés, and breakfast items. All manner of catering services are available.

GLORIOUS FOOD

504 E 74th St (bet East River and York Ave)	212/628-2320
Mon-Fri: 9-5 (by appointment)	www.gloriousfood.com

Glorious Food is at the top of many New Yorkers' lists when it comes to catering. They are a full-service outfit, expertly taking care of every detail of any event. They have met most every challenge since 1971. Give 'em a try!

Soups, salads, and sandwiches are available at an excellent *patisserie* called **Financier** (35 Cedar St, 212/952-3838; 3-4 World Financial Center, 212/786-3220; and 62 Stone St, 212/344-5600).

GOURMET GARAGE

453 Broome St (at Mercer St)	212/941-5850
1245 Park Ave (at 96th St)	212/348-5850
301 E 64th St (at Second Ave)	212/535-6271
2567 Broadway (at 96th St)	212/663-0656
117 Seventh Ave S (at 10th St)	212/699-5980
Hours vary by store	www.gourmetgarage.com

A working-class gourmet food shop is the best way to describe Gourmet Garage. These stores carry a good selection of in-demand items—including fruits and veggies, cheeses, breads, pastries, coffees, fresh meats and seafoods, and olive oils—at low prices. Organic foods are a specialty. Catering and gift baskets are available, and delivery is offered for a nominal fee. All locations offer prepared foods and a sushi bar.

GRACE'S MARKETPLACE

1237 Third Ave (at 71st St)	212/737-0600
Mon-Sat: 7 a.m.-8:30 p.m.; Sun: 8-7	www.gracesmarketplace.com

I come from a multi-generational family business where being available to customers was the key to success, so I am well aware of operations that still exhibit those values. Grace's Marketplace is a prime example. Founded in 1985 by Grace Balducci Doria and the late Joe Doria, Sr., Grace's is one of the city's finest and most popular food emporiums. The Doria family presides over this operation, and they can be seen helping customers on the floor. Products, service, and ambience are all top of the line. You'll find smoked meats and fish, cheeses, fresh pastas, homemade sauces, produce, a full range of baked goods, candy, coffee and tea, dried fruit, pastries, gourmet groceries, prepared foods, prime meats, produce, and seafood. Quality gift baskets and catering are specialties. Try their adjoining restaurant, **Grace's Trattoria** (201 E 71st St, 212/452-2323, www.gracestrattoria.com), for great Italian fare. This place is a must-visit!

GREAT PERFORMANCES
304 Hudson St (bet Spring and Vandam St)   212/727-2424
Mon-Fri: 8:30-5:30 (by appointment)   www.greatperformances.com

Great Performances has been creating spectacular events in the New York area since 1979 with the help of folks from the city's artistic community. Each division of this full-service catering company has a team of expert staff. They take pride in recruiting the best and brightest the industry has to offer. Their people bring creativity, personality, and technical expertise to each event. From intimate dinner parties to gala dinners for thousands, Great Performances is a complete event-planning resource. They also operate several cafes at cultural institutions.

Bánh mì is a flavorful Vietnamese hoagie stuffed with meats, pickled veggies, and hot sauce or peppers. Other accouterments to the warm, crackly bread might be cheese, paté, or cilantro. Order *bánh mì* at one of these eateries:

An Choi (85 Orchard St, 212/226-3700)
Bánh Mì Saigon Bakery (138 Mott St, 212/941-1541)
Baoguette (61 Lexington Ave, 212/518-4089)
Num Pang (21 E 12th St, 212/255-3271)
Paris Sandwich Bakery Cafe (113 Mott St, 212/226-7221)
Sáu Voi Corp (101-105 Lafayette St, 212/226-8184)

H&H MIDTOWN BAGELS EAST
1551 Second Ave (bet 80th and 81st St)   212/734-7441
Daily: 24 hours   www.hhmidtownbagelseast.com

Delicious bagels are made right on the premises, and if you're lucky, you'll get 'em warm! But there is more: homemade croissants, assorted Italian cookies, soups, cold cuts, sandwiches, salads, salmon, lox, sturgeon, pickled herring, jams, and honeys. The emphasis is on carryout, but tables are available for those who can't wait to dive in. Catering and shipping are offered as well.

HAN AH REUM
25 W 32nd St (bet Broadway and Fifth Ave)   212/695-3283
Daily: 9 a.m.-midnight   www.hanahreum.com

Note the late hours! Korean, Chinese, and Japanese food items are the specialties at Han ah Reum, but there are even some Mexican choices.

INTERNATIONAL GROCERY
543 Ninth Ave (at 40th St)   212/279-1000
Mon-Fri: 7:30-6:30; Sat: till 6

Ninth Avenue is one great wholesale market of international cookery.

Accordingly, International Grocery is both a spice emporium and an excellent source for rudiments on which to sprinkle the spices. You will sacrifice frills for some of the best prices and freshest foodstuffs in town. Lamb can be special-ordered.

KELLEY & PING
127 Greene St (bet Houston and Prince St)   212/228-1212
325 Bowery (at Second Ave)   212/475-8600
Lunch: Mon-Fri (11:30-5); Dinner: Daily (5:30-11)   www.eatrice.com

The exotic cuisines of Asia—Thai, Chinese, Vietnamese, Japanese, Malaysian, and Korean—are popular in restaurants and at home. Kelley & Ping specializes in groceries and housewares from this part of the world. On-premises restaurants have become a major part of the operations, serving lunch and dinner, as well as catering. You'll find lunch boxes, noodle soups, wok items, salads, wraps, and more. Delivery is available to nearby neighborhoods. If you have questions about how to prepare Asian dishes, these folks can tell you.

Located in the heart of midtown Manhattan, **Grand Central Market** (Grand Central Terminal, 42nd Street at Park Ave) has some of Manhattan's finest quality food retailers, including **Bella Cucina**, **Ceriello Fine Foods**, **Corrado Bread & Pastry**, **Dishes at Home**, **Greenwich Produce**, **Koglin German Hams**, **Li-Lac Chocolates**, **Murray's Cheese**, **Oren's Daily Roast**, **Penzeys Spices**, **Pescatore Seafood Company**, **Wild Edibles**, and **Zaro's Bread Basket**.

MANGIA
50 W 57th St (bet Fifth Ave and Ave of the Americas)   212/582-5882
16 E 48th St (bet Fifth and Madison Ave)   212/754-7600
22 W 23rd St (bet Fifth Ave and Ave of the Americas)   212/647-0200
Hours vary by store   www.mangiatogo.com

At Mangia, the old European reverence for ripe tomatoes and brick-oven bread endures. Each of these outfits offers four distinct services: corporate catering, with everything that's needed for an office breakfast or luncheon; a juice bar; a carryout shop with an antipasti bar, soups, salads, sandwiches, entrees, sweets, and cappuccino; and a restaurant with a full menu and made-to-order pastas. Prices are competitive, and delivery is offered.

NEWMAN & LEVENTHAL
45 W 81st St (bet Central Park West and Columbus Ave)
By appointment   212/362-9400

Having been a kosher caterer for nearly a century, this firm is known for unique menus and top quality. Be prepared to pay well for outstanding food.

RUSS & DAUGHTERS
179 E Houston St (bet Allen and Orchard St)
Mon-Fri: 8-8; Sat: 9-7; Sun: 8-5:30   212/475-4880, 800/RUSS-229
                                         www.russanddaughters.com

One of my favorite places! A family business in its fourth generation, Russ & Daughters has been a renowned New York shop since it first opened its doors. They carry nuts, dried fruits, lake sturgeon, salmon, sable, and herring. Russ & Daughters has a reputation for serving only the very best. Six varieties of caviar are sold at low prices. Their chocolates are premium quality. They sell wholesale and over the counter, and will ship anywhere. Many a Lower East Side shopping trip ends with a stop at Russ & Daughters. It is clean, first-rate, and friendly—what more could you ask?

SABLE'S SMOKED FISH

1489 Second Ave (bet 77th and 78th St)　　　　　212/249-6177
Mon-Fri: 8-7:30; Sat: 7 a.m.-7:30 p.m.; Sun: 7-5　www.sablesnyc.com

Kenny Sze was the appetizers manager at Zabar's for many years, and he learned the trade well. He brought that knowledge to the Upper East Side with a shop that offers wonderful smoked salmon, lobster salad, Alaskan crab salad, sturgeon, caviar (good prices), cold cuts, cheeses, coffees, salads, fresh breads, and prepared foods. Sable's catering service can provide platters (smoked fish, cold cuts, and cheese), jumbo sandwiches, whole hams, cured meats, and more. Cold cuts and chicken dishes are specialties. Free delivery is offered in the immediate area, and they'll ship anywhere in the U.S. Tables for eat-in are available.

For those New Yorkers who don't find grocery shopping a pleasant pastime, there is hope. **Fresh Direct** (212/796-8002, www.fresh direct.com) sells over 3,000 organic and prepared food items. You can place your order online from an expansive list, as well as arrange for a delivery time. They also provide useful information like recipes and cooking information. Prices are competitive, as they do not have a storefront or deal with middle men. Delivery charges are reasonable. What a great service for shut-ins!

SALUMERIA BIELLESE

378 Eighth Ave (at 29th St)　　　　　　　　　212/736-7376
Mon-Fri: 7-6; Sat: 9-5　　　　　www.salumeriabiellese.com

This Italian-owned grocery store is also the only French charcuterie in the city. If that isn't contradiction enough, consider that the loyal lunchtime crowd thinks it's dining at a hero shop when it's really enjoying the fruits of a kitchen that supplies many fine restaurants in the city. To understand how all this came about, a lesson in New York City geography is necessary. In 1945, when Ugo Buzzio and Joseph Nello came to this country from the Piedmontese city of Biella, they opened a shop a block away from the current one in the immigrant neighborhood known as Hell's Kitchen. (Today, this gentrified area is called Clinton.) They almost immediately began producing French charcuterie. Word spread among the chefs of the city's restaurants that Salumeria Biellese was producing a quality product that could not be duplicated. Buzzio's son Marc, along with partners Paul and Fouad, run the business today. Offerings include sausages (pork, game, veal, lamb, and poultry), cured meats, and specialty patés. **Biricchino** (260 W 29th St, 212/695-6690), a restaurant offering Northern Italian cuisine, is located in back.

SARGE'S
548 Third Ave (bet 36th and 37th St)   212/679-0442
Daily: 24 hours   www.sargesdeli.com

Sarge's isn't fancy, but it could feed an army, and there's much to be said for the taste, quality, and price. Sarge's will cater everything from hot dogs to hot or cold buffets for almost any size crowd, and there are remarkably reasonable package deals. Sarge's also caters deli items and has an excellent selection of cold hors d'oeuvre platters, offering everything from canapes of caviar, sturgeon, and Nova Scotia salmon to shrimp cocktail. To make the party complete, Sarge's can supply utensils, condiments, and staff. Delivery is available.

SONNIER & CASTLE
554 W 48th St (bet Tenth and Eleventh Ave)   212/957-6481
By appointment   www.sonnier-castle.com

This full-service caterer will also help with locations, flowers, entertainment, and anything else a customer might need for a memorable gathering. Russ Sonnier and David Castle are young enough to be inventive, yet mature enough to do a first-class job. Joined by a high-profile chef, they provide customized luxury catering at its best.

Scott's Pizza Tours

It doesn't get much better than a tour that combines eating pizza from some of New York's finest establishments while learning about the neighborhoods. Pizza aficionado Scott Wiener (212/209-3370, 800/979-3370) dishes out the history of pizza with four tasty stops to sample slices from brick ovens and classic New York slice counters. Since there are so many significant pizzerias, the tour itinerary changes to introduce patrons to as many eateries and styles as possible. A three-hour walking tour covers a mile-and-a-half in Little Italy and Greenwich Village. A four-and-a-half-hour bus tour leaves from Manhattan and may include Brooklyn, Queens, and The Bronx.

SPOONBREAD
Catering at specified site   212/865-0700

MISS MAUDE'S SPOONBREAD TOO
547 Lenox Ave (between 137th and 138th St)   212/690-3100
Mon-Thurs: noon-9:30; Fri-Sat: noon-10:30; Sun: 11-9:30

MISS MAMIE'S SPOONBREAD TOO   212/865-6744
366 W 110th St (between Columbus and Manhattan Ave)
Mon-Fri: noon-10; Sat: noon-11; Sun: 11-9   www.spoonbreadinc.com

If you like soul food, then go to Spoonbread. Pork chops, spoonbread (a wonderful pudding-like cornmeal bread eaten with a spoon or fork), chicken (fried, smothered, roasted, or barbecued), fried catfish, and classic sides like collard greens are prepared fresh daily at these Harlem standouts. Plan to splurge on the to-die-for banana pudding, pecan pie, or fruit cobbler with ice cream. These down-South favorites, along with more upscale selections, are offered by the catering arm of the business. Some of the dishes exhibit Asian,

Italian, and Mexican influences. Try them for wedding receptions, corporate gigs, or any other occasion and wow your guests.

TODARO BROS.
555 Second Ave (bet 30th and 31st St)　　　　　212/532-0633
Mon-Sat: 6:30 a.m.-10 p.m.; Sun: 6:30 a.m.-9 p.m.

www.todarobros.com

An icon in the Kips Bay/Murray Hill area since 1917, Todaro Bros. carries the very best in specialty foods. Great lunch sandwiches, fresh mozzarella, sausages, and prepared foods are offered daily. The fresh fish and meats are of the highest quality. The cheese department offers a huge variety of imported varieties. The shelves are stocked with artisanal oils, vinegars, pasta, condiments, coffee, fresh produce, and exquisite pastries.

If you are a pretzel lover (like your author), forget about the lousy ones sold on street corners and head to **Blaue Gans** (139 Duane St, 212/571-8880) or **Loreley** (7 Rivington St, 212/253-7077).

VINEGAR FACTORY
431 E 91st St (at York Ave)　　　　　　　　212/987-0885
Daily: 7 a.m.-9 p.m.; Brunch: Sat, Sun: 8-4　　www.elizabar.com

Located on the site of what used to be a working vinegar factory, this operation of Eli Zabar's has bearable prices on fresh produce, pizzas, fish, flowers, meats, desserts, seafood, cheeses, baked goods (including Eli's great breads), coffee, deli items, paper goods, and housewares. Breakfast and brunch (on weekends) are available on the balcony. This is one of the most intriguing food factories around! Some of the vegetables are grown in their rooftop greenhouse. Catering is offered, as is home delivery.

WHOLE FOODS MARKET
Time Warner Center, 10 Columbus Circle　　　212/823-9600
4 Union Square S　　　　　　　　　　　　212/673-5388
250 Seventh Ave (at 24th St)　　　　　　　　212/924-5969
95 E Houston (at Bowery)　　　　　　　　　212/420-1320
270 Greenwich St (bet Murray and Warren St)　212/349-6555
Hours vary by store　　　　　　　　　www.wholefoods.com

Whole Foods is big, beautiful, and busy! If you can't find a particular food item here, it probably doesn't exist. This grocery superstore has a huge deli, a seafood selection, bakery, flowers, sushi, fresh juices, and all kinds of carry-out items. Over 40 check-out stands are at the Time Warner location.

ZABAR'S
2245 Broadway (at 80th St)　　　　　　　　212/787-2000
Mon-Fri: 8-7:30; Sat: 8-8; Sun: 9-6　　　　　www.zabars.com
Mezzanine (housewares): Mon-Sat: 9-7:30; Sun: 9-6

No trip to Manhattan is complete without a visit to this fabulous store. You will find enormous selections of bread, smoked fish, coffee, prepared food, cheese, deli items, gift baskets, candy, and much more, all of the highest quality and affordably priced. A cafe next door provides snacks all day at bargain prices. Their fresh-from-the-oven rye bread is the best in Manhattan. One of the most important reasons for the success of Zabar's is that 20% of their 250 employees have been with the store for 15 years or more. Upstairs you will find the best housewares department in America, with a varied selection and good prices. Saul Zabar comes from a legendary food family in Manhattan. You will often see him wandering the aisles to make sure everything is top-notch. Assistants Scott Goldshine and David Tait provide the extra-special service for which Zabar's is renowned.

I love hot dogs! In my restaurant (Gerry Frank's Konditorei, 310 Kearney St, Salem, OR, 503/585-7070), we call them "Gerry's Franks!" For the best in Manhattan try:

Artie's Delicatessen (2290 Broadway, 212/579-5959)

Brooklyn Diner USA (212 W 57th St, 212/977-2280 and 155 W 43rd St, 212/265-5400)

Crif Dogs (113 St. Mark's Pl, 212/614-2728)

Dash Dogs (127 Rivington St, 212/254-8885)

F&B Güdtfood (269 W 23rd St, 646/486-4441 and 150 E 52nd St, 212/421-8600)

Gray's Papaya (2090 Broadway, 212/799-0243; 539 Eighth Ave, 212/904-1588; and 402 Ave of the Americas, 212/260-3532): inexpensive

Hallo Berlin (626 Tenth Ave, 212/977-1944; 744 Ninth Ave, 212/333-2372; and a stand at 54th St and Fifth Ave)

Katz's Delicatessen (205 E Houston St, 212/254-2246)

Mandler's (26 E 17th St, 212/255-8999)

Nathan's Famous Hot Dogs (stands all over Manhattan)

Old Town Bar (45 E 18th St, 212/529-6732)

Papaya King (179 E 86th St, 212/369-0648 and other locations)

2nd Avenue Deli (162 E 33rd St, 212/689-9000)

Shake Shack (Madison Square Park, Madison Ave at 23rd St, 212/889-6600 and 366 Columbus Ave): Madison Square Park location is seasonal

Cheese

ALLEVA DAIRY
188 Grand St (at Mulberry St)   212/226-7990, 800/4-ALLEVA
Mon-Sat: 9-6; Sun: 9-3   www.allevadairy.com

Alleva, founded in 1892, is the oldest Italian cheese store in America. The Alleva family has operated the business from the start, always maintaining meticulous standards. Robert Alleva oversees the production of over 4,000 pounds of fresh cheese a week, including *parmigiano*, *fraschi*, *manteche*, *scamoize*, and *provole affumicale*. The ricotta is superb, and the mozzarella tastes like it was made on a side street in Florence. Quality Italian meats, olives, and gift baskets are offered. An online catalog is available.

DIPALO FINE FOODS
200 Grand St (at Mott St)   212/226-1033
Mon-Sat: 9-6:30; Sun: 9-4   www.dipaloselects.com

The cheeses and pastas offered at DiPalo are simply superb. They carry olive oils, meats, and all things Italian. It's worth a trip to the Lower East Side for the goodies, not to mention the friendly greeting.

EAST VILLAGE CHEESE
40 Third Ave (bet 9th and 10th St)   212/477-2601
Daily: 8:30-6:30

Value is the name of the game. For years this store has prided itself on selling cheese at some of the lowest prices in town. They claim similar savings for whole-bean coffees, fresh pastas, extra-virgin olive oils, quiches, patés, and a wide selection of fresh bread. Good service is another reason to shop here. This is a cash-only operation.

IDEAL CHEESE SHOP
942 First Ave (at 52nd St)   212/688-7579
Mon-Sat: 8:30-6 (till 5 on Sat in summer)   800/382-0109
                                                                     www.idealcheese.com

Hundreds of cheeses from all over the world are sold here, and the owners are constantly looking for new items, just as is done in the fashion business. Ideal Cheese Shop has been in operation since 1954, and many Upper East Siders swear by its quality and service. They carry gourmet items: olive oils, vinegars, mustards, gourmet coffees, biscuits, preserves, specialty meats, olives, and a small line of specialty beers. A catalog is available, and they will ship anywhere in the U.S.

> Would you believe that New York's largest **Whole Foods Market** (95 E Houston St, 212/420-1320) is on the Lower East Side? This Whole Foods location features a sizable cafe and even a *fromagerie*. Its arrival is a further sign of transformation in the neighborhood. The newest Whole Foods Market (270 Greenwich St, 212/349-6555) is located downtown, as well.

JOE'S DAIRY
156 Sullivan St (bet Houston and Prince St)   212/677-8780
Tues-Fri: 9-6; Sat: 8-6

This is the best spot in town for fresh mozzarella. Anthony Campanelli makes it smoked, with prosciutto, and he also dispenses other cheese and Italian products.

MURRAY'S CHEESE SHOP
254 Bleecker St (bet Ave of Americas and Seventh Ave) 212/243-3289
Mon-Sat: 8-8; Sun: 10-7   www.murrayscheese.com

Boy, does this place smell good! This is one of the best cheese shops in Manhattan. Founded in 1940, Murray's offers wholesale and retail international and domestic cheeses of every description. Frank Meilak is the man to talk to behind the counter. There is also a fine selection of cold cuts, prepared foods, antipasti, breads, sandwiches, and specialty items. Owner Rob Kaufelt has built on the traditions of the city's oldest cheese shop. Special attractions include great party platters, gift baskets, and wholesale charge accounts for local residents. There is also a smaller Murray's outlet at Grand Central Market (in Grand Central Terminal). Ask to tour the underground cheese-curing caves! Better yet, sign up for a cheese course that includes tastings, pairings, and worthwhile information.

Chinese

GOLDEN FUNG WONG BAKERY
41 Mott St (at Pell St)   212/267-4037
Daily: 7-7

Golden Fung Wong is the real thing. Everyone from Chinatown residents to the city's gourmands extol its virtues. The pastries, cookies, and baked goods are traditional and delicious. Flavor is not compromised in order to appeal to Western tastes. The bakery features a tremendous variety of baked goods, and it has the distinction of being New York's oldest and largest authentic Chinese bakery.

For grocery shopping, don't overlook **Westside Markets** (77 Seventh Ave, 212/807-7771 and 2171 Broadway, 212/595-2536). These are first-class Lower and Upper West Side operations—immaculately clean and well-priced, with a large stock. Catering, free delivery within a ten-block radius, and food items to eat on premises are additional features. You will be very pleasantly surprised!

KAM MAN FOOD PRODUCTS
200 Canal St (bet Mott and Mulberry St)   212/571-0330
Daily: 9-8:30

Kam Man is the largest Oriental grocery store on the East Coast. In addition to Chinese foodstuffs, they carry Japanese, Thai, Vietnamese, Malaysian, and Filipino products. Native Asians should feel right at home in this store, where all types of traditional condiments are available. All of the necessities for the preparation and presentation of Asian foods can be found, from sauces and spices to utensils, cookware, and tableware. For the health-conscious, Kam Man stocks teas and Chinese herbal medicines. Prices are reasonable, and you needn't speak Chinese to shop here.

TONGIN MART
91 Mulberry St (at Canal St)   212/962-6622
Daily: 9-8

Planning a home-cooked Chinese dinner? There's no better source than this store in Chinatown. Tongin Mart boasts that 95% of its business is conducted with the Chinese community. They have an open and friendly attitude, and great care is taken to introduce customers to the wide variety of imported Oriental foods, including Japanese, Thai, and Filipino products.

Coffee, Tea

BELL BATES NATURAL FOOD MARKET
97 Reade St (bet Church St and West Broadway)   212/267-4300
Mon-Fri: 9-7; Sat: 10-6   www.bellbates.com

Bell Bates is a hot-beverage emporium specializing in organic and natural foods and all manner of teas and coffees. The selection is extensive and prices are competitive. Bell Bates considers itself a complete food source, stocking health foods, vitamins, nuts, dried fruit, spices, herbs, and gourmet items, many of which can be found in the bulk foods section. A deli features all-natural soups, salads, and sandwiches, and the salad bar includes vegan and vegetarian foods. Ask for the marvelous Mrs. Sayage.

Latte Lingo and Other Coffee Terminology

A *tall* is any 12-ounce espresso drink, while a *grande* is 16 ounces, and a *venti* is 20 ounces. A *double* is any espresso drink with a second shot added. Finally, a *skinny* is any drink made with nonfat milk.

Americano: A one- or two-ounce shot of espresso is mixed with up to seven ounces of hot water. This alternative to drip brewing yields a rich cup of gourmet coffee.

Cafe au Lait: equal portions of drip coffee and steamed milk

Cafe Breve: a latte made with half-and-half instead of milk

Cafe Coretto: espresso to which liquor, typically brandy or coffee liqueur, has been added

Caffe Latte: A two-ounce shot of espresso is combined with steamed milk and topped with a spoonful of milk froth.

Caffe Mocha: a latte with an ounce of chocolate flavoring (powder or syrup)

Cappuccino: This coffee drink consists of equal parts steamed milk, coffee, and foamed milk. It may be topped with cinnamon, nutmeg, chocolate sprinkles, or cocoa powder.

Cappuccino (dry): a cappuccino with foam but very little or no steamed milk

Cappuccino (wet): a cappuccino with less foam and more steamed milk

Con Panna: espresso topped with whipped cream

Espresso: This intense and concentrated coffee beverage is produced by using pressure to rapidly infuse finely ground coffee with boiling water.

Flavored Caffe Latte: a latte with an ounce of Italian syrup (such as almond, hazelnut, or vanilla) or liqueur

Granita: This frozen Italian drink is prepared with a granita machine (or *granitore*) and can be made with espresso and milk or fresh fruits and juices.

Shot, Straight Shot, Single Shot: a two-ounce cup of espresso served straight up, without milk or flavorings

---

EMPIRE COFFEE AND TEA COMPANY

568 Ninth Ave (bet 41st and 42nd St)　　212/268-1220
Mon-Fri: 8-7; Sat: 9-6:30; Sun: 11-5　　www.empirecoffeetea.com

Midtown java lovers have all wandered in here at one time or another. Empire carries an enormous selection of coffee (75 types of beans!), tea, and herbs. Because of the aroma and array of the bins, choosing is almost impossible. Empire's personnel are very helpful, but a perusal of their free catalog before visiting the shop might save some time. Fresh coffee beans and tea leaves are available in bulk; everything is sold loose and can be ground. Empire also carries a wide selection of teapots and coffee machines. Gourmet gift baskets, too!

ITO EN
822 Madison Ave (bet 68th and 69th St)   212/988-7111
Mon-Sat: 10-7; Sun: noon-6   www.itoen.com

Ito En is the world's leading supplier of green tea, which has won much attention for its healthy antioxidant properties. Their very gracious Japanese restaurant, **Kai**, serves lunch, dinner, and tea (closed on Sunday and Monday). It is sure to provide a soothing interlude to your day.

> No question about it: The best frozen yogurt in Manhattan is the coffee flavor at **40 Carrots**, on the 7th floor at **Bloomingdale's** (1000 Third Ave).

JACK'S STIR BREW COFFEE
138 W 10th St (bet Greenwich St and Waverly Pl)   212/929-0821
Mon-Sat: 7 a.m.-8:00 p.m.; Sun: 8-8   www.cupajack.com

Owner and brewmaster Jack Mazzola claims to serve the perfect cup of Joe (er, Jack). Behind this claim is the stir-brew process, which oxygenates the coffee, eliminating unpleasant bitterness. Steamed milk is added to the secret blend. Check the chalkboard for other favorite preparations. Certified organic and fair-trade coffees are staples, as are organic milk, brown sugar, and granola. Complete your coffee break with an oversized Oreo-type cookie or a fruit-filled muffin. Stimulating conversation and occasional live music and readings contribute to the social atmosphere at Jack's.

JAVA GIRL
348 E 66th St (bet First and Second Ave)   212/737-3490
Mon-Fri: 6:30 a.m.-7 p.m.; Sat, Sun: 8:30-6   www.javagirlinc.com

The aroma of fresh-ground coffee that greets you in this tiny place is overwhelming! For fine coffees, teas, pastries, and sandwiches, look no further. Java Girl has creative gift boxes as well.

McNULTY'S TEA AND COFFEE COMPANY
109 Christopher St (bet Bleecker and Hudson St)
Mon-Sat: 10-9 (closed Tues in July and Aug); Sun: 1-7
                              212/242-5351, 800/356-5200
                              www.mcnultys.com

McNulty's has been supplying discerning New Yorkers with coffee and tea since 1895. They carry a complete line of spiced and herbal teas, coffee blends ground to order, and coffee and tea accessories. Their blends are unique, and the personal service is highly valued. McNulty's maintains an extensive file of customers' special blend choices.

M. ROHRS' HOUSE OF FINE TEAS AND COFFEES

310 E 86th St (at Second Ave)   212/396-4456
Daily: 6 a.m.-midnight   www.rohrs.com

M. Rohrs' is over 110 years old. Owner Donald Wright carries expanded lines of tea and coffee, plus a wide variety of honey, jam, cookies, and chocolates. A tempting merchandise selection includes teapots and teaballs, coffeemakers, cups, and accessories. Rohrs' has a bar for espresso and an assortment of daily brewed coffees and teas. It truly is a village store with Old World charm in the big city. Wright, who is himself a great coffee lover, claims to drink seven cups a day! A full-service light-fare cafe offers wine, beer, salads, specialty sandwiches, and hot paninis.

The Best Natural Foods Emporiums

Bell Bates Natural Food Market (97 Reade St, 212/267-4300): herbs, coffees

Commodities Natural Market (165 First Ave, 212/260-2600): cheeses, good prices

Gary Null's Uptown Whole Foods (2421 Broadway, 212/874-4000): one of Manhattan's best; juice bar and kosher items

Health Nuts (2611 Broadway, 212/678-0054): juice bar

Integral Yoga Natural Foods (229 W 13th St, 212/243-2642): organic produce and baked items; yoga classes offered in the same building

Lifethyme Natural Market (410 Ave of the Americas, 212/420-9099): salad bar, produce

Whole Foods Market (Time Warner Center, 10 Columbus Circle, 212/823-9600; 4 Union Square S, 212/673-5388; 250 Seventh Ave, 212/924-5969; 95 E Houston St, 212/420-1320; and 270 Greenwich St, 212/349-6555): salad bar, flowers, large selection

---

NESPRESSO BOUTIQUE BAR

761 Madison Ave (bet 65th and 66th St)   212/249-4800
Mon-Fri: 8-8; Sat, Sun: 9-7

Espresso lovers will not want to miss this classy boutique bar and store. In the front you can enjoy some first-rate espresso drinks, while all manner of machines and accessories are available in the back, along with coffee capsules. The bar also serves salads, hot and cold sandwiches, pastries, and more.

PORTO RICO IMPORTING COMPANY

201 Bleecker St (main store)   212/477-5421, 800/453-5908
40½ St. Mark's Pl (coffee bar)   212/533-1982
107 Thompson St (coffee bar)   212/966-5758
Essex Street Market, 120 Essex St (coffee bar) 212/677-1210
Hours vary by store   www.portorico.com

In 1907, Peter Longo's family started a small coffee business in the Village. Primarily importers and wholesalers, they were soon pressured to serve the local community, so they opened a small storefront as well. That operation gained a reputation for the best and freshest coffee available. Since much of the surrounding neighborhood consists of Italians, the Longo family reciprocated their loyalty by specializing in Italian espressos and cappuccinos, as well as health and medicinal teas. Dispensed along with such teas are folk remedies and advice to mend whatever ails you. Today, the store remains true to its tradition. Peter has added coffee bars, making it possible to sit and sip from a selection of 150 coffees and 225 loose teas while listening to folklore or trying to select the best from the bins. All coffees are roasted daily at Porto Rico's own facility. (Hint: The inexpensive house blends are every bit as good as some of the more expensive coffees.)

SENSUOUS BEAN OF COLUMBUS AVENUE
66 W 70th St (at Columbus Ave) 212/724-7725, 800/238-6845
Mon-Wed: 8:30-6; Thurs, Fri: 8:30-7; Sat: 8-6; Sun: 9:30-6
www.sensuousbean.com

The Sensuous Bean was in business long before the latest coffee craze started. This legendary coffee and teahouse carries 72 varieties of coffee and 52 teas. Members of their coffee-of-the-month club receive one pound free after purchasing ten pounds. The bulk bean coffees and loose teas come from all around the world. Teas from England, France, Germany, Ireland, and Taiwan are featured. They carry a large variety of green, white, chai, herbal, rooibos, and blended loose teas, along with many organic and fair-trade coffees. They make lattes, cappuccinos, espressos, and chais; steep loose tea to order; and offer many sweets, biscottis, and chocolates to accompany these beverages. They specialize in gift packaging and signature presentations.

> Smoothies can be very healthy and low-calorie, too. If you're in the mood for a really good one, try **Health King** (642-A Lexington Ave, 212/593-1020), where you can create your own combination. They provide a list of remedies for almost every ailment (i.e., carrot, beet, and cucumber for headaches, and carrot, celery, and parsley for diabetes).

TEN REN TEA & GINSENG CO.
75-79 Mott St (at Canal St) 212/349-2286
Daily: 10-8 www.tenrenusa.com

This company was founded in 1953 and is the largest tea grower and manufacturer in East Asia. They sell green, oolong, jasmine, and black teas, plus tea sets and all manner of accessories. Various kinds of ginseng are also available. A delicious and chewy "bubble tea" contains tapioca pearls. Ten Ren means "heavenly love," and you will likely fall in love with one of their flavors. Be careful though, as some can set you back more than $100 a pound! Stop in next door to **Ten Ren's Tea Time**, a cozy spot to sample teas.

Foreign Foodstuffs (The Best)
British
Myers of Keswick* (634 Hudson St)
Chinese, Thai, Malaysian, Filipino, Vietnamese
Asia Market* (71½ Mulberry St)

Bangkok Center Grocery* (104 Mosco St)
Chinese American Trading Company (91 Mulberry St)
Fong Inn Too (46 Mott St)
Hong Keung Seafood & Meat Market (75 Mulberry St)
Hung Chong Imports (14 Bowery)
Kam Kuo Foods (7 Mott St)
Kam Man Food Products* (200 Canal St)
Ten Ren Tea & Ginseng Co.* (75-79 Mott St)
United Noodles (349 E 12th St)

German
Schaller & Weber* (1654 Second Ave)

Greek
Zeytuna (59 Maiden Lane and 161 Maiden Lane)

Indian
Foods of India* (121 Lexington Ave)
Kati Roll (99 MacDougal St and 49 W 39th St)
Kalustyan's* (123 Lexington Ave)

Italian
DiPalo Fine Foods* (200 Grand St)
Todaro Bros.* (555 Second Ave)

Japanese
Han ah Reum* (25 W 32nd St)
JAS Mart (2847 Broadway and other locations)
Katagiri & Company* (224 E 59th St)

Polish
East Village Meat Market (139 Second Ave)

West African
West African Grocery (535 Ninth Ave)

*Detailed write-ups of these shops can be found in this chapter.

Even if you have a favorite neighborhood market, pay a visit to these unique large Manhattan marketplaces. All are first-rate and feature a number of fine purveyors:

Chelsea Market (75 Ninth Ave, 212/243-6005, www.chelsea market.com)
Essex Street Market (120 Essex St, 212/388-0449, www.essex streetmarket.com): Lower East Side
Grand Central Market (Grand Central Terminal, 42nd St at Park

---

Fruits, Vegetables

GREENMARKET
1 Chambers St (bet Broadway and Centre St), Suite 1231 (office)
212/788-7900
www.cenyc.org

Note: The following Greenmarkets are arranged from uptown to downtown.

Inwood (Isham St bet Seaman & Cooper St)

175th St (175th St at Broadway)
Harlem Hospital (135th St bet Lenox and Fifth Ave)
Columbia (Broadway bet 114th and 115th St)
Stranger's Gate (106th St at Central Park W)
Mt. Sinai Hospital (99th St bet Madison and Park Ave)
97th St (97th St at Columbus Ave)
92nd St (First Ave bet 92nd and 93rd St)
82nd St/St. Stephens (82nd St bet First and York Ave)
77th St (Columbus Ave bet 77th and 78th St)
Tucker Square (66th St at Columbus Ave)
57th St (57th St at Ninth Ave)
Rockefeller Center (Rockefeller Plaza at 50th St)
Dag Hammarskjöld Plaza (47th St at Second Ave)
Murray Hill (Second Ave at 33rd St)
Union Square (17th St at Broadway)
Abingdon Square (12th St at Hudson St)
Stuyvesant Town (Stuy-Town Oral 14th St Loop at Ave A)
St. Mark's Church (10th St at Second Ave)
Tompkins Square (7th St at Ave A)
Grand Street (Grand St at Norfolk St)
Tribeca (Greenwich St bet Chambers and Duane St)
City Hall Park (Broadway bet Chambers and Warren St)
Cedar Street (Cedar St at Broadway)
Bowling Green (Broadway at Battery Pl)
Staten Island Ferry/Whitehall (Terminal Building)

Starting in 1976 with just one location, these unique open-air markets have sprung up in various neighborhoods. They are sponsored and overseen by a nonprofit organization. Bypassing the middle man means prices are significantly less than at supermarkets, and Greenmarkets provide small family farms in the region with a profitable outlet for their produce. All produce (over 600 varieties), baked goods, flowers, and fish come straight from the sources. Come early for the best selection. Call the office number or go online to find out the hours and address of the Greenmarket nearest you. Most are seasonal, operating from 8 to 3, although hours, days, and months of operation may vary.

Gift and Picnic Baskets

MANHATTAN FRUITIER
105 E 29th St (bet Park and Lexington Ave)
Mon-Fri: 9-5; Sat: deliveries only   212/686-0404, 800/841-5718
www.mfruit.com

Fruit baskets can be pretty bad, but this outfit makes tasty, great-looking ones using fresh seasonal and exotic fruits. You can add such comestibles as hand-rolled cheddar cheese sticks, biscotti, and individually wrapped chocolates. Locally handmade truffles, fine food hampers, fresh flowers, and organic and kosher products are also available. As a sign of the times, they have created their own stimulus package: fruit combination baskets for under $50. Delivery charges in Manhattan are reasonable, and gifts may be shipped nationwide.

SANDLER'S
530 Cherry Lane
Floral Park, NY 11001
Mon-Fri: 9-5

212/279-9779, 800/75-FRUIT
www.sandlersgiftbaskets.com

Though they are not located in Manhattan, Sandler's is a key source for scrumptious candies, delicacies, and some of the best chocolate chip cookies. They are even better known for gift baskets filled with fancy fresh fruits, natural cheeses, and gourmet delicacies. No one does it better!

The Best Places to Buy Caviar

Caviar Russe (538 Madison Ave, 212/980-5908): a luxury spot
Dean & Deluca (1150 Madison Ave, 212/717-0800 and 560 Broadway, 212/226-6800)
Firebird (365 W 46th St, 212/586-0244): housed in a re-creation of a pre-revolutionary Russian mansion
Petrossian (182 W 58th St, 212/245-2214): Providing ambience befitting the caviar set, this is also a spectacular place to dine.
Russ & Daughters (179 E Houston St, 212/475-4880)
Sable's Smoked Fish (1489 Second Ave, 212/249-6177)
Zabar's (2245 Broadway, 212/787-2000): If price is important, then make this your first stop.

Types of Caviar:

Beluga: Roe are large, firm, and well-defined, with a smooth, creamy texture.
Osetra: strong, with a sweet, fruity flavor
Sevruga: subtle, clean taste with a crunchy texture

Caviar, which is the roe of sturgeon from the Caspian and Black seas, is surely a delicacy, and a pricey one. Buy only from a trusted purveyor.

Greek

LIKITSAKOS
1174 Lexington Ave (bet 80th and 81st St)
Mon-Fri: 8 a.m.-9 p.m.; Sat, Sun: 8-8

212/535-4300

Likitsakos is one of the better places in New York for Greek and international specialties, including salads, fruits, vegetables, grains, dips, and appetizers.

MASTIHASHOP
145 Orchard St (at Rivington St)
Tues-Sat: 12-8; Sun: 11-7

212/253-0895
www.mastihashopny.com

This specialty store puts the spotlight on mastic, the aromatic resin of an evergreen that grows in the Aegean. Sisters Artemis and Kalliopi oversee a wide range of food products made with mastic, including honey, preserves, and spoonable sweets. Used in many Greek recipes, mastic is said to have anti-inflammatory and healing properties.

Health Foods

COMMODITIES NATURAL MARKET
165 First Ave (bet 10th and 11th St)   212/260-2600
Daily: 9-9   www.commoditiesnaturalmarket.com

This small East Village health-food store is just like the vitamins and supplements they sell: full of things that are good for you. They stock a full range of natural and organic meats, cheeses, produce, dairy products, bulk dry goods, canned foods, and even beauty and cleaning products, too. The helpful staff will answer questions, make suggestions, and offer tasty samples.

GARY NULL'S UPTOWN WHOLE FOODS
2421 Broadway (at 89th St)   212/874-4000
Daily: 8 a.m.-11 p.m.

This is Manhattan's premier health-food supermarket. Organic produce, fresh juices, discounted vitamins, and a full line of healthy supermarket products are featured. They will deliver in Manhattan and ship anywhere in the country. The organic and kosher takeout deli offers rotisserie chicken, vegetarian entrees, and even popcorn.

Organic Food Shops

Batch (150B W 10th St, 212/929-0250): organic dairy products and other ingredients
Birdbath—Build a Green Bakery (145 Seventh Ave S, 646/722-6570 and 223 First Ave, 646/722-6565): environmentally sound interiors and all-organic ingredients

---

HEALTH & HARMONY
470 Hudson St (bet Barrow and Grove St)   212/691-3036
Mon-Fri: 8 a.m.-8:30 p.m.; Sat: 9-7:30; Sun: 10-7

A great find for the health conscious! Health & Harmony stocks plenty of good things to eat, organic produce, vitamins and herbs, and herbal remedies. They will also deliver and ship.

INTEGRAL YOGA NATURAL FOODS
229 W 13th St (bet Seventh and Eighth Ave)   212/243-2642
Mon-Fri: 8 a.m.-9:30 p.m.; Sat: 8 a.m.-8:30 p.m.; Sun: 9-8:30
      www.integralyoganaturalfoods.com

Selection and quality abound in this clean, attractive shop, which features a complete assortment of healthy, natural foods. Vegetarian items, packaged groceries, organic produce, bulk foods, and baked items are available at reasonable prices. A juice bar, salad bar, and deli are on-premises. They occupy the same building as a center that offers classes in yoga, meditation, and philosophy. Across the street is **Integral Apothecary** (234 W 13th St, 212/645-3051), a vegetarian, vitamin, and herb shop with a nutritional consultant on staff.

KIDFRESH

1625 Second Ave (bet 84th and 85th St)   212/861-1141
Mon-Fri: 9-7:30; Sat: 10-7; Sun: 11-6   www.kidfresh.com

No additives, preservatives, or artificial colorings and flavorings here! This is a grocery store for kids that is chock full of natural, wholesome foods. Eye-appealing meals are prepared in kid-size portions using the freshest ingredients. "Grab + Go" meals are ready for little customers, or you can plan ahead and have the little ones' meals at home for the week. Kidfresh's catering department will even turn a kid's birthday party into a healthy affair. Food, games, recipes, classes, and events geared toward children emphasize the benefits of good nutrition. Kidfresh meals are available at some Whole Foods Markets and Kennedy Airport.

LIFETHYME NATURAL MARKET

408-410 Ave of the Americas (bet 8th and 9th St)   212/420-9099
Mon-Fri: 8 a.m.-10 p.m.; Sat, Sun: 9 a.m.-10 p.m.
www.lifethymemarket.com

You'll find one of the area's largest selections of organic produce at this natural supermarket. In addition, there is an organic salad table, health-related books, a deli serving natural foods, a "natural cosmetics" boutique, a complete vegan bakery, and an organic juice bar. Occupying renovated 1839 brownstones in the heart of the Village, this busy shop also sells discounted vitamins, does catering, and offers custom-baked goods for dietary needs.

> **Holyland Market** (122 St. Mark's Pl, 212/477-4440) is an excellent place for kosher cheeses and hard-to-find imported Israeli foods.

Ice Cream and Other Goodies

For more choices in this category, see the box on page 257.

CONES, ICE CREAM ARTISANS

272 Bleecker St (at Seventh Ave)   212/414-1795
Mon-Thurs, Sun: 1-11; Fri, Sat: 1-1

The D'Aloisio family brought their original Italian ice cream recipes to Manhattan . . . and boy, are they good! Cones specializes in creamy gelati made with all-natural ingredients. Thirty-two flavors (try the coffee mocha chocolate chip) and fat-free fruit flavors are available every day. All are made on-premises, ensuring creamy goodness, and can be packed for takeout. Made-to-order ice cream cakes are available, too.

Indian

FOODS OF INDIA

121 Lexington Ave (at 28th St)   212/683-4419
Mon-Sat: 10-8; Sun: 11-6

This is the place to stock up on curry leaves, rice, lentils, dried limes, mango chutney, and all kinds of fresh and dried imported Indian foods. Homemade breads and vegetarian items are also available.

KALUSTYAN'S
123 Lexington Ave (bet 28th and 29th St)

212/685-3451, 800/352-3451

Mon-Sat: 10-8; Sun: 11-7   www.kalustyans.com

In 1944, Kalustyan's opened as an Indian spice store at its present location. After all this time, it is still a great spot. Many items are sold in bins or
bales rather than prepackaged containers. The difference in cost, flavor, and
freshness is extraordinary. The best indication of freshness and flavor is the
store's aroma! Kalustyan's is both an Indian store and an export trading
corporation with a specialty in Middle Eastern and Indian items. There is a
large selection of dried fruit, nuts, mixes, coffee and tea, and accessories.

The Best Ice Cream and Gelato in Manhattan
Bussola (65 Fourth Ave, 212/254-1940)
Chinatown Ice Cream Factory (65 Bayard St, 212/608-4170)
Ciao Bella (27 E 92nd St, 212/831-5555; 285 Mott St, 212/431-3591;
   and 2 World Financial Center, 212/786-4707): gelati and sorbets
City Bakery (3 W 18th St, 212/366-1414): elegant flavors
Cones, Ice Cream Artisans (272 Bleecker St, 212/414-1795): Try
   Johnnie Walker Black Label with macerated kumquats!
E.A.T. (1064 Madison Ave, 212/772-0022)
Emack & Bolio's (389 Amsterdam Ave, 212/362-2747, summer
   only; 73 W Houston St, 212/533-5610; and 1564-A First Ave,
   212/734-0105): vanilla bean ice cream
Grom (223 Bleecker St, 212/206-1738): *real* gelato, with branches in
   Italy
Il Laboratorio del Gelato (95 Orchard St, 212/343-9922)
L'Arte Del Gelato (75 Seventh Ave S, 212/924-0803): Rent their
   party cart for a special event.
La Maison du Chocolat (1018 Madison Ave, 212/744-7117 and 30
   Rockefeller Center, 212/265-9404)
Pinkberry (7 W 32nd St, 212/695-9631; 170 Eighth Ave, 212/861-
   0574; and 41 Spring St, 212/274-8883)
Ronnybrook Farm Dairy (75 Ninth Ave, 212/741-6455): great
   flavors
Sant Ambroeus (259 W 4th St, 212/604-9254): caramel gelato
Smoochies (60 W 23rd St, 212/206-3501): lactose free

Italian
RAFFETTO'S CORPORATION
144 W Houston St (bet Sullivan and MacDougal St)   212/777-1261
Tues-Fri: 9-6:30; Sat: 9-6

You can go to a gourmet market for pasta, but why not go straight to the
source? Raffetto's has been producing fresh-cut noodles and stuffed pastas
since 1906. Though most of the business is wholesale, Raffetto's will sell their
noodles, ravioli, mini-ravioli, tortellini, manicotti, gnocchi, and fettuccine to
anyone. Variations include Genoa-style ravioli with meat and spinach, and

Naples-style ravioli with cheese. More than ten homemade sauces are personally prepared by Mrs. Raffetto. Daily bread, dry pasta, and bargain-priced olive oils and vinegars are also available.

Japanese

KATAGIRI & COMPANY
224 E 59th St (bet Second and Third Ave)   212/755-3566
Daily: 10-8 (gift shop open till 7)   www.katagiri.com

Are you planning a Japanese dinner? Do you have some important clients you would like to impress with a sushi party? Katagiri features all kinds of Japanese food, sushi ingredients, and utensils. You can get some great party ideas from the helpful personnel. Delivery in Manhattan is available.

SUNRISE MART
4 Stuyvesant St (at Third Ave), 2nd floor   212/598-3040
Sun-Thurs: 10 a.m.-11 p.m.; Fri, Sat: 10 a.m.-midnight
494 Broome St (bet West Broadway and Wooster St)   212/219-0033
Daily: 10-10

In a part of the East Village that is home to growing numbers of young Japanese and stores that cater to them, these all-purpose grocery stores do a bustling business. Japanese is spoken more often than English, and many packages bear nothing but Japanese calligraphy. In addition to snack foods and candy, they sell fruits, vegetables, meats, fish, and other grocery items. They also carry bowls, chopsticks, and items for the home. The Broome Street location stocks hard-to-find Japanese beauty products. A Japanese bake shop, **Panya Bakery** (10 Stuyvesant St, 212/777-1930), adjoins the Stuyvesant Street location.

For a delicious change, try Japanese candies. Whether your sweet tooth leans toward hard, chewy, crunchy or chocolatey, these stores have the Oriental goodies to satisfy your craving:

JAS Mart (35 St. Mark's Pl, 212/420-6370)
Katagiri (224 E 59th St, 212/755-3566)
M2M (55 Third Ave, 212/353-2698)
Sunrise Mart (4 Stuyvesant St, 212/598-3040 and 494 Broome St, 212/219-0033)
Tongin Mart (91 Mulberry St, 212/962-6622)
Yagura (24 E 41st St, 212/679-3777)

Liquor, Wine

ACKER, MERRALL & CONDIT
160 W 72nd St (bet Amsterdam and Columbus Ave)   212/787-1700
Mon-Sat: 9 a.m.-10 p.m.; Sun: noon-8   www.ackerwines.com

What a place! Acker, Merrall & Condit (AMC, for short) is the oldest operating wine and liquor store in America, having opened in 1820. There are in-store wine tastings Friday and Saturday afternoons. Wine seminars are offered to companies by the Wine Workshop. Wine parties can be arranged in private residences for special occasions. Free delivery is available in Manhattan. This service-oriented firm stocks a good inventory of American wines and also specializes in French vintages from Bordeaux and the Rhine. The Wine Workshop—Acker, Merrall & Condit's special-events affiliate—offers wine-tasting classes and dinners that range in price from $40 to $1,295. AMC is the largest independent fine-wine auction company in the United States. Check out their website for monthly online auctions.

ASTOR WINES & SPIRITS
399 Lafayette St (at 4th St)   212/674-7500
Mon-Sat: 9-9; Sun: noon-5   www.astorcenternyc.com

One of the city's largest selections of French and Italian wines is available at Astor, along with numerous sakes and sparkling wines. These folks claim to stock 10,000 labels; that's a lot of vino! Venture upstairs to one of three unique spaces for cooking and wine classes, seminars, and special events. Check their website for a schedule of events or to book a private function.

De-Vino Wines (30 Clinton St, 212/228-0073, www.devino.com) is the achievement of personable, Italian-born Gabrio Tosti di Valminuta. While Italian wines are his specialty, he is a walking encyclopedia of the entire wine industry, as well as a wonderful salesman, teacher, and "personal sommelier." Talk about service! He will even deliver a bottle to a BYOB restaurant.

BACCHUS WINE MADE SIMPLE
2056 Broadway (bet 70th and 71st St)   212/875-1200
Mon-Thurs: 11-9; Fri, Sat: 11-10; Sun: noon-9 www.bacchusnyc.com

Serious oenophiles, take note! This $1 million space has a glass-enclosed tasting room and climate-controlled area with over 800 labels. Bacchus can assist with planning and choosing wines for any event, and they provide a monthly wine club. Free daily tastings are offered evenings from 5 to 8. Private at-home tastings can be arranged, too.

BEST CELLARS
1291 Lexington Ave (at 87th St)   212/426-4200
Mon-Thurs: 9:30-9; Fri, Sat: 9:30 a.m.-10 p.m.; Sun: noon-8

2246 Broadway (bet 80th and 81st St)   212/362-8730
Mon-Thurs: 10-9; Fri, Sat: 10-10; Sun: noon-8   www.bestcellars.com

Are all those expensive wines really worth the price? If you're shopping for great-tasting wines at low prices, come to Best Cellars. They offer over 150 values, most of them are under $15. The friendly personnel are very knowledgeable and will special-order wines that are not in stock.

BOTTLEROCKET WINE & SPIRIT
5 W 19th St (at Fifth Ave)   212/929-2323
Mon-Sat: 11-8; Sun: 12-6   www.bottlerocketwine.com

Quite a place! Wines are organized by regions and by themes, such as takeout, gifts, seafood, "green," etc. These folks feature classes, special events, a children's play area, a library of food and wine books, and more.

BURGUNDY WINE COMPANY
143 W 26th St (bet Ave of the Americas and Seventh Ave)
Mon: 10-5; Tues-Fri: 10-7; Sat: 10-6　　　　　　　　　212/691-9092
www.burgundywinecompany.com

In New York, there is a store for just about every specialty. The customer is the winner because the selection is huge and the price range is broad. Such is the case with Burgundy Wine Company, a compact and attractive store in Chelsea. These folks are specialists in fine Burgundies, Rhones, and Oregon wines, with over 2,000 labels to choose from. There are some great treasures in their cellars; ask the expert personnel. Tastings are offered all day Saturday, and Monday through Friday after 5. "Wine Wednesdays" feature jazz from 5 to 7.

Boutique bottle shops offer limited selections of wines in trendy environs. Most specialize in good values for the price, with a few premium budget-busters for good measure. Look for interesting and non-traditional marketing of their products.

Appellation Wine & Spirits (156 Tenth Ave, 212/741-9474): organic and biodynamic wines and spirits

Bottlerocket Wine & Spirit (5 W 19th St, 212/929-2323): fun and user-friendly

Chambers Street Wines (148 Chambers St, 212/227-1434): European artisan wines

Embassy Wines & Spirits (796 Lexington Ave, 212/838-6551): 100 kosher vintages

Landmark Wine & Sake (167 W 23rd St, 212/242-2323): large sake selection

Moore Brothers Wine Company (33 E 20th St, 866/986-6673): Bring a sweater! A constant cellar temperature of 56 degrees is maintained throughout the shop.

Pasanella and Son Vintners (225 South St, 212/233-8383): Thursday evening and Saturday afternoon tastings

September Wines & Spirits (100 Stanton St, 212/388-0770): artisanal wines

Union Square Wines & Spirits (140 Fourth Ave, 212/675-8100): Samples are dispensed by an Enomatic automatic wine dispenser.

CROSSROADS WINES AND LIQUORS
55 W 14th St (at Ave of the Americas)　　　　　212/924-3060
Mon-Sat: 9-8:30　　　　　　　　www.crossroadswines.com

Crossroads carries 4,000 wines from all the great wine-producing countries. They stock rare, unique, and exotic liquors as well. Crossroads will special-order items, deliver, and help with party and menu planning. Their experienced staff has a passion for matching wines and foods, and their prices are as low as their attitude is low-key.

CRUSH WINE & SPIRITS
153 E 57th St (bet Third Ave and Lexington Ave)   212/980-9463
Mon-Sat: 10-9; Sun: noon-4   www.crushwineco.com

What's different about Crush Wine & Spirits is their focus on small artisanal producers. From their elegant space, they offer weekly free tastings, personal wine consultations, and a stock of rare and collectible bottles at reasonable prices. Exclusive offers and discounts are available via e-mail.

GARNET LIQUORS
929 Lexington Ave (bet 68th and 69th St)   212/772-3211
Mon-Sat: 9-9; Sun: noon-6   800/USA-VINO (out of state)
                              www.garnetwine.com

You'll love Garnet's prices, which are among the most competitive in the city for specialty wines. If you're in the market for Champagne, Bordeaux, Burgundy, Italian, or other imported wines, check here first, as selections are impressive. Prices are good on other wines and liquors, too.

IS-WINE
24 W 8th St (bet Fifth Ave and Ave of the Americas)   212/254-7800
Mon-Sat: noon-9; Sun: noon-7   www.is-wine.com

Everything is first-class at Is-Wine—the wines, the service, and the information available to customers. Specialties include informative seminars with wine tastings and food. Free delivery is available in the neighborhood.

ITALIAN WINE MERCHANTS
108 E 16th St (bet Union Square E and Irving Pl)   212/473-2323
Mon-Fri: 10-7; Sat: 11-7   www.iwmstore.com

If Italian wines are your passion, then Italian Wine Merchants should be your destination. You will find only Italian wines here, with specialties in cult and tightly allocated wines, many from undiscovered producers. This place is class personified!

K&D FINE WINES AND SPIRITS
1366 Madison Ave (bet 95th and 96th St)   212/289-1818
Mon-Sat: 9-9   www.kdwine.com

K&D is an excellent wine and spirits market on the Upper East Side. Hundreds of top wines and liquors are sold at competitive prices. Occasional ads in local newspapers highlight special bargains.

MISTER WRIGHT FINE WINES AND SPIRITS
1593 Third Ave (bet 89th and 90th St)   212/722-4564
Mon-Sat: 9 a.m.-9:30 p.m.; Sun: 1-7   www.misterwrightfinewines.com

If you are interested in Australian wines, this shop has a nice selection. A neighborhood store for over three decades, Mister Wright has a reputation for fine stock at comfortable prices and extra-friendly Aussie service. They also stock many wines from other countries. If you call ahead to place your order, they will bring it out to your car curbside. What a great service!

MOORE BROTHERS WINE COMPANY
33 E 20th St (bet Broadway and Park Ave)   866/986-6673
Mon-Fri: 10-9; Sat: 10-8; Sun: 12-6 (closed Sun in Aug)
www.moorebrothers.com

This place is unique. They sell only wine bought in their own vertically integrated supply chain from growers in France, Italy, and Germany.

MORRELL & COMPANY
1 Rockefeller Plaza (49th St bet Fifth Ave and Ave of the Americas)
Mon-Sat: 10-7   212/981-1106
www.morrellwine.com

Charming and well informed, Peter Morrell is the wine expert at this small, jam-packed store, which carries all kinds of wine and liquor. The stock is overwhelming, and a good portion of it must be kept in the wine cellar. However, it is all easily accessible, and the Morrell staff is amenable to helping you find the right bottle. The stock consists of spirits, including brandy, liqueurs, and wine vintages ranging from old and valuable to young and inexpensive. Check out the inviting menu next door at **Morrell Wine Bar Cafe** (212/262-7700).

NANCY'S WINES FOR FOOD
313 Columbus Ave (at 75th St)   212/877-4040
Mon-Sat: 10-9; Sun: noon-7   www.nancyswines.com

These folks are pros at matching wines with food. Prices are reasonable, the selection is excellent, and they offer a "wine of the month" program. German white wines, "grower" champagnes, and boutique wines are specialties. Their crew conducts in-home tasting parties; schedule well in advance.

QUALITY HOUSE
2 Park Ave (at 33rd St)   212/532-2944
Mon-Fri: 9-6   www.qualityhousewines.com

Quality House boasts one of the most extensive stocks of French wine in the city, equally fine offerings of domestic and Italian wines, and selections from Germany, Spain, and Portugal. True to their name, this is a quality house, not a bargain spot. Delivery is available and usually free.

SHERRY-LEHMANN
505 Park Ave (at 59th St)   212/838-7500
Mon-Sat: 9-7   www.sherry-lehmann.com

Sherry-Lehmann is one of New York's best-known wine shops, boasting an inventory of over 7,000 wines from all over the world. Prices run the gamut from $5 to $10,000 a bottle. This firm has been in business since 1932, and it offers many special services for their customers.

SOHO WINES AND SPIRITS
461 West Broadway (bet Prince and Houston St)   212/777-4332
Mon-Sat: 10-8   www.sohowines.com

Stephen Masullo's father ran a liquor store on Spring Street for over 25 years. When the neighborhood evolved into the Soho of today, sons Stephen,

Victor, and Paul expanded the business and opened a stylish Soho wine emporium on West Broadway. The shop is lofty. In fact, it looks more like an art gallery than a wine shop. Bottles are tastefully displayed, and classical music plays in the background. Soho Wines also has one of the largest selections of single-malt Scotch whiskeys in New York. Services include party planning and advice on setting up and maintaining a wine cellar.

VINO
121 E 27th St (bet Lexington Ave and Park Ave S)   212/725-6516
Mon-Sat: noon-9   www.vinosite.com

If you're looking for unusual varietals and love Italian wine, then come to Vino. Small-production vintners from around Italy are represented, many of them reasonably priced. The staff is extra friendly, and you might get a sample tasting.

WAREHOUSE WINES & SPIRITS
735 Broadway (bet 8th St and Waverly Pl)   212/982-7770
Mon-Thurs: 9-8:45; Fri, Sat: 9 a.m.-9:45 p.m.; Sun: noon-6:45

If you are looking to save on wine and liquor, especially for a party, Warehouse Wines & Spirits is a good place. Their selections and prices are appealing, and free delivery is available with a minimum purchase.

Meat, Poultry

FAICCO'S ITALIAN SPECIALTIES
260 Bleecker St (at Ave of the Americas)   212/243-1974
Tues-Thurs, Sat: 8:30-6; Fri: 8:30-7; Sun: 9-2

An Italian institution for over 100 years, Faicco's carries delectable dried sausage, cuts of pork, and sweet and hot sausage. They also sell equally good meat cuts for barbecue and an oven-ready rolled leg of stuffed pork. Pork loin, a house specialty, is locally famous. They carry veal cutlets, veal chops, ground veal, veal for stew, olive oils, and ingredients for antipasto. If you're into Italian-style deli, try Faicco's first. And if you're pressed for time, take home their heat-and-eat chicken rollettes: boneless breast of chicken rolled around cheese and dipped in a crunchy coating. Prepared hot foods to take home—including lasagna, baby back ribs, and eggplant parmesan—are also available. The best snack in the neighborhood is the *arancini* —fried balls of risotto. Bet you can't eat just one!

FLORENCE MEAT MARKET
5 Jones St (bet Bleecker and 4th St)   212/242-6531
Tues-Fri: 8:30-6:30; Sat: 8-6

Everything is cut-to-order by hand at Florence Meat Market. Owner Benny Pizzuco has had long relationships with his suppliers, ensuring high-quality meats. Their "Newport steak" is so delicious that many folks have it shipped to them overnight!

GIOVANNI ESPOSITO & SONS MEAT MARKET
500 Ninth Ave (at 38th St)   212/279-3298
Mon-Sat: 8-6:30

Family members still preside over an operation that has been at the same location since 1932. Homemade Italian sausages are a specialty. Every kind you can imagine—breakfast, sage, garlic, smoked, hot dogs—is available. The cold cuts selection is awesome: bologna, liverwurst, pepperoni, salami, ham, turkey breast, American and Muenster cheese, and much more. Hosting a dinner? You'll find pork roasts, crown roasts, pork chops, spare ribs, slab bacon, tenderloins, sirloin steaks, short ribs, filet mignon, London broil, corned beef brisket, leg of lamb, pheasant, quail, and venison. Free home delivery is available in midtown for "modestly minimum orders."

> Retail customers can now buy the same fresh meats as New York's top chefs by going online. Iowa pork spareribs, New York strip steaks, free range chickens, Long Island Peking duck, Rocky Mountain lamb, and seasonal meat packs are just a mouse click away. **DeBragga and Spitler** (www.debragga.com) has been around since the 1920s, supplying legendary restaurants—and now you, too!

LOBEL'S PRIME MEATS
1096 Madison Ave (bet 82nd and 83rd St)   212/737-1373
Mon-Sat: 9-6: closed Sat in July, Aug   www.lobels.com

Because of their excellent service and reasonable prices, few carnivores in Manhattan *haven't* heard of this shop. The staff has published eight cookbooks, and they are always willing to explain the best uses for each cut. It's hard to go wrong, since Lobel's carries *only* the best. They will ship all over the country. In addition to prime cuts, you'll find great ready-to-cook hamburgers, too!

L. SIMCHICK MEAT
988 First Ave (at 54th St)   212/888-2299
Mon-Fri: 8-7; Sat: 8-6

One and a half centuries in business have made these folks famous! You'll find wild game, prime meats, poultry products, wonderful homemade sausage, and a good selection of prepared foods. Delivery is provided on the East Side with a $25 minimum order.

OPPENHEIMER PRIME MEATS
2606 Broadway (bet 98th and 99th St)   212/662-0246
Mon-Fri: 9-7; Sat: 10-5   www.oppenheimermeats.com

Reliable and trustworthy, Oppenheimer is a first-rate source for prime meats in New York. Under the ownership of Robert Pence, an experienced butcher and chef, the traditions of Harry Oppenheimer have been carried forward. It's an old-fashioned butcher shop, offering the kind of service and quality you won't find at any supermarket. Prime dry-aged beef, milk-fed veal, free-range poultry, game, and fresh seafood are all sold at competitive prices. Delivery is available throughout Manhattan.

OTTOMANELLI'S MEAT MARKET
285 Bleecker St (bet Seventh Ave and Jones St)   212/675-4217
Mon-Sat: 8:30-6

Looking for something unusual? Ottomanelli's stock-in-trade is rare gourmet fare. Among the weekly offerings are boar's head, whole baby lambs, game, rabbits, and pheasant. They also stock buffalo, ostrich, rattlesnake, alligator, suckling pig, and quail. Quality is good, but service from the right person can make the difference between a serviceable cut and an excellent one. This four-brother operation gained its reputation by offering full butcher services and a top-notch selection of prime meats, game, prime-aged steaks, and milk-fed veal. The latter is cut into Italian roasts, chops, and steaks, and their preparation by Ottomanelli's is unique. Best of all, they will sell it by the piece for a quick meal at home.

PARK EAST KOSHER BUTCHER & FINE FOODS
1623 Second Ave (bet 84th and 85th St)   212/737-9800
Mon-Wed: 8-7; Thurs: 8-9; Fri: 5 a.m. till two hours before sunset;
Sun: 8-7   www.parkeastkosher.com

This is a one-stop kosher shop, carrying butcher items, cooked foods, packaged meats, bakery goods, candy, sauces and dressings, pickled products, salads and dips, frozen food, and cheeses. Park East stocks over 700 items in all! They promise delivery within three hours throughout Manhattan.

If you are looking for an excellent selection of fresh seafood at good prices, then try **Downeast Seafood** (311 Manida St, The Bronx, 212/243-5639). Check out the hours. They are open daily (except Sunday) from 6 to 5, and delivery to Manhattan is available.

SCHALLER & WEBER
1654 Second Ave (bet 85th and 86th St)   212/879-3047
Mon-Sat: 8:30-6   www.schallerweber.com

Once you've been in this store, the image will linger because of the sheer magnitude of cold cuts on display. Schaller & Weber is *Babes in Toyland* for delicatessen lovers. There is nary a wall or nook that is not covered with deli meats. Besides offering a complete line of deli items, Schaller & Weber stocks game and poultry. Try their sausage and pork items, which they will prepare, bake, smoke, or roll to your preference.

YORKVILLE MEAT EMPORIUM
1560 Second Ave (at 81st St)   212/628-5147
Mon-Sat: 8-7; Sun: 9-6   www.hungarianmeatmarket.com

Yorkville used to be a bastion of Eastern European ethnicity and culture before becoming the Upper East Side's singles playground. Here and there, remnants of Old World society remain. Yorkville Meat Emporium is patronized by Hungarian-speaking old ladies in black, as well as some of the city's greatest gourmands. The reason is simple: these prepared meats are available nowhere else in the city and possibly on the continent. The shop offers a vast variety of sausages and salami. Smoked meats include pork shoulder and tenderloin. Goose is a mainstay of Hungarian cuisine, so goose liverwurst, smoked goose, deep-fried goose rinds, and goose liver are staples here. Fried bacon bits and bacon fried with paprika (a favorite Hungarian spice) are other popular offerings. There's more: preserves, jams, spices, ground nuts, jellies, prepared delicacies, head cheese, breads, pastas and noodles, and take-out meals—all of it authentic!

Pickles

PICKLES, OLIVES, ETC.
1647 First Ave (bet 85th and 86th St)   212/717-8966
Daily: 10-8   www.picklesandolives.com

This is the only shop of its kind on the Upper East Side! All of the pickles and olives are sold the old-fashioned way—out of barrels—and in any quantity. You can buy one pickle or one gallon of them. There are ten varieties of pickles and 20 types of olives. If you can't make up your mind, between sweet, hot, or sour, ask for a sample before you buy.

Guss' Pickles was a New York legend for many years, and dipping into their barrels was one of the treats of a Lower East Side visit. Alas, they are no longer in Manhattan, but you can find them on Long Island (504-A Central Ave, Cedarhurst, 516/569-0909, www.guss pickle.com). They stock sour and half-sour pickles, sour tomatoes, and sauerkraut. If you can't make the trip, order by fax (516/569-0901) or online.

Seafood

CATALANO'S FRESH FISH MARKET
Vinegar Factory
431 E 91st St (bet York and First Ave)   212/987-0885
Daily: 7 a.m.-9 p.m.

Joe Catalano is that rare blend of knowledge and helpfulness. Catalano's customers, including many local restaurants, rely on him to select the best items for their dinner menus. He does so with a careful eye toward health, price, and preparation. Located inside the busy Vinegar Factory, Catalano's also has a good selection of poached fish, plus crawfish and soft-shell crabs in season. On cold winter days, don't miss the Manhattan clam chowder.

GRAMERCY FISH CO.
383 Second Ave (at 23rd St)   212/213-5557
Mon-Sat: 9-8; Sun: 10-6

Quality fresh seafood is the name of the game here. You'll find oysters, clams, crawfish, salmon, plus hot and refrigerated chowders and bisques. Prices are competitive and often better than at chain markets.

LEONARD'S SEAFOOD AND PRIME MEATS
1437 Second Ave (bet 74th and 75th St)   212/744-2600
Mon-Fri: 8-7; Sat: 8-6; Sun: 11-6

A family-owned business since 1910, Leonard's has expanded its inventory. You'll find oysters, crabs, striped bass, halibut, salmon, live lobsters, and squid. In addition, there are farm-fresh vegetables. Their takeout seafood department sells lobsters, codfish cakes, and crab cakes; hand-sliced Norwegian, Scottish, and Irish smoked salmon; and some of the tastiest clam chowder in Manhattan. Barbecued poultry, cooked and prepared foods, and aged prime meats (beef, lamb, and veal) round out Leonard's selection. Their homemade turkey chili, braised veal, and poached salmon are customer favorites. Leonard's also makes beautiful party platters of boiled shrimp, crab-meat, and smoked salmon. This service-oriented establishment provides fast, free delivery.

LOBSTER PLACE
75 Ninth Ave (bet 15th and 16th St)   212/255-5672
Mon-Fri: 9:30-8; Sat: 9:30-7; Sun: 10-6
252 Bleecker St (bet Ave of the Americas and Seventh Ave)
Mon-Sat: 10-8; Sun: 10-7   212/352-8063
                                                       www.lobsterplace.com

Imagine distributing one million pounds of lobster every year! The Lobster Place does just that, and they have a full line of fish, shrimp, and shellfish, too. Top hotels and restaurants take advantage of this buying power, and you, too, are assured of quality, freshness, and value.

If you can put up with periodic poor service at **Pisacane Midtown Seafood** (940 First Ave, 212/752-7560), this wholesale and retail seafood operation is worth a visit.

MURRAY'S STURGEON SHOP
2429 Broadway (bet 89th and 90th St)   212/724-2650
Sun-Fri: 8-7   www.murrayssturgeon.com

Murray's is *the* stop for fancy smoked fish, fine appetizers, and caviar. Choose from sturgeon, Eastern and Norwegian salmon, whitefish, kippered salmon, sable, pickled herring, and schmaltz. The quality is excellent, and prices are fair. Murray's also offers kosher soups, salads, cold cuts, dried fruits, and nuts.

WILD EDIBLES
535 Third Ave (bet 35th and 36th St)   212/213-8552
Mon-Sat: 11:30-9:30; Sun: noon-9   www.wildedibles.com

You can't beat these folks for fresh, high-quality seafood. Some of it is unique and imported. Many of the same foods served at Manhattan's top restaurants are sold here. A catering menu boasts that seafood caught any-where in the world can be put on your home or office table! Sustainable foods and health foods are stocked. The market also offers an oyster bar with wine and beer. You'll find another Wild Edibles location at Grand Central Market (Grand Central Terminal, 212/213-8552). Delivery is available throughout the city.

Spanish

DESPAÑA BRAND FOODS
408 Broome St (bet Lafayette and Cleveland Pl)   212/219-5050
Mon-Sat: 11-8; Sun: 11-5   www.despanabrandfoods.com

Tasty, authentic Spanish foods are available here. Try their *bocadillos* or warm *caldo gallego*. More specialties: serrano ham, blood sausage, all-natural game products, chestnuts in syrup, chocolate, cookbooks, and cookware.

Spices and Oils

APHRODISIA HERB SHOPPE
264 Bleecker St (bet Ave of the Americas and Seventh Ave)
Mon-Sat: 11-7; Sun: noon-5   212/989-6440
www.aphrodisiaherbshoppe.com

Aphrodisia is stocked from floor to ceiling with nearly every herb and spice imaginable—800 of them—all neatly displayed in glass jars. Some of the teas, potpourri, dried flowers, and oils are really not what one might expect; many are used for folk remedies. Most ingredients for ethnic cooking can be found here, as well as ingredients for body care and a variety of gift items. Aphrodisia also conducts a mail-order business.

SPICE CORNER
135 Lexington Ave (at 29th St)   212/689-5182
Daily: 10-8   www.spicecorner29.com

Indian cooking specialties can be found here in abundance. Shelves are packed with beans, grains, chutneys, and spices, plus a good selection of reasonably priced specialty foods (fresh and frozen), cookware items, and health and beauty items.

STONEHOUSE CALIFORNIA OLIVE OIL
223 Front St (bet Beekman St and Peck Slip)   212/358-8700
Daily: 11-7   www.stonehouseoliveoil.com

Organically farmed olives from California are pressed into extra virgin olive oil (EVOO), and enhancements such as Persian limes, blood oranges, chilies, and garlic are added as flavorings. Free samples and suggested uses are offered. Customers are encouraged to return with their empty EVOO bottles for discounted refills. Other products include imported balsamic vinegars and olive oil soaps.

V. Where to Find It: New York's Best Services

Most everyone needs a little help taking care of the details of their busy lives. In this chapter you'll discover a broad range of services to meet those needs: folks to clean your home, clothing, or pet; professionals to organize your closets or your life; experts to make you look and feel your best; places to rent furnishings and store out-of-season goods; and people trained to repair computers, appliances, and personal items. I've also included a number of options for where to stay in Manhattan.

Air Conditioning

AIR-WAVE AIR CONDITIONING COMPANY
2421 Jerome Ave (at Fordham Road), The Bronx   212/545-1122
Mon-Sat: 8-5   www.airwaveac.com

If the dog days of summer are getting you down or you want to plan ahead to make sure that they don't, then give these folks a call. Air-Wave has been in business since 1953 and sold, serviced, overhauled, installed, and delivered over 1 million units over the years, including top brands like Friedrich, Carrier, and Frigidaire. They offer delivery, installation, and storage of portable air conditioners.

Animal Adoptions

AMERICAN SOCIETY FOR THE PREVENTION OF CRUELTY TO ANIMALS
424 E 92nd St (bet First and York Ave)   212/876-7700, ext. 4120
Mon-Sat: 11-7; Sun: 11-5   www.aspca.org

This is one of the oldest animal protection organizations in the world, and these folks take pet adoptions very seriously. You'll need to fill out an application, go through an interview, and bring two pieces of identification (at least one with a photograph). The whole process sometimes takes longer than you might wish—but then *they're* sure that *you're* serious, and you can go home with a good pet that needs a loving home. Adoption fees for dogs and cats start at $75; puppies and kittens are higher. The fee includes a veterinarian's exam, vaccinations, microchipping, and spaying or neutering. ASPCA also enforces animal cruelty laws, and Bergh Memorial Animal Hospital is on-site.

Animal Services

ANIMAL MEDICAL CENTER
510 E 62nd St (bet FDR Dr and York Ave)   212/838-8100
Daily: 24 hours   www.amcny.org

If your pet becomes ill, try the Animal Medical Center first. This nonprofit organization does all kinds of veterinary work (domestic and exotic pets, like ferrets, lizards, and snakes) reasonably and competently. They handle over 60,000 cases a year and have more than 90 veterinarians on staff. The care is among the best in the city. They suggest calling ahead for an appointment; emergency care costs more.

BISCUITS & BATH
1535 First Ave (at 80th St)   212/419-2500
701 Second Ave (at 38th St)
41 W 13th St (at Fifth Ave)
469 Columbus Ave (at 82nd St)
160 Riverside Blvd (at 68th St)
102 Franklin St (at Church St)
Mon-Fri: 7 a.m.-10 p.m.; Sat, Sun: 8 a.m.-10 p.m.
                                www.biscuitsandbath.com

Biscuits & Bath offers grooming, training, workshops and seminars, vet care, dog walking, day and overnight care, adoption, a retail boutique, and transportation services. Even Sunday brunches for the pooches! The place is pocketbook and doggy-friendly.

CAROLE WILBOURN
299 W 12th St (bet Eighth and Ninth Ave)   212/741-0397
Mon-Sat: 9-6   www.thecattherapist.com

Would you like to talk to the author of *The Complete Guide to Understanding and Caring for Your Cat?* Carole Wilbourn is an internationally known cat therapist who has the answers to most cat problems. Carole makes house calls from coast to coast and can take care of many feline issues with just one session and a follow-up phone call. She does international consultations, takes on-site appointments at Westside Veterinary Center, and is available for speaking engagements.

EAST VILLAGE VETERINARIAN
241 Eldridge St (at Houston St)   212/674-8640
Daily: 9-3:30 (Wed, Sat till noon)

This is the only practicing homeopathic veterinary clinic in New York City. It features a complete homeopathic dispensary, with over a thousand remedies in stock. It is also a full-service animal hospital with an emphasis on prevention.

FIELDSTON PETS
                                              718/796-4541
Mon-Sat: 9-7   www.pawsacrossamerica.com

Bash Dibra is a warm, friendly man who speaks dog language. Known as the "dog trainer to the stars," Bash is an animal behaviorist. If your dog has bad manners, Bash will teach it to behave. He believes in "tandem training"—training owners to train their dogs—because it's the owner who'll be in charge. Bash's experience in training a pet wolf gave him unique insight into canine minds, and his success in bringing the most difficult pets to heel has made him a regular on the talk-show circuit. In addition to training sessions, dog and cat grooming is available.

LE CHIEN
Trump Plaza
1044 Third Ave (bet 61st and 62nd St)   212/752-2120, 800/LECHIEN
Mon-Sat: 9-6   www.lechiennyc.com

Occupying two floors of Trump Plaza, Le Chien is a luxurious pet day spa offering grooming, housebreaking, and attentive boarding services. A boutique carries a fabulous selection of custom and imported accessories, as well as Le Chien's own fragrance lines. They sell puppies directly from show breeders.

NEW YORK DOG SPA & HOTEL
32 W 25th St (bet Ave of the Americas and Broadway)   212/243-1199
415 E 91st St (bet First and York Ave)   212/410-1755
Daily: 7 a.m.-10 p.m.   www.dogspa.com

This is a full-service hotel for dogs, offering boarding, day care, massage, training, vet services, and more. They are staffed 24 hours for boarding.

Sometimes it is handy or even necessary to have a vet make a house call. One of the best is **Dr. Amy Attas** (212/581-7387).

PETS CARE NETWORK
Daily: 9-6 and by appointment   212/580-6004, 646/256-1642
                                        www.petscarenetwork.com

Pets Care Network, a kennel alternative established in 1985, offers all the comforts of home to pet dogs, cats, and birds in 35 New York apartments (the homes of the sitters). Your pet will receive individual attention from well-screened "pet people" who consider this work a treat. There are no cages. These folks are bonded and insured.

SUTTON DOG PARLOUR
311 E 60th St (bet First and Second Ave)   212/355-2850
Mon-Fri: 7-7; Sat, Sun: 9-6   www.suttonpets.com

Sutton Dog Parlour has been around for over four decades, so you know it is a responsible establishment. You will find dog grooming, boarding and day care, and supplies for dogs, cats, and birds. There's a private outdoor park for your beloved pooch to enjoy, individual dog runs, and live webcams to check up on your pet. Birds are housed in individual large cages. A TV in the bird room keeps them up-to-date on world affairs—a necessity, of course!

Antique Repair and Restoration

CENTER ART STUDIO

307 W 38th St (bet Eighth and Ninth Ave), Suite 1315   212/247-3550
Mon-Thurs: 9-6; Fri: 9-5 (by appointment)   www.centerart.com

"Fine art restoration and display design since 1919" is the motto here. The word *fine* should really be emphasized, as owners of fine paintings, sculpture, and ceramics have made Center Art Studio the place to go for restoration. The house specialty is art conservation. They will clean and restore paintings, lacquer, terra cotta, scagliola, and plaster. Their craftsmen will also restore antique furniture and decorative objects. They will even design and install display bases and mounts for sculpture. Among the oldest and most diverse restoration studios in the city, Center Art offers a multitude of special services for the art collector, dealer, or designer.

MICHAEL J. DOTZEL AND SON

402 E 63rd St (at York Ave)   212/838-2890
Mon-Fri: 8-4:30

Dotzel specializes in the repair and maintenance of antiques and precious heirlooms. They won't touch modern pieces or inferior antiques, but if your older piece is made out of metal and needs repair, this is a good choice. They pay close attention to detail and will hand-forge or hammer metal work, including brass. If an antique has lost a part or if you want a duplication, it can be re-created. Dotzel also does stripping and replating, but since it isn't always good for an antique, they may try to talk you out of it.

SANO STUDIO

767 Lexington Ave (at 60th St), Room 403   212/759-6131
Mon-Fri: 10-5 (by appointment; closed Aug)

Jadwiga Baran presides over this fourth-floor antique repair shop with an eye for excellence. That eye is focused on the quality of the workmanship and goods to be repaired. Both must be the best. Baran is a specialist who limits herself to repairing porcelain, pottery, ivory, and tortoise-shell works and antiques. She has many loyal customers.

Little Artists NYC (917/744-9930, www.littleartistsnyc.com) offers mixed media art and craft projects for toddlers to pre-teens at your location of choice. They bring all the supplies, creative suggestions, and patience. This is a great source for fun parties and rainy day activities, or for help with kids' science and school projects. Birthday party packages are available and include everything needed for a memorable event.

Art Appraisals

ABIGAIL HARTMANN ASSOCIATES

415 Central Park W (at 101st St)   212/316-5406
Mon-Fri: 9-6 (by appointment; also available on weekends)

This firm specializes in fine and decorative art appraisals for insurance, donation, or other reasons. Their highly principled and experienced staff does not buy, sell, or receive kickbacks. (This is a common practice with some auction houses, insurance companies, and galleries.) Fees are by the hour, and consultations are available. The friendly personnel can also provide restoration, framing, shipping, storage contacts, and estate disposition.

Art Services

A.I. FRIEDMAN
44 W 18th St (bet Fifth Ave and Ave of the Americas) 212/243-9000
Mon-Fri: 9-7; Sat: 10-7; Sun: 11-6   www.aifriedman.com

Those who want to frame it themselves can take advantage of one of the largest stocks of ready-made frames in the city at A.I. Friedman. Nearly all are sold at discount. In addition to fully assembled frames, they sell do-it-yourself frames that come equipped with glass and/or mats. Custom framing is also available. They are really a department store for creative individuals, providing a large assortment of tools, furniture, paints, easels, books, and other supplies and materials for the graphic artist.

ELI WILNER & COMPANY
1525 York Ave (bet 80th and 81st St)   212/744-6521
Mon-Fri: 9-5:30   www.eliwilner.com

Eli Wilner's primary business is period frames and mirrors. He keeps over 3,300 19th- and early 20th-century American and European frames in stock and can locate any size or style. Wilner can create an exact replica of a frame to your specifications. His staff of over 25 skilled craftsmen also does expert restoration and replication of frames. Boasting such clients as the Metropolitan Museum of Art and the White House, Wilner's expertise speaks for itself.

GUTTMANN PICTURE FRAME ASSOCIATES
180 E 73rd St (bet Lexington and Third Ave)   212/744-8600
Mon-Thurs: 10-4:30 (by appointment)

Though the Guttmanns have worked on frames for some of the nation's finest museums, including the Metropolitan, they stand apart from other first-class artisans in that they are not snobby or picky about the work they will accept. They will restore, regild, or replace any type of picture frame. They work with masterpieces but are equally at home framing a snapshot. Even better, they are among the few experts who don't price themselves out of the market. Bring in a broken or worn-out frame, and they will graciously tell you exactly what it will cost to fix it.

J. POCKER & SON
135 E 63rd St (bet Park and Lexington Ave)
                         212/838-5488, 800/443-3116
Mon-Fri: 9-5:30; Sat: 10-5:30 (closed Sat in summer)
                              www.jpocker.com

Three generations of this family have been in the framing business, so rest assured that you will receive expert advice from a superbly trained staff. All framing is conservation-quality. Look to them for decorative prints, custom plaques, gallery rods, and picture lights. Pickup and delivery, too.

JINPRA NEW YORK
1208 Lexington Ave (at 82nd St)   212/988-3903
Mon: 10:30-5; Tues-Sat: 10:30-6:30

The proprietor of Jinpra is Sam Chiang, and his service is unique. Jinpra provides art services like cleaning and gilding, picture framing, frame restoration, and mural reproduction. Chiang makes the high-quality frames himself; his artistry is evident in every unique piece, including his murals.

JULIUS LOWY FRAME AND RESTORING COMPANY
223 E 80th St (bet Second and Third Ave)   212/861-8585
Mon-Fri: 9-5:30   www.lowyonline.com

Serving New York City since 1907, Lowy is the nation's oldest, largest, and most highly regarded firm for the conservation and framing of fine art. Lowy's services include painting and paper conservation, professional photography, conservation framing, and curatorial work. They sell antique frames (the largest inventory in the U.S.) and authentic reproduction frames (the best selection anywhere). In addition, Lowy provides mat-making, and fitting services. Their client base includes art dealers, private collectors, auction houses, corporate collections, institutions, and museums.

KING DAVID GALLERY
128 W 23rd St (bet Ave of the Americas and Seventh Ave)
Mon-Fri: 10-8; Sun: 11-6   212/727-7184
                                         www.kingdavidgallery.com

These people provide very professional service in a number of areas: design consulting and custom framing for fine art and mirrors, canvas stretching, glass cutting, 24K gold-leaf framing, shadow boxes, glass panels for shower doors, and designing and building framed TV mirrors to cover your LCD or plasma TV. Custom glass work is really their primary specialty, but they can do almost anything in this field, beginning with designer sketches and measurements.

LEITH RUTHERFURD TALAMO
By appointment   212/535-8293

Leith Rutherfurd Talamo can restore your art to its original state. Did movers mishandle a treasured painting? Has the masterpiece that hung over the fireplace darkened with age? Do you need help hanging or lighting a collection? All of these services—plus cleaning, relining, gilding, and polishing frames—are done by Talamo with expertise and class.

Have you ever wondered how consumer products and recipes are tested or how engineers put appliances through strenuous tests? The **Good Housekeeping Research Institute** operates its test labs in the Hearst Tower (300 W 57th St, 212/649-5000). Call for a schedule of monthly tours, which includes test kitchens and the Good Housekeeping dining room.

Babysitters

BABY SITTERS' GUILD

60 E 42nd St (bet Madison and Park Ave), Suite 912   212/682-0227
Daily: 9-9   www.babysittersguild.com

The Baby Sitters' Guild was established in 1940. They charge high rates, but their professional reputation commands them. All guild sitters have passed rigorous scrutiny. Many have teaching, nursing, or nanny backgrounds, and only the most capable are sent out on jobs. Believe it or not, the sitters can speak 16 languages among them. They enforce a four-hour minimum and add on any travel expenses. Some sitters have travelled to New Jersey, Connecticut, and even abroad upon request.

BARNARD BABYSITTING AGENCY

49 Claremont Ave (at 119th St), 2nd floor   212/854-2035
Call for hours   www.barnard.edu/babysitting

Barnard Babysitting Agency is a nonprofit organization run by students at the undergraduate women's college affiliated with Columbia University. The service provides affordable child care in the New York metropolitan area. At the same time, it allows students to seek convenient employment. Live-in help is also available. A minimum registration fee is required.

The only thing worse than driving in Manhattan is finding a place to park the car. Here's one solution. Go online to **Bestparking.com** and follow the prompts to enter your destination. You'll end up with a map listing parking garages and rates in the immediate area. Information is also available for mobile phone and PDA users at www.mobile.bestparking.com.

Beauty Services

There are a myriad of beauty services in New York to help keep you feeling well and beautiful. Following are some recommended choices:

BOTOX TREATMENT
Verve Laser and Medical Spa (216 E 50th St, 212/888-3003)

CELLULITE TREATMENT
Wellpath (1100 Madison Ave, 212/737-9604): up-to-date equipment

COSMETIC SURGEONS AND CONSULTANTS
Dr. Amiya Prasad (61 E 66th St, 212/265-8877): plastic surgeon, eyelids
Dr. Neil Sadick (911 Park Ave, 212/772-7242): anti-aging treatment

DAY SPAS (by neighborhood)

Chelsea
Azure Day Spa and Laser Center (26 W 20th St, 212/563-5365): Ear-candling therapy relieves allergies, migraines, and sinus infections.
Graceful Spa (205 W 14th St, 2nd floor, 212/675-5145): budget-friendly

Spa at Chelsea Piers (Sports Center, Chelsea Piers, 23rd St at Hudson River, 2nd floor, 212/336-6780): spa parties

East Village

Great Jones Spa (29 Great Jones St, 212/505-3185): full service

Flatiron District

Completely Bare (103 Fifth Ave, 212/366-6060): one of the best laser hair-removal treatments in town; dewrinkling facial

Just Calm Down (30 W 18th St, 212/337-0032): "Peelin' Groovy" facial and chocolate treatments

Longevity Health (12 W 27th St, 9th floor, 212/675-9355): wellness center

Gramercy

Aerospa (Gramercy Park Hotel, 2 Lexington Ave, 212/920-3300)

Gloria Cabrera Salon and Spa (309 E 23rd St, 212/689-6815)

Need a quick rest in midtown Manhattan? **Yelo** (315 W 57th St, 212/245-8235, www.yelonyc.com) offers private treatment cabins, where you can rest and relax with your own choice of lighting and sounds. Options include blankets and scents to suit your mood. "Yelo-Naps" are available in five-minute increments from 20 to 40 minutes, priced from $15 to $28. Yelo reflexology treatments and full-body table massages are also available.

Greenwich Village

Acqua Beauty Bar (7 E 14th St, 212/620-4329): pedicures

Silk Day Spa (47 W 13th St, 212/255-6457): "Silk Supreme Eastern Indulgence Body Scrub and Polish"

Harlem

Turning Heads Beauty Salon and Day Spa (218 Lenox Ave, 212/828-4600)

Kips Bay

Essential Therapy (122 E 25th St, 212/777-2325): spa services with a healing bent

Oasis Day Spa (1 Park Ave, 212/254-7722)

Meatpacking District

G Spa (Hotel Gansevoort, 18 Ninth Ave, 212/206-6700): full service

Midtown

Bliss 57 (12 W 57th St, 212/219-8970)

Bloomie (44 W 55th St, 212/664-1662)

Elizabeth Arden Red Door Salon (691 Fifth Ave, 212/546-0200)

Exhale Spa (150 Central Park S, 212/249-3000): deep flow massage

Faina European Skin Care Center and Day Spa (330 W 58th St, Suite 402, 212/245-6557)

Frederic Fekkai Fifth Avenue (Henri Bendel, 712 Fifth Ave, 4th floor, 212/753-9500): the ultimate

Homme Spa (465 Lexington Ave, 212/983-0033): men's lounge, women also welcome

Ido Holistic Center (9 E 45th St, 8th floor, 212/599-5300): immune system boost

Jurlique (477 Madison Ave, 212/752-1980): facials

Juva Skin and Laser Center (60 E 56th St, 2nd floor, 212/688-5882): microdermabrasion

Juvenex (25 W 32nd St, 646/733-1330): 24-hour Korean oasis, body scrub

La Prairie at the Ritz-Carlton Spa (50 Central Park S, 2nd floor, 212/521-6135): top-drawer

Lia Schorr (686 Lexington Ave, 4th floor, 212/486-9670): efficient and reasonably priced

Metamorphosis (127 E 56th St, 212/751-6051): small but good, men and women

Nina's European Day Spa & Laser Center (5 W 35th St, 212/594-9610): skin-care treatments including "chocolate treatments"

Okeanos (211 E 51st St, 212/223-6773): coed sauna, "*Platza*" (ancient Russian technique using bundled birch leaves)

Peninsula New York Spa (Peninsula New York Hotel, 700 Fifth Ave, 21st floor, 212/903-3910)

Remede Spa (St. Regis New York, 2 E 55th St, 212/339-6715)

Salon and Spa at Saks Fifth Avenue (611 Fifth Avenue, 212/940-4000): 50th Street entrance

Salon de Tokyo (200 W 57th St, Room 1308, 212/757-2187): Shiatsu parlor, open till midnight

Smooth Synergy (686 Lexington Ave, 3rd floor, 212/397-0111): "Medspa" with a resident physician

Spa at the Four Seasons Hotel New York (57 E 57th St, 212/350-6420)

Susan Ciminelli Day Spa (Bergdorf Goodman, 754 Fifth Ave, 9th floor, 212/872-2650): highly recommended ultra spa package for men ... but if you have to ask the price....

Townhouse Spa (39 W 56th St, 212/245-8006)

Yi Pak (10 W 32nd St, 3rd floor, 212/594-1025)

Murray Hill

Elite Day Spa (24 W 39th St, 212/730-2100): "Sugar Daddy" brown sugar scrub

Hair Party (76 Madison Ave, 212/213-0056): open 24 hours a day

Murray Hill Skin Care (567 Third Ave, 2nd floor, 212/661-0777): "backcial"—i.e., a facial for the back

Oasis Day Spa (Affinia Dumont Hotel, 150 E 34th St, 212/254-7722): ask about the weekend package

Soho

Bunya CitiSPA (474 West Broadway, 212/388-1288)

Bliss Spa (568 Broadway, 2nd floor, 212/219-8970): oxygen facial

Erbe (196 Prince St, 212/966-1445)

Haven (150 Mercer St, 212/343-3515): calm and refreshing; open weekends

Iguaz Day Spa (350 Hudson St, 212/647-0007): backcials

Mezzanine Spa at Soho Integrative Health (62 Crosby St, 212/431-1600): medical spa

SkinCareLab (568 Broadway, Suite 403, 212/334-3142): body treatments, facials

Soho Sanctuary (119 Mercer St, 212/334-5550): pomegranate-infused scrub

Tribeca

Euphoria (18 Harrison St, 2nd floor, 212/925-5925): "Fresh Air Facial"

TriBeCa MedSpa (114 Hudson St, 212/925-9500): exfoliation

Upper East Side

Ajune (1294 Third Ave, 212/628-0044): full-service, Botox, superb facials

Bliss 49 (W New York Hotel, 541 Lexington Ave, 212/755-1200)

Chantecaille Energy Spa at Barneys (600 Madison Ave, 212/833-2700): facials to detoxify and decrease puffiness

Completely Bare (764 Madison Ave, 212/717-9300): sunspot removal

Dr. Howard Sobel Skin and Spa (960-A Park Ave, 212/288-0060): medical personnel on the premises

Equinox Wellness Spa (817 Lexington Ave, 212/750-4671): facials, sports massage

Institute Beauté (885 Park Ave, 212/535-0229): foot facial

Paul Labrecque Salon and Spa (171 E 65th St, 212/595-0099): facials

Yasmine Djerradine (30 E 60th St, 212/588-1771): remodeling facial

Yin Beauty and Arts (22 E 66th St, 212/879-5040): detoxifying body treatment

Upper West Side

Dorit Baxter Skin Care, Beauty & Health Spa (47 W 57th St, 3rd floor, 212/371-4542): salt scrub, lymphatic drainage massage

Ettia Holistic Day Spa (239 W 72nd St, 212/362-7109)

Paul Labrecque Salon and Spa (Reebok Sports Center, 160 Columbus Ave, 212/595-0099): Thai massages, facials

Prenatal Massage Center of Manhattan (123 W 79th St, 212/330-6846): home visits, too

Spa at Mandarin Oriental (Time Warner Center, 80 Columbus Circle, 35th floor, 212/805-8880): Lomi Lomi deep-tissue massage and holistic foot ritual

Spa Ja (300 W 56th St, 212/245-7566): Brazilian body sculpting

EYEBROW STYLING

Shobha Threading (594 Broadway, Suite 403, 212/931-8363): shaping

Borja Color Studio (118 E 57th St, 212/308-3232)

EYELASHES

Ebenezer Eyelash (10 W 32nd St, 2nd floor, 212/947-5503): extensions

HAIR CARE (best in Manhattan, by area)

Chelsea

Antonio Prieto (127 W 20th St, 212/255-3741): popular styling for women

East Village

Astor Place Hair Stylists (2 Astor Pl, at Broadway, 212/475-9854): one of the world's largest barber shops; inexpensive

Flatiron District

Sacha and Oliver (6 W 18th St, 212/255-1100): very French
Salon 02 (20 W 22nd St, 212/675-7274)

Greenwich Village

Gemini Salon and Spa (547 Hudson St, 212/675-4546): "opti-smooth" straightening treatment

Lower East Side

Laicale Salon (129 Grand St, 212/219-2424): no attitude
Snip 'n Sip (204 Waverly Pl, 212/242-3880): soda shop atmosphere
Tease Salon (137 Rivington St, 212/979-8327): extensions and relaxers

Midtown

Bumble & Bumble (146 E 56th St, 212/521-6500): no-nonsense establishment
Kenneth's (Waldorf-Astoria, 301 Park Ave, lobby floor, 212/752-1800): full service with an able staff, but a long wait for Kenneth himself
Nardi Beauty Center and Spa (Lombardy Hotel, 111 E 56th St, 212/421-4810): long hair specialists
Ouidad Hair Salon (37 W 57th St, 4th floor, 212/888-3288): curly- and frizzy hair specialists
Phyto Universe (715 Lexington Ave, 212/308-0270): specializing in French beauty
Pierre Michel (131 E 57th St, 212/593-1460): J.F. Lazartigue treatment products, eyelash extensions
Salon Ishi (70 E 55th St, 212/888-4744): scalp massages for men and women
Stephen Knoll (625 Madison Ave, 212/421-0100): highly recommended

Soho

Frederic Fekkai Salon (394 West Broadway, 212/888-2600): Wi-Fi, food from Barolo, and espresso
Ion Studio (41 Wooster St, 212/343-9060): ecologically sound
John Masters (77 Sullivan St, 212/343-9590): all-organic products
Privé (310 West Broadway, 212/274-8888): all hair services, shampoos a specialty, trendy, open Sunday

Upper East Side

Frederic Fekkai Salon (Henri Bendel, 712 Fifth Ave, 4th floor, 212/753-9500): elegant
Garren New York (Sherry Netherland Hotel, 781 Fifth Ave, 212/841-9400): customized services
John Barrett Salon (Bergdorf Goodman, 754 Fifth Ave, penthouse, 212/872-2700): top cut
Julian Farel Salon (605 Madison Ave, 2nd floor, 212/888-8988): upscale, private hair parties
Mark Garrison (108 E 60th St, 212/570-2455): popular
Oscar Blandi (746 Madison Ave, 212/988-9404): reliable
Salon A·K·S (689 Madison Ave, 10th floor, 212/888-0707)
Salon and Spa at Saks Fifth Avenue (Saks Fifth Ave, 611 Fifth Ave, concourse level, 212/940-4000): top-grade, full-service
Serge Normant at John Frieda (30 E 76th St, 212/879-1000)

Vidal Sassoon (730 Fifth Ave, 212/535-9200): popular with men and women

Yves Durif (Carlyle Hotel, 35 E 76th St, 212/452-0954): reliable

Upper West Side

Salon Above (2641 Broadway, 212/665-7149)

West Village

Whittemore House (45 Grove St, 212/242-8880): very classy; tea and wine bar

---

Inexpensive prices on beauty services are available if you are willing to try training schools. Here are some of the better ones.

Dentistry: **New York University College of Dentistry** (345 E 24th St, 212/998-9800)—initial visit and X-rays, all for $90!

Facials: **Christine Valmy International School** (437 Fifth Ave, 2nd floor, 212/779-7800)—facials start at $33

Haircut: **Mark Garrison Salon** (108 E 60th St, 212/570-2455)—training price: $40-$65!

Haircut (blow dry): **Jean Louis David** (2146 Broadway, 212/873-1850)—$41

Hairstyling: **Bumble & Bumble** (415 W 13th St, 212/521-6500)—good deals

Hairstyling and manicures: **LIBS Empire Beauty Schools** (22 W 34th St, 212/695-4555)—an old-fashioned learning institute; reasonable prices

Massage: **Swedish Institute** (226 W 26th St, 212/924-5900)—12 one-hour Swedish-shiatsu massages for $250

Men's haircuts: **Atlas Barber School** (34 Third Ave, 212/475-1360)—haircuts for $5; women are welcome, too

---

HAIR COLORING

Borja Color Studio (118 E 57th St, 212/308-3232)
Louis Licari Salon (693 Fifth Ave, 212/758-2090)
Q Hair (19 Bleecker St, 212/614-8729): brunettes
Salon A·K·S (689 Madison Ave, 10th floor, 212/888-0707)
Warren Tricomi (1 W 58th St, 2nd floor, 212/262-8899)

HAIR LOSS TREATMENT

Le Metric Hair Center for Women (124 E 40th St, Suite 601, 212/986-5620)
Philip Kingsley Trichological Clinic (16 E 52nd St, 212/753-9600)

HAIR REMOVAL

J. Sisters Salon (35 W 57th St, 3rd floor, 212/750-2485): waxing
Verve Laser and Medical Spa (216 E 50th St, 212/888-3003)

HAIRSTYLING

Discount Haircuts

Parlor (102 Ave B, 212/673-5520): check out Apprentice Monday—prices start at $20!

Salon Mingle (10 W 55th St, 2nd floor, 212/459-3320): $10 cuts on Wednesday, 7-9pm

Tease Salon (199 Second Ave, 212/725-7088): $30 for a wash and cut

Family Haircuts

Feature Trim (1108 Lexington Ave, 212/650-9746)

Hair Blow-Styling

Blow Styling Salon (342 W 14th St, 212/989-6282): for the budget conscious

Jean Louis David (2146 Broadway, 212/873-1850): good work at reasonable prices

Salon A·K·S (689 Madison Ave, 10th floor, 212/888-0707): Mika Rummo; also does house calls

Warren Tricomi (1 W 58th St, 2nd floor, 212/262-8899): for work that lasts

Men's Haircuts

Chelsea Barber (465 W 23rd St, 212/741-2254): inexpensive

Frank's Chop Shop (19 Essex St, 212/228-7442): antique barber chairs

Neighborhood Barbers (439 E 9th St, 212/777-0798): bargain haircuts at $14

Salon A·K·S (689 Madison Ave, 10th floor 212/888-0707): hair coloring

HOME SERVICES

Eastside Massage Therapy Center (351 E 78th St, 212/249-2927)

Joseph Martin (115 57th St, 212/838-3150): hair coloring, nails, and pedicures

Lady Barber (Kathleen Giordano, 212/826-8616): will come to offices

Paul Podlucky (25 E 67th St, #14E, 212/717-6622): his place or yours

SPArty! (646/736-1777): bring the spa to you

INTEGRATIVE MEDICINE

Beth Israel Medical Center Continuum Center for Health & Healing (245 Fifth Ave, 646/935-2220): *Gua Sha* Chinese healing process and other procedures

LIPOSUCTION

Taranow Plastic Surgery (169 E 69th St, 212/772-2100)

MAKEUP

Kimara Ahnert Makeup Studio (1113 Madison Ave, 212/452-4252): lessons and products

Makeup Shop (131 W 21st St, 212/807-0447): by appointment

Three Custom Color Specialists (54 W 22nd St, 888/262-7714): replication of discontinued cosmetics; bridal makeup

MASSAGE

Angel Feet (77 Perry St, 212/924-3576): reflexology

Feet Island (166 Mott St, 212/226-6328): 30-minute foot massage for $20

Graceful Services (1095 Second Ave, 2nd floor, 212/593-9904): facials, too

Relax (716 Greenwich St, 212/206-9714)

MEN'S GROOMING

Esquires of Wall Street (14 Wall St, 212/349-5064)

Frederic Fekkai Fifth Avenue (Henri Bendel, 712 Fifth Ave, 4th floor, 212/753-9500): men's lounge, L'Atelier de Frederic

John Allan's Men's Club (95 Trinity Pl, 212/406-3000): full-service

Kiehl's (109 Third Ave, 212/677-3171): toiletries

La Boîte à Coupe (38 E 57th St, 212/246-2097)

Lather Spa (127 E 57th St, 212/644-4449): manicure, pedicure

Mezzanine Spa at Soho Integrative Health (62 Crosby St, 212/431-1600): pedicure

Patrick Melville (Sports Club LA, 45 Rockefeller Plaza, 3rd floor, 212/218-8650): pedicure

Paul Labrecque (171 E 65th St, 212/595-0099): straight razor shave

Pierre Michel (131 E 57th St, 212/593-1460): manicure

SkinCareLab (568 Broadway, Suite 403, 212/334-3142): full-service for men and women

Spiff (750 Third Ave, 212/204-8720): post-shave facial and hot-oil scalp treatment

Truman's Gentlemen's Groomers (120 E 56th St, 212/759-5015): upscale men's spa

Wellness Men's Day Spa (44 W 22nd St, 212/366-9080)

Yasmine Djerradine (30 E 60th St, 212/588-1771): men's facials

---

Every home should have at least one working fire extinguisher for emergency preparedness. **Able Fire Prevention** (241 W 26th St, 212/685-8314) specializes in new fire extinguishers, as well as recharging those already in place. Able offers pickup and delivery, installation, and cabinets and hardware for mounting the cylinders.

NAILS AND PEDICURES

Angel Nails (151 E 71st St, 212/535-5333): nail-wrapping, massage, body-waxing

Dashing Diva Salon & Nail Boutique (1335 Madison Ave, 212/348-8890 and other locations): manicures, pedicures, and waxing

Grand Spa (389 Grand St, 212/253-9978)

Jin Soon Natural Hand & Foot Spa (56 E 4th St, 212/473-2047 and 23 Jones St, 212/229-1070)

Paul Labrecque Salon & Spa (160 Columbus Ave, 212/595-0099)

Pierre Michel (131 E 57th St, 212/593-1460): old-school

Rescue Beauty Lounge (34 Gansevoort St, 212/206-6409)

Sweet Lily (222 West Broadway, 212/925-5441): "natural" nail spa and boutique

Touch of East (11 W 20th St, 212/366-6333)

SAUNA

Russian and Turkish Baths (268 E 10th St, 212/674-9250): since 1892; sauna, steam, and ice pool

Spa Sol (4 W 33rd St, 212/564-2100): steam and sauna

SKIN CARE

Advanced Skin Care Day Spa (10 W 55th St, 212/758-8867)
Alla Katkov (Miano Viel, 16 E 52nd St, 2nd floor, 212/980-3222): facials
Bluemercury (2305 Broadway, 212/799-0500): makeup and facials
Christine Chin (82 Orchard St, 212/353-0503)
Glow Skin Spa (30 E 60th St, Suite 808, 212/319-6654): skin transformation
Joean Skin Care (80 Lafayette St, 212/227-5120): Chinese-style, inexpensive
Lia Schorr (686 Lexington Ave, 4th floor, 212/486-9670)
Ling Skin Care Salons (105 W 77th St, 212/877-2883 and 12 E 16th St, 212/989-8833): great skin care
Oasis Day Spa (1 Park Ave, 212/254-7722): Facials are a specialty.
Paul Labrecque East (171 E 65th St, 212/595-0099): Regina Viotto is a great facialist.
Shizuka New York (7 W 51st St, 6th floor, 212/644-7400): anti-aging facial with intense pulsed light
Tracie Martyn (59 Fifth Ave, 212/206-9333): resculpting facial

---

Interesting Manhattan Trivia

- The city's first paved road, which was actually cobblestones, is purported to be on what is now Stone Street. In 1656 paving was the result of road complaints from residents of De Hoogh Street to the city of New Amsterdam.
- In 1875 the first tattoo parlor with an electrical tattoo machine opened on East Broadway, at Chatham Square.
- Before Macy's inhabited its landmark block, it was home to Koster and Bial's Music Hall, where Thomas Edison introduced moving pictures in 1896.

TANNING

Brazil Bronze (580 Broadway, Suite 501, 212/431-0077): bronzing formula
City Sun Tanning (50 E 13th St, 212/353-9700): spray
Paul Labrecque East (171 E 65th St, 212/595-0099): air bronzing with exfoliation
Spa at Equinox (205 E 85th St, 212/396-9611): body bronzing

TATTOOS AND TATTOO REMOVAL

Dr. Roy Geronemus (317 E 34th St, 212/686-7306)
Inborn NYC (85 Ludlow St, 212/387-8480): artistic tats

TEETH WHITENING

Dr. Jan Linhart (230 Park Ave): 212/682-5180
Dr. Frederick Solomon (Tribeca Smiles, 44 Lispenard St, 212/473-4444)

Cabinetry

HARMONY WOODWORKING
153 W 27th St (bet Ave of the Americas and Seventh Ave), Room 902
By appointment   212/366-7221
www.harmonywoodworking.org

Expert woodworker Ron Rubin devotes his time to custom projects, especially kitchens, bookcases, wall units, entertainment centers, desks, and tables.

For other reliable carpenters call **R&N Construction** (914/699-0292). These folks do quality work, and they are reasonably priced and nice to deal with. Ask for Nick Alpino.

If you are interested in cabinetry, call Joe Lonigro at **European Woodworking** (914/969-5724). His custom millwork is outstanding, and believe it or not, some folks have actually claimed that he "tends to undercharge!"

JIM NICKEL
By appointment   718/963-2138

Jim Nickel, who lives in Brooklyn, is an expert in projects that use wood: cabinets, bookcases, wall sculptures, and much more. He prefers small- to medium-sized jobs and can do an entire project—from consultation and design to installation—all by himself. He has decades of experience and is budget conscious. Call in the afternoon or evening for an appointment.

MANHATTAN CABINETRY
455 Park Ave S (bet 30th and 31st St)   212/889-8808
229 E 59th St (bet Second and Third Ave)   212/750-9800
Mon-Thurs: 10-7; Fri: 10-6; Sat: 10-5:30; Sun: 12-5
www.manhattancabinetry.com

Their motto: "If you can imagine it, we can build it." Do you need a custom piece for a special nook or have a special design in mind? Visit Manhattan Cabinetry to see product samples, from French Deco reproductions to contemporary designs or somewhere in between. They will work with you from design to finish in order to create a piece of furniture reflecting your personal style. Check their website periodically to view floor samples available for sale.

Carpentry

NYcitySTUFF.com   212/242-1800
Daily: 24 hours (by appointment)   www.nycitystuff.com

Everyone needs a guy like Paul Kennedy at some time or another. Major renovations, minor handy work, even last-minute jobs are no problem for him and his friendly, resourceful crew. They'll do carpentry and sheet rock work; A/C installation, cleaning, and storage; bathroom and kitchen repairs and remodeling; wallpapering; window treatments and installation; door and lock replacement and repairs; furniture assembly; painting and color selection; and plasma TV mounting. Other services include moving, domestic cleaning, computer repair, and pre-owned furniture bargains.

Is there a spill or a stain you can't get out of the carpet? No worry, just call **ID Carpet Cleaners** (212/843-9464). They will treat floor coverings with flame retardant, too.

Carriages

CHATEAU STABLES/CHATEAU THEATRICAL ANIMALS/CHATEAU WEDDING CARRIAGES

Daily: 10-6   212/246-0520
Call for reservations   www.chateaustables.net
                                          www.chateauweddingcarriages.com

There is nothing quite as romantic as a ride in an authentic Hansom cab. If you would like to arrive at your next dinner party in a horse-drawn carriage, Chateau is the place to call. They have the largest working collection of horse-drawn vehicles in the U.S. and have been a family business for over 45 years. Although they prefer advance notice, requests for weddings, group rides, hay rides, sleigh rides, tours, funerals, movies, and overseas visitors can likely be handled at any time.

Good sliding doors can be helpful in home or office. Try the **Sliding Door Company** (230 Fifth Ave, 212/213-9350, www.slidingdoorco.com).

Cars for Hire

AAMCAR CAR RENTALS

315 W 96th St (bet West End Ave and Riverside Dr)
Mon-Fri: 7:30-7:30; Sat, Sun: 9-5   212/222-8500, 800/722-6923

506 W 181st St (at Amsterdam Ave)   212/927-7000
Mon-Fri: 9-7; Sat: 9-1   www.aamcar.com

This independent car rental company has a full line of cars including 15- and 7-passenger vans, cargo vans, and sport utility vehicles. AAMCAR has been around for several decades and offers over 200 cars.

A BETTER CHAUFFERED LIMOUSINE SERVICE

800/429-5285 (limo requests), 888/429-5780 (Town Car requests)
Customer service: 7 a.m. to 11p.m. daily   www.abcnyclimo.com

A group of experienced chauffeurs founded this limousine service in order to offer elegance, dependability, and first-class service at competitive rates. All drivers speak fluent English and proffer complimentary healthy snacks, breath mints, fresh water, and candy during the ride. Airport service starts with drivers greeting passengers at baggage claim. Their specialty is guided tours of New York City, and they offer top-notch service for shopping trips, corporate clients, and social occasions.

CAREY LIMOUSINE NY

24 hours   212/599-1122 (reservations), 800/336-4646
                                                      www.carey.com

Carey is the grandfather of car-for-hire services. They provide chauffeur-driven limousines and sedans and will take clients anywhere, at any time, in almost any kind of weather. Last-minute reservations are accepted on an as-available basis. Discuss rates before making a commitment.

> If you are having a cocktail party and want specialized bar catering, try **Cuff & Buttons** (212/625-2090, www.cuffandbuttons.com).

CARMEL CAR AND LIMOUSINE SERVICE

2642 Broadway (at 100th St)   212/666-6666, 866/666-6666
24 hours   www.carmellimo.com

These people are highly commended for good service and fair prices. Full-size and luxury sedans, minivans, passenger vans, and limos are available. Prices are by the hour, and set fees apply for airport transportation.

COMPANY II LIMOUSINE SERVICE

24 hours   718/430-6482

A good choice! Steve Betancourt provides responsible, efficient service at reasonable prices. I personally vouch that Steve's reputation for reliability is well earned.

Still More Fun Facts

- Big Apple Corner is located on the southwest corner of 54th Street and Broadway.
- The oldest standing bridge in Manhattan is High Bridge in Highbridge Park, at 155th and Dyckman Streets.
- Wyckoff House Museum in Brooklyn is the oldest building among the five boroughs.
- Manhattan encompasses a total of 22.7 square miles.
- Central Park covers a larger area than the principality of Monaco.
- The first electric subway line ran between City Hall and 156th Street in 1904.
- The Fashion Institute of Technology offers a Bachelor of Science Degree with a Major in Cosmetics and Fragrance Marketing.

Casting

SCULPTURE HOUSE CASTING

155 W 26th St (bet Ave of the Americas and Seventh Ave)
Mon-Fri: 8-5; Sat: 10-3   212/645-9430, 888/374-8665
                                            www.sculptshop.com

Sculpture House has been a family-owned business since 1918, making it one of the city's oldest casting firms. It is a full-service casting foundry, specializing in classical plaster reproductions, mold-making, and casting in all mediums and sizes. Ornamental plastering and repair and restoration work are available. Sculpting tools and supplies are sold as well.

Chair Caning

VETERAN'S CHAIR CANING AND REPAIR SHOP
442 Tenth Ave (bet 34th and 35th St)   212/564-4560
Mon-Thurs: 7:30-4:30; Fri: 7:30-4; Sat: 8-1 www.veteranscaning.com

John Bausert, a third-generation chair caner, has written a book about his craft. His prices and craftsmanship are among the best in town. Bausert believes in passing along his knowledge and encourages customers to repair their own chairs. The procedure is outlined in Bausert's book, and necessary materials are sold in the shop. If you don't want to try it yourself, Veteran's will repair your chair. For a charge, they'll even pick it up from your home. In addition to caning, Veteran's stocks materials for fixing chairs and furniture, repairs wicker, and repairs and reglues wooden chairs.

China and Glassware Repair

GLASS RESTORATIONS
1597 York Ave (bet 84th and 85th St)   212/517-3287
Mon-Fri: 9:30-5

Did you chip your prize Lalique glass treasure? These folks can restore all manner of crystal, including pieces by Steuben, Baccarat, Daum, and Waterford, as well as antique art glass. Glass Restoration is a find, as too few quality restorers are left in the country. Ask for Gus Jochec!

There's nothing like a clean, plush carpet to enhance the beauty of your home or office. The main problems with carpeting are dirt, food, pets, and those nasty red wine spills. Contact **Flat Rate Carpet** (212/777-9277, www.flatratecarpet.com) to clean up a mess or to re-stretch and Scotchguard carpeting. While you're at it, have them clean mattresses, drapes, blinds, air ducts, and other types of floor surfaces. Only organic cleaning products are used. Emergency situations can be handled at any time of day or night.

Clock and Watch Repair

FANELLI ANTIQUE TIMEPIECES
790 Madison Ave (bet 66th and 67th St), Suite 202   212/517-2300
Mon-Fri: 10-6 (Sat by appointment)

In a beautiful clock gallery, Cindy Fanelli specializes in the care of high-quality "investment-type" timepieces, especially carriage clocks. Her store has one of the nation's largest collections of rare and unusual Early American grandfather clocks and vintage wristwatches. They do sales and restoration, make house calls, give free estimates, rent timepieces, and purchase single pieces or entire collections.

J&P TIMEPIECES
1057 Second Ave (at 56th St)   212/980-1099
Mon-Fri: 10-5; Sat: 11-4 (closed Sat in summer)
                                                www.jptimepieces.com

In Europe, fine-watch repairing is a family tradition, but this craft is slowly being forgotten in our country. Fortunately for Manhattan, the Fossners have passed along this talent from father to son for four generations. You can be confident in their work on any kind of mechanical watch. They guarantee repairs for six months and generally turn around jobs within ten days.

SUTTON CLOCK SHOP
139 E 61st St (at Lexington Ave)   212/758-2260
Tues-Fri: 11-4 (call ahead)

Sutton's forte is selling and acquiring unusual timepieces, but they are equally interested in the maintenance and repair of antique clocks. Some of the timepieces they sell—even the contemporary ones—are truly outstanding, and numerous satisfied customers endorse their repair work. They sell and repair barometers and will even make house calls.

TIME PIECES REPAIRED
115 Greenwich Ave (at 13th St)   212/929-8011
Tues-Fri: 10:30-6; Sat: 11-5   www.timepiecesrepaired.com

Grace Szuwala services, restores, repairs, and sells antique timepieces. Her European training has made her a recognized expert. She has a strong sensitivity for pieces that have more sentimental than real value. She has been doing business on Greenwich Avenue since 1978.

Clothing Rentals

ILUS
248 Elizabeth St (bet Houston and Prince St)   646/454-1678
Mon-Sat: 12-7; Sun: 12-5   www.ilus-nyc.com

This business makes a lot of sense. Many ladies don't want to be seen wearing the same outfit more than once to classy parties, and investing in a large wardrobe isn't always feasible. Enter Ilus—a designer dress rental boutique with hundreds of fashionable dresses, wraps, handbags, and glitzy accessories in stock. Check out the selections in their cozy boutique or online. Three days is the standard rental term, with longer options available. A no-fee membership is required. Rental rates are very affordable.

Clothing Repair

FRENCH-AMERICAN REWEAVING COMPANY
119 W 57th St (bet Ave of the Americas and Seventh Ave), Room 1406
Mon-Fri: 10-3; Sat: 11-2   212/765-4670

Has a tear, burn, or stain ruined your favorite outfit? These folks will work on almost any garment for men or women in nearly every fabric. Often a repaired item will look just like new!

Computer Service and Instruction

ABC COMPUTER SERVICES
15 E 40th St (bet Fifth and Madison Ave), Suite 305   212/725-3511
Mon-Fri: 9-5   www.abccomputerservices.com

ABC Computer provides sales, service, and supplies for desktop and notebook computers, as well as all kinds of printers. They'll work on Apple, Microsoft, and Novell-based systems, and they are an authorized Hewlett-Packard service center. Computer instruction is offered in your home or office. They have been around for well over a decade, which is a good recommendation in itself.

TEKSERVE
119 W 23rd St (bet Ave of the Americas and Seventh Ave)
Mon-Fri: 9-8; Sat: 10-6; Sun: noon-6   212/929-3645
                                                    www.tekserve.com

For Apple Computer sales and service, TekServe will take good care of you. They carry a huge inventory of computers and peripherals, and the firm is noted for excellent customer care. A full range of services, including data recovery, in- and out-of-warranty repairs, rentals, and seminars, are available. They also sell iPods and accessories and will replace batteries while you wait.

For computer rentals, try **Business Equipment Rental** (250 W 49th St, 212/582-2020). Prices are reasonable, and pickup and delivery are available.

For excellent computer repair, try:

Data Vision (445 Fifth Ave, 212/689-1111)
Machattan (239 W 34th St, 212/242-9393): Macs only
RCS Computer Experience (575 Madison Ave, 212/949-6935)

Delivery, Courier, Messenger Services

AVANT BUSINESS SERVICES
60 E 42nd St (bet Park and Madison Ave)   212/687-5145
Daily: 24 hours   www.avantservices.com

Even before the big guys got in the business, this outfit was doing round-the-clock local and long-distance deliveries. If you have time-sensitive material, give them a call. They'll promptly pick up your item, even in the middle of the night or during a snowstorm.

If you are stymied for a fun gift idea or unique party favors, try **fill-r-up** (197 E 76th St, 212/452-3026), a gift-basket boutique. Baskets and other cute containers are brimming with items for different themes. There is also a selection of kosher gift baskets. Where this business really sparkles is with all the bits and pieces for showers—baby or wedding—monogrammed candy jars, place card holders, edibles, and party favor bags. Browse around the shop and come away with great ideas.

NEED IT NOW
153 W 27th St (bet Ave of the Americas and Seventh Ave), 1st floor
Daily: 24 hours   212/989-1919
www.needitnowcourier.com

Need It Now is set up to provide any and all courier services. They can handle everything from a crosstown rush letter (delivery completed within an hour) to delivering nearly anything worldwide.

For quick and inexpensive same-day delivery of documents or small items in Manhattan, call **Elite Courier Services** (212/696-4000) to dispatch a bicycle messenger. Rates are calculated on a base fee, and by zone. This company has been in business for almost 30 years.

Dry Cleaners, Laundries

CLEANTEX
2335 Twelfth Ave (at 133rd St)   212/283-1200
Mon-Fri: 8-4

In business since 1928, Cleantex specializes in cleaning draperies, furniture, balloon and Roman shades, vertical blinds, Oriental and area rugs, and wall-to-wall carpeting. They provide free estimates, pick up, and delivery. Museums, churches, and rug dealers are among their satisfied clients.

HALLAK CLEANERS
1232 Second Ave (at 65th St)   212/879-4694
Mon-Fri: 7-6:30; Sat: 8-5   www.hallak.com

Hallak has been a family business for four decades. Joseph Hallak, Sr., a native of France, instilled his work ethic and dedication to detail into sons John-Claude and Joseph, Jr. This no doubt accounts for the pride and personal service they offer customers. Much of their work comes from referrals by such famed boutiques as Armani and Ferragamo. Hallak does all work in their state-of-the-art plant. They will clean shirts, linens, suede (including Ugg footwear), leather, draperies, and even dog beds and dog clothing. Their specialties are museum-quality cleaning and preservation of wedding gowns and a unique couture handbag cleaning service. For those (like your author) who have trouble with stains on ties, Hallak is the place to go. Their skilled work takes time, though rush service is available at no additional cost, and they serve clients throughout the U.S. via FedEx and UPS.

LEATHERCRAFT PROCESS
Call to arrange shipping   212/564-8980, 800/845-6155
www.leathercraftprocess.com

Leathercraft will clean, re-dye, re-line, repair, and lengthen or shorten any suede or leather garment. That includes boots, gloves, clothing, and handbags, as well as odd leather items. Because leather is extremely difficult to clean, the process can be painfully expensive. However, Leathercraft has a reputation dating back to 1938, and their prices remain competitive. Call to arrange shipping to Leathercraft's facility in New Jersey.

MADAME PAULETTE CUSTOM COUTURE CLEANERS

1255 Second Ave (bet 65th and 66th St)
Mon-Fri: 7:30-7; Sat: 8-5   212/838-6827, 877/COUTURE
                                             www.madamepaulette.com

What a clientele: Christian Dior, Vera Wang, Chanel, Givenchy, Saks, and Burberry. This full-service establishment has been in business since 1959. They do dry cleaning (including knits, suedes, and leathers), tailoring (including reweaving and alterations), laundry, and household and rug cleaning. They provide seasonal storage of furs. Taking care of wedding dresses is a specialty, and they do superior hand-cleaning of cashmere, making sure that each item's shape is maintained. Experts repair garments damaged by water, bleach, and fire, do wet cleaning, and hand-clean upholstery and tapestry. Madame Paulette offers free pick up and delivery throughout Manhattan, and will set up charge accounts. One-day service is available upon request.

Other Recommended Cleaners

Chris French Cleaners (57 Fourth Ave, 212/475-5444): an East Village favorite

Fashion Award Cleaners (2205 Broadway, 212/289-5623): full-service

G-G Cleaners (46 Grand St, 212/966-9813): legendary among fashion editors and boutique owners

Orchard Tailor Services (145 Orchard St, 212/228-0429): open daily, including Sunday

Reliable Laundromat (47 Clinton St, 212/598-0381): open Sunday

---

MEURICE GARMENT CARE

31 University Pl (bet 8th and 9th St)   212/475-2778
Mon-Fri: 7:30-6 (Wed till 7); Sat: 9-6; Sun: 10-3
245 E 57th St (bet Second and Third Ave)   212/759-9057
Mon-Fri: 7:30-6; Sat: 9-6   www.garmentcare.com

Meurice specializes in cleaning and restoring fine garments. Their Eco-Care process is environmentally friendly. They handle each piece individually, taking care of details like loose buttons and tears. Special services include exquisite hand-finishing; expert stain removal; museum-quality preservation; cleaning and restoration of wedding gowns; careful handling of ultra-fragile and chemically sensitive garments; on-site leather cleaning and repairs; and smoke, fire, and water restoration. Delivery and shipping are available.

NEW YORK'S FINEST FRENCH CLEANERS & TAILORS

154 Reade St (bet Hudson and Greenwich St)   212/431-4010
Mon-Fri: 7-7; Sat: 8-5

This quality business features pick up, delivery, and one-day service. Tailoring and storage are available, as is care for fine silks and leathers.

TIECRAFTERS

252 W 29th St (bet Seventh and Eighth Ave)   212/629-5800
Mon-Fri: 9-5   www.tiecrafters.com

Old ties never fade away at Tiecrafters. Instead, they're dyed, widened, narrowed, straightened, and cleaned. They believe that a well-made tie can live forever, and they provide services to make longevity possible. In addition to converting tie widths, they restore soiled or stained ties and clean and repair all kinds of neckwear. Owner Andy Tarshis will give pointers on tie maintenance. (Hint: if you hang a tie at night, wrinkles will be gone by morning.) Tiecrafters offers several pamphlets on the subject, including one that tells how to remove spots at home. Their cleaning charge is reasonable, and they also make custom neckwear, bow ties, braces, scarves, vests, and cummerbunds.

My Fresh Shirt (212/625-3131, www.myfreshshirt.com) is an alternative to doing your own laundry. Their processes are both health and environmentally friendly (100% Perc-free). They use technologically advanced machines and recycle hangers and bags. Pick up and delivery for laundry, dry cleaning, and shoe services, with a two-day turnaround time, is offered. Laundered shirts are returned boxed or on hangers. Other laundry is returned washed and folded. Additional premium services are available.

VILLAGE TAILOR & CLEANERS
125 Sullivan St (at Prince St)   212/925-9667
Mon-Fri: 7-7; Sat: 8-6   www.villagetailor.com

They have been in business since the early 1930s! Located in the heart of Soho, Village Tailor specializes in making custom men's and ladies apparel, including leather and suede garments, and performing alterations. They specialize in tailoring Nicole Miller gowns and designs. Wash-and-fold shirt service is also available, as is same-day turnaround,

Electricians
ALTMAN ELECTRIC
283 W 11th St (at Bleecker St)   212/924-0400, 800/287-7774
Daily: 24 hours   www.altmanelectric.com

The licensed crew at this reliable outfit is available day and night. They will do small or large jobs at home or office, and rates are reasonable. Altman has been in business for over half a century.

Electronics Repair
PORTATRONICS
2 W 46th St (at Fifth Ave), 16th floor
307 W 38th St (at Eighth Ave), 8th floor
169 Thompson St (at Houston St)   646/797-2838
Mon-Sat: 11-7   www.portatronics.com

Portatronics provides on-the-spot repair of iPods, PSP (PlayStation Portable), Creative Zen, smartphones, cameras, headphones, MP3 accessories, and more. Work on portable electronics (not including laptops) is done while the customer waits or returned by mail. You'll find replacement hard drives, LCD screens, motherboards, headphone jacks, and scroll wheels.

Embroidery

JONATHAN EMBROIDERY PLUS
256 W 38th St (bet Seventh and Eighth Ave)   212/398-3538
Mon-Fri: 9-6; Sat: 9-4   www.jeplus.com

Any kind of custom embroidery work can be done at this classy workshop. Bring a photo or sketch, or just give them an idea, and they will produce a design that you can then amend or approve. They specialize in fashion embroidery on all types of fabrics, as well as embellishments with sequins, rhinestones, studs, beads, and grommets.

MONOGRAMS BY EMILY
307 Seventh Ave (bet 27th and 28th St)   212/924-4486
By appointment only

Emily is one of the few monogrammers still doing fine, detailed work on a hand-guided monogram machine. With over 30 years of experience, she guarantees that each monogram is stitched to your exact specifications on items such as wedding dress labels, men's shirts, handkerchiefs, and other delicate items. She'll even make suggestions on thread color and style to ensure perfect results.

Exterminators

ACME EXTERMINATING
365 W 36th St (at Ninth Ave)   212/594-9230
Mon-Fri: 9-5   www.acmeexterminating.com

Acme is expert at debugging homes, offices, stores, museums, and hospitals. They employ state-of-the-art integrated pest-management technology.

Fashion Schools

FASHION INSTITUTE OF TECHNOLOGY
Seventh Ave at 27th St   212/217-7999
                                                   www.fitnyc.edu

The Fashion Institute of Technology (FIT), a branch of the State University of New York, is the fashion industry's premiere educational institution. The school was founded in 1944. Its graduate roster reads like a "who's who" of the fashion world, including Jhane Barnes, Calvin Klein, and Norma Kamali. The school offers associate's, bachelor's, and master's degrees in a multitude of majors, including advertising and marketing, illustration, photography, fine arts, fashion merchandising, management, direct marketing, production management, patternmaking, jewelry, textiles, and toy design. FIT maintains a student placement service; all students are top-caliber. The **Museum at FIT** is the world's largest repository of fashion, with over a million articles of clothing.

Formal Wear

BALDWIN FORMALS
1156 Ave of the Americas (at 45th St), 2nd floor
Mon-Fri: 9-7; Sat: 10-5   212/245-8190, 800/427-0072
                                                   www.nyctuxedos.com

If you are invited to an upscale function, Baldwin can take care of the dressing details. They rent and sell all types of formal attire: suits, overcoats, top hats, shoes, and more. They will pick up and deliver for free in midtown and for a slight charge to other Manhattan addresses. Same-day service is guaranteed for rental orders received by early afternoon. Prompt alteration service (from two hours to several days) is available for an additional charge.

Funeral Service

FRANK E. CAMPBELL FUNERAL CHAPEL
1076 Madison Ave (at 81st St)   212/288-3500
Daily: 24 hours   www.frankecampbell.com

In time of need, it is good to know of a highly professional funeral home. These folks have been providing superior service since 1898.

Furniture Rental

CHURCHILL CORPORATE SERVICES
245 W 17th St (bet Seventh and Eighth Ave), 3rd floor
Mon-Thurs: 9-6; Fri: 9-5; Sun: 11-5   212/686-0444, 800/658-7366
                    www.furnishedhousing.com

Churchill carries both traditional and starkly contemporary furniture. They can furnish any size business or residence, and they offer free interior decorating advice. A customer can select what is needed from stock or borrow from the loaner program until special orders are processed. Churchill also offers a comprehensive package, including housewares and appliances. They specialize in executive relocations and will rent anything from a single chair to furnishings for an entire home. Churchill offers corporate apartments and housing on a short- or long-term basis. Their clients include sports managers, executives on temporary assignment, and actors on short-term contracts.

CORT FURNITURE RENTAL
711 Third Ave (bet 44th and 45th St)   212/867-2800
Mon-Fri: 9-6; Sat: 10-5   www.cort.com

Cort rents furnishings for a single room, an apartment, or an entire office. They show accessories as well. All furnishings (including electronics and housewares) are available for rental with an option to purchase. An apartment location service is offered, and a multilingual staff is at your service. Working with Japanese clients is a specialty. The stock is large, and delivery and setup can often be done within 48 hours. All styles of furniture and accessories are shown in their 12,000-square-foot showroom, located near Grand Central Terminal.

Furniture Repair

ALL FURNITURE AND RUG SERVICES
21 E 40th St (at Madison Ave)   646/688-4026
Mon-Fri: 10-6   www.furnitureservices.com

All Furniture will repair, restore, and clean all parts of your furniture, from leather, fabric, and vinyl, to wood and metal (including the innermost mechanisms). The same thoroughness holds true for rugs and carpets. The most intriguing part of this business is their "take apart" service. If you're trying to move a ten-foot armoire through an eight-foot door frame, these experts will assess the situation, disassemble the armoire, transport it to its new spot, and proceed with reassembly. They work with moving companies to tackle the most difficult pieces of furniture. Same day and 24/7 emergency services are offered.

Don't say I didn't warn you about outrageous phone costs when you use hotel room phones! Here is a sampling from some of the better New York hotels:

- Local calls: $1.75, plus 15 cents per minute after the first five minutes, plus 10 cents per minute after one hour
- Interstate (USA) long-distance calls: Operator-assisted day rates, plus $9.99 hotel surcharge, plus 12.5%
- International calls: Operator-assisted day rates, plus $9.99 hotel surcharge, plus 60%
- Directory assistance: $2.50 per call
- Toll Free Calls: $1.50 per call, plus 10 cents per minute after one hour

See what I mean? Remember to bring your cell phone or use a calling card.

Gardening

COUNCIL ON THE ENVIRONMENT OF NEW YORK CITY (CENYC)
51 Chambers St (bet Broadway and Centre St), Room 228
Mon-Fri: 9-5   212/788-7900
                                                www.cenyc.org

It is a little-known fact that the city will loan tools to groups involved in community-sponsored open-space greening projects. Loans are limited to one week, but the waiting period is not long and the price (nothing!) is right. You can borrow the same tools several times a season. A group can be as few as four people. CENYC also runs Greenmarket—weekly farmers markets in 45 locations around the city—and they carry a number of interesting free publications.

Haircuts

Children

COZY'S CUTS FOR KIDS
1125 Madison Ave (at 84th St)   212/744-1716
448 Amsterdam Ave (at 81st St)   212/579-2600
1416 Second Ave (at 74th St)   212/585-COZY (2699)
Mon-Sat: 10-6; Sun: 11-5   www.cozyscutsforkids.com

Cozy's takes care of kids of all ages, including the offspring of some famous personalities. What an experience: videos and videogames, themed barber chairs, balloons, candy, and free toys. They issue a "first-time" diploma with a keepsake lock of hair! Besides providing professional styling services, Cozy's is a toy boutique. There are "glamour parties" for girls, makeup and glamour art projects, and mini-manicures. Their own "So Cozy" hair-care products for children are available in-shop and online. Adults are well taken care of, too!

Family

ASTOR PLACE HAIR STYLISTS
2 Astor Pl (at Broadway)   212/475-9854
Tues-Fri: 9-9; Sat: 8-8; Sun: 9-6   www.astorplacehairnyc.com

The personnel inside what was once a modest neighborhood barbershop give some of New York's trendiest and most far-out haircuts. It all started when the Vezza brothers inherited a barbershop from their father in the East Village at a time when "not even cops were getting haircuts." Enrico took note of the newly gentrified neighborhood's young trendies and their sleek haircuts and changed the name of the shop to "Astor Place Hair Stylists." Now the shop is staffed with a resident manager, a doorman, and 50 barbers.

> **Kevin Coulthard** (917/515-8039) is a top massage therapist and personal trainer.

ATLAS BARBER SCHOOL
34 Third Ave (bet 9th and 10th St)   212/475-1360
Mon-Fri: 9-7:30; Sat: 9-5:45   www.atlasbarbersch.com

Atlas Barber School teaches general barbering and shaving techniques, refresher courses, and a correspondence course addressing contagious diseases. They've been at it since 1949. High style it isn't; great value it is!

FEATURE TRIM
1108 Lexington Ave (bet 77th and 78th St)   212/650-9746
Mon-Fri: 10-7; Sat: 10-6

Low maintenance is the key to Feature Trim's haircuts for men, women, and children. Easy care, reasonable prices, friendly faces, and more than 50 years of experience have helped them maintain an impressive clientele. Appointments are encouraged, but walk-ins are welcome.

NEIGHBORHOOD BARBERS
439 E 9th St (bet First Ave and Ave A)   212/777-0798
Mon-Sat: 8-8; Sun: 10-7   www.neighborhoodbarbersnyc.com

Even in today's economy, looking good is still important. Here's a place to keep the clean-cut look and save some dough. Owner Eric Uvaydov runs this no-frills East Village barbershop with only three chairs. Services include shampoo, shave and haircut, chest hair trim, back shave, and beard trims. You'll be pleasantly surprised by the prices. Youngsters are welcome, too.

PAUL MOLE FAMILY BARBERSHOP
1031 Lexington Ave (at 74th St)   212/535-8461
Mon-Fri: 7:30-6:30; Sat: 7:30-5:30; Sun: 9-3:30   www.paulmole.com

As the name says, this is a family business, and they have been around for over 100 years. This is a true gentlemen's barbershop, but they will cut hair for children of their long-time customers. Hours are customer-friendly and prices are affordable. Men can still get a straight-edged razor shave here, too. The place is packed after school and on weekends, so appointments are recommended.

Health and Fitness Clubs

The health craze is still alive and well! Many well-known clubs continue to thrive, with some newcomers venturing into the field. If you're considering joining a particular club, check newspapers or websites for frequent membership enticements. Be sure to thoroughly investigate a club (staff, cleanliness, equipment, price, and policies) before you sign on the dotted line. Some visitors take advantage of reciprocal arrangements through their "home" fitness centers; check before you travel. Many Manhattan hotels offer some type of exercise equipment. Some even have full-fledged facilities with personal trainers.

NEW YORK'S BEST HEALTH AND FITNESS CLUBS

Bally Sports Club and **Bally Total Fitness** (multiple locations, 800/515-2582, www.ballyfitness.com)
Clay (25 W 14th St, 212/206-9200): concierge service
Complete Body Development (60 John St, 212/248-3030)
Crunch (multiple locations, 888/310-6011, www.crunch.com)
David Barton (215 W 23rd St, 212/414-2022 and 30 E 85th St, 212/517-7577)
Dolphin Fitness (18 Ave B, 212/777-1001 and 94 E 4th St, 212/387-9500)
Equinox Fitness Clubs (multiple locations, 212/799-1818, www.equinoxfitness.com)
Hanson Fitness (multiple locations, 212/431-7682, www.hansonfitness.com)
Manhattan Plaza Health Club (482 W 43rd St, 212/563-7001)
New York Health & Racquet Club (multiple locations, 800/472-2378, www.nyhrc.com)
New York Sports Club (multiple locations, 800/666-0808, www.mysportsclubs.com)
Paris Health Club (752 West End Ave, 212/749-3500)
Printing House Fitness + Squash Club (421 Hudson St, 212/243-7600)
Reebok Sports Club NY (160 Columbus Ave, 212/362-6800)
Sports Center at Chelsea Piers (Pier 60, Twelfth Ave at Hudson River, 212/336-6000)
Sports Club/LA (330 E 61st St, 212/355-5100 and 45 Rockefeller Plaza, 212/218-8600)
24 Hour Fitness (225 Fifth Ave, 212-271-1002)

CLUBS WITH CHILD CARE

Equinox Fitness Clubs (www.equinoxfitness.com): all locations
New York Health & Racquet Club (800/472-2378, www.nyhrc.com): some locations
Paris Health Club (752 West End Ave, 212/749-3500)
Sports Club/LA (330 E 61st St, 212/355-5100)

HEALTH AND FITNESS CLUBS, BY SPECIALTY

Personal Trainers

Bodysmith (212/249-1824): in-home training for women only
Jean Pierre Cusin (917/539-7813)

Joe Massiello (212/319-3816)
La Palestra Center for Preventative Medicine (212/799-8900)
Madison Square Club (212/683-1836)
Mike Creamer (Anatomically Correct, 212/353-8834)
O-Diesel Studio (1 York Ave, 4th floor, 917/335-8103)
Sal Anthony's Movement Salon (190 Third Ave, 212/420-7242): a real exercise salon; pay by the class or service for pilates, massage, yoga, and one-on-one sessions
Shelby Grayson (212/362-3543): clinical exercise
Sitaras Fitness (212/702-9700)

Pilates

Alycea Ungaro (Real Pilates, 177 Duane St, 212/625-0777)
Power Pilates (49 W 23rd St, 2nd floor, 212/627-5852 and 920 Third Ave, 212/371-0700)
RE:AB (33 Bleecker St, Suite 2C, 212/420-9111)
Soho Sanctuary (119 Mercer St, 212/334-5550): individual sessions

Prenatal

Maternal Massage and More (73 Spring St, 212/533-3188): pre- and post-natal, labor, and with baby, too!
Patricia Durbin-Ruiz (646/643-8369): pre- and post-natal
Physique 57 (24 W 57th St, Suite 805, 212/399-0570 and 161 Ave of the Americas, 212/463-0570): prenatal workout system

Spinning

SoulCycle (117 W 72nd St, 212/787-1300): studio for spinning only

Yoga

Ashtanga Yoga Research Institute (430 Broome St, 646/509-4174)
Atmananda Yoga Sequence (324 Lafayette St, 7th floor, 212/925-4789)
Bikram Yoga (multiple locations, 212/245-2525): Hatha yoga postures
Chopra Center and Spa (Dream Hotel, 1710 Broadway, 212/246-7600)
Integral Yoga Institute (227 W 13th St, 212/929-0585)
Integral Yoga Upper West Side (371 Amsterdam Ave, 2nd floor, 212/721-4000)
Jivamukti Yoga School (841 Broadway, 2nd floor, 212/353-0214 and 853 Lexington Ave, 2nd floor, 646/290-8106)
Kula Yoga Project (28 Warren St, 4th floor, 212/945-4460): Vinyasa classes
Laughing Lotus Yoga Center (59 W 19th St, 3rd floor, 212/414-2903)
Om Yoga (826 Broadway, 6th floor, 212/254-9642)
Pure Yoga (203 E 86th St, 212/360-1888)
Yoga Works (45 Broadway, 212/965-0801 and other locations, www.yoga works.com)

Hotels

With so many hotels, each with varying amenities and locations, choosing the place you want to stay really boils down to one basic question: How much do you want to pay for the location and comforts you desire? The hotel boom days of 2006 and 2007 are over. Fewer foreign travelers and poor economic conditions have driven prices downward. Believe it or not, there are good deals to be found in Manhattan.

Study the hotels in this section carefully, noting the area and services that are important to you. Then begin the bargaining, either online or with the hotel's front desk via phone (not the toll-free number, which can land you in a central call center) or in person. Don't be embarrassed, as it is common-place to haggle for hotel rates. It used to be chic to brag about the luxury hotel where you were staying. Today, it's a sign of a travel amateur. The person who gets a good deal is the true travel pro these days.

Because it is a buyer's market, don't be afraid to ask for the little things that make for a better stay: good reading lights, extra towels, decent pillows, free continental breakfast, spa and fitness center deals, and so on. Don't be afraid to contest add-on charges or even ask to use a hotel car.

In today's economy, you are not only the guest, you are the boss!

New York Hotels with Exceptional Swimming Pools

Crowne Plaza Times Square Manhattan (1605 Broadway, 212/977-4000): 15th-floor pool in the New York Sports Club

Empire Hotel (44 W 63rd St, 212/265-7400): rooftop pool with Pool Deck menu and spa services

Hotel Gansevoort (18 Ninth Ave, 212/206-6700): in the Meatpacking District, heated outdoor glass-enclosed pool and great views

Le Parker Meridien (118 W 57th St, 212/245-5000): penthouse pool with sundeck; non-guests may purchase user passes

Mandarin Oriental (80 Columbus Circle, 212/805-8800): an indoor 75-foot lap pool in a dramatic setting on the 36th floor, with floor-to-ceiling windows

Millennium U.N. Plaza Hotel (1 United Nations Plaza, 212/758-1234): heated indoor pool, plus an indoor tennis court

Peninsula New York (700 Fifth Ave, 212/956-2888): luxurious facility with poolside lunch

Skyline Hotel (725 Tenth Ave, 212/586-3400): heated indoor pool

Trump International Hotel & Tower (1 Central Park W, 888/448-7867): 55-foot lap pool

---

Special Hotel Classifications

Extended Stays

If you are planning to be in Manhattan for awhile, check out these ex-tended-stay facilities. Some require a 30-day minimum stay. Amenities may include kitchens, daily maid service, fitness facilities, laundry facilities, business centers, and planned activities.

Bristol Plaza (210 E 65th St, 212/753-7900)
59th Street Bridge Apartments (351 E 60th St, 212/754-9388)
Greenwich Village Habitué (80 Horatio St, 212/243-6495)
Marmara-Manhattan (301 E 94th St, 212/427-3100)
Off Soho Suites (11 Rivington St, 212/979-9815)
Phillips Club (155 W 66th St, 212/835-8800)

Residence Inn New York (Times Square, 1033 Ave of the Americas, 212/768-0007)
Webster Apartments (419 W 34th St, 212/967-9000): women only

Hostels

American Dream Hostel (168 E 24th St, 212/260-9779): family-run and owned; private and dormitory rooms ($52 and up)
Big Apple Hostel (119 W 45th St, 212/302-2603): midtown location, dorms and private rooms, reservations made online
Central Park Hostel (19 W 103rd St, 212/678-0491): dorm-style rooms with shared baths ($28 and up), lockers, private rooms ($99 and up)
Chelsea International Hostel (251 W 20th St, 212/647-0010): dormitory rooms ($35 and up) and private rooms ($80 and up); need passport for check-in
Chelsea Star Hostel (300 W 30th St, 212/244-7827): hotel ($89 and up) and hostel ($35 and up)
Grace Hotel (125 W 45th St, 212/354-2323): roommate hotel
Hostelling International-New York (891 Amsterdam Ave, 212/932-2300): one of the world's largest; membership required; prices start at $30
Times Square Beds and Rooms (356 W 40th St, 2nd floor, 212/216-0642): dorms and private rooms with shared baths and lockers

Inexpensive

Affinia Dumont (150 E 34th St, 212/481-7600)
Bedford Hotel (118 E 40th St, 212/697-4800)
Belvedere (319 W 48th St, 212/245-7000)
Best Western Seaport Inn Downtown (33 Peck Slip, 212/766-6600)
Carlton Arms (160 E 25th St, 212/679-0680)
Chelsea Hotel (222 W 23rd St, 212/243-3700)
Chelsea Savoy Hotel (204 W 23rd St, 212/929-9353)
Colonial House Inn (318 W 22nd St, 212/243-9669)
Cosmopolitan Hotel-Tribeca (95 West Broadway, 212/566-1900)
Doubletree Metropolitan Hotel NYC (569 Lexington Ave, 212/752-7000)
Eastgate Tower (222 E 39th St, 212/687-8000)
Excelsior Hotel (45 W 81st St, 212/362-9200)
414 Hotel (414 W 46th St, 212/399-0006)
Gershwin Hotel (7 E 27th St, 212/545-8000)
Holiday Inn Express (232 W 29th St, 212/695-7200)
Holiday Inn Soho (138 Lafayette St, 212/966-8898)
Hotel Edison (228 W 47th St, 212/840-5000)
Hotel 57 (130 E 57th St, 212/753-8841)
Hotel Grand Union (34 E 32nd St, 212/683-5890)
Hotel Metro (45 W 35th St, 212/947-2500)
Hotel Newton (2528 Broadway, 212/678-6500)
Hotel Roger Williams (131 Madison Ave, 212/448-7000)
Hotel Stanford (43 W 32nd St, 212/563-1500)
Hotel 31 (120 E 31st St, 212/685-3060)
Hotel Thirty-Thirty (30 E 30th St, 212/689-1900)
Hudson Hotel (356 W 58th St, 212/554-6000)

La Quinta Manhattan Midtown (17 W 32nd St, 212/736-1600)
Larchmont (27 W 11th St, 212/989-9333)
Manhattan Broadway Hotel (273 W 38th St, 212/921-9791)
Marcel (201 E 24th St, 212/696-3800)
Milburn Hotel (242 W 76th St, 212/362-1006)
Milford Plaza (270 W 45th St, 212/869-3600)
Murray Hill Inn (143 E 30th St, 212/545-0879)
Off Soho Suites (11 Rivington St, 212/353-0860)
On the Avenue Hotel (2178 Broadway, 212/362-1100)
Park Central Hotel (870 Seventh Ave, 212/247-8000)
Portland Square Hotel (132 W 47th St, 212/382-0600)
Ramada Inn Eastside (161 Lexington Ave, 212/545-1800)
Super 8 Times Square (59 W 46th St, 212/719-2300)
The Time (224 W 49th St, 212/246-5252)
Union Square Inn (209 E 14th St, 212/614-0500)
Westside Inn (237 W 107th St, 212/866-0061)
Wolcott Hotel (4 W 31st St, 212/268-2900)

New on the Hotel Scene

All of these hotels are downtown, ensuring more reasonable pricing than the established properties uptown.

Ace Hotel (20 W 29th St, 212/679-2222): moderate; restaurant and cafe; well-accessorized; appeals to younger folks

Cooper Square (25 Cooper Square, 212/475-5700): moderate; smallish rooms; attractive furnishings

Gem Hotel Chelsea (300 W 22nd St, 212/675-1911): moderate; compact; handy location

Standard Hotel (848 Washington St, 212/645-4646): moderate; well-staffed; great views

Thompson LES (190 Allen St, 212/460-5300): moderately expensive; modernistic; outdoor swimming pool

---

Hotels Near Airports

The following are conveniently located, provide airport transportation, have restaurants, and are reasonably priced (ask for corporate rates). Some have recreational facilities, such as fitness rooms and pools.

John F. Kennedy International: **Anchor Motor Inn** (66 rooms, Bayside, Queens, 718/428-8000), **Doubletree JFK** (386 rooms, Jamaica, Queens, 718/322-2300), **Golden Gate Motor Inn** (150 rooms, Brooklyn, 718/743-4000), **Hampton Inn JFK** (216 Rooms, Jamaica, Queens, 718/322-7500), **Holiday Inn JFK** (360 rooms, Jamaica, Queens, 718/659-0200), **JFK Courtyard by Marriott** (166 rooms, Jamaica, Queens, 718/848-2121), and **Ramada Plaza Hotel-JFK** (478 rooms, Jamaica, Queens, 718/995-9000)

LaGuardia: **Best Western City View Inn** (71 rooms, Long Island City, 718/392-8400), **Clarion Hotel at LaGuardia** (170 rooms, East Elmhurst, Queens, 718/335-1200), **Comfort Inn LaGuardia** (50

rooms, Flushing, Queens, 718/939-5000), **Crowne Plaza New York-LaGuardia** (358 rooms, East Elmhurst, Queens, 718/457-6300), **LaGuardia Airport Hotel** (229 rooms, East Elmhurst, Queens, 718/426-1500), **LaGuardia Courtyard by Marriott** (288 rooms, East Elmhurst, Queens, 718/446-4800), **Marriott LaGuardia Airport** (437 rooms, East Elmhurst, Queens, 718/565-8900), **Sheraton LaGuardia East** (173 rooms, Flushing, Queens, 718/460-6666)

Newark Liberty International: **Four Points by Sheraton** (260 rooms, Elizabeth, NJ, 908/527-1600), **Hilton Newark Airport** (327 rooms, Elizabeth, NJ, 908/351-3900), **Hilton Newark Penn Station** (253 rooms, Newark, NJ, 973/622-5000), **Holiday Inn Newark** (412 rooms, Newark, NJ, 973/589-1000), **Marriott Newark Liberty Airport** (591 rooms, Newark, NJ, 973/623-0006), **Sheraton Newark Airport** (504 rooms, Newark, NJ, 973/690-5500), and **Wyndham Garden Hotel Newark** (347 rooms, Newark, NJ, 973/824-4000)

For young folks, bargain hunters, and groups, **Broadway Hotel & Hostel** (230 W 101st St, 212/865-7710, www.broadwayhotelnyc.com) is a winner. Rates start at about $38 a night for dormitory-style rooms. The location on the Upper West Side is convenient. They have 420 beds (some private rooms, which are a bit more expensive), no curfews or lockouts, 24-hour security, high-speed Wi-Fi and Internet access, elevator, and daily housekeeping service. The rooms are comfortable and have been renovated. Online rates may be lower.

New York's Recommended Well-Known Hotels

ACE HOTEL
20 W 29th St (bet Broadway and Fifth Ave)   212/679-2222
Inexpensive to moderate   www.acehotel.com

The construction dust has finally settled, and as promoted, Ace's guest rooms are unique! The lowest category is a bunk-bedded room for two. The next category is "cheap," which means queen or full beds and a garment rack in lieu of a closet. Spend a bit more, and rooms are larger with more amenities. All rooms have private bathrooms, mini-refrigerators, and mini-bars. Many rooms feature vintage furnishings, and turntables and records are in the "super deluxe" and "loft" accommodations. **Stumptown Coffee**—from my hometown of Portland, Oregon—has an outlet in the building.

AFFINIA HOTELS
Affinia Dumont, 150 E 34th St (bet Third and Lexington Ave)	
	212/481-7600
Affinia 50, 155 E 50th St (at Third Ave)	212/751-5710
Affinia Gardens, 215 E 64th St (bet Second and Third Ave)	
	212/355-1230
Affinia Manhattan, 371 Seventh Ave (at 31st St)	212/563-1800
Affinia Shelburne, 303 Lexington Ave (at 37th St)	
	212/689-5200
The Benjamin, 125 E 50th St (at Lexington Ave)	212/715-2500

Buckingham Hotel, 101 W 57th St (bet Second and Third Ave)
212/687-8000
Eastgate Tower, 222 E 39th St (bet Second and Third Ave)
212/687-8000
Surrey Hotel, 20 E 76th St (bet Madison and Fifth Ave)   212/288-3700
Moderate to moderately expensive   www.affinia.com

These all-suites hotels are among the most reasonably priced and conveniently located in New York. Each features 24-hour attendants and modern kitchens. Over 2,000 suites in all—studio, junior, and one- or two-bedroom suites—are available at attractive daily, weekly, or monthly rates. These are particularly convenient for long-term corporate visitors and traveling families who can economize by having the kids sleep on pull-out couches and by using the fully-equipped kitchens. The "Jet Set Kids" package has goodies for youngsters. Fitness centers are available at most properties. Food facilities vary. **Cafe Boulud** is located at the Surrey which is being renovated into a four-star property.

Hotels play a perpetual game of one-upmanship when it comes to providing new and better guest-pampering services. The latest is the "sleep menu," which might include blackout curtains, soothing room colors, luxe bedding, an in-room yoga sleep class, spa treatments, herbal teas or smoothies with lavender cookies, and even teddy bears. High on the "want" list of sleep amenities is a pillow library, with such possible choices as body pillows, eye pillows, or hypoallergenic and water-filled models. **The Benjamin** (125 E 50th St, 212/715-2500) goes so far as to offer a money-back sleep guarantee and a specialized concierge to help make a good rest a reality. Guests are called three days before their stay to plan room-service delivery of sleep-inducing foods like banana bread and to convey the 12 pillow options (from anti-snoring to one with an iPod port). Now all you need is a lullaby.

ALGONQUIN HOTEL
59 W 44th St (bet Fifth Ave and Ave of the Americas)
Moderately expensive   212/840-6800, 888/304-2047
www.algonquinhotel.com

The legendary Algonquin was designated a historic landmark by the city of New York in 1987. This home of the famous Round Table—where Dorothy Parker, Alexander Woollcott, Harpo Marx, Tallulah Bankhead, Robert Benchley, and other literary wits sparred and dined regularly—exudes the same charm and character as it did in the Roaring Twenties! There are 174 rooms, including 24 suites (some named after well-known personalities), and the atmosphere is intimate and friendly. The remodeled lobby is the best place in the city for people-watching, and the **Oak Room** is arguably the finest cabaret venue in New York. Added amenities include a 24-hour fitness center and complimentary Wi-Fi.

BOWERY HOTEL
335 Bowery (bet 2nd and 3rd St)   212/505-9100
Moderately expensive to very expensive   www.thebowery.com

A few years ago no one would have dreamed of spending a luxurious night in the Bowery, but now there's a posh newcomer in this neighborhood. All guest rooms are classically designed for comfort and timeless elegance with hardwood floors, large windows, upscale linens and toiletries, Turkish rugs, and marble bathrooms (some of which include tubs with a view). The one-bedroom suites open onto private terraces, as does the Lobby Bar in good weather. Room service is available 24 hours a day from **Gemma**, the adjoining restaurant. Hotel guests may make dinner reservations at this otherwise no-reservations restaurant. Every amenity one would expect at a tony uptown hostelry can now be found right here in the Bowery.

BRYANT PARK HOTEL
40 W 40th St (bet Fifth Ave and Ave of the Americas)   212/869-0100
Moderately expensive   www.bryantparkhotel.com

This contemporary hotel is situated right across the street from Bryant Park in the American Radiator Building. It is favored by hip fashion- and media-types. Some suites have terraces to enjoy a bird's-eye view of the park, while the upper-floor suites have views of both the park and the Empire State Building. The property boasts a 70-seat private room, which is often used for press conferences and screenings. There are two on-premises restaurants; **Koi**, a Japanese fusion restaurant, and the **Cellar Bar**. A 24-hour gym is available for guests. The spacious bathrooms are done in marble, have soaking tubs, and feature premium Molton Brown bath products.

CARLTON ON MADISON AVENUE
88 Madison Ave (at 29th St)   212/532-4100
Moderate to moderately expensive   www.carltonhotelny.com

Built in 1904 as the Seville Hotel, the Carlton lately underwent a $60 million facelift. Its 316 non-smoking rooms and suites—along with a dramatic three-story lobby, a lobby bar, and fine meeting facilities—blend modern comfort with historic preservation. For those doing business in the Madison Park, Gramercy Park, or Murray Hill neighborhoods, the Carlton is conveniently located. Their excellent restaurant, **Country**, is a real plus.

CASABLANCA HOTEL
147 W 43rd St (bet Broadway and Ave of the Americas)
Moderate   212/869-1212, 888/922-7225
                                          www.casablancahotel.com

Now that the Times Square area has been cleaned up, you might consider staying at Casablanca, an attractive, safe, and clean boutique hotel with a Moroccan flavor. It's small (48 rooms and suites), and family-owned. It offers complimentary amenities and comfortable rates, and the atmosphere is friendly. Special attractions: free European-style continental breakfast; passes to the New York Sports Club; free browsing on the lounge computer; bottled water, iced tea, and chocolates in the rooms; and a nightly wine and cheese reception for guests. Wi-Fi is available in all guest rooms. Best of all, you are right in the center of the action!

DREAM HOTEL
210 W 55th St (bet Broadway and Seventh Ave)   212/247-2000
Moderate   www.dreamny.com

If you're dreaming of a trendy, modern boutique hotel, then the Dream Hotel is for you. Dream offers pre-loaded iPods, luxurious sheets, bathrobes, and two restaurants (one Italian and one Mediterranean). The on-premises **Chopra Center and Spa** (1710 Broadway, 212/246-7600) is available for those needing relaxation and meditation.

FOUR SEASONS HOTEL NEW YORK
57 E 57th St (bet Madison and Park Ave)   212/758-5700
Expensive   www.fourseasons.com

In the hotel world, fewer names elicit higher praise or win more awards than Four Seasons. Upscale visitors to the Big Apple have an elegant, 52-story Four Seasons to make their home away from home. Designed by I. M. Pei and Frank Williams, the Four Seasons provides 368 oversized rooms and suites (some with terraces), and several fine eating places, including the top-notch **L'Atelier de Joël Robuchon** and a lobby lounge for light snacks and tea. There's also a fully equipped business center, with freestanding computer terminals and modem hookups, 6,000-square-foot fitness center and full-service spa, and numerous meeting rooms. The principal appeal, however, is the size of certain guest rooms, which run to 600 square feet, offer spectacular city views, and feature luxurious marble bathrooms with separate dressing areas. A classy staff makes this another award-winning Four Seasons property. The penthouse suite (4,300 square feet) goes for $35,000 a night, making it one of the most expensive hotel rooms in the world.

GRAMERCY PARK HOTEL
2 Lexington Ave (bet 21st and 22nd St)   212/920-3300
Expensive   www.gramercyparkhotel.com

A key to enter private Gramercy Park is part of the package here! Ian Schrager has created a one-of-a-kind resting place that can best be described as anti-establishment. The Bohemian look of the place and its guests combine to make a stay here more fun than restful, although Old World luxury abounds. The Gramercy Park Hotel's 187 rooms are served by a capable and willing staff. Artist-designer Julian Schnabel has provided a classy lobby, several watering holes, a spa, and a restaurant. The **Private Roof Club and Garden** is available for guest use. This place is eclectic and eccentric—quite a combination!

GREENWICH HOTEL
377 Greenwich St (at Moore St)   212/941-8900
Expensive   www.thegreenwichhotel.com

Owner Robert DeNiro should be very proud! Each of the 88 rooms at the Greenwich are individually decked out with Moroccan tiles, Tibetan rugs, reclaimed wood floors, English-leather settees, Swedish DUX beds, soaking tubs, and small libraries. A lantern-lit swimming pool is the focal point of the exclusive **Shibui Spa**. Services include massages, manicures and pedicures, and facials. If you really want to splurge, check into the two-level, two-bedroom North Moore Suite. At 2,030 square feet it is the size of a small home and features a chef's kitchen, wood-burning fireplace, Turkish steam room, and sauna.

HILTON NEW YORK
1335 Ave of the Americas (bet 53rd and 54th St)   212/586-7000
Moderate to moderately expensive www.newyorktowers.hilton.com

A popular business and convention hotel, the Hilton outfits its rooms with the most up-to-date communications equipment. Special features include an outstanding art collection, upscale executive floors with private lounge and large luxury suites, dozens of rooms equipped for the disabled, a highly-trained international staff, and an 8,000-square-foot state-of-the-art fitness club and spa. For leisure travelers interested in shopping, theater, Radio City Music Hall, and other midtown attractions, this location is highly desirable. The Hilton New York features two restaurants: **New York Marketplace**, an all-day dining facility, and **Etrusca**, an intimate Italian room featuring Tuscan foods and wines.

HOTEL GANSEVOORT
18 Ninth Ave (at 13th St)   212/206-6700
Moderately expensive   www.hotelgansevoort.com

In the heart of the Meatpacking District, which is known for its cool nightclubs, is a luxury full-service resort. Modern rooms and suites are outfitted with the latest electronics, featherbeds, patented steel Gansevoort bathroom sinks, and in-room safes that accommodate laptop computers. What's really impressive is the 45-foot heated rooftop pool with underwater music and colored lighting. The area is surrounded in glass for spectacular unrestricted views over the Hudson River. **Plunge**, the rooftop restaurant/bar, shares the same great vantage point.

If business or pleasure directs you to Times Square, the relatively new **Stay New York** (157 W 47th St, 212/768-3700, www.stayhotelny.com) is a good accommodation choice. Rooms are small but the price is right. Techies will love the latest in-room gadgets.

HOTEL ON RIVINGTON
107 Rivington St (bet Essex and Ludlow St)   212/475-2600
Moderate   www.hotelonrivington.com

There's never been a place like this on the Lower East Side! Rooms at this upscale 21-story glass tower hotel have floor-to-ceiling glass walls, which afford sweeping views of the city and the rivers. Some rooms also have balconies. Luxurious furnishings and oversized closets enhance the larger than-usual rooms. Bathrooms have steam showers, two-person Japanese soaking tubs, or showers with a skyline view. A complimentary continental breakfast is included. Try **Thor** for dinner or the trendy nightclub **105 Riv**. Designated floors accommodate guests with pets.

HOTEL WOLCOTT
4 W 31st St (bet Fifth Ave and Broadway)   212/268-2900
Inexpensive   www.wolcott.com

One of Manhattan's better hotel bargains, Hotel Wolcott offers a good location (just south of midtown), refurbished rooms with private baths, good security, direct-dial phones, TVs with in-room pay movies and videogames, Wi-Fi, iron and ironing boards, clock radios, and small fitness and business centers. No wonder students, foreign travelers, and savvy business people are regular patrons!

HUDSON HOTEL
356 W 58th St (bet Eighth and Ninth Ave)   212/554-6000
Inexpensive to moderate   www.hudsonhotel.com

Want a cool and stylish hotel? Hudson Hotel is an affordable hotel in an often unaffordable area. A lushly landscaped courtyard garden is open to the sky. You will find abundant amenities plus a reasonably priced restaurant and busy bars. There are 800 guest rooms and 13 suites with minimal decor and furniture, but given the good value you won't worry too much about that. There are some nice decorative touches, such as attractive wood paneling. The scene is the big thing here, especially the fabulous **Library Bar.**

JANE HOTEL
113 Jane St (bet West and Washington St)   212/924-6700
Very inexpensive   www.thejanenyc.com

For under $100 you can get a standard single room, inspired by a European train sleeper, in the West Village. The bathrooms are communal and coed. Air conditioning is individually controlled, but heat is not. Each room comes with an iPod-docking clock radio, free Wi-Fi, flat-screen TV with DVD player, and complimentary bottled water. Rooms are very small (50 square feet) in this 1908 building; however, there is plenty of built-in storage.

JOLLY HOTEL MADISON TOWERS
22 E 38th St (at Madison Ave)   212/802-0600
Moderate   www.jollymadison.com

Smack dab in the middle of Manhattan, this Italian-style boutique hotel has over 200 tastefully decorated rooms. The **Whaler Bar**, a breakfast room, the Madison Towers Health Spa, and a complete business center with meeting rooms are among the amenities. This is a great location, just blocks from the best shopping and attractions. Small pets, defined as up to twenty pounds, are welcome.

JUMEIRAH ESSEX HOUSE
160 Central Park S (bet Ave of the Americas and Seventh Ave)
Moderately expensive to expensive   212/247-0300
                                                 www.jumeirah.com

With a superb location right on Central Park and a gracious and welcoming staff, the Jumeirah Essex House remains one of the prize resting places in Manhattan. The tastefully decorated rooms and suites are equipped with every modern amenity. All-marble bathrooms add a classy flavor. The Lobby Lounge is a convenient place for cocktails or traditional afternoon tea. A health spa and a fully equipped club lounge with business center add to the attractions. The **South Gate** restaurant, designed by Tony Chi, serves contemporary American cuisine, overlooks Central Park, and can be entered from the hotel lobby or Central Park South. You'll love this place!

KIMBERLY HOTEL
145 E 50th St (bet Lexington and Third Ave)   212/755-0400
Moderate   www.kimberlyhotel.com

If big hotels turn you off, then the Kimberly may be just what you are looking for. This charming and hospitable boutique hotel in the center of Manhattan offers guests the kind of personal attention that is a rarity in today's commercial world. There are 192 luxury guest rooms with marble bathrooms and in-room safes, one- and two-bedroom suites are fully equipped with executive kitchenettes, and private terraces with most suites. There is eating at **Ferro's**, or enjoy the scene at **Nikki Beach Midtown**. Access to the New York Health and Racquet Club is complimentary, and room service is available. Ask about the summer Kimberly yacht excursions, which are also complimentary for hotel guests.

A former 1930s-era printing house in Hell's Kitchen is being transformed into a 222-room luxury hotel. **Vu Hotel** (653 Eleventh Ave, 212/757-0088) is slated to open in early 2010. Marvelous views of the Hudson River and Times Square await guests in this very relaxing, sophisticated property.

KITANO NEW YORK
66 Park Ave (at 38th St)   212/885-7000, 800/548-2666
Moderate   www.kitano.com

A tranquil hotel with Zen-like hospitality describes the first (and only) Japanese-owned hotel in Manhattan. Rooms are clean and uncluttered, and there are towel warmers in the spacious bathrooms. Premium television channels and American and Japanese newspapers are complimentary. Two Japanese-style restaurants are on the premises, and the **Bar Lounge** features live jazz. Many rooms offer views of Grand Central Terminal, the Empire State Building, or Murray Hill.

LE PARKER MERIDIEN HOTEL
119 W 56th St (bet Ave of the Americas and Seventh Ave)
Moderate to moderately expensive   212/245-5000
                                        www.parkermeridien.com

This large midtown hotel has a lot going for it: great location, ergonomically designed rooms, good eateries, excellent health club, penthouse pool, high-speed Internet access, CD and DVD players, junior suites with separate sitting areas, and baths and showers big enough for two. **Norma's** is one of New York's top breakfast rooms. You'll find one of the best burgers in town at Le Parker's well-hidden, street-level **burger joint**, or if you prefer French, try the classic bistro **Seppi's**. There is also **Knave**, an elegant espresso bar by day and alcohol bar at night. This hotel will help plan your visit through their online "New York Smart Aleck" program. (Note: If you're driving, the entrance to Le Parker Meridien is on 56th Street.)

LIBRARY HOTEL

299 Madison Ave (at 41st St)   212/983-4500
Moderate   www.libraryhotel.com

Avid readers should check out the Library, with 60 rooms individually appointed with artwork and books relating to a specific theme. Guests can also enjoy the 14th-floor Poetry Terrace, which houses volumes of verse by assorted authors. Breakfast and an afternoon wine-and-cheese reception are included in the rate. There is complimentary Wi-Fi, a business center, and 24-hour concierge service. Room numbers are uniquely based on the Dewey decimal book classification system, and floors are organized by its ten major categories.

Looking for a room with a view of the Macy's Thanksgiving Day Parade? This historic parade is re-routed beginning in 2009 and will travel down Seventh Avenue through Times Square to 42nd Street. Some hotels offer parade packages and specials as they are along the route. Make your reservations well in advance! Before plunking down a deposit, check on cancellation policies and occupancy limits, and make sure your room is positioned to see this great holiday tradition.

Michelangelo Hotel (152 W 51st St, 212/765-1900)
Renaissance New York Times Square (714 Seventh Ave, 212/765-7676)
Residence Inn New York (1033 Ave of the Americas, 212/768-0007): event spaces, too
Sheraton Manhattan (790 Seventh Ave, 212/581-3300)

LOEWS REGENCY HOTEL

540 Park Ave (at 61st St)   212/759-4100
Moderately expensive to expensive   www.loewshotels.com

With an outstanding location on Park Avenue, this contemporary and relaxed Loews hotel offers 353 spacious rooms and 84 outstanding suites. These include 10 grand suites that have housed many of the entertainment world's greats. The one-bedroom suites feature two bathrooms. Use of the fitness center and overnight shoeshine service are complimentary. Two excellent restaurants—the upscale **540 Park** and **The Library**, an intimate, residential-style lounge—offer daily meal service. **Feinstein's at Loews Regency** is a classy nightclub. Power breakfasts at the Regency are legendary. A dog-walking service is available to guests with pets.

LONDON NYC

151 W 54th St (bet Ave of the Americas and Seventh Ave)
Expensive   212/307-5000
     www.thelondonnyc.com

This midtown all-suites hotel boasts of being the tallest place to stay in Manhattan, with 54 floors. The 566 rooms and furnishings are first-class, and the service is very personal. The hotel offers a 24-hour business center, fitness facility, and complimentary newspapers. The **London Bar** and **Gordon Ramsay at the London NYC** provide excellent eating facilities and room service. **Maze** offers casual dining as well.

LOWELL HOTEL
28 E 63rd St (bet Park and Madison Ave)   212/838-1400
Moderately expensive   www.lowellhotel.com

Like an attractive English townhouse, this classy, well-located hotel features 72 suites and 21 deluxe rooms. Amenities include a 24-hour multilingual concierge service, at least two phones per room, complimentary Wi-Fi, DVRs, outlets for personal computers, marble bathrooms, complimentary shoeshines, and a fitness center. Most suites have wood-burning fireplaces, and 14 of them have private terraces. The "Hollywood Suite" has the latest entertainment gadgets and a full kitchen. Try the **Pembroke Room** for breakfast, brunch, tea, and cocktails, or go next door to the **Post House** for lunch (weekdays) and dinner (daily).

For discounted hotel rooms, try a consolidator like **Quikbook** (800/789-9887, www.quikbook.com), **Hotels.com** (800/964-6835, www.hotels.com), or **Priceline** (www.priceline.com). There are a multitude of these online businesses that buy excess rooms and pass on the savings. The best rates for Manhattan hotel rooms can generally be found at www.nycgo.com (click on "Hotels"). Bear in mind that prices can change quickly.

MANDARIN ORIENTAL NEW YORK
80 Columbus Circle (at 60th St)   212/805-8800
Expensive to very expensive   www.mandarinoriental.com

Boasting a superior location at the Time Warner Center, the Mandarin Oriental offers great views of Central Park from the 38th floor up. In its usual classy (and pricey) style, the Mandarin Oriental offers New York visitors 202 deluxe rooms (not large for the price) and 46 suites, all beautifully furnished and equipped with state-of-the-art technology. Magnificent art pieces dot the public spaces. **Asiate** (see restaurant reviews) features French-Japanese fare and room service. The 35th-floor **Mobar** is a popular spot for drinks. A beautiful ballroom is available, and a two-story spa features "holistic rejuvenation." The 75-foot lap pool has a spectacular setting.

MARITIME HOTEL
363 W 16th St (at Ninth Ave)   212/242-4300
Moderate   www.themaritimehotel.com

The Maritime is located in an area with few modern hotels, making it convenient for those doing business in Chelsea. Amenities include Italian and Japanese restaurants (**La Bottega** and **Matsuri**), a limited fitness center, flat-screen TVs, and free Wi-Fi. In good weather, you can dine and drink alfresco. The 121 rooms and bathrooms are small, but all rooms face the Hudson River and feature five-foot porthole-style windows to enjoy the view.

MORGANS HOTEL
237 Madison Ave (bet 37th and 38th St)   212/686-0300
Moderate   www.morganshotel.com

This property introduced the "boutique hotel" concept. Offering exceptional services, it is a 114-room classic beauty done-up in black, white, and gray. Guests will enjoy curling up on the sofa in the window alcove—a totally restful ambience. Rooms are equipped with desks, flat-screen televisions, and high-speed Internet connections. Bathrooms continue the monochromatic color scheme and are enlivened with Korres toiletries and gleaming modern fixtures. The on-site restaurant, **Asia de Cuba**, blends Asian and Cuban cuisines. Breakfast, lunch, and dinner are served daily.

NEW YORK MARRIOTT DOWNTOWN
85 West St (at Battery Park)   212/385-4900
Moderate   www.nymarriottdowntown.com

For those doing business in the Wall Street area, this 497-room hotel (formerly known as New York Marriott Financial Center) is ideal. It has a popular lobby lounge for lunch and dinner (**85 West**), restful Revive beds with down comforters, marble bathrooms, Internet access, and a great fitness center.

If you don't mind cozy spaces, then this hotel is for you! **The Pod Hotel** (230 E 51st St, 212/355-0300, www.podhotel.com) has 347 guest rooms, averaging about 100 square feet each. (By contrast, the average hotel room size is 325 sq. ft.) The big attraction is the price, with rates that hover around the low three figures. And you get iPod docking stations and LCD television. You *won't* find an on-site restaurant, fancy lobby, extravagant furnishings, private baths (at least in the bunk rooms), or thick walls.

NEW YORK MARRIOTT MARQUIS
1535 Broadway (bet 45th and 46th St)   212/398-1900
Moderate to moderately expensive   www.nymarriottmarquis.com

The New York Marriott Marquis has nearly 2,000 guest rooms and suites, sizable meeting and convention facilities, and one of the largest hotel atriums in the world. Times Square is just outside, putting guests in the midst of the hustle and bustle. Visitors can enjoy the two-story revolving rooftop restaurant and lounge. In addition, a legitimate Broadway theater, a fully equipped health club, six restaurants and lounges, and a special concierge level are on the property. High-speed elevators whisk guests between the 49 floors.

NEW YORK PALACE HOTEL
455 Madison Ave (bet 50th and 51st St)   212/888-7000
Expensive   www.newyorkpalace.com

Located close to Saks Fifth Avenue, the 896-room New York Palace offers commanding views of the city skyline, which are particularly enchanting in the evening. The public rooms encompass the 1882 Villard Mansion, a legendary New York landmark. Amenities include an expansive fitness center, an executive lounge, and the two-floor Villard Center (with meeting and function rooms). A multilingual concierge staff is ready to serve you, and a full-service business center is available. The casually elegant restaurant **Istana** offers New American cuisine, **Gilt** serves modern American fare, and room service is available 24 hours a day. A complimentary shuttle goes to Wall Street and the Theater District.

ON THE AVENUE HOTEL
2178 Broadway (at 77th St)   212/362-1100
Moderate to moderately expensive   www.ontheave-nyc.com

There are not many new or even particularly comfortable places to stay on the Upper West Side, making this is a great place for those who want to visit the legendary Zabar's, the American Museum of Natural History, Columbus Circle, and other attractions in the area. Among the many amenities: beautiful bed linens and towels, Italian black-marble bathrooms, suites with private balconies, room service, concierge, business center, plasma TV, and Internet connections. Open balconies on the 14th and 16th floors offer super views and comfortable chairs.

PENINSULA NEW YORK HOTEL
700 Fifth Ave (at 55th St)   212/956-2888
Expensive   www.newyork.peninsula.com

When the name "Peninsula" is mentioned, the words *quality* and *class* immediately come to mind. This is especially true of the Manhattan property, where recent renovations have freshened up the already luxurious rooms. The building is a 1905 landmark with 239 rooms, including the palatial Peninsula Suite (more than 3,000 square feet at $16,000 per night!). Room features include oversize marble bathrooms, printers, copiers, large work desks, audiovisual systems with cable, and numerous bathroom amenities. Features of the 21st-floor Peninsula Spa by Espa include an indoor pool, sun decks, modern fitness equipment, and spa services. The rooftop hot spot **Salon de Ning** offers dramatic views from its east and west terraces, and two other dining venues also call the Peninsula home.

PIERRE HOTEL
2 E 61st St (at Fifth Ave)   212/838-8000
Very expensive   www.tajhotels.com

A recent $100 million renovation has made the Pierre the flagship property for Taj Hotels in North America. Overlooking Central Park, the 189 elegant guest rooms received total makeovers. The bathrooms were enlarged to incorporate glass-walled showers and soaking tubs. The in-room entertainment and electronics are first-class. The function rooms remain a coveted venue for Manhattan's glitziest events. The distinguished London-based restaurant **Le Caprice** now has its first North American outpost in the Pierre. The new lobby lounge **2 East** is a grand watering hole and an option for light meals and afternoon tea. A fitness center and two beauty salons are on site. With a ratio of three staff members per guest, impeccable and attentive service is assured.

THE PLAZA
59th St at Fifth Ave   212/759-3000
Expensive to very expensive   www.theplaza.com

What was once the Grand Dame of New York and the city's premier uptown location, the Plaza has suffered a series of humiliations from a variety of owners, but none worse than at present. The management structure has become impossibly complex. One outfit manages the grossly overpriced and troubled residential units on Fifth Avenue and Central Park South, while Fairmont runs the several hundred hotel units in the back and another operation handles the restaurants. On that score, the **Oak Room and Bar** is striving to bring back some of the Plaza's former glory. At this writing the legendary Palm Court remains closed, after a series of unbelievable moves, like putting in chairs with backs so high that no one could see what was going on in that once glorious space. Expensive shops downstairs are mostly devoid of customers. Vienna's famous Demel's sweet shop is the exception. Room rates have plummeted from a start of $1,000. It is truly a sad situation for many of us who regarded the Plaza as home for decades. Even the staff are demoralized.

RITZ-CARLTON NEW YORK, BATTERY PARK
2 West St (at Battery Park)   212/344-0800
Expensive

RITZ-CARLTON NEW YORK, CENTRAL PARK
50 Central Park S (at Ave of the Americas)   212/308-9100
Expensive   www.ritzcarlton.com

These two properties have added luster to the Manhattan hotel scene, providing the outstanding service and amenities identified with the Ritz-Carlton name. You'll find great views, top-grade lobby-level restaurants, gym and spa services, luxurious rooms and bathrooms, and business centers. Club Level guests get special treatment, which may include unpacking and packing services, Wi-Fi, a library of children's books, and an assortment of snacks. The Battery Park location offers a romantic 14th-floor bar.

ROYALTON HOTEL
44 W 44th St (bet Fifth Ave and Ave of the Americas)   212/869-4400
Expensive   www.royaltonhotel.com

Upon stepping into the lobby of the Royalton, you know that you're in for a treat. Glass, brass, steel, wood, and even fur are combined to create a warm, sophisticated environment. The hotel features 168 rooms, banquette seating, work areas, and slate and glass showers. Some rooms have fireplaces and soaking tubs, and in-room spa services are just a phone call away. Three luxurious penthouses with private terraces have views. **Brasserie 44** serves breakfast, lunch, and dinner (plus a separate room service menu). **Bar 44** is an intimate place to meet for drinks. A fitness center and valet parking are also available.

ST. REGIS NEW YORK
2 E 55th St (at Fifth Ave)   212/753-4500
Expensive   www.starwoodhotels.com

The St. Regis, a historic landmark in the heart of Manhattan, is rightfully one of the crown jewels of the Starwood Hotels group. The hotel provides luxurious accommodations. Some rooms have been converted to condominiums. Each room has marble baths, in-room refrigerators, Pratesi linens, and round-the-clock butler service (including free pressing of two garments upon arrival) and 24/7 room service is available. Outstanding on-site restaurants include **Astor Court** (breakfast, lunch, afternoon tea, dinner, and Sunday brunch) and the **King Cole Bar** (great Bloody Marys). A recent addition to the dining scene is the **Adour Alain Ducasse**. **St. Regis' Roof** is available for private functions.

Need a short-term rental? Try **Affordable New York City** (21 E 10th St, 212/533-4001, www.affordablenewyorkcity.com). Ask for Susan Freschel.

SALISBURY HOTEL
123 W 57th St (bet Ave of the Americas and Seventh Ave)
Moderate   212/246-1300
                                                            www.nycsalisbury.com

This is one great deal! I highly recommend the Salisbury to price-savvy travelers. Capably run by Edward Oliva, it has nearly 200 rooms and suites, most of which have been redecorated. Many are outfitted with butler's pantries and refrigerators. Suites are large, comfortable, and reasonably priced. The thick walls really are soundproof! If you've waited until the last minute for reservations, the Salisbury is less well-known among out-of-towners, and therefore rooms are usually available. You'll be near Carnegie Hall and other midtown attractions. Folks here are exceedingly friendly. A continental breakfast and Wi-Fi are available for a nominal charge. Nearby parking is discounted for hotel guests with cars.

SHERATON NEW YORK HOTEL AND TOWERS
811 Seventh Ave (at 53rd St)   212/581-1000, 800/325-3535
Moderate to moderately expensive   www.starwood.com

With an outstanding location in central Manhattan and several in-house eating options (**Hudson Market** and **The Link**), the Sheraton New York is an excellent choice for tourists and business travelers. Sheraton Towers—the more luxurious upper floors—offers exclusive digs, including butler service. The exclusive **Club Lounge** on the 44th floor provides continental breakfast, Wi-Fi, and other privileges. Atlantis Fitness Center has a large selection of equipment, classes, trainers, saunas, and steam rooms. Frequent guests will appreciate Sheraton's "Travelite" program. A wide selection of package deals and seasonal specials are available.

SIX COLUMBUS
6 Columbus Cir (58th St bet Eighth and Ninth Ave)   212/204-3000
Moderately expensive   www.sixcolumbus.com

It may look like you've arrived in the 1960s with the mod-inspired furnishings, but technology like flat-screen TVs and iPod docking stations is utterly up-to-date. This 1903 building was extensively renovated, custom linens and furnishings were created, and minibars featuring Dean and DeLuca gourmet treats were added. Guests have access to the nearby Equinox gym. The in-hotel restaurant, **Blue Ribbon Sushi Bar and Grill**, will provide room service

STANDARD HOTEL

848 Washington St (at 13th St)   212/645-4646
Moderately expensive   www.standardhotel.com

This hotel was still under construction as we went to press, and it looks to be anything but standard. It will have ultramodern wall-to-wall and floor-to-ceiling windows (which actually open), providing magnificent views of the dominating skyline or the Hudson River. Continuing with the open feel, some rooms have peek-a-boo windows between the jumbo tub or shower and the rest of the room. Furnishings are sleek and décor is neutral. It's built over a defunct freight railway, the High Line, which is open as a linear park.

How to get better hotel rates

- What is a high-demand night at one hotel may be a low-demand night at another. Depending on the timing, you may be able to stay in a more luxurious hotel.

- Generally rates are cheapest on Sunday, while the most expensive nights are Wednesday and Thursday. Rates are typically lowest in January, February, late April, and May.

- Rates may go down closer to your stay. Call before your cancellation deadline to see if that is the case, and then book again at the lower rate. Rather than have a glut of empty rooms, many hotels will drastically lower rates. Bargain with the hotel's desk clerk, not with whoever answers the hotel's 800 number.

- Try the large chains' more budget-friendly brands, such as Hampton Inn (owned by Hilton), Fairfield Inn by Marriott, and Four Points by Sheraton. These outfits are typically cheaper than the big guys.

- Stay in less expensive neighborhoods. The subway is likely just a few minutes away. Often the money saved by staying in an area like Chelsea is well worth the short trip—and you are in a great shopping, dining, and walking location.

TRUMP INTERNATIONAL HOTEL AND TOWER

1 Central Park W (at 60th St)   212/299-1000
Expensive   www.trumpintl.com

Trump International is everything you'd expect from a place with The Donald's name attached. There are special amenities (fresh flowers, umbrellas, and garment bags), 24-hour room service, complete office facilities, entertainment centers in every room, a state-of-the-art fitness center, swimming pool, and marble bathrooms. They have a great program for kids: meals and drinks, robes and slippers, bath amenities—even business cards! One of Manhattan's best (and more expensive) restaurants, **Jean Georges**, will pamper your taste buds. Many rooms have wonderful views of Central Park.

W NEW YORK

541 Lexington Ave (bet 49th and 50th St)   212/755-1200
Moderately expensive   www.whotels.com

Located in midtown, this Starwood property has 688 rooms (including 10 spacious suites), a large ballroom, Bliss49 Spa, Sweat Fitness Center, and 24-hour room service. The look is strictly modern. Health-food addicts love **Heartbeat**, while trendies flock to the hip **Oasis Bar** (just off the lobby) and the **Whiskey Blue Bar**. Pets (dogs and cats) are pampered with the P.A.W. program.

Hotel bars

New York views are not necessarily only of the spectacular skyline. These hotel bars offer varying vistas:

Lobby Lounge, Mandarin Oriental (80 Columbus Circle, 212/805-8876): lobby (on the 35th floor)

mad46, Roosevelt Hotel (45 E 45th St, 212/661-9600): rooftop bar with a terrace on three sides of the building

Salon de Ning, Peninsula Hotel (700 Fifth Ave, 212/956-2888): rooftop bar offering views of the MoMA sculpture garden

Thom Bar, 60 Thompson (60 Thompson St, 212/219-3200): lobby bar packed with beautiful people

Thor, Hotel on Rivington (107 Rivington St, 212/796-8040): Check out the street action from the window seats of this ground-floor bar.

W NEW YORK—TIMES SQUARE

1567 Broadway (at 47th St)   212/930-7400
Moderately expensive   www.whotels.com

Featuring 507 recently renovated guest rooms and 43 suites in the heart of Times Square, this 57-story W flagship offers the **Blue Fin** restaurant (seafood), a classy retail store, a fitness room, 24-hour room service, and other quality amenities. Ask to stay on the highest floor possible, as the views of Times Square and the Hudson River are dramatic. **The Living Room Bar** is open until the wee hours, and **The Whiskey** is an underground watering hole and screening room with a coed bathroom!

WALDORF-ASTORIA

301 Park Ave (at 50th St)   212/355-3000
Moderately expensive   www.waldorfastoria.com

Hilton invested more than $200 million restoring their flagship property. The Royal Suite alone—used by the late Duke and Duchess of Windsor —was restored at a cost of $10 million! Renovations are ongoing and the craftsmanship is apparent. The rich, impressive lobby is bedecked with magnificent mahogany wall panels, hand-woven carpets, and a 148,000-tile mosaic floor. Management created larger spaces by reducing the number of units. Oversize executive business rooms are available. All-marble bathrooms have been installed in some suites. There is the Guerlain Spa (the city's best), a fitness center, several restaurants, and deluxe rooms and suites in the Waldorf

Towers/A Conrad Hotel. An event at the Waldorf is sure to be something special. This is a classy establishment, and appropriate attire is suggested.

WASHINGTON SQUARE HOTEL
103 Waverly Place (at MacDougal St)   212/777-9515
Inexpensive to moderate   www.washingtonsquarehotel.com

Here's a find! This hotel offers good value in rooms, a capable staff, and a nice restaurant. The location is handy for those with business at New York University or visitors who want to explore the Village. The 150 guest rooms are done in art-deco style and comfortably equipped with good bedding and complimentary high-speed Internet connections. The fitness room is convenient, and the **North Square Restaurant and Lounge** is a classy venue for cocktails or dining.

This isn't your typical inn. Each room at the **Chelsea Pines Inn** (317 W 14th St, 212/929-1023, 888/546-2700, www.chelseapinesinn. com) has a movie theme depicting a 1950s film star. All rooms in this 19th-century rowhouse have private bathrooms, flat-panel TVs, and iPod docks. (Alas, there's no elevator.) Local calls, Wi-Fi, and continental breakfast are free. As befits the eclectic Chelsea locale, the inn is gay-and lesbian-friendly.

Housing Alternatives

Many travelers and families visiting New York City prefer to stay someplace other than a hotel. The following Alternative Housing section presents options such as apartments, bed and breakfasts, townhouses, and dormitory housing.

ABINGDON GUEST HOUSE
21 Eighth Ave (bet 12th and Jane St)   212/243-5384
Moderate   www.abingdonguesthouse.com

A charming guest house located in Greenwich Village, Abingdon Guest House consists of two landmark 1850s Federal-style townhouses with fine examples of period architecture. All nine rooms are smoke-free, and some have a private bath. Abingdon offers amenities that include daily maid service, but no food is available.

ABODE
P.O. Box 20022
New York, NY 10021   212/472-2000
Mon-Fri: 9-5   800/835-8880 (outside tri-state area)
Moderate to moderately expensive   www.abodenyc.com

Would you like to stay in a delightful old brownstone? How about a contemporary luxury apartment in the heart of Manhattan? Abode selects apartments with great care, personally inspecting them to ensure the highest standards of cleanliness, attractiveness, and hospitality. All are nicely furnished. Nightly rates begin at $200 for a studio and rise to $550 for a three-bedroom apartment. Extended stays of a month or longer receive discount rates. There is a minimum stay of five nights.

AKA CENTRAL PARK
42 W 58th St (bet Fifth Ave and Ave of the Americas)   212/753-3500

AKA SUTTON PLACE
330 E 56th St (bet First and Second Ave)   212/752-8888

AKA TIMES SQUARE
123 W 44th St (bet Ave of the Americas and Broadway)   212/764-5700

AKA UNITED NATIONS
234 E 46th St (bet Second and Third Ave)   646/291-4200
www.hotelaka.com

With superb locations and gracious staffs, these facilities offer a residential respite for business and leisure travelers booking stays of a week or more. Apartments are furnished with artful designs and offer luxury hotel amenities, including concierge services and business, spa, and fitness centers.

AT HOME IN NEW YORK   212/956-3125 or 800/692-4262
www.athomeny.com

For most people, the words "bed and breakfast" connote quaint country inns, but B&Bs can also be found in Manhattan. Nightly, weekly, or long-term accommodations are available in various settings—apartments, co-ops, and condos—and rates are a fraction of those at higher-priced hotels. At Home in New York carefully screens hosted and unhosted properties. In addition to breakfasts, hosts often dish out favorite tips for a true local experience.

> Roommates can bring down the cost of housing in Manhattan. Try **Rainbow Roommates** (212/982-6265, www.rainbowroommates. com) for gay and lesbian roommate services.

BED AND BREAKFAST NETWORK OF N.Y.
130 Barrow St (bet Washington and West St), Room 508
Mon-Fri: 8-6   212/645-8134
Moderate   800/900-8134
www.bedandbreakfastnetny.com

Bed and Breakfast Network of N.Y. offers a choice of over 200 hosted and unhosted accommodations in Manhattan. The hosted rate runs from $90 to $225 a night for single or double occupancy. The weekly rate varies from $600 to $1,500. Unhosted apartments with up to four bedrooms range from $180 to $525 a night and from $1,200 to $3,500 a week. Monthly rates are also available.

HOSTELLING INTERNATIONAL–NEW YORK
891 Amsterdam Ave (at 103rd St)   212/932-2300
Inexpensive   www.hinewyork.org

Visitors over 21 are welcome here, with membership. The hostel provides over 620 beds in this renovated century-old landmark. They offer meeting spaces, Internet access, cafeteria, coffee bar, airport shuttle, catering, tours, self-service kitchens, and laundry facilities to individuals and groups. Best of all, the price is right!

INN NEW YORK CITY
266 W 71st St (bet West End Ave and Broadway)   212/580-1900
Moderate   www.innnewyorkcity.com

Situated in a restored, 19th-century townhouse, Inn New York City offers four suites behind a discreet exterior. Depending on which suite chosen, you may find a double Jacuzzi, extensive library, leaded glass skylights, fireplaces, baby grand piano, private terrace, or a fully-equipped kitchen stocked with hearty delights. Additional services include high-speed Internet, cable TV, daily newspapers, maid service, and a 24-hour concierge. Personal laundry is done on request at no additonal charge, a real plus.

Short-Term Apartment Rentals

Many travelers and families find that staying in an apartment while visiting New York City can save money, since more guests can be accommodated and meals can be prepared there. These agencies and websites are helpful in finding short-term rentals:

Affordable New York City (212/533-4001, www.affordable-newyorkcity.com): B&Bs or apartments; four-night minimum stay for B&Bs; five nights for apartments

City Sonnet (212/614-3034, www.citysonnet.com): hosted accommodations, minimum three-night stay

Radio City Apartments (877/921-9321, www.radiocityapartments.com): no minimum stay

---

INTERNATIONAL HOUSE
500 Riverside Dr (at 122nd St)   212/316-8436 (admissions)
Moderate   212/316-8473 (guest rooms and suites)
                                                www.ihouse-nyc.org

International House is a community of over 700 graduate students, interns, trainees, and visiting scholars from nearly 100 countries. Occupants spend anywhere from a day to a few years in New York City. It is located on the Upper West Side, near Columbia University and the Manhattan School of Music. Special features include a budget-friendly dining room with an international menu, 24-hour security, pub, gymnasium, and self-service laundry. Free programs for residents include ballroom dancing, lectures, a practice room for musicians, computer lab, films, recitals, and organized sports. Rates are determined by length of stay, season, and shared or private bath. Some scholarships and fellowships are available. Though catering to students and professors, International House is open to the public, depending on availability. Reasonably priced guest rooms and suites with private bath, air conditioning, daily maid service, and cable television are also available.

IVY TERRACE B&B
230 E 58th St (bet Second and Third Ave)   516/662-6862
Moderate   www.ivyterrace.com

There are six guest apartments in this century-old townhouse, two with outdoor terraces. Kitchens are stocked with breakfast goodies. Owner Vinessa (a professional actress) and innkeeper Jeff promise special care, including the possibility of tickets to TV-show tapings. The Ivy Terrace is gay-friendly. There is a three-night minimum and weekly rates are available. Local calls and Wi-Fi are free.

92ND STREET Y (DE HIRSCH RESIDENCE)

1395 Lexington Ave (at 92nd St)	212/415-5650
Mon-Thurs: 9-7; Fri: 9-5; Sun: 10-5	800-858-4692
Moderate	www.dehirsch.com

The De Hirsch Residence offers convenient, inexpensive, and secure dormitory housing for students, interns, and working men and women between the ages of 18 and 28. There are shared bathroom and kitchen facilities. Special discounts for Y health club memberships and single and double rooms are available. Lengths of stay can range from 30 days to one year. Admission is by application.

If your residential or commercial space needs a good *trompe l'oeil* (mural), call Agnes Liptak at **Fresco Decorative Painting** (324 Lafayette St, 5th floor, 212/966-0676). Decorative stucco, faux finishing, and leafing applications ($8 to $50 per square foot) are also available.

PHILLIPS CLUB

Lincoln Square	
155 W 66th St (at Broadway)	212/835-8800
Moderate to moderately expensive	www.phillipsclub.com

This 162-unit residential hotel near Lincoln Center is designed for long-term visitors but will also take nightly customers. Suites come with fully-equipped kitchens, flat-screen HDTVs, direct-dial phones, and Bose sound systems. Other impressive features include concierge, laundry and valet service, in-room safes, a handy conference room, and preferential membership at the nearby Reebok Sports Club NY.

SOLDIERS', SAILORS', MARINES', AND AIRMEN'S CLUB

283 Lexington Ave (at 37th St)	212/683-4353
Inexpensive	www.ssmaclub.org

Here is a great find in the Murray Hill area of Manhattan for American and allied servicemen and women—active, retired, veterans, reservists, military cadets, NYFD, NYPD, EMS, and Coast Guard personnel. Proof of eligibility must be shown. Rates are extremely low (with no tax) since the club rents beds rather than rooms. If you're traveling solo, you may be assigned a roommate. Rooms have two, three, four, and six beds. Communal bathroom facilities are on each floor. There are several lounges, TVs with DVD players, and a lobby canteen with refrigerator, microwave, and coffee. A complimentary continental breakfast is provided each morning.

WEBSTER APARTMENTS

419 W 34th St (at Ninth Ave)	212/967-9000
Inexpensive	www.websterapartments.org

This is one of the best deals in the city for working women with moderate incomes. It is not a transient hotel but operates on a policy developed by Charles B. Webster, a first cousin of Rowland Macy (of the department store family). Webster left the bulk of his estate to found these apartments, which opened in 1923. Residents include college students, designers, actresses, secretaries, and other business and professional women. Facilities include dining rooms, recreation areas, a library, and lounges. The Webster also has private gardens for guests, and meals can be taken outdoors. Rates are $184 to $268 per week, which includes two meals a day and maid service. The Webster is a secret find known mainly to its residents and readers of this book!

> Yes, there is a reliable pawnshop in Manhattan: **New York Pawnbrokers** (177 Rivington St, 212/228-7177).

Interior Designers

AERO STUDIOS
419 Broome St (bet Lafayette and Crosby St)   212/966-4700
Mon-Sat: 11-6   www.aerostudios.com

Thomas O'Brien's staff is well equipped to handle everything from a major commercial design project to a minor residential one. Be sure to visit his Aero, Ltd. store for home furnishings, decor, and lighting.

ALEX CHANNING
250 W 19th St (bet Seventh and Eighth Ave), Suite 11C
By appointment   212/366-4800
                                                  www.alexchanning.com

Licensed interior designer Alex Channing focuses on design and redevelopment of both residential and corporate projects. He does furniture design and custom-made furnishings, and he'll help with site selection, move-ins, and installations.

BERCELI KITCHEN & HOME DESIGN
1402 Lexington Ave (bet 92nd and 93rd St)   212/722-8811
Hours: Mon-Fri: 9-6; Sat: 10-6; Sun: 11-5   www.berceli.com

If you're ready to redo your kitchen or bathroom, give Berceli a call. For two decades they have worked with homeowners to bring function and beauty to home interiors. Whether the style is contemporary or traditional, they use the finest American and European products and appliances. They'll do the whole job, or you can choose to do portions of the work in order to save costs. Berceli has earned high marks from co-ops and condominium boards, and they are committed to customer satisfaction.

DESIGNER PREVIEWS
36 Gramercy Park E (bet 20th and 21st St)   212/777-2966
By appointment   www.designerpreviews.com

Having a problem finding the right decorator? Designer Previews keeps tabs on over 300 of the most trustworthy and talented designers, architects, and landscaping experts in Manhattan and elsewhere. They will help you select the best, based on your style and personal requirements, through office consultation or online presentation. Karen Fisher, the genius behind this handy service, is a former design editor for *Women's Wear Daily* and *Esquire* and a member of the Interior Design Hall of Fame.

Looking for an architect or decorator? Here are some of the very best:

Ashley Whittaker Design (191 E 76th St, 212/650-0024): neo-traditionalist

Bilhuber (330 E 59th St, 6th floor, 212/308-4888): Jeffrey Bilhuber has contemporary ideas.

David Anthony Harris Interiors (524 Broadway, Suite 206, 212/219-5660): an eye for detail

David Bergman Architect (241 Eldridge St, Suite 3R, 212/475-3106): eco-conscious designer

Glenn Gissler Design (155 W 19th St, 5th floor, 212/228-9880): Glenn Gissler works well with art.

Miles Redd (77 Bleecker St, Suite C111, 212/674-0902): color expert

MR Architecture & Decor (245 W 29th St, 10th floor, 212/989-9300): David Mann is very practical.

Nina Seirafi (330 E 75th St, 646/382-7547): residential and commercial interiors

Ruby (41 Union Square W, Studio 705, 212/741-3380): Bella Zakarian Mancini is mindful of budgets.

S.R. Gambrel (55 Grove St, 212/925-3380): You can't beat Steven Gambrel for detailing.

Sara Story Design (1 Gramercy Park, 212/228-6007): contemporary, eclectic

Shamir Shah Design (10 Greene St, 212/274-7476): Shamir Shah's designs are modern and clean.

Specht Harpman (338 W 39th St, 10th floor, 212/239-1150): Scott Specht and Louise Harpman are pocketbook-conscious.

Steven Holl Architects (450 W 31st St, 11th floor, 212/629-7262): residential and commercial, worldwide

---

LORE DECORATORS
2201 Third Ave (at 120th St)   212/534-2170
Mon-Fri: 9-6; Sat: 9-3   www.loredecorators.com

Owner Frank Cangelosi, Sr. is a very friendly guy who runs a reasonably priced upholstery service. Trust your heirloom furniture, thrift-shop finds, or damaged pieces to Frank and his family for an inexpensive new look. They also make drapes and slipcovers. Pick up and delivery of small and large pieces is free, which is generally unheard of in this business. All work is done on-premises.

MARTIN ALBERT INTERIORS
9 E 19th St (bet Broadway and Fifth Ave)
Mon-Thurs: 9-5:30; Fri: 9-5   212/673-8000, 800/525-4637
                                          www.martinalbert.com

Martin Albert specializes in window treatments. They measure and install their product line at considerably lower prices than most decorators. You can choose from 250,000 fabric samples, starting at $10 a yard. Custom upholstery and slipcovers, a furniture shop (bring a photo and they will re-create the piece), and a large selection of drapery hardware are also available. They'll deliver to all 50 states, too!

PARSONS, THE NEW SCHOOL FOR DESIGN
25 E 13th St (at Fifth Ave), 2nd floor   212/229-5424
Mon-Fri: 9-6   www.newschool.edu/parsons

Parsons, a division of the New School University, is one of the top schools in the city for interior design. Call for design assistance and your request will be posted on the school's career services board. Every effort is made to match clients with student decorators. Individual negotiations determine the price and length of a job, but it will be considerably less than what a practicing professional charges. Most of these students don't yet have a decorator's card, but this is a good place if you just want a consultation.

RICHARD'S INTERIOR DESIGN
1390 Lexington Ave (bet 91st and 92nd St)   212/831-9000
Mon-Fri: 10-6:30; Sat: 11-2   www.richardsinteriordesign.net

At Richard's you'll find over 10,000 imported decorator fabrics, including tapestries, damasks, stripes, plaids, silks, velvets, and floral chintzes. These are all first-quality goods at competitive prices. Richard's does upholstery, slip-covers, draperies, top treatments, shades, bedroom ensembles, custom cabinetry, custom furniture from North Carolina, and wall coverings. Interior design services, in-home consultation, and installation are available.

If you have a piece of jewelry that needs a repair, Christina at **Walter's Jewelry** (4 W 47th St, Booth 105-106, 212/840-6943) is an exceptionally helpful lady. They also sell gold, charms, colored stones, and diamonds.

Jewelry Services

GEM APPRAISERS & CONSULTANTS
608 Fifth Ave (at 49th St), Suite 602   212/333-3122
Mon-Fri: 9-5 (by appointment)   www.robaretz.com

Robert C. Aretz, who owns Gem Appraisers & Consultants, is a graduate gemologist and a certified member of the Appraisers Association of America. He is entrusted with appraisals for major insurance companies, banks, and retail jewelry stores. His specialty is antique jewelry, precious colored stones, diamonds, and natural pearls. Aretz will do appraisals and/or consultations for estate, insurance, tax, equitable distribution, and other purposes.

L AND M WATCH REPAIRS
25 W 47th St, 2nd floor (bet Fifth Ave and Ave of the Americas)
Mon-Fri: 9:30-5:30   212/221-9626
                                                   www.landmwatch.com

Is your watch losing time? Is an antique pocket watch no longer working? Check out these folks when your timepieces need help. They repair all major brands and also replace batteries and watchbands. Locman Watches trusts L and M to service and repair their timepieces.

RISSIN'S JEWELRY CLINIC
2 W 47th St (at Fifth Ave), Room 1207   212/575-1098
Mon, Tues, Thurs: 9:30-5; closed first two weeks of July

Rissin's is indeed a clinic! The assortment of services is staggering: jewelry repair and design, antique repair, museum restorations, supplying diamonds and other stones, eyeglass repair, pearl and bead stringing, restringing of old necklaces, stone identification, and appraisals. Rissins' "Earquilizer" (an earring stabilizer) has been patented, and you can try it at the store. (Bring your own earrings.) Joe and Toby Rissin run the place. Joe's father was a master engraver, and the family tradition has been passed along. *Honesty* and *quality* are their bywords. Estimates are gladly given, and all work is guaranteed.

Lamp Repair
THE LAMP SURGEON
Mon-Sat: 8 a.m.-10 p.m.   917/414-0426
www.lampsurgeon.com

Roy and Lois Schneit do lamp repairs, restoration, refinishing, and rewiring at customers' homes, offices, and apartments. Services include work on table and floor lamps, halogen lamps, chandeliers, wall sconces, and antiques. They also offer custom lampshades. Roy brings over 30 years experience to the job.

Landscape Design
AMERICAN FOLIAGE & DESIGN GROUP
122 W 22nd St (bet Ave of the Americas and Seventh Ave)
Mon-Fri: 8-5   212/741-5555
www.americanfoliagedesign.com

The focus at American Foliage is on concepts and designs for anything to do with gardens and exteriors for theater, film, and corporate or private events. These folks sell or rent live and artificial plants, props, lighting and special effects items, and party supplies. Full service is provided, including trucking and installation.

Leather Repair
FORDHAM REPAIR CENTER
39 W 32nd St, Room 604 (bet Fifth Ave and Broadway)   212/889-4553
Mon-Fri: 8:30-5

Here's a business you will want to make note of. They repair, clean, and refurbish leather luggage, handbags, wallets, briefcases, and totes—even your great-grandmother's old trunk. Ripped stitching and bindings, broken zippers and locks, missing wheels, and damaged handles receive careful attention to bring goods back to useful life.

MODERN LEATHER GOODS

2 W 32nd St (bet Fifth Ave and Broadway), 4th floor   212/279-3263
Mon-Fri: 8:30-5; Sat: 8-1:30   www.modernleathergoods.com

Is a briefcase, suitcase, or handbag looking worn? Some people regard signs of wear on leather as a mark of class, but I like to see things looking good. Modern Leather Goods, a family business for over 60 years, is the place to go for repairs and reconditioning. Ask for owner Tony Pecorella. They also do needlepoint mounting, reglaze alligator bags, clean leather and suede, and repair shoes and leather clothing.

Here is a listing of some special services to be found in Manhattan:

Ceramics: **Ceramic Restorations** (224 W 29th St, 12th floor, 212/564-8669; by appointment)

Chimney cleaning: **Homestead Chimney** (800/242-7668; Tues-Fri: 8-4, by appointment)

Clothing repairs: **Ban Custom Tailor Shop** (1544 First Ave, 212/570-0444)

Glass cutting: **Sundial-Schwartz** (159 E 118th St, 212/289-4969; Mon-Fri: 8:30-4)

Glassware: **Glass Restorations** (1597 York Ave, 212/517-3287)

Jewelry: **Murrey's Jewelers** (1395 Third Ave, 212/879-3690)

Landscape design: **Madison Cox Design** (127 W 26th St, 212/242-4631, by appointment)

Leather: **Falotico Studio** (315 E 91st St, 212/369-1217)

Silver: **Thome Silversmith** (49 W 37th St, 212/764-5426; by appointment)

Woodwork restoration: **Traditional Line** (212/627-3555, by appointment)

SUPERIOR REPAIR CENTER

141 Lexington Ave (at 29th St)   212/967-0554
Mon-Fri: 10-6; Sat: 10-3   www.superiorleathernyc.com

Do you own a fine leather garment that has been damaged? Leather repair is the highlight of the services offered at Superior. Many major stores in the city use them for luggage and handbag work. They are experts at cleaning leather (suede, shearling, and reptile) and repairing or replacing zippers on leather items. They can even remove ink spots. Superior has the answer to all leather-related problems. Just ask Gucci, Calvin Klein, Bergdorf Goodman, and Prada!

Locksmiths

AAA LOCKSMITHS

44 W 46th St (at Ave of the Americas)   212/840-3939
Mon-Thurs: 8-5:30; Fri: 8-5   www.aaahardware.com

This particular "AAA" is *not* the place to call about an automobile emergency. However, in an industry that does not often inspire loyalty or recommendations, AAA Locksmiths has been a family business for over 70 years, and that says a lot. They also discount residential and commercial door hardware.

LOCKWORKS LOCKSMITHS
By appointment   212/736-3740

Got a lock problem? Give Joel at Lockworks a call. He has been in the locksmith trade for over three decades, and there is nothing he can't unlock. Joel will install almost any type of door hardware. This honest gentleman does not advertise, but he is highly regarded by some of the top businesses in Manhattan.

NIGHT AND DAY LOCKSMITH
1335 Lexington Ave (at 89th St)   212/722-1017
Mon-Fri: 9-6 (24 hours for emergencies)

Carry Night and Day's number in case you're ever locked out! Locksmiths must stay ahead of the burglars' latest expertise and offer fast, on-the-spot service for a variety of devices designed to keep criminals out. (After all, no New York apartment has just *one* lock.) Mena Sofer, Night and Day's owner, fulfills these rigid requirements. The company answers its phone 24 hours a day, while posted hours are for the sale and installation of locks, window gates, intercoms, car alarms, safes, and keys. Welding is a specialty.

Overseas travelers can find valuable information and obtain immunizations at these places:

Travel Health Services (50 E 69th St, 212/734-3000; Mon, Wed-Fri: 9 a.m.-noon; Tues: 1 p.m.-5 p.m.

Travelers' Medical Service of N.Y. (595 Madison Ave, Suite 1200, 212/230-1020; Mon-Fri: 9-4, by appointment)

Travelers' Wellness Center (952 Fifth Ave, Room ID, 212/737-1212; available around the clock by appointment)

Marble Works

PUCCIO MARBLE AND ONYX
661 Driggs Ave, Brooklyn (main office)
Mon-Fri: 8-4:30   718/387-9778, 800/778-2246
                                                    www.puccio.info

Work of the highest quality is a tradition with Puccio. The sculpture and furniture designs range from traditional to sleekly modern. John and Paul Puccio show dining and cocktail tables, chairs, chests of drawers, buffets, desks, consoles, and pedestals. Custom-designed installations include foyer floors, bathrooms, kitchens, bars, staircases, fountains, and fireplaces. Retail orders are accepted. They are the largest distributor and fabricator of onyx in the country.

Medical Services

BIOSCRIP
197 Eighth Ave (at 20th St)   212/691-9050
Mon-Fri: 9-9; Sat: 9-6   www.bioscrip.com

Bioscrip pharmacy provides home delivery of prescription medications, comprehensive claims management, and links to community resources and national support networks. Specialties include prescriptions for patients with

HIV or transplants. All pharmaceuticals are available, as is an extensive line of vitamins and homeopathic and holistic products. Many hard-to-find items can be provided with one-day service. They will bill insurance companies directly so that customers need not pay up front. Nationwide shipping is available.

CENTER FOR HEARING AND COMMUNICATION
50 Broadway (bet Morris St and Exchange Pl), 6th floor
Mon-Fri: 9-5 (by appointment)   917/305-7700, 917/305-7999 (TTY)
www.chchearing.org

People of all ages with any degree of hearing loss are served by this not-for-profit organization. They test hearing, evaluate and dispense hearing aides, and provide speech and language therapy, and mental-health counseling. Support groups are conducted to enable people with hearing loss (and their families) in all aspects of their lives. These folks come highly recommended, and their services are a real value.

Remember when doctors made house calls? Well, in New York, some of them still do! In addition to office appointments, house calls are routine with **New York House Call Physicians** (20 Park Ave, Suite 1A, 646/957-5444, www.doctorinthefamily.com), catering to patients' schedules and their location of choice. The doctor's black bag has been expanded to include mobile medical equipment, allowing them to perform numerous procedures. They carry suture equipment, digital electrocardiogram machines, ophthalmoscopes, palm-held computers, and mobile printers.

When necessary, the doctors have admitting privileges at Beth Israel Medical Center. Costs are flat-fee based and include most testing, medication dispensing, and procedures. Insurance, Medicare, and Medicaid are not billed, so plan on using a credit card or cash. Available services include family medicine, hospice, pain management, pediatric care, psychotherapy, ultrasound, and addictions. Patients of all ages are welcome to call or visit.

C. O. BIGELOW CHEMISTS
414 Ave of the Americas (bet 8th and 9th St)   212/533-2700
Mon-Fri: 8 a.m.-9 p.m.; Sat: 8:30-7; Sun: 8:30-5:30
www.bigelowchemists.com

Bigelow touts itself as the oldest apothecary in America, and their old school approach to customer service is a testament to their longevity. The selection of signature Bigelow products and other brandnames is vast, with a treatment remedy for almost any ailment. Cruise the aisles for beauty and health-care products, plus a carefully selected assortment of gifts and fragrances.

DR WALK-IN MEDICAL CARE
1627 Broadway (at 50th St)   888/535-6963
Mon-Sat: 8-8; Sun: 11-7

125 E 86th St (at Lexington Ave)   888/535-6963
Mon-Fri: 11-7   www.drwalkin.com

Travelers take note: if you find yourself ill in New York, these convenient locations inside two Duane Reade drugstores may be able to help you get better. Licensed physicians and medical assistants are on duty to perform basic care and screenings, tend to minor sprains and lacerations, administer vaccinations, write prescriptions, and make referrals to appropriate specialists. (However, you should head for the emergency room if experiencing life-threatening conditions or broken bones.) Appointments are not necessary, making this a valuable service to New Yorkers, too.

Special pharmacies:

J. Leon Lascoff & Sons, Inc. (1209 Lexington Ave, 212/288-9500): the very best pharmacy services

The Village Apothecary (346 Bleecker St, 212/807-7566): HIV/AIDS drugs and alternative medicine

---

N.Y. HOTEL URGENT MEDICAL SERVICES
Urgent Care Center and Travelers Wellness Center   212/737-1212
952 Fifth Ave (bet 76th and 77th St), Room 1D   www.travelmd.com

This is one of the most valuable services in Manhattan! Dr. Ronald Primas, the CEO and medical director, is tops in his field. This outfit is locally based and has been in operation for over a decade. All manner of health care is available on a 24/7 basis: internists, pediatricians, obstetricians, surgeons, dentists, chiropractors, physicians-on-call service, and more. Doctors will come to your hotel or apartment, arrange for tests, prescribe medications, admit patients to hospitals, and provide nurses. They also provide travel immunizations and consultations, and they are an official WHO-designated yellow-fever vaccination site. The urgent care center is also available around the clock by appointment for patients not requiring a house call. Payment is expected at the time of service; credit cards are accepted. All physicians are board certified and have an exemplary bedside manner.

Metal Work

ATLANTIC RETINNING AND METAL REFINISHING
The Brass Lab (Manhattan dropoff location)
532 W 25th St (bet Tenth and Eleventh Ave), 3rd floor 212/243-7180
Tues-Sun: call ahead   www.retinning.com

Jamie Gibbons oversees a long-established business whose specialty is retinning. Drawing upon years of experience, Gibbons restores brass and copper antiques, repairs brass musical instruments, designs and creates new copperware, sells restored copper pieces, and restores lamps, chandeliers, and brass beds. Quality retinning work is now done out of their New Jersey plant. A convenient Manhattan dropoff and pickup location is at the Brass Lab.

Movers

BIG APPLE MOVING & STORAGE
83 Third Ave (bet Bergen and Dean St), Brooklyn
Mon-Fri: 9-5; Sat: 9-noon   212/505-1861, 718/625-1424
                                       www.bigapplemoving.com

This is a handy number for moving and storage. Even though Big Apple Moving & Storage is located in downtown Brooklyn, they do 80% of their moving business in Manhattan. They are experts with antiques, art, and high-end moves, yet manage to keep rates reasonable. Every size of box, container, and wood crate for moving or storage is stocked. They also have bubble pack, plate dividers, custom paper, and "French wraps" for crystal and delicate breakables. Many expert packers have been with Big Apple since opening in 1979. You'll find moving supplies at their "do-it-yourself" moving store. Ask for the "Gerry Frank 20% Discount Special," and get your supplies delivered free, too! For those who need overnight or short-term storage, Big Apple will keep your entire truckload of furniture inside their high-security heated warehouse. Interstate and international moving is also provided, and every item is fully wrapped and padded before leaving your residence. These folks have a good reputation and receive high marks from satisfied customers.

A dental emergency over the weekend can be both inconvenient and painful. Here are three numbers to call for relief on Saturday, as well as during normal hours.

Dr. Isaac Datikashvili (130 E 63rd St, Suite 1A, 212/486-9458): available any time

Metropolitan Dental Associates (225 Broadway, 212/732-7400; Sat: 7:30-4): across from City Hall Park; walk-ins welcome

Stuyvesant Dental Associates (430 E 20th St, 212/473-4151): open on alternating Saturdays; call for appointment

---

THE BOX BUTLER
888/881-0810
www.theboxbutler.com

You inhabit a small space, so what can you do with seasonal clothes, sports equipment, suitcases, and Christmas decorations? The Box Butler offers short- or long-term storage options. They deliver empty containers and locks to your residence or business. You box the items and inventory the contents. The containers are then transported and stored at their secure warehouse. When you need your items, contact them for delivery. The monthly rate is based upon the size of your container; other package prices are available, too. The Box Butler is also good for stowing trade-show displays, client records, and household items during a remodeling job.

BROWNSTONE BROS. MOVING
321 Rider Ave (at 140th St), The Bronx   718/665-5000
Mon-Fri: 9:30-5   www.brownstonebros.com

Since 1977 Brownstone Bros. has been offering moving and storage services with a very personal touch by head man Bill Gross. They are highly rated by customers. Here's a good tip from them: personally move your remote-control devices to your next location.

MOVING RIGHT ALONG
101-21 101st St   718/738-2468
Ozone Park, NY   www.movingrightalong.com
Mon-Fri: 9-5:30; Sat: 9-2:30

Nearly three decades of service and a top-quality reputation speak well of Moving Right Along. Moving, storage, packing, and crating are offered. A handy home cleaning and junk removal service will help get your residence ready for quick occupancy. They also sell pre-owned furniture, antiques, and imports.

WEST SIDE MOVERS
644 Amsterdam Ave (bet 91st and 92nd St)   212/874-3800
Mon-Fri: 8-6; Sat: 9-4; Sun: 9-3   www.westsidemovers.com

The late Steve Fiore started West Side Movers in the kitchen of his studio apartment more than 30 years ago, and it is now capably run by his wife, Joanne, a former psychotherapist. From its location on Amsterdam Avenue, West Side Movers offers dependable residential and office moving, specializing in fine art and antiques. Close attention is paid to efficiency, promptness, care, and courtesy. Packing consultants will help do-it-yourselfers select moving boxes and other supplies. Boxes come in a multitude of sizes, including four different options for mirrors alone. West Side Movers also provides dollies and moving pads.

Office Services

PURGATORY PIE PRESS
19 Hudson St (bet Duane and Reade St), Room 403   212/274-8228
Mon-Fri: by appointment   www.purgatorypiepress.com

Purgatory Pie Press is ideal for small printing jobs. They do graphic design and handset typography, hand letterpress printing, die-cutting, and hand bookbinding. They'll also create envelopes, do logos and other identity designs, and design handmade paper with unique watermarks. Specialties include printing and calligraphy for weddings and parties. They also carry limited-edition postcards and artists' books. Private lessons and small group classes are offered in letterpress printing.

WORLD-WIDE BUSINESS CENTRES
575 Madison Ave (at 57th St), 10th floor   212/605-0200, 800/296-9922
Mon-Fri: 9-5:30   www.wwbcn.com

Alan Bain, a transplanted English lawyer, has created a business that caters to executives who need more than a hotel room and companies that need a fully equipped, furnished, and staffed office in New York on short notice. The operation grew out of Bain's personal frustration in trying to put together a makeshift office. A full range of secretarial and telecommunication services are available. Desk space, private offices, and conference rooms may be rented on a temporary (hourly, daily, weekly, or monthly) basis. The daily rate includes a private office, telephone answering, and receptionists.

Opticians

E.B. MEYROWITZ AND DELL OPTICIANS
19 W 44th St (at Fifth Ave)   212/575-1686
Mon-Fri: 9-5:45; Sat: 10-4:30   www.ebmeyrowitz-dell.com

If you have an optical emergency in the city, E.B. Meyrowitz does on-the-spot emergency repair of eyeglasses. You're welcome to stop by for regular optical needs, too. They stock a large frame selection, made of various materials ranging from 18-karat gold to buffalo horn. They also repair binoculars.

> When it becomes necessary to look into long-term home healthcare, call **Priority Home Care** (212/401-1700).

Painting

ALLCITYPAINTING
65 Water St (at Old Slip)   917/439-5419
Mon-Fri: 8 a.m.-10 p.m.; Sat-Sun: 9-5   www.allcitypaintingnyc.com

Let the professionals at AllCityPainting take over when you're sprucing up your residential or commercial environs. They'll paint inside or out, hang wallpaper, perform tile glazing, refinish hardwood floors, and even remodel an entire kitchen or bathroom; plus they expertly patch, spackle, and repair ugly spots before getting started. Interior designers and architects are among the clients who appreciate their quick turnaround time and neat, professional workmanship. Mention this write-up to manager Damien Acevedo, and he'll offer a 10% discount.

BERNARD GARVEY PAINTING
By appointment   718/894-8272

I am often asked to recommend a reliable painter who can also do plastering and decorative finishes. Bernard Garvey Painting services residential clients, and his customers tout his reasonable prices and terrific work.

GOTHAM PAINTING COMPANY
123 E 90th St (at Lexington Ave)   212/427-5752
Mon-Fri: 9-5

If you need interior paint or wallpaper for your home, Gotham is a good resource. They do spray work, restoration, faux painting, and plastering. There are more than 50 full-time painters on staff, and all are fully licensed and bonded. They have been in business for over two decades.

> **Handy in the City Painting** (917/841-8032, www.handyinthe city.com) is a good name to keep at hand! If you need someone to paint, plaster, do skin-coating, and wall or ceiling repair, owner Mike Trupiano is the guy to call. Send him a to-do list if you're moving to or across town, and he'll provide a quote and take care of the chores before you and your belongings arrive. Think of Mike for jobs too small for a general contractor but too large for a building superintendant.

Parenting Resources

PARENTING CENTER AT THE 92ND STREET Y
1395 Lexington Ave (at 92nd St)   212/415-5611
Mon-Fri: 9-5 (office hours)   www.92y.org

Just about everything the 92nd Street Y does is impressive, and its Parenting Center is no exception. It offers every kind of class you can imagine: a newborn care class for expectant parents, a baby massage class for new parents and infants, a cooking class for preschoolers, and so on. Workshops and seminars are offered on a wide range of topics, from sleep to setting limits. They provide babysitting for 92nd Street Y users and host new parent get-togethers. Perhaps most importantly, they act as a resource and support center for members and the general public. The annual membership fee is $175 per family, and benefits include discounts and priority sign-up. Non-members are welcome to take classes, too.

PARENTS LEAGUE
115 E 82nd St (bet Lexington and Park Ave)   212/737-7385
Mon-Thurs: 9-4; Fri: 9-noon   www.parentsleague.org

This nonprofit organization is a gold mine for parents in New York. In addition to putting together a calendar of events for children of all ages, the Parents League maintains extensive files on babysitters, birthday party places, tutors, summer camps, early childhood programs, and private schools throughout the city. For a membership fee of $125 per academic year, you can access the online database of 1,500 resources, and attend workshops and other events.

At **Not Just Babysitters** (917/523-0065, www.notjustbabysitters.com), owner Zee Miller strives to make sure the person providing child care in your home is a perfect match for you and your family. She imposes a very strict application and interview process for prospective sitters and conducts home interviews with employers to match suitable caregivers with infants, older children, and the elderly. Members pay an annual fee for unlimited use of placements (short- or long-term, or as-needed basis). Rates vary by the number of children, responsibilities, sitter's experience, and qualifications.

SOHO PARENTING CENTER
568 Broadway (at Prince St), Suite 402   212/334-3744
Mon-Fri: 8-8 (by appointment)   www.sohoparenting.com

Soho Parenting Center is dedicated to the notion that parenting ought to be talked about and shared. It conducts workshops and group discussions for parents of newborns, toddlers, and older children. It offers play groups for children while parents discuss their experiences and challenges. Individual parent counseling is available, too.

Party Services

BUBBY GRAM
60 E 8th St (at Broadway)   212/353-3886
Mon-Thurs: 11-7 (Fri till 5); by phone   www.bubbygram.com

If creating fun and laughter is on your mind, then call this number. These folks have outrageous and humorous acts that run from simple singing telegrams to complete shows for parties or business meetings. They'll provide celebrity impersonators, roasts, magicians, psychics, belly dancers, hula shows, wedding officiants, and much more.

ECLECTIC ENCORE
620 W 26th St (at Eleventh Ave)   212/645-8880
Mon-Fri: 9-5   www.eclecticprops.com

Their name says it all. Eclectic Encore specializes in hard-to-find props for a party at home, a set for motion pictures or television, or a novel product announcement. They have been in business since 1986 and are known for an extensive collection of 18th-, 19th- and 20th-century furniture and accessories. You can find everything from an armoire to a zebra—even a rickshaw.

Dance Lessons
When you need to learn how to gracefully hold your own on the dance floor, contact these studios. Most classes are geared for couples.
Dance Manhattan (39 W 19th St, 5th floor, 212/807-0802, www.dancemanhattan.com): group and private lessons; wedding dance specialists
DanceSport (22 W 34th St, 212/307-1111, www.dancesport.com): group and private lessons; ballroom and Latin
Fred Astaire New York City Dance Studio (303 E 43rd St, 212/697-6535, www.fredastaireny.com): private lessons; ballroom, Latin, swing, salsa, the hustle
NY Wedding and Partner Dance (1261 Broadway, Suite 510, 646/742-1520, nyweddingdance.com): private lessons only; all genres of dance

---

EXPRESSWAY MUSIC & EVENTS
315 Madison Ave (at 42nd St), Suite 1303   212/953-9367
By appointment   www.expresswaymusic.com

If you are interested in entertainment for any kind of personal or business event, give these folks a call. Their artists include the Expressway Music Jazz Trio (modern jazz) and the Professionals (a six-piece band that plays disco, rock, dance music, swing, jazz, and more). Other ensembles include chamber music duets, trios, and quartets (for weddings, cocktail hours, and other events), and a steel drum band with up to seven pieces. They can also provide DJs for weddings and private events and karaoke services.

HIGHLY EVENTFUL
11 Fifth Ave (at 8th St), Suite 7C   212/777-3565
Daily: 10-6   www.highlyeventful.com

Since 1994, Highly Eventful has been arranging events in New York and throughout the world. These folks take charge of everything, including food, liquor, equipment rentals, tents, flowers, lighting, music, and trained personnel. They will secure prime locations, such as grand ballrooms, churches (like the Cathedral Church of St. John the Divine), museums (like the Metropolitan), and yachts. They have on-staff chefs who will handle smaller affairs, specializing in Italian or Asian cuisine.

LINDA KAYE'S BIRTHDAYBAKERS, PARTYMAKERS
195 E 76th St (bet Lexington and Third Ave)   212/288-7112
Mon-Fri: 9:45-5 (parties can be scheduled for any day)
www.partymakers.com

Linda Kaye offers children's birthday parties at two of Manhattan's most desirable locations: the Central Park Zoo and the American Museum of Natural History. Zoo parties are for children from one to ten years old. Themes include Animal Alphabet Safari, Animal Olympics, Safari Treasure Hunt, and Mystery Movie Making. The Natural History parties are for children ages four and up, with such themes as Dinosaur Discovery, Cosmic Blast-Off, Underwater Treasure, and Safari Adventure. Kaye's website serves as a resource and shopping site for birthday party needs, listing entertainers and party locations. Partymakers also specializes in creative custom cakes (including a pop-out cake) and unique corporate events.

MARCY BLUM ASSOCIATES
55 Fifth Ave (bet 12th and 13th St), 19th floor   212/929-9814
By appointment   www.marcyblum.com

What a great lady! Marcy is so well organized that no matter what the event—wedding, reception, birthday party, bar mitzvah, or dinner for the boss—she will execute it to perfection. As anyone knows, it's the details that count, and Marcy is superb at the nitty-gritty. She has organized many celebrity weddings. Utilize her for customized events and unusual gifts, too!

Fantasma Magic (421 Seventh Ave, 2nd floor, 212/244-3633) is the largest magic store in the world. The midtown shop includes two stages, flat screens, a 3D video display, a VIP room (behind a secret door and vault), magic props, and a Houdini museum with a huge collection of his original props. The VIP room can accommodate 250 to 300 guests for birthday parties or special events, or 75 seated guests for professional magic shows.

PARTY POOPERS
By appointment   212/274-9955
www.partypoopers.com

Party Poopers is a full-service party-planning company that never throws the same party twice. They can handle a job as simple as booking entertainment all the way to designing and implementing an entire event. Party Poopers' roster of top entertainers, caterers, designers, DJs, and specialty acts will ensure that you have the best possible party. Although their niche is whimsical interactive kids' parties (Pirates on the Peking is a favorite!), they are also known as a hip alternative for adult events. Established in 1991, Party Poopers is a staple in Manhattan's event-organizing world.

PROPS FOR TODAY
330 W 34th St (bet Eighth and Ninth Ave), 12th floor   212/244-9600
Mon-Fri: 8:30-5 (appointment recommended)
www.propsfortoday.com

This is the handiest place in town when you are planning a party or preparing for a trade show, TV, or movie. Props for Today has the largest rental inventory of party-furnishing decor in New York, allowing you to distinguish your events. Whether you want unique antiques, light-up sofas, or just some extra tables and stools, they've got the goods. They have children's items, books, fireplace equipment, artwork, garden furniture, and foreign items (like Moroccan-themed accessories). Over a million items are available! Phone orders are taken, and you can place your order in advance. I'd recommend checking out the three floors of inventory for yourself, since the website only shows a small sampling of the inventory.

> Guys, before you shop for clothes, check out **Glenn O'Brien** (www.men.style.com/gq/fashion/styleguy) to avoid making costly mistakes. GQ's "Style Guy" covers pretty much everything, including grooming and taking care of your garments.

Pen Repair

FOUNTAIN PEN HOSPITAL
10 Warren St (bet Broadway and Church St)
Mon-Fri: 8-6   212/964-0580, 800/253-7367
                               www.fountainpenhospital.com

Located across from City Hall, this experienced establishment sells and repairs fountain pens of all types. It also carries one of the world's largest selections of modern and vintage writing tools.

Personal Services

A. E. JOHNSON
380 Lexington Ave (at 42nd St), Suite 3810   212/644-0990
Mon-Fri: 9-5   www.aejohnsonagency.com

Dating from 1890, Johnson is the oldest licensed employment agency dealing exclusively with household help in the U.S. They specialize in providing affluent clients with highly-qualified butlers, cooks, housekeepers, chauffeurs, bodyguards, nannies, personal assistants, valets, maids, and couples. Both temporary and permanent workers are available, many on a moment's notice. Employment references, criminal records, and driver's licenses are checked by an independent firm. As a part of the Lindquist Group, they are able to assist clients with their staffing needs in other locations around the country.

AL MARTINO'S DOMESTICS
60 E 42nd St (bet Park and Madison Ave), Suite 2227
Mon-Fri: 9-5   212/867-1910
                                       www.martinodom.com

Private chefs are the specialty at Al Martino Domestics, but this agency has also been providing clientele with highly qualified butlers, housekeepers, cooks, estate managers, personal assistants, and chauffeurs since 1972. Look to Al Martino for party and seasonal help as well. Al Martino's fees are competitive and incorporate a long-term replacement service guarantee.

BIG APPLE GREETER

1 Centre St (at Chambers St)   212/669-8159
Office: Mon-Fri: 9-5   www.bigapplegreeter.org
By appointment

Big Apple Greeter is like having a new friend show you the wonders of the city! Volunteers from all five boroughs meet groups or individuals—up to six people in all—to show them New York City through the eyes of a native. On visits of two to four hours, Greeters use public transportation or travel on foot to introduce visitors to neighborhoods and the city's hidden treasures. There are over 300 Greeters, and they speak nearly 25 languages among them. They are matched with visitors by language, interest, and neighborhoods. This service is free of charge, and tipping is not permitted. At least four weeks advance notice is required.

The **United States Personal Chef Association** (800/995-2138, www.uspca.com) can provide a listing of personal chefs. Here are two of the best in New York:

Belinda Clarke (212/253-6408): Dine by Design
Bill Feldman (212/983-2952): "The Boxing Chef"; fitness regimen, too

---

CELEBRITIES STAFFING SERVICES

20 Vesey St (bet Church St and Broadway), Suite 510   212/227-3877
Mon-Fri: 9-6   www.celebrities-staffing.com

Turn to Celebrities Staffing when you are looking to hire top-of-the-line baby nurses, governesses, nannies, "mannies" (male nannies), housekeepers, ladies' maids, butlers, housemen, cooks, chefs, couples, laundresses, house managers, estate managers, personal assistants, personal shoppers, chauffeurs, bodyguards, caregivers, companions, and other types of household personnel. Their services extend across the U.S. and internationally with clients who include royalty, celebrities, dignitaries, top executives, and families looking to hire the best.

If you need a nanny at the last minute, call **A Choice Nanny** (850 Seventh Ave, Suite 706, 212/246-5437, www.achoicenanny/nyc.com) Alan and Joan Friedman carefully screen personnel. You are charged a one-time membership fee, and rates average $15 an hour.

Other highly recommended sources for nannies:

Fox Agency (212/753-2686): good record
Pavillion Agency (212/889-6609): very reliable

CROSS IT OFF YOUR LIST

60 Madison Ave (at 27th St), Suite 1020   212/725-0122
Mon-Fri: 9-6 (or by appointment)   www.crossitoffyourlist.com

Cross It Off Your List can help you do just that! These folks will do virtually anything to help busy people manage their lives: organize closets and file cabinets, oversee a move, help with daily chores, pack bags, and take care of mail. They do many other tasks, too, and have an outpost in the Hamptons.

FASHION UPDATE
Mon-Fri: 9-5   718/897-0381, 888/447-2846
                                                www.fashionupdate.com

Sarah Gardner is the "Queen of Bargains." She started her business by ferreting out substantial savings for clothing her family. She publishes *Fashion Update,* a quarterly publication that uncovers over 250 bargains per season in women's, men's, and children's designer clothing, accessories, and jewelry; furniture, home accessories, and spa services, too! She also leads shopping expeditions to designer showrooms at $175 per person for 2½ hours; group rates are available. A new service for brides-to-be is a shopping tour that includes bridal showrooms.

Here is a first-class way to see this great city! James Smythe's **My Kind of Town New York** (212/754-4500, 866/691-8687, www.my kindoftown.com) offers private and personalized custom tours in a Mercedes-Benz SUV for up to six guests. Special arrangements can be made for larger groups.

FLATIRON CLEANING COMPANY
230 E 93rd St (at Second Ave)   212/876-1000
Mon-Fri: 7-4   www.flatironcleaning.com

Can you imagine how many homes and apartments these people have cleaned since opening in 1893? Expert services include residential house and window cleaning, installing and refinishing wood floors, maid service, party help, laundry service, and carpet and upholstery cleaning. Another service, cleaning of crime and trauma scenes, is expertly performed.

FLOOD'S CLOSET
By appointment   212/348-7257

Want to be pampered? Barbara Flood will shop for clothes for or with you. She will even bring items for you to consider to your home and can also help organize closets, jewelry, decor, and other time-consuming chores.

IN TOWN RUN-A-ROUND
Mon-Fri: 9-6:30; Sat: by appointment   917/359-6688
                                                www.intownrunaround.com

Owner Henry Goldstein is the man to contact if you don't have the time or know-how for such errands as procuring an item of jewelry, shopping for groceries, organizing your home office, closet or pantry, or finding a party venue for your parents' 50th anniversary. These pleasant, efficient, and reliable folks will even wait in your apartment for a repairman! A new service: pick up from surgical procedures and transport to your home or hotel.

INTREPID NEW YORKER
220 E 57th St (bet Second and Third Ave), Suite 2D   212/750-0400
Mon-Fri: 9-6   www.intrepidny.com

Sylvia Ehrlich and her team provide one of the most complete relocation-consulting services in this area and are available at any time. Hundreds of communities are within a 75-mile radius of the city, and the network includes a hotline of resources for the first year of relocation.

Do you want to maximize your closet's potential? **California Closets** (26 Varick St, 646/486-3900 and 1625 York Ave, 212/517-7877) will reorganize, install storage systems, and, if desired, paint that dreary space!

LET MILLIE DO IT!
By appointment   212/535-1539

Millie Emory is a real problem solver! She has worked for decades as a professional organizer, saving people time, money, and stress. Millie especially likes working for theatrical folks, but she can help anyone with a broad variety of tasks. She will organize and unclutter apartments, desks, files, closets, libraries, attics, basements, garages, and storage rooms. Millie will also pay bills, balance checkbooks, and get papers in order for a tax accountant or IRS audit. She can help with paper flow, time management, and space problems. Millie is also good at finding antiques and out-of-print books and records. Seniors use her services when dismantling their homes before entering nursing facilities. When a loved one dies, Millie will handle estate liquidations, sales, and donations, leaving the space "broom clean."

NEW YORK CELEBRITY ASSISTANTS (NYCA)
459 Columbus Ave (at 82nd St), Suite 216   212/803-5444
New York, NY 10024 (mailing address only)
                                   www.nycelebrityassistants.org

Are you in need of a professional assistant? This outfit consists of current and former assistants to top celebrities in film, TV, theater, music, sports, philanthropy, fashion, business, and politics. NYCA provides educational forums, networking opportunities, and employment referrals.

NEW YORK'S LITTLE ELVES
151 First Ave (bet 8th and 9th St), Suite 204   212/673-5507
Daily: 8-6 (call for appointment)   www.nyelves.com

No need to worry about cleaning up! These little elves will do the job, whether it is a normal dusting or cleaning up after a big party—even a construction job. All kinds of modern and "green" cleaning equipment is used. They provide estimates, employ screened personnel, carry liability insurance, are fully bonded, and have an outstanding reputation. The elves will also subcontract for window, carpet, and upholstery cleaning.

PAVILLION AGENCY
15 E 40th St (bet Fifth and Madison Ave), Suite 400   212/889-6609
Mon-Fri: 9-5   www.pavillionagency.com

Pavillion has been a family business since 1962. If you are in need of nannies, housekeepers, laundresses, couples, butlers, chefs, chauffeurs, care-takers, gardeners, property managers, or personal assistants, call and ask for Keith or Clifford Greenhouse. Applicants are screened by a private firm.

PRIDE & JOY
By appointment   401/743-0814
                                        www.prideandjoynyc.com

Hilary Waterous is a former nanny to some of New York City's elite and is known for her exquisite taste. She will shop the best boutiques to find the perfect clothes for your little pride and joy or outfit the nursery. Use her expertise when it's time for kids' birthdays or new baby gifts, party favors, and gift baskets. She can also organize young ones' wardrobes and bed-rooms. Hilary can handle special requests, like finding trendy beach wear in the middle of January or the perfect tutu. She will meet with you at your home, office, or over coffee.

> Do you need a place to store art, furniture, documents, or other things? Try **Sofia Storage Centers** (475 Amsterdam Ave, 139 Franklin St and 4396 Broadway, 212/873-0700), which have been fam-ily-owned since 1910.

RED BALL WINDOW CLEANING
221 E 85th St (bet Second and Third Ave)   212/861-7686
Mon-Fri: 8-5:30   www.redballwindowcleaners.com

These people have cleaned a lot of windows since opening in 1928! Still a family business, they specialize in residential and commercial window clean-ing. The higher the windows, the happier they are.

SAVED BY THE BELL
11 Riverside Dr (bet 73rd and 74th St)   212/874-5457
Mon-Fri: 9:30-5:30 (or by appointment)

Susan Bell's goal is to take the worry out of planning and carrying out virtually any type of job for people who are too busy or need help. Bell says "doing the impossible is our specialty." They can handle weddings, bar and bat mitzvahs, fundraising and charity benefits, party planning, tag sales, relo-cations, delivery arrangements, and service referrals.

SMART START INTERIOR DESIGN
334 W 86th St (bet West End Ave and Riverside Dr)   212/580-7365
By appointment   www.smartstartny.com

There is always someone in New York to fill a special niche or need. Such a person is Susan Weinberg. She learned from experience that many ex-pectant mothers and fathers are too busy to plan for baby's arrival, so she started a consulting service to aid parents in pulling everything together. Smart Start helps to provide the basic things a newborn needs, as well as interior design, storage creation, gifts, and personal shopping. In addition, Susan sells hand-painted children's furniture—everything from table and chair sets to coat hooks and toy chests. Custom cabinet work is a specialty. She is truly the stork's assistant!

ABC NYC Concierge (718/429-5285 or 800/429-5285, www. abcnycconcierge.com) started as a limousine service, and owner Russell Figaredo expanded the offerings over time. Here's a sampling of their services: concierge, personal assistant, personal chef, mobile spa technician, trip planning, and the ever-reliable limousine service. Contact this amazing crew when you need assistance with business or domestic errands, pet sitting or care, special event tickets and restaurant reservations, personalized shopping and returns, a special night on the town, or out-of-town guests. In fact, I'd keep this number handy for just about anything!

TALKPOWER
333 E 23rd St (bet First and Second Ave)   212/684-1711
Mon-Fri: 9-5   www.talkpowerinc.com

Do you know that speaking to a group is people's single most feared experience? If you suffer from this phobia, give these folks a call. They are true professionals who train clients to make public appearances. Personal or group sessions are available for intensive weekends.

U NAME IT ORGANIZERS
629 E 11th St (bet Ave B and C)   212/598-9868
By appointment   www.masterorganizers.com

If *should've*, *could've*, and *would've* are too often part of your vocabulary, then U Name It *can* do those tasks you've been putting off. This company has been freeing up time for people who can't get certain things done themselves. They perform over 200 services, including uncluttering, providing personal assistants or clergy, feng shui, special editing, handling a traffic ticket, and even finding a soul mate. In the crowded field of organizers, U Name It has been in business for over two decades, so they must be doing something right.

FlatRate Moving and Storage (212/966-2288) uses only the most experienced and highly trained movers to perform "Elite Luxury Moving Services." Special collections, such as wine, necessitate special handling. They take extreme care in packing, padding, and labeling items; then inventory, photograph, and transport goods in secure vans.

WHITE GLOVE ELITE
39 W 32nd St (bet Fifth Ave and Broadway), Room 900
Mon-Fri: 8-8; Sat: 9-3 (cleaners available anytime)   212/684-4460

Actors Sarah and Jim Ireland started this business as an adjunct to their stage careers. They provide trained cleaners for apartments in Manhattan, The Bronx, Brooklyn, and Queens. Many of their workers are also food servers. About half of their personnel are actors between jobs.

ZOE INTERNATIONAL
20 Vesey St (bet Church St and Broadway), Suite 510   212/227-3880
Mon-Fri: 9-6 (24-hour emergency service)   www.zoehomecare.com

This agency specializes in the placement of nurses and nurses' aides, home health- and personal-care aides, companions, and housekeepers to work for the elderly, sick, and chronically ill. They work closely with doctors, hospitals, healthcare organizations, family members, friends, attorneys, estate planners, and others involved in a patient's life. Caregivers are available for live-in or live-out. They can work day or night shifts or provide 24-hour service. Specially priced packages are available for families on fixed incomes.

ZTREND

917/945-2418
www.ztrend.com

ZTrend is both a walking tour and a shopping excursion in the chic Chelsea and Meatpacking neighborhoods. Stops are scheduled at over 15 boutiques for gifts, women's clothing, shoes, purses, artisan jewelry, body care, lingerie, chocolates, and home accessories. Plan this tour at the start of your New York trip to take advantage of information on self-guided shopping tours in other areas. Private and custom tours can also be arranged.

Maid for You (718/433-1499, www.maidforyounewyork.com) claims to be the largest residential and commercial cleaning service in New York. They offer free estimates and will customize a program for your specific needs—daily, weekly, monthly, or move-in/move-out. They can do windows, floors and carpets, and pick up dry cleaning. The highly-trained and uniformed employees provide quality "green" cleaning services at competitive rates. You can even call their friendly customer service people in the middle of the night to schedule an appointment.

Photographic Services

CLASSIC KIDS, MANHATTAN
1182 Lexington Ave (bet 80th and 81st St) 212/396-1160
Tues-Sat: 8:30-5:30 www.classickidsphotography.com

Melissa O'Neal is part of a consortium of child photographers who produce black and white and hand-tinted photographs of kids and families. No stuffy formal sittings are allowed here; it's strictly fun for everyone involved. Belly laughs, mischievous grins, and monkey shines are artistically captured to evoke treasured memories.

DEMETRIAD CREATIVE MEDIA
1674 Broadway (at 52nd St), 4th floor 212/315-3400
Mon-Sat: 9-7 www.demetriad.com

These folks were trained as commercial photographers and have parlayed that expertise into commercial portrait and head-shot photography, as well as digital imaging and restoration of old and damaged photographs. They are pros at retouching and high-end portrait and editorial photography. Custom-printing and processing can be done manually or digitally, depending on a client's preference.

HAND HELD FILMS
66 White St (bet Broadway and Church St)   212/502-0900
Mon-Fri: 9-6   www.handheldfilms.com

Hand Held Films rents motion picture equipment for feature films, commercials, music videos, and documentaries. Media composers and digital video cameras are also available. You can be assured of finding the latest equipment, lenses, and "toys," including lighting. They have an impressive list of equipment—even a 20-foot truck to haul equipment to your set.

VISKO HATFIELD
Mon-Fri: 9-5   212/979-9322, 917/544-9300
                                   www.vhpictures.com

Visko Hatfield truly takes one-of-a-kind portraits. This talented photographer has captured images of celebrities from the literary, fashion, art, and sports scenes. You could be his next subject!

Need some cash? **Portero** (275 Madison Ave, Room 1201, 877/307-3767, www.portero.com) will visit your residence, catalog your quality items, and oversee online luxury auctions. You will receive payment for any sold items, minus a commission.

Plumbing and Heating

KAPNAG HEATING AND PLUMBING
150 W 28th St (at Seventh Ave), Suite 501   212/929-7111
                                                   www.kapnagplumbing.com

When a reliable plumber and/or heating expert is needed, you can't do better than this outfit. They handle plumbing renovations for kitchens and bathrooms, replace toilets, repair pipes and heating equipment, expertly diagnose plumbing system problems, and more. Two dozen professional workers have kept Kapnag at the top since 1935.

Portraits

CATHERINE STOCK
Mid-October through mid-May (by appointment)   917/915-6304
                                                 www.catherinestock.com

Catherine Stock has quite a life, traveling around the country and the world to paint subjects in their own homes. Because she is often away, it is best to arrange an appointment via her website. She is one of the best children's portrait artists. Stock usually paints in watercolors and requires just one sitting.

Psychic

JOANN SANDS
By appointment   212/465-1905

Joann Sands is a popular psychic who has a number of repeat clients and has appeared on television many times. Her fees are reasonable.

Real Estate and Relocation

SHELLEY SAXTON
Call for appointment   917/825-4195

Also known as the "Duchess of Rent," Shelley Saxton specializes in sales and high-end leasing. Her relentless energy and extensive relationships enable her to achieve outstanding results. Shelley brokers with Brown Harris Stevens and is a member of REBNY/RELO. Her clients include international banks, multinational corporations, diplomats, and celebrities.

Are relatives coming to visit? Do you need pictures framed today? One-hour framing service is available at **O.J. Art Gallery** (920 Third Ave, 212/754-0123; Mon-Sat: 10-7; Sun: 11-5).

Scissors and Knife Sharpening

HENRY WESTPFAL CO, INC.
115 W 25th St (bet Ave of the Americas and Seventh Ave)
Mon-Fri: 9:30-6   212/563-5990

The same family has been running Henry Westpfal since 1874. They do all kinds of sharpening and repair, from barber scissors and pruning shears to cuticle scissors. They'll also work on light tools. Cutlery, shears, scissors, and tools for leather workers are sold here. They even sell lefthanded scissors!

Shipping and Packaging

THE UPS STORE
Multiple locations   800/PICK-UPS
Hours vary by store   www.theupsstore.com

UPS has over 40 store locations in New York, offering professional packaging and shipping jobs. Handy document services—not all of them available at every location—include color and black-and-white copying and printing, digital printing, faxing, private mailboxes, mail forwarding, business cards, office stationery, notary and secretarial work, passport photos, binding, laminating, rubber stamps, engraving, key duplication, computer-generated letters, and money transfers. They also sell stamps, paper and office supplies, boxes, and packing and moving supplies.

UNITED SHIPPING & PACKAGING
200 E 10th St (at Second Ave)   212/475-2214
Mon-Fri: 10:30-8; Sat: 11-6   www.uspnyc.com

United Shipping will send anything, anywhere in the world! They also sell packaging supplies and boxes. Additional services include faxing, mailboxes, office supplies, and messenger services.

Shoe Repair

CESAR'S SHOE REPAIR
180 Seventh Ave (bet 20th and 21st St)   212/961-6119
Mon-Fri: 7:30-7; Sat: 9-6   www.cesarsshoerepair.com

Third generation cobbler Edward Andrade and his skilled craftsmen implement the latest technologies to repair and refurbish shoes and boots. Besides the usual sole and heel repairs, they can customize boots with calf extensions and stretching, zipper replacement, ankle tapering, and shortening the height of a boot. These and other leather-maintenance services are available at affiliated **Andrade Shoe Repair** shops, located throughout Manhattan.

JIM'S SHOE REPAIR
50 E 59th St (bet Madison and Park Ave)   212/355-8259
Mon-Fri: 8-6; Sat: 9-4 (closed Sat in summer)

This operation offers first-rate shoe repair, shoeshines, and shoe supplies. The shoe repair field has steadily been losing its craftsmen, and this is one of the few shops that upholds the tradition. Owner Jim Rocco specializes in orthopedic shoe and boot alterations. Bags and belts receive superior treatment, too!

LEATHER SPA
10 W 55th St (bet Fifth Ave and Ave of the Americas)   212/262-4823
Mon-Fri: 8-7; Sat: 10-6

Plaza Hotel Retail Boutiques (59th St at Fifth Ave)   212/527-9944
Mon-Fri: 11-8; Sat: 11-7   www.leatherspa.com

Quality work is done here—shoe repair and cleaning, bag repair and cleaning, custom work—and you will pay well for it. This handy service also offers delivery.

TOP SERVICE
845 Seventh Ave (bet 54th and 55th St)   212/765-3190
Mon-Fri: 8-7; Sat: 9-3

Shoe repair is the main business at Top Service, but there is much more. They can cut keys, repair handbags, clean suede, and dye and clean shoes. Dance shoes are a specialty, and this source is used by many Broadway theater groups. This is a great place to keep in mind for last-minute emergencies.

Silversmiths

BRANDT & OPIS
46 W 46th St (bet Fifth Ave and Ave of the Americas), 5th floor
Mon-Thurs: 8-5; Fri: 8-2   212/302-0294

If it has to do with silver, Roland Markowitz at Brandt & Opis can handle it. This includes silver repair and polishing, buying and selling estate silver, repairing and replating silver-plated items, and fixing silver tea and coffee services. They restore combs and brushes (dresser sets) and replace old knife blades. Other services include gold-plating, lamp restoration, and plating antique bath and door hardware. In short, Brandt & Opis is a complete metal restoration specialist.

THOME SILVERSMITH
49 W 37th St (bet Fifth Ave and Ave of the Americas), 4th floor
Wed, Thurs: 10-5   212/764-5426
                                              www.thomesilversmith.com

Thome cleans, repairs, and replates silver. They also buy and sell magnificent pieces. They have a real appreciation for silver and other metal goods, and it shows in everything they do. They will restore antique silver and objets d'art, repair and polish brass and copper, and repair and clean pewter, gold, and bronze. Thome can do gold-plating, too. They'll even restore the velvet backs of picture frames and velvet box linings.

Stained-Glass Design and Restoration

VICTOR ROTHMAN FOR STAINED GLASS
578 Nepperhan Ave (at Lake Ave), Yonkers

212/255-2551, 914/969-0919

With over 30 years experience, this studio specializes in museum-quality stained-glass restoration. They have worked on everything from residences to churches and public buildings. Consultation is provided, and specification reports are prepared for professional and private use. Stained-glass windows can be designed and fabricated.

Dirty windows? Call **Frank's Window Cleaning Company** (212/288-4631).

Tailors

BHAMBI'S CUSTOM TAILORS
14 E 60th St (bet Madison and Fifth Ave), Suite 610   212/935-5379
Mon-Fri: 9:30-7; Sat: 10-6   www.bhambis.com

Discover the incomparable luxury of a bespoke suit in the best British tradition at Bhambi's Custom Tailors. This four-decades-old family business combines style, quality, tradition, and skill to make suits, jackets, slacks, tuxedos, and shirts that will flatter the successful business or professional man. A distinguished list of satisfied clients attest to Bhambi's superior merchandise and fair prices.

CEGO CUSTOM SHIRTMAKER
174 Fifth Ave (bet 22nd and 23rd St), Suite 502   212/620-4512
Mon-Fri: 9:30-6; Sat: noon-4   www.cego.com

In only three weeks—faster, if it's an emergency—you can have a perfect-fitting shirt made at CEGO.

MOHAN'S CUSTOM TAILORS
60 E 42nd St (bet Park and Madison Ave), Suite 1432   212/697-0050
Mon-Sat: 10-7 (appointments appreciated)   www.mohantailors.com

Mohan's makes suits, coats, sports jackets, slacks, shirts, and formal wear from over 20,000 fabric samples. They want classy-looking, satisfied customers. For one year after a piece is made, they offer free alterations if you lose or gain weight.

NELSON TAILOR SHOP
176 Rivington St (bet Attorney and Clinton St)   212/253-7071
Mon-Sat: 9-6

Dependable and *reasonable* are the best words to describe the work at Nelson. What transpires with clothing inside this unassuming shop is almost magical. Coats are relined, pants and skirts are shortened or lengthened, waistbands are let out or nipped in, necklines are reshaped, sleeves are made to fit, and whole garments are given an updated look at a fraction of the cost for a new item. Out-of-town customers often pack their ill-fitting or damaged clothes, drop them off at Nelson when they arrive, and return home with wearable, tailored attire.

PEPPINO TAILORS
780 Lexington Ave (at 60th St)   212/832-3844
Mon-Fri: 8:30-6:30; Sat: 9-4

Peppino is a fine craftsman who has been tailoring clothes for over a quarter of a century. All types of garments, including evening wear, receive his expert attention for alterations. Delivery is offered.

Bespoke (custom) tailoring is available from these top folks:

Bespoke Tailors (509 Madison Ave, 212/888-6887)

Bruno Cosentino (Dunhill, 545 Madison Ave, 212/753-9292): English-Italian style

Cameo Cleaners of Gramercy Park (284 Third Ave, 212/677-3949): fit like a glove with your personal style

Domenico Vacca (781 Fifth Ave, 212/759-6333): He will do good things for your figure.

Dynasty Custom Tailors (6 E 38th St, 212/679-1075): dresses and wedding gowns

Eva Devecsery (201 E 61st St, Suite 1, 212/751-6091): a delightful lady whose elves can do most anything

Ghost Tailor (153 W 27th St, 11th floor, 212/253-9727): one-of-a-kind wedding gowns and heirloom dress reconstruction

Jon Green (801 Madison Ave, 4th floor, 212/861-9611): The fit is magnificent.

Leonard Logsdail (9 E 53rd St, 212/752-5030)

Lianna Lee (828 Lexington Ave, 212/588-9289): British power suits

Nino Corvato (420 Madison Ave, 212/980-4980)

Tony Maurizio (509 Madison Ave, Suite 1106, 212/759-3230)

William Fioravanti (45 W 57th St, Suite 402, 212/355-1540)

WINSTON TAILORS
11 E 44th St (bet Fifth Ave and Madison Ave), 5th floor   212/687-0850
By appointment

Paul Winston oversees the tailors at this family-owned business. The shop, also known as **Chipp 2**, was started by Paul's father. Known for highly coveted custom casual wear, Winston Tailors offers an array of brightly colored and unusual fabrics, including *tussah* silk. Another staple is conservative-appearing rep ties that, upon closer viewing, turn out to have lewd messages or images. Winston recalls that his father measured the likes of John F. and Robert Kennedy.

Attention dog owners and dog lovers! Here's a fun way to see parts of the city with your four-legged friend. **New York Dog Tours** (917/292-0680, www.doggietours.com) offers tours of Central Park, midtown Manhattan, and downtown Manhattan. Tours are designed around historical landmarks, famous sights, and intriguing pet shops—all dog-friendly. The two-hour trek includes doggie treats, entertaining and informative narratives for the human, and a stop for people-pleasing hot dogs. Call Zerve (212/209-3370) to purchase tickets which cost $30 per person and dog. These folks also operate the delicious New York Chocolate Tours.

Translation Services

THE LANGUAGE LAB
211 E 43rd St (bet Second and Third Ave), Suite 505   212/697-2020
www.thelanguagelab.com

The Language Lab is a total language solution, providing a full complement of linguistic services in over 75 languages and dialects. Services include cultural consultation, translation, desktop publishing, interpretation, website and software localization, audio and video production, and transcription.

Travel Services

PASSPORT PLUS.NET
20 E 49th St (bet Fifth and Madison Ave), 3rd floor
Mon-Fri: 9:30-5   212/759-5540, 800/367-1818
www.passportplus.net

Getting a passport and the proper visas can be a real pain in the neck. Passport Plus.Net takes care of these chores by securing business and tourist travel documents; renewing and amending U.S. passports; obtaining duplicate birth, death, and marriage certificates; and obtaining international driver's licenses. They work closely with the U.S. Passport Agency and foreign consulates and embassies. Passport Plus.Net offers assistance in case of lost or stolen passports. These folks serve customers all over the country.

Uniform and Costume Rental

I. BUSS-ALLAN UNIFORM RENTAL SERVICE
121 E 24th St (bet Lexington and Park Ave), 7th floor   212/529-4655
Mon-Fri: 9-5   www.ibuss-allan.com

Because most costumes are used only once, it is far less expensive to rent than buy. At this establishment you can rent any number of costumes: doormen, police and security, firemen, maintenance, chefs, concierges, and others. They also provide uniform rentals and sell work apparel.

Wedding Services

WEDDING CAFÉ NEW YORK
16 E 38th St (bet Fifth and Madison Ave)   212/213-2616
Mon-Fri: 10-8:30; Sat: 10-4:30   www.weddingcafeny.com

The concept at Wedding Café is to provide a place where prospective brides can meet with vendors to discuss wedding details. They offer a wedding library, a variety of wedding products, bridal shower hostings, and networking with other brides. These folks are not salespeople. A membership fee gains access to their services.

Several companies offer online discounts on airfare, car rental, and hotels. You can also call to find great deals in locations around the world.

Expedia (800/397-3342, www.expedia.com)
Hotels.com (800/246-8357, www.hotels.com)
Hotwire (866/468-9473, www.hotwire.com)
Orbitz (888/656-4546), www.orbitz.com)
Priceline (800/658-1496, www.priceline.com)
Quickbook (800/789-9887, www.quickbook.com)
Travelocity (888/872-8356, www.travelocity.com)

The best rates for Manhattan hotel rooms can often be obtained at www.nycgo.com (click on "Hotels"). Remember that prices change from day to day and even hour to hour.

If you wish to use a travel agency for assistance with complicated bookings, group tours, or emergencies, here are some established choices:

AAA Travel (1881 Broadway, 212/586-1723): AAA membership is not required to use their travel agency services.
American Express Travel (822 Lexington Ave, 212/758-6510): several Manhattan locations; provides emergency AmEx card replacements
Liberty Travel (120 Fulton St, 212/349-5610): locations around Manhattan and nearby communities

VI. Where to Buy It: New York's Best Stores

Shoppers have found their Nirvana in Manhattan! There truly is something for everyone to buy—no matter what their taste or budget. Art, clothes, shoes, electronics, jewelry, gadgets, toys—it's all in New York. Many items are only available here, while certain other items are introduced here to expectant cosmopolitan audiences who are eager to be trendsetters.

Times have changed for New York retailers. Department store sales are more frequent, discounts are deeper, and at least in the case of Henri Bendel, the clothing departments are only a memory. Boutiques are adapting to the economy and changing their product mix. This means that consumers, with a little work and planning, can get great deals. Be wary, though, of the perpetual "going out of business" sales, and if you do shop at a bona fide liquidation sale, scrutinize your purchase before buying, as you'll have no recourse afterward if you're unhappy with it.

Investigate different shopping venues—you'll see familiar brands in a variety of places, and prices are sure to vary. Check out resale shops, flea markets, and boutiques—you're sure to relish the compliments you get back home when you tell folks, "I bought it in New York!"

The Best Places to Shop for Specific Items in New York: An Exclusive List

Things for the Person (Men, Women, Children)

Accessories, fashion (vintage and contemporary): **Eye Candy** (329 Lafayette St, 212/343-4275)

Accessories, men's and women's: **Marc Jacobs Accessories** (385 Bleecker St, 212/924-6126)

Backpacks: **Bag House** (797 Broadway, 212/260-0940)

Boots, comfort and fashion: **Lord John's Bootery** (428 Third Ave, 212/532-2579)

Bridal wear (great assortment): **Kleinfeld** (110 W 20th St, 646/633-4300)

Briefcases: **Per Tutti** (49 Greenwich Ave, 212/675-0113)

Clothing and accessories, men's and women's: **Etro** (720 Madison Ave, 212/317-9096)

Clothing, children's (basics): **Lester's** (1534 Second Ave, 212/734-9292)

Clothing, children's classic: **flora and henri** (1023 Lexington Ave, 212/249-1695)

Clothing, children's French: **Catimini** (1125 Madison Ave, 212/987-0688) and **Jacadi** (1242 Madison Ave, 212/369-1616)

Clothing, children's (funky and fun): **Space Kiddets** (26 E 22nd St, 212/420-9878)

Clothing, children's party dresses and suits: **Prince and Princess** (41 E 78th St, 212/879-8989)

Clothing, denim: **G-Star** (270 Lafayette St, 212/219-2744) and **Lucky Brand Retail Store** (1151 Third Ave, 646/422-1192)

Clothing, denim, vintage: **What Comes Around Goes Around** (351 West Broadway, 212/343-9303)

Clothing, designer (resale): **Ina** (101 Thompson St, 212/941-4757)

Clothing, designer (samples): **Showroom Seven** (263 Eleventh Ave, 212/643-4810; Feb, May, Sept, and Dec)

Clothing, hip-hop: **Mr. Joe** (500 Eighth Ave, 212/279-1090)

Clothing, imported designer: **India Cottage Emporium** (221 W 37th St, basement, 212/685-6943)

Clothing, Japanese (high-end): **Uniqlo** (546 Broadway, 917/237-8800)

Clothing, men's and boys' traditional: **Jay Kos** (475 Park Ave, 212/319-2770)

Clothing, men's and women's cashmere sweaters: **Best of Scotland** (581 Fifth Ave, 212/644-0415)

Clothing, men's and women's couture: **Juicy Couture** (368 Bleecker St, 646/336-8151)

Clothing, men's and women's custom-made (good value): **Saint Laurie Merchant Tailors** (22 W 32nd St, 5th floor, 212/643-1916)

Clothing, men's and women's rain gear: **Paul & Shark** (772 Madison Ave, 212/452-9868)

Clothing, men's and women's vintage: **Reminiscence** (50 W 23rd St, 212/243-2292), **Resurrection Vintage Clothing** (217 Mott St, 212/625-1374), and **The Cube** (104 E 7th St, 212/674-7649)

Clothing, men's boutique: **Odin** (328 E 11th St, 212/475-0666)

Clothing, men's brand-name (discounted): **Century 21** (22 Cortlandt St, 212/227-9092) and **L.S. Men's Clothing** (49 W 45th St, 3rd floor, 212/575-0933)

Clothing, men's casual: **Save Khaki** (327 Lafayette St, 212/925-0134)

Clothing, men's classic: **Peter Elliot** (1070 Madison Ave, 212/570-2300)

Clothing, men's custom-made: **Alan Flusser** (3 E 48th St, 212/888-4500) and **Bhambi's Custom Tailors** (14 E 60th St, Suite 610, 212/935-5379)

Clothing, men's European suits: **Jodamo International** (321 Grand St, 212/219-0552)

Clothing, men's shirts, custom-made: **Arthur Gluck Shirtmaker** (224 W 35th St, 212/755-8165)

Clothing, men's shirts and suits, custom-made: **Ascot Chang** (110 Central Park S, 212/759-3333)

Clothing, men's vintage: **Stock** (143 E 13th St, 212/505-2505)

Clothing, outdoor wear: **Eastern Mountain Sports** (530 Broadway, 212/966-8730)

Clothing, sportswear, brand-name: **Atrium** (644 Broadway, 212/473-9200)

Clothing, T-shirts: **Eisner Bros.** (75 Essex St, 212/475-6868) and **Odin New York** (199 Lafayette St, 212/966-0026)

Clothing, "tween" girls': **Space Kiddets** (26 E 22nd St, 212/420-9878)

Clothing, unusual and custom: **Gallery of Wearable Art** (437 W 24th St, 212/425-5379; by appointment)

Clothing, women's: **TG-170** (170 Ludlow St, 212/995-8660)

Clothing, women's all-occasion dresses: **Mint Julep** (173 Ludlow St, 212/533-9904)

Clothing, women's bridal and evening wear: **Blue** (248 Mott St, 212/228-7744), **Mary Adams** (313 E 32nd St, 9th floor, 212/473-0237; by appointment), and **Reem Acra** (14 E 60th St, 212/308-8760)

Clothing, women's bridal and evening wear (made-to-order): **Jane Wilson-Marquis** (42 E 76th St, 212/452-5335; by appointment)

Clothing, women's classic designer (superior): **Yigal Azrouël** (408 W 14th St, 212/929-7525)

Clothing, women's designer (resale): **New & Almost New** (166 Elizabeth St, 212/226-6677)

Clothing, women's imported: **Roberta Freymann** (155 E 70th St, 212/585-3767)

Clothing, women's maternity (consignment): **Clementine** (39½ Washington Square S, 212/228-9333)

Clothing, women's pants: **Theory** (230 Columbus Ave, 212/362-3676)

Clothing, women's sportswear (good prices): **Giselle** (143 Orchard St, 212/673-1900)

Clothing, women's tights: **Club Monaco** (121 Prince St, 212/533-8930)

Clothing, women's vintage: **Fox & Fawn** (112 Suffolk St, 212/375-1172)

Clothing and accessories, women's: **Design in Textiles by Mary Jaeger** (17 Laight St, Suite 21, 212/625-0081)

Cuff links: **Links of London** (402 West Broadway, 212/343-8024; 535 Madison Ave, 212/588-1177; and 200 Park Ave, 212/867-0258) and **Missing Link** (Showplace Antiques Center, 40 W 25th St, Room 108, 212/645-6928)

Cuff links, vintage: **Deco Jewels** (131 Thompson St, 212/253-1222)

Eyewear (discounted): **Quality Optical** (169 E 92nd St, 212/289-2020)

Eyewear (elegant): **Morgenthal-Frederics Opticians** (944 Madison Ave, 212/744-9444; 399 West Broadway, 212/966-0099; and 699 Madison Ave, 212/838-3090), **Oliver Peoples** (755 Madison Ave, 212/585-3433), and **Vision Fashion Eyewear** (2 W 47th St, 212/421-3750)

Furs, fashion (best): **G. Michael Hennessy Furs** (345 Seventh Ave, 3rd floor, 212/695-7991)

Gloves, cashmere knit: **Meg Cohen Design Shop** (59 Thompson St, 917/805-0189)

Gloves, custom and ready-made: **La Crasia Gloves** (1181 Broadway, 8th floor, 212/803-1600; by appointment)

Gloves, Italian: **Sermoneta Gloves** (609-611 Madison Ave, 212/319-5946)

Handbags (magnificent and very expensive): **Judith Leiber** (680 Madison Ave, 212/223-2999)

Handbags, antique: **Sylvia Pines Uniquities** (1102 Lexington Ave, 212/744-5141)

Handbags, large: **Club Monaco** (160 Fifth Ave, 212/352-0936)

Handbags, men's and women's: **Longchamp** (132 Spring St, 212/343-7444)

Handbags, vintage: **Chelsea Girl Couture** (186 Spring St, 212/343-7090)

Hats: **Dae Sung** (65 W 8th St, 212/420-9745)

Hats, custom-made fur: **Lenore Marshall** (231 W 29th St, 212/947-5945)

Hats, high-end: **Eugenia Kim** (347 W 36th St, 212/674-1345; by appointment)

Hats, men's: **Arnold Hatters** (535 Eighth Ave, 212/768-3781), **Hat Corner** (145 Nassau St, 212/964-5693), **J.J. Hat Center** (310 Fifth Ave, 212/239-4368), and **Rod Keenan** (155 W 121st St, 212/678-9275)

Hats, men's (discounted): **Makin's Hats** (212 W 35th St, 212/594-6666)

Jeans (discounted): **O.M.G. Inc.** (428 Broadway, 212/925-5190)

Jeans (one-of-a-kind): **Jean Shop** (435 W 14th St, 212/366-5326)

Jeans, men's and women's (good-quality Dutch): **G-Star** (270 Lafayette St, 212/219-2744)

Jewelry, charms (baby shoe): **Aaron Basha** (680 Madison Ave, 212/935-1960)

Jewelry, costume and travel: **Lanciani** (992 Madison Ave, 212/717-2759 and 826 Lexington Ave, 212/832-2092) and **Lord & Taylor** (424 Fifth Ave, 212/391-3344)

Jewelry, custom-designed: **Sheri Miller** (205 E 83rd St, 917/836-0422; by appointment)

Jewelry, earrings: **Ted Muehling** (27 Howard St, 212/431-3825)

Jewelry, fine: **Stuart Moore** (128 Prince St, 212/941-1023)

Jewelry, handmade: **EDGE*nyNOHO** (65 Bleecker St, 212/358-0255) and **Ten Thousand Things** (423 W 14th St, 212/352-1333)

Jewelry, necklaces: **Wendy Mink Jewelry** (72 Orchard St, 212/260-5298)

Jewelry, Victorian: **Antique Source** (60 E 42nd St, 212/681-9142; by appointment)

Jewelry, vintage: **Deco Jewels** (131 Thompson St, 212/253-1222) and **Doyle & Doyle** (189 Orchard St, 212/677-9991)

Jewels (rare and historic): **Edith Weber Fine Jewelry** (987 Madison Ave, 212/570-9668 and Carlyle Hotel, 35 E 76th St, 212/470-1033)

Judaica: **Manhattan Judaica** (62 W 45th St, 212/719-1918)

Leather goods: **Dooney & Bourke** (20 E 60th St, 212/223-7444) and **Il Bisonte** (120 Sullivan St, 212/966-8773)

Leather goods, tailored: **The Leather Man** (111 Christopher St, 212/243-5339)

Leather jackets, bomber: **Cockpit USA** (652 Broadway, 212/254-4000)

Leather jackets and wallets, men's and women's: **M0851** (106 Wooster St, 212/431-3069 and 748 Madison Ave, 212/988-1313)

Lingerie (discounted): **Howard Sportswear** (69 Orchard St, 212/226-4307) and **Orchard Corset** (157 Orchard St, 212/674-0786)

Lingerie, fantasy: **Agent Provocateur** (133 Mercer St, 212/965-0229)

Lingerie, fine: **Bra Smyth** (905 Madison Ave, 212/772-9400), **Eres** (621 Madison Ave, 212/223-3550), **Jean Yu** (37 Crosby St, 212/226-0067), and **Peress** (1006 Madison Ave, 212/861-6336)

Lingerie, post-breast surgery: **Underneath It All** (444 E 75th St, 212/717-1976 and 160 E 34th St, 4th floor, 212/779-2517)

Massage oils: **Fragrance Shop** (21 E 7th St, 212/254-8950)

Millinery (one-of-a-kind): **Kelly Christy** (212/965-0686; by appointment)

Millinery (vintage): **Ellen Christine** (255 W 18th St, 212/242-2457),

Prescriptions: **J. Leon Lascoff & Sons** (1209 Lexington Ave, 212/288-9500)

Sandals (handmade): **Jutta Neumann** (158 Allen St, 212/982-7048)

Shaving products: **The Art of Shaving** (141 E 62nd St, 212/317-8436; 373 Madison Ave, 212/986-2905; and other locations)

Shoes (discounted): **DSW** (40 E 14th St, 212/674-2146 and 102 North End Ave, 212/945-7419) and **Stapleton Shoe Company** (68 Trinity Pl, 212/964-6329)

Shoes, adult: **David Z** (556 Broadway, 212/431-5450; 384 Fifth Ave, 917/351-1484; and other locations)

Shoes, athletic: **JackRabbit** (42 W 14th St, 212/727-2980)

Shoes, children's (upscale): **East Side Kids** (1298 Madison Ave, 212/360-5000), **Harry's Shoes for Kids** (2315 Broadway, 212/874-2034), and **Shoofly** (42 Hudson St, 212/406-3270)

Shoes, men's and women's custom-made: **Oberle Custom Shoes/ Mathias Bootmaker** (1502 First Ave, 212/717-4023)

Shoes, men's handmade: **E. Vogel Boots and Shoes** (19 Howard St, 212/925-2460)

Shoes, non-leather: **MooShoes** (78 Orchard St, 212/254-6512)

Shoes, sneakers (limited edition): **Alife Rivington Club** (158 Rivington St, 212/375-8128)

Shoes, walking: **Hogan** (134 Spring St, 212/343-7905)

Shoes, women's (small sizes): **Giordano's Petite Shoes** (1150 Second Ave, 212/688-7195)

Skiwear: **Bogner** (380 West Broadway, 212/219-2757; seasonal)

Soaps: **Fresh** (57 Spring St, 212/925-0099)

Sunglasses, custom and vintage: **Fabulous Fanny's** (335 E 9th St, 212/533-0637)

Swimwear, men's and boys': **Vilebrequin** (1070 Madison Ave, 212/650-0353 and 436 West Broadway, 212/431-0673)

Swimwear, women's: **Canyon Beachwear** (1136 Third Ave, 917/432-0732), **Eres** (621 Madison Ave, 212/223-3550 and 98 Wooster St, 212/431-7300), **Malia Mills Swimwear** (199 Mulberry St, 212/625-2311; 1031 Lexington Ave, 212/517-7485; and 220 Columbus Ave, 212/874-7200), and **Wolford** (619 Madison Ave, 212/688-4850; seasonal)

Ties: **Andrew's Ties** (400 Madison Ave, 212/750-5221) and **Tie Coon** (400 Seventh Ave, 212/904-1433)

Ties, custom-made and limited-edition: **Seigo** (1248 Madison Ave, 212/987-0191)

Umbrellas: **Rain or Shine** (45 E 45th St, 212/741-9650)

Uniforms, medical and housekeeping: **Ja-Mil Uniforms** (92 Orchard St, 212/677-8190)

Watchbands: **Central Watch Band Stand** (Grand Central Terminal, 45th St passageway, 212/685-1689) and **George Paul Jewelers** (1050 Second Ave, Gallery 29, 212/838-7660)

Watches: **G. Wrublin Co.** (134 W 25th St, 2nd floor, 212/929-8100), **Movado** (610 Fifth Ave, 212/218-7555), and **Swatch** (640 Broadway, 212/777-1002)

Watches (discounted): **Yaeger Watch** (578 Fifth Ave, 212/819-0088)

Watches, Swiss Army: **Victorinox Swiss Army Soho** (136 Prince St, 212/965-5714)

Wedding rings: **Wedding Ring Originals** (608 Fifth Ave, Suite 509, 212/751-3940)

Wigs: **Theresa Wigs and Eyelashes** (217 E 60th St, 212/486-1693)
Zippers: **Feibusch** (27 Allen St, 212/226-3964)

Things for the Home and Office

Air conditioners: **Elgot Sales** (937 Lexington Ave, 212/879-1200)
Appliances (discounted): **Price Watchers** (800/336-6694)
Appliances (for overseas use): **Appliances & Video Overseas** (246 Eighth Ave, 3rd floor, 212/447-2008; by appointment)
Appliances, kitchen: **Gringer & Sons** (29 First Ave, 212/475-0600) and **Zabar's** (2245 Broadway, 212/787-2000)
Art, American Indian: **Common Ground** (55 W 16th St, 212/989-4178)
Art, ancient Greek, Roman, and Near Eastern: **Royal Athena Galleries** (153 E 57th St, 212/355-2033)
Art, antique Oriental: **Imperial Oriental Art** (790 Madison Ave, 212/717-5383)
Art, erotic: **Erotics Gallery** (41 Union Square W, Suite 1011, 212/633-2241; by appointment)
Art, 19th- and 20th-century Western (and rare books): **J.N. Bartfield Galleries** (30 W 57th St, 212/245-8890)
Art, pre-Columbian: **Lands Beyond** (1218 Lexington Ave, 212/249-6275)
Art, 20th-century dadaist and surrealist: **Timothy Baum** (212/879-4512; by appointment)
Art deco, French: **Maison Gerard** (53 E 10th St, 212/674-7611)
Bakeware (discounted): **Broadway Panhandler** (65 E 8th St, 212/966-3434)
Baking supplies: **New York Cake & Baking Distributors** (56 W 22nd St, 212/675-2253)
Baskets: **Bill's Flower Market** (816 Ave of the Americas, 212/889-8154)
Baskets, fruit (custom-made): **Macres** (30 E 30th St, 212/246-1600) and **Manhattan Fruitier** (105 E 29th St, 212/686-0404)
Bath and bed items: **Bed Bath & Beyond** (620 Ave of the Americas, 212/255-3550; 410 E 61st St, 646/215-4702; 1932 Broadway, 917/441-9391; and 270 Greenwich St, 212/233-8450)
Bath fixtures (expensive): **Boffi** (31½ Greene St, 212/431-8282)
Beds (custom headboards and footboards): **Charles P. Rogers Beds** (55 W 17th St, 212/675-4400)
Beds, Murphy: **Murphy Bed Center** (20 W 23rd St, 2nd floor, 212/645-7079)
Boxes, wooden: **An American Craftsman Galleries** (60 W 50th St, 212/307-7161)
Brass hardware and accessories: **The Brass Center** (248 E 58th St, 212/421-0090)
Carpets, antique: **Art Treasury** (1185 Park Ave, 212/722-1235; by appointment)
Chandeliers, vintage Italian: **The Lively Set** (33 Bedford St, 212/807-8417)
China (bargain pieces): **Fishs Eddy** (889 Broadway, 212/420-9020)
China, English Amari: **Bardith** (901 Madison Ave, 212/737-3775)
Christmas decor: **Christmas Cottage** (871 Seventh Ave, 212/333-7380) and **Matt McGhee** (174 Waverly Pl, 212/741-3138)
Christmas decorations (discounted): **Kurt S. Adler's Santa World** (7 W 34th St, 212/924-0900; opens around Thanksgiving for sample sale)
Clocks, cuckoo: **Time Pieces** (115 Greenwich Ave, 212/929-8011)

Cookbooks (used): **Bonnie Slotnick's Cookbooks** (163 W 10th St, 212/989-8962) and **Joanne Hendricks Cookbooks** (488 Greenwich St, 212/226-5731)

Cookware: **Bed Bath & Beyond** (620 Ave of the Americas, 212/255-3550; 410 E 61st St, 646/215-4702; 1932 Broadway, 917/441-9391; and 270 Greenwich St, 212/233-8450)

Decoupaged items: **Kaas Glassworks** (117 Perry St, 212/366-0322)

Dinnerware, Fiesta (individual pieces): **Mood Indigo** (Showplace Antiques and Design Center, Gallery 222, 40 W 25th St, 212/254-1176)

Dinnerware, porcelain: **Bernardaud** (499 Park Ave, 212/371-4300)

Doorknobs: **Simon's Hardware and Bath** (421 Third Ave, 212/532-9220)

Electronics, vintage: **Waves** (Showplace Antiques and Design Center, 40 W 25th St, Galleries 107 and 216, 212/273-9616)

FDNY merchandise: **FDNY Fire Zone** (34 W 51st St, 212/698-4529)

Flags and banners: **Art Flag Co.** (8 Jay St, 212/334-1890)

Floor coverings: **ABC Carpet & Home** (881 Broadway, 212/473-3000)

Floral designs: **Country Gardens** (1160 Lexington Ave, 212/966-2015)

Flower bouquets: **Posies** (366 Amsterdam Ave, 212/721-2260)

Flowers, fresh-cut (from Europe): **VSF** (204 W 10th St, 212/206-7236)

Flowers, orchids: **Judy's Plant World** (1410 Lexington Ave, 212/860-0055)

Flowers, silk: **Pany Silk Flowers** (146 W 28th St, 212/645-9526)

Foliage, live and artificial: **American Foliage & Design** (122 W 22nd St, 212/741-5555)

Food and kitchen equipment (best all-around store): **Zabar's** (2245 Broadway)

Frames, picture: **A.I. Friedman** (44 W 18th St, 212/243-9000) and **Framed on Madison** (976 Lexington Ave, 212/734-4680)

Furniture: **Design Within Reach** (142 Wooster St, 212/471-0280; 408 W 14th St, 212/242-9449; and other locations)

Furniture and mattresses, foam: **Dixie Foam** (113 W 25th St, 212/645-8999)

Furniture, antique: **H.M. Luther Antiques** (35 E 76th St, 212/439-7919 and 61 E 11th St, 212/505-1485)

Furniture, Asian: **Jacques Carcanagues** (21 Greene St, 212/925-8110)

Furniture, children's (high end): **Kids' Supply Company** (1343 Madison Ave, 212/426-1200)

Furniture, children's handmade: **Blue Bench** (979 Third Ave, 212/267-1500)

Furniture, classic hand-carved: **Devon Shops** (111 E 27th St, 212/686-1760)

Furniture, handcrafted (expensive): **Thomas Moser Cabinetmakers** (699 Madison Ave, 2nd floor, 212/753-7005)

Furniture, handcrafted, 18th-century American reproductions: **Barton-Sharpe** (200 Lexington Ave, 646/935-1500)

Furniture, hardwood: **Pompanoosuc** (124 Hudson St, 212/226-5960)

Furniture, home and office: **Knoll** (76 Ninth Ave, 11th floor, 212/343-4000)

Furniture, infants': **Albee Baby** (715 Amsterdam Ave, 212/662-5740) and **Schneider's Juvenile Furniture** (41 W 25th St, 212/228-3540)

Furniture, modern design (pricey): **Cassina USA** (155 E 56th St, 212/245-2121)

Furniture, office (good prices): **Discount Office Furniture** (132 W 24th St, 212/691-5625)

Furniture, rental: **Props for Today** (330 W 34th St, 12th floor, 212/244-9600)

Gadgets: **Brookstone** (18 Fulton St, 212/344-8108 and other locations)

Garden accessories: **Lexington Gardens** (1011 Lexington Ave, 212/861-4390)

Glass, Venetian: **End of History** (548½ Hudson St, 212/647-7598) and **Gardner & Barr** (305 E 61st St, 212/752-0555; by appointment)

Glassware: **67th Street Wines & Spirits** (179 Columbus Ave, 212/724-6767)

Glassware, hand-blown: **Simon Pearce** (500 Park Ave, 212/421-8801)

Glassware, Steuben (used): **Lillian Nassau** (220 E 57th St, 212/759-6062)

Glassware, vintage: **Mood Indigo** (Showplace Antiques and Design Center, 40 W 25th St, 212/254-1176)

Glassware and tableware: **Avventura** (463 Amsterdam Ave, 212/769-2510)

Home accessories: **Carole Stupell** (29 E 22nd St, 212/260-3100)

Home furnishings, Indonesian: **Andrianna Shamaris** (121 Greene St, 212/388-9898)

Housewares: **Dinosaur Designs** (250 Mott St, 212/680-3523) and **Gracious Home** (1201, 1217, and 1220 Third Ave, 212/517-6300; 1992 Broadway, 212/231-7800; and 766 Ave of the Americas, 212/414-5710)

Housewares (upscale): **Lancelotti** (66 Ave A, 212/475-6851)

Ice buckets (vintage): **Mood Indigo** (Showplace Antiques, 40 W 25th St, 212/254-1176)

Kitchen gadgets: **Bed Bath & Beyond** (620 Ave of the Americas, 212/255-3550; 410 E 61st St, 646/215-4702; 1932 Broadway, 917/441-9391; and 270 Greenwich St, 212/233-8450) and **Zabar's** (2245 Broadway, 212/787-2000)

Kitchenware, professional: **Hung Chong Imports** (14 Bowery St, 212/349-3392) and **J.B. Prince** (36 E 31st St, 11th floor, 212/683-3553)

Knives: **Roger & Sons** (268 Bowery, 212/226-4734)

Lampshades: **Just Shades** (21 Spring St, 212/966-2757) and **Oriental Lampshade Co.** (223 W 79th St, 212/873-0812 and 816 Lexington Ave, 212/832-8190)

Lightbulbs: **Just Bulbs** (220 E 60th St, 212/228-7820)

Lighting, custom-made and antique: **Lampworks** (231 E 58th St, 212/750-1500)

Lighting fixtures: **City Knickerbocker** (665 Eleventh Ave, 212/586-3939) and **Lighting by Gregory** (158 Bowery, 212/226-1276)

Lighting fixtures, antique: **Olde Good Things** (124 W 24th St and 5 E 16th St, 212/989-8401)

Lighting, photographic (purchase or rental): **Flash Clinic** (164 W 25th St, 212/337-0447)

Linens: **Bed Bath & Beyond** (620 Ave of the Americas, 212/255-3550; 410 E 61st St, 646/215-4702; 1932 Broadway, 917/441-9391; and 270 Greenwich St, 212/233-8450) and **Harris Levy** (98 Forsyth St, 212/226-3102)

Linens, vintage: **Geminola** (41 Perry St, 212/675-1994)

Linoleum, vintage: **Secondhand Rose** (138 Duane St, 212/393-9002)

Locks: **Lacka Lock and Safe** (315 W 49th St, 212/391-5625)

Mattresses (good value): **Town Bedding & Upholstery** (203 Eighth Ave, 212/243-0426)

Office supplies, Muji: **MoMA Design Store** (44 W 53rd St, 212/767-1050) and **MoMA Design Store Soho** (81 Spring St, 646/613-1367)

Perfume bottles (vintage): **Gallery 47** (1050 Second Ave, 212/888-0165)

Photographs (film stars): **Movie Star News** (134 W 18th St, 212/620-8160)

Plumbing fixtures: **Blackman** (85 Fifth Ave, 2nd floor, 212/337-1000)

Portfolios, custom: **House of Portfolios** (48 W 21st St, 6th floor, 212/206-7323)

Posters, American and international movie: **Jerry Ohlinger's Movie Materials Store** (253 W 35th St, 212/989-0869)

Posters, Broadway theater: **Triton Gallery** (630 Ninth Ave, 212/765-2472)

Posters, original (1880 to present): **Philip Williams** (122 Chambers St, 212/513-0313)

Posters, vintage: **La Belle Epoque Vintage Posters** (280 Columbus Ave, 212/362-1770) and **Ross Vintage Poster Gallery** (532 Madison Ave, 4th floor, 212/223-1525)

Pottery, handmade: **Muji Studio and Gallery** (993 Amsterdam Ave, 212/866-6202)

Pottery, paint-your-own: **Make** (1566 Second Ave, 212/570-6868 and other locations)

Prints: **Charmingwall** (191 W 4th St, 212/206-8235)

Prints, botanical: **W. Graham Arader** (29 E 72nd St, 212/628-3668 and 1016 Madison Ave, 212/628-7625)

Quilts: **Down and Quilt Shop** (518 Columbus Ave, 212/496-8980)

Rugs, antique: **Doris Leslie Blau** (306 E 61st St, 212/586-5511; by appointment)

Safes: **Empire Safe** (6 E 39th St, 212/684-2255)

Screens, shoji: **Miya Shoji** (109 W 17th St, 212/243-6774)

Shelves: **Shelf Shop** (1295 First Ave, 212/988-7246)

Silver items (unusual): **Jean's Silversmiths** (16 W 45th St, 212/575-0723)

Silverware and holloware (good values): **Eastern Silver** (4901 16th Ave, Brooklyn, 718/854-5600)

Sofa beds: **Avery-Boardman** (979 Third Ave, 4th floor, 212/688-6611)

Sofas: **Classic Sofa** (5 W 22nd St, 212/620-0485)

Sofas, vintage: **Regeneration Furniture** (38 Renwick St, 212/741-2102)

Strollers and other baby equipment: **Schneider's Juvenile Furniture** (41 W 25th St, 212/228-3540)

Tabletop: **Clio** (92 Thompson St, 212/966-8991) and **Carole Stupell** (29 E 22nd St, 212/260-3100)

Teaware: **Ito En** (822 Madison Ave, 212/988-7111)

Tiles: **Mosaic House** (32 W 22nd St, 212/414-2525)

Tiles, ceramic and marble: **Complete Tile Collection** (42 W 15th St, 212/255-4450) and **Quarry Tiles, Marble & Granite** (132 Lexington Ave, 212/679-8889)

Trays: **Extraordinary** (247 E 57th St, 212/223-9151)

Typewriter ribbons: **Abalon Business Machines** (60 E 42nd St, 212/682-1653)

Vacuum cleaners: **Desco** (131 W 14th St, 212/989-1800)

Wallpaper (discounted): **Janovic Plaza** (136 Church St, 212/349-0001 and other locations)

Wallpaper, vintage: **Secondhand Rose** (138 Duane St, 212/393-9002)

Wrought-iron items: **Morgik Metal Design** (145 Hudson St, 212/463-0304)

Things for Leisure Time

Accordions: **Main Squeeze** (19 Essex St, 212/614-3109)

Art supplies: **Pearl Paint Company** (308 Canal St, 212/431-7932)

Athletic gear: **Modell's** (55 Chambers St, 212/732-8484 and other locations)

Athletic gear, team: **New York Mets Clubhouse** (11 W 42nd St, 212/768-9534) and **Yankee Clubhouse** (110 E 59th St, 212/758-7844; 393 Fifth Ave, 212/685-4693; 245 W 42nd St, 212/768-9555; and 8 Fulton St, 212/514-7182)

Balloons: **Balloon Saloon** (133 West Broadway, 212/227-3838)

Beads: **Beads of Paradise** (16 E 17th St, 212/620-0642) and **Beads World** (1384 Broadway, 212/302-1199)

Bicycles: **Bicycle Habitat** (244 Lafayette St, 212/625-1347)

Bicycles, track: **Trackstar** (231 Eldridge St, 212/982-2553)

Binoculars: **Clairmont-Nichols** (1016 First Ave, 212/758-2346)

Books (new, used, and review copies): **Strand Book Store** (828 Broadway, 212/473-1452)

Books (rare): **Imperial Fine Books** (790 Madison Ave, 2nd floor, 212/861-6620), **J.N. Bartfield Galleries** (30 W 57th St, 212/245-8890), **Martayan Lan** (70 E 55th St, 212/308-0018), and **Strand Book Store** (828 Broadway, 212/473-1452)

Books, academic: **Book Culture** (536 W 112th St, 212/865-1588)

Books, African and African-American: **Jumel Terrace Books** (426 W 160th St, 212/928-9525; by appointment)

Books, children's and parents': **Bank Street Bookstore** (2879 Broadway, 212/678-1654)

Books, comic: **Forbidden Planet** (840 Broadway, 212/473-1576)

Books, comic (vintage): **Metropolis Collectibles** (873 Broadway, Suite 201, 212/260-4147; by appointment)

Books, exam-study and science-fiction: **Civil Service Book Shop** (89 Worth St, 212/226-9506)

Books, fashion design: **Fashion Design Bookstore** (250 W 27th St, 212/633-9646)

Books, metaphysical and religious: **Quest Bookshop** (240 E 53rd St, 212/758-5521)

Books, mystery: **Partners & Crime** (44 Greenwich Ave, 212/243-0440)

Books, plates (lithographs): **George Glazer Gallery** (28 E 72nd St, Room 3A, 212/327-2598)

Books, progressive political: **Revolution Books** (146 W 26th St, 212/691-3345)

Books, publications by artists: **Printed Matter** (195 Tenth Ave, 212/925-0325)

Camping and outdoor equipment: **Tent & Trails** (21 Park Pl, 212/227-1760)

Chess sets: **Chess Forum** (219 Thompson St, 212/475-2369)

Cigarettes (luxury): **Nat Sherman International** (12 E 42nd St, 212/764-5000)

Cigars: **Davidoff of Geneva** (535 Madison Ave, 212/751-9060), **DP Cigars** (265 W 30th St, 212/367-8949), and **Midtown Cigars** (562 Fifth Ave, 212/997-2227)

Compact discs, records, tapes, and DVDs: **Disc-O-Rama** (44 W 8th St, 212/477-9410) and **St. Mark's Sounds** (20 St. Mark's Pl, 212/677-3444)

Computer software: **J&R Music & Computer World** (23 Park Row, 212/238-9000)

Computers: **RCS Computer Experience** (575 Madison Ave, 212/949-6935)

Computers, Apple: **The Apple Store** (103 Prince St, 212/226-3126; 767 Fifth Ave, 212/336-1440; and 401 West 14th St, 212/444-3400)

Costumes and makeup: **Halloween Adventure** (104 Fourth Ave, 212/673-4546)

Dance items: **World Tone Dance** (230 Seventh Ave, 2nd floor, 212/691-1934)

Dollhouses: **Tiny Doll House** (314 E 78th St, 212/744-3719)

Dolls: **Alexander Doll Company** (615 W 131st St, 212/283-5900)

Drums: **Drummer's World** (151 W 46th St, 3rd floor, 212/840-3057)

Embroidery (custom-designed): **Jonathan Embroidery Plus** (256 W 38th St, 212/398-3538)

Fabrics, decorator (discounted): **Harry Zarin** (314 Grand St, 212/925-6112)

Fabrics, decorator and upholstery: **Beckenstein Fabrics and Interiors** (5 W 20th St, 212/366-5142)

Fabrics, designer (discounted): **B&J Fabrics** (525 Seventh Ave, 212/354-8150)

Fabrics, men's: **Beckenstein Men's Fabrics** (257 W 39th St, 212/475-6666)

Fabrics and patterns: **P&S Fabrics and Crafts** (360 Broadway, 212/226-1534)

Filofax (discounted): **Altman Luggage** (135 Orchard St, 212/254-7275)

Firefighting memorabilia: **Firestore** (17 Greenwich Ave, 212/226-3142)

Fishing tackle, fly: **Orvis** (522 Fifth Ave, 212/827-0698)

Games: **Compleat Strategist** (11 E 33rd St, 212/685-3880)

Games (*Warhammer*): **Games Workshop** (54 E 8th St, 212/982-6314)

Gifts: **Mxyplyzyk** (125 Greenwich Ave, 212/989-4300)

Gifts (pop-culture curiosities): **Exit 9** (64 Ave A, 212/228-0145)

Globes, antique (world and celestial): **George Glazer Gallery** (28 E 72nd St, Room 3A, 212/327-2598)

Golf equipment (best selection): **New York Golf Center** (131 W 35th St, 212/564-2255)

Guitars: **Carmine Street Guitars** (42 Carmine St, 212/691-8400), **Dan's Chelsea Guitars** (220 W 23rd St, 212/675-4993), **Guitar Salon** (45 Grove St, Room 1C, 212/675-3236; by appointment), **Ludlow Guitars** (164 Ludlow St, 212/353-1775), and **Matt Umanov Guitars** (273 Bleecker St, 212/675-2157)

Guns: **Beretta Gallery** (718 Madison Ave, 212/319-3235) and **Holland & Holland** (10 E 40th St, 19th floor, 212/752-7755)

Harley-Davidson gear: **Harley-Davidson of New York** (686 Lexington Ave, 212/355-3003)

Holographs: **Holographic Studio** (240 E 26th St, 212/686-9397)

Home-entertainment equipment and systems: **J&R Music & Computer World** (31 Park Row, 212/238-9000)

Horseback-riding equipment: **Manhattan Saddlery** (117 E 24th St, 212/673-1400)

Knitting: **Gotta Knit** (14 E 34th St, 5th floor, 212/989-3030), **Yarn Company** (2274 Broadway, 212/787-7878), and **String** (130 E 82nd St, 212/288-9276)

Luggage and accessories: **Bag House** (797 Broadway, 212/260-0940) and **Flight 001** (96 Greenwich Ave, 212/989-0001)

Magazines: **Eastern Newsstand** (many locations) and **Universal News** (977 Eighth Ave, 212/459-0932 and 676 Lexington Ave, 212/750-1855)

Magic tricks: **Tannen's Magic** (45 W 34th St, 212/929-4500)

Maps: **Hagstrom Map and Travel Center** (51 W 43rd St, 212/398-1222)

Maps and prints (antiquarian): **Argosy Book Store** (116 E 59th St, 212/753-4455)

Maps, globes, and atlases (antique): **Martayan Lan** (70 E 55th St, 212/308-0018) and **Richard B. Arkway** (59 E 54th St, 6th floor, 212/751-8135)

Marine supplies: **West Marine** (12 W 37th St, 212/594-6065)

Musical instruments: **Music Inn World Instruments** (169 W 4th St, 212/243-5715), **Roberto's Winds** (149 W 46th St, 212/391-1315), **Rogue Music** (220 W 30th St, 212/629-5073), **Sam Ash Music Store** (160 W 48th St, 212/719-2299), and **Universal Musical Instrument Co.** (732 Broadway, 212/254-6917)

New York memorabilia: **Museum of the City of New York** (1220 Fifth Ave, 212/534-1170)

Novelties: **Gordon Novelty** (52 W 29th St, 212/696-9664)

Paper items (huge selection): **PaperPresentation.com** (23 W 18th St, 212/463-7035) and **Papyrus** (852 Lexington Ave, 212/717-0002 and other locations)

Papers (elegant): **Il Papiro** (1021 Lexington Ave, 212/288-9330)

Pens, antique and new: **Arthur Brown & Brothers** (2 W 46th St, 212/575-5555)

Pet boutique, for puppies and babies: **Raising Rover & Baby** (1428 Lexington Ave, 212/987-7683)

Pet supplies (discounted): **Petland Discounts** (312 W 23rd St, 212/366-0512 and other locations)

Pet supplies (holistic): **Spoiled Brats** (340 W 49th St, 212/459-1615)

Pets, dogs and cats: **Pets-on-Lex** (1109 Lexington Ave, 212/426-0766)

Pets, tropical fish: **New World Aquarium** (204 E 38th St, 646/865-9604)

Photo processing and frames: **Ben Ness Photo** (111 University Pl, 212/253-2313)

Photographic equipment (rental and sales): **Calumet Photographic** (22 W 22nd St, 212/989-8500)

Pool tables: **Blatt Billiards** (809 Broadway, 212/674-8855)

Quilting supplies: **City Quilter** (133 W 25th St, 212/807-0390)

Records, rare: **House of Oldies** (35 Carmine St, 212/243-0500)

Records, vintage rock and roll: **Strider Records** (22 Jones St, 212/675-3040)

Scuba-diving and snorkeling equipment: **Pan Aqua Diving** (460 W 43rd St, 212/736-3483) and **Scuba Network** (669 Lexington Ave, 212/750-9160 and 655 Ave of the Americas, 212/243-2988)

Sewing and crafts, buttons: **Tender Buttons** (143 E 62nd St, 212/758-7004)

Sewing and crafts, ribbons: **So-Good** (28 W 38th St, 212/398-0236)

Skateboards: **Supreme** (274 Lafayette St, 212/966-7799)

Skating equipment: **Blades Board & Skate** (156 W 72nd St, 212/787-3911 and 659 Broadway, 212/477-7350)

Snowboards: **Burton Snowboard Company** (106 Spring St, 212/966-8068)

Soccer supplies: **Soccer Sport Supply** (1745 First Ave, 212/427-6050)

Sports cards: **Alex's MVP Cards** (256 E 89th St, 212/831-2273)

Stationery: **Arthur's Invitations** (13 E 13th St, 212/807-6502), **Jam Paper** (135 Third Ave, 212/473-6666 and 516 Fifth Ave, 212/255-4593), **Kate's Paperie** (72 Spring St, 212/941-9816; 1282 Third Ave, 212/396-3670; 8 W 13th St, 212/633-0570; and 140 W 57th St, 212/459-0700), and **Papyrus** (852 Lexington Ave, 212/717-0002 and other locations)

Theatrical items: **One Shubert Alley** (1 Shubert Alley, 212/944-4133)

Toys (good selection): **Kidding Around** (60 W 15th St, 212/645-6337)

Toys, imported Japanese: **Image Anime** (242 W 30th St, 212/631-0966)

Toys, novelties and party supplies: **E.A.T. Gifts** (1062 Madison Ave, 212/861-2544)

Toys, vintage: **Alphaville** (226 W Houston St, 212/675-6850)

Toys, young adult: **Kidrobot** (118 Prince St, 212/966-6688)

Videogames: **GameStop** (687 Broadway, 212/473-6571 and other locations)

Videos, DVDs, CDs, rare and foreign: **Mondo Kim's** (124 First Ave, 212/533-7390)

Things from Far Away

African bowls: **Amaridian** (31 Howard St, 917/463-3719)

British clothing and shoes: **99X** (84 E 10th St, 212/460-8599)

Buddhas: **Leekan Designs** (4 Rivington St, 212/226-7226)

Chinese dinnerware: **Wing On Wo & Co.** (26 Mott St, 212/962-3577)

Chinese goods: **Chinese American Trading Company** (91 Mulberry St, 212/267-5224) and **Pearl River Emporium** (477 Broadway, 212/431-4770)

European pottery (Italian and French): **La Terrine** (1024 Lexington Ave, 212/988-3366)

Himalayan imports: **Himalayan Crafts** (2007 Broadway, 212/787-8500)

Indian imports: **Bharatiya Dress Shoppe** (83 Second Ave, 212/228-1463)

Italian shoes (exotic skins): **Cellini Uomo** (59 Orchard St, 212/219-8657)

Japanese gift items: **Katagiri** (224 E 59th St, 212/755-3566)

Mexican imports: **La Sirena** (27 E 3rd St, 212/780-9113) and **Pan American Phoenix** (857 Lexington Ave, 212/570-0300)

Scandinavian imports: **Antik** (104 Franklin St, 212/343-0471), **Clearly First** (980 Madison Ave, 212/988-8242), and **Just Scandinavian** (161 Hudson St, 212/334-2556)

Tibetan handicrafts: **Do Kham** (51 Prince St, 212/966-2404), **Tibet Bazaar** (473 Amsterdam Ave, 212/595-8487), and **Vajra** (146 Sullivan St, 212/529-4344)

Ukrainian newspapers, books, CDs, and tapes: **Surma: The Ukrainian Shop** (11 E 7th St, 212/477-0729)

Factory Outlet Centers in the Tri-State Region and Pennsylvania

Merchandise at these outlet centers is generally discounted 25% to 65% from retail prices, and special events and coupon books afford even deeper savings.

Connecticut

Clinton Crossing Premium Outlets (20 Killingworth Turnpike, Clinton; 860/664-0700, www.premiumoutlets.com): 70 upscale outlet stores

New Jersey

Harmon Cove Outlet Center (20 Enterprise Ave N, Secaucus; 201/348-4780, www.harmonmeadow.com): 150 stores, well-known names

Jackson Premium Outlets (537 Monmouth Rd, Jackson; 732/833-0503, www.premiumoutlets.com): 70 stores, top retailers

Jersey Gardens (651 Kapkowski Rd, Elizabeth; 908/354-5900, www.jerseygardens.com): over 200 stores, New Jersey's largest

Jersey Shores Premium Outlets (1 Premium Outlets Blvd, Tinton Falls; 732-918-1700, www.premiumoutlets.com): 100 stores, designer clothes and shoes

Liberty Village Premium Outlets (1 Church St, Flemington; 908/782-8550, www.premiumoutlets.com): over 60 outlets, family shopping

Marketplace Mall (Route 34, Matawan; 732-583-8700): 30 outlet and discount stores

Olde Lafayette Village (75 Route 15, Lafayette; 973/383-8323, www.lafayettevillageshops.com): 6 outlets, plus antique stores, specialty shops, eateries

New York

Tanger Outlet (152 The Arches Circle, Deer Park; 631/242-0239, www.tangeroutlet.com): over 75 shops and services

Tanger Outlet Center I & II (1770 W Main St, Riverhead; 631/369-2732, www.tangeroutlet.com): 165 shopping choices

Woodbury Common Premium Outlets (498 Red Apple Court, Central Valley; 845/928-4000, www.premiumoutlets.com): 220 upscale outlet stores

Pennsylvania

The Crossings Premium Outlets (1000 Route 611, Tannersville; 570/629-4650, www.premiumoutlets.com): over 100 stores

Franklin Mills (1455 Franklin Mills Circle, Philadelphia; 215/632-1500): nearly 200 manufacturers' and retail outlet stores

Luxury Labels

A La Vielle Russie (781 Fifth Ave, 212/752-1727): antiques

A. Testoni (781 Fifth Ave, 212/223-0909): luxury leather goods

Abercrombie & Fitch (720 Fifth Ave, 212/306-0936 and 199 Water St, 212/809-0789): preppy men's and women's clothing and accessories

Alfred Dunhill (545 Madison Ave, 212/753-9292): men's fashions and accessories

Ann Taylor (645 Madison Ave, 212/832-2010 and other locations): women's clothing and accessories

Asprey (853 Madison Ave, 212/688-1811): British luxury jewelry, leather, silver, home collection

Baccarat (625 Madison Ave, 212/826-4100): crystal

Bang & Olufsen (927 Broadway, 212/388-9792; 330 Columbus Ave, 212/501-0926; and 952 Madison Ave, 212/879-6161): home-entertainment equipment

Bernardaud (499 Park Ave, 212/371-4300): elegant tableware

Bottega Veneta (697 Fifth Ave, 212/371-5511): fashions for men and women

Botticelli (666 Fifth Ave, 212/586-7421; 620 Fifth Ave, 212/582-6313; and 522 Fifth Ave, 212/768-1430): leather goods

Brioni (55 E 52nd St, 212/355-1940 and 57 E 57th St, 212/376-5777): apparel for men and women

Brooks Brothers (1661 Broadway, 503/362-2374 and 346 Madison Ave, 212/682-8800): traditional fashions for men, women, and boys

Bulgari (730 Fifth Ave, 212/315-9000): jewelry, watches

Burberry (131 Spring St, 212/925-9300 and 9 E 57th St, 212/407-7100): plaid everything and more

Calvin Klein (654 Madison Ave, 212/292-9000): fashions for the body and home

Carolina Herrara (954 Madison Ave, 212/249-6552): wedding gowns and fine attire

Cartier (653 Fifth Ave, 212/308-0843): jewelry

Caswell-Massey (518 Lexington Ave, 212/755-2254): extravagances for the body and bath, men's shaving products

Chanel (15 E 57th St, 212/355-5050 and 139 Spring St, 212/334-0055): classic apparel and accessories

Chopard (709 Madison Ave, 212/218-7222): jewelry, watches

Christian Dior (21 E 57th St, 212/931-2950): clothing, accessories

Christofle (680 Madison Ave, 212/308-9390): silver, crystal, porcelain, jewelry

Coach (595 Madison Ave, 212/754-0041): leather goods, shoes

Crate & Barrel (650 Madison Ave, 212/308-0011 and 611 Broadway, 212/780-0004): housewares and furniture

Crouch & Fitzgerald (400 Madison Ave, 212/755-5888): luggage and leather accessories

Daum (694 Madison Ave, 212/355-2060): crystal

Dolce & Gabbana (825 Madison Ave, 212/249-4100): clothing, sunglasses

Donna Karan (819 Madison Ave, 212/861-1001): clothing

Dooney & Bourke (20 E 60th St, 212/223-7444): handbags, accessories

Emanuel Ungaro (792 Madison Ave, 212/249-4090): men's and women's clothing

Emilio Pucci (24 E 64th St, 212/752-4777 and 701 Fifth Ave, 212/230-1135): clothing for women
Ermenegildo Zegna (663 Fifth Ave, 212/421-4488): menswear
Escada (715 Fifth Ave, 212/755-2200): women's fashions
Etro (720 Madison Ave, 212/317-9096): men's and ladies' clothing and accessories
Façonnable (636 Fifth Ave, 212/319-0111): styles for men and women
Fendi (627 Fifth Ave, 212/767-0100): women's and men's fashions
Frette (799 Madison Ave, 212/988-5221): bedding, towels, pajamas
Georg Jensen (687 Madison Ave, 212/759-6457 and 125 Wooster St, 212/343-9000): silver home accessories and gifts, jewelry, sunglasses
Giorgio Armani (760 Madison Ave, 212/988-9191): men's and women's couture
Gucci (725 Fifth Ave, 212/826-2600 and 840 Madison Ave, 212/717-2619): sportswear, leather goods, accessories
Harry Winston (718 Fifth Ave, 212/245-2000): serious jewelry
Hermés (691 Madison Ave, 212/751-3181): scarves, ties, fragrances, leather goods, clothing, jewelry, home goods
Hickey Freeman (666 Fifth Ave, 212/586-6481): menswear
Hugo Boss (132 Greene St, 212/966-0152): European-cut clothing for men and women
Issey Miyake (119 Hudson St, 212/226-0100 and 802 Madison Ave, 212/439-7822): innovative apparel
Jack of Diamonds (1196 Ave of the Americas), 212/869-7272): diamonds, of course
Jil Sander (818 Madison Ave, 212/838-6100 and 30 Howard St, 212/925-2345): ladies' clothing and accessories
Jonathan Adler (47 Greene St, 212/941-8950): pottery and home furnishings
Judith Leiber (680 Madison Ave, 212/223-2999): luxury handbags and accessories
Kiehl's (109 Third Ave, 212/677-3171): skin care, toiletries
Lacoste (608 Fifth Ave, 212/459-2300 and 575 Madison Ave, 212/750-8115): polo shirts, logo gear
Lalique (712 Madison Ave, 212/355-6550): crystal, jewelry, leather goods
Leron (804 Madison Ave, 212/753-6700): linens for the home, lingerie
Lladro U.S.A. (43 W 57th St, 212/838-9356): porcelain figurines
Loro Piana (821 Madison Ave, 212/980-7961): men's and women's clothing
Louis Vuitton (1 E 57th St, 212/758-8877 and 116 Greene St, 212/274-9090): leather goods, fashions, accessories
Malo (814 Madison Ave, 212/396-4721): cashmere items for men, women, and home
Manolo Blahnik (31 W 54th St, 212/582-3007): sexy shoes for women
Michael C. Fina (545 Fifth Ave, 212/557-2500): silver, china, crystal, giftware, jewelry
Michael Kors (974 Madison Ave, 212/452-4685): women's sportswear
Mikimoto (730 Fifth Ave, 212/457-4600): cultured pearl jewelry
Missoni (1009 Madison Ave, 212/517-9339): men's and women's knit items
Montblanc (598 Madison Ave, 212/223-8888 and 120 Greene St, 212/680-1300): writing instruments

Nicole Miller (780 Madison Ave, 212/288-9779): women's clothing, evening gowns

Niketown New York (6 E 57th St, 212/891-6453): athletic wear, gear, and shoes

Oscar de la Renta (772 Madison Ave, 212/288-5810): fashions for men, women, and kids; home luxuries

Peter Elliot (1070 Madison Ave, 212/570-2300): tailored clothing and sportswear for men; women's store across the street

Piaget (730 Fifth Ave, 212/246-5555): luxury watches and snazzy jewelry

Porthault (470 Park Ave, 212/688-1660): luxurious linens, gifts

Prada (575 Broadway, 212/334-8888; 724 Fifth Ave, 212/664-0010; and 841 Madison Ave, 212/327-4200): clothing, shoes, accessories

Pratesi (829 Madison Ave, 212/288-2315): linens, towels, bathrobes

Ralph Lauren (867 Madison Ave, 212/606-2100 and 379 West Broadway, 212/625-1660): fashions and accessories for the family and home

Salvatore Ferragamo (655 Fifth Ave, 212/759-3822): shoes, clothing, handbags

Shanghai Tang (600 Madison Ave, 212/888-0111): Oriental-style family clothing

St. John (665 Fifth Ave, 212/755-5252): women's wear

Steuben (667 Madison Ave, 212/752-1441): fine glassware

Swarovski (625 Madison Ave, 212/308-1710): crystal jewelry, miniatures, figurines

Thomas Pink (520 Madison Ave, 212/838-1928 and 1155 Ave of the Americas, 212/840-9663): shirts and accessories

Tiffany & Co. (727 Fifth Ave, 212/755-8000): luxurious jewelry and gifts

Tourneau (12 E 57th St, 212/758-7300 and 500 Madison Ave, 212/758-6098): exquisite timepieces

Turnbull & Asser (42 E 57th St, 212/752-5700): custom- and ready-made classic shirts and clothes for men and women

Valentino (747 Madison Ave, 212/772-6969): formal wear and accessories

Van Cleef & Arpels (744 Fifth Ave, 212/644-9500): jewelry

Wempe Jewelers (700 Fifth Ave, 212/397-9000): jewelry and watches

---

As you might expect, the new **Armani/5th Ave** (717 Fifth Ave, 212/207-1902) clothing store is *haute moderne*, cold, black and white, and almost empty of customers. Prices are uncomfortably elevated, as is the atmosphere. But a redeeming fixture is the **Armani/Ristorante 5th Ave**, overlooking Fifth Avenue. You will find such goodies as sauteed scallops, filet mignon, carpaccio, homemade pappardelle pasta, crusted yellowfin tuna, chargrilled T-bone steak, and a super Tuscan chocolate mousse served with guava rose sorbet. Of course, all of this comes with the usual high Armani price tag!

New York Stores: The Best of the Lot

There's nothing like the excitement of shopping in the Big Apple! It seems there are just "so many places, and so little time." The following stores are but a sampling of what I consider "the best" for every category, whatever your taste or price range. So grab your wallet and your most comfortable walking shoes, and "let the shopping begin."

Anatomical Supplies

THE EVOLUTION STORE

120 Spring St (bet Greene St and Mercer St)   212/343-1114
Daily: 11-7   www.theevolutionstore.com

The Evolution Store sells unique natural history collectibles, including insects, fossils, skulls and skeletons, medical models, minerals, posters, seashells, and decorative antique taxidermy. Some merchandise is available for rental by the day, week, or month. Shopping is rarely this educational and fascinating, and kids will love the lollipops with edible crickets inside!

MAXILLA & MANDIBLE, LTD.

451 Columbus Ave (bet 81st and 82nd St)   212/724-6173
Mon-Sat: 11-7; Sun: 1-5 (closed Sun in summer)
                                                www.maxillaandmandible.com

Henry Galiano grew up in Spanish Harlem. On the days his parents weren't running their beauty parlor, the family often went to the American Museum of Natural History. His interest in things skeletal increased when he got a job at the museum as a curator's assistant. He soon started his own collection of skeletons and bones. That, in turn, led to opening Maxilla & Mandible (the scientific names for upper and lower jaw, respectively), which is the first and only such store in the world. How many people need complete skeletons—or even a single maxilla? More than you might think! The shop supplies museum-quality preparations of skulls, skeletons, bones, teeth, horns, skins, butterflies, beetles, seashells, fossils, meteorites, minerals, taxidermy mounts, and anatomical charts and models to sculptors, painters, interior decorators, jewelry manufacturers, propmasters, medical personnel, scientists, and educators. They also carry scientific equipment.

Animation

ANIMAZING GALLERY—SOHO

54 Greene St (at Broome St)   212/226-7374
Mon-Sat: 10-7; Sun: 11-6   www.animazing.com

Animazing Gallery has moved down the street to a location that better showcases its collection of fine art inspired by whimsy. They are still New York City's authorized Disney art gallery, the exclusive venue for Dr. Seuss' art works, and purveyor of vintage and contemporary cels and drawings from all major studios. New additions include bronzes of Dr. Seuss characters and contemporary glass sculptures by Susan Gott. Gallery owners Heidi Leigh and Nick Leone are extremely knowledgeable and well-connected in this arena, and their store often hosts special events featuring artists and collections.

Antiques

Bleecker Street

Les Pierre Antiques (367-369 Bleecker St, 212/243-7740): French country

Greenwich Village

Agostino Antiques, Ltd. (979 Third Ave, 15th floor, 212/421-8820): English and French 17th- to-19th-century furniture

End of History (548½ Hudson St, 212/647-7598): vintage hand-blown glass

Hyde Park Antiques (836 Broadway, 212/477-0033): 18th-century English furniture

Karl Kemp & Associates (36 E 10th St, 212/254-1877 and 833 Madison Ave, 212/288-3838): art deco and Beidermeier furniture

Kentshire Galleries (37 E 12th St, 212/673-6644): English antiques

Maison Gerard (53 E 10th St, 212/674-7611): French art deco

Ritter-Antik (35 E 10th St, 212/673-2213): early first-period Beidermeier

Lexington Avenue

Hayko (857 Lexington Ave, 212/717-5400): kilims

Sara (950 Lexington Ave, 212/772-3243): Japanese pottery and porcelain

Sylvia Pines Uniquities (1102 Lexington Ave, 212/744-5141): jewelry and handbags

Lower East Side

Billy's Antiques & Props (76 E Houston St, 917/576-6980): fun antiques

Madison Avenue

Alexander Gallery (942 Madison Ave, 212/517-4400): American and European 18th- and 19th-century paintings

Antiquarium (948 Madison Ave, 212/734-9776): jewelry, classical Near Eastern and Egyptian antiquities

Art of the Past (1242 Madison Ave, 212/860-7070): South and Southeast Asia

Bernard & S. Dean Levy (24 E 84th St, 212/628-7088): American furniture and silver

Cora Ginsburg (19 E 74th St, 3rd floor, 212/744-1352, by appointment): antique textiles

Didier Aaron (32 E 67th St, 212/988-5248): 17th-, 18th-, and 19th-century pieces

Edith Weber Fine Jewelry (987 Madison Ave, 212/570-9668 and Carlyle Hotel, 35 E 76th St, 212/570-1033): rare and historic jewels

Fanelli Antique Timepieces (790 Madison Ave, Suite 202, 212/517-2300): antique timepieces

Florian Papp (962 Madison Ave, 212/288-6770): furniture

Friedman & Vallois (27 E 67th St, 212/517-3820): high-end French art deco

George Glazer Gallery (28 E 72nd St, Room 3A, 212/327-2598): maps, globes

Guild Antiques (1089 and 1095 Madison Ave, 212/717-1810): English formal

J.J. Lally (41 E 57th St, 212/371-3380): Chinese art

L'Antiquaire & the Connoisseur (36 E 73rd St, 212/517-9176): French and Italian furniture

Linda Horn Antiques (1327 Madison Ave, 212/772-1122): late 19th-century English and French

Macklowe Gallery (667 Madison Ave, 212/644-6400): Tiffany

Ursus Books and Prints (981 Madison Ave, 212/772-8787): books

W. Graham Arader (29 E 72nd St, 212/628-3668 and 1016 Madison Ave, 212/628-7625): rare prints and furniture

Meatpacking District

Lars Bolander N.Y. (72 Gansevoort St, 212/924-1000): 17th- and 18th-century Swedish and French antiques and reproductions

Midtown

A la Vielle Russie (781 Fifth Ave, 212/752-1727): Russian art

Chameleon (223 E 59th St, 212/355-6300): lighting

Doris Leslie Blau (306 E 61st St, 212/586-5511): rugs

Gardner & Barr (305 E 61st St, 212/752-0555, by appointment): Murano glass

George N. Antiques (227 E 59th St, 212/935-4005): mirrors

Gotta Have It! (153 E 57th St, 212/750-7900): celebrity memorabilia

Gray & Davis (32 W 47th St, 212/719-4698): vintage engagement rings

Hugo, Ltd. (233 E 59th St, 212/750-6877): 19th-century lighting and decorative arts

James Robinson (480 Park Ave, 212/752-6166): silver flatware

Leo Kaplan, Ltd. (114 E 57th, 212/249-6766): ceramics and glass

Manhattan Art & Antiques Center (1050 Second Ave, 212/355-4400): 100 galleries

Martayan Lan (70 E 55th St, 6th floor, 212/308-0018): 16th- and 17th-century maps and books

Naga Antiques (145 E 61st St, 212/593-2788): antique Japanese screens

Newel LLC (425 E 53rd St, 212/758-1970): all styles and periods

Philip Colleck (311 E 58th St, 212/486-7600): 18th- and early 19th-century English furniture

Ralph M. Chait Galleries (724 Fifth Ave, 10th floor, 212/758-0937): ancient Chinese art

S.J. Shrubsole (104 E 57th St, 212/753-8920): English silver

Stephen Herdemian (78 W 47th St, 212/944-2534 and 73 W 47th St, 212/840-1271): antique jewelry

Soho/Tribeca

Alan Moss (436 Lafayette St, 212/473-1310): 20th-century furniture

Art & Industry (50 Great Jones St, 212/477-0116): items from the 1940s, 1950s, and 1960s

Bikini Bar (148-C Duane St, 212/571-6737): Hawaiian, vintage rattan, surfboards

David Stypmann (190 Ave of the Americas, 212/226-5717): eclectic, pottery, mirrors

Donzella (17 White St, 212/965-8919): 1930s, 1940s, and 1950s furnishings

Gill & Lagodich Fine Period Frames (108 Reade St, 212/619-0631, by appointment): frames

Greene Street Antiques (76 Wooster St, 212/274-1076): Scandinavian and Beidermeier

Lost City Arts (18 Cooper Square, 212/375-0500): furniture, fixtures

Secondhand Rose (138 Duane St, 212/393-9002): 19th-century Moorish antiques

Urban Archaeology (143 Franklin St, 212/431-4646): architectural antiques and reproductions

Wyeth (315 Spring St, 212/243-3661): early- to mid-20th-century antiques and custom furniture

Upper East Side

Bizarre Bazaar (130¼ E 65th St, 212/517-2100): 20th-century industrial design

Dalva Brothers (53 E 77th St, 212/717-6600): antique and reproduction French furniture

Evergreen Antiques (1249 Third Ave, 212/744-5664): European and Scandinavian furniture

Leigh Keno American Antiques (127 E 69th St, 212/734-2381): 17th-, 18th-, and 20th-century American furniture

Sentimento Antiques (306 E 61st St, 212/750-3111)

Sotheby's (1334 York Ave, 212/606-7000)

Upper West Side

La Belle Epoque Vintage Posters (280 Columbus Ave, 212/362-1770): advertising posters

---

For an insider's look at New York, tune into WOR (710 AM) to hear Manhattan's most popular radio personality, **Joan Hamburg**. Joan has been sharing her encyclopedic knowledge about the city—shopping, eating, touring—for over three decades. You'll love her! Her show airs 11 a.m. to 1 p.m., Monday through Friday.

Architectural Antiques

DEMOLITION DEPOT & IRREPLACEABLE ARTIFACTS
216 E 125th St (bet Second and Third Ave)   212/860-1138
Mon-Sat: 10-6   www.demolitiondepot.com

This is the type of business where you'll have to use your imagination to realize the possibilities. Look inside this shabby building and you'll be immersed in a treasure trove of interior and exterior vintage pieces. There is a large assortment of fixtures, lighting pieces, doors, windows, bars, shutters, railings, and even kitchen sinks, all in a variety of styles (art deco, French country, etc.). Services include demolition, reclamation, on-site liquidation, and design consultation.

OLDE GOOD THINGS
124 W 24th St (bet Ave of the Americas and Seventh Ave)
Daily: 9-7   212/989-8401

5 E 16th St (bet Fifth Ave and Union Square W)   212/989-8814
Daily: 10-7   www.oldegoodthings.com

Olde Good Things salvages significant artifacts from old buildings, offering one of the largest showings of architectural antiques and salvaged items in the country. You'll find mantels, irons, doors, stone and terra cotta, hardware, garden items, tables and other furniture, floorings, mirrors, and altered items. What a fascinating business this is!

Art Supplies

LEE'S ART SHOP
220 W 57th St (at Broadway)   212/247-0110
Mon-Fri: 9-7:30; Sat: 10-7; Sun: 11-6   www.leesartshop.com

Lee's offers four stories of materials for amateur and professional artists and kids. There are architectural, drafting, and art supplies, as well as lamps, silk screens, paper goods, stationery, pens, cards, picture frames, calendars, crafts, gifts, and much more. Same-day on-premises framing is available.

NEW YORK CENTRAL ART SUPPLY
62 Third Ave (at 11th St)   212/473-7705
Mon-Sat: 8:30-6:15   www.nycentralart.com

Since 1905 artists have looked to this firm for fine art materials, especially unique and custom-made items. There are two floors of fine-art papers, including one-of-a-kind decorative papers and over a thousand Oriental papers from Bhutan, China, India, Japan, Thailand, Taiwan, and Nepal. Amateur and skilled artisans will find a full range of decorative paints and painting materials. Their brush selection is outstanding. This firm specializes in custom priming and stretching of artists' canvas. The canvas collection includes Belgian linens and cottons in widths from 54" to 197".

Showplace Antiques and Design Center (40 W 25th St, 212/633-6063, www.nyshowplace.com) is the largest antiques center in New York, with over 200 quality galleries selling jewelry, art glass, art nouveau, art deco, bronze, pottery, paintings, furniture, silver, and more on four floors. There is even a silversmith on-premises (weekends only). They are open from 10 to 6 on weekdays and 8:30 to 5:30 on weekends.

PEARL PAINT COMPANY
308 Canal St (bet Broadway and Church St)   212/431-7932
Mon-Fri: 9-7; Sat: 10-7; Sun: 10-6   800/221-6845
                                               www.pearlpaint.com

Pearl Paint Company is the world's largest discount art supplier. The 13 retail floors at Pearl Paint contain a vast selection of fine-art supplies, graphics and crafts merchandise, plus lighting and furniture. Selections and services include fabric-paint, canvas, silk-screening and gold-leaf items, drafting and architectural goods, a fine-writing department, and custom framing. Their prices are among the best in town, and they can ship overseas. Nearby are two affiliated stores, **Pearl Paint Frame Shop** (58 Lispenard St, 212/226-6966) and **NYC Home & Craft Center** (42 Lispenard St, 212/226-3717).

SAM FLAX
900 Third Ave (bet 54th and 55th St)   212/813-6666
12 W 20th St (bet Fifth Ave and Ave of the Americas) 212/620-3000
Mon-Fri: 9:30-6:30; Sat: 10:30-6; Sun: noon-6   www.samflax.com

Sam Flax is one of the biggest and best art supply houses in the business. The stock is enormous, the service special, and the prices competitive. They carry a full range of art and drafting supplies, organizational and archival storage items, gifts, pens, classic and modern furniture, home decor items, and photographic products. Framing services are offered at both stores.

UTRECHT ART AND DRAFTING SUPPLIES
111 Fourth Ave (at 11th St)   212/777-5353
Mon-Sat: 9-7; Sun: 11-6

237 W 23rd St (bet Seventh and Eighth Ave)   212/675-8699
Mon-Fri: 9-8; Sat: 10-7; Sun: 11-6   www.utrecht.com

Utrecht is a major manufacturer of paint, art, and drafting supplies with a large factory in Brooklyn. At this retail store, factory-fresh supplies are sold at discount, and both quality and prices are superb. Utrecht also carries other manufacturers' lines at impressive discounts.

Autographs

JAMES LOWE AUTOGRAPHS
30 E 60th St (bet Madison and Park Ave), Suite 304   212/759-0775
By appointment

James Lowe is one of the nation's most established autograph houses. Regularly updated catalogs make visiting the gallery unnecessary, but in-person inspections are fascinating and invariably whet the appetite of autograph collectors. The gallery shows whatever superior items are in stock, including historic, literary, and musical autographs, manuscripts, documents, and 19th-century photographs (both signed and unsigned).

KENNETH W. RENDELL GALLERY
989 Madison Ave (at 77th St)   212/717-1776
Tues-Sat: 10-6 and by appointment   www.kwrendell.com

Kenneth Rendell has been in the business for over 40 years. He offers a fine collection of pieces from famous figures in literature, arts, politics, and science. Rendell shows autographed letters, manuscripts, documents, books, and photographs. All are authenticated, attractively presented, and priced according to rarity. Rendell also can arrange for evaluations and appraisals.

Bargain Stores

GABAY'S
225 First Ave (bet 13th and 14th St)   212/254-3180
Mon-Sat: 10-6:30; Sun: 11-6   www.gabaysoutlet.com

Gabay's sells designer overstocks of handbags, shoes, evening wear, suits, casual clothing, lingerie, and more at great prices. Goods come from some of Manhattan's best stores (like Bergdorf Goodman and Henri Bendel), with items for both men and women. Designer names include Chloe, Lanvin, Prada, Marc Jacobs, Oscar de la Renta, Yves St. Laurent, Zegna, Gucci, Ralph Lauren, and Brioni.

Where to Shop for Bargains in New York!

Asian goods: **Pearl River Mart** (477 Broadway, 212/431-4770)

Baby gear: **Buy Buy Baby** (270 Seventh Ave, 917/344-1555)

Clothing: **Old Navy** (150 W 34th St, 212/594-0115; 610 Ave of the Americas, 212/645-0663; and 503-511 Broadway, 212/226-0838)

Clothing for the family: **Daffy's** (3 E 18th St, 212/529-4477 and other locations), **H&M** (1328 Broadway, 646/473-1164; 558 Broadway, 212/343-2722; 640 Fifth Ave, 212/489-0390; 435 Seventh Ave, 212/643-6955; 3190 W 125th St, 212/665-8300; and other locations), and **Loehmann's** (101 Seventh Ave, 212/352-0856 and 2101 Broadway, 212/882-9990)

Clothing, men's and women's (Spanish): **Zara** (580 Broadway, 212/343-1725; 101 Fifth Ave, 212/741-0555; 750 Lexington Ave, 212/754-1120; and 39 W 34th St, 212/868-6551)

Designer labels for the family: **SYMS** (400 Park Ave, 212/317-8200 and 42 Trinity Pl, 212/797-1199)

Discount department store: **Century 21** (22 Cortlandt St, 212/227-9092)

Electronics: **J&R Music** (15 and 23 Park Row, 212/238-9000)

Flowers, cut: **Wholesale Flower Market** (29th St bet Ave of the Americas and Seventh Ave)—retail and wholesale

Furniture: **Room & Board** (105 Wooster St, 212/334-4343)

Home Furnishings: **Bed Bath & Beyond** (410 E 61st St, 646/215-4702; 1932 Broadway, 917/441-9391; 270 Greenwich St, 212/233-8450; and 620 Ave of the Americas, 212/255-3550)

Hosiery: **Filene's Basement** (620 Ave of the Americas, 212/620-3100; 4 Union Square S, 212/358-0169; and 2222 Broadway, 212/873-8000)

Kitchenware: **Broadway Panhandler** (65 E 8th St, 212/966-3434)

Photo: **B&H Photo-Video-Pro Audio** (420 Ninth Ave, 212/444-6600)

Sewing and upholstering notions: **M&J Trimming** (1008 Ave of the Americas, 212/391-9072)

Shoes: **Anbar** (60 Reade St, 212/227-0253), **DSW** (102 North End Ave, 212/945-7419 and 40 E 14th St, 212/674-2146), and **Payless Shoes** (187 Broadway, 212/267-2176; 415 Broadway, 212/966-9112; 513 Broadway, 212/343-1457; 600 Ave of the Americas, 212/645-1401; and other locations)

Shoes, running: **Super Runners Shop** (360 Amsterdam Ave, 212/787-7665; Grand Central Terminal, 42nd St at Vanderbilt Ave, 646/487-1120; 1337 Lexington Ave, 212/369-6010; 1246 Third Ave, 212/249-2133; 821 Third Ave, 212/421-4444; and other locations)—apparel and accessories, too!

Shoes, tennis: **Sprint Sports** (2511 Broadway, 212/866-8077)

Stationery and office products: **Jam Paper & Envelope** (135 Third Ave, 212/473-6666)

SOIFFER HASKIN
317 W 33rd St (at Eighth Ave)   718/747-1656
Hours vary; call ahead   www.soifferhaskin.com

This is an unusual operation, selling luxury merchandise at deep discounts. The varied stock of items includes clothing, silver, gifts, housewares, linens, shoes, and the like. It's a good idea to get on their mailing list for notification of special sale events.

Bathroom Accessories

A.F. SUPPLY CORPORATION
22 W 21st St (bet Fifth Ave and Ave of the Americas), 5th floor
Mon-Fri: 8-5 and by appointment   212/243-5400, 800/366-2284
www.afsupply.com

A.F. Supply offers a great selection of luxury bath fixtures, whirlpools, faucets, bath accessories, door and cabinet hardware, saunas, steam showers, shower doors, medicine cabinets, and spas from top suppliers.

SHERLE WAGNER INTERNATIONAL
300 E 62nd St (at Second Ave)   212/758-3300
Mon-Fri: 9:30-5:30   www.sherlewagner.com

If you desire elegance and originality, and price is no object, then come to Sherle Wagner for luxury hardware and bath accessories. You'll also find all kinds of bed and bath items, plus general furniture for your home. They've been around for over 60 years.

WATERWORKS
225 E 57th St (bet Second and Third Ave)   212/371-9266
7 E 20th St (bet Fifth Ave and Broadway)   212/254-6025
Mon-Fri: 9-6; Sat: 11-5 (closed Sat in summer)   www.waterworks.com

If it is for the bathroom, then Waterworks has it! You'll find bath fittings like faucets and shower heads, tubs, sinks, water closets, bidets, ceramic and glass surfacing, towels, rugs, mirrors, lighting, and a large stock of soaps, candles, and scents. There is also a selection of small furniture, including hampers, stools, etageres, and small tables.

Beads

BRUCE FRANK BEADS & FINE ETHNOGRAPHIC ART
215 W 83rd St (bet Broadway and Amsterdam Ave)   212/595-3746
Daily: 11-7:30   www.brucefrankbeads.com

You'll find one of the area's best selections of beads at this store, for example, semiprecious stones, sterling silver, gold-plated Czech and Japanese seed beads, brass beads, and contemporary glass beads. In addition to a selection of vintage and antique beads from all over the world, the store carries a large stock of supplies and findings. They also offer weekly beading classes, re-stringing, and repair. Volume discounts are available.

GAMPEL SUPPLY
11 W 37th St (bet Fifth Ave and Ave of the Americas)   212/575-0767
Mon-Fri: 8:30-5   www.elveerosenberg.com

This is the kind of esoteric business that New York does best. Request a particular kind of bead, and Gampel will invariably have it—at a cheap price, too. While single beads go for a dollar each at a department store one block away, Gampel sells them in bulk for a fraction of that price. Visit the fifth-floor showroom to view over 25,000 styles of beads. Closeouts are also available. Though they prefer to deal with wholesalers, individual customers are treated as courteously as institutions, and wholesale prices are offered to all. As for the stock—well, a visit to Gampel is an education. Pearlized beads alone come in over 20 different styles and are used for everything from bathroom curtains to earrings and flowers. Since many of its customers are craftspeople, Gampel also sells supplies for bead-related crafts. They stock needles, cartwheels, cords (in colors to match each bead), threads, chains, adhesives, jewelry tools, jewelry findings, and costume jewelry parts and pieces.

If you want to try your hand at a Martha Stewart-like craft project, you're likely to find something extra special at these shops:

Beads of Paradise (16 E 17th St, 212/620-0642): beads

Bocage Design Group (50 W 29th St, 212/779-8227): vintage inspired fabrics and accessories

City Quilter (133 W 25th St, 212/807-0390): fabrics, patterns, supplies, quilting machines

M&J Trimming (1008 Ave of the Americas, 800/965-8746): notions

Purl (137 Sullivan St, 212/420-8796): yarns

Rita's Needlepoint (150 E 79th St, 212/737-8613): stitchery

Books

Antiquarian

COMPLETE TRAVELLER ANTIQUARIAN BOOKSTORE
199 Madison Ave (at 35th St)   212/685-9007
Mon-Fri: 9:30-6:30; Sat: 10-6; Sun: noon-5   www.ctrarebooks.com

The largest collection of Baedeker Handbooks is but one feature of this store, which deals exclusively in rare, antiquarian, and out-of-print books pertaining to travel. The 12,000-book collection includes volumes on polar expeditions, adventure travel, literature, first editions, collectible children's classics, and 18th- and 19th-century maps. Fine literature, poetry, and books on New York are also available.

Architecture

URBAN CENTER BOOKS
457 Madison Ave (bet 50th and 51st St)   212/935-3595
Mon-Fri: 10-6:30; Sat: noon-5:30   www.urbancenterbooks.org

This is the Municipal Art Society's bookstore for architecture. Although it is best known for exceptionally diverse and well-conceived walking tours, the organization also runs this gallery and bookstore at its headquarters in the north end of the elegant Villard Houses. It is among the best sources in the country for books, magazines, and journals on such topics as urban and land-use planning, architecture, and interior design. Urban Center Books also carries a wide selection of guidebooks to New York City.

Art

PRINTED MATTER
195 Tenth Ave (bet 21st and 22nd St)   212/925-0325
Tues, Wed: 10-6; Thurs-Sat: 11-7   www.printedmatter.org

The name Printed Matter is a misnomer, since this store is devoted exclusively to artists' books—a trade term for portfolios of artwork in book form. They stock 15,000 titles by over 5,000 artists. The result is inexpensive, accessible art that can span an artist's entire career or focus on a particular period or theme. The store is a nonprofit operation. The idea is carried further with a selection of periodicals and audiotapes in a similar vein. Nearly all featured artists are contemporary (from 1960), so just browsing the store will bring you up-to-date on what is happening in the art world. They sell wholesale and retail, and you can browse their online catalog.

Gerry's Tips for Saving When Shopping
The retail business is highly competitive. You'll find some good money-saving hints here:

- **Pay cash, if possible**—Better prices might be available if you do.
- **Tell the shop owner you came because of this book**—If he or she is on the ball, you might get a special discount!
- **Price-check**—Know prices, if possible, before going to a store.
- **Read ads carefully**—Sometimes the fine print is misleading.
- **Look beyond brand names**—Many items without fancy labels are just as good.
- **Color-coordinate**—Buy outfits to mix and match.
- **Budget your dollars**—Know exactly what you can afford to spend.
- **Frequent thrift shops**—Some excellent values can be found at secondhand stores.
- **Shop alone**—Don't let peer pressure influence you.
- **Approach clearance racks warily**—Be leery of a series of markdown prices, as the merchandise might be undesirable.
- **Keep receipts**—Returns are much easier.
- **Buy off-season items**—Sales and markdowns can net you some real deals.
- **Avoid impulse buying**—You may regret it later.
- **Use coupons**—They can save you big bucks.
- **Check out frequent shopper programs**—Good discounts for regular customers can be had.
- **Don't be afraid to haggle**—Believe it or not, haggling is still possible in many stores!

Children's

BANK STREET BOOKSTORE
2879 Broadway (at 112th St)   212/678-1654
Mon-Thurs: 11-7; Fri-Sat: 10-6; Sun: noon-6
www.bankstreetbooks.com

A Manhattan icon for years, this store is a marvelous source of books for and about children, as well as books about education and parenting. Located adjacent to the Bank Street College of Education—a progressive graduate school for teachers and a lab school for children—it also has a great selection of tapes, videos, and CDs. It's a treasure trove of educational toys, activity books, and teacher resources. While the two-floor store is a little cramped even when it isn't full of people, the staff really knows its stock and cares enormously about quality children's literature. Make sure to check its website for a schedule of readings and other special events for children.

BOOKS OF WONDER
18 W 18th St (bet Fifth Ave and Ave of the Americas) 212/989-3270
Mon-Sat: 10-7; Sun: 11-6   www.booksofwonder.com

Books of Wonder is an enchanting spot with a special place in the hearts of New York children and their parents as they specialize in old and new children's literature. In addition to the world-famous Oz section (as in *The Wizard of Oz*), this store is known for frequent "Meet the Author" events, beautiful used and often signed children's classics, a newsletter, and a story hour for young children on Sunday at noon. A special treat is the **Cupcake Cafe** (212/465-1530), located in the same building.

SCHOLASTIC STORE
557 West Broadway (bet Prince and Spring St)   212/343-6166
Mon-Sat: 10-7; Sun: noon-6   www.scholastic.com/sohostore

One of two retail outlets for this educational publishing giant (the other being in Westchester County), this is a bright, cheerful space full of familiar titles and characters. In addition to children's books, the store stocks a range of toys, puzzles, software, CDs, DVDs, and Klutz products. There is a tremendous selection of parent/teacher resource books on the second floor. Ask for a calendar of events, which lists readings, workshops, and performances. (Note: The stroller entrance is at 130 Mercer Street.)

Comics

ACTION COMICS
345 E 80th St (bet First and Second Ave)   212/639-1976
By appointment

Action Comics presents the best selection of comic books in the city. There are new comics from all publishers and collectible comics from the 1930s to the present. They also carry sports (and non-sports) cards, action figures, magic cards, T-shirts, and collecting supplies. They will evaluate and even buy collections.

CHAMELEON COMICS & CARDS
3 Maiden Lane (at Broadway)   212/587-3411, 212/732-8525
Mon-Fri: 9-7; Sat: 10-5   www.chameleoncomics.com

Comic book fans of all ages will find the latest favorites and trade paperback books from major publishers like DC, Marvel, and Top Cow, as well as independents. You'll also find much more in this tiny shop: statues and busts of comic characters; sports and non-sports (movies, cartoons, and sci-fi) cards; comic-themed toys and action figures; and "japanime" (Japanese-

American animation). The staff is friendly and informed, and you can order books up to two months prior to publication from the preview catalog.

ST. MARK'S COMICS
11 St. Mark's Pl (bet Second and Third Ave)   212/598-9439
Mon-Tues: 10 a.m.-11 p.m.; Wed-Sat: 10 a.m.-1 a.m.; Sun: 11-11

This unique store carries mainstream and licensed products, as well as hard-to-find small-press and underground comics. They have a large selection of back issues and claim, "If it's published, we carry it." These service-oriented folks will even hold selections for you. Comic-related toys, T-shirts, statues, posters, and cards are stocked. They also carry TV- and movie-related products.

Cookbooks

KITCHEN ARTS & LETTERS
1435 Lexington Ave (at 94th St)   212/876-5550
Mon: 1-6; Tues-Fri: 10-6:30; Sat: 11-6; closed Sat in July and Aug
                         www.kitchenartsandletters.com

Cookbooks traditionally are strong sellers, and with all the interest in health, fitness, and natural foods, they are more popular than ever. It should come as no surprise that Nachum Waxman's Kitchen Arts & Letters found immediate success as a store specializing in food- and wine-related books and literature. Imported books are a specialty. Waxman claims his store is unique in the city and that there are fewer than ten like it in the entire country. He formerly edited cookbook projects at Harper & Row and Crown. Wanting to start a specialty bookshop, he identified a demand for out-of-print cookbooks. So while his cozy shop stocks more than 10,000 current titles, much of the business consists of finding deleted and want-listed books.

Foreign

FRENCH AND EUROPEAN PUBLICATIONS
Dictionary Store/Learn-a-Language Store
Rockefeller Center   212/581-8810
610 Fifth Ave (bet 49th and 50th St)   www.frencheuropean.com
Mon-Sat: 10-6 (open Sun during holiday season)

A short stroll through Rockefeller Center Promenade takes you to this unique foreign-language bookstore, which has occupied the same location since 1934. Inside you will find an interesting collection of French magazines and newspapers, children's books, cookbooks, best sellers, greeting cards, and recorded French music. It is on the lower level, however, where most of the treasures are found. Books and videos in French and Spanish are available on almost every topic. There are also books on cassette, a multimedia section, books and recordings for learning more than a hundred languages, and a specialized foreign-language dictionary section covering engineering, medicine, business, law, and other fields.

KINOKUNIYA BOOKSTORE
1073 Ave of the Americas (bet 40th and 41st St)   212/869-1700
Mon-Sat: 10-8; Sun: 11-7:30   www.kinokuniya.com

Japanese and English reading materials coexist in this bookstore. There are books, CDs, DVDs, comics, hard-to-find magazines, and beautiful pictorial books. Subjects cover all aspects of Japanese culture: art, cooking, travel, language, literature, history, business, economics, martial arts, comic books, and more. The bilingual staff can help all customers. New stock arrives about three times a week.

General
BARNES & NOBLE
105 Fifth Ave (at 18th St)	212/675-5500
555 Fifth Ave (at 46th St)	212/697-3048
160 E 54th St (at Third Ave)	212/750-8033
1972 Broadway (at 66th St)	212/595-6859
33 E 17th St (bet Broadway and Park Ave)	212/253-0810
2289 Broadway (at 82nd St)	212/362-8835
240 E 86th St (at Second Ave)	212/794-1962
396 Ave of the Americas (at 8th St)	212/674-8780
97 Warren St (at Greenwich Ave)	212/587-5389
Hours vary by store	www.barnesandnoble.com

For value and selection, you can't beat Barnes & Noble. Their stores are beloved by book buyers and browsers in virtually every area of the city. Generations of New York students have purchased textbooks at Barnes & Noble's flagship store at 105 Fifth Avenue. A number of newer superstores have enormous stocks of books (including bargain-priced remainders), comfortable shopping conveniences (including cafes), a large magazine selection, and gift items. Best of all, they continue to offer deep discounts on best sellers and other popular titles.

BORDERS
461 Park Ave (at 57th St)	212/980-6785
2 Penn Plaza (bet Seventh Ave and 33rd St)	212/244-1814
576 Second Ave (at 32nd St)	212/685-3938
100 Broadway (bet Pine and Wall St)	212/964-1988
10 Columbus Circle (Time Warner Building)	212/823-9775
Hours vary by store	www.bordersstores.com

Borders is one of the major national bookstore chains, offering books, CDs, DVDs, periodicals, calendars, gift items, reading areas, and cafes. The stock at Borders is wide and deep. There is plenty of well-informed help, and in-person author events draw crowds. Customer kiosks allow access to their extensive inventory via computerized searches by author, title, and keyword.

MCNALLY JACKSON BOOKS
52 Prince St (bet Lafayette and Mulberry St)	212/274-1169
Daily: 10-10	www.mcnallyjackson.com

Sarah McNally is a brave lady. "Brave" because opening an independent bookstore is a daring endeavor! But she has been successful. The store is chock full of titles in every category, and personal, informed service will help lead you to the right book. Author appearances are frequent. There is a tearoom on-premises, too.

RIZZOLI BOOKSTORE
31 W 57th St (bet Fifth Ave and Ave of the Americas)   212/759-2424
Mon-Fri: 10-7:30; Sat: 10:30-7; Sun: 11-7   www.rizzoliusa.com

When you talk about class in the book business, Rizzoli tops the list. For more than 40 years they have maintained an elegant atmosphere that makes patrons feel as if they are browsing a European library rather than a midtown Manhattan bookstore. The emphasis is on art, architecture, foreign language, literature, photography, fashion, and interior design. There is a good selection of paperbacks, children's books, sports, and collectors' editions. You'll discover book finds in every nook and cranny on all three floors of this historic townhouse.

STRAND BOOK STORE
828 Broadway (at 12th St)   212/473-1452
Mon-Sat: 9:30 a.m.-10:30 p.m.; Sun: 11-10:30

STRAND BOOK KIOSK
Fifth Ave at 60th St
April-Dec (weather permitting)   www.strandbooks.com

This is the largest and best used bookstore in the world. Need I say more? Family-owned for eight decades, it is a fascinating place to visit and shop. The store has over 2.5 million titles in stock—that's 18 miles of books—tagged at up to 85% off list prices. They sell secondhand, out-of-print, and rare books. Thousands of new books and quality remainders are sold at 50% off publisher prices. An outstanding rare book department is located on the third floor. You'll find 20th-century first editions, limited signed editions, fine bindings, and much more. Their mail-order and Internet business is huge. (A personal connection: Knowledgeable owner Fred Bass and daughter Nancy now have ties to my home state, as Nancy is the wife of Oregon Senator Ron Wyden.)

THREE LIVES & CO.
154 W 10th St (at Waverly Pl)   212/741-2069
Mon-Tues: noon-8; Wed-Sat: 11-8:30; Sun: noon-7
www.threelives.com

Three Lives is one of New York's best remaining independent bookstores. Founded in 1978, it specializes in literary fiction and nonfiction, with good sections on poetry, art, New York, cooking, and gardening. The staff is knowledgeable and helpful.

Music

JUILLIARD BOOKSTORE
60 Lincoln Center Plaza (66th St bet Broadway and Amsterdam Ave)
Mon-Sat: 10-6   212/799-5000, ext 237
www.bookstore.juilliard.edu

With an extensive selection of sheet music and scores, and hard-to find books on classical music, this bookstore claims to carry every classical music book in print! You will also find CDs, DVDs, musicians' accessories, and imprinted apparel and gifts. Due to renovations at Lincoln Center, the store is temporarily housed in a big blue trailer. A permanent address will be announced in 2010.

Mystery

MYSTERIOUS BOOKSHOP
58 Warren St (bet West Broadway and Church St)   212/587-1011
Daily: 11-7   www.mysteriousbookshop.com

Otto Penzler is a Baker Street Irregular, a Sherlock Holmes fan extraordinaire (an elementary deduction!), and the Mysterious Bookshop's owner. The expanded shop stocks new hardcover and paperback books that deal with all types of mystery, and it is also filled floor-to-ceiling with out-of-print, used, and rare books. Amazingly, the staff seem to know exactly what is in stock. If it is not on the shelves, they will order it. There is as much talk as business conducted here, and you can continue the conversation with authors who sign their works from time to time. Mysterious carries thousands of autographed books, and several store-sponsored book clubs provide autographed first editions to members.

Around the World

Across the street from Bryant Park is **Around the World** (28 W 40th St, 212/575-8543), a magazine shop featuring fashion publications and books from all over the world. There are periodicals devoted to knits, lingerie, kids' clothes, models' accessories, and menswear—an amazing source of information for the fashionista or fashion designer.

New York

CITYSTORE
1 Centre St (at Chambers St), north plaza of Municipal Bldg
Mon-Fri: 9-4:30   212/669-8246
                                    www.nyc.gov/citystore

This city government bookstore provides access to more than 120 official publications, all of which are dedicated to helping New Yorkers cope with their complex lives. *The Green Book* is the official directory of the city of New York, listing phone numbers and addresses of more than 900 government agencies and 6,000 officials. It includes state, federal, and international listings, as well as courts and a section on licenses. There is also a unique collection of New York memorabilia: city-seal ties, pins, official merchandise for NYPD, FDNY, DSNY, NYC Parks, NYC Taxi, NYC Subway, and more. You can purchase NYC parking cards here as well.

Rare and Out-of-Print

ALABASTER BOOKSHOP
122 Fourth Ave (bet 12th and 13th St)   212/982-3550
Mon-Sat: 10-10; Sun: 11-10   www.abebooks.com

There was a time when Fourth Avenue was known as "Bookshop Row." Back then, it was *the* place for used books in Manhattan. All that has changed with the advent of franchised superstores and the demise of smaller entrepreneurs. Alabaster's owner, Steve Crowley, has bucked the trend, offering a great selection of used and rare books in all categories while focusing on literature and the arts. Prices range from $2 paperbacks to a $1,000 first edition. Specialities include New York City, photography, and the arts.

ARGOSY BOOK STORE
116 E 59th St (bet Park and Lexington Ave) 212/753-4455
Mon-Fri: 10-6 www.argosybooks.com

In its third generation of ownership, Argosy Book Store houses six stories of antiquarian and out-of-print items. They specialize in Americana, modern first editions, autographs, art, antique maps and prints, and the history of science and medicine.

Some Independent Bookstores

Look to independent bookstores for personalized services and special events. Most also stock used books, and some are purveyors of rare volumes.

Books of Wonder (18 W 18th St, 212/989-3270): children's

Complete Traveller Antiquarian Bookstore (199 Madison Ave, 212/685-9007): travel

Crawford and Doyle (1082 Madison Ave, 212/288-6300): general bookstore

Drama Book Shop (250 W 40th St, 212/944-0595): plays, musicals, theater

East West Living (78 Fifth Ave, 212/243-5994): spirituality, holistic health, and esoteric philosophy

Forbidden Planet (840 Broadway, 212/473-1576): sci-fi, fantasy, and Japanese animation and comics

Librairie de France (610 Fifth Ave, 212/581-8810): French and Spanish books

McNally Jackson Books (52 Prince St, 212/274-1160): general bookstore

Mysterious Bookshop (58 Warren St, 212/587-1011): thrillers and killers

Posman Books (9 Grand Central Terminal, 42nd St at Vanderbilt Ave, 212/983-1111)

Quest Bookshop (240 E 53rd St, 212/758-5521): spirituality and esoterica

St. Mark's Bookshop (31 Third Ave, 212/260-7853): eclectic stock, books on culture, foreign and domestic periodicals

Strand Book Store (828 Broadway, 212/473-1452): 18 miles of new and used books; something for everyone

Three Lives & Co. (154 W 10th St, 212/741-2069): specializes in literary fiction and nonfiction

---

BAUMAN RARE BOOKS
535 Madison Ave (bet 54th and 55th St) 212/751-0011
Mon-Sat: 10-6 www.baumanrarebooks.com

Bauman offers a fine collection of books and autographs dating from the 15th through the 20th centuries. Included are works of literature, history, economics, law, science, medicine, nature, travel, and exploration. First editions and children's books are a specialty. They also provide services from designing and furnishing libraries to locating books for customers.

IMPERIAL FINE BOOKS
790 Madison Ave (bet 66th and 67th St), 2nd floor   212/861-6620
Mon-Fri: 10:30-6; Sat: 10:30-5   www.imperialfinebooks.com

If you are in the market for books that look as great as they read, Imperial is the place to visit. You will find fine leather bindings, illustrated books, vintage children's books, unique first editions, and magnificent sets of prized volumes. Their inventory includes literary giants like Twain, Dickens, Brontë, and Shakespeare. An outstanding Oriental art gallery features Chinese ceramics and antiques. (They will purchase fine pieces.) Services include complete restoration and binding of damaged or aged books, as well as custom bookbinding and library projects. A search office will locate titles and make appraisals.

J.N. BARTFIELD GALLERIES AND FINE AND RARE BOOKS
30 W 57th St (bet Fifth Ave and Ave of the Americas), 3rd floor
Mon-Fri: 10-5; Sat: 10-3, or by appointment (closed Sat in summer)
212/245-8890
www.bartfield.com

For lovers of fine paintings and rare books and manuscripts, this shop is a spectacular place to browse. Since 1937 Bartfield has specialized in fine-press books, Americana, and better books in all fields. You'll also find American Western and sporting and wildlife art from the 1800s to the present. I have purchased outstanding collections of leatherbound books from them and can vouch for their expertise. First editions, sporting books, and high-quality antiquarian books in virtually every collecting category are featured. Who wouldn't be excited to explore elegantly bound volumes that once graced the shelves of old family libraries?

Religious

J. LEVINE BOOKS & JUDAICA
5 W 30th St (bet Fifth Ave and Broadway)   212/695-6888
Mon-Wed: 9-6; Thurs: 9-7; Fri: 9-2; Sun: 10-5 (closed Sun in July)
www.levinejudaica.com

The history of the Lower East Side is reflected in this store. Started back in 1905 on Eldridge Street, J. Levine was a fixture in the area for many years. Now it operates farther uptown, just off Fifth Avenue. Being one of the oldest Jewish bookstores in the city, Levine is a leader in the Jewish book market. Though the emphasis is still on the written word, they also carry many gift items, tapes, coffee-table books, and thousands of Judaica items. You can also browse and order online.

ST. PATRICK'S CATHEDRAL GIFT STORE
15 E 51st St (bet Fifth and Madison Ave)   212/355-2749, ext 400
Daily: 10-6   www.saintpatrickscathedral.org

This store is an oasis of calm in midtown. Lovely music plays in the background as you browse books on Catholicism, displays of rosary beads, statues of saints, music, wall decor, medals, and related items. Proceeds benefit the cathedral and its upkeep.

Theater

DRAMA BOOK SHOP

250 W 40th St (bet Seventh and Eighth Ave) 212/944-0595
Mon-Sat: 10-6 (Thurs till 8) www.dramabookshop.com

Since 1923 this shop has been providing a valuable service to the performing arts community. Its stock includes publications dealing with theater, film, dance, music, puppetry, magic, design, and costumes. You'll also find biographies, cooking, crafts, health, philosophy, sports, and other subjects. The Drama Book Shop is well known for courteous and knowledgeable service.

RICHARD STODDARD—PERFORMING ARTS BOOKS

43 E 10th St (bet University Pl and Broadway), Room 6D
By appointment 212/598-9421
www.richardstoddard.com

Richard Stoddard runs a one-man operation dedicated to rare, out-of-print, and used books, and to memorabilia relating to the performing arts. Equipped with a Ph.D. from Yale in Theater History and three decades of experience as a dealer and appraiser of performing arts materials, Stoddard offers a broad range of items. He has the largest collection of New York playbills (about 20,000) for sale in the U.S., as well as books, autographs, souvenir programs, and original stage designs.

Used

HOUSING WORKS BOOKSTORE CAFE

126 Crosby St (bet Houston and Prince St) 212/334-3324
Mon-Fri: 10-9; Sat, Sun: noon-7 www.housingworks.org/usedbookcafe

Housing Works has it all: new and rare used books, collectibles, out-of-print titles, first editions, DVDs, CDs, and audiobooks. The cafe features baked goods, seasonal soups, soft drinks, beer and wine, and catering services. Proceeds go to Housing Works, providing social services for homeless New Yorkers with HIV/AIDS.

Buttons

TENDER BUTTONS

143 E 62nd St (bet Lexington and Third Ave) 212/758-7004
Mon-Fri: 10:30-6; Sat: 10:30-5:30

You'll find buttons ranging in price from 60 cents to $12,000 at Tender Buttons. Millicent Safro's retail button store is complete in variety as well as size. One antique wooden display cabinet shows off the selection of original buttons, many imported or made exclusively for the store. There are buttons of pearl, wood, horn, silver, leather, ceramic, bone, ivory, pewter, and semiprecious stones. Many are antiques. Some are as highly valued as artwork; a French enamel button, for instance, can cost almost as much as a painting! Unique pieces can be made into special cuff links—real conversation pieces for the lucky owner. Blazer buttons are a specialty. They also have a fine collection of antique and period cuff links and men's stud sets. I am a cuff-links buff and have purchased some of my best pieces from this shop. They also have wonderful small antiques.

China, Glassware

CRATE & BARREL
650 Madison Ave (at 59th St)   212/308-0011
Mon-Fri: 10-8; Sat: 10-7; Sun: noon-6

611 Broadway (at Houston St)   212/780-0004
Mon-Sat: 10-9; Sun: noon-7   www.crateandbarrel.com

The folks at Crate & Barrel are professional merchants in the best sense. Even if you aren't in the market for china, glassware, cookware, home accessories, bedroom furnishings, or casual furniture, the displays will make shopping hard to resist. The place is loaded with attractive, quality merchandise at sensible prices. With its creative displays, employing effective lighting and signage, the store layout makes for enjoyable shopping. Quick, no-fuss checkout, too!

FISHS EDDY
889 Broadway (at 19th St)   212/420-9020
Mon: 10-9; Tues-Sat: 9-9; Sun: 10-8   www.fishseddy.com

Besides being a treasure trove for bargain hunters, this shop is fun to browse for some of the most unusual industrial strength china and glassware items available anywhere. Nearly everything is made in America, and the stock of dinnerware, flatware, and glassware changes on a regular basis. Fishs Eddy is ideal for young people setting up a new residence or a business looking for unique pieces. You'll find interesting accessory selections of linens, T-shirts, coasters, and more. Their tabletop collection is carried in some of the Gracious Home locations as well.

Clothing and Accessories

Antique and Vintage

CIRCA NOW
238 E 6th St (bet Second and Third Ave)   212/254-2555
Daily: noon-8   www.circanownyc.com

What's old is new again at this East Village boutique. Vintage clothing is spruced up and made ready for a new era of wearers. The friendly owners choose quality women's dresses, pants and jeans, shoes and boots, hats, purses, eyewear and other accessories. Prices are affordable, the boutique is well-organized, and the selection is tastefully displayed.

FAMILY JEWELS
130 W 23rd St (bet Ave of the Americas and Seventh Ave)
Sun-Mon: 11-7; Tues-Sat: 11-8   212/633-6020
                                          www.familyjewelsnyc.com

Family Jewels is the place to go for vintage clothing and accessories from the Victorian era through the 1980s. The stock is well organized, the selections are huge, the service is excellent, and shopping is fun! Prices are reasonable, too. The decor is 1940s, and appropriately retro music plays. A costume and styling service is available.

FROM AROUND THE WORLD
209 W 38th St (bet Seventh and Eighth Ave), Suite 1201
Mon-Fri: 9:30-5:30 (by appointment)   212/354-6536

This is a vintage clothing archive, wardrobe lending library, and retail outlet specializing in unique, quality vintage apparel and accessories from all over the world. The continually replenished selection of designer, ethnic, military, Western, Hawaiian, work, and athletic wear includes collectible and never-worn dead-stock pieces. Items range from the 1890s to 1990s for men, women, and children.

LAUREL CANYON
63 Thompson St (bet Broome and Spring Sts)   212/343-1658
Daily: noon-7   www.laurelcanyon.com

There's old merchandise in this new store—and that is exactly the point! The goods are vintage wear from the 1960s and 1970s, which means hippie and bohemian clothing and accessories. Laurel Canyon is the premiere shopping source for worn-in Western boots, and they carry an amazing selection of vintage Western wear, too. Head around the corner to their affiliated store, **Chelsea Girl Couture** (186 Spring St, 212/343-7090), for 1920s-to-1980s vintage clothes, handbags, and accessories.

LEGACY
109 Thompson St (between Prince and Spring St)   212/966-4827
Daily: 12-7   www.legacy-nyc.com

Here's another winner in Soho! Vintage women's fashions from the 1940s join with original new designs, some made with vintage fabrics. Big name designers like Gucci, Chanel, and Ungaro are represented in this eclectic shop, which shows an assortment of suits, dresses, separates, outerwear, shoes, handbags, and accessories. Rita Brookoff, the owner, will help pair a vintage blouse with a current fashion suit or select the perfect timeless black dress for a *tres chic* look.

REMINISCENCE
50 W 23rd St (bet Fifth Ave and Ave of the Americas)   212/243-2292
Mon-Sat: 11-7:30; Sun: noon-7   www.reminiscence.com

It's fun to revisit the 1950s through the 1980s at this hip emporium, created by Stewart Richer on lower Fifth Avenue. Although he is a product of this era, most of Richer's customers are between the ages of 13 and 30. The finds are unusual and wearable, with large selections of colorful vintage clothing and attractive displays of jewelry, hats, gifts, and accessories. Richer's goods, although vintage in style, are mostly new, and the company also sells what it makes to outlets all over the world. Because of its vast distribution, Richer can produce large quantities and sell at low prices.

SCREAMING MIMI'S
382 Lafayette St (bet 4th and Great Jones St)   212/677-6464
Mon-Sat: noon-8; Sun: 1-7   www.screamingmimis.com

Screaming Mimi's is a landmark vintage emporium founded in 1978. It is known for its excellent selection of clothing and accessories for men and women from the 1940s through the 1980s. There is an excellent showing of handbags, shoes, jewelry, sunglasses, lingerie, and sportswear. One department also features designer and vintage couture.

TRASH & VAUDEVILLE
4 St. Mark's Pl (bet Second and Third Ave)   212/982-3590
Mon-Thurs: noon-8; Fri: 11:30-8:30; Sat: 11:30-9; Sun: 1-7

This place is hard to pin down since the stock changes constantly and seems to have no boundaries. Trash & Vaudeville describes its inventory as punk and goth clothing, accessories, and original designs. "Punk clothing" means rock and roll styles from the 1950s to the present, including outrageous footwear.

WHAT COMES AROUND GOES AROUND
351 West Broadway (bet Broome and Grand St)   212/343-9303
Mon-Sat: 11-8; Sun: noon-7   www.whatcomesaroundgoesaround.com

This Soho boutique offers a wide range of high-end vintage garments and accessories. The shop is best known for concert T-shirts, leather purses, and a large collection of denim apparel. The W.C.A.G.A. Collection, comprising vintage-inspired clothing for men and women, is also available in such upscale stores as Bergdorf Goodman, Bloomingdale's, and Neiman Marcus.

Athletic

LULULEMON ATHLETICA
1928 Broadway (at 64th St)   212/712-1767
Mon-Sat: 10-8; Sun: 11-7

1127 Third Ave (at 66th St)   212/755-5019
Mon-Sat: 10-7; Sun: 11-6

481 Broadway (bet Broome and Grand St)   212/334-8276
15 Union Square W (bet 14th and 15th St)   212/675-5286
Mon-Sat: 10-8; Sun: 11-7   www.lululemon.com

Founded in Canada, this yoga-inspired clothing store shows attractive and offbeat wear for active people. You'll find clothing for yoga, dancing, running, and other sweaty pursuits. Check out in-store events, including free yoga classes and self-defense instruction.

Bridal

HERE COMES THE BRIDESMAID . . .
213 W 35th St (bet Seventh and Eighth Ave), Room 502
By appointment   212/647-9686

Stephanie Harper decided it was time that bridesmaids had a store of their own. Her establishment carries designer bridesmaid gowns available in every size from After Six, Bill Levkoff, Bari Jay, and others. She also features gowns that can be hemmed and worn again to occasions other than weddings. Weekend hours make Here Comes the Bridesmaid especially convenient for working women.

KLEINFELD
110 W 20th St (bet Ave of the Americas and Seventh Ave)
By appointment   646/633-4300
                                                  www.kleinfeldbridal.com

Experience the magic! From beginning to end, the Kleinfeld experience sets the standard for all brides-to-be. The bridal business has changed a great deal, yet little has changed at the legendary Kleinfeld. A 35,000-square-foot location features the most exclusive bridal- and evening-wear designers anywhere. They are tops in the business, and the Manhattan salon is a wonder to experience. Brides will enjoy a private dressing room with an experienced consultant to review 1,500 styles of American and European designer bridal gowns, including Amsale, Carolina Herrera, Monique Lhuillier, and Pnina Tornai. The perfect Kleinfeld fit will be achieved with experienced professional stylists, bridal consultants, custom fitters, seamstresses, beaders, embroiderers, and pressers.

Children's

Before describing what I consider to be the best children's clothing stores in New York, let me be clear about what I'm *not* including: big chains and the haughty "just so" boutiques that line Madison Avenue. That is not to say some of the chains don't have great stores here. **Baby Gap** and **Gap Kids**, **The Children's Place**, **Gymboree**, and even Europe's **Oilily** all have good selections, as does the cavernous "big-box" **buybuy Baby**. But unlike the stores listed below, they sell very little that isn't available in any other city. As for the haughty boutiques, I see no reason to patronize wildly overpriced and unwelcoming places.

BONNE NUIT
1193 Lexington Ave (at 81st St)   212/472-7300
Mon-Fri: 9-7; Sat: 10-7; Sun: noon-5

What a fun place to shop! You'll find mother and daughter pajamas, robes, and slippers; European children's wear for boys and girls (up to preteen sizes); old-fashioned children's books; wool and cashmere blankets; baby gifts; and fine lingerie and boudoir accessories. Very personal service is another plus.

BU AND THE DUCK
106 Franklin St (bet Church St and West Broadway)   212/431-9226
Mon-Sat: 10-6; Sun: 11-5   www.buandtheduck.com

Quality is the byword here. Come to Bu and the Duck for outstanding handmade sweaters, clothing, shoes, and accessories for infants up to eight-year-olds. The fabrics are gorgeous, the designs unique, and the prices less than you might think, given the quality.

giggle
120 Wooster St (bet Spring and Prince St)   212/334-5817
Mon-Sat: 10-7; Sun: noon-6
1033 Lexington Ave (at 74th St)   212/249-4249
Mon-Sat: 10-7; Sun: 11-6   www.giggle.com

For those about to be parents, as well as those who already are, giggle is a godsend! You'll find most every item needed to take care of the little one(s), including furniture for the nursery. In addition, there are toys, books, music, bath and spa items, and information on keeping baby healthy and happy. Helpful personal shoppers are available. Customized delivery is available (that is, for the merchandise—not the baby!), and in-store parenting activities are a plus.

LESTER'S
1534 Second Ave (at 80th St)   212/734-9292
Mon-Fri: 10-7 (Thurs till 8); Sat: 10-6; Sun: 11-6   www.lestersnyc.com

If you're looking for basic clothes, shoes, campwear, and/or accessories for children and don't want to leave the East Side, Lester's is your best bet. It is large and inviting, including a downstairs section dedicated entirely to boys. In fact, you can clothe everyone from infants to teenagers, and even moms, with a selection of women's contemporary clothing. You will also find a good selection of shoes. While its stock is not unique and might not win any fashion awards, Lester's is just stylish enough to keep East Side moms and kids coming back.

LILLIPUT
265 Lafayette St (bet Spring and Prince St)   212/965-9567
Mon-Thurs: 11-6; Fri, Sat: 11-7   www.lilliputsoho.com

Children's clothing stores have multiplied in New York's hot shopping neighborhoods, and a lot of them start to look alike after awhile. Sometimes a good buyer with a sharp eye can set a store apart, however. In certain respects Lilliput resembles a lot of other relatively upscale children's stores, and some of what you'll find here is neither unusual nor well-priced. But look a little closer and you'll see certain items, including a wide selection from Lili Gaufreete, that make a trip here worthwhile. Some items are offered for rental. In addition to a wide and varied selection of infant clothes, Lilliput has a great shoe selection, unusual accessories, a few toys, and a diverse range of clothes for young children to size 8. **Lilliput Soho Kids** (240 Lafayette St, 212/965-9201), a sister store right down the block, offers clothes for girls to size 18.

LUCKY WANG
799 Broadway (bet 10th and 11th St)   212/353-2850
LUCKY WANG 2
82 Seventh Ave (bet 15th and 16th St)   212/229-2900
Mon-Sat: 11-7; Sun: noon-6   www.luckywang.com

Are you looking for something unusual or unique in children's wear? These sister stores showcase colorful contemporary kimonos and karate pants for babies and kids that are as fashionable as they are practical. A few other labels are featured as well, as are accessories from shoes to blankets.

SPACE KIDDETS
26 E 22nd St (bet Park Ave S and Broadway)   212/420-9878
Mon-Sat: 10:30-6 (Wed, Thurs till 7)   www.spacekiddets.com

This cheerful store is overflowing with funky children's clothes, shoes, and accessories. Although the selection always seems fresh and fun, Space Kiddets actually has been around for a long time. The prices may seem a bit high if you're from out-of-town, but they're reasonable compared to some of the boutiques in trendier neighborhoods. Moreover, the sales staff is welcoming and helpful. Check out **Space Kiddets Toys** (46 E 21st St), just around the corner, for a wild assortment of playthings.

RealKidz Clothing (www.realkidzclothing.com) taps into one of the hottest areas of retail—fashion for plus-size girls from 5 to 12. They do not yet have a storefront, but their website guarantees sales with a 60-day return policy.

Costumes

ABRACADABRA
19 W 21st St (bet Fifth Ave and Ave of the Americas) 212/627-5194
Tues-Sat: 11-7; Sun: 5-7   www.abracadabrasuperstore.com

Abracadabra can transform you into almost anything! They rent and sell costumes and costume accessories, magician's supplies, theatrical makeup, and props for magic tricks. It is a gagster's heaven! Come to the free magic show on Sunday afternoon. The Halloween season brings extended hours.

CREATIVE COSTUME
242 W 36th St (bet Seventh and Eighth Ave), 8th floor 212/564-5552
Mon-Fri: 9:30-4:30 (open Sat in Oct)   www.creativecostume.com

With thousands of costumes for purchase or rental, Creative Costume likely has a suitable outfit for the occasion. They will even manufacture a special look. Alterations are included with every sale.

HALLOWEEN ADVENTURE
104 Fourth Ave (bet 11th and 12th St)   212/673-4546
Mon-Sat: 11-8; Sun: noon-7 (extended hours in Oct)
                              www.newyorkcostumes.com

You and your family will be the talk of the neighborhood after a visit here. You'll find wigs, costumes for adults, kids, and pets, hats, gags, magic items, props, and all manner of games, and novelties. In addition, a professional makeup artist is on hand most of the time.

PARAMOUNT
52 W 29th St (bet Broadway and Ave of the Americas) 212/696-9664
Mon-Fri: 9-5

Crowns, tiaras, headpieces, false teeth, wigs, beards, eyepatches, eyelashes, swords, fake blood—name the prop or theatrical accessory, and chances are good this fading old store sells it either singly or by the dozen. The collection of masks is extensive.

Family

BLUE TREE
1283 Madison Ave (at 91st St)   212/369-2583
Mon-Fri: 10-6; Sat, Sun: 11-6   www.bluetreenyc.com

You never know what you might find at this unusual boutique! The street floor has merchandise for kids and gifts and trinkets for almost any occasion, while the second floor displays a rather exclusive collection of clothing and accessories for men and women. A number of big name clothing designers are represented at Blue Tree.

Furs and Leather

BARBARA SHAUM
60 E 4th St (bet Bowery and Second Ave)   212/254-4250
Wed-Sat: 1-6

Barbara Shaum has been doing magical things with leather since 1963. She's a wonder with sandals, bags, sterling silver buckles, and belts (with handmade brass, nickel-silver, inlaid wood, and copper buckles). Everything is designed in the shop, and Shaum meticulously crafts each item using only the finest materials. She is regularly featured in leading fashion magazines.

G. MICHAEL HENNESSY FURS
345 Seventh Ave (bet 29th and 30th St), 5th floor   212/695-7991
Mon-Fri: 9:30-5; Sat by appointment

You'll find an abundance of beautiful, affordable furs here. Fur lovers should get to know Rubye Hennessy, a former fashion editor. Hennessy furs and service are famous worldwide; the label assures you of superior pelts, great designs, and low prices. Their showroom in the wholesale fur district stocks hundreds of furs, ranging from highly coveted minks and sables to sporty boutique furs and shearlings. You'll find all the newest fashion looks, colors, shapes, and techniques. A spectacular Italian fur collection is exclusive to Hennessy. Today's fur technology is evident in skillfully executed sheared and grooved minks, "double-face" reversible styles, and furs that weigh next to nothing but still keep you warm. No wonder the Hennessy name commands such a large international following. They have a huge remodeling business, turning furs that are a few years old into brand-new styles. That classic mink you've worn for years can have a second life as a sheared swingcoat or *blouson*. While this is a sizable operation, you can count on Rubye being available to assist you.

GOODMAN COUTURE FURS
224 W 30th St (bet Seventh and Eighth Ave), Suite 902   212/244-7422
Mon-Fri: 10-6; Sat by appointment   www.buonuomo.com

Since 1918 the Goodmans have been creating fine fur styles. Third-generation furrier David Goodman offers a quality collection of fur-lined and reversible fur coats and jackets for men and women. You may choose from an array of furs, including mink, sheared mink, and fine sables. Your out-of-date or unused fur coats can be brought back to life with a new all-weather design. The Goodmans offer a custom cashmere knit collection under the label Buonuomo ("good man"), made in an Italian cashmere factory and trimmed with luxurious furs. Additionally, they have developed an innovative line of fur accessories, including scarves, collars, hats, and handbags. A full-time staff designer specializes in custom designs. Their hottest new items are feather-weight, fur-lined reversible coats.

HARRY KIRSHNER AND SON
307 Seventh Ave (bet 27th and 28th St)   212/243-4847
Mon-Fri: 9-5; Sat: 10-5

Kirshner should be one of your first stops for any kind of fur product, from throw pillows to full-length mink coats. They will re-line, clean, alter, and store any fur at rock-bottom prices. They are neither pushy nor snobbish. Harry Kirshner offers tours of the factory. If nothing appeals to a customer, a staff member will design a coat to specifications. Often, however, the factory stocks a collection of restored secondhand furs in perfect and fashionable condition. Many customers come in for a new fur and walk out with a slightly worn one for a fraction of what they expected to spend.

LIBRA LEATHER
259 W 30th St (bet Seventh and Eighth Ave), 7th floor 212/695-3114
Mon-Fri: 9-5:30   www.libraleather.com

For over a half century this family-owned business has been the ultimate source for fashionable fur and leather skins from the best-known designers. You'll find leather, suede, and shearling skins, as well as novelty items and accessories for the home, such as pillow and blanket covers, all in sheepskin and Mongolian lamb. The inventory is breathtaking, with luxurious skins from Italy, France, and Spain displayed in a beautiful space in the Garment District with a European *haute couture* feel.

Hosiery
FOGAL
515 Madison Ave (at 53rd St)   212/355-3254
Mon-Sat: 10-6:30   www.fogal.com

Before Fogal came to New York from Switzerland, the thought of a Madison Avenue boutique devoted to hosiery was, well, foreign. But since opening in 1982, it's hard to imagine Manhattan without it. If it's fashionable and different leg wear you're after, Fogal has it. Plain hosiery comes in nearly a hundred hues. The designs and patterns make the number of choices almost incalculable. You might say that Fogal has a leg up on the competition! Fogal also carries lingerie, bodywear, swimming suits, and men's socks.

Men's and Women's—General
BILLY REID
54 Bond St (at Bowery)   212/598-9355
Mon-Sat: 11-8; Sun: 11-7   www.billyreid.com

One might describe the style of clothes sold here as "Southern comfort." An Alabama gentleman, William Reid, designs tailored apparel in easy-to-wear moleskin, hopsack, tweeds, and plaids. Men and women will find outerwear, jackets, sweaters, pants, shirts, dresses, and tops. A custom-tailoring department will make you look extra sharp. It's worth a trip to Reid to see the decor, as recommissioned items from down South have taken on creative new uses up North.

CHRISTOPHER FISCHER
80 Wooster St (bet Broome and Spring St)   212/965-9009
Mon-Sat: 10-6; Sun: noon-6   www.christopherfischer.com

Fischer is a homestyle store which carries luxurious cashmere and leather goods for men, women, and children, including sweaters, blankets, shawls, and cushions. Accessories from Henry Beguelin are also available, as well as cashmere items for your dog.

COCKPIT USA

652 Broadway (bet Bleecker and Bond St) 212/254-4000
Mon-Thurs: 11-7:30; Fri, Sat: 11-8; Sun: noon-7 www.cockpitusa.com

This bustling emporium features clothing from authentic contemporary flight jackets to reproductions of World War II jackets. You'll find premium contemporary Americana items, vintage clothing, antique furniture, and accessories, including Fortis watches, boots, footwear, and sunglasses from various makers.

COURT BOUTIQUE

178 Mulberry St (bet Broome and Kenmare St) 212/925-1022
Daily: noon-8 www.courtshop.com

Beyond the black façade of this tidy shop in Little Italy is a hip collection of clothing for men and women, wild fashion accessories, and funky shoes. Seasonal trends are reflected in the ever-changing roll call of designers. The experienced shop owners have introduced their own leather collection, and they round out the mix with a selection of vintage clothing. Court Boutique is definitely something different for this neighborhood.

DAFFY'S

3 E 18th St (bet Fifth Ave and Broadway)	212/529-4477
335 Madison Ave (at 44th St)	212/557-4422
1311 Broadway (at 34th St)	212/736-4477
462 Broadway (at Grand St)	212/334-7444
125 E 57th St (bet Lexington and Park Ave)	212/376-4477
1775 Broadway (at 57th St)	212/294-4477
50 Broadway (bet Exchange Pl and Beaver St)	212/422-4477
Hours vary by store	www.daffys.com

Daffy's describes itself as a bargain clothing outlet for millionaires. Since a lot of folks got to be millionaires by saving money, perhaps Daffy's has something going for it! Great bargains can be found in better clothing (including unusual European imports) for men, women, and children. Fine leather items are a specialty. This is not your usual "off-price" store, as they have done things with a bit of flair.

GARGYLE

16-A Orchard St (bet Canal and Hester St) 917/470-9367
Mon-Fri: 10-6 www.gargyle.com

Leisure attire doesn't get any better than at Gargyle, purveyors of upscale country-club clothing, shoes, and classy accessories for men and women. They carry tops, bottoms, shoes, swimwear, and accessories from some of the world's best designers. Even if you're not part of the country-club set, you'll leave here dressed to impress.

H&M

125 W 125th St (bet Lenox Ave and Adam Clayton Powell, Jr Blvd)
212/665-8300

731 Lexington Ave (at 59th St)	212/935-6781
640 Fifth Ave (at 51st St)	212/489-0390
435 Seventh Ave (at 34th St)	212/643-6955
1328 Broadway (at 34th St)	646/473-1164
111 Fifth Ave (at 18th St)	212/539-1741
558 Broadway (bet Prince and Spring St)	212/343-2722
515 Broadway (bet Spring and Broome St)	212/965-8975
Hours vary by store	www.hm.com

From the day it opened, H&M has been packing customers in, and it's no secret why! In a convivial atmosphere, up-to-date men's and ladies' clothing and accessories for the young—as well as those who want to remember their carefree days—can be found at very reasonable prices. Don't come looking for pricey labels; what you will find are knockoffs of items that sell for much more at boutiques and department stores. The Swedes learned quickly that American yuppies like nothing better than to fill their closets with clothing that doesn't cost very much. This is the place to get it!

Jeans come in all manner of styles, colors, fabrics, prices, and comfort levels. For the best selection try:

Anik (1122 Madison Ave, 212/249-2417 and 1355 Third Ave, 212/861-9840)

Atrium (644 Broadway, 212/473-9200)

Bloomingdale's (1000 Third Ave, 212/705-2000 and 504 Broadway, 212/729-5900)

Levi's Store (750 Lexington Ave, 212/826-5957; 536 Broadway, 646/613-1847; 1501 Broadway, 212/944-8555; and 25 W 14th St, 212/242-2128)

Scoop (473 Broadway, 212/925-3539; 861 Washington St, 212/691-1905; and 1275 Third Ave, 212/535-5577)

HARLEM UNDERGROUND
20 E 125th St (bet Fifth and Madison Ave)   212/987-9385
Mon-Thurs: 10-7; Fri, Sat: 10-8; Sun: noon-6

www.harlemunderground.com

This is a good stop for comfortable, reasonably priced, and "cool" urban wear. Guys will like the Spike Lee Collection. The merchandise has the feel of the historic area it represents. Personal or corporate embroidery is available for denim shirts and jackets, T-shirts, sweats, and caps.

HOUSE OF MAURIZIO
509 Madison Ave (at 53rd St), Room 1106   212/759-3230
Mon-Fri: 8-5

Tony Maurizio caters to men and women who like the functional and fashionable look of tailored suits. Although almost any kind of garment can be copied, this house is known for coats; two-, three-, and four-piece suits; and mix-and-match combinations. This look is favored by busy executives and journalists who have to look well-dressed but don't have hours to spend dressing. House of Maurizio's tailors create blazers and suits in a range of 500 fabrics, and those in silk, linen, cotton, and solid virgin wool are sensational. In addition to women's garments, they design and create coats and suits for men in the same broad range of fabrics. Tony promises fast service and expert tailoring. Expect to pay prices in the range of the rich-and-famous.

JEAN SHOP
425 W 14th St (bet Ninth and Tenth Ave)   212/366-5326
424 West Broadway (bet Prince and Spring St)   212/334-5822
Mon-Sat: 11-7; Sun: noon-6   www.worldjeanshop.com

These are not ordinary jeans. Each pair is created to a customer's specifications using high-quality Japanese selvedge denim (woven on projectile looms in Japan). Choose from classic, relaxed fit, and rocker styles in short, medium, or long lengths, and show your personality with custom distressing and dyeing. Create a one-of-a-kind denim outfit from a selection of jackets, shirts, belts, and accessories. These are quality goods, so expect to pay accordingly.

Here is a novel shop! **Nom de Guerre** (640 Broadway, 212/253-2891) can only be reached by going underground (at the Bleecker Street station of the #6 Lexington Avenue subway line). Once there you will find unusual men's T-shirts, sweat shirts, jeans, and sneakers. It's worth a visit.

JEFFREY—NEW YORK
449 W 14th St (bet Ninth and Tenth Ave)   212/206-1272
Mon-Fri: 10-8 (Thurs till 9); Sat: 10-7; Sun: 12:30-6

You wouldn't expect to find a store like Jeffrey Kalinsky's in Manhattan's Meatpacking District! It offers men's and women's clothing, accessories, cosmetics, and a large selection of shoes. His Atlanta operation has been successful, and now he's brought such fashion names as Pucci, Prada, Gucci, Manolo Blahnik, and Yves St. Laurent to Manhattan.

LOUIS VUITTON
1 E 57th St (at Fifth Ave)   212/758-8877
Mon-Sat: 10-7 (Thurs till 8); Sun: noon-6   www.louisvuitton.com

In spectacular quarters at 57th and Fifth, Louis Vuitton has nearly everything you might expect: a dramatic exterior, compelling windows, a tasteful assortment of merchandise, snobby service, and inflated prices. Vuitton designer Marc Jacobs has certainly polished the label. If the LV signature is important to you, then this is the place to shop. Just know that you are paying for four floors of very expensive real estate at Louis Vuitton.

RALPH LAUREN
867 Madison Ave (at 72nd St)   212/606-2100
872 Madison Ave (bet 71st St and Madison Ave), layette/girls
                                                         212/434-8099
878 Madison Ave (at 72nd St), boys' store   212/606-3376
888 Madison Ave (bet 71st and 72nd St)   212/434-8000
379 West Broadway (bet Spring and Broome St)   212/625-1660

381 Bleecker St (bet Charles and Perry St), men's   646/638-0684
383 Bleecker St (bet Charles and Perry St), women's   212/645-5513
Hours vary by store   www.polo.com

Ralph Lauren has probably done as much as anyone to bring a classic look to American fashion and furnishings. His Manhattan showcase store, housed in the magnificent Rhinelander mansion at 867 Madison Avenue, is fabulous. Four floors of merchandise for men, women, and home are beautifully displayed and expertly accessorized. You will see a much larger selection than in the many specialty boutiques in department stores. There are several things to be aware of, however. One is the haughty way some of the staff greet customers who don't look like they have big bucks. Moreover, although the clothes and furnishings are classy, one can find items of equal or better quality elsewhere at considerably lower prices. The purple-label merchandise is grossly overpriced. But shopping here does mean you can carry out your purchase in one of those popular green bags, if that matters to you.

REPLAY STORE
109 Prince St (at Greene St)   212/673-6300
Daily: 11-7   www.replay.it

This very attractive Soho store carries dozens of different washings and fits in jeans and a variety of shirt styles and accessories. Outdoor clothing is featured. This is one of the better-stocked stores in the area, and prices are as comfortable as the merchandise.

STEVEN ALAN
229 Elizabeth St (bet Prince and Houston St)   212/226-7482
69 Eighth Ave (at 14th St)   212/242-2677
103 Franklin St (bet Church St and West Broadway)   212/343-0692
465 Amsterdam Ave (bet 82nd and 83rd St)   212/595-8451
Hours vary by store   www.stevenalan.com

Steven Alan is the place for men and women who have difficulty finding small or large sizes in designer merchandise. They also stock accessories, outerwear, and toiletries. The Franklin Street location is the largest.

TOPSHOP
478 Broadway (bet Broome and Grand St)   212/966-9555
Mon-Sat: 10-9; Sun: 11-8   www.topshop.com

This Soho store is the first U.S. affiliate of this trendy British retail chain. Ladies sized from zero to 12 have lots to choose from in apparel, accessories, and shoes from British designers like Kate Moss, Barbara Hulanicki, Christopher Kane, and Marios Schwab. Guys will find plenty of shirts, pants, sweaters, coats, and hoodies to fill their wardrobes, too. Personal stylists are on hand to help customers pull together the right look. The experience is spread over three floors, where new merchandise constantly arrives.

UNIQLO
546 Broadway (at Spring St)   917/237-8800
Daily: 11-9   www.uniqlo.com

This is a branch of one of Japan's largest retailers, started in 1984 in Hiroshima, Japan. You'll find high-quality casual wear for men, women, and children in a wide range of fabrics and prices. Denim and cashmere items with matching accessories are featured.

Men's Formal Wear

CUSTOM MEN
140 W 57th St (bet Ave of the Americas and Seventh Ave), Suite 4C
Mon-Fri: 9-8; Sat, Sun: 10-5   212/767-0545, 866/611-0545
                                                www.custommen.com

The choices here are almost limitless! Men's suits, sport coats, slacks, tuxedos, top coats, and shirts are individually tailored. There are about 15,000 fabrics to peruse, including Scabal, Georgio Armani, and Ermenegildo Zegna for suits; Japanese silk, Italian Tessitura, and pinpoint Oxford shirtings; and a wide variety of linings. Choose from double- or single-breasted jackets. Pants can be made in any style to fit all shapes and sizes. There are dozens of shirt collar, cuff, and front- and back-style combination options. Of course, you can add special details, like hidden pockets in coats and pants. Prices are competitive (especially sale prices), free alterations are offered within two years of purchase, and home or office appointments are available. The company is family-owned and -operated, and all articles are crafted by skilled tailors.

A visit to **R.M. Williams** (46 E 59th St, 212/308-1808) is like going "down under" without leaving the city! High-quality Australian jeans, belts, saddlery, and boots are specialties. The denim is like no other you have seen or felt. Prices are not bargain oriented, as this place is for the discerning shopper.

DANTE ZELLER TUXEDOS
201 E 23rd St (at Third Ave), 2nd floor   212/532-7320
459 Lexington Ave (at 45th St), 3rd floor   212/286-9786
Hours vary by store   www.dantezeller.com

Dante Zeller Tuxedos is Manhattan's largest locally owned formal-wear specialist, offering over 75 years of experience. Their wide selection includes the newest styles and colors from Calvin Klein, Ralph Lauren, Hugo Boss, Tallia Uomo, and others.

TED'S FORMAL WEAR
155 Orchard St (bet Rivington and Stanton St)   212/966-8029
Daily: 10-6   www.tedsrocktshirts.com

Ted's is an institution on the Lower East Side. They offer reasonable prices for tuxedo sales or rentals. You'll also find a large selection of rock and roll T-shirts for all ages.

Men's—General

BONOBOS
59 W 19th St (bet Ave of the Americas and Fifth Ave), Suite 6B
By appointment   646/710-3700, 877/294-7737
                                            www.bonobos.com

The mainstays of this business are men's casual or office-worthy trousers in cotton twill, corduroy, wool, and seersucker fabrics. Styles are made to fit guys with athletic builds. All pants are finished in one length with a slight flare to the leg and a curved waist. A limited number of each color and style are produced. Call for a showroom appointment or order online. They have a very liberal return policy, encouraging shoppers to try different sizes. They also carry shorts, logo T-shirts, and belts fashioned from designer woven silk ties.

I'm often asked where to go for French cuffed shirts and a good selection of links. Here are my answers:

Links of London (535 Madison Ave, 212/588-1177)
Missing Link (40 W 25th St, Room 108, 212/645-6928)
Thomas Pink (520 Madison Ave, 212/838-1928; 1155 Ave of the Americas, 212/840-9663; 10 Columbus Circle, 212/812-9650; and 63 Wall St, 212/514-7683)

CAMOUFLAGE
141 Eighth Ave (at 17th St) 212/741-9118
Mon-Fri: noon-7; Sat: 11:30-6:30; Sun: noon-6

At Camouflage you'll find men's brandname clothing, plus private label trousers, shirts, ties, and accessories. Considering some of the designers represented, prices range from reasonable to good. Camouflage can attire customers with a dignified but unique look. You definitely won't blend into the wallpaper!

EISENBERG AND EISENBERG
16 W 17th St (bet Fifth Ave and Ave of the Americas) 212/627-1290
Mon, Wed, Fri: 9-5:45; Tues: 9-5:30; Thurs: 9-6:45; Sat: 9-5; Sun: 11-5
www.eisenbergandeisenberg.com

Things have changed at Eisenberg and Eisenberg. You'll find the same great service and men's dress attire since 1898, but now their main business is the sale and rental of designer tuxedos, dinner jackets, and elegant accessories.

FAÇONNABLE
636 Fifth Ave (at 51st St) 212/319-0111
Mon-Sat: 10-8; Sun: 11-6 www.faconnable.com

Façonnable (a French outfit) has made a name for itself in the fashion world with clothes that appeal to conservative dressers. Their New York store—which admittedly does not match the class or selection of the Beverly Hills operation—carries a good showing of men's and women's sportswear, tailored clothing, suits, and shoes.

J. PRESS
380 Madison Ave (at 47th St) 212/687-7642
Mon-Sat: 9-7; Sun: noon-6 www.jpressonline.com

As one of New York's classic conservative men's stores, J. Press takes pride in its sense of timelessness. Its salespeople, customers, and attitude have changed little from the time of the founder. Styles are impeccable and distinguished; blazers are blue, and shirts are button-down and straight. Even when button-down collars were out, they never went away at J. Press.

JOHN VARVATOS

122 Spring St (at Greene St)   212/965-0700
Mon-Sat: 11-7; Sun: noon-6

315 Bowery (at Bleecker St)   212/358-0315
Mon-Sat: 12-9; Sun: noon-7   www.johnvarvatos.com

Elegance is a tradition at John Varvatos, which features an outstanding collection of leather and shearling outerwear, sportswear, accessories, and skin care and fragrance items. Men of all ages will feel comfortable with the Old World detailing of a line that exudes class. The Bowery location shows an edgier mixture of retro clothes and accessories, as well as audio equipment and vintage records. Varvatos, himself, is a music buff. The stores reek of atmosphere, and the salespeople couldn't be more helpful.

MZ Wallace (93 Crosby St, 212/431-8252 and 102 Christopher St, 212/206-1192) is the name to remember for women's handbags and totes. The enterprising ladies behind this company have developed a quality line in a variety of sizes for different purposes. Plain or fancy, they are made of nylon, twill, linen, and raffia with Italian leather trim and custom hardware. The boutiques are reminiscent of galleries, with merchandise carefully shown in uncluttered displays.

L.S. MEN'S CLOTHING

49 W 45th St (bet Fifth Ave and Ave of the Americas), 3rd floor
Mon-Thurs: 9-6:30; Fri: 9-3; Sun: 10-4   212/575-0933
                                          www.lsmensclothing.com

L.S. Men's Clothing bills itself as "*the* executive discount shop." I would go further and call them a must for fashion-minded businessmen. For one thing, the expansive midtown location means one needn't trek down to Fifth Avenue in the teens, which is the main area for men's discount clothing. Better still, as owner Israel Zuber puts it, "There are many stores selling $400 suits at discount, but we are one of the few in mid-Manhattan that discount the $550 to $1,500 range of suits." The main attraction, though, is the tremendous selection of executive-class styles. Within that category, a man could outfit himself almost entirely at L.S. Men's. Natural, soft-shoulder suits by name designers are available in all sizes. A custom-order department is available, with over 2,500 bolts of Italian and English goods in stock. Custom-made suits take four to six weeks and sell for around $595; sport coats are priced at $445. Custom suits by H. Freeman range from $595 to $880. H. Freeman shirts can be ordered ready-made or through the made-to-measure department at L.S. Men's, with 300 swatches priced from $70 to $95. This is one of the very best destinations for top-drawer names.

PAUL STUART

10 E 45th St (at Madison Ave)   212/682-0320
Mon-Fri: 8-6:30 (Thurs till 7); Sat: 9-6; Sun: noon-5
                                            www.paulstuart.com

You'll find classy merchandise, especially in the furnishings area, at Paul Stuart. A great selection of sweaters, ties (bow ties, too!), socks, shirts, and more is shown, with ready-to-wear for women, too. The men's clothing section is extensive but not exciting. As a matter of fact, the whole store is very sedate and nontrendy. Be selective when choosing a salesperson, as some of them have haughty attitudes that should be retired.

RIFLESSI
289 Madison Ave (bet 40th and 41st St)   212/679-4875
Mon-Sat: 10-7

47 W 57th St (bet Fifth Ave and Ave of the Americas) 212/935-4747
Mon-Sat: 10-7; Sun: 11-6

Beautiful, well-priced Italian suits, jackets, shirts, ties, sweaters, trousers, and outerwear are sold at Riflessi by pleasant salespeople. They stock a wide variety of clothes for men of different shapes and sizes; no worries for the entry-level guy who wears a trim-fit suit or the man who only has a memory of his once slim physique. Alterations are complimentary. Suit prices range between $300 and $1,200. Sales events bring prices down further.

Freemans Sporting Club (8 Rivington St, at Freeman Alley, 212/673-3209) is a source for classic work shirts, custom suiting, and high-quality outerwear. The entire F.S.C. brand is built around the vanishing trade of handmade clothing for stylish guys. Pieces are durable and meant to be worn day in and day out. Upstairs is an old-school barbershop to keep you looking ruggedly handsome. You can enjoy a delicious meal at nearby **Freemans Restaurant** (end of Freeman Alley, off Rivington St, bet Bowery and Christie St, 212/420-0012).

ROTHMAN'S
200 Park Ave S (at 17th St)   212/777-7400
Mon-Fri: 10-7 (Thurs till 8); Sat: 9:30-6; Sun: noon-6
www.rothmansny.com

Harry Rothman's grandson, Ken Giddon, runs this classy men's store, which offers a huge selection of quality clothes at discounts of up to 40%. In a contemporary and comfortable atmosphere, he carries top names like Canali, Hickey-Freeman, Corneliani, Joseph Aboud, Calvin Klein, Zegna, Theory, Ben Sherman, Scotch & Soda, and Hugo Boss. Sizes at Rothman's range from 36 to 50 in regular, short, long, and extra long. Raincoats, slacks, sport jackets, and accessories are also sold at attractive prices.

SAINT LAURIE MERCHANT TAILORS
22 W 32nd St (bet Fifth Ave and Ave of the Americas), 5th floor
Mon-Fri: 9-6; Sat: 9-5:30 (closed Sat in summer)   212/643-1916
www.saintlaurie.com

These folks have created many items for Broadway shows and movies! For four generations Saint Laurie has been providing quality made-to-order handmade clothing for men and women at rack prices. Also offered is a fine selection of shirts, blouses, and accessories. A laser body scanner ensures accurate measurements. They buy directly from weavers, resulting in price savings for customers. Saint Laurie's showroom and manufacturing facility occupy the same location.

SEIZE SUR VINGT
243 Elizabeth St (bet Houston and Prince St)   212/343-0476
Mon-Sat: 11-7; Sun: noon-6

SEIZE SUR VINGT AT THE PLAZA
1 W 58th St (at Fifth Ave)   212/832-1620
Mon-Sat: 11-6; Sun: noon-5   www.16sur20.com

The translation of *seize sur vingt* is "16 out of 20," as in a French homework score. Everything about this store is first-class: the elegant materials from Switzerland, Spain and Italy; the quality craftsmanship and styles; and the faultless fit. Ready-made shirts, suits, and sportswear are proportioned for the lean, well-toned man or woman. If you want to splurge, order a bespoke suit of the finest imported wool, linen, or cashmere. Shirts, sportswear, and accessories are also custom-made. Made-to-order cashmere sweaters are offered in 200 glorious colors.

Men's Hats

J.J. HAT CENTER
310 Fifth Ave (at 32nd St)   212/239-4368, 800/622-1911
Mon-Fri: 9-6; Sat: 9:30-5:30   www.jjhatcenter.com

This outfit stocks over 10,000 brandname hats and caps (to size 8) from all over the world. This classy shop offers a super selection, from fedoras to porkpies and safari helmets. Founded in 1911, it is New York's oldest hat shop. Special services include free brush-up, hat stretching or tightening, custom orders, and a free catalog.

WORTH & WORTH
45-47 W 57th St (bet Fifth Ave and Ave of the Americas)
Mon, Tues: 10-6; Wed-Sat: 10-7   800/428-7467
www.hatshop.com

Worth & Worth has specialized in men's hats since 1922. You'll find a good selection of fedoras, panamas, felts, caps, and berets at reasonable prices. You *won't* find baseball caps here!

Men's Shirts

CEGO CUSTOM SHIRTMAKER
174 Fifth Ave (bet 22nd and 23rd St), Room 502   212/620-4512
Mon, Tues: 9-7:30; Wed-Fri: 9-5:30; Sat: 10-3:30   www.cego.com
By appointment

For over two decades, service-oriented owner Carl Goldberg has been making quality shirts for regular people and media types. Delivery usually takes two to three weeks. If time is important, he can produce shirts in as little as two days. Prices start at less than $100 for Pima cotton broadcloth and go up for superb materials from Italy and Switzerland. CEGO also sells boxer shorts and pillow cases from their large fabric collection.

SHIRT STORE
51 E 44th St (bet Vanderbilt and Madison Ave)   212/557-8040
Mon-Fri: 8-6:30; Sat: 10-5   www.shirtstore.com

The appeal of the Shirt Store is that you're buying directly from the manufacturer, so there's no middle man to hike prices. The Shirt Store offers all-cotton shirts for men in sizes from 14½x32 to 18½x37. Although the ready-made stock is great, they also do custom work for men and women, even coming to your office with swatches. Additional services include mail order, alterations, and monogramming.

STATS
331 W 57th St (bet Eighth and Ninth Ave), Suite 280   212/262-5844
Mon-Fri: 8-7; weekends by appointment   www.statscustom.com

What does STATS stand for? Shirts, Ties, And Terrific Service, of course! Julie Manis sells custom-dress and casual shirts, neckwear, braces, and accessories, all custom-made and in the convenience of one's office or home. She carries tailoring tools and fabrics, and can special order fabrics not in stock. Julie also takes the extra step of a sample shirt fitting.

Men's Ties
ANDREW'S TIES
400 Madison Ave (bet 47th and 48th St)   212/750-5221
30 Rockefeller Plaza (50th St), Room 11   212/245-4563
Mon-Fri: 8:30-7; Sat: 10-7; Sun: noon-6   www.andrewstiesusa.com

There are not many really good tie stores left in New York. It's certainly not like it used to be, with great selections and bargains on the Lower East Side. But Andrew's Ties has some nice handmade Italian ties, along with ascots, pocket squares, belts, shirts, men's and women's scarves, and the like. Prices are reasonable.

Tie Care
- Always hang up ties.
- Don't rub spots.
- Use soda water to remove small spots.
- Don't iron ties.
- Don't send ties to the cleaners.
- Don't use water on stains.
- Roll ties when packing.

GOIDEL NECKWEAR
100 Clinton St (at Delancey St)   212/475-7332
Mon-Fri: 9:30-3

Since 1935 Goidel has been *the* place for bargains on ties, cummerbunds, men's jewelry, and accessories. They triple as manufacturers, wholesalers, and retailers, so savings are passed on to customers. These folks will match most items brought in, usually within a week or two.

Resale Clothing
ALLAN & SUZI
416 Amsterdam Ave (at 80th St)   212/724-7445
Mon-Sun: noon-7   www.allanandsuzi.net

This "retro clothing store" is quite an operation. You'll find current designer and vintage clothing for men and women, old and new shoes, and accessories under one roof. There are big names (like Galliano, Lacroix, Ungaro, and Versace) and newer cutting-edge labels. Some outfits are discounted. They dress a number of Hollywood and TV personalities. Ask for Allan Pollack or Suzi Kandel.

DESIGNER RESALE
324 E 81st St (bet First and Second Ave)   212/734-3639
Mon-Fri: 11-7 (Thurs till 8); Sat: 10-6; Sun: noon-5
          www.resaleclothing.net, www.designerresaleconsignment.com

"Gently worn" is the concept here. Designer Resale offers previously owned ladies' designer clothing and accessories at moderate prices. Most major fashion names are represented. You might find Chanel, Armani, Hermes, or Valentino garments on the racks. If items do not sell, prices are marked down further. Call to ask about the latest bargains.

ENCORE
1132 Madison Ave (bet 84th and 85th St), upstairs   212/879-2850
Mon-Fri: 10:30-6:30 (Thurs till 7:30); Sat: 10:30-6;
Sun: noon-6 (closed Sun in July, Aug)   www.encoreresale.com

Founded in 1954, Encore can honestly be billed as a "resale shop of gently worn clothing of designer/couture quality." When you see the merchandise and clientele, you'll know why. For one thing, it is a consignment boutique, not a charity thrift shop. Its donors receive a portion of the sales price, and according to owner Carole Selig, many of the donors are socialites and other luminaries who don't want to be seen in the same outfit twice. Selig can afford to be picky, and so can you. The fashions are up-to-date and sold at 50% to 70% off original retail prices. There are over 6,000 items in stock. Prices range from reasonable to astronomical—but just think about the original tags!

GENTLEMEN'S RESALE
322 E 81st St (bet First and Second Ave)   212/734-2739
Mon-Fri: 11-7; Sat: 10-6; Sun: noon-5
          www.gentlemensresaleclothing.com

Gentlemen interested in top-quality designer suits, jackets, and sportswear can save a bundle at this resale operation. Shopping here is like a treasure hunt, and that is half the fun. Imagine picking up a $1,000 Armani suit for $200! You might even earn some extra bucks by consigning items from your own wardrobe.

INA
101 Thompson St (bet Prince and Spring St), women   212/941-4757
Sun-Thurs: noon-7; Fri, Sat: noon-8

21 Prince St (bet Mott and Elizabeth St), women   212/334-9048
Sun-Thurs: noon-7; Fri, Sat: noon-8

208 E 73rd St (bet Second and Third Ave), women   212/249-0014
Mon-Sat: noon-7; Sun: noon-6

262 Mott St (bet Prince and Houston St), men   212/334-2210
Sun-Fri: noon-7; Sat: noon-8

15 Bleecker St (bet Lafayette St and Bowery), men and women
Mon-Sat: noon-8; Sun noon-7   212/228-8511
                                               www.inanyc.com

It is possible to wear the latest designer clothing, shoes, handbags, and accessories at a fraction of the original cost. These consignment shops routinely carry gently worn Gucci, Louis Vuitton, Dior, and Pucci couture for both men and women. Hundreds of savvy shoppers showed up for their *Sex and the City* wardrobe sale. You can get a heads up on such events by joining their online mailing list. Consider consigning your still-stylish fashions, as Ina stores are always looking for more great merchandise,

---

Notable Consignment and Thrift Shops in New York

Consignment shops have become busier during these dismal economic times. Many folks who had never shopped for clothes, home furnishings, or collectibles in these types of stores are amazed at the bargains to be found. Others have turned to consigning as a way to bring cash to their pocketbooks. Everything from *haute couture* (some brand new) to coffee mugs find their way onto the shelves and racks. Some items are undiscovered treasures worth big bucks.

Chelsea
Fisch for the Hip (153 W 18th St, 212/633-9053): high-end consignment
Goodwill (103 W 25th St, 646/638-1725)
Housing Works Thrift Shop (143 W 17th St, 718/838-5050): There are other locations on the Upper East Side, Upper West Side, West Village, Soho, and Tribeca, too.

East 20s
City Opera Thrift Shop (222 E 23rd St, 212/684-5344)
Goodwill (220 E 23rd St, 212/447-7270)
Salvation Army Thrift Shop (212 E 23rd St, 212/532-8115)

Soho
Ina (101 Thompson St, 212/941-4757)

Upper East Side
A Second Chance Designer Resale (1109 Lexington Ave, 2nd floor, 212/744-6041): designer handbags
Arthritis Foundation Thrift Shop (1430 Third Ave, 212/772-8816)
Bis Designer Resale (1134 Madison Ave, 2nd floor, 212/396-2760)
Cancer Care Thrift Shop (1480 Third Ave, 212/879-9868)
Council Thrift Shop (246 E 84th St, 212/439-8373)
Memorial Sloan-Kettering Thrift Shop (1440 Third Ave, 212/535-1250)
Michael's (1041 Madison Ave, 212/737-7273): consignment, ladies' designer attire
Spence-Chapin Thrift Shop (1473 Third Ave, 212/737-8448)

Upper West Side
Ina (208 E 73rd St, 212/249-0014)

MICHAEL'S, THE CONSIGNMENT SHOP FOR WOMEN
1041 Madison Ave (at 79th St)   212/737-7273
Mon-Sat: 9:30-6 (Thurs till 8)   www.michaelsconsignment.com

Are you dying to own one of those gowns you have seen in the papers or on TV? Would you like to dress up like a star? Here's the source for pieces from top designers. Evening wear is just part of Michael's stock. You'll also find pant suits, skirts, suits, bags, shoes, and more. Personal attention is assured, and prices are right.

ROUNDABOUT
31 E 72nd St (bet Park and Madison Ave), ground floor 646/755-8009
Mon-Sat: 10-6; Sun: noon-5

High-end clothing, shoes, handbags and accessories can be found at this new and resale women's clothing boutique. The owners started their business in Connecticut and branched into the Upper East Side. Some of the finds bear brand names like Pucci, Prada, Gucci, Hermes, and Chanel, with savings up to 70% off retail. Add a little green to your pocketbook by consigning your designer couture with Roundabout.

TATIANA DESIGNER RESALE
767 Lexington Ave (bet 60th and 61st St)   212/755-7744
Mon-Fri: 11-7; Sat: noon-6   www.tatianas.com

This is a unique designer consignment boutique for contemporary and vintage couture. For consigners, Tatiana offers free estimates and pickup service. For retail customers, she will try to find whatever outfit they may want. The stock is top-grade, with clothing, jewelry, bags, shoes, hats, and furs bearing well-known names.

Shoes—Children's

EAST SIDE KIDS
1298 Madison Ave (bet 92nd and 93rd St)   212/360-5000
Mon-Fri: 10-6; Sat: 11-8   www.eastsidekidsshoes.com

East Side Kids stocks classic footwear items up to women's size 12 and men's size 13. They can accommodate older children and juniors, plus adults with small- to average-sized feet. Of course, there is also a great selection of children's shoes in both domestic and imported styles. The store is known for helpful service.

HARRY'S SHOES FOR KIDS
2315 Broadway (bet 83rd and 84th St)   212/874-2034
Mon, Thurs: 10-7:45; Tues, Wed, Fri, Sat: 10-6:45; Sun: 11-6
                                             www.harrys-shoes.com

This popular Upper West Side shoe store is not fancy and is often wildly busy. Every single person working here knows how to fit shoes. The inventory is terrific, lots of big name brands, and the prices are often more reasonable than those at other Manhattan shoe stores. Just bring along some patience, particularly on weekends and in summer. Down the street is **Harry's Shoes** (2299 Broadway, 212/874-2035), with footwear for the rest of the family.

LITTLE ERIC

1118 Madison Ave (bet 83rd and 84th St)   212/717-1513
Mon-Sat: 10-6; Sun noon-6

There's a big difference between a shoe store and a shoemaker. Little Eric is an Italian shoemaker. Everything in this shop is designed and manufactured by them under their private label. They specialize in dressy and casual shoes, boots, and sandals for infants and children. They also indulge grownups with women's sizes to 10½ and men's to 8½. Kids love to come to ride the coin-operated horse and play with the toys. Parents like the welcoming family atmosphere and great customer service. Beautiful Italian shoes and knowledgeable staff to fit children's fast-growing feet make shoe buying pleasurable at Little Eric.

If you have large feet, these outfits have shoes that will fit them.
Johnston & Murphy (345 Madison Ave, 212/697-9375 and 520 Madison Ave, 212/527-2342): men's shoes to size 15
Stapleton Shoe Company (68 Trinity Pl, 212/964-6329): men's shoes to size 18

SHOE GARDEN

152 W 10th St (at Waverly Pl)   212/989-4320
Mon-Sat: 10-6 (Thurs till 7); Sun: noon-5   www.shoegardennyc.com

This West Village newcomer has Astroturf on the floor in a terrarium. It also has a great assortment of fashionable and funky children's shoes. You'll find familiar brands like Merrell, Ecco, and Converse, as well as more unusual European names. Price takes a back seat to fashion at the Shoe Garden, although sales can be quite good. The proprietors are committed to being "green," and they carry eco-friendly shoes. They recycle worn-out sneakers, which are ground up and used in playground materials.

SHOOFLY

42 Hudson St (bet Duane and Thomas St)   212/406-3270
Mon-Sat: 10-7; Sun: noon-6   www.shooflynyc.com

Shoofly carries attractive and reasonably priced European shoes for infants to 14-year-olds. Women with tiny feet will appreciate the chic selection of footwear as well. Shoofly will take care of your shoewear needs with styles both funky and classic. The selection of tights, socks, and fun accessories is great, too!

Shoes—Family

E. VOGEL BOOTS AND SHOES

19 Howard St (one block north of Canal St, bet Broadway and
    Lafayette St)   212/925-2460
Mon-Fri: 8-4; Sat: 8-2 (closed Sat in summer)   www.vogelboots.com

Hank and Dean Vogel and Jack Lynch are the third- and fourth-generation family members to join this business, which has operated since 1879. They will happily fit and supply made-to-measure boots for everyone and shoes for men. Howard is one of those streets that even native New Yorkers don't know exists. Still, many beat a path to Vogel for top-quality shoes and boots (including equestrian boots). While not inexpensive, prices are reasonable for the service involved. Made-to-measure shoes may not always fit properly, but they do at Vogel. Once your pattern is on record, they can make new shoes without a personal visit. For craftsmanship, this spot is top-drawer. There are more than 500 Vogel dealers throughout the world, but this is the original store and the people here are super.

Shopping in Chinatown

Here are some top choices for shopping in Chinatown:

CoCo Fashion (5-7 Doyers St, 917/669-0993): reasonable prices for teen fashions

GLS (Girls Love Shoes) (29 Ludlow St, 917/250-3268): thousands of vintage shoes

---

KENNETH COLE

595 Broadway (at Houston St)	212/965-0283
353 Columbus Ave (bet 76th and 77th St)	212/873-2061
95 Fifth Ave (at 17th St)	212/675-2550
107 E 42nd St (bet Vanderbilt and Park Ave)	212/949-8079
610 Fifth Ave (at 49th St)	212/373-5800
130 E 57th St (at Lexington Ave)	212/688-1670
Hours vary by store	www.kennethcole.com

In addition to signs that induce hearty laughter at the expense of some well-known personalities, Kenneth Cole offers quality shoes, belts, scarves, watches, outerwear, and accessories at sensible prices. Most stores also carry men's and women's sportswear.

LORD JOHN'S BOOTERY

428 Third Ave (bet 29th and 30th St)	212/532-2579

Mon-Fri: 10-8; Sat: 10-7

Lord John's Bootery has been family-owned and -operated for three generations. Renovated and expanded, the store carries one of the largest selections of dress, casual, and comfort shoes in the area. They offer footwear for men and women from such manufacturers as Ecco, Mephisto, Rockport, Sebago, Birkenstock, Merrell, Pikolinos, Santana, and Dansko.

SHOE MANIA

853 Broadway (bet 14th St and Union Square W)	212/253-8744
654 Broadway (bet Bleecker and Bond St)	212/673-0904
331 Madison Ave (bet 42nd and 43rd St)	212/557-6627
30 E 14th St (bet University St and Fifth Ave)	212/627-0420
11 W 34th St (bet Fifth Ave and Ave of the Americas)	212/564-7319
Hours vary by store	www.shoemania.com

Shoe Mania carries men's and women's shoes for fashion, comfort, and sport at great prices. Most major brands—Adidas, Birkenstock, Kenneth Cole, Mephisto, Rockport, Steve Madden, Via Spiga, and others—are stocked in a broad range of sizes.

T.O. DEY CUSTOM SHOE MAKERS
9 E 38th St (bet Fifth and Madison Ave), 7th floor   212/683-6300
Mon-Fri: 9-5   www.todeyshoes.com

T.O. Dey is a solid jack-of-all-trades operation. Though their specialty is custom-made shoes, they can also repair any kind of shoe. These folks will create men's or women's shoes based on a plaster mold of a customer's feet. Their styles are limited only by a client's imagination. They make arch supports, cover shoes to match a garment, and sell athletic shoes for football, basketball, cross-country, hockey, boxing, and running.

Christopher Street

Greenwich Village has an ever-expanding selection of intriguing places to shop and dine. Within the Village, Christopher Street offers several notable choices.

I Sodi (105 Christopher St, 212/414-5774): Tuscan cuisine

Jane Hotel (113 Jane St, 212/924-6700): inexpensive accommodations; shared bathrooms

Kesner (524 Hudson St, 212/206-6330): high-end clothing for guys

Leffot (10 Christopher St, 212/989-4577): luxury shoes for men

Rag & Bone (100 Christopher St, 212/727-2999): edgy menswear; women's and kids' collection two doors down at 104 Christopher Street

---

YORKE FASHION COMFORT CENTRE
140 E 55th St (at Lexington Ave)   212/753-5151, 800/746-3397
Mon-Sat: 10-6; Sun noon-5   www.comfortable-shoes.com

Do you have problem feet but still want to wear fashionable dress, leisure, and sport shoes? For over 40 years Yorke Fashion Comfort has made custom Italian leather footwear for hard-to-fit feet—women's sizes 3 to 13, narrow to extra wide, and men's sizes 7 to 15, narrow to extra wide. All shoes have removable insoles and are made for orthopedic comfort as well as fashion. Certified experts are on hand for consultation, and the on-premise lab fabricates orthotics. Foam casting kits are available for out-of-town clients.

Shoes—Men's

CHURCH'S ENGLISH SHOES
689 Madison Ave (at 62nd St)   212/758-5200
Mon-Sat: 10-6 (Thurs till 7); Sun: noon-4

Anglophiles feel right at home here, not only because of the *veddy* English atmosphere but also for the pure artistry and "Englishness" of the shoes. Church's has been selling English shoes for men since 1873 and is known for classic styles, superior workmanship, and fine leathers. The styles basically remain unchanged year after year, although new designs are occasionally added as a concession to fashion. All shoes are custom-fitted, and if a style or size does not feel right, they will special order a pair that does.

STAPLETON SHOE COMPANY
68 Trinity Pl (at Rector St)   212/964-6329
1 Rector St (bet Broadway and Trinity Pl)   212/425-5260
Mon-Fri: 8:15-5:15

Their motto is "better shoes for less," but that doesn't begin to describe this superlative operation. Gentlemen, these stores offer Bally, Alden, Allen-Edmonds, Cole-Haan, Timberland, Rockport, Johnston & Murphy, and a slew of other top names at discount. There isn't a better source for quality shoes. They are size specialists, carrying men's sizes 5-18 in widths A-EEE.

Shoes—Women's

ANBAR SHOES
60 Reade St (bet Church St and Broadway)   212/227-0253
Mon-Fri: 9-6:20; Sat: 11-5:45

Bargain hunters, rejoice! Anbar customers will find great deals on brand-name styles at discounts up to 80% on over 12,000 pairs of shoes. This is a good place to save money.

GIORDANO'S PETITE SHOES
1150 Second Ave (at 60th St)   212/688-7195
Mon-Fri: 11-7; Sat: 11-6 (call ahead) www.petiteshoes.com

This place has a very special clientele. Partners Susan Giordano and Alan Gonzalez stock a fine selection of women's designer shoes in small sizes (a range that is virtually nonexistent in regular shoe stores). If you're a woman who wears shoes in the 4 to 5½ medium range, you are probably used to shopping in children's shoe departments or having shoes custom-made, either of which can cramp your style. For these women, Giordano's is a godsend. Brands carried include Anne Klein, Stuart Weitzman, Donald Pliner, Via Spiga, and Rangoni.

Sportswear

FOOTACTION USA
430 Seventh Ave (at 34th St)   646/473-1945
Mon-Sat: 9-10; Sun: 9-9   www.footaction.com

Major sports clothing and accessories can be found here! A nice selection of athletic shoes (like Michael Jordan's Nike line) and big name brands like Jordan Clothing, Rocawear, and David Beckham are also available.

GERRY COSBY AND COMPANY
11 Pennsylvania Plaza (at 31st St, east of Seventh Ave)
Mon-Sat: 9:30-6   212/563-6464, 877-563-6464
                     www.cosbysports.com

There's a lot to like about this company. Located at the famous Madison Square Garden, they are a professional business in an appropriate venue for "team sportswear"—that is, what athletes wear. They remain open until game time for all Rangers home games. Gerry Cosby designs and markets protective equipment and is a top supplier of professionally licensed products. The protective equipment and bats are designed for pros but are available to the general public as well. They accept mail, phone, and online orders for everything, including personalized jerseys and jackets.

NAPAPIJRI
149 Mercer St (at Broadway)   212/431-4490
Mon-Sat: 11-7; Sun: 11-6   www.napapijri.com

The name is almost impossible to pronounce, spell, or remember, but don't let that stop you from coming here. Napapijri actually means "Arctic Circle" in Finnish. Travel and adventure are built into their men's and women's sportswear apparel and accessories. Some children's wear is also shown. Soho style is paramount here.

NBA STORE
666 Fifth Ave (at 52nd St)   212/515-6270
Mon-Sat: 10-7; Sun: 11-6   www.nbastore.com

The National Basketball Association does a tremendous job of marketing itself. (I wish the same could be said for all of the NBA players!) This two-level store, occupies a prime location on Fifth Avenue, and is always busy with people buying team jerseys and equipment, and watching NBA videos.

Where to Buy Yoga Wear

Of course you can purchase yoga attire at almost any clothing retailer. However, these shops sell yoga wear endorsed by the pros.
East West Yoga (78 Fifth Ave, Room 2, 212/243-5994)
Jivamukti Yoga School (841 Broadway, 2nd floor, 212/353-0214)
Lululemon (1928 Broadway, 212/712-1767)
Puma (521 Broadway, 212/334-7861)
Realpilates (177 Duane Street, 212/625-0777)

NIKE SPORTSWEAR
21 Mercer St (at Grand St)   212/226-5433
Mon-Sat: 11-7; Sun: noon-6   www.nikesportswear.com

Nike Sportswear is the flagship store for cutting-edge athletic and workout apparel. This flashy space is a maze of rooms with flat-screens TVs. You'll find nylon jackets and hoodies, but Nike shoes are the top feature. Their Nike iD service sets them apart from NikeTown. For $225, serious Nike addicts can customize their Air Force 1 shoes.

NIKETOWN NEW YORK
6 E 57th St (bet Fifth and Madison Ave)   212/891-6453
Mon-Sat: 10-8; Sun: 11-7   www.niketown.com

Product innovation and Nike's sports heritage are the foundations of Niketown New York. They offer a huge selection of Nike products, including footwear, apparel, items for timing and vision, and hot new tech-lab products. The fifth floor has been completely redesigned, dedicating the entire space to Nike Sportswear. Their newest apparel line, NSW, is featured.

PATAGONIA

101 Wooster St (bet Prince and Spring St)   212/343-1776
Mon-Sat: 11-7; Sun: noon-6

426 Columbus Ave (bet 80th and 81st St)   917/441-0011
Mon-Sat: 10-7; Sun: 11-6   www.patagonia.com

If you ask an outdoors type about their favorite brand of attire for hiking, climbing, surfing, or skiing, you'll often hear the name Patagonia. This environmentally-friendly company designs family clothing, packs and totes, blankets, and books. They make wetsuits from organic cotton and sturdy man-made fabrics. The company takes great pains to assure that their clothing allows freedom of movement, is durable, looks good, and feels good against the skin. Even those who don't spend much time in the great outdoors appreciate Patagonia clothing for those same qualities.

Surplus

KAUFMAN'S ARMY & NAVY

319 W 42nd St (bet Eighth and Ninth Ave)   212/757-5670
Mon-Fri: 11-6:30 (Thurs till 7); Sat: noon-6
www.kaufmansarmynavy.com

Kaufman's has long been a favorite of New Yorkers and city visitors for its extensive selection of genuine military surplus from around the globe. Since 1938, they have outfitted dozens of Broadway and TV shows and supplied a number of major motion pictures with military garb. The store is a treasure trove of military collectibles, hats, helmets, uniforms, and insignias. Over a thousand military pins, patches, and medals from armies the world over are on display.

UNCLE SAM'S ARMY NAVY OUTFITTERS

37 W 8th St (bet Fifth Ave and Ave of the Americas)   212/674-2222
Mon-Sat: 10-9; Sun: noon-8:30   www.armynavydeals.com

There are a lot of Army-Navy surplus stores, but this is the only outlet in the city that gets its stock straight from the U.S. government. The quality at Uncle Sam's is very good. You'll find an excellent selection of pants, shirts, tank tops, flight jackets, watches, flags, pins, patches, and more. They will even loan goods for a 48-hour period for various production needs—such as for school plays and church groups—at no cost.

Sweaters

BEST OF SCOTLAND

581 Fifth Ave (bet 47th and 48th St), penthouse
Mon-Fri: 10-6; Sat: 10-4   212/644-0403, 800/215-3864
www.cashmerenyc.com

These folks are among the very best purveyors of cashmere goods. There is a big difference in the quality of cashmere from Scotland and the Far East. At Best of Scotland you will find luxurious sweaters, baby blankets, ladies' capes, scarves, mufflers, and throws. Don't worry about sizes: you'll find ladies' sweaters up to size 48 and gentlemen's to size 59. In addition to beautiful classic styles, you'll find multiple-ply styles with zippers and cables. Nice people, too!

GRANNY-MADE
381 Amsterdam Ave (bet 78th and 79th St)　　　212/496-1222
Mon-Fri: 12:30-6:30; Sat: 10-6; Sun: 12:30-5:30　www.grannymade.com

Michael Rosenberg (grandson of Bert Levy, the namesake "Granny") has assembled an extensive collection of sweaters for infants, children up to 6X/7, and women. These include handmade sweaters from all over the world, as well as some hand-loomed right here at home. The collection of women's sweaters, knitwear, soft items, and accessories is unique. They have an extensive selection of infant and toddler clothing, toys, hats, gifts, and accessories. Granny-Made has an extremely service-oriented, knowledgeable staff. During the holidays (Thanksgiving to New Year's) they sell "Moon and Star" cookies, made from a recipe passed down three generations!

JULIE ARTISANS' GALLERY
762 Madison Ave (bet 65th and 66th St)　　　212/717-5959
Mon-Sat: 11-6　　　　　　　　　　　　　　www.julieartisans.com

One look inside this shop and you will realize that nothing is mass-produced. Innovative artists from around the world create colorful and wearable art garments. Sweaters come to life with distinctive graphics, and jewelers fashion pieces using conventional metals and gems, as well as unexpected components. Wonderful scarves are made from a variety of fabrics and traditional and nontraditional techniques. Jackets, dresses, skirts and tops are attractively displayed. Yes, the gallery has a few non-wearable pieces of art, too.

Swimwear

CANYON BEACHWEAR
1136 Third Ave (bet 66th and 67th St)　　　917/432-0732
Mon-Fri: 10-8; Sat: 10-7; Sun: 11-6　　www.canyonbeachwear.com

Before you dive into a pool, visit a beach, or take a cruise, come to this store. Canyon Beachwear is the ultimate in swim, sun, and vacation wear. You'll find over a thousand swimsuits, with most major manufacturers represented. Great salespeople, also!

PARKE & RONEN
176 Ninth Ave (at 21st St)　　　　　　　212/989-4245
Mon-Sat: noon-8; Sun: noon-6

If you're a man looking for a new swimsuit, Parke & Ronen is a great Chelsea destination. The store focuses on four styles: bikini briefs, four-inch boxers, eight-inch surfer shorts, and something the shop calls snap shorts. All are folded neatly underneath a table in an array of stripes, plaids, and paisley patterns. After designing for six years, Ronen Jehezkel and Parke Lutter decided to feature their unique creations in their own store (although Parke & Ronen designs are also found in other stores). You will find T-shirts, trousers, and a collection of women's clothing, all with refined details, quality fabrics, and exquisite fits.

Teens

BILLIONAIRE BOYS CLUB & ICE CREAM
456 West Broadway (at Houston St)   212/777-2225
Mon-Sat: noon-7; Sun: noon-6   www.bbcicecream.com

I walked into the Billionaire Boys Club & Ice Cream expecting to find an ice-cream store. Well, there was no ice cream, but I did find a novel collection of clothing under that unique name. The first floor has sneakers and more. The dark stairs to the second floor reveal a unique clothing line.

T-Shirts

EISNER BROS.
75 Essex St (bet Broome and Delancey St)   212/475-6868
Mon-Thurs: 9:30-6; Fri: 8:30-2; Sun: 9:30-4   www.eisnerbrothers.com

Eisner Bros. carries a full line of licensed NBA, NFL, NHL, MLB, collegiate, and other sports, character, and novelty T-shirts and sweat shirts. Major quantity discounts are offered. Personalizing is available on all items. They are the largest source in the area for printable corporate sportswear, T-shirts, sweat shirts, caps, jackets, work clothing, uniforms, reflective vests, tote bags, towels, aprons, umbrellas, gym and exercise equipment, team uniforms, and much more.

Uniforms

JA-MIL UNIFORMS
92 Orchard St (bet Delancey and Broome St)   212/677-8190
Mon-Thurs: 10-5 (or by appointment)

This is *the* bargain spot for those who must wear uniforms for work but do not want to spend a fortune on them. There are outfits for doctors, nurses, and technicians, as well as the finest domestic uniforms and chef's apparel. Clogs, Nurse Mates, and SAS shoes are available in white and colors. Mail orders are accepted.

Western Wear

BILLY MARTIN'S
1034 Third Ave (bet 61st and 62nd St)   212/861-3100
Mon-Fri: 10-7; Sat: 10-6; Sun: noon-5   www.billymartin.com

If unique, upscale Western wear is on your shopping list, then head to Billy Martin's! They have a great selection of deerskin jackets, shirts, riding pants, skirts, hats, and parkas. They also boast one of the best collections of cowboy boots for men and women in the city. Great accessory items like bandannas, jewelry, silver buckles, and belt straps complete the outfit. The items are well-tooled and well-designed, and they are priced accordingly.

WESTERN SPIRIT
395 Broadway (at Walker St)   212/343-1476
Daily 10:30-7:30   www.weseternspiritnyc.com

You don't have to ride into town on a horse to shop here for authentic Western fashions. Alongside cowboy hats, shirts, jeans, moccasins, jackets, and stylish boots are colorful selections of Native American jewelry, leather belts, and silver belt buckles. Interspersed among the clothing and leather saddles are Western furniture and artistic home decor items befitting a bunkhouse, kid's room, or your own home on the range.

Women's Accessories

ARTBAG
1130 Madison Ave (at 84th St)   212/744-2720
Mon-Fri: 9:30-5; Sat 10-4   www.artbag.com

European-trained artisans craft purses, wallets, belts, accessory cases, briefcases, and even pet accessories from a large selection of exotic skins, leathers, and fine fabrics. Choose from ready-made, beautifully beaded bags and handsome wallets, or supply your own quality materials for a unique accessory. They also do all types of umbrella, luggage, and handbag repairs, from minor stitching to total renovations.

BLUE BAG
266 Elizabeth St (bet Prince and Houston St)   212/966-8566
Mon-Sat: 11-7:30; Sun: noon-7

Every month you'll find a different stock of small designer bags from all over the world at Blue Bag. You likely won't find these bags in any other stores, and Blue Bag never reorders the same bag. Prices range from $50 to $700 for suedes, leathers, and other materials.

DESIGN IN TEXTILES BY MARY JAEGER
17 Laight St (bet Varick St and Ave of the Americas)   212/625-0081
Tues-Fri: 10-4 (or by appointment)   www.maryjaeger.com

Mary Jaeger has relocated from Nolita to a gallery adjacent to her Tribeca design studio. Handcrafted women's items available at her shop include capes, shawls, limited-edition shibori tees, tunics, and 3D textured wool wraps. You'll also find such custom interior accessories as pillows, throws, and wall panels.

JIMMY CHOO
716 Madison Ave (bet 63rd and 64th St)   212/759-7078
Mon-Sat: 10-6 (Thurs till 7); Sun: noon-5   www.jimmychoo.com

Follow the celebrities to Jimmy Choo, where you can find classic boots, daytime and evening bags, small leather goods, fabulous designer footwear, and jeweled sandals. Bring your goldest credit card!

SUAREZ
5 W 56th St (bet Fifth Ave and Ave of the Americas)   212/315-3870
Mon-Sat: 10-6; Sun: 11-5   www.suarezny.com

Suarez has been in business for more than a half-century. In that time, they have cultivated a reputation for quality merchandise, good service, excellent selection, and reasonable prices. For years the Suarez name has been whispered by women-in-the-know as a resource for fine leather goods. They offer a great selection of exotic skin bags in a variety of colors.

Women's—General

ABBY Z.
57 Greene St (bet Spring and Broome St)   212/944-8886
Mon-Sat: 11-7; Sun: noon-6   www.abbyz.homestead.com

Bright, fun, and *glitzy* describe these contemporary fashions for ladies who wear sizes 12 and up. Abby selects clothing and accessories to enhance a woman's inner and outer beauty and raise self-confidence, which gives credence to her motto: "It's Good to Be Me." Offering fashion seminars and makeovers, this is a must-visit shopping stop. In addition, there is an in-house tailor to make necessary adjustments.

ANNELORE
636 Hudson St (at Horatio St)   212/255-5574
Mon-Sat: 11-7; Sun: 11-6

Timeless fashion defines the clothes at Annelore. The well-edited collection is inspired by and made in New York City. This gem of a shop also highlights local one-of-a-kind jewelry and accessories.

Shopping Abbreviations
Be sure to read the fine print in sales ads and in-store promotions. Some are sprinkled with abbreviations. Here are a few common ones:

AR: after rebate
BOGO: buy one, get one
CPN: coupon
MIR: mail-in rebate
S&H: shipping and handling

BENEATH
265 E 78th St (near Second Ave)   212/288-3800
Tues-Fri: noon-8; Sat-Sun: noon-6; Mon: noon-8 (summer only)

Stuffed into a tiny shop that is the size of some ladies' closets is an assortment of casual, comfortable, and elegant women's clothing. Think fun-in-the-sun Southern California styles in dresses, separates, and accessories. New merchandise in a full range of sizes arrives weekly and turns over quickly.

BETSEY JOHNSON
248 Columbus Ave (bet 71st and 72nd St)   212/362-3364
138 Wooster St (bet Prince and Houston St)   212/995-5048
251 E 60th St (at Second Ave)   212/319-7699
1060 Madison Ave (at 80th St)   212/734-1257
Hours vary by store   www.betseyjohnson.com

In the 1960s and 1970s, Betsey Johnson was *the* fashion designer. While her style is always avant-garde, it's never *too* far out. Her lacy, demure frocks are perfect for parties. Johnson believes in making her own statement, and each store is unique, despite the fact that she has over 60 of them in this country and abroad. Prices are bearable, particularly at the Soho store (which started as an outlet). Incidentally, it's hard to overlook the shops: pink with neon accents, yellow floral with gold accents, great windows, and funky, personable staff.

CALYPSO

815 Madison Ave (bet 68th and 69th St)	212/585-0310
935 Madison Ave (at 74th St)	212/535-4100
654 Hudson St (bet 13th and Gansevoort St)	646/638-3000
280 Mott St (bet Prince and Houston St)	212/965-0990
191 Lafayette St (bet Broome and Grand St)	212/941-6512
137 West Broadway (bet Duane and Thomas St)	212/608-2222
Hours vary by store	www.calypso-celle.com

This chain of upscale stores features casual resort-like fashions that are high in color and trendiness. You'll find women's and children's attire, accessories, and some home items. You will understand the bohemian-chic merchandise when you realize that the store started in the West Indies and the designer was born in the south of France.

EDGE*nyNOHO

65 Bleecker St (bet Broadway and Lafayette St)	212/358-0255
Wed-Sun: noon-8 (Sun till 7)	www.edgeny.com

This is *the* place for new fashion items, accessories, and other merchandise by 50 designers. Some are just getting into the New York market, while others are now well-known names. Located in the historic Louis Sullivan building, Edge is a fun place for those in their 20s and 30s to shop. Prices range broadly from $25 to $6,000.

EILEEN FISHER

314 E 9th St (bet First and Second Ave)	212/529-5715
521 Madison Ave (bet 53rd and 54th St)	212/759-9888
341 Columbus Ave (bet 76th and 77th St)	212/362-3000
10 Columbus Circle (at 58th St), Suite 205	212/823-9575
166 Fifth Ave (bet 21st and 22nd St)	212/924-4777
1039 Madison Ave (at 79th St)	212/879-7799
395 West Broadway (bet Spring and Broome St)	212/431-4567
Hours vary by store	www.eileenfisher.com

For the lady who likes her clothes cool, loose, and casual, look no further than Eileen Fisher. This talented designer has assembled a collection of easy-care, mostly washable natural-fiber outfits in earthy colors. They travel well and are admired for their simple and attractive lines. There are also accessories, sleepwear, outerwear, and shoes to round out your wardrobe. From a small start in the East Village to seven units all over Manhattan and space in some of the top stores, Eileen has produced a winner. The East Village store features discounted merchandise and first-quality goods.

ELENY

152 W 36th St (bet Seventh Ave and Broadway), Suite 504	
Mon-Sat: 10-6 (by appointment)	212/564-1515

Have you dreamed about designing a dress for yourself? Well, at Eleny, this is possible. The customer-oriented personnel enjoy receiving input from clients, and you can rest assured your evening gown will not be seen anywhere else. They will send sketches and finished gowns anywhere, and Eleny (who has been designing clothes for over three decades) gives each client her undivided attention. All fabrics are imported from Europe.

ELIZABETH CHARLES
639½ Hudson St (bet Gansevoort and Horatio St)   212/243-3201
Tues-Sat: noon-7; Sun: noon-6:30   www.elizabeth-charles.com

Flirty original clothes for all occasions from Australia, New Zealand, and other international designers make this a very special shop. Ladies can bring their husbands or significant others, as the shop provides a great antique couch for patient partners!

GEMINOLA
41 Perry St (bet Seventh Ave and 4th St)   212/675-1994
Tues,Wed: noon-7;Thurs-Sat: noon-8; Sun: noon-6   www.geminola.com

Geminola has an eclectic assortment of styles for the home and self. All of their clothing is made from vintage pieces, and the original designs are adapted to customer specifications.

Little-Known Neighborhood Gems

Lower East Side

Bacaro (136 Division St, 212/941-5060):Venetian tavern
Main Squeeze (19 Essex St, 212/614-3109): accordions!
Still Life (77 Orchard St, 212/575-9704): haberdashery
Wendy Mink Jewelry (72 Orchard St, 212/260-5298): handmade
   costume jewelry

Soho

Amarcord (252 Lafayette St, 212/431-4161): vintage European clothing and accessories for men and women
Mango (561 Broadway, 212/343-7012): Spanish line of men's and
   women's clothing

Upper West Side

Laytner's Linen and Home (2270 Broadway, 212/724-0180):
   essentials for the home; affordable

GISELLE
143 Orchard St (bet Delancey and Rivington St)   212/673-1900
Sun-Thurs: 9-6; Fri: 9-5 (till 3 in winter)   www.giselleny.com

Women's European designer sportswear, current-season goods, a large selection (sizes 4 to 20), and discount prices are among the reasons Giselle is one of the more popular shopping spots on the Lower East Side. All merchandise is first quality. Factor in excellent service and four floors of merchandise, and Giselle is well worth a trip.

LEA'S DESIGNER FASHIONS
125 Orchard St (at Delancey St)   212/677-2043
Sun-Thurs: 9:30-5:30; Fri: 9:30-4 (till 3 in summer)

You don't have to pay full price for your Louis Feraud, Valentino, or various European designer clothes. Lea's, a popular Lower East Side outlet, discounts merchandise up to 30% and sells the previous season's styles for 50% to 60% off. Don't expect much in the way of amenities, but you'll save enough to afford a special night out to show off your new outfit!

MIRIAM RIGLER
41 E 60th St (bet Park and Madison Ave)   212/581-5519
Mon-Sat: 10-6 (Thurs till 7)   www.miriamrigler.com

Miriam Rigler is the quintessential ladies' dress shop. They have it all: personal attention, expert alterations, wardrobe coordination, custom designing (including bridal), and a large selection of sportswear, knits, suiting, and evening gowns in sizes 4 to 20. Also featured: custom headpieces, traditional and nontraditional bridal gowns, mother-of-the-bride ensembles, and debutante dresses. A newer department shows original paintings described as "gently priced." Despite the location, all items are discounted, including special orders. Don't miss the costume jewelry!

Tips for Shopping Sample Sales

As I've said elsewhere, shopping in New York is expensive. However, with a little legwork, dressing in classy clothes does not have to mean paying full retail prices. Designer sample sales are held on a regular basis with deep discounts.

Here are a few tips:

- Know your size, as dressing rooms are sometimes nonexistent.
- Bring cash, since checks and plastic are not always accepted.
- Scrutinize your intended purchases, as all sales are final.
- Be prepared for disarray; many locations are temporary sales rooms located up several flights of stairs.
- Scout out sample-sale shopping websites. **Daily Candy** (www. dailycandy.com) gives heads-ups on sales for clothing, home goods, and beauty products, as well as other fun shopping tidbits.

OWL'S LAB
20 E 12th St (bet University Pl and Fifth Ave)   212/633-2672
Mon-Sat: 11-8; Sun: noon-6   www.owlslab.com

This shop is stocked with everyday clothing and accessories for the everyday gal. Each season they offer a large selection of brands from all over the world. Trendy, classic items are carefully selected with an entire outfit or look in mind.

PALMA
463 Broome St (bet Mercer and Greene St)   212/966-1722
Tues-Sat: 11-7; Sun: noon-6   www.palmasoho.com

Palma has remained in business in Soho for over three decades, and that is a tribute to sound retailing. This store carries clothing from American and occasionally English, Italian, Canadian, French, and Spanish designers. Lenny Variano loves working with lesser-known American designers. They also provide personal wardrobe consultations.

PIXIE MARKET
100 Stanton St (bet Ludlow and Orchard St)   212/253-0953
Daily: noon-8   www.pixiemarket.com

Young, fun, and *funky* describe Pixie Market's clothing and accessories. Only a few of the cute women's separates and dresses are stocked in each size, and they are generally priced under $100. A limited selection of special finds costs more, but still won't break the budget. Check out their private label totes and shoes to flatter your newest outfit.

PRADA

575 Broadway (at Prince St)	212/334-8888
841 Madison Ave (at 70th St)	212/327-4200
45 E 57th St (bet Park and Madison Ave)	212/308-2332
724 Fifth Ave (bet 56th and 57th St)	212/664-0010
Hours vary by store	www.prada.com

Prada is one of the most revered high-end brands in the world! Their Soho location is glamorous and attracts well-heeled fashionistas and tourists. The distinctive, coveted label embellishes chic clothing, knock-out shoes, and trendy leather goods and accessories for men and women. A Prada handbag is an essential fashion statement for many ladies, and there is an ample assortment of sizes, shapes, and colors. A line of fragrances complements any attire.

PROJECT NO. 8

138 Division Street (bet Orchard and Ludlow St)	212/925-5599
Tues-Sat: noon-7; Sun: noon-6	www.projectno8.com

You could say that partners Brian Janusiak and Elizabeth Beer are "project oriented." This is their eighth project together, hence the name. In this venture, they've created a boutique of clothing and accessories from international and local designers. The lineup includes affordable dresses, separates, and knits for women, and a small selection of men's shirts and knits. Also expect the unexpected, such as German fountain pens, designer shoes, and eclectic trinkets.

REALLY GREAT THINGS

284 Columbus Ave (bet 73rd and 74th St)	212/787-5354
300 Columbus Ave (at 74th St)	212/787-5868
Tues-Sat: 11-7; Sun: 1-6	

There are not many stores on the Upper West Side like these! The store at 284 Columbus Avenue is filled with high couture merchandise, while the one at 300 Columbus Avenue has a more casual feel and lower prices. Both are indeed full of really great things: clothing, bags, shoes, and accessories from the hottest European designers.

REBECCA TAYLOR

260 Mott St (bet Houston and Prince St)	212/966-0406
Daily: 11-7	www.rebeccataylor.com

Here you'll find clothing, shoes, handbags, hosiery, and accessories. The Nolita location is a popular stop for the young (and young-at-heart) who are looking for whimsical merchandise.

ROBERTA FREYMANN

153 E 70th St (bet Lexington and Third Ave)	212/585-3767
Mon-Fri: 10:30-6:30; Sat: 11-6	www.roberta-freymann.com

No need to buy an around-the-world airplane ticket. Just grab a cab to this vibrant shop to hear Roberta tell you all about the clothes and accessories she has assembled from all over the world. The colorful and unique wine drop necklace is sure to bring rave reviews any time it's worn. Check out the cruise wear, beaded handbags, warm scarves, and fashion jewelry.

SAN FRANCISCO CLOTHING
975 Lexington Ave (at 71st St)   212/472-8740
Mon-Sat: 11-6; Sun: noon-5   www.sanfranciscoclothing.com

The women's and children's items at San Francisco Clothing are just right for a casual weekend. Their merchandise is comfortable, colorful, and classy. The mature woman will find an especially good selection. Separates, like taffeta blouses to go with your evening clothes, are also a specialty.

TEMPERLEY LONDON
453 Broome St (at Mercer St)   212/219-2929
Mon-Sat: 11-7; Sun: noon-6   www.temperleylondon.com

This distinctive shop was created by London fashion designer Alice Temperley. Plenty of big names shop here for women's ready-to-wear and hand-beaded bridal dresses, as well as leather and suede accessories. Champagne, wine, and accompaniments are served, as you might expect at a classy shop like this. If you want to splurge, then this is a good place to start.

TG-170
170 Ludlow St (bet Houston and Stanton St)   212/995-8660
Mon-Sun: noon-8   www.tg170.com

You won't see the clothes carried here in any other store. That is because most of the merchandise is made in small quantities especially for this store. TG-170 started as a studio where baseball hats and T-shirts were made but has grown into a retail showroom that displays unique items from young, emerging designers and some well-known ones. Freitag bags, too!

Women's—Maternity

BELLY DANCE MATERNITY
548 Hudson St (bet Charles and Perry St)   212/645-3640
Mon-Thurs: 11-7; Fri, Sat: 11-6, Sun: noon-5
www.bellydancematernity.com

Hip and fashionable moms-to-be definitely need to know about Belly Dance Maternity, a bright and funky store that's taken the West Village by storm. It is a branch of a store that started in Chicago. This is a great source for affordable jeans, T-shirts, lingerie, swimsuits, and cool dresses —even ultra-hip diaper bags.

Women's Millinery

BARBARA FEINMAN MILLINERY
66 E 7th St (bet First and Second Ave)   212/358-7092
Mon-Sat: 12:30-8; Sun: 1-7   www.barbarafeinmanmillinery.com

Although accessories are carried here, the big draw is the hats, made on-premises from original designs. If you are looking for something really funky—or, by contrast, very classy—try this spot first. Costume jewelry is also a specialty. Custom orders are welcome!

THE HAT SHOP
120 Thompson St (at Prince St)   212/219-1445
Mon-Sat: noon-7; Sun: 1-6 (closed Mon in summer)
                                        www.thehatshopnyc.com

Owner Linda Pagan has quite a background. The boss at the Hat Shop was formerly a Wall Street broker, bartender, and world traveler. The stock reflects her diverse history, with showings from 30 local milliners. Sewn and knit hats are priced from $20 to $125; blocked hats run from $125 to $700. Custom orders are welcome.

SUZANNE COUTURE MILLINERY
27 E 61st St (bet Park and Madison Ave)   212/593-3232
Mon-Fri: 10-6; Sat: 11-5   www.suzannehats.com

The Kentucky Derby, Easter, and weddings are just a few of the special occasions that call for the perfect hat. Suzanne and her talented staff create stunning bridal headpieces and high fashion hats. Exotic feathers, Austrian crystals, gleaming pearls, and quality trims embellish classic and contemporary hat shapes to form one-of-a-kind designs. A Suzanne bridal headpiece is a work of art, be it a simple tiara or a long flowing veil with a fresh-flower band.

Women's Undergarments

A.W. KAUFMAN
73 Orchard St (bet Broome and Grand St)
Sun-Thurs: 10:30-5; Fri: 10:30-2   212/226-1629, 212/226-1788

For three generations A.W. Kaufman has combined excellent merchandise with quality customer service. They specialize in European designer lingerie for women and men. Among the wonderful labels you will find are Hanro, Chantell, Wolford, LaPerla, Zimmerli, Joelle, Fantasy, Pluto, and many more.

HOWARDS SPORTWEAR
69 Orchard St (at Grand St)   212/226-4307, 888/974-2727
Sun-Fri: 9-5:30   www.shopatshellys.com

Howard transformed itself from a typical Lower East Side shop into a fashionable boutique without sacrificing the bargain prices. They carry an excellent selection of women's underwear, including top names like Hanes, Bali, Vanity Fair, Warners, Maidenform, Wacoal, Olga, Lilyette, Chantell, and Jockey.

IMKAR COMPANY (M. KARFIOL AND SON)
294 Grand St (bet Allen and Eldridge St)   212/925-2459
Mon-Thurs: 10-5; Fri: 9:30-2; Sun: 10-5 (till 3 in summer)

Imkar carries pajamas, underwear, and shifts for women at roughly a third off retail prices. A full line of Carter's infants' and children's wear is also available at good prices. The store has a fine line of women's lingerie, including dusters and gowns. Featured names include Model's Coat, Vanity Fair, Arrow, Jockey, Lollipop, and Munsingwear. Gold Toe hosiery and Arrow and Van Heusen shirts for men are also stocked.

LA PETITE COQUETTE
51 University Pl (bet 9th and 10th St)   212/473-2478
Mon-Sat: 11-7 (Thurs till 8); Sun: noon-6   www.thelittleflirt.com

Interested in a male-friendly lingerie store that will take care of your gift needs? La Petite Coquette offers a large, eclectic mix of lingerie from around the world in a diverse price range. I like their description of the atmosphere: "Flirtatious!" You'll find everything from classic La Perla to edgy designers like Aubade. There are also old standbys like Cosabella, Hanky Panky, Mary Green, On Gossamer, and Eberjey.

UNDERNEATH IT ALL
444 E 75th St (at York Ave)   212/717-1976
Mon-Thurs: 10-6

160 E 34th St (at Lexington Ave), 4th floor   212/779-2517
Mon-Fri: 9-4:30   www.underneathitallnyc.com

Underneath It All is a one-stop shopping service for women who have had breast surgery. You can be assured of attentive, informed, and personal service from the staff, some of whom are breast cancer survivors. The store carries a large selection of breast forms in light and dark skin tones and in a variety of shapes, sizes, and contours. They specialize in breast equalizers and enhancers to create body symmetry in your bra. There is also a complete line of mastectomy and brandname bras; mastectomy and designer swimwear; sleepwear, loungewear, and body suits; and wigs and fashionable head accessories.

VICTORIA'S SECRET
565 Broadway (at Prince St)   212/274-9519
19 Fulton St (South Street Seaport)   212/962-8122
115 Fifth Ave (bet 18th and 19th St)   212/477-4118
901 Ave of the Americas (bet 32nd and 33rd St)   646/473-0950
1328 Broadway (at 34th St)   212/356-8380
34 E 57th St (bet Park and Madison Ave)   212/758-5592
722 Lexington Ave (bet 58th and 59th St)   212/230-1647
1240 Third Ave (at 72nd St)   212/717-7035
2333 Broadway (at 85th St)   212/595-7861
165 E 86th St (bet Lexington and Third Ave)   646/672-9183
Hours vary by store   www.victoriassecret.com

These are some of the sexiest stores in the world! The beautiful lingerie and bedroom garb, bridal peignoirs, exclusive silks, and accessories are displayed against the most alluring backdrops. The personnel are absolutely charming as well.

Coins, Stamps

STACK'S RARE COINS
123 W 57th St (at Ave of the Americas)   212/582-2580
Mon-Fri: 10-5   www.stacks.com

Established in 1858, Stack's is the country's oldest and largest rare-coin dealer. Moreover, it is still a family operation. Specializing in coins, medals, bullion, and paper money of interest to collectors, Stack's has a solid reputation for individual service, integrity, and knowledge of the field. In addition to walk-in business, Stack's conducts ten or so public auctions a year. Both neophytes and experienced numismatists can do well at Stack's.

Computers
(See also "Electronics")

RCS COMPUTER EXPERIENCE
575 Madison Ave (at 56th St)   212/949-6935
Mon-Fri: 10-7; Sat, Sun: 10-6   www.rcsnet.com

RCS is the best name to know for computers, phones and accessories, radios, and all the latest gadgets. The personnel are well-informed, the selections are vast, and the gift possibilities are endless. Customers enjoy the hassle-free environment. For those who like high-tech toys for adults (like your author), RCS is heaven!

TEKSERVE
119 W 23rd St (bet Ave of the Americas and Seventh Ave)
Mon-Fri: 9-8; Sat: 10-6; Sun: noon-6   212/929-3645
                                                               www.tekserve.com

Tekserve sells and services Macintosh computers and other Apple products. They also have a pro audio and video department, and sell all kinds of Mac accessories. On-site service and equipment rentals are offered. In business since 1987, their interest in individual customers is evidenced by the fact that Tekserve is busy all the time.

If Mac computers, iPhones, iPod players, and related gizmos are the "Apple" of your eye, don't miss **Apple Fifth Avenue** (767 Fifth Ave, 212/336-1440). This retail store on Fifth Avenue is identified by a stunning 32-foot tall glass tower in front of the General Motors Building. It is open 24/7 and is crowded with fascinated shoppers of all ages.

Cosmetics, Drugs, Perfumes

C.O. BIGELOW CHEMISTS
414 Ave of the Americas (bet 8th and 9th St)   212/533-2700
Mon-Fri: 8 a.m.-9 p.m.; Sat: 8:30-7; Sun: 8:30-5:30
                                                        www.bigelowchemists.com

Bigelow touts itself as the oldest apothecary in America, and the old-school approach to customer service helps explain its longevity. The selection of signature Bigelow products and other brandnames is vast, with treatments for almost any condition from acne to obesity. Cruise the aisles for beauty and health-care products for every member of the family. A carefully selected assortment of gifts and fragrances is available, too.

KIEHL'S
109 Third Ave (bet 13th and 14th St)   212/677-3171, 800/543-4571
Mon-Sat: 11-8; Sun: 11-6

154 Columbus Ave (bet 66th and 67th St)   212/799-3438
Mon-Sat: 10-8; Sun: 11-7   www.kiehls.com

Kiehl's has been a New York institution since 1851. Their special treatments and preparations are made by hand and distributed internationally. Natural ingredients are used in their full lines of cleansers, scrubs, toners, moisturizers, eye-area preparations, men's creams, masks, body moisturizers, bath and shower products, sports items, ladies' leg-grooming formulations, shampoos, conditioners, and treatments. Express interest in a particular product and you'll receive a decent-size sample and advice about using it. Kiehl's counters are located in Bloomingdale's and Barneys, too.

Crafts

ALLCRAFT JEWELRY & ENAMELING CENTER
135 W 29th St (bet Ave of the Americas and Seventh Ave), Room 205
Mon-Fri: 9:15-5:30 (open late some evenings)
212/279-7077, 800/645-7124

Allcraft is *the* jewelry-making supply store. Their catalog includes a complete line of tools and supplies for jewelry making, silver- and metalsmithing, lost-wax casting, and much more. Out-of-towners usually order from their catalog, but New Yorkers shouldn't miss an opportunity to visit this gleaming cornucopia. Call for a catalog.

> Over the years, the cost of Cool Water—my favorite brand of aftershave lotion—has steadily climbed. I was delighted to find this product at **M&R Perfumes** (1178 Broadway, 212/481-4680) for less than half-price. You, too, may find your favorite fragrance at deep discount.

CITY QUILTER
133 W 25th St (bet Ave of the Americas and Seventh Ave)
Tues-Fri: 11-7; Sat: 10-6; Sun: 11-5   212/807-0390
www.cityquilter.com

This is the only shop in Manhattan that's completely devoted to quilting. They serve everyone from beginners to professionals with classes, books, notions, thread, gifts, New York-themed fabrics, patterns and kits, and 3,000 bolts of all-cotton fabrics, many hand-dyed.

CLAYWORKS POTTERY
332 E 9th St (bet First and Second Ave)   212/677-8311
Tues-Thurs: 3-7; Fri: 3-8:30; Sat: 1-8:30; Sun: 2-8:30;
and by appointment   www.clayworkspottery.com

Since 1974, talented Helaine Sorgen has been at work here. If you are interested in stoneware and porcelain, then you will love Clayworks, which has a wide range for tabletop and home decor. All of Clayworks' pottery is lead-free and dishwasher- and microwave-safe. Everything is individually produced, from teapots to casseroles, mugs, and sake sets. One-of-a-kind decorative pieces include honey pots, garlic jars, pitchers, cream and sugar sets, vases, goblets, platters, and bowls. Small classes in wheel-throwing are given for adults. Bridal registry and commission work are available by appointment.

GOTTA KNIT!
14 E 34th St (bet Fifth and Madison Ave), 5th floor
Mon-Fri: 11-6 (Wed, Thurs till 7); Sat, Sun: 11-4   212/989-3030
(closed Sun in summer)   www.gottaknit.net

At Gotta Knit! you will find luxury yarns for hand-knitting, crocheting, and custom pattern-writing for unique garments, as well as a selection of accessories, books, and buttons. Individual instruction and knitting classes are offered, too.

KNITTY CITY
208 W 79th St (bet Broadway and Amsterdam Ave)   212/787-5896
Mon, Fri, Sat: 11-6; Wed, Thurs: 11-8; Sun: noon-5   www.knittycity.com

Knitty City stocks a fine selection of yarn for knitting and crocheting., and an assortment of free patterns. There are also books, notions, classes, and a sampling of finished items.

WOOLGATHERING
318 E 84th St (bet First and Second Ave)   212/734-4747
Tues-Fri: 10:30-6; Sat: 10:30-5; Sun: noon-5

Woolgathering is a unique oasis dedicated to the fine art of knitting. You'll find a big selection of quality European woolen, cotton, and novelty yarns. They carry many exclusive classic and contemporary designs, a complete library of knitting magazines and books, and European-made knitting implements and gadgets. They also provide very professional finishing services, as well as crocheting and needlepoint. They will even help with your project if purchases are made at the store and will loan books to customers.

THE YARN COMPANY
2274 Broadway (bet 81st and 82nd St), 2nd floor
Tues-Sat: noon-6 (Wed till 8)   212/787-7878, 888-927-6265
                                       www.theyarnco.com

The largest selection of unique high-end knitting yarns in the city can be found here. You'll find cashmeres, merino wools, silks, linens, rayons, and more. The best part of this second-floor operation is the personal interest shown by the owners, who have written five knitting books. There are many samples to look at, and these folks are up to date on new yarns and designs. Workshops and classes are available to learn to purl, cast-on, and bind-off.

Dance Items

CAPEZIO DANCE THEATRE SHOPS
1650 Broadway (at 51st St), 2nd floor   212/245-2130
136 E 61st St (at Lexington Ave)   212/758-8833
201 Amsterdam Ave (at 69th St)   212/586-5140
1651 Third Ave (bet 92nd and 93rd St), 3rd floor   212/348-7210
Hours vary by store   www.capeziodance.com

Capezio Dance Theatre Shops offer one-stop shopping for all your dance, theater, and fitness needs. These dance emporiums stock the Capezio brand's full line, including sections for men, Flamenco, Skatewear, and a variety of shoes and accessories. You don't have to be a performer to appreciate the wares. The Third Avenue location carries only children's goods.

ON STAGE DANCEWEAR

197 Madison Ave (bet 34th and 35th St)   212/725-1174, 866/725-1174
Mon-Fri: 10-6:30; Sat: 11-6   www.onstagedancewear.com

On Stage serves professional ballet and theater companies across the world, including the New York City Ballet. Individuals are welcome, too! You'll find everything in dancewear for ballet, tap, and ballroom. They specialize in discount dancewear and are an authorized dealer for Capezio. This is also your source for bodywear for yoga and cheerleading.

Time Warner Center (10 Columbus Circle, 212/823-6300) is a vertical mall. In a dramatic setting on the corner of Central Park West and Central Park South, the complex offers much for well-heeled shoppers, diners, and lodgers. Assembled under one roof are The Art of Shaving, bebe, Borders Books & Music, Coach, Cole Haan, Davidoff of Geneva, Equinox Fitness Club, L'Occitane, Montmarte, Stuart Weitzman, Swarovski, Thomas Pink, Williams-Sonoma, and more. For a quick bite to eat or a leisurely, memorable dining experience, try Porter House New York, Stone Rose Lounge, Asiate, Bouchon Bakery, per se, Godiva Chocolatier, and the fabulous Whole Foods Market.

The magnificent Mandarin Oriental New York (see Services) is a deluxe place to rest your head. All of this luxury comes at a price, and only time will tell whether New Yorkers and visitors will support the various venues. No expense has been spared to bring a mall to Manhattan that compares with the very best in America.

Department Stores (An Overview)

Many of us remember when department stores were *the* gathering place for folks to meet friends, have lunch, and make a day of shopping and browsing. Then came the malls, huge and impersonal, which attracted the crowds. Now, believe it or not, the pendulum is slowly swinging back, but this time mostly to smaller specialty stores like the ones you will find in this book. New York is no different, except that we are blessed in this grand city with some truly great department stores, probably more than in any other city in the world. Having been raised in a department-store family, I watch them closely and now present my impressions of the current operations.

A little history is pertinent. Some great names in the merchandising field have disappeared: Gimbel's at Herald Square was always on par with its neighbor, Macy's. Abraham & Strauss was a popular venue. B. Altman & Co., now a library site, was a very classy and "proper" store.

Probably no one person has done more to change the landscape of retailing in recent years than the very talented Terry Lundgren, CEO of Macy's. He was the driving force behind the consolidation of the former May Company and Federated Department Stores into the Macy's group, which is over 850 stores strong. Along with Bloomingdale's (now also a part of Macy's), they are a dominant power all across America.

It is exciting also to see the revitalization of Lord & Taylor, once headed by Dorothy Shaver, one of the most dynamic women ever in the retail world. Long established as the epitome of American style, this Fifth Avenue store has recently rebounded and is once again a major power in the New York retailing experience.

Also on the upper end, Bergdorf Goodman—which has separate stores across Fifth Avenue for men and women—is probably at the top of the heap, both in quality and price. Next down is Saks, once a great operation but now struggling to find an identity (and make a profit). Century 21 remains the personification of bargain shopping in New York.

Barneys New York (660 Madison Ave, at 60th St, 212/826-9800, www. barneys.com): High-class and high-priced men's and women's clothing and accessories; cold atmosphere and pushy salespeople; many top brand names; periodic sales are the best times to shop; unique window displays.

Barneys Co-Op (236 W 18th St, bet Seventh and Eighth Ave, 212/593-7800; 116 Wooster St, bet Spring and Prince St, 212/965-9964; and 2151 Broadway, at 75th St, 646/335-0978, www.barneys.com): Younger customers feel more at home with the selections and the more comfortable pricing; young designers' clothing is a specialty (with clothing only at the Wooster Street location); these stores have a much friendlier attitude.

Bergdorf Goodman (754 Fifth Ave, at 57th St, 212/753-7300, www. bergdorfgoodman.com): Nearly every top designer is represented in the various women's sections; not an easy store to shop in, due to vertical transportation system; high prices and spotty service (good if the salesperson knows you and quite dismal if not); beautiful gift and home accessories sections; fully represented cosmetic section in the downstairs store; windows are always a precursor of what is new (and expensive).

Bergdorf Goodman Men (745 Fifth Ave, at 58th St, 212/753-7300, www.bergdorfgoodman.com): The ritziest and classiest men's operation in the city, with every top men's designer represented; wonderful selection of suits and formal wear; accessory departments not spectacular; wait for sales or special ads; competent salespeople; hold on to your wallet.

Bloomingdale's (1000 Third Ave, at 59th St, 212/705-2000 and 504 Broadway, 212/729-4900, www.bloomingdales.com): Once the trendsetter in fashion and home decor, Bloomie's is still very good but a shadow of its former greatness; very good women's sections; men's accessories are adequate but men's clothing not too hot; huge cosmetics operation with pushy personnel; excellent home furnishings sections; the Art of Shaving Barber Spa; good eating places; handy services available, but when will they bring back their once-great model rooms?

Century 21 (22 Cortlandt St, at Church St, 212/227-9092, www.c21 stores.com): Located downtown near Ground Zero; not fancy; busy; great values if you know where to look; shoes, clothing, and accessories for men and women; designer labels at a discount; the fitting rooms are unique and busy, with scenes that could be out of a comedy show.

Henri Bendel (712 Fifth Ave, at 56th St, 212/247-1100, www.henri bendel.com): Gone are the fashion departments! Accessories and beauty products remain and a food balcony is new; don't miss the historic Rene Lalique windows; service is spotty (especially by telephone).

Lord & Taylor (424 Fifth Ave, at 38th St, 212/391-3344, www.lordand taylor.com): Rejuvenated and highly regarded again; famous for emphasis on American designers; check their windows and ads; outstanding women's clothing and accessory departments; larger women and petites will find good selections; men's sections could stand some sprucing up; give them an "A" for effort.

Macy's (151 W 34th St, at Herald Square, 212/695-4400, www.macys.com):
You don't want to miss shopping at the world's largest department store,
with huge selections in every department; prices are family-oriented;
service has improved considerably; a number of eating places throughout
the Manhattan store; great housewares and food operations in the Cellar; men's department has been vastly improved; don't miss the flower
show at Easter; the store is visitor-friendly. A great place to shop!

Saks Fifth Avenue (611 Fifth Ave at 49th St, 212/753-4000, www.saks
fifthavenue.com): These folks change managers and direction too often;
what used to be a quality-predictable store with well-trained sales personnel has turned into just another department store, although women's
clothing and accessory departments are still excellent; pushy personnel
in cosmetics area; pricey but good eating spot on eighth floor; men's
clothing department carries most major names (at major prices).

Takashimaya (693 Fifth Ave, bet 54th and 55th St, 212/350-0100, www.
takashimaya.com): An unusual operation, more like a museum than a
store; classy Japanese merchandise at respectable prices; especially good
for home accessory items; refreshment facility at the Tea Box Restaurant.

Domestic Goods

BED BATH & BEYOND

620 Ave of the Americas (bet 18th and 19th St)	212/255-3550
410 E 61st St (at First Ave)	646/215-4702
1932 Broadway (at 65th St)	917/441-9391
270 Greenwich St (bet Warren and Murray St)	212/233-8450
Hours vary by store	www.bedbathandbeyond.com

Bed Bath & Beyond does things in a big way while still making every
customer feel important. The selection is huge. The quality is unquestioned.
The service is prompt and informed. The store on Avenue of the Americas
has over 103,000 square feet of sheets, blankets, rugs, kitchen gadgets, towels, dinnerware, hampers, furniture, cookware, kiddie items, pillows, paper
goods, and appliances. The fine-china department is superb. Several locations
now have health and beauty departments. The store on 61st Street has three
levels jam-packed with great merchandise. The layout of the store on Broadway makes it a shopper's paradise. Prices are discounted.

BOUTIQUE D. PORTHAULT

470 Park Ave (at 58th St)	212/688-1660
Mon-Sat: 10-6	www.dporthault.com

Porthault, the French queen of linens, needs no introduction. Custom-
made linens are available in a wide range of designs, scores of colors, and
weaves of luxurious density. Wherever the name Porthault appears—for
instance, on the linens at some fancy hotels—you know you're at a top-
notch operation. Their printed sheets seem to last forever and are handed
down from one generation to another. Porthault can handle custom work
of an intricate nature for odd-sized beds, baths, and showers. Specialties
include signature prints (hearts, clovers, stars, and *mille fleurs*), printed terry
towels, children's special-occasion clothing, and unique gift items. The Porthault brand is available at Bergdorf Goodman as well.

HARRIS LEVY
98 Forsyth St (bet Grand and Broome St)   212/226-3102
Mon-Sat: 10-6; Sun: 10-5   www.harrislevy.com

Over a century old, Harris Levy has moved into a space that was originally a premier downtown catering hall called "Pearl's Mansion," built in 1900. The building has been completely renovated, and this outstanding retailer of luxury home furnishings now includes all manner of quilts, pillows, bed linens, table accessories, bath products, candles, and fragrances —even stuffed animals for the kids. Harris Levy is a must-visit for those who want to outfit their home or apartment with goods at sensible prices.

> Leave it to **David Burke at Bloomingdale's** to be at the right place at the right time! On the 59th Street side of Bloomingdale's (1000 Third Ave, 212/705-3800), the hungry shopper will find a delicious array of goodies for coffee and pastries, lunch, and early evening at two adjacent operations. One is a sit-down cafe and the other a takeout facility. You'll find soups and dumplings, salads, hot sandwiches and cheeseburger sliders, hot lunches, pizzas, and complete dinners.

PRATESI
829 Madison Ave (at 69th St)   212/288-2315
Mon-Sat: 10-6   www.pratesi.com

Pratesi claims to carry the finest linens the world has to offer, and that is no idle boast. In 2006 they celebrated a century in business. Families hand down Pratesi linens for generations. Customers who don't have affluent ancestors will wish to avail themselves of the new collections that arrive in spring and fall. The Pratesi staff will help you coordinate linens to decor and create a custom look. This three-story store has a garden that sets a mood for perusing luxurious bed and bath linens. Towels are made in Italy exclusively for Pratesi and are of a quality and thickness that must be felt to be believed. Bathrobes are magnificent, plush, and quietly understated. Cashmere pillows, throws, and blankets are available, and baby boutique items can be special ordered.

Electronics and Appliances

DALE PRO AUDIO
22 W 19th St (bet Fifth Ave and Ave of the Americas)   212/475-1124
Mon-Fri: 9:30-5:30   www.daleproaudio.com

A family business for over half a century, this professional audio dealership carries the largest selection of merchandise for recording, broadcast, DJ, and sound-contracting in the country, including hundreds of brands from A Design to Zoom. They know their stuff and are respected by customers.

GRINGER & SONS
29 First Ave (at 2nd St)   212/475-0600
Mon-Fri: 8:30-5:30; Sat: 8:30-4   www.gringerandsons.com

Come to Gringer & Sons for brandname major appliances at good prices. Gringer's informed personnel sell refrigerators, microwaves, ranges, and other appliances to residential and commercial customers.

J&R MUSIC & COMPUTER WORLD
I-34 Park Row (across from City Hall)   212/238-9000, 800/221-8180
Mon-Sat: 9-7:30; Sun: 10:30-6:30   www.jr.com

This operation prides itself on being one of the nation's complete electronics and home entertainment department stores. They carry cameras, printers and other photo accessories; iPods and other personal music players; TVs and home-theater components; one of New York's largest selections of music and movies; and home office gear, including smartphones, iPhones, phones, PDAs, faxes, multi-function printers, and desktop and laptop computers (both PCs and Macs). The place is well organized, though it can get rather hectic at times. Prices are competitive and merchandise is guaranteed. In the middle of the block, J&R has other stores with more small appliances, kitchenware, and personal care items.

For bathroom and kitchen fix-ups, these firms stand out:
Krup's Kitchen & Bath (11 W 18th St, 212/243-5787): good source for appliances
Simon's Hardware & Bath (421 Third Ave, 212/532-9220): everything you need for the bathroom

---

P.C. RICHARD & SON
120 E 14th St (bet Third and Fourth Ave)	212/979-2600
205 E 86th St (bet Second and Third Ave)	212/289-1700
2372 Broadway (at 86th St)	212/579-5200
53 W 23rd St (bet Ave of the Americas and Fifth Ave)	212/924-0200

Mon-Fri: 9 a.m.-9:30 p.m.; Sat: 9-9; Sun: 10-7   www.pcrichard.com

For nearly a century this family-owned and -operated appliance, electronics, and computer store has been providing superior service to customers. They offer a large inventory, good prices, delivery seven days a week, and in-house repair service. P.C. Richard started as a hardware outfit, and the dedication to personalized service has successfully passed from one generation to the next. They also get an A+ for friendliness.

STEREO EXCHANGE
627 Broadway (bet Bleecker and Houston St)   212/505-1111
Mon-Fri: 11-7:30; Sat: 10:30-7; Sun: noon-7 www.stereoexchange.com

For high-end audio-video products, you can't do better than this outfit! They carry top names like Integra, McIntosh, and B&W, and trained, certified engineers will work with architects and designers on in-home installations. Moreover, the personnel really care about their products.

WAVES
Showplace Antiques and Design Center
40 W 25th St (bet Fifth Ave and Ave of the Americas), Spaces 107, 216
Wed-Sun: noon-5; other times by appointment   212/273-9616
www.wavesllc.com

Bruce and Charlotte Mager allow the past to live on with their collection of vintage record players, radios, receivers, and televisions. They favor the age of radio over the high-tech present. The shop is a virtual shrine to the 1930s and before. At Waves you'll find the earliest radios (still operative!) and artifacts. There are promotional pieces, such as a radio-shaped cigarette lighter. Gramophones and virtually anything dealing with the radio age are available. Waves also rents phonographs, telephones, and neon clocks, and they will repair and appraise items.

I've long been a fan of Sony products—they are top of the line and dependable. Inside **Sony** (550 Madison Ave, 212/833-8800) are all sorts of high-tech electronics to educate, communicate, and amuse. They feature the latest computers, cameras, TV and home entertainment systems, portable electronics (MP3 players, iPods, and all types of accessories), and the most popular movies, music, and games. This mecca appeals to all ages. Be prepared to spend some bucks, as these items are tagged to fetch top dollar. (Prices on Sony goods are cheaper elsewhere.) I only wish their in-store customer service was as good as their products.

Eyewear and Accessories

THE EYE MAN
2264 Broadway (bet 81st and 82nd St)   212/873-4114
Mon, Wed: 10-7; Tues, Thurs: 10-7:30; Fri, Sat: 10-6; www.eyeman.com
Sun: noon-5 (closed Sun in summer)

Dozens of stores in Manhattan carry eyeglasses, but few take special care with children. The Eye Man carries a great selection of frames for young people, as well as specialty eyewear for grownups.

FABULOUS FANNY'S
335 E 9th St (bet First and Second Ave)   212/533-0637
Daily: noon-8 p.m.   www.fabulousfannys.com

I like the slogan of this outfit: "If you have to wear them, make it fun!" What they are referring to are glasses. This store has the largest and best selection of antique and vintage eyewear in the country. Both men and women will be dazzled by the stock.

GRUENEYES
599 Lexington Ave (bet 52nd and 53rd St)   212/688-3580
1076 Third Ave (bet 63rd and 64th St)   212/751-6177
1022 Madison Ave (bet 78th and 79th St)   212/439-8590
2009 Broadway (at 69th St)   212/874-8749
1225 Lexington Ave (bet 82nd and 83rd St)   212/628-2493
2384 Broadway (at 87th St)   212/724-0850
Hours vary by store   www.grueneyes.com

The same faces and quality care can be found at Grueneyes year after year. The firm enjoys a reputation for excellent service. They can do emergency fittings and one-day turnaround, and they carry a superb selection of specialty eyewear. Their sunglasses, theater glasses, sports spectacles, and party eyewear are noteworthy.

ILORI
138 Spring St (bet Greene and Wooster St) 212/226-8276
Mon-Sat: 10-8; Sun: 11-6 www.iloristyle.com

Ilori carries over 1,400 pairs of sunglasses in limited-edition designs and from the classic companies. All are temptingly displayed in this Soho gallery-like boutique. The knowledgeable staff can recommend the best shape and color of shades to best play up your facial features. Spring for a couple of unusual pairs to change your persona. Be sure to check out the seasonal art work in the front window.

JOËL NAME OPTIQUE DE PARIS
448 West Broadway (at Prince St) 212/777-5888
Tues-Fri: 11-7; Sat: noon-6

Service is the name of the game at this shop. Owner Joël Nommick and a crew of professionals stock some of the most fashionable specs in town. While you won't find other brand names here, the selection is good if you are looking for frames for prescription glasses, readers, sunglasses, and contact lenses. Vision exams are not offered, so bring your optical prescription.

LIGHTHOUSE STORE
110 E 60th St (bet Park and Lexington Ave) 212/821-9384
Mon-Fri: 10-6 www.lighthouse.org

This is a wonderful place for the blind or partially sighted. The vast selection includes CCTVs (desktop and pocket models), specialty lighting, magnifying mirrors, talking products, watches, clocks, and household items. Open houses and hands-on demonstrations allow customers to learn about state-of-the-art technology.

MORGENTHAL-FREDERICS OPTICIANS
699 Madison Ave (bet 62nd and 63rd St) 212/838-3090
944 Madison Ave (bet 74th and 75th St) 212/744-9444
399 West Broadway (at Spring St) 212/966-0099
1 W 58th St (at Plaza Hotel) 212/829-1100
10 Columbus Circle 212/956-6402
Hours vary by store www.morgenthalfrederics.com

If you're looking for unique eyewear and accessories, then put Morgenthal-Frederics high on your list. Owner Richard Morgenthal displays innovative styles, including exclusive designs. With Morgenthal-Frederics' various locations and attentive staff, clients are truly well serviced. The Soho location on West Broadway offers eye exams on the weekend; otherwise, they'll make appointments for you with some of New York's best ophthalmologists.

20/20 EYEWEAR
1592 Third Ave (bet 89th and 90th St) 212/876-7676
57 E 8th St (bet Broadway and University Pl) 212/228-2192
Mon-Fri: 10-7:30; Sat: 10-6 www.twentytwentyeyewear.com

Whether you see glasses as a simple necessity, a statement of style, or both, the large selection at 20/20 will likely suit your needs. For over two decades 20/20 has offered trendsetting eyewear in a casual, appealing atmosphere. They provide overnight delivery, eye exams, and prescription fulfillment.

Fabrics, Trimmings

A.A. FEATHER COMPANY
(GETTINGER FEATHER CORPORATION)
16 W 36th St (bet Fifth Ave and Ave of the Americas), 8th floor
Mon-Thurs: 9-6; Fri: 9-3   212/695-9470
www.gettingerfeather.com

Do you need an ostrich plume, feather fan, or feather boa for your latest ensemble? Have you made a quilt that you'd like to stuff with feathers? Well, you're in luck with A.A. Feather (a.k.a. Gettinger Feather Corporation). The Gettingers have been in business since 1915, and first grandson Dan Gettinger runs it today. There aren't many family-owned businesses left, and there are almost no other sources for fine quality feathers. This is a find!

A. FEIBUSCH—ZIPPERS & THREADS
27 Allen St (bet Canal and Hester St)   212/226-3964
Mon-Fri: 9-4:30; Sun: 10-2 (closed Sun in summer)
www.zipperstop.com

A. Feibusch boasts of having "one of the biggest selections of zippers in the U.S.A.," as if they really believe there are zipper stores throughout the country! They stock zippers in every size, style, and color (hundreds of them), and can make zippers to order. Feibusch carries matching threads to sew in a zipper, webbing, ribbons, elastic, seam binding, and other sewing supplies. Eddie Feibusch assures me that no purchase is too small or large, and he gives each customer prompt, personal service.

B&J FABRICS
525 Seventh Ave (at 38th St), 2nd floor   212/354-8150
Mon-Fri: 8-5:45; Sat: 9-4:45   www.bandjfabrics.com

B&J started in the fabric business in 1940. In this well-organized space, they carry high-quality fashion fabrics, many imported directly from Europe. Specialties of the house: natural fibers, designer fabrics, bridal fabrics, ultrasuede, Liberty of London, and silk prints (over a thousand in stock!). Swatches are sent free of charge by specific request. You will also find a wonderful selection of hand-dyed batiks, brocades, and faux furs.

BARANZELLI SILK SURPLUS
938 Third Ave (bet 56th and 57th St)   212/753-6511
Mon-Fri: 10-6; Tues-Thurs: 10-8; Sat, Sun: noon-5

Silk Surplus is the exclusive outlet for Scalamandre close-outs of fine fabrics and trimmings, as well as Baranzelli's own line of imported and domestic informal fabrics and trimmings. Scalamandre sells for half of retail, and a choice selection of other luxurious fabrics is offered at similar savings. There are periodic sales, even on already discounted fabrics, at this elegant fabric store. They also have custom workrooms for upholstery, drapery, pillows, and furniture.

BECKENSTEIN FABRIC AND INTERIORS
4 W 20th St (bet Fifth and Ave of the Americas)   212/366-5142
Mon-Sat: 10-6   www.beckensteinfabrics.com

Beckenstein's has a rich history as purveyors of fine fabrics for window treatments, bedding, pillows, and home accessories, and now they have added a new furniture department. Custom upholstery work is their specialty—restoration, restyling, or reupholstery to spruce up a new decor. Impressive selections, reliable service, and excellent workmanship have kept them in business since 1918.

BECKENSTEIN MEN'S FABRICS
257 W 39th St (bet Seventh and Eighth Ave)   212/475-6666
Mon-Sat: 9-6   800/221-2727
                                           www.fabricczar.com

Beckenstein is the finest men's fabric store in the nation. Proprietor Neal Boyarsky and his son Jonathan have been called "the fabric czars of the U.S." These folks sell to a majority of custom tailors in the country and to many top manufacturers of men's clothing, so you know the goods are best-quality. Their customer list reads like a who's who of film stars, sports figures, and politicians, including President Obama. You will find every kind of fabric, from goods selling for $10 a yard to fabulous pieces at $1,000 a yard. There are pure cashmeres, fine English suitings, silks, camel hair, and more. Beckenstein will custom-make trousers, skirts, and shirts on-premises.

HYMAN HENDLER AND SONS
21 W 38th St (bet Fifth Ave and Ave of the Americas)   212/840-8393
Mon-Fri: 9-5   www.hymanhendler.com

Although Hyman Hendler passed away, the store that proudly bears his name is in the capable hands of his son-in-law. In the trimmings world, it is one of the oldest businesses (established in 1900) and the crown head of the ribbon field. This source is used by dressmakers, milliners, and crafters alike. Hyman Hendler manufactures, retails, imports, and acts as a wholesaler for every kind of ribbon. It's hard to believe as many variations exist as are jammed into this store.

LIBRA LEATHER
259 W 30th St (bet Seventh and Eighth Ave), 7th floor 212/695-3114
Mon-Fri: 9-5:30   www.libraleather.com

This family-owned business is one of the best-kept secrets of the fashion world. Since 1977, Libra Leather has imported the finest leather skins from Italy, France, and Spain. An extensive inventory of breathtaking skins in all colors and textures is displayed in a beautiful showroom. Competent staff walk you around to find just the right choice. A line of novelty items and home accessories, including pillow and blanket covers, is also available in selected leathers.

LONG ISLAND FABRIC WAREHOUSE
406 Broadway (bet Canal and Walker St)   212/431-9510
Daily: 9-7

Long Island Fabric Warehouse has one huge floor of every imaginable kind of fabric and trimming. Since all are sold at discount, it's one of the best places to buy fabrics. There is an extensive wool collection and such dressy fabrics as chiffon, crepe, silk, and satin. Most amazing are the bargain spots, where remnants and odd pieces go for so little it's laughable. They carry an excellent selection of patterns (only $2), notions, trimmings, and dollar-a-yard fabrics.

M&J TRIMMING/M&J BUTTONS
1006 and 1008 Ave of the Americas (bet 37th and 38th St)
Mon-Fri: 9-8; Sat: 10-6; Sun: noon-6   212/391-9072
www.mjtrim.com

These folks claim to have the largest selection of trims at one location, and I'm inclined to believe them! You will find everything from imported trims, buckles, buttons, and decorator trims to various fashion accessories. One area specializes in clothing and fashion trims like sequins, bridal beading and crystals, and rhinestone appliques. The other features interior decor trim. They have over a half-century of experience in this business.

MARGOLA IMPORT CORP.
48 W 37th St (bet Fifth Ave and Ave of the Americas)
Mon-Fri: 9-5:30; Sat: 10-4 (closed Sat in summer)   212/564-2929
www.margola.com

You'll find an outstanding showing of beads, rhinestones, crystals, pearls, crocheted items, settings, and jewelry findings. They stock labor-saving machines for attaching beads and other embellishments, and will help with any phase of beading.

PARON WEST
206 W 40th St (at Seventh Ave)   212/768-3266
Mon-Thurs: 8:30-7; Fri: 8:30-5:45; Sat: 9-4:30; Sun: 11-4
www.paronfabrics.com

Paron carries an excellent selection of contemporary designer fabrics suitable for clothing, home decor, theatrical set design, and costumes, all at discount prices. Many of the goods are available only in their store. A full line of patterns is also stocked. This is a family operation, so personal attention is assured. **Paron Annex**, their half-price outlet, adjoins Paron West.

ROSEN & CHADICK FABRICS
561 Seventh Ave (at 40th St), 2nd and 3rd floors
Mon-Fri: 8:30-5:45; Sat: 9-4:30   212/869-0142, 800/225-3838
www.rosenandchadickfabrics.com

For over a half-century this family-owned business has been offering customers (including the theatrical trade), a huge selection of high-end quality fabrics: silks, wools, cashmeres, linens, cottons, laces, velvets, brocades, and more. With so much interest in cashmere these days, I was particularly impressed with the selection. You can be assured of personal, attentive, and knowledgeable service. Ask for David Chadick, the hands-on owner.

TINSEL TRADING
1 W 37th St (at Fifth Ave)   212/730-1030
Mon-Fri: 9:45-6; Sat: 11-5   www.tinseltrading.com

Tinsel Trading claims to be the only firm in the United States specializing in antique gold and silver metallics from the 1900s. They have everything from gold thread to lamé fabrics. Tinsel Trading offers an amazing array of tinsel threads, braids, ribbons, fringes, cords, tassels, gimps, medallions, edging, banding, gauze lamés, bullions, fabrics, soutache, trims, and galloons. All are genuine antiques, and many customers buy them for accenting modern clothing. The collection of military gold braids, sword knots, and epaulets is unsurpassed.

TOHO SHOJI
990 Ave of the Americas (bet 36th and 37th St)   212/868-7466
Mon-Fri: 9-7; Sat: 10-6; Sun: 10-5   www.tohoshoji-ny.com

Have you ever heard of a beads supermarket? Only in New York will you find an establishment like Toho Shoji, which stocks all manner of items for designing and making custom jewelry: earring parts, metal findings, chains, and every kind of jewelry component. Beads are made of every imaginable material—ceramic, shell, CZ (cubic zirconia), wood, and glass. Items are well displayed for easy selection.

Walking into this sunny boutique will brighten any day! Fabulous striped cotton fabrics associated with the French Riviera are now available at **Les Toiles du Soleil** (261 W 19th St, 212/229-4730) as throw pillows, computer cases, tote bags, aprons, deck chairs, espradilles, and other useful items. These French-made fabrics are woven on traditional looms and are sun-, stain-, and water-resistant, making them ideal for outdoor use and as custom-made goods (window or shower curtains, cushions, etc.). The "cloth of the sun"—the store name translated into English—sums up their products!

ZARIN FABRIC WAREHOUSE
314 Grand St (at Allen and Orchard St)   212/925-6112
Mon-Thurs: 9-7; Fri: 9-6; Sat, Sun: 10-6   www.zarinfabrics.com

Founded in 1936, Zarin is the largest and oldest drapery and upholstery fabric warehouse in Manhattan. This "fabric heaven" occupies an entire city block stocked with thousands of designer fabrics and trims at below wholesale prices. With the largest selection of designer fabrics in New York, Zarin is a favorite inside source for decorators, set designers, and celebrity clientele. Zarin also carries some of the finest ready-made collections of window panels, custom lampshades, lamps, and other home furnishings. Another worthy Zarin operation, **BZI Distributors** (314 Grand St, 212/966-6690), sells trimmings, fringe, and drapery and upholstery hardware.

Fireplace Accessories

DANNY ALESSANDRO
308 E 59th St (bet First and Second Ave)   212/421-1928
Mon-Fri: 9-5 (open weekends by appointment)

New Yorkers have a thing for fireplaces, and Danny Alessandro caters to that infatuation. Alessandro has been in business for more than four decades. Just as New York fireplaces run the gamut from antique brownstone to ultramodern blackstone, Alessandro's fireplaces and accessories range from antique pieces to a shiny new set of chrome tools. The shop also stocks antique marble and sandstone mantelpieces, andirons, and an incredible display of screens and tool kits. In the Victorian era, paper fans and screens were popular for blocking fireplaces when not in use. The surviving antique pieces at Alessandro are great for modern decorating. They will also custom order mantels, mantelpieces, and fireplace accessories; however, they do not repair or clean fireplaces. Ask for Peter, as there is no Danny Alessandro!

WILLIAM H. JACKSON COMPANY
18 E 17th St (bet Fifth Ave and Broadway)   212/753-9400
Mon-Thurs: 9:30-5; Fri: 9:30-4   www.wmhj.com

In real estate ads "wbfp" stands for "wood-burning fireplace," and they remain the rage in New York. In business since 1827, William H. Jackson is familiar with the various types of fireplaces in the city. In fact, they orginally installed many of those fireplaces. Jackson has hundreds of mantels on display in its showroom. They range from antiques and reproductions (in wood or marble combinations) to starkly modern pieces. There are also andirons, fire tools, and screens. In addition, they provide advice on how to enjoy your fireplace. Jackson does repair work (removing and installing mantels is a specialty), but they're better known for selling fireplace accessories.

Flags

ACE BANNER FLAG AND GRAPHICS
107 W 27th St (at Ave of the Americas)   212/620-9111
Mon-Fri: 7:30-4   www.acebanner.com

If you need a flag, Ace is the right place. Established in 1916, Ace prides itself on carrying the flags of every nation, as well as New York City and New York State flags in all sizes. Custom flags can be made to order. They range in size from 4" by 6" desk flags to bridge-spanning banners. Ace also manufactures custom banners, from podium to building size. Portable trade show graphics and large-format digital prints are available on a quick turnaround. They will ship anywhere. Ask for owner Carl Calo.

Floor Coverings

COUNTRY FLOORS
15 E 16th St (bet Fifth Ave and Union Square W)   212/627-8300
Mon-Fri: 9-6; Sat: 11-4   www.countryfloors.com

Country Floors is one of New York's biggest retail success stories, no doubt because they offer a magnificent product. Begun in 1964 in a tiny, cramped basement under the owner's photography studio, Country Floors has grown to include huge stores in New York and Los Angeles. There are nearly 80 affiliates worldwide, including Canada and Australia. Country Floors carries the finest floor and wall tiles, made of stone, glass, porcelain, and terra cotta. Sources include artisans from all over the world. A visit—or at least a look at their website—is necessary to appreciate the quality and intricacy of each design. Even the simplest solid-color tiles are beautiful.

ELIZABETH EAKINS
21 E 65th St (bet Fifth and Madison Ave)   212/628-1950
Mon-Fri: 10-5   www.elizabetheakins.com

Elizabeth Eakins is a first-class source for wool, cotton, and linen rugs. She custom-designs and makes hand-woven and hand-hooked rugs in standard and hand-dyed colors. Since this is a small shop, it is best to call ahead for an appointment.

JANOS P. SPITZER FLOORING CONSULTANTS
131 W 24th St (bet Ave of the Americas and Seventh Ave)
Mon-Fri: 8-4:30   212/627-1818
www.janosspitzerflooring.com

Janos Spitzer, a Hungarian craftsman, has over four decades of experience. His top-notch flooring headquarters features installation of high-end (read: pricey) wooden floors in high-rise residences, as well as expert restoration and repair. You'll find many unusual finishes as they source wood from around the world—domestic, imported, and exotic tree species. The selection ranges from simple to elegant, with unique borders and parquets. Spitzer offers highly reliable and experienced craftspeople and the finest products. Consultations on large projects include follow-up to ensure that specifications have been met.

LOOM & WEAVE
43 W 33rd St (bet Fifth Ave and Broadway), 3rd floor   212/779-7373
Mon-Thurs: by appointment   www.loomweave.com

Loom & Weave stocks one of the largest collections of antique and semi-antique Oriental rugs in the city—over 2,000 of them! They work exclusively with decorators, designers, and private clients.

NEMATI COLLECTION
Art and Design Building
1059 Third Ave (bet 62nd and 63rd St), 3rd floor   212/486-6900
Mon-Fri: 9-6; Sat: by appointment   www.nematicollection.com

The Nemati Collection was founded by Parviz Nemati, author of *The Splendor of Antique Rugs and Tapestries*. He has been dealing in antique Oriental rugs and tapestries for four decades. The tradition is carried on by his son, Darius Nemati. In addition to an extensive collection of antique Oriental rugs and period tapestries, the gallery also features modern and contemporary rugs, as well as an exclusive collection of custom carpeting and natural-fiber flooring. Services includes a full restoration and conservation department, consulting, insurance appraisals, and professional cleaning.

PASARGAD CARPETS
180 Madison Ave (bet 33rd and 34th St)   212/684-4477
Mon-Fri: 9-6; Sat: 10-6; Sun: 11-5   www.pasargadcarpets.com

Pasargad is a fifth-generation family business established in 1904. They have one of the largest collections of antique, semiantique, and new Persian and Oriental rugs in the country. Decorating advice, repair, cleaning, and pickup and delivery services are offered. Pasargad will also buy or trade quality antique rugs.

SAFAVIEH CARPETS
153 Madison Ave (at 32nd St)	212/683-8399
238 E 59th St (at Second Ave)	212/888-0626
Mon-Sat: 10-6; Sun: noon-5	
902 Broadway (bet 20th and 21st St)	212/477-1234
Mon-Sat: 10-7; Sun: 11-6	www.safavieh.com

There was a time when it was possible to visit the teeming markets of Tehran and find some real rug bargains. At Safavieh one can still see a vast selection of these beautiful works of art, even if the setting is a little less authentic. Safavieh has one of the finest collections of Persian, Indian, Pakistani, and Chinese rugs in this country. They're displayed in a showroom spacious enough for customers to visualize how the prized pieces would look in their homes or places of business. These rugs are truly heirlooms, and you will want to spend time hearing about their exotic origins. The Broadway store also carries furniture. Prices, although certainly not inexpensive, are competitive for the superior quality represented. (Hint: It doesn't hurt to do a little haggling.)

Prudence Designs (231 W 18th St, 212/691-1356, Mon-Fri: 9-6; Sat: noon-6) is a florist shop with down-to-earth prices. They specialize in weddings, bar mitzvahs, and other special events. Delivery is available, and you won't be disappointed in the exotic arrangements.

Flowers, Plants, and Gardening Items

BELLE FLEUR
134 Fifth Ave (bet 18th and 19th St), 4th floor	212/254-8703
Mon-Fri: 8:45-5:45	www.bellefleurny.com

This mother-daughter team defines floral style as refined, abundant, and luxurious. (I would add "expensive" to that description.) Their gift bouquets and wedding displays are absolutely gorgeous works of art, using exotic blooms from around the globe. If you'd like to make your own floral arrangement, hands-on private classes are held. Belle Fleur has developed a private label line of room fragrance sprays and candles for lasting enjoyment.

BLOOM
541 Lexington Ave (at 50th St)	212/832-8094
Mon-Fri: 8-6; Sat: 9-6	www.bloomflowers.com

When price is no object, you can do no better in the floral department than Bloom. Come here for a superb bouquet or arrangement when you have a special occasion to celebrate. If you're fortunate enough to have an outdoor space, their landscape architecture experts do wonders with rooftop gardens, poolside areas, and country estates.

CHELSEA GARDEN CENTER HOME
580 Eleventh Ave (at 44th St)	212/727-7100
Mon-Sat: 9-6; Sun: 10-6	www.chelseagardencenter.com

These folks have combined their home store and outdoor garden center into one large operation. For the urban gardener this place is a dream, offering a wide selection of plants and flowers, soil, fertilizers, containers, tabletop items, candles, holiday decor, tools, garden books, and much more. Statuary, fountains, and outdoor furniture can be special-ordered through the catalog.

COUNTRY GARDENS
1160 Lexington Ave (at 80th St)   212/966-2015
Mon-Fri: 8:30-6; Sat: 9-3 (closed July and Aug in summer)

The service at Country Garden is highly personalized, and they show a great selection of cut flowers and plants. Nosegays and English garden style are their specialties. They arrange everything to order and will deliver up to 125th Street.

GROVE
617 Hudson St (bet Jane and 12th St)   212/673-8300
Tues-Sat: 11-8; Sun noon-5   www.grovenyc.com

Sarah Tallman has assembled a pleasant mix of fresh flowers, casual- chic home decor, and fragrance items. Select a bunch of posies from the more than 20 varieties at the fresh-flower bar, or place an order for a special event. A signature arrangement may include flowers in a Ball jar placed inside a replica of an orange crate with fresh oranges. More lasting merchandise choices include pillows, vases, decorative objects, desk accessories and other fun objects to liven up your dwelling.

JAMALI GARDEN SUPPLIES
149 W 28th St (bet Ave of the Americas and Seventh Ave)
Mon-Sat: 6:30-5   212/244-4025
                                                    www.jamaligarden.com

This store in the Flower Market carries just about everything except live plants and fresh flowers. The stock includes colorful accouterments to create stunning arrangements for any occasion. Event planners, brides, and floral designers shop here for party lights, candles and holders, plant ferti- lizers, tabletop items, curtains, pillows, baskets, ribbons, floral picks, and all sorts of other objects to exercise their creative bent.

JONATHAN FLORIST
36 W 56th St (bet Fifth Ave and Ave of the Americas) 212/586-8414
Mon-Sat: 9-6

Jonathan's boasts the most beautiful Christmas floral display in the city. The designers use top quality, exotic fresh flowers and gifts and accessories from private collections to create one-of-a-kind artistic arrangements. Birthdays, weddings, anniversaries, or any other occasion are more spectac- ular and memorable with florals from Jonathan's. Major events with distinc- tive themes and elegant styles are a specialty.

SIMPSON & CO. FLORISTS
457 W 56th St (at Tenth Ave)   212/772-6670
Mon-Fri: 9-5   www.simpsonflowers.com

Simpson specializes in unusual baskets, cut flowers, plants, and orchids. They will decorate for gatherings of all sizes, and their prices are very com- petitive. Affable Ted Simpson is a delight to work with!

TREILLAGE

418 E 75th St (at York Ave)   212/535-2288
Mon-Fri: 10-6

1015 Lexington Ave (at 73rd St)   212/988-8800
Mon-Fri: 10-6; Sat: 11-5   www.treillageonline.com

New Yorkers have gardens, too, although out of necessity they are small. Many times they are just patio blooms, but still they add special charm to city living. Treillage can help make an ordinary outside space into something special. They carry furniture and accessories for indoors and out, with a great selection of unusual pieces to set your place apart. They sell everything except plants and flowers! The Lexington Avenue store carries smaller tabletop items and decorative accessories. Prices are not inexpensive, but why not splurge to enhance your little corner of the world?

VSF

204 W 10th St (bet 4th and Bleecker St)   212/206-7236
Mon-Fri: 11-5:30; Sat: 11-4   www.vsfnyc.com

If you want a special look when it comes to fresh-cut flowers and dried or silk creations, you can't do better than VSF. Unusual fresh flowers are shipped in daily from flower markets around the world. Their top-drawer list of clients attests to their talents for weddings and other special events. Ask for owners Jack Follmer or Todd Rigby.

ZEZÉ FLOWERS

938 First Ave (at 52nd St)   212/753-7767
Mon-Sat: 8-6 (also open holiday weekends)   www.zezeflowers.com

Zezé came to New York several decades ago from Rio de Janeiro, a city known for its dramatic setting, and he brought a bit of that drama to the flower business in Manhattan. Zezé's windows reflect his unique talent. The exotic orchid selection is outstanding. You'll find premium fresh-cut flowers, topiaries, ceramics and glassware, gift items, and antiques. They offer the ultimate in personalized service, including same-day deliveries and special requests. A small cafe around the corner on 52nd Street (212/758-1944) is a delightful setting for a small catered affair.

Frames

HOUSE OF HEYDENRYK

601 W 26th St (bet Eleventh and Twelfth Ave), Suite 304B-305
Mon-Fri: 10-6; Sat: by appointment only   212/206-9611
                                                    www.heydenryk.com

These folks have been doing frame reproductions of the highest quality since 1845 in Amsterdam (and since 1936 in Manhattan). They stock reproductions, contemporary moldings, and over 3,000 European and American antique frames dating from the 15th through the 20th centuries. They also feature exclusive original frame designs created during the lifetime of such artists as Picasso, Dali, Hopper, O'Keeffe, and Wyeth.

Furniture, Mattresses

General

CHARLES P. ROGERS

55 W 17th St (bet Fifth Ave and Ave of the Americas)   800/561-0467
Mon-Fri: 9-8; Sat: 10-7; Sun: noon-6   www.charlesprogers.com

Rogers has been allowing folks to sleep comfortably in handcrafted beds since 1885! Their brass beds are made from heavy-gauge brass tubing with solid brass castings. Iron beds are hand-forged, making them exceptionally heavy and sturdy. Wooden and leather beds are available, too. Rogers stocks bed linens made from the finest materials, including European linen.

COVE LANDING

995 Lexington Ave (bet 71st and 72nd St)   212/288-7597
Mon-Fri: 11-6

A collector's paradise! This miniature jewel shows carefully selected 18th- and 19th-century English and continental furniture, plus tasteful Chinese art objects from the same period.

Resource Furniture (969 Third Ave, 212/753-2039) is known for contemporary European space-saving furniture. Of course, there are wall beds modeled after the familiar Murphy beds. What's really impressive is a sofa that transforms into a bunk bed set. Beautiful fabrics and quality structural materials combine good looks with functionality. Other furniture categories include tables, seating, and executive office pieces.

FLOU

42 Greene St (bet Broome and Grand St)   212/941-9101
Mon-Fri: 11-7; Sun: noon-5   www.flou.it

In its U.S. flagship store, the Italian retailer Flou shows everything for the bedroom, from designer beds, mattresses, and furniture to sleepwear. This outfit is well known in Europe and Japan, where they tout the brand as promoting "the art of sleeping."

GRANGE

New York Design Center Building
200 Lexington Ave (at 32nd St), 2nd floor   212/685-9057
Mon-Fri: 9-6   www.grange.fr

French furniture and accessories fill this stylish showroom. The pieces range from classic period designs to the exotic and contemporary. All of them emphasize form, function, and comfort.

KENTSHIRE GALLERIES

37 E 12th St (bet University Pl and Broadway)   212/673-6644
700 Madison Ave (bet 62nd and 63rd St)   212/421-1100
Mon-Fri: 9-5   www.kentshire.com

Kentshire presents eight floors of English furniture and accessories, circa

1690–1870, with a particular emphasis on the Georgian and Regency periods. This gallery has an excellent international reputation, and the displays are a delight to see, even if prices are a bit high. A Kentshire boutique at Bergdorf Goodman features antique and estate jewelry.

LOST CITY ARTS
18 Cooper Square (Bowery at 5th St)   212/375-0500
Mon-Fri: 10-6; Sat, Sun: noon-6   www.lostcityarts.com

Established in 1982, Lost City Arts shows mid 20th-century (1950s and 1960s) furniture and lighting fixtures, plus many other vintage objects. Owner James Elkind travels the world in search of unique pieces.

OFFICE FURNITURE HEAVEN
22 W 19th St (bet Fifth Ave and Ave of the Amercas), 7th floor
Mon-Fri: 9-6   212/989-8600
www.officefurnitureheaven.com

This place has bargains in first-quality contemporary pieces for the office. Some are new merchandise, while others are manufacturers' closeouts and discontinued or used items that have been refurbished to look almost new. You'll find a large showroom display of refurbished Knoll Morrison work stations and new ones by HON Initiate. There are conference tables, chairs, bookcases, file cabinets, accessories, and much more.

Expecting? Fill your closet with designer maternity fashions at **Clementine** (39½ Washington Square S, 212/228-9333), a consignment store. Other consigned goods include gift items and children's clothing to size 4T. Look for hand-knit, one-of-a-kind baby hats by Myrle, one of the shop owners.

SLEEPY'S
176 Ave of the Americas (at Spring St)   212/966-7002
874 Broadway (at 18th St)   212/995-0044
Hours vary by store   www.sleepys.com

Sleepy's sells bedding below department store prices. The byword is *discount*. Sleepy's features mattresses from Stearns & Foster, Sealy, Simmons, Serta, Kingsdown, and more. They claim to beat competitors' prices by 20%. Check the website for other locations in Manhattan.

Infants and Children

ALBEE BABY
715 Amsterdam Ave (at 95th St)   212/662-5740
Mon-Sat: 9-5:30 (Thurs till 7)   www.albeebaby.com

Albee has one of the city's best selections of basics for infants and toddlers. This longtime family-owned and -operated store has everything from strollers and car seats to cribs and rocking chairs—and the staff can be very helpful. Organizationally, however, it's a disaster area, and it is sometimes hard to get anyone's attention in the chaos, particularly on weekends. That said, Albee Baby is very popular with Manhattan parents (and grandparents), and it's worth a visit.

GRANNY'S RENTALS
231 E 88th St (bet Second and Third Ave), Suite 4W   212/876-4310
By appointment   www.grannysrental.com

This is a great spot to know about! Granny's rents all sorts of things for babies and children, including strollers, cribs, breast pumps, car seats, games for kids, and popcorn, snow cone, and cotton candy machines. They also rent tables and chairs for parties (children's and adults'). The minimum rental is one week, and they'll deliver to you from their Bronx warehouse.

SCHNEIDER'S JUVENILE FURNITURE
41 W 25th St (bet Broadway and Ave of the Americas)
Mon-Sat: 10-6 (Tues till 8)   212/228-3540
                                                  www.schneidersbaby.com

This Chelsea store is a find for those interested in children's furniture at comfortable prices. Bedroom suites are fit for a princess or young gent. You'll also find cribs, car seats, strollers, diaper bags, backpacks, and most everything else for infants through teens.

WICKER GARDEN'S CHILDREN
1300 Madison Ave (bet 92nd and 93rd St), 2nd floor   212/410-7000
Call for hours   www.wickergarden.com

Pamela Scurry has a great sense of style and competitive prices! If you like wicker furniture, hand-painted detail, and unusual, often whimsical designs, you'll love the baby and juvenile furniture on the second floor of this East Side institution. Moms-to-be, take note: Wicker Garden's selection of comfortable, nice looking gliders is the best in the city.

Games—Adult

COMPLEAT STRATEGIST
11 E 33rd St (at Fifth Ave)   212/685-3880, 800/225-4344
Mon-Sat: 10:30-6 (Thurs till 9)   www.thecompleatstrategist.com

The Compleat Strategist was established over a quarter of a century ago as an armory of sorts for military games and equipment. As the only such place in the city, it was soon overrun with military strategists. As time went on, the store branched into science fiction, fantasy, and murder-mystery games, as well as adventure games and books. Today, people who are re-enacting the Civil War browse the shelves alongside Dragon Masters. The stock is more than ample, and the personnel are knowledgeable and friendly. For more cerebral sorts, they have chess and backgammon sets—even good old Monopoly! Free shipping is offered. There are special events for gamers every Saturday; call or go online for details.

VILLAGE CHESS SHOP
230 Thompson St (bet Bleecker and 3rd St)   212/475-9580
Daily: noon-midnight   www.chess-shop.com

People who enjoy playing chess do so at the Village Chess Shop for a small fee. Those searching for unique chess pieces patronize this shop as well. Chess sets are available in pewter, brass, ebony, onyx, and more. Village Chess has outstanding backgammon sets, too. In short, this should be your first stop if you're planning on moving chess pieces—either from one square to another or from the store to your home!

Gifts, Accessories

ADRIEN LINFORD
927 Madison Ave (bet 73rd and 74th St)   212/628-4500
1339 Madison Ave (at 93rd St)   212/426-1500
Daily: 11-7

At Adrien Linford you will find an eclectic mixture of gifts, decorative home accessories, occasional furniture, lighting, jewelry, and whatever else Gary Yee finds interesting and exciting. The atmosphere and price tags are definitely upscale. You'll be impressed with the tasteful stock.

BIZARRE BAZAAR
130¼ E 65th St (bet Lexington and Park Ave)   212/517-2100
Mon-Sat: noon-6 (call for appointment)   www.bzrbzr.com

Some people collect baseball cards, while others find political buttons fascinating. I collect "Do Not Disturb" signs from hotels where I have stayed. For the discerning and serious collector, Bizarre Bazaar offers antique toys, aviation and automotive memorabilia, vintage Louis Vuitton luggage, enamel glassware, French perfume bottles, Lalique pieces, artists' mannequins, architectural miniatures, and much more of good quality.

CAROLE STUPELL
29 E 22nd St (bet Park Ave and Broadway)   212/260-3100
Mon-Fri: 10:30-6; Sat: 11-6   www.carolestupell.com

In my opinion, Carole Stupell is the finest home accessories and gifts store in the country. The taste and thought that has gone into the selection of merchandise is simply unmatched. Keith Stupell, a second generation chip-off-the-old-block, has assembled a fabulous array of china, glassware, silver, tabletop, and imported gift treasures. European vases, bowls, candlesticks, and ice buckets are but a few of the choices. All are displayed in spectacular settings. In addition, they carry a large selection of china and glassware replacement patterns dating back over 30 years. Prices are not in the bargain range, but the quality is unequaled.

DE VERA
1 Crosby St (at Howard St)   212/625-0838
Tues-Sat: 11-7   www.deveraobjects.com

Federico de Vera travels the world, purchasing whatever catches his eye. The result is a unique operation, with decorative arts, antiques, Asian lacquerware, Venetian glass, and other unusual items. There's an emphasis on jewelry (vintage, one-of-a-kind, and some even designed by Federico). A craftsman as well as a merchant, he does wonders with the most unusual items. A De Vera outlet is located on the seventh floor of Bergdorf Goodman (745 Fifth Ave).

ESTELLA
493 Ave of the Americas (bet 12th and 13th St)
Mon-Fri: 11-7; Sat: 11-6; Sun: noon-5   212/255-3553, 877/755-3553
                                                              www.estella-nyc.com

The husband-and-wife team of Jean Polsky and Chike Chukwulozie operate this great shop. They go out of their way for those interested in special
and unusual gifts for youngsters six and under. Service is given with a smile,
and they will even make house calls to deliver a present.

EXTRAORDINARY
247 E 57th St (bet Second and Third Ave)   212/223-9151
Daily: 11-10   www.extraordinaryny.com

Quite a unique jewel! An international gift selection is the draw at Extraordinary. Owner J.R. Sanders has a background in museum exhibition design,
and it shows. You'll find boxes, bowls, trays, candle holders, lamps, jewelry,
and other items for the home. The round-the-world theme includes merchandise from the Philippines, Japan, Thailand, China, Vietnam, India, Morocco,
Ghana, Peru, and other stops. Local artists are also featured.

FELISSIMO DESIGN HOUSE
10 W 56th St (bet Fifth Ave and Ave of the Americas)   212/247-5656
Mon-Sat: 11-6   www.felissimo.com

Constructed with the senses in mind, Felissimo Design House is a venue
for "design experiences in everyday life." They sell not just products but
"space, inspiration, experience, and opportunity." The first four floors
showcase the latest in everyday product design, while the fifth floor is an
ever-changing exhibition space.

GLOBAL TABLE
107 Sullivan St (bet Prince and Spring St)   212/431-5839
Mon-Sat: noon-7; Sun: noon-6   www.globaltable.com

Affordable. Different. Fun. Worldwide in scope. These all describe inventory at this crowded tabletop and accessory store, where you will find
pottery, ceramic, wood, and plastic gifts. You might find a thoughtful surprise
for mom or the perfect gift to take to your next dinner party.

KIRNA ZABÊTE
96 Greene St (bet Prince and Spring St)   212/941-9656
Mon-Sat: 11-7; Sun: noon-6   www.kirnazabete.com

If you're looking for something different, Kirna Zabête surely qualifies.
With a mixture of high-end designer items, jewelry, shoes, candy, dog accessories, and much more, *color* and *imagination* are the bywords!

MICHAEL C. FINA
545 Fifth Ave (at 45th St)   212/557-2500, 800/BUY-FINA
Mon-Thurs: 11-8; Fri: 10-7, Sat: 10-6; Sun: 11-6

www.michaelcfina.com

A New York tradition since 1935, Michael C. Fina is a popular bridal gift
registry firm with an extensive selection (over 200 brand names) of sterling
silver, china, crystal, jewelry, stationery, and housewares. Prices are attractive,
quality is top-notch, and the store is well organized.

ONLY HEARTS
386 Columbus Ave (bet 78th and 79th St)   212/724-5608
Mon-Sat: 11-7:30; Sun: 11-6:30

230 Mott St (bet Prince and Spring St)   212/431-3694
Mon-Sat: noon-8; Sun: noon-7   www.onlyhearts.com

At this heart-themed boutique, Helena Stuart offers romantics an extraordinary collection of European designer accessories, posh scents, soaps, and candles. She also shows a beguiling array of intimate apparel, lingerie, and women's wear.

SUSTAINABLE NYC
139 Ave A (bet 8th and 9th St)   212/254-5400
Mon-Sat: 8 a.m.-11 p.m.; Sun: 9 a.m.-10 p.m.
                                                 www.sustainable-nyc.com

We're all trying to be responsible stewards of our planet, and this store offers local, organic, recycled, fair-trade, re-purposed, and biodegradable products and gifts. There are a variety of books, jewelry, clothing, toiletries, and solar-powered gadget chargers. One recent workshop showed how to convert plastic soda bottles into useful home accessories or bracelets. Even the store sign is solar-powered.

> Some say the dollar store is a relic of the past. Not so! Try **Jack's World** (110 W 32nd St, 212/268-9962 and 45 W 45th St, 212/354-6888) and **Jack's 99 Cent Store** (16 E 40th St, 212/696-5767).

WORKS GALLERY
1250 Madison Ave (bet 89th and 90th St)   212/996-0300
Mon-Thurs: 10-6:30; Fri, Sat: 10-6   www.worksgallery.com

Do you need a unique gift for a special person or occasion? At Works Gallery you will find one-of-a-kind jewelry, art-glass items, and wall art handmade by talented artists. You can also have a personal piece made from your own stones. They have been in business for two decades.

YOYA
636 Hudson St (at Horatio St)   646/336-6844
Mon-Sat: 11-7; Sun: noon-5   www.yoyashop.com

What an eclectic place! You will find toys, furniture, clothing, and books for newborns to age eight. Choose from handmade and one-of-a-kind pieces by local artists and Yoya's own line of clothing and toys. This appealing potpourri makes Yoya a fun store to shop.

Greeting Cards

UNICEF CARD & GIFT SHOP
3 United Nations Plaza (44th St bet First and Second Ave)
Mon-Fri: 10-6   212/326-7054
                                                 www.unicefusa.org

For nearly 60 years the United Nations Children's Emergency Fund (UNICEF) has been improving the lives of the world's children. One way this tremendous organization raises money for its life-saving projects and programs is through the sale of cards and gifts. If you've never seen UNICEF products before, then you're in for a treat at this well-planned and friendly store, which carries fabulous calendars, greeting cards, stationery, books and games for children, apparel, and a fascinating assortment of Nepalese paper products. It also sells cards chosen for sale in Asia, Africa, Europe, and South America. In fact, it's the only store in the U.S. that stocks these exotic cards!

Hearing Aids

EMPIRE STATE HEARING AID BUREAU
25 W 43rd St (bet Fifth Ave and Ave of the Americas)   212/921-1666
Mon-Thurs: 9-5:30; Fri: 9-5

Baby boomers are adjusting to the annoyances of aging, and hearing loss is a common complaint. Fortunately, the latest hearing aids are so small that most people cannot even tell they're being worn. Empire State products are up-to-date and state-of-the-art. They have been in the business for over half a century and carry all of the major manufacturers in the field: Siemens, Starkey, Oticon, and GN ReSound. Skilled personnel will test and fit quality hearing aids in a quiet, unhurried atmosphere.

Hobbies

JAN'S HOBBY SHOP
1435 Lexington Ave (bet 93rd and 94th St)
Mon-Sat: 10-7; Sun: noon-5   212/987-4765, 212/861-5075

Jan's is one of my favorite examples of New York retailing! When Fred Hutchins was young, he was obsessed with building models and dioramas, particularly on historical themes. Eventually, his parents bought his favorite source of supply. Now he runs the shop, keeping Jan's stocked with everything a serious model builder could possibly want. The store has a superb stock of plastic scale models, model war games, paints, books, brushes and all kinds of model cars, trains, planes, RC helicopters, ships, and tanks. It also carries remote-controlled planes and boats. Fred himself creates models and dioramas for television, advertising, and private customers. He is noted for accurate historical detailing and can provide information from his vast library of military subjects. Because any hobbyist likes to show his wares, Fred also custom-makes wood, Plexiglas, glass, and mahogany showcases.

Home Furnishings

ABC CARPET & HOME
881 and 888 Broadway (at 19th St)   212/473-3000
Mon-Fri: 10-7 (Thurs till 8); Sat: 11-7; Sun: 11-6   www.abchome.com

If you can visit only one home furnishings store in Manhattan, ABC should be it! Starting in 1897 as a pushcart business, ABC expanded into one of the city's most unique, exciting, and well-merchandised emporiums. (It's actually two buildings located across the street from each other.) ABC is the Bergdorf Goodman of home furnishings. There are floors of great-looking furniture, dinnerware, linens, gifts, accessories, and antiques. You will see many one-of-a-kind pieces as you explore corner after corner. There is an entire floor of fabrics by the yard and an extensive selection of carpets and rugs at reasonable prices. Don't miss their restaurant, **Pipa** (38 E 19th St, 212/677-2233), serving tapas and more. An ABC outlet store is located in The Bronx (1055 Bronx River Ave, 718/842-8772).

ADELAIDE

702 Greenwich St (at 10th St)   212/627-0508
Wed-Sun: noon-7   www.adelaideny.com

The elegant interior of this shop belies its former life as a trucking garage. Furniture, interesting decor pieces, and artwork from the 1930s to the 1960s are attractively displayed. Classy vignettes incorporate gleaming aluminum, glass, brass tables, and interesting accessories alongside upholstered chairs, settees, and sofas.

It used to be that only those holding designer's cards were admitted to some trade buildings. These days, a number of design outfits will take care of individual customers, even if the signs on their doors say "Trade Only." Listed below are some of the trade buildings worth checking out. Each has a multitude of shops where you can find just about anything you need to fix up an apartment or home.

Architects & Designers Building (150 E 58th St, 212/644-2766; Mon-Fri: 9-5)

Decoration & Design Building (979 Third Ave, 212/759-5408; Mon-Fri: 8:30-5:30)

Manhattan Art & Antiques Center (1050 Second Ave, 212/355-4400; Mon-Sat: 10:30-6; Sun: noon-6)

AUTO

803-805 Washington St (bet Gansevoort and Horatio St)
Mon-Fri: noon-7; Sat: 11-7; Sun: 11-6   212/229-2292
                                                www.thisisauto.com

The stock at oddly-named Auto includes specially designed and hard-to-find home furnishings such as pillows, ceramics, glassware, throws, and home accessories. Most are handmade and one-of-kind. Next door is a similarly unique selection of jewelry, hats, scarves, and wallets.

CALYPSO HOME

199 Lafayette St (at Broome St)   212/925-6200
Mon-Sat: 11-7; Sun: noon-7

Bedrooms will look casual and breezy with merchandise from this outfit. Calypso Home specializes in beautiful pillows, throws, textiles, furniture, and other home items, including some designer originals. Many items are loungey, but there is a real mix of modern and coastal decor.

HOME DEPOT

980 Third Ave (bet 58th and 59th St)   212/888-1512
Mon-Sat: 6 a.m.-7 p.m.; Sun: 8-8

40 W 23rd St (bet Fifth Ave and Ave of the Americas) 212/929-9571
Mon-Sat: 6 a.m.-10 p.m.; Sun: 8-8   www.homedepot.com

Home Depot has two huge stores in Manhattan that feature every modern convenience. Flat-panel touch screens will display inventories and print out product lists and how-to instructions. Expert salespeople can customize products for small spaces in Manhattan apartments. You'll find kitchen and bath items, appliances, window treatments and moldings, lighting fixtures, phones and accessories, paint, cleaning supplies, lumber, building materials, tools, plants, and patio furniture. Same- and next-day delivery are offered.

KARKULA

48 Walker St (bet Church St and Broadway)   212/645-2216
Mon-Fri: 10-6; Sat: 11-6

Karkula is synonymous with modern furniture, lighting, and flooring (indoor and outdoor), that's sexy and urban. The international roster of designers respresented includes Paola Lenti, Oluce, Fritz Hansen, Bill Katavolos, Tobias Grau, Omikron, Carpet Sign, Gubi, and Carl Hansen & Sons. Many of these collections are exclusive to Karkula. Designs feature such natural materials as bronze, wood, leather, and felt.

MACKENZIE-CHILDS

14 W 57th St (bet Fifth Ave and Ave of the Americas) 212/570-6050
Mon-Sat: 10-6 (Thurs till 7); Sun: 11-5   www.mackenzie-childs.com

Style, color, and quality intersect inside this marvelous boutique. Stripes, checks, plaids, floral, and black-and-white patterns adorn the handcrafted and hand-painted tableware, kitchen accessories, gifts, home decor, lighting, unique furniture pieces, and stunning accessories. This same theme carries over to the selection of apparel and holiday items. There are even whimsical bathroom sinks! A visit to MacKenzie-Childs will brighten any day.

SURPRISE! SURPRISE!

91 Third Ave (bet 12th and 13th St)   212/777-0990
Mon-Sat: 10-7; Sun: 11-6   www.surprisesurprise.com

Surprise! Surprise! offers a complete line of reasonably priced items for the home. With all their stock and know-how, you can have your new apartment looking like a home in no time. You'll find a large selection of kitchenware, furnishings, patio furniture, and lamps.

TRIBBLES HOME & GARDEN

217 West Broadway (at Franklin St)   212/965-8480
Mon-Sat: 10-6; Sun: 11-6   www.tribbleshomeandgarden.com

When you're in Tribeca, check out the wonderful collection of home and garden items at Tribbles, run by the sister team of Cara and Elizabeth. This store is a real gem, with a nice assortment of essentials for the home and garden, including furniture, trendy desktop items and stationery, fragrant bath and personal-care articles, and cookware, serveware, tableware, and other thoughtful things for the kitchen. There is also a section for kids and an eco-friendly household products line. No home and garden store is complete without fresh plants and flowers. The display of floralscapes is beautiful!

WEST ELM

112 W 18th St (bet Ave of the Americas and Seventh Ave)
212/929-4464
1870 Broadway (bet 62nd St and Broadway)   212/247-8077
Mon-Sat: 11-8; Sun: noon-7   www.westelm.com

West Elm is like a Crate & Barrel store with slightly lower prices. You'll find furniture, shelving, mirrors, lamps, quilts, bedding, shower curtains, bath accessories, towels, clocks, room accents, dinnerware, glassware, and flatware. The store is attractive and merchandise is well displayed.

Housewares, Hardware

BASICS PLUS

2315 Broadway (bet 84th and 83rd St)	212/873-7837
86 Christopher St (at Seventh Ave)	212/620-9000
194 Third Ave (at 18th St)	212/620-9000
845 Second Ave (at 45th St)	212/682-6311
1621 First Ave (at 84th St)	212/620-9000
121 University Pl (at 13th St)	212/228-4950
386 Canal St (at West Broadway)	212/620-9000
148 Church St (at Chambers St)	212/791-6269
Mon-Fri: 8 a.m.-9 p.m.; Sat: 9-9; Sun: 10-9	www.basicsplusny.com

Zvi Cohen is a real entrepreneur. Upon starting his first locksmith company on the Upper East Side, he realized he needed merchandise on the shelves; so he asked his customers what they would buy, and the rest is history. Zvi opened additional locations, with more outlets planned. Every location has a New York Locksmith service counter, as well as hardware store essentials like tools, cleaning supplies, automotive needs, housewares, paint, and fasteners, and basic items needed to keep a home in good repair.

One of the very best design stores in Manhattan is **Moss** (150 Greene St, 866/888-6677). This emporium is internationally known for the quality and presentation of its merchandise. You'll find furniture, lighting, watches, jewelry, books, and a large showing of tabletop items. For a complete selection, visit www.mossonline.com.

BROADWAY PANHANDLER

65 E 8th St (bet Broadway and University Pl)
Mon-Sat: 11-7 (Thurs till 8); Sun: 11-6   212/966-3434, 866/266-5927
www.broadwaypanhandler.com

Broadway Panhandler maintains a tradition of great assortments and low prices! These folks are a pleasure to deal with. Thousands of cutlery, bakeware, tabletop items, and cookware pieces are available at sizable savings. Guest chefs make periodic appearances, and a fine selection of professional items is offered to walk-in customers and restaurant and hotel buyers.

DICK'S CUT-RATE HARDWARE

9 Gold St (at Maiden Lane)   212/425-1070
Mon-Fri: 7:30-6:30; Sat: 9-4; Sun: 10-3

Really complete hardware stores like Dick's are a great convenience for shoppers. In a Lower Manhattan location where there are few such stores, Dick's provides good prices and informed service. You will find great selections of electrical and plumbing supplies, tools, plus more. They also make duplicate keys.

DOMUS NEW YORK

413 W 44th St (at Ninth Ave)   212/581-8099
Tues-Sat: noon-8; Sun: noon-6   www.domusnewyork.com

What fun it is shopping at this eclectic Hell's Kitchen housewares store! Luisa Cerutti and Nicki Lindheimer have excellent taste. They have picked out one-of-a-kind European imports (many handcrafted), including pottery, tabletop, vintage glassware, linens, china, furniture, and unusual pieces that will catch everyone's attention. By working directly with international artisans, they are able to trim costs by eliminating middle men. Domus (which is Latin for *home*) is a super place to shop for wedding gifts. Free gift wrapping and delivery in Manhattan are available.

GARBER HARDWARE

710 Greenwich St (bet 10th and Charles St)   212/929-3030
Mon-Thurs: 8-8; Fri, Sat: 8-5; Sun: 10-4   www.garberhardware.com

This unique family business has become a New York institution. The Garbers have been operating since 1884 with this appealing motto: "Either we have it or we can get it for you." You will find a complete inventory of paints, hardware, home and garden, plumbing and electrical supplies, housewares, locks, tools, and building materials. Custom window shades, key-cutting, and pipe-cutting are among the many handy services offered.

Top Button is a web-based company (www.topbutton.com) that informs consumers about sample, warehouse, outlet, clearance, and promotional sales. Categories include apparel, housewares, and accessories. Information can be accessed by company name, product type, and date. The service is free.

GEORGE TAYLOR SPECIALTIES

76 Franklin St (bet Church St and Broadway)   212/226-5369
Mon-Thurs: 7:30-5; Fri: 7:30-4

Taylor stocks replacement plumbing parts to fit all faucets, and custom faucets can be fabricated via special order. They also offer reproduction faucets and custom designs of fittings for unique installations. Antique-style towel bars, bath accessories, and pedestal sinks are among Taylor's specialties. Founded in 1869, Taylor remains a family-run operation. Ask for father Chris, daughter Valerie, or son John.

GRACIOUS HOME

1201, 1217 and 1220 Third Ave (bet 70th and 71st St) 212/517-6300
1992 Broadway (at 67th St)   212/231-7800
1201 Third Ave (at 70th St)   212/414-5710
Hours vary by store   www.gracioushome.com

Since 1963 Gracious Home has been popular with savvy New Yorkers. These stores are must-visits for anyone interested in fixing up their home, establishing a new one, looking for gifts, or just browsing stores that typify the New York lifestyle. The style, expertise, and service are outstanding. You'll find appliances, wall coverings, gifts, hardware, decorative bath accessories, lighting, china, casual furniture, bedding, shelving, pots and pans, and heaven knows what else! They install window coverings, large appliances, and countertops; offer tool rental and repair services; provide a special order department; and will deliver in Manhattan for $10.

P.E. GUERIN
23 Jane St (bet Greenwich and Eighth Ave)   212/243-5270
Mon-Fri: 9-5:30 (by appointment)   www.peguerin.com

Andrew Ward, P.E. Guerin's president, is the fourth generation to run the oldest decorative hardware firm in the country and the only foundry in the city. It was founded in 1857 and has been on Jane Street since 1892. In that time, the firm has grown into an impressive worldwide operation. The main foundry is now in Valencia, Spain (although work continues at the Village location), and there are branches and showrooms across the country. The Jane Street location is still headquarters for manufacturing and importing decorative hardware and bath accessories. Much of it is done in brass or bronze, and the foundry can make virtually anything from those materials, including copies and reproductions. The Gueridon table has garnered design and production awards and enjoys an international reputation. No job is too small for Guerin, which operates like the hometown firm it thinks it is. They offer free estimates and can help with any hardware problems. They have a wonderful color catalog.

There's no excuse to set a boring table! Whether you are outfitting an undersized efficiency kitchenette or a sprawling penthouse kitchen and dining room, **Sur la Table** (75 Spring St, 212/966-3375) is the place to shop. You'll find a large colorful, well-displayed assortment of essentials for cooking and entertaining with name brands such as Weber, Le Creuset, Cuisinart, and Viking, not to mention their own quality Sur la Table merchandise. Attractive displays change seasonally.

RESTORATION HARDWARE
935 Broadway (at 22nd St)   212/260-9479
Mon-Sat: 10-8; Sun: 11-7   www.restorationhardware.com

If you prefer a classic, quality look, then come to Restoration Hardware. You'll find a large selection of furniture, bed and bath items, home decor, drapery, lighting, bathware, and hardware; a good selection of cleaning and maintenance supplies, too! This operation is among the best in its field.

SAIFEE HARDWARE
114 First Ave (at 7th St)   212/979-6396
Mon-Sat: 8:30-7:30; Sun: 10-6:30

Everyone needs a good neighborhood hardware store for the little things it takes to run an apartment or home. Saifee has the usual supplies for plumbing, electrical, gardening, and small building projects, as well as housewares, tools, and other gadgets. Although prices are not as good as they are at big box stores, the expertise you'll find here makes it worth the stop.

S. FELDMAN HOUSEWARES
1304 Madison Ave (at 92nd St)   212/289-7367
Mon-Sat: 9-6; Sun: 11-5   www.wares2u.com

Keep this name and address on your refrigerator door! Founded in 1929 during the Depresson, Feldman was originally a five-and-dime store. Over the years it has changed dramatically, but it still is family-owned and -operated. You'll find housewares, cookware, home decor, gifts, tabletop items, appliances, toys, and more. Customer service is a big plus; they even provide free espresso for shoppers. With over 12,000 items to choose from, this can be a true one-stop shopping spot. They also repair vacuum cleaners.

SIMON'S HARDWARE & BATH
421 Third Ave (bet 29th and 30th St)   212/532-9220, 888/274-6667
Mon, Tues, Wed, Fri: 8-5:30; Thurs: 10-7; Sat: 10-5

Simon's is really a hardware supermarket, offering one of the city's finest selections of quality decorative hardware items and bath and kitchen fixtures and accessories. Woodworkers will find myriad tools, supplies, and materials. The personnel are patient, even if you just need something to fix a broken handle on a chest of drawers.

Remodelers and builders, take note! For lumber, plywood, Masonite, bricks, cork, paint, and more, **Metropolitan Lumber and Hardware** (175 Spring St, 212/966-3466 and 617 Eleventh Ave, 212/246-9090) is a good name to remember.

WILLIAMS-SONOMA
1175 Madison Ave (at 86th St)	212/289-6832
110 Seventh Ave (at 17th St)	212/633-2203
121 E 59 St (bet Park and Lexington Ave)	917/369-1131
10 Columbus Circle (Time Warner Building)	212/823-9750
Hours vary by store	www.williams-sonoma.com

From humble beginnings in the wine country of Sonoma County, California, Williams-Sonoma expanded across the nation and is referred to as the "Tiffany of cookware stores." The serious cook will find a vast display of quality cookware, bakeware, cutlery, kitchen linens, specialty foods, cookbooks, small appliances, kitchen furniture, glassware, and tableware. Only the Columbus Circle location carries a home furniture collection. The stores also offer a gift and bridal registry, cooking demonstrations, free recipes, gift baskets, and shopping assistance for corporations or individuals. Especially at holiday time, the candy assortment is first-class. Ask for their attractive catalog, which includes a number of excellent recipes.

Imports
Afghan

NUSRATY AFGHAN IMPORTS
113 W 10th St (bet Greenwich and Ave of the Americas) 212/691-1012
Daily: 12-8   www.nusratyafghanimports.com

Nusraty is one of the best sources of Afghan goods on the continent. There are magnificently embroidered native dresses and shirts displayed alongside semiprecious stones mounted in jewelry or shown individually. One area of the store features carpets and rugs, while another displays antique silver and jewelry. Nusraty has an unerring eye; all of his stock is of the highest quality and is often unique. The business operates on both a wholesale and retail level.

Chinese

CHINESE PORCELAIN COMPANY
475 Park Ave (at 58th St)   212/838-7744
Mon-Fri: 10-6; Sat: 11-5 (closed Sat in summer)
www.chineseporcelainco.com

Come here for Chinese ceramics, furniture, and works of art. There are Chinese, Tibetan, Indian, Khymer, and Southeast Asian sculptures, as well as French and continental furniture.

CQ ASIAN FURNITURE
37 W 20th St (bet Fifth Ave and Ave of the Americas) 212/366-1888
Daily: 10:30-7:30   www.cqasianantiquefurniture.com

Whether you decorate with an Asian theme or need the perfect accent piece, check out the vast selection at CQ. Antiques, good-looking reproductions, and a few accessories (like vases and ginger jars) have been imported from Korea, Mongolia, Tibet, and Beijing. Choose from a variety of table styles, armoires, buffets, chairs, and desks. Talk to the store personnel if you don't find exactly what you're looking for, as they have a huge warehouse and take custom orders.

The Best of Britain!

British sweets: **Carry On Tea & Sympathy** (108-110 Greenwich Ave, 212/807-8329)

Clothes and toiletries: **Eskandar** (33 E 10th St, 212/533-4200 and Bergdorf Goodman, 754 Fifth Ave, 6th floor, 212/872-8659)

Fashion designer: **Alexander McQueen** (417 W 14th St, 212/645-1797)

Handbags: **Lulu Guinness** (394 Bleecker St, 212/367-2120)

Leather goods and stationery: **Smythson of Bond Street** (4 W 57th St, 212/265-4573)

PEARL RIVER MART
477 Broadway (bet Broome and Grand St)   212/431-4770
Daily: 10-7:30   www.pearlriver.com

This is a true Chinese department store, with many items made in China. Pearl River is busy and well-stocked, and even with a language barrier, most everyone can understand what you want. A home department has been added.

WING-ON TRADING
145 Essex St (bet Delancey and Houston St)   212/477-1450
Mon-Sat: 10-6

There's no need to go to the Orient to get your Chinese porcelain or earthenware. Wing-On has a complete and well-organized stock of household goods. One of their specialties is Chinese teas at low prices.

Eskimo / Native American

ALASKA ON MADISON

1065 Madison Ave (bet 80th and 81st St) 2nd floor   212/879-1782
Tues-Sat: 11:30-6 (or by appointment)   www.alaskaonmadison.com

This gallery is New York's most complete collection of Inuit and North-west Coast artifacts and sculptures. Periodic shows highlight aspects of these cultures. A number of contemporary artists whose works have been shown here have gained international acclaim.

General

JACQUES CARCANAGUES

21 Greene St (bet Grand and Canal St)   212/925-8110
Tues-Sun: 11:30-7   www.jacquescarcanagues.com

After a stint in the diplomatic service, Frenchman Jacques Carcanagues decided to assemble and sell the finest artifacts he had encountered in his world travels. So while the goods are mostly Southeast Asian, this empo-rium is, in Jacques own words, "a complete ethnic department store, not a museum." Textiles and *tansus* (dressers) are everywhere, as are jewelry and lacquerware. It is also very appealing to Soho shoppers, who can choose among Indian, Myanmarese, and Thai sculptures of many periods and unusual household objects not seen elsewhere in New York. The overall effect is that of an Eastern bazaar, yet all pieces are of museum quality.

KATINKA

303 E 9th St (at Second Ave)   212/677-7897
Tues-Sat: 4-7 (call ahead, as hours can vary)

Katinka is an import paradise, with jewelry, natural-fiber clothing, shoes, scarves, belts, hats, musical instruments, incense, and artifacts from India, Thailand, Pakistan, Afghanistan, and South America. The most popular items are colorful shoes and embroidered silk skirts from India. The place is small, and prices are reasonable. Jane Williams and Billy Lyles make customers feel like they have embarked on a worldwide shopping safari!

KIOSK

95 Spring St (bet Mercer St and Broadway), 2nd floor   212/226-8601
Tue-Sat: 1-7   www.kioskkiosk.com

The owners of this eclectic Soho shop travel to a different foreign coun-try every couple of months to select a few dozen more items for their self-described collection of "simple everyday anonymous things." These include ordinary and unique personal care items, home accessories, kitchenware, stationery, toys, clothing, gifts, jewelry, and some custom-made products. An area within Kiosk is designated for mini-exhibits of carefully chosen artists and designers. They've chronicled a couple of their trips in small, eclectic guidebooks.

KISAN CONCEPT STORE

125 Greene St (bet Prince and Houston St)   212/475-2470
Mon-Sat: 11-7; Sun: noon-6   www.kisanstore.com

Look for really cool merchandise in this shop, thanks to the Icelandic owners. This is their first store in the States; the original opened in Reykjavik in 2005. Vanessa Bruno, Sonia Rykiel, and Flora and Henri are among classy brands of women's and kids' clothing and accessories. Designers worldwide contribute to the mix of household goods, travel items and exclusive gifts. Kisan shows a nice, eclectic selection in one locale.

PIER I IMPORTS

71 Fifth Ave (at 15th St)	212/206-1911
1550 Third Ave (at 87th St)	212/987-1746
Mon-Sat: 10-9; Sun: 11-7	www.pier1.com

At Pier 1, you will find imported dining room sets, occasional furniture, bathroom accessories, picture frames, brassware, china and glassware, floor coverings, bedding, and pillows. The goods come from exotic lands throughout Asia and the rest of the world. The selections are inviting, the prices are right, and the stores are fun to visit.

Japanese designer Nigo has created **A Bathing Ape** (91 Greene St, 212/925-0222) for lovers of things Japanese. Offerings include unusual clothing and shoes. Fans of rock star couture will be blown away by the merchandise.

SHEHERAZADE IMPORTS

121 Orchard St (bet Delancey and Rivington St)	212/539-1771
Daily: 11-7	www.sheherazadenyc.com

Sheherazade features handcrafted merchandise imported from a number of countries. You'll find home furnishings from North Africa, the Middle East, and Asia, including antique and contemporary furniture, carpets, tapestries, chandeliers, lanterns, jewelry, and gifts. Islamic art and Oriental decorative furnishings are also featured. Custom-made furniture can be ordered.

Indian

INDIA COTTAGE EMPORIUM

221 W 37th St (bet Seventh and Eighth Ave), basement 212/685-6943
Mon-Fri: 10-5

India Cottage features clothing, jewelry, handicrafts, and gifts imported directly from India. Moti R. Chani has a sharp eye for the finest details; the Indian clothing he sells reflects his taste and expertise. The clothing is prized by Indian nationals and neighborhood residents for its sheer beauty. The garments are made of cotton and feature unique madras patterns.

Japanese

SARA JAPANESE POTTERY

950 Lexington Ave (bet 69th and 70th St)	212/772-3243
Mon-Fri: 11-7; Sat: noon-6	www.saranyc.com

Looking for something with a Japanese flair? Sara is the place to go for modern Japanese ceramics, glassware, tableware, cast iron, and gifts. Check out the colorful lacquerware, textiles, and bamboo products. Artist exhibitions are occasionally held at Sara.

THINGS JAPANESE

800 Lexington Ave (bet 61st and 62nd St), 2nd floor	212/371-4661
Mon-Sat: 11-5	www.thingsjapanese.com

Things Japanese believes that the Japanese "things" most in demand are prints. So while there are all sorts of Japanese artworks and crafts, prints highlight the selection. They know the field well and will help collectors establish a grouping or assist decorators in finding pieces to round out decor. There are also original 18th- to 20th-century Japanese woodblock prints, porcelains, baskets, chests, lacquers, and books. Prices range from $10 to several thousand dollars, and every piece is accompanied by a certificate of authenticity. Things Japanese will help you appreciate both the subject matter and the artistry in the works it sells.

Middle Eastern

PERSIAN SHOP
534 Madison Ave (bet 54th and 55th St)   212/355-4643
Mon-Fri: 10-6; Sat: 10-6 (call ahead in summer)

Since 1940, the Persian Shop has featured unusual Middle Eastern items: end tables, chairs, frames, mirrors, and brocades sold by the yard or made into magnificent neckties. The jewelry selection is especially noteworthy. You'll find precious and semiprecious items, silver and gold cuff links, rings, earrings, bracelets, necklaces, and heirloom pieces. All will add a special air of interest to any setting.

Ukrainian

SURMA (THE UKRAINIAN SHOP)
11 E 7th St (at Third Ave)   212/477-0729
Mon-Fri: 11-6; Sat: 11-4   www.surmastore.com

Since 1918, Surma has functioned as the "general store of the Slavic community in New York City." Quite honestly, it seems capable of serving the entire hemisphere. This bastion of Ukrainianism makes it difficult to believe you're still in New York. The clothing is pure ethnic opulence. There are dresses, vests, shirts, blouses, and accessories. All are hand-embroidered with authentic detailing. For the home, there are accent pieces (including an entire section devoted to Ukrainian Easter egg decorating), brocaded and hand-embroidered linens, and Surma's own Ukrainian-style honey (different and very good). Above all, Surma is known for its educational tapes and books. Pay particular attention to the artwork and stationery, which depict ancient Ukrainian glass paintings.

Jewelry

CATWALK COUTURE
933 Lexington Ave (bet 71st and 72nd St)   212/249-5066
Mon-Fri: 10:30-6; Sat: 11-6 (or by appointment)
                                        www.catwalkcouturenyc.com

Catwalk Couture offers one of the largest selections of couture costume jewelry in the city. Featured designers include Chanel, Armani, Valentino, YSL, and more.

CHROME HEARTS
159 E 64th St (bet Lexington and Third Ave)   212/327-0707
Mon-Sat: 11-7   www.chromehearts.com

If you're looking for unique accessories, Chrome Hearts is the place to go! They show a broad selection of handmade jewelry in sterling silver, 22-karat gold and platinum, and precious stones; clothing in leather and fabric; gadgets for people who think they have everything; handcrafted furniture in exotic woods; great-looking eyewear; and much more.

DIAMONDS BY RENNIE ELLEN

15 W 47th St (bet Fifth Ave and Ave of the Americas), Room 503
Mon-Fri: 10-4:30 (by appointment)   212/869-5525
                                                  www.rennieellen.com

Rennie Ellen is a wholesaler offering the sort of discounts for which the city's wholesale businesses are famous. She was the first female diamond dealer in the male-dominated Diamond District. Rennie personally spent so much time and effort keeping the district straight and honest that she earned the title "Mayor of 47th Street." In other words, Ellen's reputation is impeccable. Her diamond-cutting factory deals exclusively in diamond jewelry. There are pendants, wedding bands, engagement rings, and diamonds to fit all sizes, shapes, and budgets. All sales are made under Ellen's personal supervision and are strictly confidential. Call for her $3 mail-order catalog or look online.

DOYLE & DOYLE

189 Orchard St (bet Houston and Stanton St)   212/677-9991
Tues-Sun: 1-7   www.doyledoyle.com

Two sisters operate this shop specializing in antique and estate jewelry, with an emphasis on treasured engagement rings. You'll find Georgian, Victorian, Edwardian, art deco, art nouveau, and retro pieces.

FRAGMENTS

116 Prince St (bet Greene and Wooster St)   212/334-9588
Mon-Sat: 11-7; Sun: noon-6

997 Madison Ave (bet 77th and 78th St)   212/537-5000
Daily: 10-6   www.fragments.com

Fragments shows the latest jewelry collections from some of the country's top designers. You'll find Annie Fensterstock, Erica Molinari, Mizuki, and a number of others represented in their large collection. Much of the credit for the success of this outfit goes to Janet Goldman, its talented founder and CEO. A special area named **Fragments Fine Jewelry** features high-end items with precious stones and gem-quality pearls.

HERMAN ROTENBERG & BILL SCHIFRIN

National Jewelers Exchange
4 W 47th St (bet Fifth Ave and Ave of the Americas), Booth 86
Mon-Fri: 10-5:30   212/944-1713, 800/877-3874
                                        www.unusualweddingrings.com

From a booth in the National Jewelers Exchange—better known for its collection of gold, platinum, and diamond wedding and engagement rings—Bill Schifrin and son-in-law Herman Rotenberg preside over a collection of over 2,000 unusual wedding rings. Prices range from under $100 to several thousand dollars, depending upon the work's complexity and the types of metal and stones used. Bill has been doing this for over 60 years and knows the story behind each ring.

JENNIFER MILLER JEWELRY
972 Lexington Ave (bet 70th and 71st St)　　　212/734-8199
Mon-Sat: 10:30-6　　　　　　　　　　　　www.jewelsbyjen.com

Jennifer Miller is the ultimate jewelry store! Miller specializes in contemporary, classic, and estate jewelry, in both fine and faux. The varied selection changes daily, almost guaranteeing that you will find something you can't leave without. Classically chic diamond chain necklaces in 14-karat yellow or white gold range from $200 to $1,800 with man-made stones and up to $61,000 with genuine diamonds. Handbags, shoes, and decorative home items round out the mix.

MAX NASS
118 E 28th St (bet Park Ave S and Lexington Ave)　　212/679-8154
Mon-Fri: 9:30-6; Sat: 9:30-4

The Shah family members are jewelry artisans. Araceli is the designer and Parimal ("Perry") is the company president. Together they make and sell handmade jewelry, service and repair clocks and watches, and restore antique jewelry. They deal in virtually every type of jewelry: antique (or merely old), silver and gold, as well as semiprecious stones. Two special sales each year bring Max Nass's already low prices down even further. One is held the last three weeks in January (33% discount), and the other runs for two weeks in July (25% discount). In between, Araceli will design pieces on a whim or commission. His one-of-a-kind necklaces are particularly impressive. The store also restrings, restores, and redesigns necklaces.

MURREY'S JEWELERS
1395 Third Ave (bet 79th and 80th St)　　　　212/879-3690
Mon-Sat: 9:30-6

I heartily recommend this shop! Family jewelers since 1936, Murrey's sells fine jewelry, watches, and giftware. In the service area, they do fine-jewelry repair, including state-of-the-art laser repair, and expert special-order design and manufacturing, European clock repair, engraving, pearl-stringing, and watch repair. Most watch batteries are replaced while the customer waits, as well as steam cleaning of engagement and wedding rings. Scrap gold is purchased or taken in as trade. The talented staff includes three goldsmiths, three watchmaker/clockmakers (including one of the world's best), one stringer, and one setter.

Ladders

PUTNAM ROLLING LADDER COMPANY
32 Howard St (bet Lafayette St and Broadway)　　212/226-5147
Mon-Fri: 8:30-4　　　　　　　　www.putnamrollingladder.com

Putnam is an esoteric shop on an esoteric street! Why, you might ask, would anyone in New York need those magnificent rolling ladders traditionally used in formal libraries? Could there possibly be enough business to keep a place like this "rolling" since 1905? The answer is that clever New Yorkers turn to Putnam to improve access to their lofts (especially sleeping lofts). Ladders come in many hardwoods and range from rolling ladders (custom-made, if necessary) to folding library ladders.

Lighting Fixtures and Accessories

CITY KNICKERBOCKER
665 Eleventh Ave (at 48th St), 2nd floor   212/586-3939
Mon-Fri: 8:30-5   www.cityknickerbocker.com

The fourth generation of the Liroff family operates this outfit, which has been in business since 1906. These folks are completely reliable when it comes to all aspects of lighting, including quality antique reproductions, glassware, and first-rate repair. The large sales inventory includes contemporary art-glass lamps. Rentals are available.

JUST BULBS
220 E 60th St (bet Second and Third Ave)   212/888-5707
Mon-Sat: 10-7; Sun: noon-6   www.justbulbsnyc.com

This store stocks almost 25,000 types of bulbs, including some that can be found nowhere else. In addition to all the standard sizes, Just Bulbs has lightbulbs for use in old fixtures. The shop looks like an oversized backstage dressing room mirror. Everywhere you turn, bulbs are connected to switches that customers can flick on and off. They also "refresh" light fixtures, changing bulbs and cleaning fixtures at your home or office.

JUST SHADES
21 Spring St (at Elizabeth St)   212/966-2757, 888/898-4058
Tues-Fri: 9:30-6; Sat: 9:30-5   www.justshadesny.com

Just Shades has specialized in lampshades for over 40 years. They are experts at matching shades to lamps and willingly share their knowledge with retail customers. They have lampshades of silk, hide, parchment, and other materials. You'll also find a large selection of finials. No job, residential or commercial, is too large or too small.

LAMPWORKS
231 E 58th St (bet Second and Third Ave)   212/750-1500
Mon-Fri: 9-6   www.lampworksinc.com

You will find an extensive selection of table lamps, antiques, imports, custom lampshades, and exterior lighting fixtures at Lampworks. Over 45 lines are available, and they specialize in custom lighting. Discounts are given to those in the interior design and architectural trades.

LIGHTING BY GREGORY
158 Bowery (bet Delancey and Broome St)   212/226-1276
Daily: 9-5:30   www.lightingbygregory.com

This full-service discount lighting store claims to be the most technically knowledgeable in the country, and counts celebrities, museums, and film companies as satisfied customers. It is the largest contemporary and traditional lighting and ceiling fan distributor in America. They are major dealers of Lightolier, Tech Lighting, and Monte Carlo ceiling fans, and are also experts in track lighting.

LIGHTING PLUS
680 Broadway (bet Great Jones and Bond St)   212/979-2000
Mon-Sat: 10-6:30; Sun: 11-6:30

Lighting Plus is a very handy neighborhood lighting store, featuring floor and table lamps, all kinds of bulbs, and extension cords.

SCHOOLHOUSE ELECTRIC
27 Vestry St (at Hudson St)   212/226-6113
Tues-Fri: 10-6; Sat: 11-5   www.schoolhouseelectric.com

You'll find period lighting fixtures and glass shades at this unique store. Styles range from art deco to mid-20th century. Also available are hand-crafted solid brass lighting fixtures, made to order in many different finishes.

TUDOR ELECTRICAL SUPPLY
222-226 E 46th St (bet Second and Third Ave)   212/867-7550
Mon-Thurs: 8:30-5; Fri: 8:30-4:30

At first glance you may feel like you need an engineering degree to patronize Tudor Electrical. However, the staff is trained to explain everything in stock. Lightbulbs are the store's forte. They are cataloged by wattage, color, and application, and the staff can quickly locate the right bulb for your needs. Some basic knowledge: quartz, tungsten, and halogen bulbs offer undistorted light, while incandescent and fluorescent lamps are best for desk work. Tudor discounts by at least 20%.

Luggage and Other Leather Goods

DEAN LEATHER
822 Third Ave (at 50th St)   212/583-0461
Mon-Fri: 8:30-7:30; Sat: 9-7:30; Sun: 9-6

If it is leather, you can probably find it here: briefcases, wallets, luggage, watchbands, and gift items. The prices are right on many top names like Hartmann, Swiss Army, Samsonite, Briggs & Riley, Bosca, Tumi, and more.

LEXINGTON LUGGAGE
793 Lexington Ave (bet 61st and 62nd St)   800/822-0404
Daily: 9-6   www.lexingtonluggage.com

If you are in the market for luggage, don't miss this place! Lexington Luggage has been family-owned and -operated for over 30 years. They carry nearly every major brand—Samsonite, Delsey, Travelpro, Kipling, Hartmann, and Briggs & Riley—at almost wholesale prices. Luggage and handbag repairs can be done the same day. Other pluses: free same-day delivery, free monograms, and friendly personnel. You'll also find attaché cases, pens, poker sets, trunks, and a nice gift selection.

T. ANTHONY
445 Park Ave (at 56th St)   212/750-9797
Mon-Fri: 9:30-6; Sat: 10-6   www.tanthony.com

T. Anthony handles luxurious luggage of distinction. Anything purchased here will stand out in a crowd. Luggage ranges from small overnight bags to massive steamer trunks. Their briefcases, jewelry boxes, desk sets, albums, key cases, and billfolds make terrific gifts, individually or in matched sets. Don't come looking for discount prices; however, T. Anthony's high quality and courteous service are well-established New York traditions. Exclusive products are also available through the store's website. Repair service on their products is available.

Magic

ENCHANTMENTS
424 E 9th St (bet First Ave and Ave A)   212/228-4394
Wed-Mon: 1-9   www.enchantmentsincnyc.com

This business claims to be the largest and oldest witchcraft and goddess supply store in the city, and one best not argue with them! There is a great selection of essential and fragrance oils, lotions, potions, and incense. Many of these items are custom-blended. Ask for guidance when purchasing magical candles, talismans and charms in order to ensure the desired outcome.

TANNEN'S MAGIC
45 W 34th St (bet Fifth Ave and Ave of the Americas), Suite 608
Mon-Fri: 10-5 (Thurs till 7); Sat, Sun: 10-4   212/929-4500
                                        www.tannens.com

Tannen is one of the world's largest suppliers of magician's items, stocking more than 8,000 magic tricks, books, and DVDs. They have all that a magician of any skill level could possibly need. Since 1925 Tannen's showroom has been patronized by the finest magicians in the country. The floor demonstrators are some of the best in the business—always friendly, helpful, and eager to share their knowledge with those willing to study the art of magic. Tannen also runs a "Magic Summer Camp" for boys and girls age 12 to 20. It has spawned some of today's greatest working magicians.

Maps

HAGSTROM MAP AND TRAVEL CENTER
51 W 43rd St (at Ave of the Americas)   212/398-1222
Mon-Fri: 8:30-6; Sat: 10:30-4:30

Hagstrom is the only complete map and chart dealer in the city, highlighting the maps of major manufacturers and three branches of government. There are also nautical, hiking, global, and travel guides, plus globes, atlases, and foreign-language phrase books. The staff are experts when it comes to maps and travel information.

Memorabilia

CBS STORE
1691 Broadway (at 53rd St)   212/975-8600
Mon-Sat: 10-8; Sun: noon-6   www.cbs.com

Just down the street from the Ed Sullivan Theater (where *The Late Show with David Letterman* is filmed), this store stocks T-shirts, mugs, and other merchandise with the CBS logo and images from the network's past and present shows, such as *I Love Lucy* and *Survivor*.

FIRESTORE
17 Greenwich Ave (bet Christopher and 10th St)   212/226-3142
Mon-Thurs: 11-7; Fri, Sat: 11-8; Sun: noon-6   www.firestore.com

Firefighters, cops, and their fans can find everything under the sun relating to these first responders. Patches, pins, T-shirts, turnout coats, caps, work shirts, FDNY memorial shirts, firefighter jackets, and even toys are available at this fascinating shop!

GOTTA HAVE IT! COLLECTIBLES
153 E 57th St (bet Lexington and Third Ave)   212/750-7900
Mon-Fri: 10:30-6; Sat: 11-5   www.gottahaveit.com

Do you have a favorite sports star, Hollywood personality, musical entertainer, or political figure? Gotta Have It features original and unique products in these categories. There are signed photos, musical instruments, baseball bats, used sports uniforms, documents, and movie props. All items are fully authenticated and guaranteed.

New York City-Themed Merchandise

CityStore (Manhattan Municipal Building, 1 Centre St, 212/669-8246, www.nyc.gov/citystore): official City of New York merchandise

FDNY Fire Zone (34 W 51st St, 212/698-4520, www.fdnyfirezone. org): officially licensed FDNY products

Harlem Underground (20 E 125th St, 212/987-9385, www.harlem underground.com): sleek sportswear with Harlem logos and uptown attitude

Macy's Herald Square Arcade (151 W 34th St, 212/695-4400): unique and classy items

Metropolitan Museum of Art (Fifth Ave at 82nd St, 212/535-7710, www.metmuseum.org): posters of recent art exhibits

Museum of the City of New York (1220 Fifth Ave, 212/534-1672, www.mcny.org): ties, scarves, and umbrellas with New York-themed designs

New York City Police Museum (100 Old Slip, 212/480-3100, www.nycpolicemuseum.org): gift items, including stuffed bears and books

New York Gifts (729 Seventh Ave, lobby, 212/391-7570)

New-York Historical Society (2 W 77th St, 212/873-3400, www. nyhistory.org): posters, prints, and holiday cards featuring scenes of old New York

Statue of Liberty Gift Shop (212/363-3180, www.statueof liberty.com): mini statues, books, postcards, glassware, and holiday ornaments

Steuben (667 Madison Ave, 212/752-1441, www.steuben.com): gorgeous crystal apple and the Manhattan skyline etched in crystal

Tiffany & Co. (727 Fifth Ave, 212/755-8000, www.tiffany.com): Big Apple-themed items, including an apple key ring and Elsa Peretti-designed silver apple earrings, necklaces, and bracelets

---

MOVIE STAR NEWS
134 W 18th St (bet Ave of the Americas and Seventh Ave)
Mon-Fri: 10:30-6:30; Sat: 10:30-4:30   212/620-8160
www.moviestarnews.com

Movie Star News may be the closest thing to Hollywood on the East coast! It claims to have the world's largest collection of movie photos. Stars past and present shine brightly in this shop, which offers posters and other movie memorabilia. The store is laid out like a library. Ira Kramer, who runs the shop, does a lot of research for magazines, newspapers, and other media.

NBC EXPERIENCE STORE
30 Rockefeller Plaza (49th St bet Fifth Ave and Ave of the Americas)
Mon-Sat: 8-8; Sun: 9-6   212/664-3700
                                www.nbcuniversalstore.com

The NBC Experience Store offers walking tours that take visitors behind the scenes of NBC's studios and around one of New York's most recognizable landmarks, Rockefeller Center. The 20,000-square-foot facility is located directly across from Studio 1A, home of the *Today Show*. It stocks T-shirts, mugs, keychains, and other merchandise with the NBC logo or images from such television shows as *The Biggest Loser, 30 Rock,* and *Saturday Night Live*.

ONE SHUBERT ALLEY
One Shubert Alley (45th St bet Broadway and Eighth Ave)
Tues-Sat: noon-8; Sun: noon-7:30   212/944-4133
                                www.broadwaynewyork.com

Shubert Alley is often used as a shortcut between Broadway theaters, and One Shubert Alley is the only retail establishment in the alley. It's a fascinating place to browse for T-shirts, posters, recordings, buttons, and other paraphernalia from current shows on and off Broadway.

Mirrors

SUNDIAL-SCHWARTZ
159 E 118th St (bet Lexington and Third Ave)
Mon-Fri: 8-4   800/876-4776, 212/289-4969
                                www.sundialschwartz.com

Sundial-Schwartz supplies "decorative treatments of distinction." Anyone who has ever seen a cramped New York apartment suddenly appear to expand with the strategic placement of mirrors will understand. They deal with professional decorators and do-it-yourselfers, and both benefit from the staff's years of experience. They carry tabletop glass, shower doors, and mirrors for the home, office, and showroom. In addition, Sundial-Schwartz will remodel, re-silver, and antique mirrors. They also custom design window treatments, blinds, shades, and draperies, and offer measuring and installation of all their products.

Movies

VIDEOROOM
1403 Third Ave (bet 79th and 80th St)   212/879-5333
Mon-Thurs: 10-10; Fri, Sat: 10-11; Sun: noon-10   www.videoroom.net

VideoRoom stocks a large selection of foreign, classic, and hard-to-find films in both VHS and DVD. The highly competent staff—all students of film —are motivated to help inquiring customers. There is also an in-depth selection of new releases and a special-order department. Silver, gold, and platinum memberships offer such privileges as free delivery and special discounts. Check the website for details.

Museum and Library Shops

Whether you're looking for a one-of-a-kind gift or unusual books and posters, I especially recommend shopping in the following unique and large museums where you'll find classy, artistic, well-made items. In most cases, at least some of the wares relate directly to current and past exhibits or the museum's permanent collection. Even at museums that charge an admission fee, you need not pay if you're only shopping. You might save money with a museum membership, which may offer store discounts.

AMERICAN FOLK ART MUSEUM
45 W 53rd St (bet Fifth Ave and Ave of the Americas)
Daily: 10-6 (Fri till 8)   212/265-1040
2 Lincoln Square (Columbus Ave bet 65th and 66th St)
Tues-Sat: noon-7:30; Sun: noon-5   212/595-9533
www.folkartmuseum.org

Both at its beautiful new home on 53rd Street and its homey branch location across from Lincoln Center, the American Folk Art Museum runs great gift shops stocked with handcrafted items such as stationery, jewelry, and kids' toys in various price ranges. The 53rd Street store has a nice selection of quilting books.

AMERICAN MUSEUM OF NATURAL HISTORY
Central Park West bet 77th and 81st St   212/769-5100
Daily: 10-5:45   www.amnh.org

The museum's amazing three-level store features a wide selection of unusual merchandise related to the natural world, diverse cultures, and exploration and discovery. You'll find plenty of children's books and toys on the first floor, a huge selection of natural history books for all ages on the second floor, and merchandise related to human cultures, the natural world, and the universe on the third floor. Five smaller satellite shops throughout the museum offer children's toys, space-themed merchandise, and dinosaur-related items. Temporary shops are often set up to accompany the museum's special exhibits.

ASIASTORE
725 Park Ave (at 70th St)   212/327-9217
Daily: 11-6 (Fri till 9); closed on Mon in July and Aug
www.asiasociety.org

The Asia Society and Museum's fabulous AsiaStore showcases the best in Asian design. Offerings include hundreds of unique items from Asia and Asian-American artists: jewelry, fashion accessories, home accents, stationery, gifts, and novelty items. A selection of books includes scores of titles on Asian art, culture, politics, religion, and philosophy.

EL MUSEO DEL BARRIO
1230 Fifth Ave (at 104th St)   212/831-7272
Call for hours   www.elmuseo.org

The charming shop at El Museo del Barrio is a great source for unique jewelry and handicrafts; art from local artists, Latin America, and the Caribbean; children's books in Spanish and English; and books for adults about the history, art, and culture of Latin America, the Caribbean, and immigrants from these regions.

FRICK COLLECTION

1 E 70th St (bet Fifth and Madison Ave)   212/547-6848
Tues-Sat: 10-5:45; Sun: 11-4:45   www.frick.org

The Frick's gift shop makes the most of its small space by concentrating on exquisite cards, stationery, prints, and art books. You will also find a small collection of paperweights, scarves, porcelains, museum-inspired gifts, and the like. Note that the shop closes 15 minutes before the museum.

GUGGENHEIM MUSEUM STORE

1071 Fifth Ave (bet 88th and 89th St)   212/423-3615
Sun-Tues: 10-5:45; Wed, Fri: 9:30-6; Thurs: 11-5:30; Sat: 8:30-7:45
    www.guggenheimstore.org

Although much for sale here is typical gift shop fare—including scarves, T-shirts, prints and posters, tote bags, umbrellas, note cards and stationery, jewelry, and children's toys—the design and craftsmanship are anything but ordinary. If you're looking for an unusual clock, a great wedding present, or the right pair of earrings to set you apart from the crowd, try this store. Just be aware that prices are often through the roof. Of course, the store also carries books on modern art and exhibition catalogs. It has a great online shop as well. Unlike many other museum stores, this one is actually open before and after the museum itself closes. It is also open on Thursday, when the museum is closed.

INTERNATIONAL CENTER OF PHOTOGRAPHY

1133 Ave of the Americas (at 43rd St)   212/857-9725
Daily: 10-6 (Mon till 5, Fri till 8)   www.shopping.icp.org/store

This store is definitely worth a look if you're shopping for a photography buff with high-quality gifts in mind. It has an excellent collection of books about the history and technology of photography and photojournalism, plus coffee-table books of collected works by photographers, as well as prints, picture frames, unusual postcards, toy cameras, and monographs.

JEWISH MUSEUM'S COOPER SHOP

1109 Fifth Ave (at 92nd St)   212/423-3211
Sun-Wed: 11-5:45; Thurs: 11-8; Fri: 11-3
    www.jewishmuseum.org/jmuseum

This relatively large store is an excellent source for Jewish literature, decorative art, and Judaica. Its selection of menorahs is among the classiest in the city. The store also sells cards, coffee-table books, and numerous children's books with Jewish themes and characters. **Celebrations**, the Jewish Museum's design shop, is housed in a brownstone next to the museum. It is worth a look if you're interested in high-quality ceremonial objects, jewelry, and things for the home.

METROPOLITAN MUSEUM OF ART

1000 Fifth Ave (bet 80th and 84th St)   212/570-3894
Macy's (Herald Square, 34th St at Ave of the Americas), mezzanine
    212/268-7266

Rockefeller Center (15 W 49th St, bet Fifth Ave and Ave of the Americas)
212/332-1360
The Cloisters (Fort Tryon Park)   212/650-2277
Hours vary by store   www.metmuseum.org/store

The two-floor store inside the Metropolitan Museum of Art is the grand-father of all museum gift shops. It specializes in reproductions of paintings and other pieces in the Met's incredible collection, as well as from museum collections around the world. (For limited-edition prints, go to the mezzanine gallery or call 212/650-2910.) You can find jewelry, statues, vases, scarves, ties, porcelains, prints, rugs, napkins, and scores of other beautiful gift items. They also carry books relating to special exhibits and the museum's exten-sive holdings, as well as umbrellas, tote bags, and other things with the Met-ropolitan name emblazoned on them. Prices are reasonable and the sales-people are generally patient and helpful. Smaller "remote" shops can be found throughout the museum, and satellite shops are located at LaGuardia and Kennedy airports, as well as the locations in Manhattan listed above. The sec-ond floor of the main store in the Met and the satellite shop in Rockefeller Center have particularly good children's sections.

METROPOLITAN OPERA SHOP
Metropolitan Opera House   212/580-4090
Lincoln Center (Columbus Ave at 65th St)   www.metoperashop.org
Mon-Sat: 10-10; Sun: noon-6

Remodeling at Lincoln Center brought renovations to the Metropolitan Opera Shop, and the store added new merchandise to celebrate the Met's 125th anniversary! Opera lovers will be in heaven. In addition to operas on video, compact discs, and other media, you'll find books, mugs, umbrellas, sta-tionery, T-shirts, and pillows for the opera buff. And if you're looking for posters and prints from various seasons, visit The Gallery on the lower con-course.

MoMA DESIGN AND BOOK STORE
11 W 53rd St (bet Fifth Ave and Ave of the Americas)   212/708-9700
MoMA DESIGN STORE
44 W 53rd St (bet Fifth Ave and Ave of the Americas)   212/767-1050
Daily: 9:30-6:30 (Fri till 9)
MoMA DESIGN STORE, SOHO
81 Spring St (at Crosby St)   646/613-1367
Daily: 10-8 (Sun till 7)   www.momastore.org

These magnificent stores—one inside the Museum of Modern Art, one across the street from the museum, and a satellite shop in Soho—are ded-icated to what the curators consider the very best in modern design. Fur-niture, textiles, books, vases, ties, kitchen gadgets, silverware, frames, watches, lamps, and toys and books for children are among the things you'll find. These items are not cheap, but the selection is truly exceptional.

NATIONAL MUSEUM OF THE AMERICAN INDIAN
1 Bowling Green (at the foot of Broadway)
Museum Shop   212/514-3766
The Gallery   212/514-3767
Daily: 10-5   www.nmai.si.edu

Like everything else about the National Museum of the American Indian, its gift shops are classy operations. The Gallery—located on the main floor to the right of the entrance—has a wide selection of books and high-quality Native American weavings, jewelry, and other handicrafts. The Museum Shop—down the grand marble staircase from the main entrance—is focused more on kids and families. Children's books, videos, toys, and craft kits, along with T-shirts and some moderately priced jewelry, are among the offerings. Because the museum is part of the Smithsonian Institution, both stores offer discounts to Smithsonian associate members.

NEUE GALERIE BOOKSTORE AND DESIGN SHOP
1048 Fifth Ave (at 86th St)   212/628-6200
Mon, Wed-Sun: 11-6   www.neuegalerie.org

The Neue Galerie Bookstore is clearly *the* source for books on art, architecture, and cultural life in Germany, Austria, and Central Europe in the 19th and 20th centuries. The Design Shop has a small but well-chosen selection of beautiful high-end jewelry, tableware, textiles, and other decorative arts by modern German and Austrian designers. Most merchandise is related to past or current exhibits.

NEW YORK PUBLIC LIBRARY SHOP
Fifth Ave bet 41st and 42nd St   212/930-0641
Mon-Sat: 11-6   www.thelibraryshop.org

If ever there was a perfect gift shop for book lovers, this is it. Located just off the main lobby of the New York Public Library's main branch, it features a high-quality selection of unusual merchandise. You'll find magnets with provocative messages like "I Think, Therefore I'm Dangerous" and "Think for Yourself, Not for Me," and books about the library's history, and catalogs of past library shows. The staff is particularly pleasant and helpful. The online store is a great spot to shop if you can't make it to New York.

NEW YORK TRANSIT MUSEUM STORE
Grand Central Terminal (42nd St at Vanderbilt Ave)   212/878-0106
Mon-Fri: 8-8; Sat, Sun: 10-6   www.transitmuseumstore.com

This little shop and gallery make train and subway buffs downright giddy. Items for sale include books, clever T-shirts, replicas of old station signs, banks for children in the shape of city buses, jewelry made from old tokens, and very classy mirrors made by an artist involved with restoration of the subway system's mosaics. Bus and subway maps, as well as other MTA information, are also available. Note that this shop is a branch of the much larger main store at the **New York Transit Museum** in Brooklyn (Boerum Place at Schermerhorn Street, 718/694-1868).

PICKMAN MUSEUM SHOP AT THE MUSEUM OF JEWISH HERITAGE
36 Battery Pl (in Battery Park City)   646/437-4213
Sun-Thurs: 10-5:45 (Wed till 8); Fri: 10-3   www.mjhnyc.org

This store is a fitting companion to the museum in its celebration of Jewish art, crafts, and culture. The selection is diverse, and many items are related to the museum's collection. Everything is high quality, and much of it is quite unusual. A carefully chosen section includes books and gifts for children of various ages. Elegant jewelry and Judaica are also available. The prices are extremely good. Note that the store and the museum are closed on all major Jewish holidays.

THE SHOP AT COOPER-HEWITT NATIONAL DESIGN MUSEUM

2 E 91st St (bet Fifth and Madison Ave)   212/849-8355
Mon-Fri: 10-5; Sat: 10-6; Sun: noon-6   www.cooperhewittshop.org

The Cooper-Hewitt, a subsidiary of the Smithsonian, is the only museum in the nation devoted exclusively to historic and contemporary design. At the museum shop, you'll find products by a range of established and emerging contemporary designers, from exclusive limited editions to tableware, jewelry, accessories, and glassware. The shop sells items relating to the museum's current exhibitions and extensive permanent collections. You'll also find a wide selection of books on design, including many rare and hard-to-find titles.

THE SHOP AT SCANDINAVIA HOUSE

58 Park Ave (bet 37th and 38th St)   212/847-9737
Mon-Sat: noon-6; Sun: noon-5   www.scandinaviahouse.org

Nestled in Scandinavia House—the Nordic Center in America is a lifestyle shop showcasing both the leading modern designers and the legends from this part of the world. Luxurious home-design items, tableware, art glass, textiles, fashion, jewelry, and accessories range from trendy to classic. Gift registries, corporate promotions, custom baskets, special orders, and gift certificates are available.

THE STORE AT THE MUSEUM OF ARTS AND DESIGN

2 Columbus Circle (at Eighth Ave)   212/299-7700
Mon-Sat: 10-7 (Thurs till 9); Sun: 10-6   www.madmuseum.org

This museum store is one of the most attractive in town, thanks to its relocation to Columbus Circle. The work of exceptional artisans from around the United States is displayed with a constantly changing collection of beautifully designed jewelry, textiles, housewares, and more.

STUDIO MUSEUM

144 W 125th St (bet Malcolm X and Adam Clayton Powell, Jr. Blvd)
Wed-Fri, Sun: noon-6; Sat: 10-6   212/864-0014
                                         www.studiomuseum.org

Located just inside the museum's entrance on the right, this store sells a wide and generally high-quality selection of jewelry, textiles, crafts, note cards, and calendars created by African and African-American artists. It also carries an unusually broad selection of cookbooks, fiction, biographies, children's books by and about Africans and African-Americans, museum logo merchandise, and the usual tourist gift items.

UKRAINIAN MUSEUM

222 E 6th St (bet Second and Third Ave)   212/228-0110
Wed-Sun: 11:30-5   www.ukrainianmuseum.org

This store is well worth a visit if you want to find Ukrainian Easter eggs (already made and kits for do-it-yourselfers), embroidery, art books, jewelry, and other handicrafts.

UNITED NATIONS

First Ave at 44th St   212/963-7680
Mon-Fri: 9-5:15; Sat, Sun: 10-5 (closed weekends in Jan, Feb)
www.un.org

On the lower level of the main UN building is a bookstore, post office (a real treat for stamp collectors), small UNICEF shop, and an even smaller shop run by the UN Women's Guild. That's in addition to the main gift shop, also on the lower level. The bookstore features calendars, postcards with the flags of member nations, holiday cards in dozens of languages, and a wide variety of books about the UN and related subjects. The main gift shop features a wonderful array of carvings, jewelry, scarves, dolls, and other items from all over the world. The better imports can get pricey, but it's definitely going to a good cause! One final thought: if you are interested in UNICEF cards and gifts but find the selection at the UN rather thin, visit the well-stocked store in the lobby of the nearby **UNICEF House** (3 United Nations Plaza, 44th St bet First and Second Ave, 212/326-7054).

Music

ACADEMY RECORDS & CDs

12 W 18th St (at Fifth Ave)   212/242-3000
415 E 12th St (bet First Ave and Ave A)   212/780-9166
Mon-Sat: noon-8; Sun: noon-6   www.academylps.com

Academy Records & CDs has Manhattan's largest stock of used, out-of-print, and rare classical LPs, CDs, and DVDs. They emphasize opera, contemporary classical, and early music (through the Baroque period). Academy boasts an international reputation, and the staff is knowledgeable. The 12th Street location is strictly devoted to vinyl and doesn't carry classical recordings.

BLEECKER BOB'S GOLDEN OLDIES RECORD SHOP

118 W 3rd St (bet MacDougal St and Ave of the Americas)
Mon-Thurs: 11 a.m.-1 a.m.; Fri, Sat: 11 a.m.-3 a.m.   212/475-9677
www.myspace.com/bleeckerbobs

Name another store that's open till **3 a.m.** on Christmas Day! Although there is a real Bleecker Bob (Plotnik, the owner), the store isn't on Bleecker Street. This place is an institution to generations of New Yorkers who have sifted through his vast selection of rock, punk, and heavy-metal recordings. They stock vintage rock, pop, soul, funk, and jazz, including rarities. You'll find 45s, too, some with collectible picture sleeves. Bleecker Bob's also serves as a gathering place in the wee hours of the morning in the Village. It's a great source for out-of-print, obscure, and imported compact discs and DVDs.

FRANK MUSIC

244 W 54th St (bet Broadway and Eighth Ave), 10th floor
Mon-Fri: 11-5 (hours vary in summer)   212/582-1999
www.frankmusiccompany.com

Founded in 1938, this professional business has never advertised, relying instead on word of mouth. They sell classical sheet music from European and American publishers, in-store and via mail order. There is an aisle for voice and violin, another for piano, and so on.

JAZZ RECORD CENTER
236 W 26th St (bet Seventh and Eighth Ave), Room 804   212/675-4480
Mon-Sat: 10-6   www.jazzrecordcenter.com

Jazz Record Center is run by Frederick Cohen, a charming guy who really knows his business. It is the only jazz specialty store in the city. They deal in out-of-print and new jazz records, CDs, videos, books, posters, photos, periodicals, postcards, and T-shirts. The store buys collections, fills mail orders, and offers appraisals. They auction jazz rarities on eBay, too.

OTHER MUSIC
15 E 4th St (bet Broadway and Lafayette St)   212/477-8150
Mon-Fri: 11-9; Sat: noon-8; Sun: noon-7   www.othermusic.com

If you can't find it elsewhere, try Other Music. They stock CDs and vinyl, hard-to-find releases, and a wide variety of imports, and offer downloadable music for purchase. They will purchase or give store credit for used CDs and records.

WESTSIDER RECORDS
233 W 72nd St (at Broadway)   212/874-1588
Mon-Thurs: 11-7; Fri, Sat: 10-9; Sun: noon-6
www.westsiderbooks.com

Westsider remains one of the few stores specializing in rare and out-of-print LPs. Compact discs have been added to the stock of 80,000 LPs. You'll also find printed music and books on the performing arts. There are all genres: classical jazz, rock, pop, blues, country, folk, and spoken word. A short walk away is their sister store, **Westsider Rare & Used Books** (2246 Broadway, 212/362-0706). These places buy, sell, and trade records and books, respectively.

Musical Instruments

DRUMMER'S WORLD
151 W 46th St (bet Ave of the Americas and Seventh Ave), 3rd floor
Mon-Fri: 10-6; Sat: 10-4   212/840-3057
www.drummersworld.com

This is a great place, unless the patron is your teenager or an upstairs neighbor! Barry Greenspon and his staff take pride in guiding students and professionals through one of the best percussion stores in the country. Inside this drummer's paradise is everything from commonplace instruments to one-of-a-kind antiques and esoteric imports. All are high-quality percussion items. The store also offers instructors and how-to books. Customers receive the same attention whether they are members of an orchestra, rock band, or rap act. Drummer's World has a catalog and will ship anywhere in the country.

GUITAR SALON
45 Grove St (at Bleecker St)   212/675-3236
By appointment   www.theguitarsalon.com

Beverly Maher's Guitar Salon NY is a unique one-person operation located in a historic brownstone in Greenwich Village. Outstanding personal service is provided by Beverly, who specializes in 19th- and 20th-century vintage instruments. You will find handmade classical and flamenco guitars for students, professionals, and collectors. Appraisals are available, and lessons are given on all styles of guitars. Paul Simon and the Rolling Stones have been known to shop here!

SAM ASH
160 W 48th St (between Ave of the Americas and Seventh Ave)
Mon-Sat: 10-8; Sun: noon-6   212/179-2299
                                              www.samashmusic.com

Under three roofs—the guitar and brass/woodwinds shops are across the street—you'll find a full selection of musical instruments, recording equipment and software, lighting, music books, amplifiers, DJ gear, and more. Sam Ash has just about anything that a band, orchestra, or single musician might need.

Pets and Accessories

BARKING ZOO
172 Ninth Ave (bet 20th and 21st St)   212/255-0658
Mon-Fri: 11-8; Sat: 10-6; Sun: noon-5   www.barkingzoo.com

You'll find quality items for your favorite canine, including knitwear and pet food. They offer valuable information on the care of dogs and cats and a list of dog runs.

> Are you ready to get a dog? Here are a couple of suggestions. If it is a purebred you want, call the **American Kennel Club** (919/233-9767) and tell them the breed you have in mind. Another good bet is **Bide-a-Wee** (410 E 38th St, 212/532-4455). If you need to train your dog, try **Follow My Lead** (212/873-5511).

DOGGYSTYLE
73 Thompson St (bet Spring and Broome St)   212/431-9200
Mon-Sat: noon-7; Sun: noon-6

There's no fancy stuff here—just good, practical items for your pet at sensible prices. Doggystyle features boutique collars, leashes, coats, and feeding bowls, plus handy products for traveling with a pet. Dog and cat grooming is available.

PACIFIC AQUARIUM & PET
46 Delancey St (bet Forsyth and Eldridge St)   212/995-5895
Daily: 10-7   www.pacificaquarium.com

Goldfish are their specialty, but Pacific Aquarium & Pet also carries all types of freshwater and saltwater fish, aquatic plants, and every kind of aquarium and supply you could imagine. Custom-made tanks (up to 500 gallons) are installed in homes, businesses and restaurants. Tank maintenance packages are available.

PETCO
147-149 E 86th St (at Lexington Ave)   212/831-8001
560 Second Ave (at 30th St)   212/779-4550
860 Broadway (at Union Square W)   212/358-0692

2475 Broadway (at 92nd St)   212/877-1270
Hours vary by store   www.petco.com

With a selection of over 10,000 items—including food, toys, treats, and pet-care products—this store is a pet owner's treasure trove. There are sections for cats, dogs, birds, fish, and even reptiles! Services vary slightly by location and may include low-cost vaccine clinics, pet photography, DNA breed testing, dog training, and grooming.

PETLAND DISCOUNTS
132 Nassau St (bet Beekman Pl and John St)   212/964-1821
530 E 14th St (at Ave B)   212/228-1363
312 W 23rd St (bet Eighth and Ninth Ave)   212/366-0512
137 W 72nd St (bet Columbus and Amsterdam Ave)   212/875-9785
389 Ave of the Americas (bet 8th St and Waverly Pl)   212/741-1913
734 Ninth Ave (at 50th St)   212/459-9562
2708 Broadway (at 104th St)   212/222-8851
304 E 86th St (bet First and Second Ave)   212/472-1655
56 W 117th St (bet Malcolm X Blvd and Fifth Ave)   212/427-2700
167 E 125th St (bet Ave of the Americas and Lexington Ave)
                                                        212/426-7193
1954 Third Ave (bet 107th and 108th St)   212/987-6714
Hours vary by store   www.petlanddiscounts.com

The pros at the New York Aquarium recommend this chain for fish and aquarium accessories. Petland also carries discount food and accessories for dogs, cats, birds, reptiles, and other pets.

RAISING ROVER & BABY
1428 Lexington Ave (at 93rd St)   212/987-7683
Daily: 10:30-7 (11-6 in summer)   www.raisingroverltd.com

Have you ever heard of a boutique catering to both pets and children? This one does, selling all manner of puppies. Merchandise includes matching clothing for puppy and baby, diaper bags and dog carriers, collars and leashes, toys, booties and sneakers, layettes, beds for dogs, and designer clothes for kids. They will babysit your pets during your visit, even giving them a bath and "pawdicure!"

TRIXIE + PEANUT PET EMPORIUM
23 E 20th St (bet Broadway and Park Ave)   212/358-0881
Mon-Sat: 11-8; Sun: noon-5   www.trixieandpeanut.com

If you want your four-legged friend to become a fashionista, here's the spot to make it happen. Practical apparel, accessories, collars and leashes, and cute costumes and special-occasion garb make a real statement. There's a variety of amusing toys and gifts, as well as treats, bedding, carriers, and other provisions for pets large or small.

Photographic Equipment and Supplies
ADORAMA CAMERA
42 W 18th St (bet Fifth Ave and Ave of the Americas)   212/741-0052
Mon-Thurs: 9-7; Fri: 9-2; Sun: 9:30-5:15   www.adorama.com

Adorama is one of the largest photographic mail-order houses in the country. They carry a huge stock of equipment and supplies, a showcase of astronomy equipment, iPods and cell phones, stockroom accessories, frames and albums, and video paraphernalia, all sold at discount. Workshops for all skill levels are frequently offered, and they have quite an array of equipment for rent.

B&H PHOTO-VIDEO-PRO AUDIO
420 Ninth Ave (bet 33rd and 34th St)   212/444-6600, 800/606-6969
Mon-Thurs: 9-7; Fri: 9-2; Sun: 10-6   www.bhphotovideo.com

This is a superstore in more ways than one! You'll find departments for video, pro audio, pro lighting, darkroom, film and film processing, books, used equipment, and accessories. Trade-ins are welcome. The store has been in operation since 1974 and is staffed by informed personnel. Inventory levels are high (about 200,000 products), prices are reasonable, and hands-on demo areas make browsing easy. Check out their catalog!

CALUMET PHOTOGRAPHIC
22 W 22nd St (bet Fifth Ave and Ave of the Americas) 212/989-8500
Mon-Fri: 8:30-5:30; Sat: 9-5   www.calumetphoto.com

In business for over 60 years, this firm provides start-to-finish photographic service. Professional camera equipment, film, digital cameras and accessories, printers, and scanners are all available at good prices. There's no need to haul items you're purchasing throughout the store, as an overhead trolley system moves merchandise up to the register. The service-oriented repair technicians are factory-trained.

LAUMONT
333 W 52nd St (bet Eighth and Ninth Ave)   212/245-2113
Mon-Fri: 9-5:30 (evenings and weekends by appointment)
                                www.laumont.com

Whether you're a professional or amateur, Laumont can take care of your photographic needs. They do excellent work producing exhibition-quality color and black-and-white prints. They are patient and understanding with those who need advice. Laumont's staff are experienced digital re-touchers and duplicators, and they repair damaged originals or create new images on state-of-the-art computers. Lamination, print mounting, and framing are done on-premises.

WILLOUGHBY'S KONICA IMAGING CENTER
298 Fifth Ave (at 31st St)   212/564-1600, 800/378-1898
Mon-Fri: 9-7; Sat, Sun: 10-6   www.willoughbys.com

Established in 1898, this is New York's oldest camera store. Willoughby's has a huge stock, an extensive clientele, and a solid reputation. They can handle almost any kind of camera order, either in person or by mail. They service cameras, supply photographic equipment, and recycle used cameras. Moreover, they sell video cameras, cell phones, camcorders, binoculars and telescopes, medical and dental digital cameras, and other high-tech equipment.

Pictures, Posters, and Prints

JERRY OHLINGER'S MOVIE MATERIALS STORE
253 W 35th St (bet Seventh and Eighth Ave)   212/989-0869
Mon-Sat: 11-7   www.moviematerials.com

Jerry Ohlinger stocks a huge selection of movie posters (from the 1930s to the present) and photographs from film and TV. He also researches these items and will gladly provide a catalog.

OLD PRINT SHOP
150 Lexington Ave (bet 29th and 30th St)   212/683-3950
Tues-Fri: 9-5; Sat: 9-4 (closed Sat in summer) www.oldprintshop.com

Established in 1898, the Old Print Shop exudes an old-fashioned charm, and its stock only reinforces the impression of timelessness. Kenneth M. Newman specializes in Americana, including original prints, town views, Currier & Ives prints, and original maps that reflect America's yesteryear. Many of the nostalgic pictures that have adorned calendars and stationery were copies of prints found here. Amateur and professional historians have a field day in this shop. Newman also does "correct period framing," and prints housed in his custom frames are striking. Everything bought and sold here is original. Newman purchases estate and single items.

PAGEANT PRINT SHOP
69 E 4th St (bet Bowery and Second Ave)   212/674-5296
Tues-Sat: noon-8; Sun: 1-7   www.pageantprintshop.com

Antique maps and prints are among the treasures you will find at this cozy, enchanting shop. The daughter of the original founder (Sidney Solomon) now runs Pageant, which houses over 10,000 items.

PHILIP WILLIAMS POSTERS
122 Chambers St (bet Church St and West Broadway) 212/513-0313
Mon-Sat: 11-7   www.postermuseum.com

This is the largest poster gallery in the world, with over 50,000 original posters for sale from 1870 to the present. Philip Williams features prints in a variety of categories, including travel, food, drink, transportation, autos, bicycles, trains, sports, magic, and films. Southern folk art, books, maps, and magazines are also carried, and custom framing and poster restoration are available.

PHYLLIS LUCAS GALLERY & OLD PRINT CENTER
981 Second Ave (at 52nd St)   212/755-1516
Mon-Fri: 10-5; Sat, Sun: 2-5   www.phyllislucasgallery.com

Inside Phyllis Lucas Gallery & Old Print Center is a treasure trove of antique and contemporary engravings, prints, and photographs. As one of the oldest antiquarian print galleries in the city, this place is known for its fine decorative art and superior framing services. Owner Michael (the son of the founder) suggests calling ahead, as they may be relocating.

TRITON GALLERY
630 Ninth Ave (bet 44th and 45th St)   212/765-2472
Mon-Sat: 10-6   www.tritongallery.com

Theater posters are presented at Triton like nowhere else. Posters of current Broadway shows join a stock of older show posters. U.S. Show cards—which are the most readily available items—are the standard 14" x 22" size. Posters range in size from 23" x 46" to 42" x 84" and are priced according to rarity, age, and demand. Triton also does custom framing.

Rubber Goods

CANAL RUBBER SUPPLY COMPANY
329 Canal St (at Greene St)   212/226-7339, 800/444-6483
Mon-Fri: 9-4:45; Sat: 9-3:45   www.canalrubber.com

"If it's made of rubber, we have it" is the motto at this wholesale-retail operation, which has occupied this same location since 1954. There are foam mattresses, bolsters, cushions, pads cut to size, hydraulic hoses, rubber tubing, vacuum hoses, floor matting, tiles, stair treads, and sheet-rubber products. Looking for rubber boots? They have those, too.

Safes

EMPIRE SAFE
6 E 39th St (bet Fifth and Madison Ave)   212/684-2255, 800/543-5412
Mon-Fri: 9-5 or by appointment   www.empiresafe.com

Empire shows the city's largest and most complete selection of safes. Their safes are used in residences and businesses, with delivery and installation offered. They also offer specialized burglary protection safes with jewelry and watch drawers. Whether you want to protect jewelry and valuables at home or documents in an office building, you can rely on these folks.

TRAUM SAFE
946 Madison Ave (at 74th St)   212/452-2565
Mon-Fri: 10-6; Sat: by appointment   www.traumsafe.com

Traum Safe can design and construct a secure vault to protect your collection. Contemporary or classic, bold or subdued, their safes include interior lighting and electronic locks. From consultation to installation, Traum can analyze your needs and recommend the right size and finish. For $90,000 you can get a safe with custom-made drawers that will even wind your watches!

Sexual Aids and Items

COME AGAIN
353 E 53rd St (at First Ave)   212/308-9394
Mon-Sat: 11-7:30

Come Again is a one-stop shop for sexual paraphernalia. There's exotic lingerie for men and women to size 4XL, bachelorette items, adult books, magazines, DVDs, oils and lotions, adult games, gift baskets, party gifts, and toys and equipment of a decidedly prurient nature. They offer a 20% discount for readers of this book!

EVE'S GARDEN INTERNATIONAL
119 W 57th St (bet Ave of the Americas and Seventh Ave), Suite 1201
Tues-Sat: 11:30-6:45   212/757-8651, 800/848-3837
                              www.evesgarden.com

This is not your usual sex shop; it is particularly geared to women who wish to shop in a pleasant atmosphere. Eve's Garden is a pleasure chest of games, books, and videos to seduce the mind. A vast array of sensuous massage oils, candles, and incense will help realize your wildest fantasies. Mail orders are welcome.

Signs

LET THERE BE NEON
38 White St (bet Broadway and Church St)   212/226-4883
Mon-Fri: 9-5   www.lettherebeneon.com

While the flashing neon sign has become the ultimate urban cliché, here it is rendered as artistic fine art. Let There Be Neon operates as a gallery with a variety of sizes, shapes, functions, and designs to entice the browser. Almost all their sales are custom pieces. Even a rough sketch is enough for them to create a literal or abstract neon sculpture. Some vintage pieces are available.

Silver

JEAN'S SILVERSMITHS
16 W 45th St (at Fifth Ave)   212/575-0723
Mon-Fri: 9-4:45   www.jeanssilversmiths.com

Having a problem replacing a fork that went down the disposal? Proceed directly to Jean's, where you will find over a thousand discontinued, obsolete, and current flatware patterns. They specialize in antique and second-hand silver, gold, and diamond jewelry, and they also sell watches.

TIFFANY & CO.
727 Fifth Ave (at 57th St)   212/755-8000, 800/843-3269
Mon-Fri: 10-7; Sat: 10-6; Sun: noon-5

37 Wall St (bet Broad and William St)   212/514-8015
Mon-Fri: 10-7; Sat: 11-5   www.tiffany.com

Despite the fact that Tiffany has appeared in plays, movies, books, and songs, this legendary store really isn't that formidable or forbidding, and it can be an exciting place to shop. Yes, there really is a Tiffany diamond, and it can be viewed on the first floor. That floor also houses the watch and jewelry departments. While browsing is welcome, salespeople are quick to approach loiterers. The store carries clocks, silver jewelry, sterling silver, bar accessories, centerpieces, leather accessories, fragrances, knickknacks, china, crystal, glassware, flatware, and engraved stationery. The real surprise is that Tiffany carries an excellent selection of reasonably priced items. Many are emblazoned with the Tiffany name and wrapped in the signature blue box.

Sporting Goods
Bicycles and Accessories

BICYCLE HABITAT
244 Lafayette St (bet Spring and Prince St)   212/431-3315
Mon-Wed: 10-7; Thurs: 10-8; Fri: 10-6:30; Sat, Sun: 10-6
                                                www.bicyclehabitat.com

These customer oriented folks are "geared" toward cycling buffs. They really want to get more people interested in biking! They sponsor bike repair classes, including one on roadside emergencies. There's something for everyone at Bicycle Habitat—tricycles for the little ones, very expensive racing bikes, and all the accessories for riding, transporting, and storing bikes. If you don't find what you want, they will special order it or have a bike custom-built to your specifications.

BICYCLE RENAISSANCE
430 Columbus Ave (at 81st St)   212/724-2350
Mon-Fri: 10:30-7; Sat, Sun: 10-5   www.bicyclerenaissance.com

Biking is a way of life at Bicycle Renaissance. Services include custom-building bikes and bicycle repair, and mechanics aim for same-day service on all makes and models. They carry racing and mountain bikes by Cannondale, Jamis, and Specialized, as well as custom frames for Guru and Calfee Designs, and others. Prices are on par with so-called discount shops.

CITY BICYCLES
315 W 38th St (bet Eighth and Ninth Ave)   212/563-3373
Mon-Fri: 9-6:30; Sat: 10-5   www.citybicycles.net

These folks have a huge selection of bicycles and will design and construct a custom bike for the ultimate ride. They also have commuter, road, mountain, and BMX models from manufacturers such as Bianchi, Schwinn, Haro, and Pake. The informed staff will help you decide which kind of bike is best for your needs—classic, suspension, or hybrid. See them for bike rentals and repairs, including welding.

LARRY'S SECOND AVENUE BICYCLES PLUS
1690 Second Ave (at 87th St)   212/722-2201
Daily: 10-8   www.larrysbicyclesplus.com

Larry Duffus started fixing bicycles at age 15. He has been operating this unique retail and repair shop since 1977. Bikes range in price from $200 to $7,500 (and up!), and plenty of parts and accessories are stocked, too. Special services include lifetime free tuneups with the purchase of a new bicycle, bike rentals for rides through Central Park, and free local delivery.

Billiards
BLATT BILLIARDS
809 Broadway (bet 11th and 12th St)   212/674-8855
Mon-Fri: 9-6:30; Sat: 10-5   www.blattbilliards.com

Blatt's six floors are outfitted from top to bottom with everything for billiards. The variety inside this shop is amazing: custom and antique billiard tables, jukeboxes, an art gallery, arcade games, table games, bars and accessories. and other items. They also carry everything you need to play these games or furnish your game room.

Exercise Equipment
GYM SOURCE
40 E 52nd St (bet Park and Madison Ave)   212/688-4222
Mon-Fri: 9-7; Sat: 10-6; Sun: noon-5   www.gymsource.com

This is the largest exercise equipment dealer in the Northeast. They carry new and pre-owned treadmills, bikes, stair-steppers, weight machines, rowers, and more. Top brands are available at good prices, and Gym Source's skilled technicians provide competent servicing. They have a design and consultation service for fitness facilities, home gyms, and rehab centers; rent equipment; and will deliver items for use in Manhattan hotel rooms.

Fishing

CAPITOL FISHING TACKLE COMPANY
132 W 36th St (bet Seventh Ave and Broadway)   212/929-6132
Mon-Fri: 10-7; Sat: 10-5   www.capitolfishing.com

Anglers will find the store of their dreams right in the heart of Manhattan! Established in 1897, these folks carry a full line of fishing gear from names like Penn, Shimano, Garcia, and Daiwa. Specials and closeouts offer good values, as these folks buy surplus inventories from bankrupt dealers and liquidators.

URBAN ANGLER
206 Fifth Ave (bet 25th and 26th St), 3rd floor
Mon-Fri: 10-6 (Wed till 7); Sat: 10-5   212/689-6400, 800/255-5488
                                           www.urbanangler.com

Urban Angler is the only pro fly fishing shop in Manhattan. You'll find fly-fishing tackle, high-end spin and surf tackle, and travel clothing. They offer casting and fly-tying lessons. They will also plan fishing trips to anywhere you want to go.

General

EASTERN MOUNTAIN SPORTS (EMS)
530 Broadway (bet Prince and Spring St)   212/966-8730
Mon-Fri: 10-9; Sat: 10-8; Sun: noon-6   www.ems.com

EMS is *the* place for outdoor clothing and gear. Although prices can be bettered elsewhere, it is an excellent source for one-stop shopping, and the merchandise is of a higher quality than that carried in department stores. EMS covers virtually all outdoor sports, including mountain climbing, backpacking, skiing, hiking, kayaking, and camping.

G&S SPORTING GOODS
43 Essex St (at Grand St)   212/777-7590, 800/215-3947
Mon-Fri: 9-6; Sun: 10-6   www.gsboxing.com

If you are looking for a place to buy a birthday or Christmas gift for a sports buff, I recommend G&S. They have a large selection of brandname sneakers, in-line skates, boxing equipment, balls, gloves, toys, games, sports clothing, and accessory items. Prices reflect a 20% to 25% discount.

MODELL'S
150 Broadway (bet Maiden Lane and Liberty St)   212/227-0560
55 Chambers St (at Broadway)   212/732-8484
607 Ave of the Americas (at 18th St)   212/989-1110
1293 Broadway (at 34th St)   212/244-4544
51 E 42nd St (bet Madison and Vanderbilt Ave)   212/661-4242

234 W 42nd St (bet Seventh and Eighth Ave)   212/764-7030
1535 Third Ave (bet 86th and 87th St)   212/996-3800
300 W 125th St (at Eighth Ave)   212/280-9100
606 W 181st St (at St. Nicholas Ave)   212/568-3000
Hours vary by store   www.modells.com

You can't beat this outfit for quality and value! Founded in 1889, Modell's is America's oldest family-owned sporting goods chain. They carry a large selection of footwear and apparel for men, women, and children. Make note of Modell's low-price guarantee.

NBA STORE
666 Fifth Ave (at 52nd St)   212/515-NBA1
Mon-Sat: 10-8; Sun: 11-6   www.nba.com/nycstore

This attractive and well-designed store has the largest assortment of basketball merchandise in the nation. A winding ramp allows full exposure to areas featuring apparel and accessories, jewelry, watches, photographs, collectibles, headwear, practice gear, basketballs, and more. The store also features multimedia presentations of game action and highlights of historic moments. An actual half-court surrounded by bleachers is a popular spot for a quick pickup game.

PARAGON SPORTS
867 Broadway (at 18th St)   212/255-8036
Mon-Sat: 10-8; Sun: 11-7   www.paragonsports.com

Paragon is truly a sporting goods department store, with over 100,000 square feet of specialty shops devoted to all kinds of sports and fitness equipment and apparel. The stock is arranged for easy shopping. There are departments for team equipment, athletic footwear, skateboards, ice skates, in-line skates, racquet sports, aerobics, swimming, golf, skiing and snowboarding, hiking, camping, diving, biking, watersports, and anything else that can be done in the great outdoors. They also carry gift items.

Golf

NEW YORK GOLF CENTER
131 W 35th St (bet Seventh Ave and Broadway)   212/564-2255
Chelsea Piers, Pier 59 (West Side Hwy at 18th St) 212/242-8899
Mon-Fri: 10-8; Sat: 10-7; Sun: 11-6   888/465-7890
                                                www.nygolfcenter.com

New York Golf Center is the Big Apple's only golf superstore, offering goods at prices that average 20% below list. There are clubs, bags, clothing, shoes, accessories, and novelties . . . everything except one's own hard-won golfing expertise. They carry pro-line equipment by such names as Callaway, Taylor Made, Cleveland, Titleist, Ping, and Nike. Golfers can test demo clubs at the Chelsea Piers Driving Range. Employees couldn't be more helpful. Mention this book and receive a free sleeve of golf balls with any $20 purchase.

Guns

JOHN JOVINO GUN SHOP
183 Grand St (at Mulberry St)   212/925-4881
Mon-Sat: 10-6; Sun: 2-6   www.johnjovinogunshop.com

These folks have been in business since 1911 and are recognized leaders in the field. They carry all major brands of handguns, rifles, and shotguns, as well as ammunition, holsters, bulletproof vests, knives, and scopes. Major brands include Smith & Wesson, Colt, Ruger, Beretta, Browning, Remington, Walther, Glock, Winchester, and Sig Sauer. Jovino is an authorized warranty repair station for gun manufacturers, with a licensed gunsmith on-site.

Marine

WEST MARINE
12 W 37th St (bet Fifth Ave and Ave of the Americas) 212/594-6065
Mon-Fri: 10-6 (Thurs till 7); Sat. Sun: 10-4   www.westmarine.com

West sells marine supplies as if it were situated in the middle of a New England seaport rather than the heart of Manhattan. The staff sometimes looks like a ship's crew on leave in the Big Apple, and they actually are that knowledgeable. They carry marine electronics, sailboat fittings, gamefish tackle, lifesaving gear, ropes, anchors, compasses, clothing, clocks, barometers, and books. You'll also find foul-weather suits and a line of clothing for yachters.

Outdoor Equipment

TENT AND TRAILS
21 Park Pl (bet Broadway and Church St)   212/227-1760
Mon-Sat: 9:30-6 (Thurs, Fri till 7); Sun: noon-6   800/237-1760
                                                     www.tenttrails.com

Whether you are outfitting yourself for a weekend camping trip or an ascent of Mt. Everest, Tent and Trails is the place to go! In the urban canyons near City Hall, this 6,000-square-foot store is devoted to camping. The staff is experienced and knowledgeable. There are boots from Asolo, Garmont, Lowa, Merrell, Vasque, Hi Tec, and Scarpa Footwear. They carry camping gear from top makers like North Face, Patagonia, ArcTeryx, Canada Goose, and Osprey Packs. You'll find backpacks, sleeping bags, tents, down clothing, and much more. Tent and Trails also rents camping equipment.

Running

SUPER RUNNERS SHOP
1337 Lexington Ave (at 89th St)   212/369-6010
360 Amsterdam Ave (bet 77th and 78th St)   212/787-7665
1246 Third Ave (bet 71st and 72nd St)   212/249-2133
821 Third Ave (bet 50th and 51st St)   212/421-4444
745 Seventh Ave (at 49th St)   212/398-2449
51 W 42nd St (bet Fifth Ave and Ave of the Americas) 212/997-9112
Grand Central Terminal (42nd St at Vanderbilt Ave)   646/487-1120
Hours vary by store   www.superrunnersshop.com

Co-owner Gary Muhrcke won the first New York City Marathon in 1970, and his passion became his livelihood. The stock at Super Runners Shop includes a superb selection of men's and women's running and racing shoes, as well as performance running clothes. The informed staff, who are themselves runners, believe that each person should be fitted individually, based on sizing and need. You can also pick up entry blanks for local races at these stores.

Skating

BLADES BOARD & SKATE

120 W 72nd St (bet Amsterdam and Columbus Ave)	212/787-3911
659 Broadway (at Bleecker St)	212/477-7350

Mon-Sat: 10-7 (Sun hours vary by store)

Founded in 1990 by Jeff Kabat, Blades Board & Skate has become the largest action-sports retail company in the nation. There are a number of reasons for this: a great selection of equipment for snowboarding, skateboarding, and in-line skating; a good stock of lifestyle apparel; informed service; and a 30-day price guarantee.

Soccer

SOCCER SPORT SUPPLY

1745 First Ave (bet 90th and 91st St)	212/427-6050, 800/223-1010
Mon-Fri: 10-6; Sat: 10-4	www.homeofsoccer.com

Hermann and Jeff Doss are the proprietors of this 70-year-old soccer and rugby supply company. Half their business involves importing and exporting equipment around the world. Visitors to the store have the advantage of seeing the selection in person, as well as receiving guidance from a staff that knows the field (pardon the pun) completely.

Tennis

MASON'S TENNIS

56 E 53rd St (bet Park and Madison Ave)	212/755-5805
Mon-Fri: 10-7; Sat: 10-6; Sun: noon-6	www.masonstennis.com

Mason's is the oldest tennis specialty store in Manhattan. Mark Mason offers a superb collection of clothing by Fila, Polo, Nike, Ralph Lauren, and more. U.S. Open products are carried from May to December. You will also find ball machines, bags, and other tennis paraphernalia. They sell racquets and shoes at the minimum prices allowed by the manufacturers and will special order any tennis product. Same-day stringing is offered. A yearly half-

---

Looking for security and surveillance equipment? **Spy Tec** (44 W 55th St, 3rd floor, 212/957-7400) offers video surveillance and countersurveillance items, network cameras, digital and analog recorders, wireless camera detection and location, metal detectors, and infrared sensors. All are available for residential or corporate installation. Spy Tec's trained personnel will discreetly take care of any need.

---

price clothing sale (excluding children's wear) takes place in mid-January.

Stationery

BOWNE & CO. STATIONERS

211 Water St (at Beekman St)	212/748-8651
Tues-Sun: 10-5	www.southstseaport.org

Bowne is tucked between two galleries in a restored 19th-century print shop. The gift shop sells affordable note cards and stationery that are printed on antique treadle-powered platen presses using hand-set, historic types from their collection. The equipment doesn't stay idle, as they welcome custom orders for wedding invitations, announcements, stationery, and other items. If nothing else, stop by to see how an old-time print shop operates!

JAM PAPER & ENVELOPE
135 Third Ave (bet 14th and 15th St)   212/473-6666, 800/801O-JAM
Mon-Fri: 8:30-8 (Fri till 7); Sat, Sun: 10-6   www.jampaper.com

At 7,000 square feet, this is the largest paper and envelope store in the city and perhaps the world! They stock over 150 kinds of paper, with matching card stock and envelopes. You will find a vast selection of presentation folders, plastic portfolios, plastic envelopes and folders, cello sleeves, translucents, bags, tissue, and raffia—all in matching colors. Close-outs and discounted items provide excellent bargains. Ask for their free catalog.

Do you want to create a little desk accessory envy in your office? Head over to **Muji** (455 Broadway, 212/334-2002; 620 Eighth Ave, 212/382-2300; Muji at MoMA Design Store, 44 W 53rd St, 212/708-9700; and Muji at MoMA Design Store Soho, 81 Spring St, 646/613-1367). This Japanese newcomer stocks eye-catching and unique desk, office, and stationery items as part of their no-name generic line. They also carry tempting jewelry and watches, personal accessories, housewares and home accessories, and books—even furniture and lighting! Great stuff at affordable prices.

KATE'S PAPERIE
72 Spring St (bet Crosby and Lafayette St)   212/941-9816
8 W 13th St (bet Fifth Ave and Ave of the Americas)   212/633-0570
140 W 57th St (bet Ave of the Americas and Seventh Ave)
                                                   212/459-0700
1282 Third Ave (at 74th St)   212/396-3670
Hours vary by store   www.katespaperie.com

Kate's Paperie has one of the largest selections of decorative and exotic papers in the country. You'll find thousands of papers, including papyrus, hand-marbled Italian, Japanese lace, and recycled papers from Zimbabwe. There are also leatherbound photo albums and journals, classic and exotic stationery, boxes, wax seals, rubber stamps, pens, and desk accessories. Kate's will do custom printing and engraving, personal and business embossing, and custom and corporate gift selection and wrapping.

PAPERPRESENTATION.COM
23 W 18th St (bet Fifth Ave and Ave of the Americas)   212/463-7035
Mon-Fri: 9-7; Sat, Sun: 11-6   www.paperpresentation.com

Come here for a huge selection of quality paper goods. Business cards, writing paper, invitations, brochures, postcards, envelopes, folders, Oriental laser paper, bags, labels, and more are shown in quantity. Certificate plaques are also available.

PURGATORY PIE PRESS
19 Hudson St (bet Duane and Reade St), Room 403   212/274-8228
Mon-Fri: by appointment   www.purgatorypiepress.com

The people at Purgatory Pie are experts at letterpress printing from hand-set metal and wood type. In addition, they do book production, albums, custom hand bookbinding, yearly datebooks, invitations, coasters, artists' books, and handmade paper with uniquely designed watermarks. Classes are taught in hand-making books and typography.

Papyrus is a chain of upscale paper goods stores that carry Schurman Fine Papers and Marcel Schurman creations. You will find an attractive and friendly environment, superior service, custom printing, stationery, gift wrap, gift products, and a great selection of greeting cards in every outlet.

- 852 Lexington Ave (bet 64th and 65th St), 212/717-0002
- 1270 Third Ave (at 73rd St), 212/717-1060
- Grand Central Terminal, 42nd St at Vanderbilt Ave, 212/490-9894 and 212/682-9359
- 2157 Broadway (bet 75th and 76th St), 212/501-0102
- 1250 Ave of the Americas (at 50th St), Suite 1, 212/265-9003
- 11 W 42nd St (bet Fifth Ave and Ave of the Americas), 212/302-3053
- 940 Broadway (bet 22nd and 23rd St), 212/228-2877
- 641 Ave of the Americas (bet 19th and 20th St), 212/741-7890
- 753 Broadway (bet Astor Pl and 8th St), 212/533-6039
- 233 Broadway (at Park Pl), 212/608-3180
- 73 Spring St (bet Crosby and Lafayette St), 212/625-0912

Tiles

BISAZZA MOSAICO
43 Greene St (bet Broome and Grand St)   212/334-7130
Tues-Sat: 11-7 (Mon-Fri: 10-6 in summer)   www.bisazzausa.com

Bisazza Mosaico claims to be the world's leading glass mosaic company, with high design standards and outstanding solutions. They have large stocks of glass mosaic tiles, custom mosaics, and tiles for residential, commercial, indoor, and outdoor use. They have been in business for over a half-century and carry recognized quality products.

COMPLETE TILE COLLECTION
42 W 15th St (bet Fifth Ave and Ave of the Americas) 212/255-4450
Mon-Fri: 10-6:30; Sat: 11-6   www.completetile.com

If you are shopping for quality tiles, come to Complete Tile. They carry American art tiles; glass, ceramic, concrete, metal, slate, granite, and molded tiles; marble and limestone mosaics; and a large assortment of handmade tiles. Design services are available, and the selection (800 varieties of natural stone and 400 colors of ceramic tile) is tops. They fabricate stone countertops, too!

IDEAL TILE
405 E 51st St (at First Ave)   212/759-2339
Mon-Fri: 9-5; Sat: 10-3   www.idealtile.com

Ideal Tile imports ceramics, porcelain, marble, granite, and terra cotta from Italy, Spain, and Brazil. They have absolutely magnificent hand-painted Italian ceramic pottery as well. This outfit guarantees installation of tiles by skilled craftsmen. They also offer marble and granite fabrication for fireplaces, countertops, window sills, and tables.

I've never seen a shop like this! **Manhattan Wardrobe Supply** (245 W 29th St, 8th floor, 212/268-9993, www.wardrobesupplies.com) has all sorts of items having to do with clothes (making, storing, cleaning, and displaying), theatrical makeup and hair, jewelry maintenance and storage, and miscellaneous bits and pieces like location set bags and fabric dyes or distressing kits. If you're a wardrober, you'll definitely want to shop here. If not, you'll learn the secrets of the professionals.

Tobacco and Smoking Accessories

BARCLAY-REX
75 Broad St (bet Beaver and William St)   212/962-3355
70 E 42nd St (bet Madison and Park Ave)   212/692-9680
570 Lexington Ave (at 51st St)   212/888-1015
Hours vary by store   www.barclayrex.com

Established in 1910, Barclay-Rex is the product of three generations of the Nastri family. They cater to devotees of fine cigars, pipes, tobaccos, and smoking-related gifts and accessories. Their shops are stocked with more than 200 brands of imported and domestic tobaccos. The finest tobaccos from all over the world are hand-blended and packaged under the Barclay-Rex label, and custom blending is one of their specialties. Cigars are housed in walk-in humidors at controlled temperatures. They have one of the city's best selections of pipes. You'll also find a large selection of Borsalino hats in felt, straw, and beaver.

MIDTOWN CIGARS
562 Fifth Ave (at 46th St)   212/997-2227
Mon-Fri: 9-7; Sat: 10-5; Sun: 11-4   www.mid-towncigar.com

Midtown Cigars showcases over 200 brands of domestic and handmade imported cigars, plus quality humidors and cigar accessories. Manager Marie Jeune suggests checking their website for special events that periodically features specific cigars.

OK CIGARS
383 West Broadway (bet Spring and Broome St)   212/965-9065
Daily: noon-7 (sometimes later)   www.okcigars.com

Looking for a really good cigar? Len Brunson carries some of the best in a pleasant atmosphere. Unique accessories are available, including some of the finest and most peculiar antique tobacciana to be found.

> Gentlemen! Tired of searching for a place where cigar smoking is not only allowed but encouraged? At **De La Concha** (1390 Ave of the Americas, 212/757-3167), you can enjoy your stogie, a cup of coffee, and good conversation, too. High-quality imported and domestic cigars, cigarettes, pipes, and tobacco are carried here.

Toys and Children's Items

General

DINOSAUR HILL
306 E 9th St (bet First and Second Ave)   212/473-5850
Daily: 11-7   www.dinosaurhill.com

Dinosaur Hill is a really enchanting toy store that seems to be thriving even as some of its competitors are struggling or have closed. Maybe it's because of the diverse and consistently high-quality stock. There are brightly colored toys, solid wood blocks, globes, and a wonderful assortment of games, gadgets, hats, music boxes, monkeys, rattles, and board games. In addition, there is handmade clothing, quilts, bibs, and T-shirts in natural-fiber fabrics.

F.A.O. SCHWARZ
767 Fifth Ave (at 58th St)   212/644-9400
Mon-Thurs: 10-7; Fri, Sat: 10-8; Sun: 11-6   www.fao.com

Shopping here can be a special experience! In the competitive (and sometimes unprofitable) field of toy retailing, F.A.O. Schwarz's flagship store has had its problems. Following a makeover, shopping has become a bit easier, and prices are somewhat more comfortable. You'll find some merchandise that is not readily available elsewhere, and the mere fact that your purchase came from this store makes it special for many youngsters (and adults). This is a great place for birthday parties!

KID O
123 W 10th St (at Ave of the Americas)   212/366-5436
Mon-Sat: 10-7; Sun: 11-6   www.kidonyc.com

Lisa Mahar has gathered products that have both a design and educational focus; she has designed many herself. Lisa believes such items can accelerate children's development. You'll find play objects, kids' furniture, artwork, nursery items, and books. Educational materials include Montessori and Froebel gifts.

KIDDING AROUND
60 W 15th St (bet Fifth Ave and Ave of the Americas)   212/645-6337
Mon-Sat: 10-7; Sun: 11-6   www.kiddingaround.us

This bright, spacious emporium in the heart of Greenwich Village is arguably the city's best toy store. Books, toys, puzzles, balls, games, craft supplies, birthday party favors—you name it, they've got it. In addition to a wide selection of Playmobil, Brio, and Corolle dolls, Kidding Around stocks an amazing assortment of quality wooden toys for riding, building, and just having fun. The clothing section is small but well chosen, and the dress-up clothes are great, too.

MARY ARNOLD TOYS
1010 Lexington Ave (at 72nd St)   212/744-8510
Mon-Fri: 9-6; Sat: 10-5; Sun: 11-5

You won't find any great bargains and likely won't see anything you haven't seen before, but Mary Arnold Toys is a spacious, well-organized, and well-stocked source for the basics. There are separate sections for games, early-development toys, puzzles, books, videos, stuffed animals, craft kits and supplies, Playmobil, and Madame Alexander dolls. The dress-up collection deserves a close look.

SONS & DAUGHTERS
35 Ave A (at 3rd St)   212/253-7797
Mon-Tues: noon-7; Wed-Sun: 10-7   www.sonsanddaughtersinc.com

This is a toy store with a conscience! Instead of the cheap plastic toys made on assembly lines in China, you'll find all sorts of wonderful toys made from recycled cardboard and other sustainable resources by people working in decent conditions for fair wages. A trip here will prove that you can buy great gifts and feel good about it, too.

TOYS "R" US
1514 Broadway (at 44th St)   800/869-7787
Mon-Thurs: 10-10; Fri, Sat: 10-11; Sun: 10-9   www.toysrus.com

No family trip to Manhattan is complete without a visit to Toys "R" Us! Set in Times Square, this marketing marvel features a huge stage set with a giant *Tyrannosaurus rex* and a 60-foot tall ferris wheel at the entrance. Each car of the ferris wheel models a different toy. The "R" zone entertains with its showcase of the latest electronic games, DVDs, CDs, and a huge plasma screen. Barbie's Dollhouse features two floors of the latest toys and fashions. Every square inch of this busy store is filled with kid-pleasing merchandise.

ZITTLES
969 Madison Ave (at 76th St), 3rd floor   212/737-5560
Mon-Fri: 9-8; Sat: 9-7; Sun: 10-6   www.zitomer.com

Housed on the third floor of Zitomer—an amusingly snobby drugstore-cum-department-store on Madison Avenue—Zittles has one of the most extensive selections of toys, games, stuffed animals, dolls, books, party balloons, software, and videos for children in the city. There are neither bargains nor much imagination shown here, but there is a lot of space, and every inch—from floor to ceiling—is filled with all the basics and more. They have added an arcade, too.

Specialty and Novelty

ALPHABETS
115 Ave A (bet 7th and 8th St)   212/475-7250
47 Greenwich Ave (bet Charles and Perry St)   212/229-2966
Mon-Thurs: noon-8; Fri: noon-10; Sat: 11-10; Sun: 11-7
www.alphabetsnyc.com

Take a walk down memory lane in these crowded spaces. In what is a combination toy store and novelty shop, you'll find funky items like a Desi Arnaz wristwatch, a Gumby and Pokey piggybank, kitschy ceramics, and a T-shirt with the Velveeta logo on it. Alphabets is the place to visit if you want to relive your childhood.

BALLOON CENTER OF NEW YORK
5 Tudor City Pl (bet First and Second Ave)
By appointment   212/682-0122, 212/682-3803

The Balloon Center of New York sells balloons individually or in quantities. There are graduations in diameter, thickness, style, and type (including Mylar balloons). Sizes range from peewees to three feet and extra-long shapes. Balloon clips, ribbon, and imprinting are available, as is helium. They do balloon arches, special events, and street fairs.

DISNEY STORE
711 Fifth Ave (at 55th St)   212/702-0702
Mon-Sat: 10-8; Sun: 11-6   www.worldofdisney.com

This store can be a fun place to shop. Unlike the staff at many of the huge stores that have popped up all over New York, these folks really know their stock and are personable, to boot. If you don't have a Disney Store back home and are looking for kids' luggage emblazoned with Mickey Mouse, backpacks in the shape of Winnie the Pooh, or other Disney-related items, visit this three-floor maze of merchandise. Their gallery offers authentic Disney art from past and present.

Once among the most famous areas of Manhattan, "Ladies' Mile" is again on the itineraries of wise shoppers. Some terrific stores are grouped along Avenue of the Americas between 18th and 19th streets:

Bed Bath & Beyond: a wonderful store, with huge selections of bed, bath, and home furnishings at good prices

Filene's Basement: famous for clothing bargains

Old Navy: very "in," especially with the young anti-yuppie set; clothing is fashionable and priced right

T.J. Maxx: values in clothing and accessories for the family

FORBIDDEN PLANET
840 Broadway (at 13th St)   212/473-1576
Sun-Tues: 10-10; Wed: 9 a.m.-midnight; Thurs-Sat: 10 a.m.-midnight
                                                    www.fpnyc.com

This unique shop is a shrine for science-fiction artifacts. Forbidden Planet stocks sci-fi comic books and publications, videos, posters, T-shirts, cards, toys, and games.

IMAGE ANIME
242 W 30th St (bet Seventh and Eighth Ave)   212/631-0966
Mon-Fri: 11-7; Sat: noon-6   www.imageanime.com

Image Anime specializes in imported Japanese toys and collectibles. If that category interests you—and a great many children and adults are fanatically devoted to it—then this packed little store will thrill you. Lines include Gundam, Pokémon, Transformers, Robotech, Anime, and just about every other popular Japanese line.

MANHATTAN DOLLHOUSE

767 Fifth Ave (bet 58th and 59th St)   212/644-9400, ext 3041
Mon-Sat: 10-7; Sun: 11-6   www.manhattandollhouse.com

The Manhattan Dollhouse occupies a historic location—the former General Motors Building. I was sorry to learn that they no longer carry or repair dolls. However, they still carry a large selection of dollhouses, miniature furniture, and accessories. If you collect and decorate dollhouses, put this place on your list.

RED CABOOSE

23 W 45th St (bet Fifth Ave and Ave of the Americas), basement
Mon-Fri: 11-7; Sat: 11-5   212/575-0155
www.theredcaboose.com

Owner-operator Allan J. Spitz says that 99% of his customers are not wide-eyed children but sharp-eyed adults who are dead serious about model railroads. The Red Caboose claims to have 100,000 items on hand, including a line of 300 hand-finished, imported brass locomotives. The five basic sizes—1:22, 1:48, 1:87, 1:161, and 1:220, in a ratio of scale to actual size—allow model railroaders to build layouts sized to fit everything from a desk drawer to an entire room. They stock an extensive line of plastic kits, paints, tools, and model supplies. Red Caboose also carries die-cast airplanes (military and commercial), autos, and military vehicles.

TOY TOKYO

121 Second Ave (at 7th St), 2nd floor   212/673-5424
Daily: 1-9   www.toytokyo.com

This store is a great example of why I love New York! Started in 2000, Toy Tokyo sells toys and collectibles from every genre, including wonderful Japanese action figures and *Star Wars* collectibles. The stock changes a bit every week, and many items come straight from Hong Kong, Japan, and other points east. If you're a collector or just a curious browser, put this overflowing walkup on your list. You must see it to believe it!

Travel Items

FLIGHT 001

96 Greenwich Ave (bet Jane and 12th St)   212/989-0001
Mon-Sat: 11-8; Sun: noon-6   877/FLIGHT1
www.flight001.com

Traveling these days isn't always fun, but a trip to Flight 001 will make it more bearable. You will find novel and useful travel aids, including cosmetics, bags, wallets, luggage tags, cameras, guidebooks, stationery, luggage, and more.

Watches

TEMPVS FVGIT AT THE SHOWPLACE

40 W 25th St (bet Ave of the Americas and Broadway)   212/633-6063
Thurs-Sun: 10-5   www.tempvsfvgit.com

If you're looking for a vintage Rolex, this is the place! They also carry other top brands and watchbands at considerable savings. Services offered include watch repair and restoration.

YAEGER WATCH
578 Fifth Ave (at 47th St)   212/819-0088
Mon-Fri: 10-4:45; Sat: 10-3 (closed Sat in summer)

www.yaegerwatch.com

Over 2,000 discounted watches are carried at Yaegar. Choose from the latest styes and classic in name brands retailing from $100 to $150,000. Watch repair and warranties are offered, and prices are quoted over the phone. Yaeger Watch has been owned by the same family since 1973.

Other reliable New York watch stores include:

Cellini Fine Jewelry (509 Madison Ave, 212/888-0505)
Kenjo (40 W 57th St, 212/333-7220)
Tourneau (500 Madison Ave, 212/758-6098; 12 E 57th St, 212/758-7300; and 200 W 34th St, 212/563-6880)
Wempe (700 Fifth Ave, 212/397-9000)

VII. Where to "Extras"

As I research each new edition of this book, I'm always struck by the amount of information that doesn't fit neatly into any of the other chapters. That's why I came up with this chapter of "Extras": where to play, take kids, spend a romantic evening, or host a special event. Those are just four of the more than a dozen subjects this chapter addresses.

ANNUAL EVENTS

While stores, museums, restaurants, and the like are open all year, some special events are held only during certain seasons or once a year. Keep in mind that since some of these events are seasonal, dates and venues frequently change.

JANUARY
Polar Bear Club New Year's Dip (Coney Island)
Ice skating (Rockefeller Center, Central Park, and Bryant Park)
Winter Antiques Show (Seventh Regiment Armory)
Chinese New Year (January or February)

FEBRUARY
Westminster Kennel Club Dog Show (Madison Square Garden)
Empire State Run-Up (Empire State Building)
National Antiques Show (Madison Square Garden)
International Art Expo
Valentine's Day wedding ceremony (Empire State Building)

MARCH
St. Patrick's Day Parade (Fifth Ave)
International Cat Show (Madison Square Garden)
Spring Armory Antiques Show (Seventh Regiment Armory)
Big East and NIT college basketball tournaments (Madison Square Garden)
Ringling Brothers and Barnum & Bailey Circus (Madison Square Garden)
Macy's Spring Flower Show
Radio City Easter Show (Radio City Music Hall)

APRIL
Major League Baseball season opens (Yankees and Mets)
New York Antiquarian Book Fair (Seventh Regiment Armory)
New York International Auto Show (Jacob K. Javits Convention Center)
Tribeca Film Festival

MAY
Ninth Avenue International Food Festival (Ninth Ave)
Ukrainian Festival (7th St in the East Village)
Fleet Week (week before Memorial Day)
River to River Festival (Lower Manhattan)
Washington Square Outdoor Art Exhibit

JUNE
Salute to Israel Parade (Fifth Ave)
Free concerts and performances (Central Park and other city parks)
Lesbian and Gay Pride March
Jazz festivals (Bryant Park, Carnegie Hall, and other locations)

JULY
Free concerts and performances (Central Park and other city parks)
Free movies (Bryant Park and other locations)
Fourth of July fireworks (East River and other locations)
Asian American International Film Festival
Mostly Mozart (Avery Fisher Hall)
Midsummer Night Swing (Lincoln Center)

AUGUST
Free concerts and performances (Central Park and other city parks)
Free movies (Bryant Park and other locations)
New York City Triathlon
Lincoln Center Out-of-Doors Festival (Lincoln Center)
Festival Latino (Public Theater and other locations)
U.S. Open tennis tournament begins (USTA Billie Jean King National Tennis
    Center in Flushing Meadows, Queens)
Harlem Week

SEPTEMBER
Autumn Crafts Festival (Lincoln Center)
National Football League season opens (Giants and Jets)
Big Apple Performing Arts Festival (Seventh Ave)
Feast of San Gennaro (Little Italy)
New York Film Festival (Lincoln Center)

OCTOBER
Columbus Day Festival and Parade
National Basketball Association season opens (Knicks and Liberty)
Hockey season opens (Rangers and Islanders)
Union Square Autumn Fair
Fall Antiques Show (Pier 92, Twelfth Ave at 52nd St)
Halloween Parade (Greenwich Village)
New York Marathon (late October or early November)
New York City Oktoberfest (Lexington Ave)

NOVEMBER
New York Comedy Festival
Margaret Mead Film Festival (American Museum of Natural History)
Macy's Thanksgiving Day Parade
Christmas tree lighting (Rockefeller Plaza)

DECEMBER
Christmas windows (Saks Fifth Avenue, Macy's, Lord & Taylor, and other
   locations)
Messiah Sing-In (Avery Fisher Hall)
Radio City Christmas Show (Radio City Music Hall)
Holiday bazaar (Grand Central Terminal)
New York National Boat Show (Jacob K. Javits Convention Center)
Christmas Day walking tour (Big Onion Walking Tours)
New Year's Eve celebrations (Times Square and other locations)
First Night celebrations (Grand Central Terminal, Central Park, and other
   locations)

'Tis the Season

   Some things can only be done in New York if you're in town at the
right time. If you are planning a trip in spring or summer, get tickets to
a baseball game at the new **Yankee Stadium** (www.yankees.com)
or **Citi Field**, the new home of the Mets (www.mets.mlb.com). If
you're in town during the summer, find out what's going on in **Central Park** (www.centralparknyc.org). In the fall, get tickets to the
Metropolitan Opera (www.metoperafamily.org). And if you're in
town around Christmas, take the family to see the Christmas Show at
Radio City Music Hall (www.radiocity.com).

WHERE TO PLAY
Films

   Like any city, New York has a multitude of theaters for first-run movies.
Indeed, most movies debut in New York and Los Angeles before opening
anywhere else. (Depending on the size of the crowds they draw, some never
open elsewhere.) You can call 212/777-FILM (3456) for information about
what movies are showing at virtually every theater in Manhattan and to purchase tickets by credit card at many of those theaters. If you're online, go to
www.moviefone.com or www.newyork.citysearch.com.
   If you're looking for an old movie, a foreign film, an unusual documentary,
a 3D movie, or something out of the ordinary, try calling one of the following theaters. Most numbers connect you with a recording that lists current
movies and times, ticket cost (some places accept cash only), and directions.

American Museum of Natural History's IMAX Theater (Cen-
   tral Park West and 79th St, 212/769-5100)
Angelika Film Center and Cafe (18 W Houston St, 212/995-2000)
Anthology Film Archives (32 Second Ave, 212/505-5181)
Asia Society (725 Park Ave, 212/327-9276)
Austrian Cultural Forum (11 E 52nd St, 212/319-5300)
Film Forum (209 W Houston St, 212/727-8110)

Florence Gould Hall at the French Institute (55 E 59th St, 212/355-6160)
Japan Society (333 E 47th St, 212/832-1155)
Lincoln Plaza Cinema (1886 Broadway, 212/757-2280)
Millennium (66 E 4th St, 212/673-0090)
Paley Center for Media (25 W 52nd St, 212/621-6600)
Quad Cinema (34 W 13th St, 212/255-8800)
Symphony Space (2537 Broadway, 212/864-5400)
Walter Reade Theater at Lincoln Center (165 W 65th St, 212/875-5600)
Whitney Museum of American Art (945 Madison Ave, 212/570-3676)

Like everything else, the price of movie tickets in New York tends to be higher than elsewhere in the country. The second-run theaters, film societies, and museums usually charge a little less, and Bryant Park, Central Park, and other parks throughout the city host free movies in the summer. What fun it is to sing "Somewhere Over the Rainbow" with a thousand other people!

Of course, New York is home to dozens of popular film festivals. The best known is the Film Society of Lincoln Center's **New York Film Festival**, held in late September and early October. This annual event showcases 20 films and gets more popular every year. Call the Walter Reade Theater box office for more information.

Kid-Friendly Places

Taking little ones along to see the sights or to restaurants can be trying, as they can easily get bored with adult activities. Here are a couple of spots that are sure to delight kids:

City Hall New York—The Restaurant (131 Duane St, 212/227-7777): Saturday morning is "Kiddie Hall," with 'toons at the bar and a special menu.

Jewish Museum (1109 Fifth Ave, 212/423-3200): Don 19th-century Turkish costumes and dig for artifacts in the Archaeology Zone on the second Sunday of the month.

Museum of American Finance (48 Wall St, 212/908-4110): Kids can design their own currency and talk to active Secret Service agents; call for a schedule.

Nightlife

Whether you want an evening of elegant dining and dancing, rocking and rolling till the wee hours, dropping in on a set of jazz, or catching some stand-up comedy, New York's club scene offers endless choices. I've listed several popular places in each category to get you started. Most levy a cover charge, many offer at least a light menu, and a very few require reservations and jackets for men. (Don't worry if you don't have one, as they'll have "loaners.") As with so many other things, it is wise to call in advance.

Cabaret Rooms
Cafe Carlyle, Carlyle Hotel (35 E 76th St, 212/744-1600)

Don't Tell Mama (343 W 46th St, 212/757-0788)
Feinstein's at Loews Regency, Regency Hotel (540 Park Ave, 212/339-4095)
Metropolitan Room (34 W 22nd St, 212/206-0440)
Oak Room, Algonquin Hotel (59 W 44th St, 888/304-2047 and 212/840-6800)

Comedy Clubs

Caroline's on Broadway (1626 Broadway, 212/757-4100)
Comedy Cellar (117 MacDougal St, 212/254-3480)
Comix (353 W 14th St, 212/524-2500)
Dangerfield's (1118 First Ave, 212/593-1650)
Gotham Comedy Club (208 W 23rd St, 212/367-9000)
Stand-Up New York (236 W 78th St, 212/595-0850)

Dancing

China Club (268 W 47th St, 212/398-3800): live music and DJs on weekends
SOB (204 Varick St, 212/243-4940): selected weekends

> Lots of dancing and singles action at **bOb Bar** (235 Eldridge St, 212/529-1807; closed Mondays). DJs keep the music going all night, but the party really kicks into high gear around midnight. Check with the bar for a roster of guest DJs and cover charges.

Gay and Lesbian Clubs

Boiler Room (86 E 4th St, 212/254-7536): gay
g Lounge (225 W 19th St, 212/929-1085): gay
Henrietta Hudson (438 Hudson St, 212/924-3347): lesbian
Posh (405 W 51st St, 212/957-2222)
Stonewall (53 Christopher St, 212/488-2705): historic, mostly gay

Jazz Clubs

B.B. King's Blues Club (237 W 42nd St, 212/997-4144)
Bill's Place (148 W 133rd St, 212/281-0777)
Birdland (315 W 44th St, 212/581-3080)
Blue Note (131 W 3rd St, 212/475-8592)
Iridium (1650 Broadway, 212/582-2121)
Jazz Standard (116 E 27th St, 212/576-2232)
Showman's Jazz Club (375 W 125th St, 212/864-8941)
Smoke (2751 Broadway, 212/864-6662)
Village Vanguard (178 Seventh Ave S, 212/255-4037)

Rock and Folk Clubs

A Happy Ending (302 Broome St, 212/334-9676): two floors of music, drinks, and partygoers
Bitter End (147 Bleecker St, 212/673-7030): one of the original Greenwich Village folk clubs, with rock and blues as well

Bowery Ballroom (6 Delancey St, 212/533-2111): the city's premier rock showcase

"Let's Have a Drink"
Aquavit (65 E 55th St, 212/307-7311)
Campbell Apartment (Grand Central Terminal, 42nd St at Vanderbilt Ave, 212/953-0409)
Grand Bar, Soho Grand Hotel (310 West Broadway, 212/965-3000)
21 Club (21 W 52nd St, 212/582-7200)
Ty Lounge, Four Seasons Hotel New York (57 E 57th St, 212/758-5757)

Jazz at Lincoln Center

Well, it isn't actually at Lincoln Center anymore. **Jazz at Lincoln Center** has relocated just down the street in the Time Warner Center at Columbus Circle. Jazz trumpeter Wynton Marsalis and his orchestra are featured regularly. Look for **Dizzy's Club Coca-Cola** (212/258-9800 or www.jalc.org), too.

Music in the Museums
Brooklyn Museum (200 Eastern Parkway, Brooklyn, 718/638-5000): free music and entertainment from 5 to 11 on the first Saturday of each month
The Cloisters (Fort Tryon Park, 212/923-3700): frequent concerts
Frick Collection (1 E 70th St, 212/288-8700): concerts some Sundays at 5 p.m.
Guggenheim Museum (1071 Fifth Ave, 212/423-3500): live jazz on Friday and Saturday evening in the warmer months
Metropolitan Museum of Art (Fifth Ave bet 80th and 84th St, 212/535-7710): classical music on Friday and Saturday from 5:30 to 8:30 in the Balcony Bar
Morgan Library and Museum (225 Madison Ave, 212/685-0008): lots of concerts, mostly classical; tickets required

---

Keep the **Garage Restaurant & Cafe** (99 Seventh Ave S, 212/645-0600) in mind if you're looking for live jazz. You can hear jazz seven days a week, over a relaxing brunch on the weekends, nightly during dinner, and into the wee morning hours. If you're a people-watcher, opt for a table on the balcony or a sidewalk cafe table in the summer.

Recreation

Visitors sometimes see Manhattan as nothing but concrete and can't imagine what those who live here do for exercise other than walking. The people who live here, however, know that you can do just about anything in New York that can be done anywhere else—and then some! Whether it's batting cages, tennis courts, riding stables, or a driving range, chances are that New York has it. You just have to know where to look.

Baseball
Baseball Center NYC (202 W 74th St, 212/362-0344)
Field House at Chelsea Piers (23rd St at Hudson River, 212/336-6500)

Basketball
BasketBall City (3100 47th Ave, 212/924-4040)
Field House at Chelsea Piers (23rd St at Hudson River, 212/336-6500)

For Young Athletes

   If you have a child who wants to climb a wall, take batting practice, or kick a soccer ball, then go to the **Field House at Chelsea Piers**. Located on the far west side of Manhattan between 17th and 23rd streets, this remarkable complex has it all. Call 212/336-6500 or go to www.chelseapiers.com for more information. They offer plenty of sports programs for adults, too

---

Billiards
Amsterdam Billiards and Bar (110 E 11th St, 212/995-0333)
Slate Billiards (54 W 21st St, 212/989-0096)

Bowling
Bowlmor Lanes (110 University Pl, 212/255-8188)
Leisure Time Bowl (Port Authority Bus Terminal, 625 Eighth Ave, 212/268-6909)
300 New York (Chelsea Piers, 23rd St at Hudson River, 212/835-2695)

Chess, Checkers, and Backgammon
Bryant Park (Ave of the Americas bet 40th and 42nd St)
Chess Shop (230 Thompson St, 212/475-9580)
Washington Square Park (foot of Fifth Ave, below 8th St)

Climbing
Field House at Chelsea Piers (23rd St at Hudson River, 212/336-6500)
North Meadow Recreation Center (Central Park at 97th St, 212/348-4867)

Golf
Golf Club at Chelsea Piers (Pier 59, 23rd St at Hudson River, 212/336-6400)
Split Rock (public course in The Bronx, 718/885-1258)

Horseback Riding
River Ridge Equestrian Center (914/633-0303, www.riverridgestable.com)

Ice Skating
Lasker Rink (Central Park at E 107th St, 917/492-3856)
The Pond at Bryant Park (Ave of the Americas at 42nd St, 866/221-5157)

Rockefeller Center (Fifth Ave bet 49th and 50th St, 212/632-3975)
Seaport Ice (South Street Seaport, South St at Fulton St, 212/661-6640)
Sky Rink at Chelsea Piers (Pier 61, 23rd St at Hudson River, 212/336-6100): year round
Trump Wollman Rink (Central Park, W 59th St at Ave of the Americas, 212/439-6900)

Soccer
Field House at Chelsea Piers (23rd St at Hudson River, 212/336-6500)

What a Deal!

For $75 a year (just $10 for senior citizens over 55 and free for children under 18), you can use the city's wonderful recreation centers, including indoor pools and excellent facilities, and sign up for all sorts of classes. Go to www.nycgovparks.org and then click on "Recreation Centers" for descriptions of each center and its offerings.

Swimming
All-Star Fitness Center (75 West End Ave, 212/265-8200)
Asphalt Green (1750 York Ave, 212/369-8890)
Carmine Street Recreation Center (1 Clarkson St, 212/242-5418)
Vanderbilt YMCA (224 E 47th St, 212/912-2500)

Tennis
Midtown Tennis Club (341 Eighth Ave, 212/989-8572)
Sutton East Tennis Center (488 E 60th St, 212/751-3452)
Tennis Club at Grand Central (Grand Central Terminal, 42nd St at Vanderbilt Ave, 212/687-3841)
USTA Billie Jean King National Tennis Center (Flushing Meadows, Queens, 718/760-6200)

Spectator Sports

Some people associate New York with fine food and expensive stores, while others link the city with the Yankees, the Mets, the Knicks, the Rangers, and other professional sports teams. The New York area is home to more than half a dozen professional sports teams—although only basketball's Knicks and Liberty and hockey's Rangers actually play in Manhattan. (Home field for the city's two pro football teams, the Jets and the Giants, is across the river in New Jersey).

If you want tickets to a professional sporting event, plan as far in advance as possible. Diagrams of all the area's sports stadiums appear near the front of the Manhattan Yellow Pages, and each team's website has detailed information about schedules, tickets, and how to get there.

A word of warning: New York sports fans are like no others. They are loud, rude, and typically very knowledgeable about their teams and sports in general. If you're cheering against the home team, keep your voice down—and your head, too!

Baseball
New York Mets (Citi Field, Queens, www.mets.com)

New York Yankees (Yankee Stadium, I E 161st St, The Bronx, www. yankees.com)

Basketball

New York Knicks (Madison Square Garden, www.nba.com/knicks)
New York Liberty (Madison Square Garden, www.wnba.com/liberty)

Football

The Giants and the Jets share Meadowlands Stadium and they'll have a new facility for the 2010 NFL season.

New York Giants (The Meadowlands, East Rutherford, New Jersey, www. giants.com)
New York Jets (The Meadowlands, East Rutherford, New Jersey, www. newyorkjets.com)

Hockey

New York Rangers (Madison Square Garden, www.newyorkrangers. com)

The **U.S. Open** returns to the Billie Jean King National Tennis Center in Flushing, Queens, at the end of every summer. One of four Grand Slam tournaments in professional tennis, the U.S. Open draws tennis fans from around the world. The finals are held over Labor Day weekend. If you're interested in learning more about the National Tennis Center or getting tickets for the U.S. Open, go to www.usta.com.

WHERE TO GO
For Great Views and Photo Ops

There are thousands of great views and photo opportunities in every part of New York. If you're a photographer or just want a memorable "only in New York" photo for your album, then here are some of my favorite views and backdrops:

Battery Park Esplanade (length of Battery Park City along the Hudson River)
Brooklyn Bridge (anywhere along its length)
Central Park rock outcrops (just inside the park's southwest corner)
The Cloisters (Fort Tryon Park)
LOVE Sculpture (Ave of the Americas at 55th St)
Morris-Jumel Mansion grounds (65 Jumel Terrace, in Harlem Heights)
New York Harbor (particularly from the Staten Island Ferry)
Patience and Fortitude (lion statues in front of New York Public Library, at Fifth Ave and 42nd St)
Prometheus Statue (Rockefeller Plaza, west of Fifth Ave bet 49th and 50th St)
Roosevelt Island (anywhere on the west side, particularly Lighthouse Park)
Statue of Liberty (off Battery Park in New York Harbor)
Wall Street Bull (bronze sculpture, Broadway at Bowling Green)
Washington Arch (Washington Square Park, foot of Fifth Ave in Greenwich Village)

Nothing can compare to Central Park in size or attractions, but here are several other relaxing spots throughout the city:

Greenacre Park (51st St bet Second and Third Ave): A beautiful waterfall is surrounded by lush greenery.

Jefferson Market Garden (Greenwich Ave bet 10th St and Ave of the Americas): best viewed May through October; one-third acre

Paley Park (53rd St bet Fifth and Madison Ave): An enticing waterfall occupies the former site of the legendary Stork Club.

Shakespeare Garden (Central Park, bet 79th and 80th St): Be sure to read the plaques with Shakespearean quotes at this romantic and rustic spot.

Sutton Place Park (57th St along East River): five tiny parks, wild boar statue, kids' sandbox

Teardrop Park (River Terrace between Murray and Warren St): Battery Park City; lots of rocks for sitting, walking, and climbing.

1251 Avenue of the Americas (between 49th and 50th St): two-story waterfall, free summer concerts

West Side Community Garden (89th St bet Amsterdam and Columbus Ave): floral amphitheater, massive spring tulip display

In the Middle of the Night

New York bills itself as "the city that never sleeps," and many who live here are night people. They include not only actors and artists, but also those who clean and maintain the huge office buildings, work for answering services, put together morning newspapers and newscasts, work the night shift at hospitals and other businesses that never close, and secretaries, transcribers, and editors who must make sure paperwork is ready overnight.

In general, stores and restaurants in Soho, Tribeca, and Greenwich Village stay open later than those in the rest of the city. The restaurants and mom-and-pop operations along Broadway on the Upper West Side and on Lexington and Third avenues on the Upper East Side also tend to keep late hours. As with everything else, call before setting out.

Up Late and Looking for Something to Do?

Barnes & Noble (2289 Broadway, 212/362-8835 and other locations)
Bowlmor Lanes (110 University Pl, 212/255-8188)
Cafeteria (119 Seventh Ave, 212/414-1717)
Chess Shop (230 Thompson St, 212/475-9580)
Crunch Fitness (404 Lafayette St, 212/614-0120)
Slate Billiards (54 W 21st St, 212/989-0096)

Need Help in the Middle of the Night?

Animal Medical Center (212/838-8100)
Doctors on Call (212/737-2333)
Moonlight Courier (212/473-2246)

With Kids

When I first began writing this book, I did so from the perspective of an adult who comes to New York without children. I quickly learned that many people bring kids to New York, whether they're coming for business or pleasure. That's more true now than ever before. The number of kids living in New York has also increased dramatically over the years. Restaurants, hotels, museums, theaters, and other tourist venues have noted this trend and adjusted their offerings to this growing audience. Always ask about special deals and events for children and families.

Remember that New York can be totally overwhelming for children. (The same is true for adults!) Don't push too hard and retreat to quiet spaces from time to time. Remember, too, that New York can be a wonderland for all ages, if you know where to go. Look inside toy stores and bookstores for seasonal calendars, and get hold of *New York Metro Parents* (www.nymetro parents.com) or one of the other free parenting magazines published in New York. Here are some good websites for families and children in New York:

- www.gocitykids.com
- www.newyorkkids.net
- www.ny.com/kids
- www.parentsknow.com

I've listed some suggestions for things to do with kids in several categories: entertainment, museums, and sights; restaurants; and toy and bookstores. In many cases, these places are described in detail in other parts of this book. Of course, children's interests can vary dramatically, so I've inevitably included places that one child will love and another might find boring. I'll let you be the judge of that! I also recommend looking under Children's Books, Children's Clothing Stores, and Toy Stores in Chapter VI.

Skating on Non-Ice

The **American Museum of Natural History** brought ice skating to the Arthur Ross Terrace in 2008. The seasonal **Polar Rink** (79th St at Columbus Ave) is composed of synthetic ice, with a 17-foot polar bear statue in the middle. According to skaters, the surface makes for softer landings and it's not wet or cold; however, it does take more leg strength to skate on artificial ice. Equipment rental and hot cocoa are available. Check with the museum for seasonal hours (212/769-5100).

Entertainment, Museums, and Sights

Busy Little Ones

Bryant Park Carousel (Ave of the Americas at 42nd St)
Central Park Carousel (behind The Arsenal in Central Park at E 64th St)
Central Park Zoo (behind The Arsenal in Central Park at E 64th St, 212/439-6500)
Children's Museum of the Arts (182 Lafayette St, 212/941-9198)
Heimbold Family Children's Learning Center (Scandinavia House, 58 Park Ave, 212/879-9779)
92nd Street Y (Parenting Center, 1395 Lexington Ave, 212/415-5611)

Museums with a Family Focus

American Museum of Natural History (Central Park West bet 77th and 81st St, 212/769-5100)
Children's Museum of Manhattan (212 W 83rd St, 212/721-1234)
Dyckman Farmhouse Museum (4881 Broadway, 212/304-9422)
Fraunces Tavern Museum (54 Pearl St, 212/425-1778)
Liberty Science Center (Liberty State Park, Jersey City, NJ, 201/200-1000)
Lower East Side Tenement Museum (90 Orchard St, 212/431-0233)
Madame Toussaud's (234 W 42nd St, 212/512-9600)
Museum of the City of New York (1220 Fifth Ave, 212/534-1672)
New York City Fire Museum (278 Spring St, 212/691-1303)
New York City Police Museum (100 Old Slip, 212/480-3100)
Sony Wonder Technology Lab (550 Madison Ave, 212/833-8100)
South Street Seaport Museum (12 Fulton St, 212/748-8600)

Circus Arts Academy

Have you ever thought about joining the circus? Here's a way to make it happen! The **New York Circus Arts Academy** (646/291-6364, www.nycircusarts.com) trains performers for outfits like **Cirque du Soleil**. They also offer classes to the public that are great for improving body alignment, flexibility, and stamina. Two-hour trial courses include tumbling, trampoline and vaulting, aerial acrobatics, hand balancing, pyramids, and juggling. Doesn't that sound like fun?

For Tweens and Teens

Dylan's Candy Bar (1011 Third Ave, 646/735-0078)
Field House at Chelsea Piers (23rd St at Hudson River, 212/336-6500)
Leisure Time Bowl (Port Authority Bus Terminal, 625 Eighth Ave, 212/268-6909)
Madame Toussaud's (234 W 42nd St, 212/512-9600)
On Location Tours (www.sceneontv.com)
Shark Speedboat Harbor Ride (South Street Seaport, 866/925-4631, www.circlelinedowntown.com)
Sony Wonder Technology Lab (550 Madison Ave, 212/833-8100)

New York Classics

Bronx Zoo (2300 Southern Blvd, The Bronx, 718/367-1010)
Ellis Island (New York Harbor, 212/363-3200)
Empire State Building (Fifth Ave bet 33rd and 34th St, 212/736-3100)
New York Hall of Science (4701 111th St, Queens, 718/699-0005)
Statue of Liberty (New York Harbor, 212/363-3200)
United Nations (First Ave bet 42nd and 47th St, 212/963-4440)
Yankee Stadium (1 E 161st St, The Bronx, 718/579-4594)

Plays, Movies, and TV

IMAX Theater (American Museum of Natural History, Central Park West at 79th St, 212/769-5100)

The Lion King (Minskoff Theater, 1515 Broadway)
NBC Experience Studio Tour (49th St bet Fifth Ave and Ave of the Americas, 212/664-3700)
Paley Center for Media (25 W 52nd St, 212/621-6800)

Boats and Other Transportation

Circle Line Sightseeing Tours (Pier 83, 42nd St at Hudson River, 212/563-3200)
New York Transit Museum (Boerum Pl at Schermerhorn St, Brooklyn, 718/694-1600)
Roosevelt Island Tram (Second Ave bet 59th and 60th St)
Staten Island Ferry (Whitehall Terminal, south end of Manhattan)

Sailing

Yes, there is a way to enjoy the waters around Manhattan without having to share the ride with hundreds of others. The 82-foot **Shearwater** (212/619-0885) is a restored 1929 sailboat that holds up to 48 passengers. The Moët & Chandon (as in the bubbly wine) **America II** (www.bigapplesailing.com) is 65 feet long and competed in the America's Cup in Australia in 1987. Both of these boats have scheduled and charter trip options and sail out of North Cove Marina in Battery Park City.

Restaurants

Good for Grownups, Too

Mars 2112 and Bar (1633 Broadway, 212/582-2112)
Shake Shack (Madison Square Park, Madison Ave at 23rd St)
Tavern on the Green (Central Park West at 67th St, 212/873-3200)
Union Square Cafe (21 E 16th St, 212/243-4020)

Great Basics

EJ's Luncheonette (447 Amsterdam Ave, 212/873-3444 and 1271 Third Ave, 212/472-0600)
Jackson Hole Burgers (232 E 64th St, 212/371-7187 and several other locations)
John's Pizzeria (278 Bleecker St, 212/243-1680 and other locations)
Lombardi's (32 Spring St, 212/941-7994)
Two Boots Pizza (42 Ave A, 212/254-1919 and other locations)

Ruby-Red Stairs

There's a new landmark in Times Square: the glowing **Ruby-Red Stairs** which are built mostly of structural-strength glass. The 27 wide steps seat 1,500 (if everyone gets cozy) and offer a commanding view down Broadway. It's a great place to meet friends or enjoy solo. Don't forget your latte or lunch, as eating and drinking are welcome here. L.E.D. lights bring the stairs to life at night, and an innovative heating system keeps them snow- and ice-free. The **TKTS** ticket windows face 47th Street, underneath the stairway.

Great Desserts

Blue Smoke (116 E 27th St, 212/447-7733)
Bubby's (120 Hudson St, 212/219-0666)
Cafe Lalo (201 W 83rd St, 212/496-6031)
Peanut Butter & Co. (240 Sullivan St, 212/677-3995)
Serendipity 3 (225 E 60th St, 212/838-3531)

Theme Restaurants

Barking Dog Luncheonette (1678 Third Ave, 212/831-1800 and other
  locations)
Brooklyn Diner USA (212 W 57th St, 212/977-1957)
ESPN Zone (1472 Broadway, 212/921-3776)
Hard Rock Cafe (1501 Broadway, 212/489-6565)
Jekyll & Hyde (1409 Ave of the Americas, 212/541-9505 and other loca-
  tions)

Toy Stores and Bookstores

Bookstores

Bank Street Bookstore (2875 Broadway, 212/678-1654)
Scholastic Store (557 Broadway, 212/343-6166)

Toy Stores

E.A.T. Gifts (1062 Madison Ave, 212/861-2544)
F.A.O. Schwarz (767 Fifth Ave, 212/644-9400)
Kid O (123 W 10th St, 212/366-KIDO)
Kidding Around (60 W 15th St, 212/645-6337)
Toys "R" Us (Times Square, 1514 Broadway, 646/366-8858)
West Side Kids (498 Amsterdam Ave, 212/496-7282)

Bicycling Basics

New York's parks are full of bike paths, including a 6.2-mile loop in
Central Park and a 5.5-mile route that runs along the Hudson River
down to Battery Park. Go to www.transalt.org/info/bikeshop.html for
an extensive list of shops throughout the city that rent bikes. This website belongs to **Transportation Alternatives**, a terrific advocacy
group that supplies extensive maps and useful information to bicyclists,
pedestrians, and mass-transit riders.

Just as some things are fun to do with kids, there are others that you
should *not* do with them. Check your destination's age requirement before
bringing the kids. If you're going shopping at a perpetually crowded place like
Zabar's or Fairway, don't take kids or keep a firm grip on their hands if you
do. The latter holds true just about everywhere in New York—it's easy for
a young one to get lost in a crowd! And remember that kids tire more
quickly than adults. Chances are you'll do a lot of walking, and they're taking
two or three steps for every one of yours! As the *New York Times* once put
it, "Baby miles are like dog years."

Finally, it's a real challenge to tote an infant or toddler in New York. While
hundreds of thousands of children are born and raised in the city, visitors
who are accustomed to carting children through malls in strollers and

around town in car seats may have trouble here. Many places, including the subway system, are not exactly stroller-accessible. Taxis with functioning seatbelts have become much easier to find in recent years, but ones with car seats are a rarity.

Roller Skating

Looking for a roller-skating rink in Manhattan? You'll need to look a little farther. The last of the hardwood rinks has closed, but head over to Staten Island to **Roller Jam USA** (236 Richmond Valley Road, 718/605-6600). Check the schedule for sessions and classes; DJs keep the pace moving with lively tunes. For special events, book the party room, which serves beer and wine to the over-21 crowd.

For Free

Even the most frugal and resourceful visitors often feel as if they're bleeding money. ("Didn't we just get $200 out of the ATM!?") Still, you can find some good deals and do a lot of sightseeing for free.

Museums and Sights

The Museum of Modern Art broke through the $20 ceiling for admission several years ago, and now other museums are following suit. Still, you can find some free museums and sights in New York. They include:

Cathedral Church of St. John the Divine
Drawing Center
Federal Hall National Memorial
Forbes Magazine Galleries
General Grant National Monument (Riverside Park)
Museum at FIT
National Museum of the American Indian (Alexander Hamilton U.S. Custom House)
New York Public Library
Sony Wonder Technology Lab
Tibet House
Transit Museum Gallery Annex (Grand Central Terminal)
Trinity Church

Picnicking

Picnicking in New York City can be as simple as takeout food eaten on a park bench; a couple of made-at-home sandwiches with a few extra goodies tossed in a backpack; or an elaborately catered affair with elegant china, fine linens, and cushy chairs and tables. The locations are limitless: rooftops, parks, marinas, gardens, and more. Perhaps you already have a favorite spot. If not, check with the New York City Department of Parks and Recreation (www.nycgovparks.org) for a list of available locales and facilities. What to eat? Chapter IV lists food stores that are chock full of possibilities to fill a picnic basket. A perfect way to spend a sunny day in the city!

It used to be that all the museums along Museum Mile on Fifth Avenue offered free admission one night a week. Unfortunately, that tradition lives on only one night a year, in late June. Still, some museums do offer pay-as-you-wish admission on certain evenings. They include:

Brooklyn Museum
China Institute
Guggenheim Museum
International Center of Photography
Jewish Museum
Morgan Library and Museum (including Mr. Morgan's Library and Study)
Museum of Arts and Design
Museum of Modern Art
New Museum of Contemporary Art
Studio Museum
Whitney Museum of American Art

Many places admit children under 12 for free. Active-duty military personnel in uniform are admitted free to the Empire State Building, and Smithsonian Associates are admitted free to the Cooper-Hewitt. Although it definitely isn't free, you can tour both The Cloisters and the Metropolitan Museum of Art on the same day for one admission price. You can also get a discount on admission to the Jewish Museum if you show a ticket stub from the Museum of Jewish Heritage (and vice versa).

Note: If you're interested in visiting any of the places listed here, you will find addresses, phone numbers, and more information in Chapter III.

I'm often asked about reliable ticket brokers. For over 80 years **Americana Tickets** (800/833-3121, 212/581-6660, www.americana tickets.com) has been cited over and over for outstanding service. The third generation of the Radler family is outstanding to deal with! Just a few of the advantages: premium seating for theater, entertainment, concert, and sporting events in New York and worldwide; expert, professional agents; unique cancellation and exchange privileges; special offers for individuals and groups; a conveniently located ticket desk in the Marriott Marquis; great hours (Mon-Sat: 8:30-8; Sun: 9-5); and complimentary hotel, restaurant, limousine, and sightseeing reservations.

You can also rely on **Surftix.com** (877-SURFTIX, www.surftix. com) for all of your worldwide entertainment needs. They have sold over 16 million tickets and offer more than 10,000 events worldwide at any given time.

For Tickets

Nowhere else in the world will you find such a wealth of performing arts. And no trip to New York is complete without taking in at least one play, musical, ballet, concert, or opera.

The trick, of course, is getting tickets. People have written entire books about how and where to get tickets, while others have made lucrative careers out of procuring them for out-of-towners. I've provided a variety of approaches for getting theater tickets and to find out about other performances. Keep your eye out for student and other discounts, but be aware that good deals for the best shows and performances are few and far between.

Hot Deals

Every theater does things differently, so you really need to get accurate, up-to-date information if you want to get hot tickets at a lower price. Some theaters have lotteries a couple of hours before each performance for seats in the first few rows. Some have Standing Room Only (SRO) tickets available. Some give discount tickets only to students, while others have so-called rush tickets available for certain performances. To make sense of it all, go to www.talkingbroadway.com and click "On the Boards." Be sure to bring lots of patience and enough cash to cover the cost of whatever tickets you end up buying.

BROADWAY

People often have different things in mind when they say they want to see a show. Some may have their hearts set on great seats at a Saturday night performance of the hottest show on Broadway, while others are willing to sit anywhere to see anything. A lot of people fall somewhere between those extremes. In addition, some are willing to pay whatever it takes to see the show they want, while others just won't go if they can't pay less than full price. If the main purpose of your visit to the city is to see a particular show (or shows), make sure you have the tickets you want before leaving home so you're not disappointed. The **Broadway Line** (888/276-2392 or 212/302-4111) tells what is playing and where, and also gives plot summaries.

Bring the Kids!

It used to be that everyone dressed up for the theater and nobody would think of bringing a young child. Disney's *The Lion King* changed all that, and now the pre-teen set is often seen in almost every Broadway theater. Some even supply booster seats! One word from this adult: Please try to choose productions your child will appreciate and leave promptly if your little one behaves disruptively. I know you paid a lot for that ticket, but so did the rest of us!

Box Offices and Phone Orders—If you want to save money and pick your seat, go directly to the theater's box office with cash or a major credit card. Ask to see a diagram of the theater if it isn't posted, although most theaters are small enough to ensure that every seat has a good view. The best time to try is midweek. You can also ask the box office if it releases day-of-performance cancellations or rush tickets (see "Hot Deals" box, top of page 507).

If you're willing to spend a little extra and let a computer pick what is in theory the "best available" seat, call the number or go to the website listed and have your credit card ready. Most numbers will be for **Telecharge** (212/239-6200, www.telecharge.com) or **TicketMaster's Broadway Performance Line** (212/307-4100, www.ticketmaster.com). Both services charge a handling fee in addition to the ticket price.

Be forewarned: full-price tickets to Broadway shows typically cost $100 and sometimes fetch well over $250. Moreover, if the play or musical you want to see is really hot, it may be sold out the entire time you're in New York. In fact, a few really hot shows may be sold out months in advance.

Care-Tix—If you have your heart set on a particular show and cost is no obstacle, Broadway Cares/Equity Fights AIDS sells house seats for sold-out Broadway and off-Broadway shows for twice the box-office price. The extra money goes to a good cause and is a tax-deductible contribution. Call 212/840-0770 and ask for Care-Tix.

What Are Those Unique Flags Flying Over New York?

The presence of the United Nations means that flags of many countries fly in New York. However, two flags flown over the city can't be found in any world atlas. The white one with the green maple leaf is the New York City Parks and Recreation Department's flag, while the blue, white, and orange one is the official flag of New York City.

TKTS Outlets—If you want to see a Broadway show, are flexible, and have some free time, go to one of the TKTS outlets in Manhattan. Operated by the Theater Development Fund, these outlets sell whatever tickets happen to be left for various shows on the day of performance for half price or less (plus a $3 per-ticket charge). The most popular TKTS outlet is now easily located as a result of some snazzy construction. Look for the red glass stairs at 47th Street and Broadway; tucked underneath the steps are 12 ticket booths. It's open from 3 to 8 Monday through Saturday, from 10 to 2 for Wednesday and Saturday matinees, from 11 to 3 for Sunday matinees, and from 3 until half an hour before the latest curtain time of a ticket being sold that day. A less crowded TKTS outlet is located at the intersection of Front and John streets, just below South Street Seaport's main plaza. It's open Monday through Saturday from 11 to 6, and Sunday in summer months from 11 to 6. Matinee tickets at this location go on sale the day *before* a performance. The problem with the TKTS outlets is that you won't know until you get there what is available. A list of available shows is posted at each outlet, and chances are that the hottest tickets won't be among them. You can go to the Theater Development Fund's website (www.tdf.org) to see which tickets were available *last* week. The really good news is that both outlets now accept major credit cards, as well as cash and travelers' checks.

The Theater Development Fund also offers extremely good deals to its members on tickets to theater and other performances. If you're a student, member of the clergy or armed forces (serving or retired), teacher, union member, or performing artist, go to the Fund's website for more information. All Broadway theaters offer a small number of deeply discounted tickets to people in wheelchairs and their companion or attendant. Call the theater box office directly for more information.

Swedish Cottage

The **Swedish Cottage Marionette Theatre** is a whimsical structure in Central Park (79th St at West Dr, 212/988-9093) that now serves as a puppeteer's venue for kids' classics like *Jack and the Bean Stalk* and *Peter Pan*. The charming theater seats 100, and a party room accommodates 30 special guests. Reservations are required and show times vary. The cottage has an interesting past. It was imported in 1876 as Sweden's exhibit for the Centennial Exposition in Philadelphia and brought to Central Park a year later. It has served as a tool shed, comfort station, and entomological lab. The current use is by far its best role!

Off-Broadway and off-off-Broadway—In part because staging a Broadway production has become almost prohibitively expensive, off-Broadway and off-off-Broadway theaters have really taken *off*. Thanks to a glut of talented actors and actresses in New York, such theater is typically excellent and often innovative. Tickets for off-Broadway and off-off-Broadway productions tend to be significantly less expensive. TKTS outlets sometimes offer discounts, and "twofers"—two tickets for the price of one—may be available.

Online Tickets

Here are some better-known websites for event tickets in the city (and sometimes elsewhere). Check for discount programs associated with Costco, AAA, and other membership cards. Compare prices from a couple of sites to make sure you are getting the best deal.

www.BroadwayBox.com (discounted theater, sports events, and concerts)

www.ilovenytheater.com (theater, restaurants, hotels, other events)

www.kidsnightonbroadway.com (Kids from 6-18 attend free with a full-paying adult on the first Tuesday and Wednesday of each month at participating shows.)

www.StubHub.com (Buy or sell any tickets to any event, anywhere.)

OPERA AND CLASSICAL MUSIC

No other city in the world has as many musical events to choose from as New York! Contact the **92nd Street Y** (212/996-1100, www.92y.org) if you're interested in chamber music or recitals by top performers. Otherwise, here's how to find schedule and ticket information at New York's top venues:

Carnegie Hall—Individual musicians, out-of-town orchestras, and chamber music ensembles perform at Carnegie Hall all year. For detailed information about performances, go to www.carnegiehall.org. For information about rush tickets and same-day student and senior discounts, call 212/247-7800. A limited number of partial-view seats are available for $10 at noon on the day of each performance.

Metropolitan Opera—The internationally renowned Met's season runs from fall through spring, and ticket sales are broken into three periods. Try the Met's box office (212/362-6000, www.metopera.org) at Lincoln Center between 10 and 8 (noon to 6 on Sunday). Be aware that choice seats can cost as much as $375! If you have a little time on your hands, there are bargains to be had. Two hundred orchestra seats are sold for $20 two hours before curtain time for performances during the week. Full-time students under 30 with identification can buy tickets for $25 ($35 for Friday and Saturday performances) at 10 on the day of a performance. Standing Room Only ("SRO") tickets are also often available. No more than two discounted tickets can be purchased at a time.

New York City Opera—The season for this exceptional but often overshadowed opera runs through summer and early fall. For schedule and ticket information, visit the opera's website (www.nycopera.com) or go to the New York State Theater's box office at Lincoln Center. Special student discounts are often available, including a limited number of rush tickets sold at 4 on the day of each performance for $16. Call in advance (212/870-5630) to learn about availability.

New York Philharmonic—The Philharmonic's season runs from September through June at Avery Fisher Hall in Lincoln Center. For schedule and ticket information, go to the Philharmonic's website (www.nyphil.org) or call 212/875-5656. If you would rather attend a performance during the day and save a bit, ask about reduced tickets to open rehearsals. Rush tickets may also be available.

Take My Money . . . Please!

    American Girl Place (609 Fifth Ave, at 49th St) is a restaurant, theater, store, and giant credit-card bill all wrapped up into one. A relative newcomer, you'll know it by the line of dressed-up little girls coming and going. If you're familiar with the American Girl Doll phenomenon, I need explain no more. If you're not, you don't want to know! A whole-day dream package starts at $270 for one child over six and an accompanying adult. Call 877/247-5223 or go to www.amer icangirl.com for more information. You might also try the wildly popular **Build-a-Bear Workshop** on the corner of Fifth Avenue and 46th Street for a less expensive excursion. Call 212/871-7080 or go to www.buildabear.com/nyc.

DANCE AND BALLET

    Ballet and dance companies have experienced tough times financially, but New York is still home to several world-class companies and a great many smaller ones. They include:

    Alvin Ailey American Dance Theater (212/405-9000, www.alvin ailey.org)
    American Ballet Theater (212/477-3030, www.abt.org)
    Dance Theater Workshop (212/691-6500, www.dtw.org)
    Dance Theatre of Harlem (212/690-2800, www.dancetheatreof harlem.org)

New York City Ballet (212/870-5570, www.nycballet.com)
Paul Taylor Dance Company (212/431-5562, www.ptdc.org)

A number of major companies perform at the **New York City Center** (131 W 55th Street). The Alvin Ailey American Dance Theater is now in the **Joan Weill Center for Dance** (405 W 55th St). Contact **CityTix** (212/581-1212, www.citytix.org), or visit an individual dance company's website for information about tickets and upcoming performances.

What's Happening?

There really is something always happening in New York! It's impossible to list everything in one place, so I suggest consulting the following publications for the most current list of activities. You'll find complete listings for cultural events, festivals, activities for kids, comedy clubs, gallery and museum exhibits (and free admission periods), sporting events, parades, movies, and lots more. Dates, times, and costs are usually included.

New York magazine, www.nymag.com

New York Times, Friday Weekend section and Sunday Arts and Leisure section, www.nytimes.com

New Yorker, www.newyorker.com

Time Out New York, www.timeout.com/newyork

These publications are generally available out of town as well as online. Many New York-related websites offer this comprehensive information, too.

TELEVISION SHOW TAPINGS

Fine arts aside, there is one other kind of ticket everybody wants to get in New York: those that allow you to become part of the television studio audience for one of the many talk shows filmed here. I've listed some of the most popular shows and rules for getting free tickets.

The Daily Show with Jon Stewart—These tickets must be ordered well in advance, but the system for getting them is wonderfully straightforward. Simply go to www.thedailyshow.com and complete the online reservation form. The website for **The Colbert Report** is www.colbertnation.com, and the method is the same. Standby tickets are sometimes available, so check when you are online. Bring identification, as audience members must be at least 18 years of age.

Late Show with David Letterman—These remain among the hottest tickets in town, and you must be at least 18 to qualify. You can apply by filling out a form at www.lateshow.cbs.com or go in person to the Ed Sullivan Theater box office (1697 Broadway between 53rd and 54th St) between 9:30 and 12:30 on weekdays or 10 to 6 on weekends. Expect to wait at least six to eight months and probably longer. Standby tickets are sometimes distributed at 11 on the morning of a show by calling 212/247-6497. If you hear a recording, you'll know tickets have run out. Shows are taped Monday through Thursday. Bring a picture ID and jacket, as Dave insists that the theater be kept at a chilly 52° all year! They are sticklers for the rules, and tickets are non-transferable.

Saturday Night Live—Year in and year out, these are the hardest tickets of all to get. A lottery is held every August from emails collected during the preceding 12 months, and each winner gets two tickets. If you want to be included in the lottery, send an e-mail to snltickets@nbc.com. Send only one email per household, and realize there is no guarantee that you will get tickets in the following year. Standby tickets for the 8 p.m. dress rehearsal and the 11:30 p.m. live show are available at 7 a.m. on the day of the show (but show up around 5 a.m. if you really want them) at the 49th Street entrance to 30 Rockefeller Plaza. Be sure you're certain there's a live show planned for the time you are in New York, and expect a long line if there's a popular host. They do not guarantee entrance, and only one ticket is distributed per person over age 16.

Look for NBC's **Today Show** crowd on the sidewalk along 49th Street between Fifth Avenue and Avenue of the Americas. People show up before dawn, although cameras don't starting rolling until 7 a.m. ABC's **Good Morning America** welcomes audiences Monday through Friday for their 7 to 9 live show. See their website (www.abc news.go.com/gma) for ticket information. A standby line forms outside the Times Square studio (44th St and Broadway) alongside those with tickets. Fans of CBS's **The Early Show** may stop by the Early Show plaza (Fifth Ave and 59th St) before 7:15 a.m. to join the audience. Backstage tours of the studio are conducted after the show. No tickets are needed.

The View—This women's gabfest is taped Monday through Thursday at the ABC Studios on Manhattan's Upper West Side (320 W 66th St). If you're planning well in advance and live outside of New Jersey, New York, Connecticut, and Pennsylvania, go to www.abc.go.com/daytime/theview/tickets to request tickets for a specific date at least three months in advance. (If you live in one of those four states, ABC will simply assign a date to you.) If you're in town and feel lucky, go by the studio between 8:30 and 10 on a morning they're taping and pick up a standby number. When you return at 9:30, they'll let you know what numbers they're taking that day. You must be at least 16 years old to attend. The show airs from 11 to noon.

For a Romantic Interlude

Whether you're falling in love for the first time or celebrating a wedding anniversary, New York can be one of the most romantic places in the world to celebrate. If you're in the mood for love or want to create a mood that's just right for romance, try the following:

- Drinks by the fireplace followed by dinner at **One if by Land, Two if by Sea** (17 Barrow St)
- A summertime dinner in the garden at **Barbetta** (321 W 46th St)
- Dinner at the discreet and classy **Le Périgord** (405 E 52nd St)

- Dinner at **Tavern on the Green**'s sparkling Crystal Room (in Central Park off 67th St)
- Drinks at **Campbell Apartment**, an elegant spot tucked away in Grand Central Terminal (just east of Vanderbilt Ave)
- A late-night visit to the **Empire State Building Observation Deck** (Fifth Ave between 33rd and 34th St)
- A walk across the **Brooklyn Bridge** is a must!
- Watching the sun rise from the **Brooklyn Bridge**, the **Battery Park Esplanade**, **Lighthouse Park** on Roosevelt Island, or the deck of the **Staten Island Ferry**
- A visit to the restored **Winter Garden** (World Financial Center)
- A picnic lunch looking out over the Hudson River from **The Cloisters**
- A stroll through the splendid lobby of the **Waldorf-Astoria**
- An early evening spent listening to classical music from the balcony of the **Metropolitan Museum of Art**'s Great Hall or jazz at the **Guggenheim Museum**
- A rowboat or gondola ride on **Central Park Lake** or a nighttime sail around Manhattan
- An evening carriage ride through **Central Park** after a fresh snow has fallen or a springtime stroll on some of the park's less traveled paths

---

Test Your New York IQ

Here's an eclectic list of questions about New York that even a native New Yorker probably wouldn't know:

1. Where was George Washington's inauguration held in 1789?
2. When was the first ticker-tape parade and why was it held?
3. What do Ella Fitzgerald, the Rolling Stones, Mark Twain, and Eleanor Roosevelt all have in common?
4. Why are triads, nautiluses, and Poseidon himself carved in stone outside the Bowling Green Post Office?
5. Where does the red star associated with Macy's come from?

Answers: 1. In a building on the corner of Wall and Nassau streets that is now home to the Federal Hall National Memorial. 2. The throwing of a ticker tape happened spontaneously in October 1886 during a parade to celebrate the dedication of the Statue of Liberty. 3. They all appeared in front of sold-out crowds at Carnegie Hall. 4. The building (on Broadway at Bowling Green), was home of the Cunard Steamship Line. 5. Rowland Hussey Macy, who started the store in 1858, had a red star tattooed on his hand from his days as a Nantucket whaler.

For Parties and Special Events

If you're looking for the perfect place to hold a wedding reception, bar mitzvah, or gala event for thousands, New York inevitably has the right place …and the people to put it together. The trick, of course, is finding them. The other trick is paying for them!

Note that you will not find museums, restaurants, or hotels in the following list. Many museum spaces, including the **Mount Vernon Hotel**

Museum and Garden, the **Cooper-Hewitt National Design Museum**, and the Theodore Roosevelt Rotunda at the **American Museum of Natural History** (complete with its dinosaur display) can be rented for parties and other events. Many restaurants have spaces for private parties, as do most hotels.

Some of my favorite private party rooms in New York are at **Barbetta** (321 W 46th St), **Firebird** (365 W 46th St), **Four Seasons** (99 E 52nd St), **Gramercy Tavern** (42 E 20th St), **Le Périgord** (405 E 52nd St), **One if by Land, Two if by Sea** (17 Barrow St), **Primavera** (1578 First Ave), **Serendipity 3** (225 E 60th St), **Tavern on the Green** (Central Park W at 67th St), **Terrace in the Sky** (400 W 119th St), and **Tribeca Grill** (375 Greenwich St). If you want to throw a party at your favorite museum, restaurant, hotel, or bar, by all means ask.

Some venues available for special events take care of all the catering, while others simply provide the space. This list should give you an idea of the breadth of spaces available: **New York Public Library** (Fifth Ave at 41st St), the **Puck Building** (295 Lafayette St, at Houston St), **Studio 450** (450 W 31st St), **Astra** (979 Third Ave), **The Boathouse** (in Central Park), **Glorious Foods** (522 E 74th St), the **Museum Club at Bridgewaters** (South Street Seaport), **Pier 60** (at Chelsea Piers), and **Upper Crust 91** (91 Horatio St). Catering is optional at the **New York Botanical Garden** (in The Bronx) and the **Pratt Mansion** (1027 Fifth Ave).

Before forging ahead with planning a party in New York, make note that it's going to cost a great deal of money. I'm talking *really* big bucks. You can save money by avoiding Saturday evening, holding your numbers down, and throwing your party in the off months of July and August or between January and early April. Some venues and services may negotiate on price, but don't expect any great or even particularly good deals. Make your reservations at least two months and as far as two years in advance.

Going Underground?

Manhattan has some interesting below-ground spots for you to visit! One of the best known is the **Grand Central Oyster Bar Restaurant** (Grand Central Terminal, 42nd St at Vanderbilt Ave, 212/490-6650), and there are also other eateries in the Food Court in the same building. **Sake Bar Decibel** (240 E 9th St, 212/979-2733) is a restaurant and sake bar, but because of the loudness, it is not the kind of place you would want to spend a whole evening. **Pravda** (281 Lafayette St, 212/226-4944) is a bit more visitor friendly, with plenty of vodka available. For good jazz, the **Village Vanguard** (178 Seventh Ave, 212/255-4037) is the place to go "down under." A surprise underground venue is **Zankel Hall** (Carnegie Hall, 881 Seventh Ave, 212/247-7800). It is a 600-seat concert theater that even most New Yorkers have never even heard of!

For Restrooms

Nothing can ruin a trek around New York more quickly than not being able to find a bathroom when one is needed. By law, public buildings are required to have public restrooms. They are not, however, required to be clean and safe.

Following is a list of bathrooms that meet at least minimal standards of safety and cleanliness. You may need to ask for directions or a key, but all are free to the public. As a general rule, try hotel lobbies, department stores, schools, theaters, municipal goverment buildings, churches, libraries, and even hospitals. **Barnes & Noble** and **Starbucks** locations throughout the city are also good bets. Of course, if you have small children in tow, just about any store or restaurant will likely take pity.

Wherever you end up, be sure to follow a few safety tips. Leaving anything on the floor in a public restroom is a mistake, as purses and packages have a bad habit of disappearing while you're occupied! The same is true of items left hanging on the back of a stall door. Avoid deserted bathrooms, as well as those in parks (unless listed below) and most subway stations.

Comfort Stations

New York's Parks Department has placed more than 600 "comfort stations" inside its parks. While many languish in disrepair, several dozen have been significantly improved, thanks in part to revenue from selling advertising space in some of them. By far the nicest is in Bryant Park, behind the main branch of the New York Public Library.

Below 14th Street

- **Castle Clinton** (inside Battery Park)
- **National Museum of the American Indian** (1 Bowling Green)
- **Trinity Church** (Broadway at Wall St)
- **Federal Hall National Memorial** (Wall St at Nassau St)
- **South Street Seaport** (Fulton St at Water St)
- **The Hotel on Rivington** (107 Rivington St)
- **Essex Street Market** (120 Essex St)
- **New York City Fire Museum** (278 Spring St, bet Hudson and Varick St)
- **Strand Book Store** (Broadway at 12th St)

Between 14th and 42nd streets

- **Loehmann's** (Seventh Ave at 17th St)
- **ABC Carpet & Home** (Broadway at 19th St)
- **Macy's** (Herald Square, Broadway at 34th St)
- **Science, Industry, and Business Library** (Madison Ave at 34th St)
- **New York Public Library** (Fifth Ave bet 40th and 42nd St)
- **Bryant Park** (Ave of the Americas bet 40th and 42nd St)
- **Grand Hyatt New York** (42nd St bet Park and Lexington Ave)
- **Grand Central Terminal** (42nd St at Vanderbilt Ave)

Midtown

- **United Nations** (First Ave bet 45th and 46th St)
- **Waldorf-Astoria** (Park Ave at 50th St)

- **Saks Fifth Avenue** (611 Fifth Ave, bet 49th and 50th St)
- **Rockefeller Center** (concourse level, bet Fifth Ave and Ave of the Americas from 49th to 51st St)
- **Fendi** (677 Fifth Ave, bet 53rd and 54th St)
- **Park Avenue Plaza** (55 E 52nd St, at Madison Ave)
- **Henri Bendel** (712 Fifth Ave, at 56th St)
- **Park Central New York** (870 Seventh Ave, at 56th St)
- **Sony Wonder Technology Lab** (550 Madison Ave, at 56th St)

Upper East Side

- **McDonald's** (Third Ave bet 57th and 58th St)
- **Bloomingdale's** (1000 Third Ave, at 59th St)
- **Asia Society** (725 Park Ave, at 70th St)
- **Ralph Lauren** (867 Madison Ave, at 72nd St)
- **Marimekko** (1262 Third Ave, at 73rd St)
- **92nd Street Y** (1395 Lexington Ave, at 92nd St)
- **Charles A. Dana Discovery Center** (in Central Park, Fifth Ave at 110th St)

Upper West Side

- **Avery Fisher Hall** (Lincoln Center, at 65th St and Columbus Ave)
- **New York Public Library for the Performing Arts** (Lincoln Center, 65th St at Broadway)
- **Barnes & Noble** (Broadway at 82nd St)
- **Cathedral Church of St. John the Divine** (Amsterdam Ave at 112th St)

---

311 is New York City's all-purpose information number. Do you need to know how to rent a baseball field in Central Park, how to sign up for a tour of Gracie Mansion, or how to pay a parking fine? Operators are standing by!

For More Information

I suggest doing a few things before packing your bags for New York. Contact **NYC & Company** (800/692-8474, 212/484-1222, www.nyc visit.com), the city's marketing arm, to request a free copy of the official **NYC Guide**. Second, look through both the "Tours" section of Chapter III and the "Tickets" section of this chapter to find out which things you want to do that require advance reservations.

If you don't have everything planned when you arrive, drop by one of several visitor information centers in Manhattan. They include:

- **Chinatown Visitor Kiosk**—Walker, Canal, and Baxter streets
- **NYC Heritage Tourism Center**—Broadway at Park Row
- **Times Square Information Center**—1560 Broadway, bet 46th and 47th St
- **Federal Hall National Memorial "Gateway to America"**—This is a great source for information about National Parks and other federally run attractions in New York. Located at 26 Wall Street, it's open weekdays (except federal holidays).

- **Harlem Visitor Information Center**—Located in Studio Museum, 144 W 125th St, bet Adam Clayton Powell, Jr. Blvd and Malcolm X Blvd
- **NYC & Company**—810 Seventh Ave at 53rd St

The front section of the Manhattan Yellow Pages is a good place to look for information and ideas. In addition to useful telephone numbers, it includes diagrams of major concert halls and sports stadiums. It also includes a short calendar of major annual events and maps of the subway and bus systems.

Finally, the Internet has made accessing tourist information about New York as easy as clicking a mouse. Typing "New York City" into a search engine will generate several million hits. Here are some useful sites:

- **www.ci.nyc.ny.us**: The official site of the city of New York has helpful information for residents and visitors alike, including transportation resources, links to attractions and events, and the New York Yellow Pages.
- **www.centralparknyc.org**: The official site of the Central Park Conservancy offers a great deal of information about this remarkable park.
- **www.cityguidemagazine.com**: restaurant reviews and numerous links to tours, museums, discounts, and other sites
- **www.mta.nyc.ny.us**: The official site of the Metropolitan Transportation Authority has helpful information about the bus and subway systems.
- **www.newyork.citysearch.com**: current schedules for plays, concerts, and movies; good descriptions of clubs and lots of opinions
- **www.nycgovparks.org**: extensive information about parks and recreation centers in all five boroughs

---

Over the Bridge

As I explained in the first chapter, New York to me means Manhattan. The moment I leave "the city," I'm definitely out of my element. For many years, no self-respecting Manhattanite would even think of crossing the bridge to any other burrough. But in recent years, Brooklyn has become increasingly appealing and lots of folks, even tourists, are heading that way.

The **Brooklyn Museum** (718/638-5000, www.brooklynmuseum.org) is a world-class art museum that's well worth a visit. The **Brooklyn Botanic Gardens** (718/623-7200, www.bbg.org) and **Prospect Park** are within walking distance of each other and the Brooklyn Museum. Of course some folks come to Brooklyn for the great shops and restaurants in Park Slope, Carroll Gardens, Williamsburg, and other Brooklyn neighborhoods. Among those I recommend are **Blue Ribbon Brooklyn** (278 Fifth Ave, 718/840-0408), **Beast** (638 Bergen St, 718/399-6855), and the amazing **Brooklyn Ice Cream Factory** (1 Water St, 718/246-3963). If you want a taste of what makes Brooklyn so appealing that folks are willing to take the F train out of Manhattan, take a walk along Smith and Court streets south of Atlantic Avenue.

If you're coming to New York in a wheelchair, you ought to know about a couple of resources. First, get a copy of "Access for All," an exceptional guide to the city's cultural institutions that describes in detail facilities for people in wheelchairs, as well as the blind and deaf. This invaluable guide is available from **Hospital Audiences** (www.hospaud.org). This organization also runs a hotline (212/575-7676) on weekdays. Second, the **Metropolitan Transportation Authority** has a special phone number (718/596-8585) for information about routes accessible to people in wheelchairs and postage-paid fare envelopes for disabled riders. The **Mayor's Office for People with Disabilities** (212/788-2830, www.nyc.gov/html/mopd) is also a great resource. Finally, many Broadway theaters offer deeply discounted tickets for people in wheelchairs and their companions. Call individual theaters for more information.

Are you short on cash but still want to enjoy fun and interesting entertainment? Fire up your computer and check out **FreeNYC.net**. Each day FreeNYC publishes a list of free or cheap activity options, and an online subscription costs nothing. Museums, movies, concerts, dances and dance classes, club and gallery openings, book signings, and the ever-popular happy hours and free tastings are routinely included.

Index

(Note: Bolded page numbers indicate major listings' main entries. The index is in strict alphabetical order, ignoring spacing and punctuation, and treating numerals as if spelled out.)

NOTES